Naval Order of the United States

Past - Present - Future

TURNER PUBLISHING COMPANY
Paducah, Kentucky

TURNER PUBLISHING COMPANY
Publishers of America's History
412 Broadway • P.O. Box 3101
Paducah, KY 42002-3101
270-443-0121

NOUS Editor:Capt. John C. Rice, Jr.
Publishing Consultant: Douglas W. Sikes
Book Designer: Elizabeth Sikes

Library of Congress Catalog No.: 2003101755

ISBN: 978-1-68162-158-6

Limited Edition, First Printing 2003 A.D.
Additional copies may be purchased from Turner Publishing
Company

Table of Contents

Introduction

My Fellow Companions,

As the title suggests, this volume will take you back in time to 4 July 1890, the day the idea of organizing our Naval Order first surfaced as the Naval Commandery of the US. You will read in their own words what our three Founders said and did. What is presented here is taken directly from their Minutes. As you read it, you will see the care which they took to define why they were organizing, what the membership would be made up of, and what they expected to accomplish. The objects of the society they established are the bases of our Mission to this day. Reference will be made to it throughout.

The various categories of _Membership_ are described followed by an overview of the _Application_ process.

Next in sequence is the _General Commandery_, the national body consisting of the General Congress and the General Council. The Congress, made up of representatives of all local units, is the final authority.

Following the General Commandery Governance structure, are two sections: one dealing with _Initiatives_ conducted on a national scale and a second describing the Order's National _Recognition and Awards_ programs. Space constraints pose limitations, so both these sections should be viewed as representative and not all-inclusive.

Next you read about the _Local Commandery_. Three sections discuss _Governance, Local Initiatives_ and _Local Awards_ Programs. It is said that one picture is worth a thousand words, so the narrative purposely has been curtailed to permit more photos of the Local Commanderies in action. Here again they are not all-inclusive (see photos illustrated in the Register section).

Next there is a separate section entitled _Significant Civil War Engagements_. As you will have learned by the time you read this section, the Civil War and its aftermath were the catalysts leading the Founders to act.

This is followed by a _Future Initiative Section_. Its focus is our Mission. It suggests what are appropriate endeavors for the General Commandery and the Local Commanderies. You will read the word "you" many times here, for it is an invitation to you to become an active contributor in the work.

Special Interests contributed by your fellow Companions are next followed by _Biographies_ provided by Companions.

I would be remiss if I failed to identify those who have labored in our research over these many years. They are my Historian Predecessors CAPT Emile Bonnot and LCDR Russ Miller, the indefatigable Recorder LCDR Lee Douglas, RADM Win Weese who helped on selections and choices, the Lupo Foundation for secretarial support and many others whose ears I bent and whose counsel I sought including past Recorder General CAPT Jan Armstrong and our incumbent Mr. Timothy "Chris" Cummings. Two others deserve special mention. They are Companion Craig Cheramie, who volunteered in excess of 200 hours verifying the Register data; and Mrs. Patricia Catania of the Lupo Foundation staff who labored through the heavily annotated worksheets to assemble the complete _Register of Companions_, Insignia numbers 0001 through 8155.

Lastly, the book differs from many descriptive ones of organizations in that every effort was made to keep the presentation light and flowing and still be informative. Enjoy – especially our _Register of all Companions_ and the illustrations included within it!

John C. Rice Jr.
Captain, USNR (Ret)
Historian General Emeritus

The Russian Admiral

Exemplifying the informative, read the item from the Naval Order Newsletter "Scuttlebutt" issued by then Recorder A. Fred Kempe, 23 July 1970:

"Quick, now! What Russian admiral was dug up in Paris and reburied at Annapolis? You'll think I'm funning when I say John Paul Jones, but facts are facts, unless in a political speech, and our naval hero, John Paul Jones, was a Russian admiral.

"This week, on the 18th, we mark the anniversary of his death in 1792. He was born John Paul, the son of a Scotch gardener. His career began as third mate on a slave ship. At 22 he was captain of a West Indies merchantman. Then in 1771 he fatally flogged a carpenter for neglect of duty. In England he was tried for murder.

"Unlike Capt. Kidd who was hanged for killing one of his men, Paul (as he was then known) was acquitted. Then in 1773 he killed another man, an alleged mutineer. This time the captain took no chances on jail or worse, but fled the West Indies to Virginia and added Jones to his name to hide his trail.

"He was an out-of-work sea captain when the new American Navy commissioned him a lieutenant in 1775. This was his cup of tax-free tea. No English lover, he! For two years he lambasted English shipping on our coast, then began sailing out of France.

"His fight with the *Serapis* was his most famous. Louis XVI of France, our ally, had put him in command of the *Bonhomme Richard* and a squadron of French ships under jealous and near-mutinous French captains (an American-mon Dieu!). In the *Serapis* fight, the *Richard's* guns blew up at the first broadside.

"Then the *Serapis* drifted close enough for Jones to lash the two ships together. With the *Richard* on fire, Jones bawled his famous "I have not yet begun to fight!" defiance to a demand for surrender. Finally it was the *Serapis* that gave up, even though the *Richard* sank with the help of two broadsides fired into her by one of the jealous French captains.

"After the war we gave Jones a medal, but Russia hired him as a rear admiral in its Black Sea fleet where he served from 1788 to 1790. Even then the Russians were difficult, and he quit to live in Paris, where he died and was buried. Then, 113 years later, in 1905, the once-lost body of the former Russian admiral was returned to the United States for burial with honors at Annapolis."

Naval Order of the U. S.
An Overview

The Naval Commandery

4 July 1890 – 4 July 1893

Every organization is founded to address an unmet need. The Naval Order of the United States is no exception. On July 4, 1890 in Boston the first meeting of our Founders was held. It included three persons, namely Charles Calhoun Philbrook, Charles Frederick Bacon Philbrook, and Franklin Senter Frisbie. They are identified in the Record Book of the Massachusetts Commandery of the Naval Order of the United States Volume I as "interested in the naval arm of the service, and while citizens of Massachusetts were descended in the paternal line from New Hampshire families who had, since 1636, been identified with their occupation as mariners."

Hereditary societies were already in vogue and a mark of distinction. In the ensuing discussion, Charles F.B. Philbrook observed:

"I have many times been at a loss to understand why a Naval society hereditary in character and confined to the survivors and descendants of those who performed Naval service in wars or battles in which the United States Navy has participated, has never been organized.

"I believe that such an organization if correctly formed, would be a success as the Navy has many supporters, who would be interested in and eligible to such a society and would be glad to become members of it. Such a society composed of men who were survivors or descendants of those who, from 1775 to 1865 in times of war maintained the dignity of this government on the high seas, would have a great and commendable work in seeking to perpetuate the glorious achievements of the Navy and could demand the full justice and recognition due the same which has unquestionably been denied to a deplorable extent on many occasions."

Mr. Philbrook continued:

"There should be just a good field to work in though not so extensive perhaps, as there is for societies composed of descendants of soldiers of the Colonial and Revolutionary Wars and descendants of soldiers of the War of 1812, the Mexican and Civil War."

Thus it was that the following Agreement was drafted and signed by the three aforementioned gentlemen.

"We the undersigned, believing there to be strong reasons for the existence of a society composed of survivors and descendants of those who as officers, sailors, or marines performed service in any of the wars or in any battle in which the United States Navy has participated, hereby associate ourselves by the following articles of agreement as a temporary society (pending permanent establishment) (sic) to be known as the Naval Commandery of the United States of America."

The Articles are brief and speak for themselves:

"1. The name of this society shall be as above stated.

"2. The objects of the society shall be to perpetuate the glorious names and memories of the great Naval Commanders and their companion officers in arms and their subordinates; to collect and preserve documents and relics relating to the Navy and the men who have composed it; to promote the spirit of good fellowship among the members of the society.

"3. The membership shall be limited to male persons above the age of eighteen (18) years who have served or who is (sic) descended from one who served as an officer or enlisted man in any of the wars or in any battle in which the United States Navy or Marine Corps has participated or who served as above in connection with the Revenue or Privateer services.

"Gentlemen prominent in Military, Naval, or Civil affairs may be elected, provided that the number of members shall at no time exceed the ratio of one to five (1-5) (sic) active members.

"4. The officers of the society shall consist of a Commander, Recorder and Treasurer."

Mr. Philbrook continued:

"The Recorder considers it well to place on record the fact that in the organization of the Commandery as above the society enjoyed at least the following distinctive (sic) features:

"1. As the first society hereditary in character to recognize Naval service exclusively as qualifying for membership;

"2. As the first society to recognize service in all of the wars in which the United States participated from 1775 to 1865;

"3. As the first to recognize performance in the Wars with France and Tripoli."

The group set a date for the first annual meeting for the permanent organization; the agenda to include consideration of the proposed Constitution and election of permanent officers. The date chosen was November 10, 1890, the 115th anniversary of the organization of the United States Marine Corps. It was noted as such in the Minutes. This is the first specific mention of the fact that a meeting date was chosen because it had some specific historical significance.

On November 10 the Constitution Committee presented its report which was unanimously adopted. It is reproduced in its entirety here both as a matter of record and to demonstrate evidence of refinement in the various aspects of the society.

Constitution

ARTICLE I–NAME

"The name style and title of this Society is the Naval Commandery of the United States of America."

Commodore Jacob W. Miller, N. M. N. Y. Vice-Commander, New York Commandery, 1902-1906. Jacob Miller was instrumental in organizing the first Naval Militia in the State of New York. It is active to this day. Naval Militias were the source of much of navy manpower in war of 1812 and WW I. It preceded the U. S. Naval Reserve

ARTICLE II–OBJECTS

"The objects of the society (to be known as a Commandery) are to **perpetuate and transmit to posterity** (emphasis added) the glorious names and memories of the great commanders, their companion officers and their subordinates; to collect and preserve documents and relics relating to the Navy and the men who have composed it, and to promote the spirit of good fellowship among the members (to be known as Companions) (sic) of the Commandery."

The words "and to transmit to posterity" were added to Article II to ensure that the Order would not only collect and preserve but **it would publicize, communicate, and assume an advocacy** role for the naval forces. Subsequent correspondence makes it clear that the Founders were anxious to bring to the attention of the Executive Branch of our Government, of the Congress, and also of the American people what services mariners had performed and to solicit funding needed for the maritime services. Their frustration simply put, was that years after the Civil War ended, Congress was addressing the needs of the Grand Army of the Republic to the great detriment of the maritime arm.

In Article II also, we first find the members of the society identified as Companions. The wording appears in the third purpose to promote the spirit of good fellowship, a time honored objective at the core of Local Commandery Affairs to this day.

ARTICLE III–MEMBERSHIP

"Any male person above the age of 18 years who served, or who is descended from one who served as an officer or enlisted man in any of the wars or in any battle in which the United States Navy or Marine Corps has participated, or who served as above in the authorized Revenue or Privateer services, is eligible to membership in the Commandery.

"No person shall be elected to membership in the Commandery unless he is of good moral character and is endorsed by the Committee of Membership, after their careful investigation.

"The Commandery may elect to honorary membership, gentlemen prominent in Naval, Military, or Civil affairs, provided, however, that the number of honorary members shall at no time exceed the rate of one to five (1 to 5) (sic) active members.

"The total membership shall not exceed the number of forty unless the cooperation of the Commandery is desired by similar societies in the other states, in the matter of organization of a National Society or Commandery."

This Article III is an expansion from the original. While service eligibility criteria remain the same, the concept of Commandery right of refusal is introduced in the paragraph requiring good moral character and verification of that by the Commandery's Membership Committee.

Note also that from the onset the founders recognized the **need** and **potential** of a **society** of **national scope** (emphasis added).

ARTICLE IV–OFFICERS

"The officers of the Commandery shall be a Commander, Recorder, Treasurer, Chancellor and a Council consisting of four Companions of which Council the other officers shall be members ex officio."

The Council concept introduced here endures today at the Local Commandery and General Commandery levels (see Article V below).

ARTICLE V–MEETINGS

"The Commandery shall meet quarterly, as follows, November 10, February 22, June 19 and September 9.

"The (annual) (sic) meeting for the election of officers shall be the meeting of November 10, that being the anniversary of the organization of the Marine Corps (November 10, 1775).

"Companions attending the meetings shall on each occasion subscribe his (sic) proportion of the expenses of a quarterly dinner."

It is worth noting that the Founders were anxious to establish a routine which could easily be identified in the minds of the Companions. They chose **permanent dates of known naval significance** for the quarterly meetings and elections.

ARTICLE VI–COUNCIL

"The Council shall conduct the entire affairs of the Commandery and shall, from time to time, specify and announce the duties of the several officers of the Commandery."

ARTICLE VII–AMENDMENTS

"This Constitution shall not be amended unless notice to amend is mailed to each Companion at least one week before the meeting at which the said amendment is to be considered and then adopted by a majority vote."

Mr. Charles F.B. Philbrook closes the Minutes with this statement. "Interesting remarks relating to the Commandery, its objects and proposed line of work" were made by the Commander, Recorder and Treasurer, the three Founders. This brainstorming process was to become an integral part of future meetings.

One additional precedent was set, for the group then adjourned to the First Annual Dinner of the Commandery thereby implementing object #3 "to promote the spirit of good fellowship among the members of the society."

Quarterly meetings become the rule. Formal business of which advance notice was given was completed followed by election of new Companions. In some instances formal papers were presented; at other times informal discussion was entertained. The Recorder took pains to record the significance of the meeting date, e.g., June 9 1891 was the 27th anniversary of the battle between the USS *Kearsarge* and the Confederate Cruiser *"Alabama"* and also the 79th anniversary of the Declaration of War by the United States against Great Britain.

November 10, 1891 was an Annual Meeting, Here the next change to the Constitution was made adding a Vice Commander.

Charles Philbrook gave personal reminiscences of the expedition against Port Royal, S.C. and foundering of the transport steamer *Governor* and rescue of Marines on board of which he was one. Willson Elliot addressed the topic of privateers of the American Revolution.

Charter cruises were common as were visits to Historical Societies and Museums in nearby states, e.g., the yacht *Liberty* and the New Hampshire Historical Society.

Commander John C. Soley, U. S. N. Commander General, 1893-1895

The Annual Meeting of November 10, 1892 is of particular import for it was at this meeting that "The Recorder suggested the appointment of a Committee to **investigate** and report as to the advisability of extending the Commandery by the **organization of a** National or **General Commandery** and of other Commanderies throughout the States (emphasis added)."

The motion passed and a Committee of 3 headed by the Recorder was appointed.

On February 22, 1893 Recorder Philbrook reported that his Committee had met with a Committee from the Naval Legion of the United States (formerly Society of Naval Sons). The sum of thirty-five dollars was subscribed to cover whatever expenses the Committee might incur.

June 1, 1893 saw a Special Meeting of the Commandery at Tremont House in Boston. The Committee on organization reported meeting with representatives of the Naval Legion and the two were working out plans for a National Naval hereditary Society.

The proposed plan would provide for a General Commandery of the Naval Legion of the United States and in it, future State Commanderies which would have equal delegate representation.

The Constitution's statements of objects or purposes and rules of eligibility would closely parallel the Naval Commandery's own.

For purposes of orderly procedure the two groups resolved themselves into one Committee. Its chairman "out of courtesy to the Naval Legion" was the President of that Society; the Secretary was the Naval Commandery Recorder Charles F.B. Philbrook.

A convention to organize the new General Commandery was called for June 19, 1893 at the Armory of the Ancient and Honorable Artillery Company in the Faneuil Hall Building in Boston.

Recorder Philbrook reported that the Organization had even approached "a number of prominent Naval officers" who had agreed to accept nomination to the various offices. The

Naval Order of the United States

Founded 4 July 1890
MEMBERSHIP APPLICATION

Insignia # _____

Please print or type: _____

First Name	Full Middle Name	Last Name	Suffix

☐ Navy   ☐ NOAA

By:
- ☐ Personal
- ☐ Ancestral
- ☐ Spouse's

Commissioned and /or Enlisted service in the...

- ☐ Marine Corps
- ☐ Coast Guard
- ☐ US Maritime Service

- ☐ Public Health Service
- ☐ Allied Sea Services
- ☐ Associate

I was born in (community) _____ State _____ on _____

I/My ancestor/spouse was commissioned/enlisted on _____

And served on active duty from: _____ to _____

Now holding (or when discharged, if applicable) the rank/rate of: _____ with addl. specialty: _____
Off. Designator/NEC/Other

AND
- ☐ Am/Is still on active duty or
- ☐ Am/Is active in the reserve
- ☐ Am/Is in a retired status
- ☐ Was honorably discharged

Mailing Address: Street: _____ Apt # _____

City: _____ St. _____ ZIP+4 _____ - _____

Telephone
Home: ( ) _____ My Occupation: _____

Business: ( ) _____ Spouse's Name: _____

Fax: ( ) _____ E-Mail address: _____

Military applicants should complete the reverse side in detail, giving an account of military service, in ALL ARMED FORCES, both as ENLISTED and/or COMMISSIONED. Continuation sheets may be appended. Note: An appropriate military biography or record of assignments may be substituted as the "Record of Service", however, please note that ALL APPLICANTS MUST SIGN AND DATE THE DECLARATION ON THE REVERSE SIDE.

Registration Fee for New Members: $_____ 10.00
Membership Dues:
____ 1-Year................................$ 35.00 *
____ Student (Undergraduate)......$ 15.00
____ Life Member.....................$375.00 ** $_____
(*3 Year Payment Option:* $225.00[1st year], $100.00 [2nd & 3rd years] Total $425.00)
Total Enclosed: $_____
Make check payable to Naval Order of the United States or NOUS

* Regular Dues include a one year subscription to the Naval History Magazine
** Life Dues, when paid in full, includes a life subscription to the Naval History Magazine

---

(This section to be completed by the Local Commandery) *(please print or type)*
This applicant ☐ is   recommended for membership   PROPOSER_____
         ☐ is not   *(Please print/type AND sign your name)*

SECONDER_____
Dues and initial fees paid:_____, transmitted herewith to the General Commandery. The applicant was elected to the Naval Order of the United States through the _____ Commandery as of _____, 20____ The applicant requests primary affiliation with the _____ Commandery, and secondary affiliation(s) with the _____ Commandery(s).

_____
Local Commandery Commander or Representative

Naval Order Web Site: http://www.navalorder.org

Revised: 21 January 2001

Naval Order of the United States

Web Site: http://www.navalorder.org

RECORD OF SERVICE OF APPLICANT

(Complete both sides of this application)

Please Print or Type_____

| First Name | Full Middle Name | Last Name | Suffix |

(NOTE: : An appropriate military biography or record of assignments may be substituted as the "Record of Service"; continuation sheets may be appended)

SHIPS/STATIONS/UNITS Indicate under * whether A (active duty) or R (reserve duty)	*	INCLUSIVE DATES	DUTIES

ENGAGEMENTS AND CAMPAIGNS_____

_____

_____

CITATIONS AND DECORATIONS:_____

_____

OTHER EXPERIENCES AND PERTINENT DATA:_____

_____

_____

I DECLARE, upon honor, that the facts herein given by me are true to the best of my knowledge and belief, and that, if admitted to the Naval Order of the United States, I will observe the CONSTITUTION of this Order and endeavor to promote its purposes; and that I will support the Constitution of the United States of America.

Signed, this _____day of _____, 20

_____   Applicant _____

Application registered by the General Commandery:

INSIGNIA NUMBER _____   _____

DATE RECORDED_____   Registrar General

11

Naval Commandery accepted the report and agreed to attend in a body.

Before adjourning for dinner the Commandery inaugurated another tradition when it elected CAPT James Hooper of Baltimore, MD the only surviving Naval veteran of the War of 1812 to active membership "without financial obligation."

The Commandery set its next meeting, for July 4, 1893 to receive the report of the June 19 Convention meeting. They took trouble to note it would be the third anniversary of the organization of the Naval Commandery as well as the one hundred and seventeenth anniversary of the Declaration of Independence, again emphasizing the group's history purpose.

Faneuil Hall was the site of the July 4th meeting. The Organization Committee reported:

1. That a National or General Commandery had been organized on June 19th.

2. Provisional officers were elected pending a Special Congress to be held August 15th at which permanent officers would be elected;

3. The name chosen was General Commandery of the Naval Order of the United States in preference to Naval Legion of the United States.

The report was accepted to be followed immediately by a petition addressed to the General Commandery which requested that the Naval Commandery of the United States be "warranted, constituted and recognized by the General Commandery as the Massachusetts Commandery of the Naval Order of the United States."

The petition continues:

"The present Naval Order of the United States having derived its existence from a convention called by the society (i.e. the Naval Commandery of the U.S.) and the Naval Legion of the United States held on June 19th last, and as the last named society has since disbanded, the undersigned pray, that the petition will meet with the approval of the General Commandery."

This petition was formally presented to the General Commandery at the Special Congress, where it was granted on 15 August 1893.

Thus while the General Commandery as such dates its origin from the Congress of 19 June 1893 (the Order's first General Congress), the Naval Order and the Massachusetts Commandery share a common date of origin, 4 July 1890.

Membership

Our Founders provided that any male person above the age of eighteen years who either served himself, was still presently serving, or was descended from an officer or enlisted man who served in any of the wars which the U.S. Navy, Marine Corps, or Revenue or Privateer services was engaged was eligible for Regular membership. This was amended to include midshipmen as well.

Medal of Honor recipients constituting a special category (originally enlisted only) were admitted without fees. When Congress later extended MOH to officers too, and the Congressional Medal of Honor Society established, this special category was dropped.

Another amendment required that enlisted be subsequently commissioned although all current members were grandfathered in. Membership would evolve into three classes: Regular as described above with this category expanded to include U.S. citizens who served with an Allied force; Associate which was made up of citizens of Allies who served with U.S. forces. Both categories were limited to male personnel. In 1985 at the Williamsburg Congress Associate membership was opened also to spouses of Regular Companions.

Mrs. Patricia (Pat) Cucullu wife of CAPT Irwin Cucullu, then Resolutions Committee Chairman, was attending. During the lunch break her application was approved and she became the first Associate Life Member.

The third category, Honorary, was retained to accommodate persons of outstanding reputation not eligible for regular nor Associate status. The Congress specified that Honorary status was not to be offered to anyone eligible for Regular or Associate status. It was not a dues payment issue but rather the fact that only Regular and Associate Companions could become voting delegates or hold office.

On several occasions it was suggested that persons eligible by reason of lineal descent who were mostly civilians with no maritime military experience should be Associate not Regular members. On each such occasion the Congresses adamantly insisted that voting rights of these personnel must be safeguarded. This was the Founders' intent. Then in 1999 the National Capitol Commandery proposed that Regular membership with full voting rights be extended to enlisted personnel as well. The issue was tabled for one year to allow Local Commandery input and to allow an Ad Hoc Committee to research the matter. Minutes of Congresses and Council meetings and texts of all amendments to the Constitution were examined. No written reason for the earlier deletion was found in any of the Order's files. Therefore at the 2000 Annual Congress it was determined the issue was not one of extending but restoring eligibility and this was done.

Today, the Order also extends eligibility to cadets, midshipmen and ROTC students in their third and final year. A Posthumous membership was also enacted.

Companions may elect either annual pay or life payment. All persons seeking membership must submit a written application signed by two Companions. The application must include proof of eligibility. Official military records are either extracted or attached. In the early years, anyone not a commissioned officer was required to have the application notarized with seal affixed.

These applications are historical treasures because they are autobiographical, written in a straight forward manner. The applications, based on lineal descent, are particularly revealing. Individuals not only provide data about themselves, if eligible in their own right, but they will also attest eligibility based on service of ancestors, some going back four, five and six generations. They will also identify family histories, annals of various agencies, and state historical archives. To a genealogist the many leads are invaluable. In the hustle and bustle of today's pace, we frequently don't stop to record what future historians and descen-

dants might consider priceless and we ourselves are largely unaware of what our early companions did. See sample Certificate of Membership.

For the record, it must be stated that the Order is a "by invitation only" society, involving a dual status. Thus the applicant becomes a Companion of the Naval Order and an affiliate of one or more of its Local Commanderies. Just as the Founders sought persons of influence, so does the Order today. The Naval Commandery limited itself to a "select few," namely 40 members. Today the Order still seeks to attract persons of influence to assist in accomplishing its Mission, however, selectivity still exists as it has throughout the Order's history. Repeatedly we read in Minutes and Reports of successive Commanders General and Recorders General that while growth was desirable it must be based on quality not quantity.

The Naval Order Mission

"To encourage research and writing on naval and maritime subjects; preserve documents, portraits and other records of prominent figures, deeds and memories of our naval and maritime history; and through fellowship of our members advance the Naval Order's unselfish service and worthy aims for the security and enduring well-being of our country.

To foster, among all American Citizens, informed interest in the Navy, Marine Corps, Coast Guard and Merchant Marine, with the understanding that their efficiency is essential to national security and that readiness to make victory in war certain and speedy, will deter aggression and minimize dangers to world peace.-

General Commandery Governance

The Naval Order is administered nationally by the General Commandery through two "constituted bodies" established in the Naval Order CONSTITUTION: First of these is the General Congress which is the supreme governing body and final reviewing authority in all matters affecting the Order. It establishes policy, amends the Constitution, authorizes awards and insignia, establishes dues and fees, sets date and place of Annual Congress and elects National Officers. Its Chief Executive Officer is the Commander General.

All members in good standing have the privilege of the floor to speak on any matter under discussion at the Congress sessions. Voting privileges are exercised by three designated delegates (each having one vote), who must be present to cast the vote. No proxies are allowed.

In addition, each local Commandery is entitled to one vote for each fifty Companions. Past Commanders General in recognition of past services each have one personal vote if present.

At least 40% of the chartered local Commanderies must be represented. Further the total number of voting delegates must be at a minimum equal twice the number of Local Commanderies. The intent is obvious-to ensure a broaf base of consensus. When this is reported by the Credentials Chairperson, a quorum is declared and the Congress is ready to receive the reports of its National Officers, National

Committees, which are made up of voting delegates, and the reports of the Local Commanderies. Parliamentary procedure is in accordance with *Robert's Rules of Order (Newly Revised)*, designed by Colonel Robert to ensure the right of minority to be heard, and the vote of majority to prevail.

The second constituted body is the General Council. The Council is made up of some elected National Officers and four Companions at Large representing the Local Commanderies. It functions as an Executive Committee between Annual Congresses.

In lieu of a formal meeting the Council may use a telephone poll subject to a written ballot in confirmation. All Council actions must be affirmed by the next Annual Congress. This process has been utilized very well to expedite approval for and chartering of new Local Commanderies. The Council is also specifically charged with publishing a national newsletter to all Companions.

Provision also exists for the calling of a Special Congress. This was necessary in the early days when Congresses only met tri-annually and later bi-annually, due primarily for recognized need of Constitutional revision and establishment of additional National Officers to accommodate the Order's growth. 1940 was an off-year, so a Special Congress was called that year to commemorate the 50th anniversary of the Order's founding. A special 50th anniversary Roster was published: 9 Honorary, 10 Life, 331 Regular Companions for a total of 350. Planning for the 100th anniversary began several years in advance. 1990 was also an off-year, however, by this time the Congress was already set in an annual cycle, so the designation of Special Congress was changed to Centennial Congress.

The General Commandery through the Congress and Council has established its own distinctive Seal which will be found on all certificates and many awards, e.g. Certificate of Membership.

Both a large and a miniature Medal were designed by Bailey, Banks and Biddle, makers of military insignia. The obverse and reverse of the Order's Medal are reproduced on the covers of this book. Subsequently, a blazer patch, tie and rosette were authorized

General Commandery Initiatives

From its very inception, it was obvious that the three Founders of the Naval Commandery of the United States of America in Massachusetts had in mind an organization that would become national in scope.

They sought to educate the American public and the United States Congress concerning the accomplishments of Mariners in support of the original colonies and subsequently of the individual states and of the Federal Union.

In the early Colonial period ships were brought into service by the individual colonies by writs or letters of Marque employing privately owned vessels involved in the mercantile trade.

Just as Fulton's invention of the steam engine eclipsed the age of sail, so the appearance of the iron clads would signal the end of the wooden vessel. The machine age had now reached the maritime industry and this bustling young new nation needed the means of protecting its shores and commerce from foreign aggressors.

Even though the city of Boston was well known as a Maritime center, Massachusetts could not alone sway public opinion and the government. Persons sympathetic to this cause had to be located in other states and brought into this attempt to win funds to build and maintain a naval force capable of defending American interests adjacent to our shores and also capable of the same on the high seas or in foreign waters. The isolationism of the Monroe Doctrine was no longer tenable in the closing years of the 19th century. Yet federal funds were so concentrated on the Grand Army of the Republic and its triumph in 1865, that for some 30 years, it seemed as though the nation either forgot or never knew that decisive victory was only achieved by effective blockade of the Confederate ports.

When the Naval Commandery became a national organization in Boston in 1893, the lantern of Old North Church shone once again and led to the organization of state Commanderies in Pennsylvania, New York, District of Columbia, Illinois and California by 1899. Thanks to their work, funds finally began to flow for the new iron-clads, their machinery and weaponry.

With success comes opposition and criticism, in this instance from the Grand Army of the Republic veterans who from 1860 to 1895 got the lion's share. Conflict of interest was heard, i.e. persons on active duty cannot lobby the Congress. It is interesting to note that of the first 100 companions enrolled, 49 were descendants, 5 were honorary, and even of the 46 who were eligible by virtue of personal service almost all were retired. An examination of original applications for membership will verify that those holding elected office in the Order were indeed retired, but the men of the Order were made "of sterner stuff." Having succeeded in raising national awareness of maritime services rendered and present needs, they stepped forth with a new initiative. Based on what Herbert Satterlee had seen in Britain, 11 Naval Order Companions with the strong encouragement of Vice President Theodore Roosevelt, joined with six others including representatives of the New York Naval Militia and the U.S. Naval Academy Alumni Association to charter on 30 December 1902 the Navy League of the United States. Its membership excludes active duty personnel. Navy League has become the official lobbying voice of the sea services. The Naval Order therefore focuses on the historical aspects of our Mission. Here is the Resolution from the Navy League presented to the Naval Order on the occasion of its Centennial Congress held in San Francisco 4 July 1990.

"The Navy League of the United States Salutes The Naval Order of the US on its 100th Anniversary

"WHEREAS the Naval Order of the United States was founded July 4, 1890; and;

"WHEREAS following the turn of the century, the Naval Order of the United States, having seen the need for a volunteer civilian organization to both create a better understanding and awareness in the public of the vital need to maintain a strong Navy, assumed the major role in the founding of the Navy League of the United States; and;

"WHEREAS two thirds of the directors named in the Certificate of Incorporation of December 29, 1902 to serve until the first annual meeting were members of the Naval Order, now therefore

"Be it resolved that the Navy League of the United States in National Convention assembled June 4, 1990, salutes the Naval Order of the United States on the occasion of its 100th anniversary."

In Boston, Companion CAPT John C. Soley, the Order's first Commander General, and in New York Commodore Jacob W. Miller and CAPT Herbert L. Satterlee, also a Past Commander General, led the organization of the first two State Naval Militias. The movement rapidly spread such that when war was declared with Spain in 1898, fifteen states furnished 4,094 uniformed and trained naval militia officers, petty officers and junior enlisted men.

Subsequently, these organized militias became the nucleus of the Naval Reserve Force answering the call in 1917. World War I would also find the General Commandery in the foreground of support for Navy Clubs for active duty personnel.

Resolution Passed at Triennial Convention, November 14, 1922:

WHEREAS the Naval Order of the United States has always had at heart the welfare of the Country and the Navy, and the records show that it has in the past been of considerable public service; and believing that there was never a time when the Government needed more urgently the support of all patriotic citizens.

NOW THEREFORE BE IT RESOLVED that the Naval Order of the United States in Congress assembled in New York on the 14th day of November 1922, call upon the various State Commanderies of the Order, and upon all Companions individually, to do all in their power to support the Secretary of the Navy in his efforts to secure from Congress appropriations great enough to maintain the 5-5-3 ratio as between the United States, Great Britain, and Japan, both as to personnel and ships, and be it further

RESOLVED that the Naval order do everything within its power to combat all movements and propaganda directed against the integrity of our Government; and be it further

RESOLVED that a copy of this resolution be sent to the Secretary of the Navy.

Attest

JOHN CONSTABLE MOORE,

Recorder General

The booklet published by the Order in 1927 describes two major undertakings. First was the lead role taken by the Order to raise the funds needed to refurbish the USF Constitution. Witness the letter of solicitation.

In the same time frame $3,000 was raised to procure a Bronze Bust of Admiral David Farragut, hero of the Civil War and in particular of the Mobile Bay action which closed the last southern port still functioning. The bust rests today in the Hall of Fame at New York University.

Annex N. Protocol

The appropriate Naval Order insignia to be worn at any function is determined by the military uniform/civilian dress code prescribed and the organizations hosting the function.

A. Hosting organizations. Naval Order Insignia can be worn at functions hosted by

1. Any Naval Order group.

2. A Naval Order group and another paramilitary organization.

3. Another paramilitary organization.

4. The Navy Department, but only if acting in a official capacity representing the Naval Order, e.g. an award presentation.

B. Military uniform/civilian dress code

1. The **Miniature Cross** is worn on the left breast with the formal dress, dinner dress blue jacket, dinner dress white jacket, dinner dress blue, dinner dress white, and tropical dinner dress blue uniform; or with civilian formal white or black tie. Except: present and past Commanders General, National Officers, and Local Commandery Commanders wear the Large Cross with Neck Suspension Ribbon instead of Miniature.

2. The **Large Cross** is worn only with the full dress blue or full dress white uniforms. It is not used with civilian attire, except as noted above.

3. The **Campaign Ribbon** is worn only with service dress blue, service dress white or service dress Yankee.

4. The **Patch** is worn on civilian informal attire, either blazer or suit coat, never on a military uniform nor on formal civilian wear. Present and past Commanders General, National Officers, and Local Commandery Commanders wear the Patch with crown.

5. The **Tie** may be substituted for the Patch. Since both depict the Naval Order Cross, they are never worn at the same time.

6. The **Rosette** may be worn with civilian informal attire only, in lieu of the Patch or Tie; or it may be worn with the Tie; it is not, however, worn with the Patch.

Number of Medals to be worn	Prescribed Number of Rows	Number of Medals Per Row			
		Top Row	2nd Row	3rd Row	4th Row
1-5	1 row only	1-5			
6	2	3	3		
7	2	3	4		
8	2	4	4		
9	2	4	5		
10	2	5	5		
11	3	3	4	4	
12	3	4	4	4	
13	3	3	5	5	
14	3	4	5	5	
15	3	5	5	5	
16	4	4	4	4	4
and so on					

TABLE FOR WEARING LARGE OR MINIATURE MEDALS

WEARING OF LARGE MEDALS

Full Dress Blue
(Men)

Full Dress White
(Men - Officer &
CPO) (CPOs wear
collar insignia)

Full Dress White/Blue
(Women - Officer & CPO)

WEARING OF MINIATURE MEDALS

Dinner Dress Jacket
(Men)

Dinner Dress Blue
(Men)

Dinner Dress White
(Men - Officer &
CPO) (CPOs wear
collar insignia)

Dinner Dress
(Women)

Dinner Dress Jacket
(Women)

Jumper Style
(Men - E1-E5)

15

The United States Frigate Constitution: *This picture was printed on the back of the 1820 edition of Durand's narrative. It was engraved on wood and sterotypes were sold to printers by some New York type-founder. The present illustration is from a photograph of a type-founder's specimen, furnished by courtesy of the Typographic Library and Museum, Jersey City.*

U.S.S. Constitution

Launched 1797

"Old Ironsides", as she is familiarly and affectionately called, typifies the ideals of the Naval Order of the United States. She is the very embodiment of the best naval traditions–the victor in more single-ship sea fights than any ship of which we have authentic record. She was not only the flagship of squadrons, but the ship that whipped the Tripolitan pirates; first planted the American flag on foreign soil and captured in hard-fought battles the ships *Guerrierre, Java, Pictou, Cyane* and *Levant*. Gallant officers have trod her quarter-deck, brave Yankee sailors have swarmed up her shrouds, manned her halyards and braces and fought her canonades. She has made history, for she won America's independance on salt water. After her victories the unfamiliar flag of a young, loose-built Union of sparsely populated states floated on the seven seas, respected by the strongest nations of the world.

The Naval Order is pledgeed to aid in her reconditioning as a patriotic shrine for the inspiration of generations of American citizens.

Checks for contributions to the "Old Ironsides Fund" should be sent to the Treasurer General.

A spirited picture of the old battleship under full sail (in color, suitable for framing) will be mailed to every Companion who contributes one dollar or more.

Rear Admiral Philip Andrews, U.S.N., says of "Old Ironsides", "Her fighting record has never been equalled by any single ship of any navy in the world. She was almost a navy in herself and, like her own great name, the names of her Commanders are bound up with our early and hazardous national life."

Commodore William Bainbridge, U.S.N., who commanded "Old Ironsides" when she captured His British Majesty's man-of-war "Java" in the war of 1812, said of her in 1831, when she was badly in need of repairs–*"Her name is an inspiration. Not only do her deeds belong to our naval record, but she herself is possessed of a brave personality. In light weathers, in storm or hurricane, or amid the smoke of battle, she repsonded with alacrity and obedience, and seemed ever eager to answer the will of her commander. May the citizens of this country, in gratitude, see that she, like her namesake and prototype, will never be forgotten. Her commanders in the future, as in the past, will see to it that her flag shall never be lowered. She was conceived in patriotism, gloriously has she shown her valor. Let her depart in glory, if the fates so decree; but let her not sink and decay into oblivion."*

Annually on Pearl Harbor Day the Order places a wreath at the Tomb of the Unknowns in Arlington National Cemetery where it also has its own commemorative stone marker in tribute to our brother Mariners.

In 1991 at the Fort Lauderdale Annual Congress, two seminars of major import were conducted. The morning panel consisting of the top planners of the Maritime Administration, Navy, Marine Corps and Coast Guard Forces who designed the Persian Gulf strategy we commonly refer to as Desert Shield. In the afternoon the officers of the Maritime Administration, Navy, Marine Corps and Coast Guard charged with executing the plan, addressed Desert Storm implementation. The testimony of these officers is preserved in our files for future research and publication. Panels such as these have become annual highpoints of our Congress. Our Mission is not just to collect and preserve but also to disseminate.

Another major undertaking was support for the U.S. Navy Memorial in Washington DC where a Bronze Bas Relief was erected. The design chosen depicts the great White Fleet whose feat in the Pacific occurred shortly after the Order was established. See photos of the dedication ceremony in register section.

In 1994 on the occasion of the 50th anniversary of the landing on the Normandy beaches, through the efforts of the San Francisco Commandery, we were able to have a Naval Order recognition plaque placed aboard the SS *Jeremiah O'Brien*, the only World War II Liberty Ship surviving today. It is now a registered National Historical Landmark.

And when the Naval Order met in Annual Congress in Newport, Rhode Island in 1995, Companions first gathered in the armory of the Ancient and Honorable Artillery Company, commonly known as Faneuil Hall in Boston, where then Commander General William Bremer presented a plaque commemorating the historic meeting held there on Monday 19 Jun 1893 – the meeting? Why the establishment of the Naval Order of the United States, of course!

General Commandery Recognition/Awards

Our human experience is such that there lies innately in our make-up the capacity to recognize our own and others needs, and a willingness to take action required. This same ability applies to our organizations and other groups with which we are affiliated.

Just as we hold "no evil deed should go unpunished" so we believe "every good deed deserves a pat on the back or some form of thank you."

This applies equally to services to affiliated groups – for services rendered, recognition is due. Thus, the General Commandery has sponsored several internal awards, which are presented to Companions for service to the Order.

Initially, formal Resolutions of Appreciation were authorized by either the General Congress or the General Council.

In 1969 then Recorder General and later Commander General A. Fred Kempe would design an 11" x 14" scroll, multi-colored and hand painted, first on parchment and later heavy bond paper. It is entitled General Commandery Certificate of Appreciation, reserved for presentation by the Commander General to Companions "who have rendered outstanding and exceptional service to the Order." This design is presently under revision since procurement of the original item is not currently possible and its hand preparation a tedious process. It is anticipated a suitable computer designed product will replace it. See attached Douglas Award.

A second award, also a Certificate of Appreciation was designed in 1989. This certificate depicts the Order's Cross and ribbon in color with the seal of the Order in gold. It is intended for Local Commandery use, or for General Commandery use in lieu of a second General Commandery Certificate of Appreciation. See Sample.

Internal recognition may also take the form of specially designed awards. Companions rendering exemplary service have received Bronze Plates depicting the Order's Medal, desk clocks, wrist watches, distinctive plaques and most recently a medal designed by past Commander General William R. Bremer, USMC (Ret) consisted of the NOUS Medal on a bronze disc inscribed "commitment – service – excellence." See illustrations.

In addition to internal awards, the General Commandery also sponsors annually an external awards program.

Oldest of these is the United States Naval Academy Political Science Awards. Initially conceived and funded by the New York Commandery, these competitive awards are presented "to the midshipmen, who in competitive examination show the broadest knowledge of national and international political and military events." First place is choice of a USN or USMC sword or gold wristwatch. Second and third place receive a gold watch also. All three receive a small plaque bearing a 5-inch reproduction of the Order's seal and an engraved plate listing name, award and date.

The second oldest award is the Rear Admiral Thurston H. James Memorial Award established in 1965 in honor of the late Commander General T.H. James. The award, which consists of a 9x12 inch plaque bearing the Order's seal mounted onto a brass plate on which are etched the obverse and the reverse of the Order's Medal is presented annually to the outstanding graduate of the Naval Flight Officer (NFO) Program. A 12 x 15 inch wall plaque describing the award with seal and medals attached is maintained by the Chief of Naval Air Training, the award's co-sponsor. Individual small plates bearing the winners name are added annually. See presentation by Capt. Roy Williams of San Diego Commandery.

In 1989 in cooperation with superintendent of the United States Coast Guard Academy, the Order introduced an annual award entitled the U.S. Coast Guard Junior Officer Instructor Award "to recognize the personal, professional and academic leadership exhibited by a junior officer of the rotating faculty." Unique to this award is that cadets, as well as department heads, participate in the selection process. A personal and a wall plaque similar in format to the T.H. James plaques are given to the individual and the academy respectively.

In 1998 Captain John Brasel of New York Commandery proposed an annual award be given "to recognize the exemplary service of a senior flag officer of one of the Maritime Services, who is finishing a continuous career of active service." This is the Distinguished Sea Service Award inaugurated in 1990 and always presented at a formal ceremony, preferably at the Order's Annual Congress. See award and Admiral William J. Crowe Jr., USN (Ret) the first Honoree and list of succeeding recepients.

Distinguished Sea Service Award

Year	Recipient
1990	Admiral William James Crowe Jr., USN (Ret)
1991	General Alfred Mason Gray Jr., USMC (Ret)
1992	Admiral Paul Alexander Yost Jr., USCG (Ret)
1993	Admiral Carlisle Albert Herman Trost, USN (Ret)
1994	Vice Admiral John H. Fetterman Jr., USN (Ret)
1995	Admiral David E. Jeremiah, USN (Ret)
1996	General Walter E. Boomer, USMC (Ret)
1997	Admiral Stanley R. Arthur, USN (Ret)
1998	Admiral Leighton W. Smith, USN (Ret)
1999	Admiral Robert E. Kramek, USCG (Ret)
2000	Admiral Joseph W. Prueher, USN (Ret)
2001	General Anthony C. Zinni, USMC (Ret)

At the 2001 Annual Congress, Past Commander General RADM William F. Merlin, USCG (Ret), proposed the establishment of a new award to honor a United States citizen acting in a civilian capacity as a Senior Federal Government Official for unique achievements by that individual "based on exceptional insight, persistent effort and firm determination to continually advance the paramount interests of the United States and its Sea Services." This award is entitled The Admiral of the Navy George Dewey Award. The award consists of a 12 x 15 inch plaque with plate bearing the Naval Order Seal in the center flanked by obverse and reverse large Naval Order Crosses. Presentation is made at a formal ceremony preferably the Annual Congress. Past U.S. President George Bush was the first recipient.

Local Commandery Governance

At the first Special Congress, the Naval Commandery (the original group founded in 1890) petitioned the General Commandery to be recognized as the Massachusetts Commandery of the Naval Order of the United States. Petition was granted and the Massachusetts group continued as before.

But in 1894, a new wrinkle popped up. Interest had surfaced in and around Philadelphia to establish a State Commandery in Pennsylva-

Memorial plaque erected at Fanevil Hall to commemorate founding meeting site.

nia. The Constitution authorized the General Commandery to charter State Commanderies made up of a specific number of Companions, i.e. only Companions could petition for a charter, but the General Commandery could not admit eligible persons to membership, only a State Commandery could do that. Thus, Massachusetts was directed to admit certain eligible persons for membership on one day, for transfer as Founders of a new Commandery the next day!

In 1985 groups in New York and the District of Columbia presented their petitions. The General Commandery directed that the same procedure be followed, but by Pennsylvania which was closer, or did this have to be by Massachusetts since a precedent was already set? Wiser heads prevailed and eligible persons could be admitted by either Commandery "not later than___" since the chartering date was one day later. This would task Massachusetts and New York to hold unscheduled Committee and Council meetings to formally process the applications so action was taken at the next Triennial Congress whereby the General Commandery was also able to admit eligible persons. Eventually the authority to charter and also to admit was also given to the General Council.

The Naval Commandery had specified what officers the Commandery would have including makeup of its Council. Succeeding amendments detailed job descriptions for each office. One simple paragraph stated the General Commandery would have the same officers with same duties but extended scope. It was only in 1981 in a major overhaul authored by RADM Alban Weber, Past Commander General, that the Constitution described national officers and duties stating that Commanderies now designated by city vice state, i.e. Local Commanderies would be similarly structured.

Today the Local Commanderies are free to pursue interests identified by the membership. Local Commandery Programs require long range planning and early notification. San Francisco uses

a very thorough and efficient communication device – a simple postcard with a full year schedule. San Diego uses a large postcard detailing 6 months of schedule. Many others use a full page flyer. See insert in Register Section. Included here is a complete listing of all States or Local Commanderies and their chartering dates.

Commissioning Dates of Local Commanderies

Naval Commandery/	4 July 1890/
Massachusetts	15 August 1893
Pennsylvania	8 August 1894
New York *	22 September 1895
District Of Columbia	22 September 1895
Illinois	26 November 1895
California	1 November 1899
Aviation	29 May 1928
San Francisco *	4 July 1950
Southwest *	23 January 1952
Western New York	18 September 1952
Santa Barbara	18 May 1958
Washington, D.C.	1 February 1959
Illinois	1 July 1959
Colorado	15 August 1959
Seattle	10 November 1959
Arizona *	23 October 1973
National Capitol *	3 October 1979
New Orleans *	3 October 1979
Western New York *	3 October 1979
San Diego *	20 October 1981
Texas *	4 July 1986
Atlanta *	13 October 1986
Florida Keys *	21 May 1988
Long Beach *	7 December 1988
Southeast Florida *	9 April 1989
Massachusetts *	28 September 1989
Hampton Roads *	28 September 1989
Philadelphia - Del. Valley *	4 July 1990
Raleigh *	13 July 1991
New Mexico *	1 October 1992
Monterey	19 February 1995
Pensacola	February 1997
First Coast (Jacksonville)	7 December 1997
Annapolis *	20 July 1998

* Commanderies currently in commission

Sample Charters – The Constitution prescribed the exact wording of the charter. See New York and Illinois charter, the latter more elaborate. When the supply was exhausted an interim format was produced to be followed by a re-designed format. See samples in Register Section. This new format remains in use today.

Local Commandery Initiatives

The second paragraph of the <u>Preamble</u> to the Naval Order Constitution reads "It is well and fitting that the illustrious deeds of the great naval commanders, their Companion officers in arms and their subordinates in the wars of the United States should be forever honored and respected."

In keeping with this statement, the General Commandery has encouraged the local Commanderies to conduct suitable programs to memorialize major engagements in our nation's history.

Paramount among these memorials is the annual observance of <u>Pearl Harbor Day</u> or the anniversary of the December 7th attack in 1941. President Franklin Roosevelt's famous declaration to the nation that "This is a day that will live in infamy" will never be forgotten. It was and continues to be a rallying cry of the American people. Uppermost in our recollections must be the importance of ETERNAL VIGILANCE.

Observance is conducted by all Commanderies. The form of memorial varies with Local Commandery customs and interests. Most common is a memorial including music, wreath laying and one or more addresses on aspects of that day and subsequent naval engagements.

Illinois, for example, has a wreath laying ceremony at the site of the Eternal Flame Memorial in Daley Plaza. Texas uses the site of the USS *Texas* for its programs. Western New York uses Servicemen's Park where its ceremonies are conducted aboard the USS *Little Rock*. Cer-

emonies are held at Navy Landing in Woldenberg Park on the banks of the Mississippi River in downtown New Orleans.

Suffice to say where appropriate maritime facilities are made available and where possible these ceremonies are conducted in public to maximize impact and foster sustained understanding and patriotism. Parades made up of veterans, ROTC, active duty, and inactive duty personnel are out wearing the uniform with pride. Patriotic marches provide background, colors are presented, our National Anthem is sung with audience participation. At the close "God Bless America" will resound in the area.

Another common approach is an evening formal dinner, uniform preferred. This usually includes a guest speaker, and in many cases, is held under sponsorship jointly of the Local Commandery and other para-military groups. Again, see the Register Section.

While there were numerous naval battles and encounters in all waters of the earth including the numerous amphibious assaults, the Battle of Midway on 1 June 1942 stands out as the decisive engagement, the turning point of World War II, in the Pacific. Many of our fellow citizens do not realize that the emergence of naval air power made it possible for surface ships to engage in mortal combat-sight unseen. With the passing of time and research work, dedicated naval historians have caused renewed and well deserved but long overdue attention to Midway.

Another case in point is the Battle of Manila Bay on 1 June 1898, when the Commodore George Dewey surprised the Spanish fleet, captured the colony, without loss of single American life, and ended Spanish dominance in the Pacific. The grateful nation raised him to the rank of Admiral. He served as Commander of the New York Commandery and then Commander General from 1907 through 1917. Currently renewed awareness of the true significance of Dewey's contributions is dawning.

The writer some years ago visited the U.S. Library of Congress Archives section with then Historian General Russell Miller, one of the

Founders of the National Capitol Commandery. The Archives Index lists some 55 containers as Dewey documents. Knowing that Dewey's family had placed his awards, etc. there for safe keeping, we searched in vain for his Membership Certificate. The collection is most impressive among which Russ even found two 2 x 3 foot parchments highly adorned naming the admiral and his lady, Duke and Duchess of Manila! Turns out the awards were from the Land of Make Believe." The Admiral and Mrs. Dewey were honored guests at the Mardi Gras in New Orleans the year after his Manila feat. Rex, who rules the city of New Orleans on that one day, made the presentation at the formal ball. See copy of Invitation in Register Section – A Bit of Local Elasticity!

There are also programs under the aegis of other groups such as Toys for Tots, Blood Bank, medical research foundations i.e., the American Cancer Society, Heart Fund and Veterans programs which local Commanderies endorse and to which many donate in addition to cash, time, talent and support personnel.

Then there is another dimension to our Order. Article II of the Original Constitution of the Naval Commandery states in part ""The objects of the society…are…to promote the spirit of good fellowship among the members (to be known as Companions) (sic) of the Commandery." We have seen how this objective was implemented immediately with the "first Annual Dinner." This same social dimension was adopted for the quarterly meetings as well.

This practice became standard for all Commanderies whether they meet monthly, quarterly or annually. Both Dining In and Dining Out programs are conducted, golf tournaments, trips to dinner theater, seafood extravaganzas, cruises of various durations, trips to historical sights, lectures by historians, updates by U.S. Congressmen and our own active duty military are routine. Visits to NASA facilities, to military campuses, museums, hosting visiting ships are all commonplace. In truth, while

ever mindful of our history mission, it can be said that our gatherings are pleasant occasions for Companions and their guests. In sum, we meet, we greet, we eat.

Local Commandery Recognition/Awards

Just as each Local Commandery is free to establish its own traditions for its local affairs, so also it will design its own recognition and awards programs. Most common is use of the Certificate of Appreciation presented to guest speakers, and Commandery officers at the end of their terms.

Local circumstances, however, tend to warrant something more. In the early thirties, New York, the Order's 3rd oldest Commandery and longest in continuous active status, numbered among its Companions several who had personal dealings with the U.S. Naval Academy. They therefore established the awards program which today is under General Commandery auspices. Today New York sponsors the Rear Admiral Samuel Eliot Morison Award for Naval Literature in memory of the Admiral who was a Companion and is considered the country's leading naval historian of World War II. See the 1989 program cover commemorating the presentation of this award to Secretary of the Navy, The Honorable John F. Lehman, Jr. This award is presented at a formal dinner held annually.

The former Pennsylvania Commandery rejuvenated as the Philadelphia-Delaware Valley Commandery has two major awards: the Annual Admiral David Glasgow Farragut Award given in recognition of leadership, courage and gallantry above and beyond the call of duty and the CAPT Emile Louis Bonnot, USNR, Memorial Award for naval writing. See photo.

Captain Bonnot was formerly Historian General of the Order and a dedicated research historian in his own right. Having served during World War II in the Pacific Theater, he was keenly interested in its naval history, even to the point of challenging RADM Samuel E. Morison's account of the Battle of Savo Island.

Admiral William James Crowe, Jr., recipitent of the first Distinguished Sea Service Award.

Large Plaque.

19

Certificate of Appreciation
Presented to

in recognition of and appreciation
for outstanding service rendered the
Naval Order of the United States
Your inspired leadership and dedication
to the Mission and precepts of the Order
is in keeping with the finest traditions
of American patriotism and loyalty.
Presented this   day of

Morison's position was that the disaster suffered by the Americans there could have been averted if the two Australian Hudson planes which has sighted the movement of the Japanese fleet had followed orders to break radio silence and report the sightings. It was alleged they went on to complete the scheduled search mission with the result that the sightings were only reported after the aircraft returned to base *in toto* some eight hours after the first sightings.

Captain Bonnot working with friends and spouses of the disgraced pilots, after in-depth research, clears the two pilots of any wrong doing or negligence. Those interested might want to read the Bonnot Report entitled "Guadalcanal – The First Three Days" appearing in the January 1993 issue of *Guadalcanal Echoes,* the official quarterly publication of the Guadalcanal Campaign Veterans, PO Box 181, Coloma, MI 49038-0181. Copy will also be available soon through General Commandery Archives.

Several Commanderies also sponsor awards to outstanding NROTC midshipmen. Illinois sponsors three annually. A plaque and stipend is given to the top cadet in the three universities of the area. These awards were established by the then Illinois Commandery Companion CDR Maurice L. Horner Jr.

San Francisco sponsors two such awards similar in design to the national ones, i.e. a smaller plaque to the midshipman and a larger 15 x 18 wall plaque on which annual winners names are engraved. As is often the case, universities with long standing ROTC units have multiple awards so the NOUS award may be limited to a particular NROTC program. See the photo of the individual plaque presented at Tulane University to the top achiever in the Surface Warfare Program. Commanderies also sponsor recognition awards for cadets in the Junior Naval ROTC Program. Medals similar to the Order's own are awarded for years of service. Commanderies also sponsor essays on topics of naval interest sometimes limited exclusively to cadet of the N or MC JROTC, or are open to entire student body of schools having a JROTC Program as a recruiting device. Lastly,

space does not permit a detailed listing here of the many specialized awards, but photos of many are included among the pages of the *Register* section. Some are one of a kind designed to recognize the Maritime contributions of individuals and organizations. And, of course, this being an organization with strong emphasis on the social side, it is not unlikely that a Companion may be honored for her/his performance of one or more extraordinary feats surpassed in creativity only by the elasticity of the imaginations of the Honor Committee!

Future Initiatives

With some knowledge of how the Naval Order came into being and with a broad brush view of who we are; how we presently operate and what we do, the question arises "What lies ahead?"

Listed here are ideas the writer has acquired not just through research of our own records, but primarily from discussions with fellow Companions, some living, some deceased. The items are not listed in any order or priority, nor should they be viewed as solely General Commandery initiatives. Some can become Local Commandery efforts, others may more aptly be done by one or two Companions working in concert. As you read on, ask yourself what can I individually or my Commandery do to sponsor this project? Or some part of it? Here goes:

Our Mission includes collection of records of accomplishments of fellow Companions. The records of the General Commandery were placed in historical/research collections for safe-keeping usually located near the domicile of the successive incumbent Recorders General. It was only in the preparation for the Order's Centennial Congress of July 1990 that a concerted effort was made to collocate records from Boston, New York, Washington DC, Chicago and San Francisco. While many records thought to have been lost were uncovered in the "moleing" process; others still, if they exist, are buried in archives. The Order is establishing a permanent archive site at the Maritime Center of Excellence (MCE), a long Beach Maritime Foundation, where all General Commandery files will be maintained. Local Commanderies are invited to use the same repository, or one of their own choosing DO archive and DO leave a written record of where it is.

So ask yourself. Can you help collect and organize the Order's records.

Examples: Minutes of First Congress in 1893 thought to be in Massachusetts or in New Hampshire Archives; and records of Defunct Local Commanderies (see list under Local Commandery Governance). We need trackers to ferret things out. You will see that in the introduction of the *Register* section which follows this *Future Initiatives* section, there is still research needed. We have unassigned Insignia Numbers and names of persons thought to have been Companions, but no supporting data, i.e. applications. We need search done in Local Commandery Records, Register Books, Museums, Public Libraries.

Why do we want these? First of all this is our Mission, the accomplishments of our con-

temporaries and predecessors, remember? The final objective is to have as complete a file as possible. While the significance of the accumulated list in the *Register* section is of major import, it was and is only an intermediate step to the ultimate publication of a Register as designed in 1995 based on some 58 possible items gleaned from the original applications and supplemented by sources listed in the Register Intro.

How can you help?

Task I Take a look at your copy of your Original Application. Have your rank, Commandery affiliations, commands, experiences, list of awards earned changed? What maritime activities services have you rendered since joining? On active duty or in retired status? SHOULDN'T YOU CONSIDER UPDATING YOUR APPLICATION? The update will be filed with the original under your Insignia Number. If you've misplaced your original Application, your local Commandery should have it. If you changed affiliation either Commandery may have it.

The second aspect of collecting relates to Local Commandery files. Were you, are you an officer? Do you or others have document copies of which should be in your Local Commandery files?

Task II is to preserve and house original records. The oldest ones have seen the ravages of time and moisture. Sometimes they are beyond restoration. Because of this, efforts have been underway for some years to transcribe and authenticate working copies. These copies (also on diskette) will be used for actual research. Research librarians will tell you the best approach is to copy the originals which are then stored in fire and moisture proof environments. You will also be told to wear cotton gloves to prevent oil from the skin being absorbed by the document. Can you help your local Commandery to (a) copy its original documents, and (b) preserve those originals in fire proof hermetically sealed containers? Preservation is an urgent need.

Task III is a big one. We cannot be satisfied with collecting and preserving alone, we must disseminate! As the collected records were studied in the 1988-1990 time frame, Historian General Miller expressed the wish that we could publish an updated Register. None had been attempted since the 50th Anniversary Congress. Recorder General Lee Douglas, based on information then in hand, authored the Centennial Register of Companions 1890-1990.

The Thomas J. Lupo Foundation has agreed to underwrite the cost of preparing an in depth history of the Order's First 100 years. The "Commodore" was that impressed when he saw what had been amassed in 1989-90. The collection was stored in a bank vault accessible only to us. Work has been ongoing ever since: locate, collect, preserve and copy a working file.

The history is a detailed account replete with quotations from source documents, all of which will be identified by footnote entries. Not only will it lay out the History of the General Commandery, it will include also the History of each Local Commandery. The same outline used here will be followed:

A) Local Commandery Governance – 1) A copy of your charter and statement of location of the original, i.e., in the custody of the incumbent Commander or in some Historical Archive Facility; 2) Names of all charter members; 3) Lists of successive Commandery Officers.

B) Local Commandery Recognition/Awards. 1) Photo of the actual award; 2) History of the Award and its purpose; 3) Eligibility criteria; and 4) Recipients – photos of presentations along with consecutive list. Particularly needed are photographs of each Local Commandery Award itself, of award presentations and group shots of attendees at Commandery Evolutions. Please be certain to identify persons in the photos, date, location and occasion. Do not write on front or back of photo with a pen of any kind. The ink bleeds through. Use a separate tack-on sheet.

C) Local Initiatives – one-time and recurring. Please document. You may well have a great idea others can easily adopt and use. Incidentally, some Commanderies have adopted the practice of passing of the original charter from the retiring to the incoming Commandery Commander. It replaces the transfer of the gavel concept. A handout has also been developed to aid in identifying any accompanying photographs.

Then there are some instances in which very early members have no Application because they once belonged to a similar organization whose application design our Founders adopted. It appears that these folks wanted to recopy their App on the printed form which read Massachusetts Commandery, but unfortunately, being human they never got around to it. Right now we have a team of National Capitol Commandery volunteers researching those individuals in the genealogy section of the Library of Congress.

Presently under consideration is the issuance of a document printed and online detailing procedure steps for doing genealogy work.

Task 3. Recalling that we seek to honor our illustrious Companions, it seems appropriate to focus files on Medal of Honor Recipients this can be done by recording the text of their citations, perhaps one per issue of our NOUS Newsletter. We need help to identify all of them. This can be an individual or small team effort. Interested?

Task IV. Another desirable objective is living history – oral interviews with Companions themselves. When one reads early written applications, the value of first hand auto-biographical accounts is unmistakable. This is a virtually untouched arena of possible NOUS endeavor. In the mid-1980s it was suggested that Companions prepare taped bios which could then be used for a live one-on-one interview. Past Commander General Stan Majka immediately went to work on his and duly submitted it to then Recorder General Russ Miller. However, the tape carefully packed in Russ's bag was erased by the airport security system. Why detail this here? Because all was not lost, Stan Majka had a printed copy an extract of which appeared in the History Book. Advertisement. So What? Well, it was only when Stan's two sons read the brochure that they learned of this sensational occurrence in their father's life! How about you? What experiences have you encountered that would cause your kinfolk's breasts to swell up with pride?

Another venue totally in keeping with our purpose is looking carefully at the Applications of those eligible by descent. Remember these all require signature and seal of a notary. This writer has probably spent more time

in examining these records than any other Companion living today. It was stated earlier that some applicants traced their ancestry back three, four, five and even six generations. But just who were those ancestors? Why, Governors of States, signers of the Declaration of Independence, crew members of John Paul Jones to cite just a few. I venture to postulate that through these descendants, we have linkage to every maritime leader and patriot of the Revolution. It's a big order but good project perhaps for doctoral research dissertation.

Addressing dissemination, the ideal would be an accurate Register of all past and present Companions that can be continuously updated. Our options are to scan everything on diskette, or publish in a series or printed volumes. If funding can be found, both merit consideration

In this light, you are asked: Have you any contacts who can assist with funding or preparing requests for funding from private and public foundation sources?

One final example of what success you can have. When the original Pennsylvania Commandery became inactive, the General Commandery directed that all records be sent to the Recorder General, but this never happened. Were they lost? They were not in any other Depository we used. Well CDR Don Baker Organizer of the Philadelphia-Delaware Valley Commandery in 1990 found them safe and sound in the Pennsylvania Historical Society. Important? You bet, the accounts of the Monitor vs Merrimac and Monitor's coastal crises which are contained in this volume were found there!

My fellow Companions, the future is Now! Let's get on with it!

Register of Companions 1890 – 2002

Presented here is a chronological listing of all <u>known</u> Companions in Insignia Number Order. Sources used were: Original <u>Applications;</u> Official USCG, USMC, and USN <u>Retired Officer Registers:</u> <u>WHO WAS WHO IN AMERICA,</u> and its successor, <u>WHO'S WHO,</u> applicable <u>Correspondence,</u> and Historical Society <u>Archives.</u> Establishing and accurate total count is impeded by several factors. Initially Insignia Numbers were assigned in blocks to Local Commanderies, with local Recorders making actual number assignments to applicants. However, where numbers "ran out" a letter suffix was sometime used, e.g. 1421, and 1421A. Additionally 188 numbers are not known to have ever been assigned (we had previously tracked down 232 others from Sources indicated). Further 7 were cancelled because Applicant did not qualify – our Predecessors were diligent. Also identified were 168 duplications, i.e. Companion due to relocation acquired a second number. Finally there remain 435 names without numbers. Here then are our best efforts, especially those of Recorder General Lee W. Douglas. See last page for Commandery codes.

INSIG	COMPANION	RANK	CDRY
0001	PHILBROOK, CHARLES FEDRK BACON	MR	MAS
0002	PHILBROOK, CHARLES CALHOUN	MR	MAS
0003	FRISBIE, FRANKLIN SENTER	MR	MAS
0004	ELLIOTT, WILLSON CLOUGH	MR	MAS
0005	PHILBROOK, CLARK BACON	MR	MAS
0006	SENTER, GEORGE ALBERT	MR	MAS
0007	TAPPAN, CHARLES LANGDON	REV	MAS
0008	TARBELL, LUTHER LEWIS	MR	MAS
0009	BOWEN, GEORGE HENRY	MATE	MAS
0010	JAMES, GEORGE FRANK	MR	MAS
0011	BOWEN, HOSEA EMERY	MR	MAS
0012	CLAPP, FREDERICK WALTER	MR	MAS
0013	WEST, THEODORE PARKER	MR.	MAS
0014	PHILBROOK, ALFRED SPOONER	MR	MAS
0015	CLARK, ARTHUR WELLINGTON	DR	MAS
0016	BARBOUR, CHARLES JUSTIN	MR	MAS
0017	BARTLETT, EDWARD JOSIAH	MR	MAS
0018	WILLEY, WILLIAM LITHGOW	CAPT	MAS
0019	BEATTY, FRANKLIN THOMASON	MR	MAS
0020	NICHOLS, FRANK WILLIAM	LCDR	MAS
0021	CURRIER, JOSEPH HILTON ALLEN	MR	MAS
0022	HOOPER, JAMES, JR	MR	MAS
0023	SOLEY, JOHN CODMAN	CAPT	MAS
0024	WORDEN, JOHN LORIMER	RADM	MAS
0025	TAYLOR, HENRY CLAY	RADM	MAS
0026	ROE, FRANCIS ASBURY	RADM	MAS
0027	DEBLOIS, THOMAS AMORY	LT	MAS
0028	MASON, THEODORUS BAILY MYERS	LCDR	MAS
0029	LOWRY, HORATIO BERNARD	Maj.	DOC
0030	MILLER, JACOB WILLIAM	COMO	NYC
0031	THOMPSON, THEODORE STRONG	RADM	CAL
0032	PAUL, WILLIAM MELVILLE	LT	MAS
0033	CHURCHILL, THOMAS LORING	IAENG	MAS
0034	GATLEY, RICHARD KENT		MAS
0035	HARRIS, WILLIAM HERY	ADM	MAS
0036	MERRY, JOHN FAIRFIELD	RADM	MAS
0037	HARRINGTON, FRANCIS HENRY	Maj.	MAS
0038	SAVAGE, MINOT JUDSON	REV	NYC
0039	PISHON, HIRAM LEANDER	MR	MAS
0040	WARD, PRESCOTT TEMPLE	MR	MAS
0041	COLLAMORE, JOHN HOFFMAN	MR	MAS
0042	BLUNT, STANHOPE ENGLISH	Col.	MAS
0043	KELLEY, JAMES DOUGLAS JERROLD	CAPT	MAS
0044	MCCURLEY, FELIX (N)	CDR	PEN
0045	FARRAGUT, LOYALL (N)	1ST Lt	NYC
0046	HENRY, MORRIS HENRY	ASURG	MAS
0047	ROBINSON, FRANK TRACY	LT	MAS
0048	SHUBRICK, EDWARD RUTLEDGE	LT	PEN
0049	NICHOLS, HENRY KUHL	MR	PEN
0050	PERRY, WILLIAM STEVENS	REV	MAS
0051	WETMORE, WILLIAM BOERUM	Maj.	MAS
0052	WOODHULL, WILLIAM WATERS	PAY.I	PEN
0053	HUMPHREYS, FRANK LANDON	CDR	NYC
0054	MILLER, HENRY WILLIAM	CDR	MAS
0055	JONES, ROGER CATESBY	CAPT	CAL
0056	SIMS, CLIFFORD STANLEY	APAYM	MAS
0057	BICKFORD, JOHN FAIRFIELD	MMATE	MAS
0058	STEVENS, DANIEL DICKINSON	QMC	MAS
0059	WEBSTER, LEROY CHARLES	Capt	MAS
0060	CHAUNCEY, HENRY (N) JR.	Col	NYC
0061	WYLIE, GEORGE SANFORD	MR	NYC
0062	GALLOUPE, CHARLES WILLIAM	DR	MAS
0063	FRISBEE, OLIVER LIBBY	MR	MAS
0064	BELLAS, HENRY HOBART	CAPT	PEN
0065	JAMES, JOHN FARADAY	MR	MAS
0066	KEYES, ALEXANDER BROOKS	Maj.	MAS
0067	HEYL, EDWARD MILES	Col	PEN
0068	HEYL, CHARLES HEATH	CAPT	PEN
0069	TURNER, JAMES VARNUM PETER	MR	PEN
0070	PORTER, JONN BIDDLE	Col	PEN
0071	HOFF, WILLIAM BAINRIDGE	CAPT	PEN
0072	COLLUM, RICHARD STRADER	Maj	PEN
0073	HAYDEN, HORACE EDWIN	REV	PEN
0074	DILLARD, HENRY KUHL	MR	PEN
0075	MARSTON, JOHN (N)	MR	PEN
0076	TRENCHARD, EDWARD E.	MR	NYC
0077	BULLUS, WILLIAM ELLISON	MR	PEN
0078	HOFF, ARTHUR BAINBRIDGE	CDR	PEN
0079	DORCY, BEN HOLLADAY	LT	PEN
0080	DENIS, AUGUSTUS HENRY	MR	MAS
0081	MACOMB, DAVID BETTON	RADM	MAS
0082	SEAWARD, RICHARD HENRY	MR	MAS
0083	DAHLGREN, CHARLES BUNKER	MASTR	PEN
0084	FARQUAHAR, NORMAN VON HELDRICH	RADM	PEN
0085	FORSYTH, JAMES MC QUEEN	RADM	PEN
0086	FRAZER, REAH (N)	PAY.D	PEN
0087	HADDOCK, STANLEY BRICKET	MR	PEN
0088	POTTER, EDWARD EERG	COMO	PEN
0089	RICHARDS HENRY MELCIOR MUHNBRG	LT	PEN
0090	GILL, WILLIAM HARRISON	MR	PEN
0091	SEELY, HENRY BATES	CAPT	PEN
0092	WALKER, JOHN GRIMES	RADM	PEN
0093	MORRELL, EDWARD DEVEAUX	MR	PEN
0094	REITER, GEORGE COOK	RADM	PEN
0095	HART, ABRAHAM ELLIOTT	MR	MAS
0096	HOOKER, EDWARD (N)	CDR	MAS
0097	PARKER, MONTGOMERY DAVIS	1ST Lt	MAS
0098	RUSCHENBERGER, CHARLES WISTER	LT	PEN
0099	ROBINSON, LEWIS WOOD	RA	PEN
0100	BLEECKER, JONN VAN BENTHUYSEN	RA	MAS
0101	BINNEY, AMOS (N)	MR	MAS
0102	ALLEN, LOUIS JOSEPH	RADM	CAL
0103	LADNER, JAMES LAWRENCE	MR	PEN
0104	HENRY, HUGH HASTINGS	MR	MAS
0105	ROSS, HENRY SCHUYLER	CAPT	NYC
0106	LOYD, JOHN (N)	1AENG	NYC
0107	BULLUS, ALBERT (N)	MR	NYC
0108	COWIE, GEORGE (N) JR	CAPT	NYC

INSIG	COMPANION	RANK	CDRY	INSIG	COMPANION	RANK	CDRY
0109	EDSON, JARVIS BONESTEEL	3AENG	NYC	0184	LEUTZE, EUGENE HENRY COZZENS	RADM	ILL
0110	SALTER, WILLIAM TIBBITS	MR	NYC	0185	GREENE, LEVI RAWSON	1AENG	MAS
0111	LOW, PHILIP BURRIL	ENS	NYC	0186	FOSTER, FRANCIS ARTHORP	MR	MAS
0112	MONTGOMERY, JAMES MORTIMER	MR	NYC	0187	BURNS, CHARLES MARQUEDANT	PAYM	PEN
0113	DAVIDSON, MARSHALL TEN BROECK	CHENG	NYC	0188	BURNS, FRANK (N)	MR	PEN
0114	PARKER, JAMES (N)	LCDR	NYC	0189	FORNEY, JAMES (N)	BGEN	PEN
0115	REID, GEORGE CROGHAN	BGEN	DOC	0190	BREESE, EDWARD YARD	MR	PEN
0116	MELVILLE, GEORGE WALLACE	RADM	DOC	0191	MORRIS, HENRY (N)	DR	PEN
0117	PORTER, THEODORIC (N)	CDR	DOC	0192	WHARTON BENJAMIN		
0118	CADLE, HENRY (N)	MR	NYC		BRADFORD HARRIS	CHENG	NYC
0119	TILTON, MCLANE (N) JR	Lt Col	DOC	0193	ATKINS, JAMES (N)	1AENG	NYC
0120	DENNY, FRANK LEE	Col	DOC	0194	FORBES, CHARLES WILLIAM	3AENG	NYC
0121	COLAHAN, CHARLES ELWOOD	CDR	DOC	0195	PERKINS, GEORGE HAMILTON	COMMO	MAS
0122	LOCKWOOD, JOHN ALEXANDER	SURG	DOC	0196	HILL, FREDERIC STANHOPE	Vol Lt	MAS
0123	OLIVER, PAUL AMBROSE	BGEN	DOC	0197	CLITZ, RANDOLPH (N)	MR	NYC
0124	CRITCHELL, ROBERT SIDERFIN	MMATE	ILL	0198	HUBBARD, SOCRATES (N)	LCDR	NYC
0125	WAIT, HORATIO LOOMIS	PAYM	ILL	0199	GILLIS, JAMES HENRY	COMMO	NYC
0126	FRANKLIN, JOHN (N)	2AENG	ILL	0200	HIGBY, JOHN HENLEY	Lt Col	NYC
0127	SULLIVAN, JAMES JOSEPH	2AENG	ILL	0201	POST, ALFRED SETON	MATE	NYC
0128	PLATTENBERG, CYRUS BOSWORTH	ENS	ILL	0202	WRIGHT, EDEN (N)	MR	NYC
0129	DAMON, ORISON BENJAMIN	ASURG	ILL	0203	TAYLOR, EDWARD GRAHAM	MR	NYC
0130	STRONG, FRANK LEE	PAENG	ILL	0204	WOODS, GEORGE WORTH	MED.D	CAL
0131	ORR, WILLIAM LINDSAY	AENG	ILL	0205	LONGACRE, ORLEANS (N)	1ARENG	NYC
0132	HUBBARD, DANIEL BROOKS	ENS	ILL	0206	THOMPSON, ROBERT MEANS	MASTR	NYC
0133	POTTER, JAMES BOYD	LT	ILL	0207	DEWEY, GEORGE (N)	ADM	NYC
0134	STEADMAN, EDWARD MARSHALL SR	CDR	ILL	0208	GREENE, DAVID MAXSON	ENGR	NYC
0135	DAYTON, JAMES HENRY	RADM	ILL	0209	BUTLER, GEORGE HENRY	PASRG	NYC
0136	DECHERT, HENRY MARTYN	MR	PEN	0210	SKELDING, HENRY TITUS	PAYM	NYC
0137	ENGARD, ALBERT CORION	CHENG	PEN	0211	VINTON, CHARLES HARROD	DR	PEN
0138	FEASTER, JOSEPH (N)	NCONS	PEN	0212	CASE, DANIEL ROGER	MR	NYC
0139	FRIFFING, GEORGE H.	PAY.I	PEN	0213	TUCKER, PREBLE (N)	MR	NYC
0140	MACAULEY, CARTER NELSON BERKLEY	MR	PEN	0214	VANDERBILT, ARRON (N)	ENS	NYC
0141	CARNODY, JOHN RANDOLPH	PAYM	DOC	0215	BELL, WILLIAM HAYWOOD	APAYM	NYC
0142	LITTLE, WILLIAM MCCARTY	LT	MAS	0216	MORSE, JEROME EDWARD	LCDR	NYC
0143	HICKEY, JAMES BURKE	BGEN	NYC	0217	BOUGHTER, FRANCIS (N)	LT	PEN
0144	HYDE, JAMES NEVINS	PASRG	ILL	0218	COHEN, NEWCOMB HARRY RADCLIFF	LT	PEN
0145	CALLENDER, ELIOT (N)	ENS	ILL	0219	JOHNSON, MORTIMER LAWRENCE	RADM	MAS
0146	CALLENDER, JOSEPH ELIOT	MR	ILL	0220	PURDY, WARREN FREDERICK	ENS	ILL
0147	HUBBARD, LYMAN JOSIAH	MR	ILL	0221	FLOOD, SAMUEL DOUGLAS	ENS	ILL
0148	MORRIS, WILLIAM GABRIEL	MASTR	ILL	0222	STRATTON, SAMUEL WESLEY	LT	ILL
0149	MACDONOUGH, RODNEY (N)	MR	MAS	0223	KIMBALL, GRANVILLE (N)	PAENG	CAL
0150	PHILIP, JOHN WOODWARD	COMMO	MAS	0224	KNOWLES, CHARLES ROBERT	MASTR	NYC
0151	WILSON, THEODORE DELAVAN SR	NCONS	MAS	0225	SCHUYLER, MONTG'Y ROOSEVELT	MR	NYC
0152	POTTS, ROBERT (N)	RADM	MAS	0226	MCGOWAN, JOHN (N)	RADM	NYC
0153	ELDRIDGE, JOSHUA HAMBLIN	Vol Lt	MAS	0227	SMITH, GEORGE WILLIAMSON	CDR	NYC
0154	SCOFIELD, WALTER KEELER	RADM	PEN	0228	SCHLEY, WINFIELD SCOTT	RADM	NYC
0155	STAMM, WILLIAM SEAMAN	CHENG	PEN	0229	GLASSFORD, HENRY AUGUSTUS	Vol Lt	NYC
0156	REARICK, PETER A	RADM	PEN	0230	PHOENIX, LLOYD (N)	LT	NYC
0157	FRAZER, JAMES PATRIOT WILSON	MR	PEN	0231	THURSTON, ROBERT HENRY	1AENG	NYC
0158	LYON, HENRY WARE	RADM	MAS	0232	APGAR, ALLEN STODDARD	APAYM	NYC
0159	BELKNAP, GEORGE EUGENE	RADM	MAS	0233	STEBBINS, LEONARD C.	APAYM	NYC
0160	JORDAN, JOHN WOOLF	MR	PEN	0234	PRINCE, THOMAS CLAYTON	Lt Col	PEN
0161	KAISER, JULIUS ADAM	PAENG	PEN	0235	WILLIAMSON, JOHN DUNLAP	CHENG	PEN
0162	SLACK, CHARLES HENRY	1AENG	ILL	0236	WILLIAMSON, WILLIAM CORKEN	1AENG	PEN
0163	JONES, SAMUEL J.	SURG	ILL	0237	DEACON, HOWARD RIDGWAY	MR	PEN
0164	STEADMAN, EDWARD MARSHALL JR	MR	ILL	0238	THORNTON, JAMES BROWN	DR	MAS
0165	BARTON, WILLIAM HENRY	LCDR	PEN	0239	WISE, FREDERICK MAY	CDR	MAS
0166	DAHLGREN, JOHN ADOLPH	MR	PEN	0240	PECK, GEORGE (N)	MED.D	NYC
0167	JORDAN, WILLIAM MESERVE	MR	MAS	0241	TURNER, THOMAS JEFFERSON	MED.D	NYC
0168	EDSON, HERMAN ALDRICH	MR	NYC	0242	KELLOGG, WAINWRIGHT (N)	LCDR	NYC
0169	CROIN, CORNELIUS (N)	GUNNER	NYC	0243	ZEREGA, THEODORE CLINTON	LT	NYC
0170	BENJAMIN, PARK (N)	ENS	NYC	0244	TOBIN, JOHN ALBERT	PAENG	NYC
0171	WILSON, FRANK STEADMAN	MR	MAS	0245	SATTERLEE, HERBERT LIVINGSTON	CAPT	NYC
0172	EMANUEL, JONATHAN	CHENG	PEN	0246	SLOANE, ROBEFT SAGE	LT	NYC
0173	WINGATE, GEORGE E.	CDR	PEN	0247	CARTER, ERNEST (N)	PAYM	NYC
0174	JOY, WILLIAM FRANCIS	MR	MAS	0248	DIXON, ALBERT FIRMAN	CAPT	NYC
0175	CLAY, ANTHONY ALEXANDER	MR	PEN	0249	DUNCAN, WILLIAM BUTLER JR	CAPT	NYC
0176	MCMASTER, GILBERT TOTTEN	MR	PEN	0250	GREENE, SAMUEL DANA	LT	NYC
0177	SELFRIDGE, GEORGE SHEPLEY	CDR	MAS	0251	IVERSON, ANDREW JOHAN	CDR	MAS
0178	NEWLAND, WILLIAM DAVENPORT	MMATE	MAS	0252	HALL, MARTIN ELLSWORTH	CDR	MAS
0179	COLBY, HARRISON GRAY OTIS	RADM	MAS	0253	MCCLURG, WALTER AUDUBON	MED.D	PEN
0180	HOYT, LOWELL DALTON	MR	MAS	0254	RUSSELL, BENJAMIN REEVES	Lt Col	PEN
0181	OLIPHANT, ALEXANDER COULTER	Col	PEN	0255	BARNES, JOHN SANFORD	LCDR	NYC
0182	CHENERY, LEONARD (N)	LCDR	NYC	0256	MAYER, WILLIAM GODFREY	LT	NYC
0183	JAQUES, WILLIAM HENRY	LT	MAS	0257	COWLES, WILLIAM SHEFFIELD	RADM	NYC

INSIG	COMPANION	RANK	CDRY	INSIG	COMPANION	RANK	CDRY
0258	WELLING, RICHARD WARD GREENE	LT	NYC	0333	WISE, WILLIAM CLINTON	RADM	NYC
0259	ANDERSON, FRANK BARTOW	LT	CAL	0334	MCCAWLEY, CHARLES LAURIE	BGEN	NYC
0260	TRYON, JAMES RUFUS	RADM	NYC	0335	ASTON, RALPH (N)	RADM	NYC
0261	TOPPAN, FRANK WINSHIP	ENS	NYC	0336	HUNTINGTON, FRANKLIN BACHE	MR	NYC
0262	PLOTTS, REZEAU BROWN	CHENG	NYC	0337	BRAINE, LAWRENCE FULTON	MR	NYC
0263	DUANE, ALEXANDER (N)	LTJG	NYC	0338	EVANS, CHARLES (N)	LT	CAL
0264	WILSON, THEODOR DELAVAN JR	MR	NYC	0339	MAHAN, ALFRED THAYER	RADM	NYC
0265	WOOD, THOMAS CLARK	LT	NYC	0340	WILSON, JONN CLARK	CDR	NYC
0266	BEVINGTON, MARTIN (N)	LCDR	PEN	0341	BARTLETT, JOHN RUSSELL	RADM	NYC
0267	MICHLER, AMBROSE KIRTLAND	PAYM	PEN	0342	DENNY, ARTHUR BRIGGS	CAPT	MAS
0268	HARRISON, THOMAS SKELTON	PAYM	PEN	0343	MACKAY, WILLIAM ESHORNE	LT	MAS
0269	MACCONNELL, CHARLES JENKINS	RADM	NYC	0344	GHERARDI, BANCROFT (N)	RADM	NYC
0270	BATTLE, SAMUEL WESTRAY	SURG	NYC	0345	STOCKTON, CHARLES HERBERT	RADM	NYC
0271	RHOADES, HENRY ECKFORD	PAENG	NYC	0346	THOMAS, WILLIAM STURGIS	MED.D	NYC
0272	RIDGATE, THOMAS HOWE	LT	DOC	0347	WILSON, GEORGE (N)	APAYM	NYC
0273	CHENERY, LEONARD EDWIN	MR	CAL	0348	DAHLGREN, ERIC BERNARD	MR	NYC
0274	AMES, PELHAM WARREN	APAYM	CAL	0349	BAILEY, EDMUND SMITH	MR	NYC
0275	AMES, WORTHINGTON (N)	MR	CAL	0350	BRECK, EDWARD (N)	LCDR	MAS
0276	DAY, ARTHUR HERBERT	LT	NYC	0351	STEMBEL, ROGER NELSON	RADM	NYC
0277	SEBREE, URIEL (N)	RADM	CAL	0352	SELFRIDGE, THOMAS OLIVER	RADM	NYC
0278	WELCH, CHARLES PAINE	ENS	CAL	0353	RUHM, THOMAS FRANCIS	CDR	NYC
0279	ETTING, EMLEN POPE	APAYM	PEN	0354	BLAKEMAN, ALEXANDER NOEL	APAYM	NYC
0280	RUSSELL, ALEXANER WILSON JR	ENS	PEN	0355	POTTER, CHARLES (N)	MASTR	CAL
0281	MUCKLE, JOHN SEISER	LT	PEN	0356	MITCHELL, GEORGE JUSTICE	LT	CAL
0282	MIDDLEBROOK, LOUIS FRANK	ENS	NYC	0357	WHITING, WILLIAM HENRY	RADM	CAL
0283	MAYO, HENRY THOMAS	ADM	CAL	0358	LEFAVOR, FREDERIC HERBERT	LT	CAL
0284	TURNER, LOUIS HORATIO	LT	CAL	0359	SAMPSON, WILLIAM THOMAS	RADM	MAS
0285	GLASS, HENRY (N)	RADM	NYC	0360	ALLEN, GARDNER WELD	SURG	MAS
0286	STONE, GEORGE LORING PORTER	LT	CAL	0361	BRANTINGHAM, CHARLES HAWLEY	MASTR	NYC
0287	WALL, FRANCIS RICHARDSON	LT	CAL	0362	GREENE, GEORGE DEBOKETON	MR	NYC
0288	RAE, CHARLES WHITESIDE	RADM	CAL	0363	DIMOCK, WILLIAM DEWOLF	ENS	NYC
0289	PRINDLE, FRANKLIN COGSWELL	RADM	CAL	0364	WILLIAMS, WILLIAM HENRY H.	PAYM	NYC
0290	BAGG, CHARLES PERRY	SURG	CAL	0365	ARMS, FRANK THORNTON	RADM	NYC
0291	BURNETT, JEREMIAH CUTLER	LT	CAL	0366	BARRY, THOMAS GLOVER	MR	NYC
0292	HATHAWAY, WILLIAM RUSSELL	MR	CAL	0367	JOSEPHTHAL, LOUIS MAURICE L.	APAYM	NYC
0293	ISAACS, WALLER GILBERT	CHAPL	CAL	0368	ARMORY, EDWARD LINZEE	LCDR	NYC
0294	MORONG, JOHN CAMPBELL	CAPT	CAL	0369	CAMPBELL, NICHOLAS LAFAYETTE	PASRG	NYC
0295	MCNUTT, WILLIAM FLETCHER	ASURG	CAL	0370	YOUNG, LUCIEN (N)	RADM	NYC
0296	HOWARD, HORACE ZERAH	ENS	CAL	0371	MATTHEWS, JOSEPH HENRY	AENG	CAL
0297	JEWETT, HENRY E.	PAYM	CAL	0372	MONTAGUE, JAMES PETER	ENS	CAL
0298	DILL, ALBERT FREEMAN	ENS	CAL	0373	GRAY, HARRY PAUL	PAENG	CAL
0299	SMILTEN, CHARLES H.	ENS	CAL	0374	DRAKE, FRANKLIN JEREMIAH	RADM	CAL
0300	RAYNOLDS, EDWARD VILETTE	LT	NYC	0375	MCNUTT, MAXWELL (N)	DR	CAL
0301	GILLIS, IRVIN VAN GORDER	CDR	NYC	0376	HODGES, HARRY MARSH	CAPT	NYC
0302	ALLEN, EDWIN STANTON	MR	NYC	0377	MORRELL, HENRY	CDR	NYC
0303	TAYLOR, ALBERT OTIS	MASTR	NYC	0378	BARRY, EDWARD BUTTEVANT	RADM	NYC
0304	BALDWIN, LELOYD BYON	SURG	PEN	0379	SIMS, GARDINER CARLETON	CHENG	NYC
0305	MCFARLAND, WALTER MARTIN	CHENG	PEN	0380	INGERSOLL, ROYAL RODNEY	RADM	NYC
0306	SIMPSON, GEORGE WASHINGTON	PAY.I	PEN	0381	PLUME, JOSEPH WILLIAMS	MR	NYC
0307	CLAY, RANDOLPH (N)	MR	PEN	0382	SINGER, FREDERICK	RADM	NYC
0308	MILLER, JAMES (N)	JM	PEN	0383	FIELD, MAUNSELL BROADHURST	LT	NYC
0309	WELLS, WILLIAM STITELER	2AENG	NYC	0384	NORTH, JOSEPH WATSON	ENS	NYC
0310	POST, CHARLES ALFRED	CLRK	NYC	0385	STAYTON, WILLIAM HENRY	LT	NYC
0311	ROCKWELL, CHARLES HENRY	RADM	NYC	0386	EATON, CHARLES PHILLIPS	LT	NYC
0312	EDIE, JOHN RUFUS	LCDR	NYC	0387	HUGHES, EDWARD MERRITT	CDR	MAS
0313	CRAWFORD, MILLARD HENRY	SURG	NYC	0388	BUFFINTON, GEORGE ROBERT H.	LT	MAS
0314	LAMOTTE, HENRY (N)	PASRG	NYC	0389	POPE, PERCIVAL CLARENCE	BGEN	MAS
0315	HIGBEE, WILLIAM HOWELL	APAYM	NYC	0390	EDGAR, WILLIAM BORDEN	LT	MAS
0316	BARTON, GEORGE DEFOREST	PAYM	NYC	0391	BERNADOU, JOHN BAPTISTE	CDR	PEN
0317	SHACKFORD, WILLIAM GARDNER	ENS	NYC	0392	HANSCOM, JOHN FORSYTH	RADM	PEN
0318	SHACKFORD, CHAUNCEY (N)	CAPT	NYC	0393	CUTHBERT, MAYLAND (N)	2AENG	PEN
0319	HEYWOOD, CHARLES (N)	MGEN	NYC	0394	MILLER, FREDERICK AUGUSTUS	CDR	NYC
0320	WHIPPLE, NAPOLEON DANA	MR	NYC	0395	IRVING, WASHINGTON (N)	LT	CAL
0321	KENT, GEORGE EDWARD	CDR	NYC	0396	SCOTT, JOSEPH ALVAH	PAENG	CAL
0322	READ, JOHN (N)	APAYM	MAS	0397	WILDES, FRANK (N)	RADM	NYC
0323	BROWNSON, WILLARD HERBERT	RADM	NYC	0398	HIGGINSON, FRANCIS JOHN	MASTR	NYC
0324	WINSLOW, CAMERON MCRAE	RADM	NYC	0399	GAGER, EDWIN VLIE	MASTR	NYC
0325	JACKSON, ORTON PORTER	LT	NYC	0400	CHADWICK, FRENCH ENSOR	RADM	NYC
0326	MAGEE, GEORGE WILLIAM	CHENG	NYC	0401	ROOSEVELT, HENRY LATROBE	Lt Col	CAL
0327	HOSLEY, HARRY HIBBARD	CDR	NYC	0402	GETLIFFE, FREDRICK CHARLES	PAENG	CAL
0328	HARRIS, HENRY TUDOR BROWNELL	RADM	NYC	0403	COFFIN, RUFUS (N)	APAYM	MAS
0329	CHIDWICK, JOHN PATRICK	CHAPL	NYC	0404	STANTON, OSCAR FITZ ALAN	RADM	NYC
0330	TREADWELL, THOMAS CONRAD	Col	NYC	0405	UPSHUR, JOHN HENRY	RADM	NYC
0331	CURTIS, LLOYD WOLLEY	SURG	NYC	0406	HAMMATT, CHARLES HOWLAND	APAYM	NYC
0332	STAUFFER, DAVID MCNEELY	ENS	NYC	0407	ROANE, SAMUEL BERTRAND	AENG	NYC

INSIG	COMPANION	RANK	CDRY	INSIG	COMPANION	RANK	CDRY
0408	BARKER, ALBERT SMITH	RADM	NYC	0483	MACFARLANE, JAMES JR. (N)	LT	NYC
0409	ISHAM, CHARLES	MR	NYC	0484	MULDAUR, GEORGE BARTON	LTJG	NYC
0410	MCKEEVER, JAMES LAWRENCE	MR	NYC	0485	NEWCOMB, FRANK H.	CAPT	NYC
0411	MORGAN, JAMES HENRY	MR	NYC	0486	TOPPAN, JOHN DAVID	1AENG	NYC
0412	HALL, REYNOLD THOMAS	RADM	NYC	0487	WEST, CLIFFORD HARDY	RADM	NYC
0413	PEAR, CHARLES MERIAM	MR	MAS	0488	WORDEN, DANIEL S.	MR	NYC
0414	SUGHRUE, DANIEL HENRY	ENS	MAS	0489	DUBOIS, BARRON POTTER	PAYM	MAS
0415	STOTESBURY, LOUIS WILLIAM	MR	NYC	0490	WILDE, GEORGE FRANCIS FAXEN	RADM	MAS
0416	AVERILL, FREDERICK LAWTON	APAYM	NYC	0491	KUCHMEISTER, HERMAN WILLIAM	CPL	MAS
0417	PARSONS, WILLIAM DECATUR	MR	NYC	0492	GILBERT, DANIEL DUDLEY	ASURG	MAS
0418	HOWARD, ZERAH YATES	MR	CAL	0493	HASWELL, CHARLES H.	LT	NYC
0419	SYMONDS, FREDERICK MARTIN	RADM	ILL	0494	CHASMAR, JAMES HENRY	CHENG	NYC
0420	DAIGH, CHARLES A.	PAENG	ILL	0495	BARKER, EDWARD TOBY	APAYM	MAS
0421	GELM, GEORGE EARLE	LT	ILL	0496	BASSETT, THOMAS HENRY	2AENG	NYC
0422	TUTTLE, CHARLES W.	ENS	ILL	0497	HARRIS, IRA (N)	LCDR	NYC
0423	WILSON, WILLIAM JOSEPH	LT	ILL	0498	BARNETT, THOMAS G.	MR	NYC
0424	BRIGGS, WILLIAM CHURCHILL	MR	MAS	0499	LEVY, JEFFERSON MONROE	MR	NYC
0425	MACY, NELSON (N)	AENG	NYC	0500	PROCTOR, THOMAS REDFIELD	MR	NYC
0426	SAWYER, FRANK EZRA	CAPT	NYC	0501	WALKER, JOHN MCKEAN	MR	NYC
0427	WRIGHT, ROBERT KEMP	LCDR	NYC	0502	JENKINS, STEPHEN (N)	LT	NYC
0428	THORPE, GEORGE CYRUS	Col	NYC	0503	EDWARDS, WILLIAM DRESSER	AENG	CAL
0429	WADHAUS, ALBION VARETTE	CDR	NYC	0504	KNOWLES, CHARLES PLATT	DR	NYC
0430	STANTON, JOSIAH RUMBLE	PAY.D	CAL	0505	WARE, JOSPEH (N)	AENG	NYC
0431	PERKINS, CHARLES PLUMMER	COMO	ILL	0506	DRIPPS, WILLIAM A	2AENG	PEN
0432	HOWE, CHALES MELVILLE	ENGR	ILL	0507	PURDY, WILLIAM BOTTER	APAYM	NYC
0433	ROBINSON, EUGENE NUGENT	ENS	NYC	0508	RILEY, REUBEN (N)	2AENG	NYC
0434	NEWBERRY, TRUMAN HANDY	LCDR	NYC	0509	SLOANE, THOMAS DONALDSON	MR	NYC
0435	CHADWICK, FRANCIS LAIRD	LCDR	NYC	0510	KOTZSCHMAR, HERMANN JR (N)	RADM	NYC
0436	SHAW, THOMAS MONTAGUE	ENS	CAL	0511	LIND, ERIC G	LTJG	NYC
0437	COLLUM, JAMES WALTER	MR	PEN	0512	ROLLER, JOHN EMIL	CAPT	NYC
0438	POWELL, WILLIAM GLASGOW	Maj	PEN	0513	COHEN JACOB SOLIS SR	ASURG	PEN
0439	BRAINE, CLINTON ELGIN	MR	NYC	0514	MURPHY, PAUL ST. CLAIR	Col	PEN
0440	DUPE OF 0431 (CHARLES PLUMMER PERKINS)			0515	WILLIAMS, HARRISON (N)	MR	NYC
0441	ELLIOTT, WILLIAM HENRY	LT	ILL	0516	LEONARD, JOHN CALVIN	CDR	PEN
0442	DUPE OF 0432 (CHARLES MELVILLE HOWE)			0517	STOUT, GEORGE CLYMER	LT	PEN
0443	COOK, WILLIAM CROWELL	PAYM	NYC	0518	DILLARD, HENRY KUHL JR	DR	PEN
0444	MCGOWAN, JOHN PATRICK	SURG	NYC	0519	SMITH, JOHN ADDISON BAXTER	RADM	PEN
0445	TOWNSEND, GERARD BOSTWICK	LT	NYC	0520	FULMER, DAVID MATTHEYS	PAENG	PEN
0446	GIBBS, LUCIUS TUCKERMAN	AENG	NYC	0521	PRENTISS, NATHANIEL APPLETON	MR	NYC
0447	UNDERHILL, FREDERIC EDGAR	MR	NYC	0522	ADDICKS, WALTER ROBARTS	LT	NYC
0448	LEONARD, HENRY (N)	Lt Col	NYC	0523	BECKWITH, GEORGE ERNEST	LTJG	NYC
0449	KENDRICKEN, PAUL HENRY	2AENG	MAS	0524	PORTER, WILLIAM BOARDMAN	LTJG	NYC
0450	DANKER, ALBERT (N)	REV	MAS	0525	SMITH, WILLIAM A. F.	ENS	NYC
0451	MORONG, FREDERIC LINCOLN	MR	CAL	0526	PENDLETON, EDWIN CONWAY	RADM	PEN
0452	PLEADWELL, FRANK LESTER	CAPT	PEN	0527	THOMAS, JOSEPH H.	2AENG	PEN
0453	HUGHES, WALTER SCOTT	CAPT	CAL	0528	SMITH, JOHN ADDISON BAXTER, JR	PAYM	PEN
0454	ZANE, ABRAHAM VANHOY	RADM	PEN	0529	WILLIAMSON, JOHN DUNLAP JR	MR	PEN
0455	PERKINS, HAMILTON (N)	LT	MAS	0530	ABLE, AUGUSTUS HENRY	MR	PEN
0456	WINSLOW, GEORGE F.	RADM	MAS	0531	CLAGHORN, WILLIAM CRUMBY	MR	PEN
0457	RODGERS, FREDERICK (N)	RADM	NYC	0532	CHESSMAN, TIMOTHY MATLOCK	MR	NYC
0458	WEEKS, JOHN WINGATE	RADM	MAS	0533	WALKER, ISAAC HENRY	MR	NYC
0459	WILSON, THOMAS STANLY	MIDN	CAL	0534	MCILVANE, HENRY C. JR	MR	PEN
0460	KEMPFF, LOUIS (N)	RADM	CAL	0535	FAGAN, LOUIS ESTELL JR	MR	PEN
0461	PERRY, OLIVER HAZARD	MR	NYC	0536	MCELWELL, THOMAS A.	MR	PEN
0462	PARKER, CHARLES HAMILTON	LT	MAS	0537	COHEN, JACOB DASILVA SOLIS JR	MR	PEN
0463	BALL, RICHARD THOMASON MASON	PAY.I	CAL	0538	JONES, WALTER RYSAM	MR	NYC
0464	EAGLE, CLARENCE HENRY	MR	NYC	0539	CRAWFORD, ROBERFT (N)	CHENG	PEN
0465	COGHLAN, JOSEPH BULLOCK	RADM	NYC	0540	TAYLOR, ROBERT D.	CHENG	PEN
0466	CRONIN, WILLIAM PIGOTT	LCDR	NYC	0541	TULLY, HENRY RONALD	MR	PEN
0467	BROWN, FRANCIS KISSAM	MR	NYC	0542	KINGSBURY, JEROME (N)	Col	NYC
0468	HENRY, JAMES MALCOLM	MR	DOC	0543	SMITH, HENRY EAGLE	MR	PEN
0469	SMITH, REGINALD KNIGHT	SURG	CAL	0544	HOLSTEIN, OTTO (N)	MR	PEN
0470	JONES, GARDNER IRVING	CAPT	MAS	0545	RAYNOR, RUSSELL (N)	ENS	NYC
0471	BAILEY, THODORUS (N)	MR	NYC	0546	FRIELE, DANIEL E	ENS	CAL
0472	BATES, WILLIAM HENRY	PASRG	NYC	0547	MORRISON, GEORGE AUSTIN JR	MR	NYC
0473	COYE, CHARLES SIBLEY	Vol Lt	NYC	0548	KING, GUY (N)	MR	PEN
0474	COOPER, PHILIP HENRY	RADM	NYC	0549	PRATT, WILLIAM HENRY	PAENG	PEN
0475	HOWISON, HENRY LYCURGUS	RADM	NYC	0550	PENHALLOW, THOMAS W.		MAS
0476	WALKER, THOMAS DIXON	MMATE	NYC	0551	TARBELL, ARTHUR P	MR	MAS
0477	BROWN, GEORGE WASHINGTON (#1)	Vol Lt	NYC	0552	KENDRICKEN, JOHN MARTIN	MR	MAS
0478	BULKLEY, ERASTUS BRAINERD	MR	NYC	0553	CANDLER, DUNCAN (N)	MR	NYC
0479	COLBY, ARTHUR H.	PAPAY	NYC	0554	PERRY, JOHN MOORE	MR	NYC
0480	CORNWELL, FRANK STANLEY	LT	NYC	0555	TERHUNE, TEN BROECK MONROE	MR	NYC
0481	HEMPHILL, JOSEPH NEWTON	RADM	NYC	0556	ADAE, CHARLES FLAMERO	PAY.I	NYC
0482	DUPE OF 0143 (JAMES BURKE HICKEY, JR)			0557	GILBERT, WILLIAM MORRIS JR	ENS	NYC

25

INSIG	COMPANION	RANK	CDRY	INSIG	COMPANION	RANK	CDRY
0558	COHEN, ISIDOR SOLIS JR	SK3	PEN	0633	HALL, ALEXNADER MITCHELL 2ND.	LT	NYC
0559	PALMER, WILLIAM HENRY	LT	NYC	0634	POGGI, RICHARD HARRISON	LT	NYC
0560	BROOKS, EDWIN C	3AENG	MAS	0635	MCCLOY, JOHN (N)	LT	NYC
0561	DERBY, WILLIAM MINER	LT	PEN	0636	COX, STANLEY MIRICK	CDR	NYC
0562	NAILE, FREDERICK RAYMONDE	CAPT	PEN	0637	FRY, GEORGE GARDINER	CDR	NYC
0563	SHIRLEY, RUFUS GEORGE	MR	NYC	0638	HAWKS, WELLS (N)	LCDR	NYC
0564	KNEASS, EDWARDS (N)	LTJG	PEN	0639	DUPE OF 0336 (FRANKLIN BACHE HUNTINGTON)		
0565	LUCE, STEPHEN BLEECKER JR	LTJG	MAS	0640	RAYMOND, JOHN WILLIAM	MR	NYC
0566	HOGAN, REGINALD ROCKWOOD	Maj	PEN	0641	FISHER, MILTON MARSHALL	LTJG	NYC
0567	ODIORNE, WALTER JONES	MR	PEN	0642	SIMONPIETRI, WILLIAM LUCIUS F.	CAPT	NYC
0568	ROBINSON, DEWITT C	MR	PEN	0643	HENDRICKS, HENRY S.	ENS	NYC
0569	BURKHARDT, WALTER MILLER	LTJG	PEN	0644	WINN, JOHN GREELEY	CDR	NYC
0570	AUSTIN, HENRY SLOAN	LT	PEN	0645	BELDON, JOSEPH WILLARD	ENS	NYC
0571	WASHBURN, GEORGE HITTINGER	LT	MAS	0646	POST, CHARLES KINTZING	CDR	NYC
0572	ALKER, JAMES WARD	LTJG	NYC	0647	JACKSON, JAMES ADELBURT	CAPT	NYC
0573	CHESTER, ARTHUR TREMAINE	LCDR	NYC	0648	SCHERMERHORN, ARTHUR F.	MR	NYC
0574	STEPHENSON, GRANT THOMAS	LT	NYC	0649	JONES, FREDERICK WILLIAM	CAPT	MAS
0575	MONTGOMERY, JOHN SEYMOUR	ENS	NYC	0650	THEBAUD, PAUL GILBERT	MR	NYC
0576	MASTICK, SEABURY CONE	LCDR	NYC	0651	BRUMMER, HAROLD MAX	ENS	NYC
0577	PHELPS, JOHN JAY	LT	NYC	0652	JUNKIN, GEORGE (N)	ENS	NYC
0578	MOORE, JOHN CONSTABLE	LTJG	NYC	0653	DUANE, ROBERT LIVINGSTON	Maj	NYC
0579	EDSON, MARMOUNT (N)	MR	NYC	0654	GALOW, AUGUST HENRY	ENS	NYC
0580	FLAGG, MONTAGUE (N)	LTJG	NYC	0655	BERRY, JOHN GIVEEN	CDR	NYC
0581	FISK, HARVEY EDWARD JR.	ENS	NYC	0656	DUPE OF 0177(GEORGE SHEPLEY SELFRIDGE)		
0582	FISK, KENNETH (N)	LTJG	NYC	0657	PARKER, JAMES PHILLIPS	CAPT	MAS
0583	PHILLIPS, ROBERT (N)	CDR	NYC	0658	MOFFAT, ROBERT TUCKER	LT	MAS
0584	TOVELL, JOSEPH WILBUR	ENS	NYC	0659	DRAPER, ERNEST GALLAUDET	LT	NYC
0585	MORGAN, JUNIUS SPENCER JR.	LT	NYC	0660	BELKNAP, REGINALD ROWAN	RADM	NYC
0586	TAINTOR, STARR (N)	CDR	NYC	0661	KIMBALL, CLEVELAND CADY	CDR	NYC
0587	BURROUGH, LEWIS FAIRBROTHER	LT	NYC	0662	WISEMAN, LAWRENCE (N)	ENS	NYC
0588	MOORE, THEODORE CLEMENT	MR	NYC	0663	ELDRIDGE, DAVID GORHAM	CDR	MAS
0589	HANN, CHARLES JR. (N)	CDR	NYC	0664	ADAMS, PORTER H.	LCDR	MAS
0590	LORILLARD, GRISWOLD (N)	ENS	NYC	0665	HUBBARD, GORHAM (N)	LT	MAS
0591	MOYES, WINCHESTER (N)	CDR	NYC	0666	WILBUR, CURTIS DWIGHT	HONOR	
0592	CARR, ELMENDORF LESTER	ENS	NYC	0667	MCLEAN, NORMAN THOMAS	CAPT	NYC
0593	TERRELL, HEGE DOUD	LT	NYC	0668	SULLIVAN, J. DELEON	LT	NYC
0594	BURGOYNE, WILLIAM WALLING	LT	NYC	0669	EPPLEY, MARION (N)	CAPT	NYC
0595	MATHEWS, CLARENCE HERBERT	CDR	NYC	0670	STOKES, WILLIAM EARL DODGE JR.	LCDR	NYC
0596	PATTEN, WILLIAM HENRY	LCDR	NYC	0671	DUPE OF 0329(JOHN PATRICK CHIDWICK)		
0597	MAN, ELLERY ANDERSON	LTJG	NYC	0672	BARR, MICHAEL PHILLIP	LT	NYC
0598	STRAND, ERNEST GORDON	LT	NYC	0673	HEARN, CORNELIUS (N), JR.	LTJG	NYC
0599	CONDON, RICHARD (N)	LCDR	NYC	0674	LASPIA, JOHN (N)	LTJG	NYC
0600	GOELLER, FREDERICK WILLIAM JR.	LT	NYC	0675	DILLON, EDWARD J. JR.	LT	NYC
0601	STOKER, FLOYD WATROUS	LT	NYC	0676	HUGHES, GEORGE W. R.	LTJG	NYC
0602	MARCEAU, THEODORE JR.	LTJG	NYC	0677	MADEIRA, DASHIELL LIVINGSTON	RADM	NYC
0603	BARNEY, WILLIAM JOSHUA	MR	NYC	0678	SESSELBERG, ARHTUR WALTERS	CAPT	NYC
0604	BRADY, JOHN WILLIAM	CAPT	NYC	0679	HAMMOND, STEPHEN HOWLAND	LTJG	NYC
0605	DEAN, GERALD JACKSON	ENS	NYC	0680	MORAN, EUGENE FRANCIS	COMMO	NYC
0606	HAFFENDEN, CHARLES RADCLIFFE	LT	NYC	0681	MCEWAN, HENRY D.	MR	PEN
0607	HUNTINGTON, JOHN CALDWELL	CAPT	NYC	0682	CLAGHORN, STUART (N)	MR	PEN
0608	KNAUER, RANSOM LEONARD	LT	NYC	0683	DUPE OF 0078(ARTHUR BAINBRIDGE HOFF)		
0609	BAYNE, CARROLL S.	LT	NYC	0684	SWINBURNE, WILLIAM THOMAS	ADM	NYC
0610	LEE, GERALD ALBERT	LTJG	NYC	0685	JESSOP, EARL PERCY	CAPT	NYC
0611	MASON, CHARLES ALONSO	CDR	NYC	0686	DAVIS, JOHN F. A.	CDR	MAS
0612	MOORE, CLARENCE AMBROSE	LCDR	NYC	0687	MONTGOMERY, ROBERT LANGFORD	LTJG	NYC
0613	PELL, HOWLAND HAGGERTY	LCDR	NYC	0688	PERRY, FRNCIS WILLIAM	Col	NYC
0614	RABBAGE, LEWIS HENRY	CAPT	NYC	0689	HAINES, JOHN ALLEN	LCDR	NYC
0615	ROMAINE, RALPH BENJAMIN	LCDR	NYC	0690	BAINBRIDGE, WILLIAM SEAMAN	CAPT	NYC
0616	SAWYER, WARREN LOCKHART	LCDR	NYC	0691	BROOMALL, WILLIAM BOOTH JR.	MR	NYC
0617	YARD, RAYMOND CARTER	LT	NYC	0692	MITCHELL, FREDERIC MASON	MR	MAS
0618	MILLER, ROSWELL (N)	ENS	NYC	0693	SCOTT, ANDREW (N) JR.	ENS	NYC
0619	ROOT, CHARLES STEVENS	CAPT	NYC	0694	PELL, HOWLAND HAGGERTY JR.	MR	NYC
0620	FOUNTAIN, EUGENE JAMES	ENS	NYC	0695	RIDDLE, TRUMAN POST	CDR	NYC
0621	BIEL, WILLIAM (N)	ENS	NYC	0696	FROST, AARON V.	LT	NYC
0622	HAMMOND, PAUL LYMAN	CAPT	NYC	0697	GARRISON, DANIEL MERSHON	CAPT	NYC
0623	MARSDEN, CHRISTOPHER (N)	LCDR	NYC	0698	WHEAT, GEORGE SEAY	LT	NYC
0624	ASTOR, WILLIAM VINCENT	LCDR	NYC	0699	OREILLY, PETER S.	LT	NYC
0625	BOONE, CHARLES (N)	CAPT	NYC	0700	STRASSBURGER, RALPH BEAVER	LT	NYC
0626	WISE, ALFRED LEO	ENS	NYC	0701	BOYD, WILLIAM HENRY	LCDR	NYC
0627	MEYER, ROBERT BENSEN	LTJG	NYC	0702	HUNTLEY, EDWARD S.	ENS	NYC
0628	STAVEY, ERNEST (N)	LT	NYC	0703	HUGER, DANIEL ELLIOTT	LCDR	AVN
0629	ROOSEVELT, ROBERT B.	LT	NYC	0704	WILLARD, EUGENE SANDS	LTJG	NYC
0630	BURBANK, JAMES ARCHER	LT	NYC	0705	TOD, ROBERT E.	CDR	NYC
0631	REIMER, AUGUSTUS CHARLES	CDR3	NYC	0706	MCDONNELL, EDWARD ORRICK	RADM	AVN
0632	BASSETT, PRENTISS PECK	CDR	NYC	0707	GATES, ARTEMUS L.	LCDR	AVN

INSIG	COMPANION	RANK	CDRY	INSIG	COMPANION	RANK	CDRY
0708	TAYLOR, JAMES BLACKSTONE JR.	LTJG	AVN	0783	BRISTOL, LEE HASTINGS	ENS	AVN
0709	DWYER, MARTIN JOSEPH JR.	LTJG	AVN	0784	BROWNE, HAROLD J.	ENS	AVN
0710	BIGGS, JAMES ROY	LTJG	AVN	0785	BRUSH, MILTIMORE WITHERELL	CAPT	AVN
0711	KING, FREDERICK ELMER	LTJG	AVN	0786	CLAYTON, HENRY COMYN	LT	AVN
0712	LANGE, KARL LINWOOD	RADM	AVN	0787	COOMBE, REGINALD GASTON	LT	AVN
0713	BIZZELL, CASEY KINCHEN	ENS	AVN	0788	DALRYMPLE, FITZWILLIAM (N)	LTJG	AVN
0714	BERTINE, EDWIN KELLOGG	CDR	AVN	0789	DAVISON, FREDERICK TRUBEE	LTJG	AVN
0715	POST, GEORGE B.	LCDR	AVN	0790	DAVISON, HENRY POMEROY	LT	AVN
0716	WHITNEY, PAUL LEBROCQUE	ENS	AVN	0791	DEMONET, GREGORY FAURE	CDR	AVN
0717	BRYAN, WALTER CHARLES	LT	AVN	0792	DONNELLY, THORNE (N)	LT	AVN
0718	NORDHOUSE, STERLING MORTON	CDR	AVN	0793	DOUGLAS, GILBERT WILSON	LTJG	AVN
0719	INGALLS, DAVID SINTON	RADM	AVN	0794	ELMER, ROBERT EMMETT P.	LCDR	AVN
0720	DRISCOLL, LEON FRANCIS	1ST Lt	AVN	0795	FALVEY, WALLACE (N)	LTJG	AVN
0721	SWEETSER, GEORGE THEODORE	ENS	AVN	0796	FARWELL, JOHN V. 3RD	LTJG	AVN
0722	ROGERS, WILLIAM ANDERSON	LCDR	AVN	0797	GARRETT, ROBERT M.	ENS	AVN
0723	GIBBONS, DOUGLAS (N)	LCDR	NYC	0798	GEST, JOSEPH HEYWOOD	LCDR	AVN
0724	SAUNDERS, GEORGE AUGUSTUS	LCDR	NYC	0799	GOULD, ERL CLINTON BAKER	RADM	AVN
0725	DOLAN, RICHARD VINCENT	CAPT	NYC	0800	GUGGENHEIM, HARRY FRANK	CAPT	AVN
0726	FITZGERALD, EDWARD THOMAS	LT	NYC	0801	HAHN, FREDRICK HALSTED	LTJG	AVN
0727	DOMINICK, GAYER GARDNER	LT	NYC	0802	HARDER, HUBERT (N)	ENS	AVN
0728	HARVEY, CHARLES WESLEY	ENS	NYC	0803	HAWKINS, ASHTON W.	LT	AVN
0729	HARRINGTON, WILSON HEMPFIELD	CAPT	NYC	0804	HENRY, CHARLES THOMAS	ENS	AVN
0730	WOODHOUSE, HARTLAND (N)	ENS	NYC	0805	HEWLETT, JAMES AUGUSTUS	ENS	AVN
0731	LEE, ROBERT CORWIN	COMMO	NYC	0806	HOLLOWAY, THOMAS FORSYTHE	ENS	AVN
0732	ELLSBERG, EDWARD (N)	RADM	NYC	0807	HOLTHAM, EARL A.	ENS	AVN
0733	GUNDLACH, F. KENNETH	LT	NYC	0808	DUPE OF 0703(DANIEL ELLIOTT HUGER)		
0734	DENTON, EDWARD LOUIS	CDR	NYC	0809	GRELAND, R. LIVINGSTONE	LT	AVN
0735	EVANS, EARLE REMINGTON	ENS	NYC	0810	JAMES, OLIVER BURR	LT	AVN
0736	LEMKE, FREDERICK GODFREY	CDR	NYC	0811	LYON, ROBERT G.	ENS	AVN
0737	FAGAN, JAMES (N)	LCDR	NYC	0812	MARTIN, MATTHEW SCOVELL	ENS	AVN
0738	HASLER, THOMAS BANYARD	LCDR	NYC	0813	MCADOO, ROBERT HAZELHURST	ENS	AVN
0739	WAINWRIGHT, STUYVESANT (N) SR.	LTJG	NYC	0814	MCCORMACK, JAMES STANLEY	ENS	AVN
0740	CRANDALL, RAND PERCY	CAPT	NYC	0815	MCMILLAN, HERMON GEORGE	ENS	AVN
0741	CRONIN, GERALD ELLIS	MR	NYC	0816	PACKARD, WILLIAM GUTHRIE	ENS	AVN
0742	MASURY, JOHN MILLER	LCDR	NYC	0817	PAINE, BRYSON (N)	LTJG	AVN
0743	BIGELOW, ANSON ALEXANDER	LT	NYC	0818	PALMEDO, ROLAND (N)	LCDR	AVN
0744	VAN VOORHIS, ROBERT ARTHUR	CDR	NYC	0819	PHILLIPS, ELLIOT SCHUYLER	ENS	AVN
0745	CONE, HUTCHINSON INGHAM	RADM	NYC	0820	PURDY, HERBERT MCLEAN	LT	AVN
0746	LANSING, SANFORD GREENE	LTJG	NYC	0821	READ, RUSSELL BARTOW	LTJG	AVN
0747	WAIT, WILLIAM BELL	CAPT	NYC	0822	READ, WILLIAM AUGUSTUS	VADM	AVN
0748	NICOLL, DELANCEY (N) JR.	LT	NYC	0823	RICE, ALBERT FTELEY	CAPT	AVN
0749	SULLIVAN, ARTHUR CAMPBELL	LT	MAS	0824	ROBINSON, GLEN E	LTJG	AVN
0750	MICHLER, GORDON HUNT	MR	NYC	0825	ROSENDAHL, CHARLES EMERY	VADM	AVN
0751	RUSSELL, FREDERICK	LT	NYC	0826	ROSS, JOHN WILLIAM	ENS	AVN
0752	SMALL, JOHN DAVIS	LT	NYC	0827	RUST, HARRY LEE JR.	LT	AVN
0753	RISDON, CHARLES SECOR	ENS	NYC	0828	SLADE, PENTRICE (N)	ENS	AVN
0754	JONES, HOWLAND BARTON	LTJG	NYC	0829	STANTON, GEORGE HAROLD	ENS	AVN
0755	HOLLYDAY, RICHARD CARMICHAEL	CAPT	NYC	0830	TALLMAN, FRANK GIFFORD JR.	LTJG	AVN
0756	GLEAVES, ALBERT (N)	ADM	NYC	0831	TRIPPE, JUAN TERRY	ENS	AVN
0757	PITTMAN, GEORGE HARRISON	ENS	NYC	0832	URNER, GORDON (N)	ENS	AVN
0758	VAIL, LOUIS RICHARDSON	CAPT	NYC	0833	WHITCOMB, HAROLD DAVIS	LTJG	AVN
0759	LONG, WILLIAM HENDERSON JR.	LTJG	NYC	0834	WHITE, WALTER (N)	ENS	AVN
0760	ROTHSCHILD, WALTER N.	LTJG	NYC	0835	WHITE, HENRY JAMES	LCDR	AVN
0761	MILLER, MORRIS (N)	ENS	NYC	0836	WILLCOX, WESTMORE JR.	LT	AVN
0762	BURK, SAMUEL BENNETT	CAPT	NYC	0837	GLENNAN, WILLIAM SHIELD	LCDR	NYC
0763	CARVER, CLIFFORD NICKELS	LT	NYC	0838	JEWETT, EDWARD HULL JR.	LCDR	NYC
0764	MAYER, JOHN ADAMS	ENS	NYC	0839	SCHIFF, WILLIAM (N)	LTJG	AVN
0765	MARTIN, MULFORD (N)	ENS	NYC	0840	WARD, ELIOT LEE	LTJG	NYC
0766	HOFF, ARTHUR BAINBRIDGE, JR.	MR	NYC	0841	FOLEY, PAUL (N)	CAPT	NYC
0767	ELDREDGE, CHARLES (N)	ENS	NYC	0842	WELL, JOHN (N)	LT	NYC
0768	WAINWRIGHT, LOUDON SNOWDON	MR	NYC	0843	HESSELMAN, LEO WILLIAM	CDR	NYC
0769	WAINWRIGHT, CARROLL L. JR.	MR	NYC	0844	FRANKLIN, WILLIAM BUEL	RADM	NYC
0770	FARWELL, EARLE (N)	CDR	NYC	0845	STONE, ELLERY WHEELER	RADM	NYC
0771	CONSTEIN, EDWARD THEODORE	CAPT	NYC	0846	BLADES, LAWRENCE (N)	CDR	NYC
0772	BAKER, GEORGE BARR	CDR	NYC	0847	CORNING, EDWARD PARSONS	ENS	NYC
0773	WAINWRIGHT, STUYVESANT (N) JR.	LTJG	NYC	0848	ANDREWS, CHARLES LEE	RADM	NYC
0774	WAINWRIGHT, JOHN HOWARD	MR	NYC	0849	ALLEN, WILLIAM SEWARD	ENS	NYC
0775	MCILWAINE, ARCHIBALD GRAHAM JR	LT	AVN	0850	MORGAN, CASEY BRUCE	RADM	NYC
0776	ALLEN, FRDERICK STEVENS	LT	AVN	0851	POOR, STEARNS (N)	ENS	MAS
0777	BARR, JOSEPH SYDNEY	ENS	AVN	0852	HEALY, THOMAS RAYMOND	LCDR	MAS
0778	BARR, THOMAS T. JR.	LTJG	AVN	0853	WEEKS, SINCLAIR (N)	CAPT	MAS
0779	BARR, WILLIAM MANNING	LTJG	AVN	0854	DOSIS, CHARLES THORNTON	MR	MAS
0780	BENEDICT, HORCE GUION.	CAPT	AVN	0855	PARKER, WILLIAM STANLEY	GEMC	MAS
0781	BEVIER, RICHARD B.	LTJG	AVN	0856	BLAKE, ROBERT FULTON	LTJG	MAS
0782	BLAKE, OCTAVE (N) JR	LTJG	AVN	0857	JACKSON, HERBERT W.	LT	MAS

Wreath Laying at the Lone Sailor Statue during dedication of NOUS Bas Relief.

VADM Philip Quast, USN; RADM William Thompson, USN (Ret.); and Commander General Col William R. Bremer, USMCR (Ret.)

INSIG	COMPANION	RANK	CDRY	INSIG	COMPANION	RANK	CDRY
0858	HOFF, NICHOLAS ROOSEVELT	MR	NYC	0933	MACKAY, WILSON ESHORNE	MR	MAS
0859	STUART, WALTER HARCOURT	LT	NYC	0934	PYNE, FREDERICK GLOVER	RADM	MAS
0860	ATWOOD, KIMBALL C. JR.	LTJG	NYC	0935	FINN, WILLIAM ALBERT	CAPT	MAS
0861	WILDMAN, CYRIL KENNIN	CAPT	NYC	0936	DAVIS, GEORGE PHILIP	LCDR	MAS
0862	DYER, LEONARD HUNTRESS	LT	NYC	0937	HUMPHREYS, HAROLD ELLIOTT	CDR	NYC
0863	LONG, BRYON ANDREW	CAPT	NYC	0938	LYON, MELVILLE WALTER	ENS	MAS
0864	KOBBE, FREDERICK WILLIAM	LTJG	NYC	0939	EPPLE, LOUIS (N)	ENS	MAS
0865	BEHN, HERNAND (N)	LT	NYC	0940	SMITH, RENSHAW (N) JR.	ENS	MAS
0866	FISKE, BRADLEY ALLEN	RADM	NYC	0941	WALTERS, HENRY CUTTER	CDR	MAS
0867	WILEY, HENRY A.	RADM	NYC	0942	HOOPER, ROGER FELLOWES	ENS	MAS
0868	DESTEIGUER, LOUIS RODOLPH	ADM	NYC	0943	WYLDE, JOHN IRTON	LTJG	MAS
0869	SCANDRETT, RICHARD B. JR.	ENS	NYC	0944	MOFFAT, ALEXNADER WHITE	CAPT	MAS
0870	GIRDNER, FREDERIC W.	LT	NYC	0945	BROWN, WALDO HAYWARD	LT	MAS
0871	CRAVEN, FREDERICK BERNARD	CDR	MAS	0946	COLLIDGE, AMORY (N)	LTJG	MAS
0872	LANE, J. ALEX	ADM	MAS	0947	ALLEN, THOMAS LAMB	LTJG	MAS
0873	FALES, DE COURSEY (N)	LT	NYC	0948	MCCAFFERTY, WILLIAM JOHN	CDR	NYC
0874	LEMMON, JOHN UHLER, JR	LTJG	MAS	0949	BRADFORD, GERARD (N)	CDR	NYC
0875	TOMB, JAMES HARVEY	CAPT	NYC	0950	LEHMAN, MORTIMER B	LT	NYC
0876	WILLARD, ARTHUR LEE	VADM	NYC	0951	GUILD, HENRY R.	LTJG	MAS
0877	QUEN, WALTER KERR	LCDR	NYC	0952	BARBER, ARETAS OSMOND	LTJG	MAS
0878	HASTINGS, ALTON BRUCE JR.	ENS	MAS	0953	KING, FRANKLIN (N)	LT	MAS
0879	CURRIER, ROSS HAMILTON	CDR	MAS	0954	BEAMAN, JONN ALDEN	CDR	MAS
0880	BONNE, WILLIAM RAMIAR	CAPT	NYC	0955	MOULTON, FRANCIS SEVERN	CDR	MAS
0881	BEHN, SOSTHENES (N) II	MR	NYC	0956	SHARP, ALTON B	LTJG	MAS
0882	SAUNDERS, CHARLES CYRIL	MR	NYC	0957	SHANLEY, THOMAS ANDREW	CDR	MAS
0883	SAGE, DARROW (N)	LT	NYC	0958	HATCH, FREDERICK SOUTHARD	CDR	MAS
0884	BERTSCHMANN, JEAN JACQUES	ENS	NYC	0959	RUDD, HENRY W. DWIGHT	ENS	MAS
0885	SCOTT, FORRESTER HOLMES	LT	NYC	0960	DAVIS, WILLIAM SEWALL GARDNER	LCDR	MAS
0886	DUPE OF 0708(JAMES BLACKSTONE TAYLOR JR)			0961	BOWDITCH, RICHARD LYON	MR	MAS
0887	DARLINGTON, GILBERT STERLING B.	LT	NYC	0962	CLAUSON, ANDREW GUSTAVE JR	ENS	MAS
0888	ANDREWS, RICHARD SNOWDEN	MR	NYC	0963	COADY, EDWARD A.	ENS	MAS
0889	PRAY, DUDLEY MALCOLM	LCDR	MAS	0964	CURRIER, GEORGE CRANDALL	CAPT	MAS
0890	MADDEN, ALPHONSUS LIGOURI	CAPT	MAS	0965	KALER, HAROLD VINCENT	ENS	MAS
0891	DOW, HARRY EDWARD	LT	MAS	0966	CURTIS, CHARLES PELHAM	LT	MAS
0892	EVANS, RALPH PALMER	LT	MAS	0967	KEITH, HENRY HIRAM WHEATON	LCDR	MAS
0893	SHAW, FREDERICK JOSELYN	LCDR	MAS	0968	MILLER, CHARLES HORACE K.	RADM	MAS
0894	WALLER, STEWART (N)	ENS	NYC	0969	HAYCOCK, WARREN ELMER	RADM	MAS
0895	POWELSON, WILFRID VAN NEST	LCDR	NYC	0970	DUNWOODY, KINGSLAND (N)	LT	MAS
0896	MOE, HENRY ALLEN	LTJG	NYC	0971	BORDEN, WALTER E.	LT	MAS
0897	RALSTON, BYRON BROWN	CDR	NYC	0972	FLANNIGAN, ERNEST JORDAN	LCDR	MAS
0898	MACKENZIE, MALCOLM	LTJG	NYC	0973	SOULE, CHARLES CARROLL JR.	CAPT	MAS
0899	FRANCIS, TAPPAN E.	LT	MAS	0974	HAYDEN, ARTHUR HOLDEN	ENS	MAS
0900	FERGUSON, DAVID (N)	LCDR	MAS	0975	SEWARD, HERBERT LEE	CDR	MAS
0901	MOULTON, STANLEY WINDSOR	ENS	MAS	0976	JOHNSON, CARL CUSTAVUS A.	CAPT	MAS
0902	WEBB, JOHN CRAWFORD	LT	MAS	0977	BOYER, WILLIAM FRANCIS	LT	MAS
0903	HOOPER, CHARLES FREDERICK	CAPT	MAS	0978	KILDUFF, WILLIAM DOUGLAS	CDR	MAS
0904	SULLIVAN, JOSEPH B.	LCDR	MAS	0979	MERWIN, HENRY CHESTER	CAPT	MAS
0905	EVANS, HERBERT SMITH	LT	MAS	0980	SHEPHEARD, HALERT CLIFFORD	LCDR	MAS
0906	MAJOR, EARL MELVIN	CAPT	MAS	0981	FENNESSY, FRANK EDWARD JR.	ENS	MAS
0907	POWELL, JOSEPH WRIGHT	LT	MAS	0982	BAKER, ROLAND HENRY	CAPT	MAS
0908	MARASPIN, DAVIS GOODWIN	LT	MAS	0983	SALTMARSH, SHERMAN WHIPPLE	LCDR	MAS
0909	WAMBAUGH, MILES (N)	LT	MAS	0984	HOLCOMB, THOMAS (N)	GEN	MAS
0910	BOLSTER, CHARLES STEPHEN	LTJG	MAS	0985	WILLIAMS, ROY FOSTER	LTJG	MAS
0911	ABELE, CLARENCE ARTHUR	CAPT	MAS	0986	DALLIN, EDWIN BERTRAM	ENS	MAS
0912	VARNEY, JOHN EDWARD	CDR	MAS	0987	SMITH, FREDERICK HORTON	CDR	MAS
0913	PAUL, HOWARD CHANDLER	LCDR	MAS	0988	FARRELLY, RICHARD LLOYD	CAPT	AVN
0914	ELLIS, HERBERT ALOYSIUS	LCDR	MAS	0989	WAESCHE, RUSSELL RANDOLPH	ADM	MAS
0915	PICKERING, LANGDON DOMINIQUE	LCDR	MAS	0990	MURRAY, JOSEPH DANIEL	Maj.	MAS
0916	ROHRMAN, HORATIO WRAY	CDR	MAS	0991	TARRANT, WILLIAM THEODORE	VADM	MAS
0917	WHITE, WILFRED O.	LT	MAS	0992	WALSH, DAVID IGNATIUS	HONOR	MAS
0918	COX, THOMAS GEORGE JR.	CAPT	MAS	0993	JONES, DAMON EVERETT	MR	MAS
0919	FRANSWORTH, HAROLD VINCENT	ENS	MAS	0994	BAKER, MYERS ELLIOTT	LCDR	AVN
0920	PERRY, HOWARD RUSSELL (PRATT)	ENS	MAS	0995	JENNEY, THACHER (N)	LTJG	MAS
0921	HOGG, FRANK TREVOR	LCDR	MAS	0996	COOK, BOYD LEE	ENS	MAS
0922	ADAMS, CHARLES FRANCIS	HONOR	MAS	0997	SPAULDING, PAUL PICKERING	CAPT	MAS
0923	SIMS, WILLIAM SNOWDEN	ADM	MAS	0998	SHEA, ALFRED ALONZO	LCDR	MAS
0924	GHERARDI, WALTER R.	RADM	MAS	0999	WALKER, ROBERT JOHN	CDR	MAS
0925	FLANNERY, JONN WILLIAM	LT	MAS	01000	MIDDLETON, THOMAS HAZELHURST	ENS	NYC
0926	THACKABERRY, MARK W	ENS	NYC	01001	JUPP, WILLIAM BRADFORD	LCDR	NYC
0927	KNOWLES, HERBERT PIPER	ENS	MAS	01002	STANDLEY, WILLIAM HARRISON	ADM	NYC
0928	RUSSELL, HENRY EASTIN	CDR	MAS	01003	CAPSHAW, HULON (N)	ENS	NYC
0929	BRIGGS, GEORGE KENNEDY	CDR	MAS	01004	STONE, JOHN GILBERT MARSHALL	LT	NYC
0930	ZUKOR, EUGENE JAMES	CDR	NYC	01005	DUNCAN, WILLIAM JAMES	LT	NYC
0931	CUNNINGHAM, ALAN (N)	LTJG	MAS	01006	LANIER, BERWICK BRUCE	LT	NYC
0932	BLAKE, FORDYCE TURNER	ENS	MAS	01007	MORAN, EDMOND JOSEPH	RADM	NYC

INSIG	COMPANION	RANK	CDRY	INSIG	COMPANION	RANK	CDRY
01008	BLOCK, WESLELY STEELE JR.	LT	NYC	01083	CONDON, FREEMAN JAMES	LT	MAS
01009	JEFFERS, LEON HENRY	LT	MAS	01084	BOTHFELD, HENRY SOULE	LTJG	MAS
01010	MUDGE, RAYMOND CORWIN	LTJG	MAS	01085	MARSHALL, JOHN ROSS	LCDR	MAS
01011	MANNING, GEORGE CHARLES	LCDR	MAS	01086	CLARK, ELLERY HARDING JR.	CAPT	MAS
01012	WEST, JOHN DORMAN	ENS	MAS	01087	BENNETT, EDWIN CLARK	ENS	MAS
01013	HEALY, JAMES KNOPP	MR	MAS	01088	HURLEY, CHARLES HENRY	LT	MAS
01014	SCARBOROUGH, EUGENE WESLEY	ENS	NYC	01089	TAUSSIG, JOSEPH KNEFLER SR.	VADM	MAS
01015	EUBANK, GERALD ABNER	RADM	NYC	01090	FAXON, FRANCIS BRADFORD	ENS	MAS
01016	WORRELL, MALCOLM LEE	CAPT	NYC	01091	ASHLEY, RAYMOND ELLIOTT	LTJG	MAS
01017	RINEHART, EVAN URNER	LT	NYC	01092	PILSBURY, ELMER KNAPP	ENS	MAS
01018	HOOD, VANCE ROBERT	ENS	NYC	01093	MCLEISH, JONN RULE	ENS	MAS
01019	DILLON, SCHUYLER (N)	LT	MAS	01094	WYNNE, WALKER MOAKLER	CDR	NYC
01020	LYMAN, CHARLES F. JR.	ENS	MAS	01095	CHAMBERLAIN, WARREN MILLER	ENS	AVN
01021	DECELLES, FRANCIS JOSEPH	CAPT	MAS	01096	CLAPP, KENNETH HERBERT	LT	AVN
01022	BRANNAN, WILLIAM FORREST	ENS	MAS	01097	CRAFTS, LEWIS HENRY	ENS	AVN
01023	STOWE, IRVING ELMER	LCDR	MAS	01098	STITT, WILLIAM BRITTON	ENS	AVN
01024	GIBSON, FRANCIS STEPHENSON	CAPT	NYC	01099	STANSBURY, JOHN ALEXANDER	LCDR	MAS
01025	HAAG, JOSEPH (N) JR.	LT	NYC	01100	POSEY, ERNEST LAMONT	CDR	MAS
01026	TODD, JAMES HERBERT	LTJG	NYC	01101	DUPE OF 0748(DELANCEY NICHOLL JR)		
01027	ALDRICH, THOMAS ROSS	ENS	MAS	01102	DANIELS, GEORGE COLUMBUS	CDR	MAS
01028	COPELAND, HOWARD GREYDON	CAPT	MAS	01103	COHEN, ALBERT MORRIS	CDR	MAS
01029	ADEE, GRAHAM MONTROSE	CAPT	MAS	01104	MERRILL, JONN LEE	LT	MAS
01030	RHODES, JOHN BARCLAY	CDR	NYC	01105	GILKINSON, JAMES FRANKLIN	ENS	NYC
01031	SADLER, EVERIT JAY	LCDR	NYC	01106	GRIDLEY, JAMES VERNON	ENS	MAS
01032	OSBURN, FRANKLIN WAYNE JR.	CDR	NYC	01107	LANE, FRANKLIN JOHNSON	ENS	MAS
01033	SCOTT, THOMAS ALBERTSON	CDR	NYC	01108	MERRIT, MELVILLE PETTENGILL	ENS	MAS
01034	LAMB, SCOTT GRISELL	LT	MAS	01109	CUNNINGHAM, JONN JAY	LT	NYC
01035	HORNER, HALSEY BOARDMAN	ENS	MAS	01110	DRAKE, FREDERICK ELLIS JR.	LCDR	MAS
01036	QUARLES, SHERROD HADLEY	LCDR	NYC	01111	TWOMBLY, LEO WALLACE	ENS	MAS
01037	MOUNT, DAVID A.	LT	AVN	01112	HOGAN, EDWARD JOSEPH	LCDR	MAS
01038	CHADWICK, JOHN CAMPBELL	LT	AVN	01113	WYLIE, JAMES WILLIAM	LT	NYC
01039	HARRIS, FREDERICK MACK	ENS	AVN	01114	JENNINGS, ALBERT GOULD JR.	ENS	AVN
01040	JOHNSON, WARREN FORREST	ENS	AVN	01115	POTTER, HAMILTON FISH	CDR	NYC
01041	WERFELMAN, DIETRICK JOHN	ENS	AVN	01116	COBB, BOUGHTON (N)	LTJG	NYC
01042	RYAN, HAROLD LYMAN	LT	AVN	01117	FOLEY, THOMAS RUSSELL	CDR	MAS
01043	WHITE, WILLIAM MERRILL	LCDR	MAS	01118	MORRIS, COLTON GROSS	CDR	MAS
01044	SCHIEFFELIN, JOHN JAY	RADM	NYC	01119	HILL, ELMER ROBERT SR.	CAPT	MAS
01045	HAVENS, BECKWITH (N)	LCDR	AVN	01120	BRIGHAM, CHARLES H.	LTJG	MAS
01046	WARREN, ALFRED KENNEDY JR	LT	WNY	01121	DELAND, FRANK STANTON JR.	CDR	MAS
01047	PECK, LYMAN STANNARD	LT	AVN	01122	HUNT, EMERSON WILSON	CAPT	MAS
01048	LEIGHTON, BRUCE G.	LCDR	AVN	01123	SAUNDERS, JOHN FRANCIS	LT	MAS
01049	ADAMS, ASHLEY DAY	LCDR	MAS	01124	HUTCHINSON, EARL GRANVILLE	CDR	NYC
01050	DEKAY, ECKFORD CRAVEN	LCDR	NYC	01125	QUINBY, JONN GURLEY	LTJG	NYC
01051	HINES, JOHN WILLIS	ENS	AVN	01126	COOPER, MORRIS (N) JR.	CDR	NYC
01052	FINNEGAN, JAMES JOSEPH	LT	AVN	01127	TUNNEY, JAMES JOSEPH (GENE)	CAPT	NYC
01053	BARNEY, WILLIAM JOSHUA JR.	CAPT	NYC	01128	SIDES, ANDREW BENJAMIN	LCDR	MAS
01054	KENWORTHY, JESSE LLOYD JR	CAPT	MAS	01129	RUDDY, STEPHEN A., JR.	CDR	NYC
01055	TUTTLE, ALBERT EDWARD (NED)	CAPT	MAS	01130	BLAKE, FORDYCE TURNER JR.	LCDR	MAS
01056	CRAVEN, FRANCIS SANDERSON	CAPT	MAS	01131	GOULD, RICHARD KENELM	LTJG	MAS
01057	HODGKINSON, HAROLD DANIEL	LTJG	MAS	01132	HOLMSTROM, ANDREW BIRGER	LCDR	MAS
01058	WOODWARD, CLARK HOWELL	VADM	NYC	01133	STERNFELT, CARL WALTER	CDR	MAS
01059	PECK, FREDERICK CARLETON	ENS	AVN	01134	MITCHELL, THOMAS HENRY	CAPT	MAS
01060	MORSE, HUNTINGTON TOMLINSON	LT	MAS	01135	SKUSE, PAUL HOWARD	CDR	MAS
01061	PENNIMAN, JOHN GRISCOM	LT	MAS	01136	CORNWELL, KIRKHAM RANDOLPH	LT	NYC
01062	NELSON, JOHN THACKERAY	CAPT	MAS	01137	ALDRICH, THOMAS ROSS JR.	LT	MAS
01063	ANDERSON, WILLIAM COLFORD	ENS	AVN	01138	WALKER, FREDERICK STEWART	CDR	MAS
01064	WILCOX, ROBERT BARTLES	CDR	AVN	01139	HATHAWAY, EDWIN REYNOLDS	LT	MAS
01065	TAYLOR, HENRY CALHOUN	LT	NYC	01140	DUFFILL, HUGH PERRINS	ENS	MAS
01066	HARVEY, MURRAY CHEEVER	ENS	MAS	01141	GOODRICH, RICHARD I.	ENS	MAS
01067	DELANO, MERRILL POTTER	LT	MAS	01142	SEAVER, WALTER ENWRIGHT	ENS	MAS
01068	SMITH, DAVID ALLEN	LT	MAS	01143	HOVEY, CARLETON BEECHER	CDR	MAS
01069	TRAVER, CLARENCE HOFFMAN	CDR	MAS	01144	TOLMAN, GILBERT (N) JR.	ENS	MAS
01070	BOWERS, ANDERSON (N)	ENS	AVN	01145	HIBLER, EDWARD BARDEN	LT	MAS
01071	FLYNN, GEORGE DANIEL JR.	ENS	MAS	01146	RANDALL, LARCOM (N)	ENS	MAS
01072	SHAW, HOWARD RUTHERFORD	RADM	MAS	01147	LEMAY, GEORGE HENRY	CDR	MAS
01073	WEST, THOMAS ALFRED	LTJG	MAS	01148	ROBERTSON, RURIC RITCHIE	CDR	MAS
01074	WOOD, CORNELIUS AYER	LCDR	MAS	01149	KIRK, WILLIAM JOHNSON	CDR	MAS
01075	CUSHMAN, RUFUS CUTLER	LTJG	MAS	01150	BREWER, EDWARD SOLCUM	CDR	MAS
01076	MCMILLAN, HERMON GEORGE	ENS	AVN	01151	KEATING, LEO ALBERT	CDR	MAS
01077	RIIS, ROGER WILLIAM	ENS	NYC	01152	MEALS, FRANK MICHAEL	CAPT	MAS
01078	FOX, WILLIAM VINCENT	RADM	NYC	01153	ARNOLD, WALTER RICHMOND	LT	MAS
01079	WYLIE, WALKER GILL JR.	LCDR	NYC	01154	MCCRACKEN, DWIGHT MASON	LTJG	MAS
01080	ATWOOD, RAYMOND LORING	LT	MAS	01155	MOSHER, CURTIS HOWARD	ENS	MAS
01081	UPTON, JOHN (N)	LCDR	MAS	01156	SHANKS, ROBERT MCFARLANE	ENS	MAS
01082	CLOUGH, WILLIS BARTON	ENS	MAS	01157	LEWIS, HOWARD WILLIAM	LTJG	MAS

INSIG	COMPANION	RANK	CDRY	INSIG	COMPANION	RANK	CDRY
01158	HORNER, MERRITT (N)	ENS	MAS	01233	GRACE, WILLIAM WALLACE	LCDR	MAS
01159	METCALF, ERNEST CLIFFORD	CDR	MAS	01234	EDDY, BURTON HENRY	LCDR	MAS
01160	STUDLEY, LINNELL EDWARDS	ENS	MAS	01235	DOANE, CLARENCE EASTMAN	LT	MAS
01161	WHIPPLE, SHERMAN LELAND JR.	LTJG	MAS	01236	FARR, JAMES FRANCIS	LT	MAS
01162	MACQUARRIE, KENNETH GODFREY	ENS	MAS	01237	BORGESON, OLAF BERNARD	LCDR	MAS
01163	DERBY, WILFRID NEVILLE	RADM	MAS	01238	BRADY, JAMES FRANCIS	LCDR	MAS
01164	PEIRCE, GEORGE LEIGHTON	ENS	MAS	01239	LEONARD, JOHN T.	LCDR	MAS
01165	REGAN, JAMES JOSEPH	CAPT	NYC	01240	RICHARDSON, PAUL BEDFORD	ENS	MAS
01166	STATTER, HUMPHREY (N) JR.	LCDR	NYC	01241	GAUTHIER, ROYAL HENRY	ENS	MAS
01167	BOARDMAN, ELLIOT SHEFFELD	ENS	MAS	01242	MCINTIRE, ALLYN BREWSTER	ENS	MAS
01168	FRANKS, WILLIAM HUNT	ENS	MAS	01243	WHITE, GEORGE AVERY	LT	MAS
01169	GEROULD, RUSSELL (N)	ENS	MAS	01244	CHAMBERLIN, HARMON PAINE	LCDR	MAS
01170	HALL, HENRY ALFRONSO JR.	LTJG	MAS	01245	DONLEY, HOWARD LEE	LT	MAS
01171	KNIGHT, ELLIOT PRESTON	CDR	MAS	01246	AWALT, THOMAS YOUNG	CAPT	MAS
01172	LANDERS, JOHN JAMES	ENS	MAS	01247	BURGER, FRANKLYN DONALDSON	LT	MAS
01173	MOORE, LEO JOSEPH	LTJG	MAS	01248	DURFEE, THOMAS (N)	CAPT	MAS
01174	PAUL, DAVID HUME	LCDR	MAS	01249	GIFFORD, ROBERT LINDLEY	CDR	MAS
01175	PRENTICE, HOWARD ANDERSON	CDR	MAS	01250	HALL, ARTHUR GRAHAM	CAPT	MAS
01176	TELLIER, AUGUSTUS NAPOLEON	ENS	MAS	01251	LAWRENCE, PHILIP EUGENE	CDR	MAS
01177	WILDE, ALFRED ALLAN	ENS	MAS	01252	LOVELACE, RICHARD SHRIVER	LT	MAS
01178	WICHERT, STUART KIMBALL	LTJG	MAS	01253	MAGNUSSON, MAGNUS B.	LCDR	MAS
01179	RICHARDS, JOHN KELVEY JR.	COMMO	MAS	01254	MUNZERT, GEORGE MARTIN	ENS	MAS
01180	ALLEN, HUGH	CDR	MAS	01255	SULLIVAN, JAMES FITZGERALD	ENS	MAS
01181	ANDERSON, WINFIELD CARL	LTJG	MAS	01256	WOLLEY, SUMNER ROBINSON	ENS	MAS
01182	ARION, HARRY FRANK	ENS	MAS	01257	HARRIMAN, FRANK WESLELY	CDR	MAS
01183	BROWN, RALPH HORACE KINGSLEY	ENS	MAS	01258	FRYE, JAMES EDWIN	CDR	MAS
01184	DRUMMOND, JOSIAH HAYDEN	LT	MAS	01259	WILLIAMS, WHEELER (N)	LCDR	NYC
01185	FALVEY, GEORGE HENRY	ENS	MAS	01260	RAE, GENE GEORGE	LT	NYC
01186	GEARY, JOHN ALOYSIUS	LCDR	MAS	01261	CANCELLED (WILLIAM THOMAS MAST)		
01187	GREGG, JAMES DOUGLAS	ENS	MAS	01262	ROTHWELL, WILLIAM HERBERT 2ND	CDR	MAS
01188	HANRON, FRANCIS BENEDICT	LCDR	MAS	01263	HAMILTON, DONALD GRAHAM		
01189	HUNTINGTON, PAUL OSBORNE	ENS	MAS	01264	LORTON, SPENCER DIXON		
01190	KIMBALL, CHAS EDGAR L.	LCDR	MAS	01265	TUTTLE, DONALD STEWART	ENS	NYC
01191	KIMBALL, WHITEFIELD FROST	LCDR	MAS	01266	MCKEAN, JONN FERGUSON	CDR	NYC
01192	LINDSAY, RALPH HAILBURTON	LT	MAS	01267	BISHOP, CLAUDE ULYSSES JR.	CAPT	MAS
01193	LITCHFIELD, ROLAND MOORE	LCDR	MAS	01268	BARRY, EDMUND HALEY	CAPT	MAS
01194	MACGILLIVRAY, EARLE PAUL	ENS	MAS	01269	BREITMAN, ARNOLD (N)	LCDR	NYC
01195	MCMULLIN, ROBERT DRUMMOND	LT	MAS	01270	PETERKIN, DEWITT JR.	CAPT	NYC
01196	MORTON, HOWARD MILLER	ENS	MAS	01271	HADDEN, ALBERT BYRON JR.	LCDR	NYC
01197	PENNIMAN, JONN GRISCOM JR.	2ND Lt	MAS	01272	MAGUIRE, CHARLES FRANKLIN	ENS	NYC
01198	RAYNER, ARTHUR WARREN	ENS	MAS	01273	WILLS, ARTHUR EDWARD	CDR	NYC
01199	SCOBIE, JAMES PORTER	LT	MAS	01274	HORTON, FREDERICK LYMAN	LCDR	NYC
01200	SHAFFER, STUART (N)	ENS	MAS	01275	DUPE OF 0800 (HARRY FRANK GUGGENHEIM)		
01201	SHUNWAY, CARL ELLIOT	LCDR	MAS	01276	SEELER, MARCEL KLEINERT	ENS	NYC
01202	SMITH, FREDERIC BURGESS	LTJG	MAS	01277	FARR, HENRY BARTOW	LT	NYC
01203	SMITH, WILLIAM THOMAS	ENS	MAS	01278	MASTER, ARTHUR MATTHEW	CAPT	NYC
01204	STAVREDES, THEODORE JONN	ENS	MAS	01279	BARRY, ARTHUR JOHN JR.	CDR	NYC
01205	STENGEL, PETER (N)	LTJG	MAS	01280	KLEIMAN, JACOB JULIUS (JACK)	LCDR	NYC
01206	SULLIVAN, WALTER LOUIS	LT	MAS	01281	DEBOER, LEE (N)	LCDR	NYC
01207	USINA, MICHAEL NELIGAN	CAPT	MAS	01282	FRAVELL, JAMES E. G.	LCDR	NYC
01208	WEBBER, ROBERT KENDALL	ENS	MAS	01283	BYRNE, JAMES JOSEPH	LT	NYC
01209	WILLOUGHBY, MALCOLM FRANCIS	ENS	MAS	01284	LEARY, HERBERT FAIRFAX	VADM	NYC
01210	WILSON, CHARLES J.A.	LCDR	MAS	01285	BLACK, ALEXANDER LESLIE	LT	NYC
01211	WILSON, CHESTER WORCESTER	ENS	MAS	01286	DAY, FAIRFIELD POPE	LCDR	NYC
01212	WING, HAROLD EDWARD	ENS	MAS	01287	FULLERTON, JOHN SHERON	LT	NYC
01213	BAKENHUS, REUBEN EDWIN	RADM	NYC	01288	POTTER, THOMAS W.	CDR	NYC
01214	HARRIS, FREDERIC ROBERT	RADM	NYC	01289	HARDER, F. KENNETH	ENS	NYC
01215	ROCK, GEORGE HENRY	RADM	NYC	01290	SCHANZER, BENJAMIN M.	LCDR	NYC
01216	CAHILL, WILLIAM THOMAS	1ST Lt	MAS	01291	ENGLIS, JONN (N)	LT	NYC
01217	VENTURA, AMERICO BENEDICT	ENS	MAS	01292	CENDO, JONN CHARLES	LCDR	NYC
01218	BORDEN, MILTON ELWOOD	CAPT	MAS	01293	HARLOW, ARTHUR BROOKS	CAPT	NYC
01219	RUDD, CHARLES ALFRED	ENS	MAS	01294	HARDING, THEODORE PASCUAL	LT	NYC
01220	STEPHENSON, CHARLES S.	RADM	NYC	01295	HEMPHILL, CLIFFORD (N) JR.	LCDR	NYC
01221	EVANS, EARLE REMINGTON JR.	LT	NYC	01296	SEIDEL, HARRY GEORGE JR.	LT	NYC
01222	DANIELS, MILTON ROCKWOOD	CAPT	MAS	01297	KLEPAC, THADDEUS BERNARD	LCDR	NYC
01223	MOBERG, ALEXANDER GUSTAF	LCDR	MAS	01298	ERSKINE, FRED STODDARD NEVILLE	Maj.	NYC
01224	MACPHERSON, ROY GAY	LCDR	MAS	01299	CLICK, DAVID GORMAN	CAPT	NYC
01225	ROACH, RICHARD ALFRED	LCDR	MAS	01300	GRIFFIN, ROBERT HAMILTON	CAPT	NYC
01226	ABBOTT, NATHANIEL WALES	LCDR	MAS	01301	STRONG, DONALDSON (N)	CDR	NYC
01227	LAURIAT, GEORGE REYNOLDS JR.	LCDR	MAS	01302	TOBEY, JULIAN ELNATHAN SR.	ENS	NYC
01228	ELDER, PAUL B.	LCDR	MAS	01303	DOWNS, FREDERICK SHELDON	LT	NYC
01229	MARTIN, CLARENCE AMBROSE	LCDR	MAS	01304	CLOGSTON, ROY B.	CDR	NYC
01230	FAUNCE, CALVIN BARSTOW	CAPT	CDAS	01305	O'CONNELL, JOSEPH MICHAEL JR.	ENS	NYC
01231	RUSSELL, DONALD BURTON	CDR	MAS	01306	HURD, JAMES DOUGLAS	LT	NYC
01232	KIMBALL, PETER REED	1ST Lt	MAS	01307	CAHILL, ROBERT LIVINGSTON	LCDR	NYC

Completion Of Nous Navy Memorial Pledge Urged By Time Of Cen. Congress

In his report to the Galveston Congress in 1987, then Commander General-Elect Fred D. Carl, reminding delegates of their Mission to encourage research and preserve documents and other records of naval and maritime history, first suggested that the NOUS as a whole actively support the U.S. Navy Memorial being constructed in Washington DC at the time. Accordingly, the Congress voted to do so by sponsoring one of the bronze bas-reliefs to be placed on either side of the entrance area to the amphitheater. The panel, "The Great White Fleet" was chosen because of its world prominence at a time close to the time the Order was founded.

Naval Order Sponsered Bronze Sculpture Ceremony At U.S. Navy Memorial

On the bright Saturday morning of the 24th of September, a sculpture depicting the sailor of the *Great White Fleet* from Hampton Roads was dedicated at the Navy Memorial.

The ceremony on Pennsylvania Avenue, attended by several hundred Naval Order companions and members of the general public, culminated a five-year project by the Naval Order. During that period the sponsership goal of $50,000 was raised and contributed to the Navy Memorial Foundation. More than 350 companions participated in the sponsorship.

INSIG	COMPANION	RANK	CDRY	INSIG	COMPANION	RANK	CDRY
01308	CHECKOW, STANLEY (N)	LT	NYC	01383	GROSSMAN, LOUIS (N)	LCDR	NYC
01309	HUMRICHOUSE, JAMES WALKER	CDR	NYC	01384	FOSCATO, DONALD A.	LT	NYC
01310	LE MAIRE, EDWARD (N)	LT	NYC	01385	PERLBERG, HARRY JAMES JR.	LCDR	NYC
01311	PRYIBIL, PAUL (N)	ENS	NYC	01386	DAVIS, HORACE WEBBER 2ND	LCDR	NYC
01312	GALLAGHER, FREDERICK AUGUSTINE	CDR	NYC	01387	ZOLLER, ERNEST KUHRT	CAPT	NYC
01313	SLAY, ROBERT C.	LTJG	NYC	01388	SCULLY, VINCENT A.	LT	NYC
01314	PAPE, WILLIAM BOLTON	LCDR	NYC	01389	IRWIN, ROBERT HEILBRON	LT	NYC
01315	GORDON, HAROLD LEON	CDR	NYC	01390	STARKS, RUSSELL NASH	CWO2	NYC
01316	BARTLETT, FREDERICK EUGENE	ENS	MAS	01391	ALLEN, HARRISON HARMON	LCDR	NYC
01317	ROBERTSON, JOESPH MILTON	LCDR	MAS	01392	RUDDY, THOMAS A.	LCDR	NYC
01318	HILL, EDGAR CECIL	LT	MAS	01393	DOTTERER, PAUL REIGNER	LCDR	NYC
01319	GATES, PHILIP BRACKETT	LT	MAS	01394	ABRAHAMS, NOBLE WAYNE	CAPT	NYC
01320	PEAVEY, NEWELL ALPHONSO	CDR	MAS	01395	KOOISTRA, ABBO HENRY	CDR	NYC
01321	GOSSELIN, JOSEPH WILLIAM	CDR	MAS	01396	SMOOT, HOPE MASSIE	CDR	NYC
01322	DONNELL, RAYMOND HERBERT	CDR	MAS	01397	BARUCH, SAILING PRINCE	ENS	NYC
01323	WILMARTH, FRANKLIN (N)	LCDR	MAS	01398	GORDON, RALPH CARSON	LT	NYC
01324	WILDMAN, JONN (N)	CAPT	MAS	01399	HART, FRANK CHARLES JR.	LCDR	NYC
01325	LEWIS, EARL MALCOLM	LCDR	MAS	01400	HIGGINS, GEORGE EDWARD	CAPT	NYC
01326	EATON, CHARLES SHURTLEFF	LT	MAS	01401	HARRISON, ROBERT BRUCE	LCDR	NYC
01327	FOSTER, LEONARD MELVIN	LTJG	MAS	01402	MULLALLY, JOSEPH WILSON	LT	NYC
01328	MAGNUSON, HAROLD ERIC	LCDR	MAS	01403	ANDERSON, CLARENCE EDWARD	CW04	NYC
01329	BURKE, JONN THOMAS	CDR	MAS	01404	DEGARMO, GEORGE JAY	CDR	NYC
01330	WALKER, FREDERICK BURGESS	CW04	MAS	01405	HAGENBUCH, JOHN DANIEL	LT	NYC
01331	BURKE, EDMUND JAMES	CDR	MAS	01406	BROWN, GEORGE ESTABROOK JR	CDR	NYC
01332	BARTLETT, CHARLES WILLIAM	LCDR	MAS	01407	THOMPSON, MATTHEW EMBLETON	CDR	NYC
01333	LEMMON, JOHN UHLER 3RD	ENS	MAS	01408	PAULSON, CHARLES (N)	LT	NYC
01334	WILSON, ORME (N) JR.	LCDR	NYC	01409	BAKEWELL, HENRY PALMER	LCDR	NYC
01335	PERRY, MARSDEN J.	CDR	NYC	01410	FARLEY, EDWARD I.	LCDR	NYC
01336	WILSON, SAMUEL KOOMES	CAPT	NYC	01411	BARTLEY, ARTHUR MCLEAN	LCDR	NYC
01337	FOX, HOWARD ALFRED	LT	NYC	1411A	MCGURL, DANIEL MICHAEL	RADM	NYC
01338	HOWLEY, ROBERT VINCENT	LCDR	NYC	01412	WALSH, GEORGE JOQUES	LT	NYC
01339	STRAUSS, STUART M.	CAPT	NYC	1412A	BELL, FREDERICK JACKSON	RADM	NYC
01340	DEDDISH, MICHAEL RAYMOND	LT	NYC	01413	OKEEFEE, JOHN ARTHUR FRANCIS	LCDR	NYC
01341	EWING, JAMES HALSTED	CAPT	NYC	1413A	KENDERICK, MERCATOR COOPER	LCDR	NYC
01342	CLARK, LEROY (N) JR.	CDR	NYC	01414	MORRISON, JONN EMERSON JR	LT	NYC
01343	REBHAN, JULIUS VICTOR	ENS	NYC	1414A	RCE, HARRY MILTON	CDR	NYC
01344	COSDEN, EDWARD D.	LT	NYC	01415	SHETTLER, WALTER ROBERT	ENS	NYC
01345	BADOLATO, ANGELO CARMINE	LT	NYC	1415A	KNAPP, ARTHUR ALEXANDER	CAPT	NYC
01346	CAREY, JAMES PAUL II	CDR	NYC	01416	ROBINSON, JAMES WATSON	CDR	NYC
01347	SMOLIANOFF, ANDRE V.	LCDR	NYC	1416A	CORDELL, JOSEPH EDWARD	CDR	NYC
01348	ROBBINS, ROBERT MORRILL	LT	NYC	01417	LEBARON, WILLIAM FLOYD JR.	LT	NYC
01349	TANANBAUM, SAMUEL STANLEY	ENS	NYC	1417A	LUDLUM, SAMUEL ALLEN	LCDR	NYC
01350	TROONIN, ALEXANDER EMILIAN	LCDR	NYC	01418	STAUDT, ALBERT RAYMOND	CAPT	MAS
01351	REID, JACK BATEMAN	LCDR	NYC	1418A	SCHOLLY, FRANCIS ROYDON	CAPT	NYC
01352	ZITENFIELD, ABRAHAM (N)	LCDR	NYC	01419	MCGUIRE, EDWARD PERKINS	CDR	MAS
01353	SOBEL, ALBERT (N)	CAPT	NYC	1419A	KITTLER, FRED WARREN	CAPT	NYC
01354	POULSON, JOHN WILSON	LCDR	NYC	01420	GREENOUGH, MALCOLM WHELEN	CDR	MAS
01355	KOECHEL, JOSEPH BERNARD	LCDR	NYC	1420A	STERN, GARDNER HENRY	CDR	NYC
01356	TIM, LOUIS DE JONGE	LCDR	NYC	01421	PERRY, HOWARD RUSSELL JR.	LCDR	MAS
01357	DUFFY, HUGH ALPHONSE	LCDR	NYC	1421A	MAGENNIS, EDWARD GEORGE	CAPT	NYC
01358	RAYMOND, JOHN HOWARD	LCDR	NYC	01422	THOMPSON, CHARLES ARTHUR	LCDR	MAS
01359	PENNA, NICHOLAS CHARLES R.	LCDR	NYC	1422A	HEPPENHEIMER, WILLIAM C JR.	ENS	NYC
01360	MCKINNEY, JOHN MCDOWELL	CDR	NYC	01423	DAVIS, EDMUND STEUART	VADM	NYC
01361	LYON, ALEXANDER BOGART JR	LCDR	AVN	01424	PETIX, CHARLES ALBERT	LCDR	NYC
01362	FLETCHER, WILLIAM BARTLETT	RADM	NYC	01425	BACKE, NILS PETER ANDREW	ENS	MAS
01363	KENNY, LEONARD (N)	CDR	NYC	1425A	JUNKERMAN, WILLIAM JOSEPH	CDR	NYC
01364	VAUGHN, ANTHONY JOSEPH	LCDR	NYC	01426	ALLEN, CLYDE EDGAR	CW03	MAS
01365	KNOX, WILLIAM HENRY	LCDR	NYC	1426A	STARBUCK, WILSON (N)	CAPT	NYC
01366	STUART, WESTON MELVILLE	LCDR	NYC	01427	CROSBIE, ARTHUR WILLIAM JR.	LCDR	MAS
01367	MULLEN, JAMES JOSEPH	LT	NYC	1427A	SCHAPIRO, SAMUEL KRAMER	LTJG	NYC
01368	MACK, WALTER STAUNTON JR.	ENS	NYC	01428	DUNTON, LEWIS WARREN JR.	RADM	MAS
01369	WILDE, JONN (N)	CDR	NYC	1428A	TRAPNELL, FREDERICK MACKAY	VADM	NYC
01370	SMITH, ROBERT TORSLEFF	LCDR	NYC	01429	FLAHERTY, EDWARD BROMLEY	CAPT	MAS
01371	HECHT, KALMAN HENRY	LCDR	NYC	1429A	ANSEL, WALTER CHARLES	RADM	NYC
01372	SWEENY, CAREY PORTER	CAPT	NYC	01430	MCGLONE, LOUIS GERARD	CAPT	MAS
01373	WORTENDYKE, JOHN JACOB	LCDR	NYC	1430A	RINKIN, JOHN GEORGE JR	LT	NYC
01374	VETLESEN, F.W. GEORG UNGER	CDR	NYC	01431	MERENDA, PETER FRANCIS	CAPT	MAS
01375	MCAFEE, ROBERT (N)	CAPT	NYC	1431A	HORAN, JOHN JOSEPH	CDR	NYC
01376	DUNNE, FRANCIS EDWARD	LT	NYC	01432	MCINTYRE, JOSEPH W.	CDR	MAS
01377	NOLAN, JAMES JOSEPH	LT	NYC	1432A	HOTES, JOHN LAWRENCE	CDR	NYC
01378	MORGAN, HENRY STURGIS	CDR	NYC	01433	RUSSELL, LAWRENCE BRADFORD	CDR	MAS
01379	SHEARER, JOHN ALEXANDER	LT	NYC	1433A	WELS, RICHARD HOFFMAN	LT	NYC
01380	HARRIS, LLOYD ELVIN	ENS	NYC	01434	BENE, EDMUND GEORGE	ENS	NYC
01381	WALSMAN, EVERETT CHARLES	LCDR	NYC	1434A	BRUCE, GORDON MURPHY	RADM	NYC
01382	POWELSON, ROGER VAN NEST	CDR	NYC	01435	RIKER, WILLIAM CHANDLER	LCDR	NYC

INSIG	COMPANION	RANK	CDRY	INSIG	COMPANION	RANK	CDRY
1435	AHODGKINSON, THOMAS HENRY	CDR	NYC	01500	MCNAMARA, WILLIAM PATRICK	Capt	MAS
01436	BARRUCH, HERBERT RAYMOND	LT	NYC	01501	MACDONALD, MALCOLM ALEXANDER	CDR	MAS
1436A	LIBONATI, PHILIP (N)	LT	NYC	01502	FORSELL, HERBERT G.	CAPT	MAS
01437	WIRTH, HERBERT PAUL	CAPT	NYC	01503	TRACHTENBERT, FRANK (N)	ENS	MAS
1437A	SCHNEIDER, WARREN JEROME	LCDR	NYC	01504	BUCKLEY, CHARLES PETFORD JR	LCDR	NYC
01438	FISHER, GEORGE GORDON	CDR	NYC	01505	LOWDEN, FRANCIS VIELE	CAPT	NYC
1438A	JANSS, EDWIN (N)	LT	NYC	01506	RUDDY, STEPHEN A. III	CDR	NYC
01439	WAUGH, ALEXANDER PAUL	LCDR	NYC	01507	KRUTH, ARTHUR A.	LCDR	NYC
1439A	ENGLISH, WILLIAM HAMILTON, JR	CDR	NYC	01508	PARKINSON, JONN (N) JR.	CDR	NYC
01440	TOWNSEND, GREENOUGH (N)	LCDR	NYC	01509	BOWDOIN, GEORGE TEMPLE	LCDR	NYC
1440A	JONES, GUSTAV (N)	LCDR	NYC	01510	TELSEY, LEON GERSONI	RADM	NYC
01441	LEWIS, KASSEL (N)	LT	NYC	01511	STEELE, JOHN RUDOLPH	LT	NYC
1441A	EBERHARDT, RAYMOND EDWARD	LT	NYC	01512	DOWNES, MELVIN RICE	CDR	NYC
01442	YOUNG, ALBERT A., JR.	LT	NYC	01513	LABRANCHE, GEORGE MICHEL L JR.	CDR	AVN
1442A	JORDON, JOHN JERMIAH	LT	NYC	01514	HUNT, PETER FRANCIS	CDR	NYC
01443	DERMAN, CARL LOUIS	LT	NYC	01515	HAMILTON, FRANCIS JOSEPH	CDR	NYC
1443A	SIMPSON, RICHARD FULTON	1ST Lt	NYC	01516	MURRAY, ALEXANDER (N) JR.	CAPT	NYC
01444	KING, DUDLEY WALTER	CAPT	NYC	01517	LATHROP, JOHN CLARKE	LCDR	NYC
1444A	LAKE, MICHAEL (N)	CAPT	NYC	01518	FARRELL, JAMES AUGUSTINE JR.	LCDR	NYC
01445	MCMAHON, HENRY EASTON	CAPT	NYC	01519	EMMONS, KINTZING BLYTH	CDR	NYC
1445A	SIEDENBURG, FRANK CHARLES	LCDR	NYC	01520	LAFFEY, HOWARD JAMES	LCDR	NYC
01446	GRENING, PAUL C.	CAPT	NYC	01521	BECKWITH, CHARLES LAKE	LCDR	NYC
01447	STUTZMAN, FREDERIC HENRY	LT	NYC	01522	WILLIAMS, PAUL WHITCOMB	CDR	NYC
01448	HAWKINS, JAMES HARVEY	CW04	NYC	01523	KUBACKI, EDWARD LEONARD	CDR	NYC
01449	BRIGHT, HENRY RALSTON	CDR	NYC	01524	TACK, OSCAR CHARLES	LCDR	NYC
01450	LIDDY, JAMES J.	CDR	NYC	01525	DAY, BERNARD POPE	CAPT	NYC
01451	COLEMAN, CHARLES ALBERT	LT	NYC	01526	DUGAN, DANIEL CALLAHAN	LCDR	NYC
01452	AUSTIN, NORRIS HOWE	LCDR	NYC	01527	GEORGE, JACK FORREST	LT	NYC
01453	HOOKER, JOHN C.	LCDR	MAS	01528	MCKEAN, HUGH FERGUSON	LCDR	NYC
01454	PETERSON, HERBERT AUGUSTUS	CAPT	MAS	01529	EWALD, LOUIS PHILIP III	LT	NYC
01455	MUNZERT, GEORGE CLIFFORD	ENS	MAS	01530	BROWN, WILLARD WILKINS	CDR	NYC
01456	HALL, ARTHUR HARMON	LCDR	NYC	01531	WOODLAND, HENRY THOMPSON	CDR	NYC
01457	MANGANO, RICHARD FARNHAM	CDR	NYC	01532	OGLE, HENRY LANE	CDR	NYC
01458	LIVINGSTON, JOHN HORWOOD	LT	NYC	01533	WILLIAMS, GORDON ALFRED JR	CDR	NYC
01459	WILKES, LLOYD FRANK	LT	NYC	01534	WILLIAMS, FREDERICK FRANCIS	LT	NYC
01460	WHEELWRIGHT, JERE H. JR	LCDR	NYC	01535	ULEN, FRANCIS GRAEME	CAPT	NYC
01461	HUBBELL, DANIEL SOUTHWICK	CDR	NYC	01536	AMELOTTE, NAPOLEON ROMEO	LT	NYC
01462	JONES, WILLARD EDMUND	LCDR	NYC	01537	COSTER, GERARD HOLSMAN JR	CAPT	NYC
01463	STORER, CYRIL VICTOR	LT	NYC	01538	MACK, HARRY R.	CDR	NYC
01464	KUPCHAK, WALTER (N)	LT	NYC	01539	STUHR, WILLIAM SEBASTIAN	CDR	NYC
01465	SAVARESE, LAWRENC ALTON	CAPT	NYC	01540	BROSS, STEWARD RICHARD	LCDR	NYC
01466	MASLINE, JOHN RANDOLPH	LCDR	NYC	01541	WHITLOCK, HERBERT VERNET	LCDR	NYC
01467	HENERSON, DOUGLAS RICHARD JR	LT	NYC	01542	BESKIN, GERALD S.	LCDR	NYC
01468	SHAFER, JUDSON BELL	LT	NYC	01543	LEBOUTILLIER, PETER (N)	LT	NYC
01469	ALDERDICE, JOSEPH JAMES	LCDR	NYC	01544	CUMINGS, THAYER (N)	LCDR	NYC
01470	STONE, FRED D. JR.	LCDR	NYC	01545	BUEHLER, HOWARD (N)	LCDR	NYC
01471	ALLEN, DAVID EVANS	CDR	NYC	01546	CONNORS, RAYMOND JOSEPH	CAPT	NYC
01472	JUDGE, CYRIL BATHURST	CAPT	NYC	01547	CULBERT, WILLIAM LEDLIE JR.	LCDR	NYC
01473	FITZ-PATRICK, JOSEPH PAUL	CDR	NYC	01548	CRAMP, GEORGE WALTER	CAPT	NYC
01474	MCGANN, ELVIN MICHAEL	LT	NYC	01549	HARTFORD, GEORGE HUNTINGTON	LT	NYC
01475	BULLWINKEL, HENRY GRIFFIN	CAPT	NYC	01550	BALL, HERBBERT MORTON	LCDR	NYC
01476	MOTT, JORDAN LAWRENCE	LCDR	NYC	01551	EVANS, FRANCIS JOSEPH	LT	NYC
01477	PHILLIPS, ROLAND VIVIAN	LCDR	NYC	01552	ERMILIO, DOMINICK JOSEPH	CAPT	NYC
01478	DUNBAR, CHARLES ENOCH	LCDR	NYC	01553	HOGUET, PETER W.	LCDR	NYC
01479	BACON, EDWARD ALSTED	CDR	NYC	01554	FISH, RAYMOND TREADWELL	CDR	NYC
01480	MASON, WILLIAM AMBROSE JR.	LCDR	NYC	01555	SCHMIDT, FRANK WHALEN	CAPT	NYC
01481	RICHARDSON, GEORGE SELDEN	LCDR	NYC	01556	ARMEL, LYLE OLIVER	CAPT	NYC
01482	CAMPBELL, VERNON WILLIAM H.	CAPT	NYC	01557	HUGHES, HAROLD KNIGHT	CAPT	NYC
01483	WALSH, JOHN JOSEPH	LCDR	NYC	01558	HARRIS, HAROLD JEROME	CAPT	NYC
01484	MAZZEI, RALPH ALFRED	LT	NYC	01559	GARDNER, CARL (N)	1ST Lt	NYC
01485	WHITE, MARTIN JOSEPH	LCDR	NYC	01560	GREER, BERTRAND CALVERT	LCDR	NYC
01486	HAVENS, JUSTIN ELY	LCDR	NYC	01561	GLIDDEN, JONN CHENEY	CAPT	NYC
01487	HARDING, JOHN MITCHELL	CW03	NYC	01562	ESCHER, ROBERT ALEXANDER	LT	NYC
01488	MERRY, REMINGTON (N)	LCDR	NYC	01563	SMITH, FRANK EDWARD JR	CDR	NYC
01489	WEIL, CHARLES SAMUEL	LCDR	NYC	01564	GRIFFIN, JOHN JOSEPH JR.	LT	NYC
01490	HENDERSON, WYATT COLLIER	LCDR	NYC	01565	KAZMANN, HAROLD AARON	CDR	NYC
01491	MCARDLE, HENRY ROY	LCDR	NYC	01566	DIEFENDORF, FLOYD KINGSLEY	LT	NYC
01492	DOWNING, ARNOLD ANDREW	CAPT	NYC	01567	WEINTROB, MORRIS (N)	CDR	NYC
01493	GUEST, RAYMOND RICHARD	CDR	NYC	01568	VON LEDEN, HANS VICTOR	CDR	NYC
01494	THOMPSON, JESSE PRESTON	CW0	NYC	01569	FERGUSON, ADLAI LIVINGSTONE	LT	NYC
01495	STILLMAN, CHAUNCEY DEVEREUX	LCDR	NYC	01570	WHITLOCK, WILARD PALMER III	LT	NYC
01496	ALLEN, CHANNING (N)	LT	NYC	01571	PELLISIER, EDWARD ARTHUR	LT	NYC
01497	HEMPHILL, JULIAN	LT	NYC	01572	SMITH, WILLARD LYNWOOD JR	CDR	NYC
01498	LOCKMAN, WILLIAM HARWOOD	LCDR	MAS	01573	MEYER, IRA ROY	LT	NYC
01499	STEVENS, CHAUNCEY SYLVANUS	LCDR	MAS	01574	TRAPNELL, RICHARD WATKINS III	CDR	NYC

INSIG	COMPANION	RANK	CDRY	INSIG	COMPANION	RANK	CDRY
01575	PILLER, MARCEL NELSON	CDR	NYC	01650	SARGENT, JON FRANCIS	CDR	NYC
01576	MADDEN, JOHN FITZPARTICK	CAPT	NYC	01651	YEAGER, HOWARD AUSTIN	VADM	NYC
01577	ZANGG, JONN VAN WIE	LT	NYC	01652	BALLARD, WALTER ALEXANDER	LCDR	NYC
01578	WALKER, HAROLD GILLMORE	CAPT	NYC	01653	SULLIVAN, JOHN LAWRENCE	HONOR	
01579	MCEWEN, WILLIAM HENRY JR.	LCDR	NYC	01654	HOULE, DONALD JOSEPH	CAPT	MAS
01580	VAUGHAN, JOHN PHILLIP	LCDR	NYC	01655	BURCHETT, EUGENE CARROLL	CAPT	MAS
01581	FREEMAN, HAROLD DUDLEY	LCDR	NYC	01656	MARE, VICTOR SOCRATES	LCDR	NYC
01582	DUPE OF 1450 (JAMES J. LIDDY)			01657	CARR, WILLARD HERBERT	CDR	NYC
01583	DUPE OF 1481 (GEORGE SELDEN RICHARDSON)			01658	CARZOLINI, ALECHI F.	LT	NYC
01584	GAUDREAUX, LAURENCE FRANK	CAPT	NYC	01659	MC NAMARA, JOSEPH VINCENT	CAPT	NYC
01585	MERWARTH, HAROLD RUSSELL	CAPT	NYC	01660	CAMP, ROBERT CLIFTON JR	LT	NYC
01586	ROBERTSON, HUGH (N)	CDR	NYC	01661	BREEN, CLAYTON CHARLES	LT	NYC
01587	O'CONNOR, EDWARD FRANCIS	CDR	NYC	01662	POMEROY, STUART EIBERT	LCDR	NYC
01588	ADAMS, ROBERT LEE	CAPT	NYC	01663	LITTLEFIELD, WILLIAM EMERY	LCDR	NYC
01589	JOERG, ROBERT CONRAD III	CDR	NYC	01664	FEARON, HENRY DANA	CDR	NYC
01590	ZOTTI, FRANK (N) JR.	CAPT	NYC	01665	SHIELDS, M. LAWRENCE	CDR	NYC
01591	PAPE, CHARLES GEORGE	CDR	NYC	01666	BLOOMINGDALE, LYMAN GUSTAVE	LT	NYC
01592	RAPHAELIAN, GEORGE A.	LCDR	NYC	01667	MANN, CHARLES FRANK	CAPT	NYC
01593	COLLISON, PERCE BRAWN	LCDR	NYC	01668	SIMET, FRANKLIN M.	LCDR	NYC
01594	HASLER, ARTHUR RICHARD JR.	ENS	NYC	01669	CAREY, JOHN STANLEY	LCDR	NYC
01595	MICHLER, GORDON BOURNE	MR	NYC	01670	ABBOTT, PAUL (N)	CAPT	NYC
01596	STEWART, ALEXANDER (N)	LCDR	NYC	01671	GRISWOLD, GEORGE (N) JR	CDR	NYC
01597	TOCCO, CAJETAN ANTHONY	LT	NYC	01672	HANRAHAN, JOSEPH PATRICK	LCDR	NYC
01598	DINGWALL, HERBERT ALLAN JR.	LT	NYC	01673	SHIFRIN, LEO ARTHUR	CDR	NYC
01599	STERN, JESSE N.	CAPT	NYC	01674	GREENE, RAYMOND THOMAS	LT	NYC
01600	GRAY, KIMBALL (N)	LCDR	NYC	01675	BOYNTON, ELWOOD DADMUN	CDR	NYC
01601	NEUBERGER, JULIUS FREDERICK	CAPT	NYC	01676	BURKE, ROBERT GRANVILLE	CAPT	NYC
01602	MULHEARN, THOMAS JOSEPH	LCDR	NYC	01677	TABOR, FORDHAM DODGE	LCDR	NYC
01603	DUPE OF 0725 (RICHARD VINCENT DOLAN)			01678	NELIGH, HOWARD CHARLES	LT	NYC
01604	SNYDER, ELDREDGE (N)	CDR	NYC	01679	PIERPOINT, POWELL (N)	LT	NYC
01605	SHAW, WILFRED ERNEST	CDR	NYC	01680	HEMPSTEAD, EMERSON PEASE	LCDR	NYC
01606	CROUCH, CHARLES RAE	CDR	NYC	01681	STEELE, THEODORE MANNING	LCDR	NYC
01607	PERCY, GEORGE ALMY	Col	NYC	01682	MORRIS, RICHARD BOWERS	LCDR	WNY
01608	MARE, JOHN (N)	LCDR	NYC	01683	FAGAN, WILLIAM EDWARD	LCDR	NYC
01609	RAYMOND, GORDON (N)	LCDR	NYC	01684	GULBERTSON, JOSEPH LIVINGSTON	ENS	NYC
01610	GOULD, JOHN HURST PURNELL	CDR	NYC	01685	CANCELLED (JAMES ALEXANDER FOWLER JR)		NYC
01611	CLIFT, WILLIAM ORRIN	LT	NYC	01686	SMITH, MASON ROSSITER	LT	NYC
01612	WALKER, CHARLES M.	LT	NYC	01687	DEVAUGHN, WILLIAM (N)	CW02	NYC
01613	BERNER, WILLIAM (N)	ENS	NYC	01688	HASSAN, HARRY A.	CAPT	NYC
01614	STOUT, CHARLES HOLT	CDR	NYC	01689	GILLIES, LOUIS ARCHIBALD	RADM	NYC
01615	MALSTROM, ALVIN INGERSOLL	RADM	NYC	01690	VANBERGEN, GEORGE LORING	LCDR	NYC
01616	DINGWALL, HERBERT ALLAN	ENS	NYC	01691	MOODY, JOSEPH NESTOR	CDR	NYC
01617	COCRANE, EDWARD LULL	VADM	MAS	01692	MC WILLIAMS, ALFRED REEVES JR	CAPT	NYC
01618	BURACKER, WILLIAM HOUCK	RADM	MAS	01693	GRAIG, PHILIP YAWMAN	CAPT	NYC
01619	MCCLURE, JOHN FRANCIS W.	LCDR	NYC	01694	BRYAN, ROBERT CONGER	CDR	NYC
01620	THACKARA, CHARLES VAN ZANDT JR	LT	NYC	01695	HOLDEN, CARL FREDERICK	RADM	NYC
01621	SLATER, EDWARD WILLIAM	LT	NYC	01696	GOODWIN, HUGH HILTON	VADM	NYC
01622	ACKERMAN, GEORGE HENRY	LCDR	NYC	01697	NICHOLSON, JOHN ELLIOT	ENS	NYC
01623	JEWITT, DAVID WILLARD PENNOCK	LT	NYC	01698	GOODWIN, MAUURICE (N) JR	LT	NYC
01624	STONEMETZ, PHILIP THAYER	CAPT	AVN	01699	DALE, ORTON GOODWIN JR	LCDR	NYC
01625	SEAKWOOD, HERBERT JOSEPH	CAPT	NYC	01700	BERNARD, RICHARD JACQUES	LCDR	NYC
01626	SHETLER, JULIUS FREDERICK JR	ENS	NYC	01701	HAUERWAAS, JOHN CONRAD, JR.	ENS	NYC
01627	BLAKE, MONTGOMERY STEPHENSON	LCDR	NYC	01702	HOLMES, WALTER STEPHEN JR	LT	NYC
01628	DUPE OF 0677(DASHIELL LIVINGSTON MADEIRA)			01703	HERSEY, JONN DICKSON	CAPT	NYC
01629	RODGERS, LEON J.	CDR	NYC	01704	TRAFFORD, PERRY DAVIS JR	LCDR	NYC
01630	TELL, MEYER EDWARD	CDR	NYC	01705	JENNINGS, RALPH EDWARD	VADM	NYC
01631	LOW, FRANCIS HINE	LCDR	NYC	01706	ROBBINS, THOMAS HINCKLEY SR	RADM	NYC
01632	CASSIDY, JONN DINGEE	CDR	NYC	01707	MC LEAN, HEBER HAMPTON	VADM	NYC
01633	CLINCHY, DONALD STAGG	CDR	NYC	01708	PUGSLEY, EDMOND BREWSTER	CAPT	NYC
01634	MASSEY, JOHN FLOYD JR.	Capt	NYC	01709	SHERIDAN, WILLIAM P.	LT	NYC
01635	MASSEY, JOHN FLOYD SR.	LCDR	NYC	01710	PUDER, ROBERT STUARD	LT	NYC
01636	BENNETT, JOEL RICE II	LCDR	NYC	01711	MC DONALD, WILLIAM LAW	CAPT	NYC
01637	TORMA, STEPHEN (N)	LCDR	WNY	01712	BONNOT, EMILE LOUIS	CAPT	NYC
01638	STAFFORD, PAUL TUTT	CDR	NYC	01713	CATES, VINCENT KACZYNSKI	CDR	MAS
01639	LENZNER, JOSEPH B.	LCDR	NYC	01714	MC GINTY, DOUGLAS TORNOW	CAPT	MAS
01640	JOHNSTON, HERBERT ROBERT	CAPT	NYC	01715	LOWE, THOMAS JULIUS	LT	MAS
01641	ELLIS, GEORGE ELLWOOD	LCDR	NYC	01716	GARVEY, EDMOND PETER	CAPT	MAS
01642	BRONSON, JAMES FERDINAND	CDR	NYC	01717	BOURNE, KENNETH BARNES	LCDR	NYC
01643	STRONG, JAMES MERLIN	CAPT	NYC	01718	STERN, HENRY ROOT JR	LT	NYC
01644	WOODELL, JONN HENDERSON	LT	NYC	01719	MAXON, THOMAS RODGERS	LT	NYC
01645	OSHEA, JAMES CORNELIUS	LCDR	NYC	01720	KORN, EDWARD JOHN	CW03	NYC
01646	ACKEN, HENRY S. JR.	CAPT	NYC	01721	FLECK, HAROLD R.	LCDR	NYC
01647	BREWER, ARTHUR DOUGLASS	CDR	NYC	01722	RAMSEY, HOBART COLE	LCDR	NYC
01648	MEYERSON, HAROLD ISIDOR	LCDR	NYC	01723	MACWHINNIE, DONALD THOMAS	LCDR	NYC
01649	STEEPER, WILLIAM PURDY	LT	NYC	01724	SIMONS, ROBERT BENTHAM	RADM	NYC

Desert Shield/Desert Storm Review Panel 1: Planning and Logistics - (l to r) CAPT Warren Leback, Administrator, U.S. Maritime Service; RADM Arthur E. Henn, USCG, recent Commander, Maintenance and Logistics Command Atlantic Area; BGen James A. Brabham, Jr., USMC, Commanding General, 1st Force Service Support Group; and VADM Francis R. Donovan, USN, Commander Military Sealift Command. The moderator (not pictured) was RADM William F. Merlin, USCG (Ret.), Vice Commander General.

Desert Shield/Desert Storm Review Panel 2: Implementation and Execution - (l to r) VADM James D. Williams, USN, Deputy Chief of Naval Operations, Naval Warfare; RADM Walter T. Leland, USCG, former Chief of Law Enforcement and Defense Operations; RADM Riley D. Mixson, USN, former Commander, Carrier Group TWO; and MGen Harry W. Jenkins, Jr., USMC, Director Intelligence Division, HQMC. The moderator (not pictured) was MGen Ronald J. Beckwith, USMC (Ret.), Vice Commander General.

INSIG	COMPANION	RANK	CDRY	INSIG	COMPANION	RANK	CDRY
01725	HOLBROOK, WALTER SCOTT	LCDR	NYC	01790	DOYLE, JAMES HENRY	VADM	NYC
01726	GOELET, ROBERT GUESTIER	LT	NYC	01791	WILLCUTTS, MORTON DOUGGLAS	VADM	NYC
01727	MORRIS, ROBERT JOHN	CDR	NYC	01792	SWITZER, WENDELL GRAY	VADM	NYC
01728	PUDER, RICHARD K.	LT	NYC	01793	WHITEHEAD, RICHARD FRANCIS	VADM	ILL
01729	WEINER, JOSEPH (N)	CDR	NYC	01794	LIBBY, RUTHVEN ELMER	VADM	NYC
01730	RIMINGTON, CRITCHELL (N)	ENS	NYC	01795	KEMPE, ALBERT FREDERICK	CDR	ILL
01731	DAVIS, JOHN JOSEPH JR.	CDR	NYC	01796	TOMKINSON, KENNETH DREYER	CDR	NYC
01732	DOYLE, AUSTIN KEVIN	ADM	NYC	01797	COWDREY, ROY THOMAS	RADM	NYC
01733	JACKSON, WILLIAM BARTRUM	CDR	NYC	01798	AGNEW, WILLIAM JOHN CLARKE	RADM	NYC
01734	HARRIS, FIELD (N)	MGEN	NYC	01799	ROPER, JOHN WESLEY	RADM	NYC
01735	BULLOCK, HARVEY READE, JR.	LT	NYC	01800	PUGH, HERBERT LAMONT	RADM	NYC
01736	MC MASTER, JOHN DENNIS	LCDR	NYC	01801	ANDERSON, THOMAS CARLYLE	RADM	NY
01737	THEOBALD, JOSEPH BURHEIM	CDR	NYC	01802	CARSON, JOSEPH MALCOLM	RADM	NY
01738	RUSSELL, ALLEN (N)	CDR	NYC	01803	CRUISE, EDGAR ALLEN	VADM	NY
01739	MEEK, SAMUEL W.	CAPT	NYC	01804	HERRMANN, ERNEST EDWARD	RADM	NY
01740	CROSS, JAMES JEFFERSON JR	CDR	NYC	01805	HUNT, DANIEL (N)	RADM	NY
01741	OCONNELL, GEORGE ALBERT JR	CAPT	NYC	01806	MC QUISTON, IRVING MATTHEW	RADM	NY
01742	RASMUSSEN, RICHARD GEORGE	LT	NYC	01807	FULTON, JAMES MURDOCK	CDR	NY
01743	FROELICH, LOUIS B	LCDR	NYC	01808	ROBB, MAJOR WILLIAM	CDR	NY
01744	TOLLNER, THOMAS HOWLETT	LT	NYC	01809	LOVETTE, LELAND PEARSON	VADM	NY
01745	VEITCH, JAMES (N) JR.	LCDR	NYC	01810	STONE, JACOB CHAUNCEY	LCDR	NY
01746	HUGHES, JAMES JOSEPH	LCDR	NYC	01811	VINCENT, HARRY BARTLETT	CDR	NY
01747	MURPHY, WILLIS A.	CAPT	NYC	01812	HARTMAN, WILLIAM NORMAN	LT	NY
01748	NORTHROP, ROBERT WRIGHT	LT	NYC	01813	ROBARDS, WILLIAM CAMP FITZHUGH	CAPT	NY
01749	MC COMB, MARSHALL FRANCIS	LCDR	NYC	01814	BOURNE, ROBERT CUSHMAN	CAPT	NY
01750	JONES, FRANK JOHNSTON	LCDR	NYC	01815	WILDE, FRANCIS E. J. JR.	LT	NY
01751	BLANCHARD, THEODORE (N)	RADM	NYC	01816	DONEHUE, FRANCIS MCGARVEY	CAPT	NY
01752	STRETCH, DAVID ALBERT	CDR	NYC	01817	CULLMAN, HUGH (N)	LT	NY
01753	LEINWAND, IRVING (N)	LT	NYC	01818	LEVINGS, NELSON TRIMBLE	CDR	NY
01754	STEPHENSON, HUGH ROBERT	ENS	NYC	01819	DETZER, AUGUST J.	CAPT	NY
01755	WOLBARST, BERNARD PAUL E.	LCDR	NYC	01820	MEADE, EDWARD GRANT	CDR	NY
01756	BENJAMIN, JOSEPH FRANCIS	CDR	NYC	01821	MAHONEY, STEPHEN PATRICK	CDR	NY
01757	MACINNES, JOHN NEALON	CDR	NYC	01822	EAGAN, JAMES K, JR.	LT	NY
01758	BEARD, JEFFERSON DAVIS	RADM	NYC	01823	MARTIN, CHARLES FRANCIS	CAPT	NY
01759	PRESTON, IRVING SHERWOOD	LCDR	NYC	01824	HAWKE, ERIC ALEXANDER	LT	NY
01760	VALLDEJULI, JEROME KEARNEY	LT	NYC	01825	COGSWELL, JAMES KELSEY III	RADM	NY
01761	RINGDAHL, ESKIL BERG	LT	NYC	01826	EYER, GEORGE ALEXANDER JR.	LCDR	NY
01762	JACOB, LEONARD (N) II	LT	NYC	01827	LEARY, LEO HENRY JR.	LT	NY
01763	FOLLAND, WILLIAM RUSSELL	LT	MAS	01828	BAYLIS, CHESTER (N) JR.	LCDR	NY
01764	ADAMS, CHARLES FRANCIS JR.	LT	MAS	01829	HENRY, LINDSAY RUTHVEN	CAPT	NY
01765	MATHESON, ELMER CARL	LT	MAS	01830	HYDE, WILLIAM ALFRED	LCDR	NY
01766	CONNOOLY, JOSEPH VINCENT JR.	LTJG	NYC	01831	BROWN, ROBERT GOULD	CDR	NY
1766A	FAHEY, EDMUND EUGENE	CDR	NYC	01832	SHERMAN, FREDERICK CARL	ADM	NY
01767	SCOTT, JOHN WILLIAM JR.	CDR	NYC	01833	MC MAHON, FREDERICK WILLIAM	VADM	NY
1767A	HORGAN, THOMAS PATRICK	CDR	MAS	01834	GANO, CHARLES WILLIAM	LCDR	NY
01768	DARLINGTON, HENRY (N) JR.	LT	NYC	01835	MURPHY, JOHN DAMIAN	RADM	NY
1768A	PARCELL, ALVA DEAL	CDR	MAS	01836	MOORE, DONALD LEIGH	CDR	NY
01769	SULLIVAN, FRANCIS JOHN	LCDR	NYC	01837	DUNN, CHARLES JOHN	CAPT	NY
1769A	SHERRILL, GIBBS WLYNNKOOP	CDR	MAS	01838	CUTLER, SHIRLEY YOUNGS	CAPT	NYC
01770	BURKE, ANDREW JOOSEPH JR.	ENS	NYC	01839	JOHNSON, JOTHAM (N)	LCDR	NYC
1770A	HUTCHINS, ROBERT DALTON	CDR	MAS	01840	KALES, ROBERT GRAY	CAPT	NYC
01771	MOORE, JAMES BIGGS JR.	LCDR	NYC	01841	REINICKE, FREDERICK GEROGE	COMMO	NYC
1771A	MILLAR, JAMES (N)	LT	MAS	01842	PERDUE, CHARLES HIRAM	CAPT	NYC
01772	KAYDOUH, GEORGE MICHAEL	CAPT	NYC	01843	KNIGHT, PAGE (N)	CAPT	NYC
1772A	BROOKS, FREDERICK HIESTER JR.	CDR	MAS	01844	LAMBORN, RICHARD LAFORGE	LCDR	NYC
01773	TAYLOR, THEODORE LANGHANS	LTJG	NYC	01845	HUBBARD, MILES HUNTER	RADM	NYC
1773A	DUNLAP, LINNCOLN MEAD	LCDR	NYC	01846	MACROBERT, RUSSELL GALBRAITH	CAPT	NYC
01774	FOLK, WINSTON ESTES PILCHER	RADM	NYC	01847	TEMPLETON, THOMAS HARRY	CAPT	NYC
1774A	LOWELL, HENRY TRUE JR.	LT	MAS	01848	POWELL, PAULLUS PRINCE	RADM	NYC
01775	DUPE OF 0820(HERBERT MCLEAN PURDY)			01849	KRIENDLER, IRVING ROBERFT	Maj.	NYC
1775A	PRATT, MORTON SAUNDERS	CAPT	MAS	01850	COLEMAN, SHELDON TOWNSEND	CDR	NYC
01776	HINES, ARTHUR JAMES	LT	NYC	01851	LASHMAN, SHELLEY BORTIN	CAPT	NYC
01777	WELLS, CHARLES RAYMOND	CAPT	NYC	01852	BISSELL, FREDERICK OLDS	CDR	NYC
01778	MC GOVERN, EDWARD GERARD	CDR	NYC	01853	HILL, NATHANIEL MAURICE JR.	LT	NYC
01779	MC KAY, ZACHARY S.	LCDR	NYC	01854	AILES, JOHN WILLIAM III	RADM	NYC
01780	DOWNEY, CHARLES STANLEY	CAPT	ILL	01855	BEYER, MALCOLM KELLER	BGEN	NYC
01781	ENGELS, WALTER DONIHEE	LT	NYC	01856	NIXON, JON LEON	CAPT	NYC
01782	ROSS, LELAND HAMILTON JR.	LCDR	NYC	01857	FULLER, FREDERIC JAMES JR..	CDR	NYC
01783	MC KEE, WALDO MCCUTCHEON	MR	NYC	01858	SELDEN, JOHN TAYLOR	BGEN	NYC
01784	TAUSSIG, FRANCIS BREWSTER	CDR	NYC	01859	HUDSON, HOMER BERNARD	CAPT	NYC
01785	ENTWISTLE, FREDERICK IRVING	RADM	NYC	01860	ATWOOD, GEORGE DICKINSON	LT	NYC
01786	MILLER, THORNTON CHARLES	RADM	NYC	01861	NEBOLSIN, EUGEN ARCADI	LCDR	NYC
01787	ROYAR, MURREY LEVERING	VADM	DNYC	01862	BROOKS, MORRIS (N)	CAPT	NYC
01788	DIETZ, HOWARD JOSEPH	LT	NYC	01863	JAME, OLIVER BURR JR.	CDR	NYC
01789	GREENMAN, GARRETT WILLIAM	COMMO	NYC	01864	DONAHUE, CHARLES WILLIAM	LCDR	NYC

INSIG	COMPANION	RANK	CDRY
01865	MOREHOUSE, ALBERT KELLOGG	RADM	NYC
01866	MC KEE, LOGAN (N)	RADM	NYC
01867	TYRREL, RANDOLPH E.	LCDR	NYC
01868	BITTNER, WALTER WILLIAM	CDR	NYC
01869	STRANG, WALTER DANIEL JR.	CDR	NYC
01870	GROSS, ROBERT FRANK	CDR	NYC
01871	VONHERBULIS, JOHN WILLIAM	LT	NYC
01872	FREILE, ORMOND	CDR	NYC
01873	SWANWICK,, L. VAUGHAN	LT	NYC
01874	GANO, ROY ALEXANDER	VADM	NYC
01875	SCHOONOVER, CORTLANDT	LT	NYC
01876	PINNEY, HENRY JULIUS JR.	LCDR	NYC
01877	SHIFLEY, RALPH LOUIS	VADM	NYC
01878	MAAS, MELVIN JOSEPH	MGEN	NYC
01879	STEPHENS, JAMES COLLINS	ENS	NYC
01880	ELLSWORTH, THOMAS THORPE	CDR	NYC
01881	GREENBERG, JACK	LCDR	NYC
01882	REICHNER, MORGAN STEPHENS A.	LCDR	NYC
01883	RING, STANHOPE COTTON	CAPT	NYC
01884	SPELLMAN, HOWARD HILTON	LCDR	NYC
01885	EDWARDS, HAROLD MARION	CAPT	NYC
01886	IRWIN, CHARLES JAMES JR.	Maj.	NYC
01887	ROBINSON, SAMUEL MURRAY	ADM	NYC
01888	O'HARA, "H" RICHARD	LCDR	NYC
01889	HICKS, FREDERICK STEVENS	MR	NYC
01890	JEROME, CLAYTON CHARLES	LGEN	NYC
01891	HOWLAND, JOHN (N)	LTCol	NYC
01892	CLARKE, RICHARD WARNER	LCDR	NYC
01893	TOWERS, HAROLD REYNOLDS	LT	NYC
01894	CANCELLED (CHESTER M. LAWSON, DESCNT)		
01895	MURRAY, JOHN RINGLAND	LCDR	AVN
01896	LEMKIN, EDWIN HERBERT	LT	NYC
01897	WREN, HAROLD GWYN	CAPT	NYC
01898	ZOLLER, CARL A. JR.	CAPT	NYC
01899	GREELEY, HAROLD DUDLEY	LT	NYC
01900	FREELAND, ROBERT WILLIAM	LCDR	NYC
01901	DRAIN, DAN THOMAS	CAPT	NYC
01902	HAVEN, HUGH ELLIOTT	RADM	NYC
01903	VICKREY, CLAUDE CLAIRE	CDR	NYC
01904	BESSIE, EVERETT MORTIMER	CAPT	NYC
01905	KINNEY, RONALD EARL JR.	CDR	NYC
01906	BARNUM, ROBERT HUDSON	RADM	NYC
01907	ARMSTRONG, JOHN TILT	CDR	NYC
01908	ZIMMERMAN, JAMES JOSHUA	LT	NYC
01909	ROBISCH, IRVING CARL	CDR	NYC
01910	HARDING, HAROLD JESSE	CDR	NYC
01911	LONG, RALPH WALDO	LCDR	NYC
01912	MOUKAD, JOSEPH ELIAS	LCDR	NYC
01913	STEVENSON, ROBERT JAMES JR.	CDR	NYC
01914	WELCH, PHILIP PINDELL	RADM	NYC
01915	HICKMAN, NORMAN GILBERT	LT	NYC
01916	BLAKE, WILLIAM GARDNER	LCDR	NYC
01917	BURKE, ARLEIGH ALBERT	ADM	NYC
01918	NELSON, HARRY BURTON	LT	NYC
01919	MC CORMACK, JONN (N)	LT	NYC
01920	DAVIES, THOMAS DANIEL	RADM	NYC
01921	SELDIN, HERMAN MARTIN	LT	NYC
01922	MCINNES, HECTOR JOSEPH ALLEN	CAPT	NYC
01923	LEITH, STANLEY (N)	RADM	AVN
01924	OGORMAN, THEODORE ARTHUR	CAPT	NYC
01925	EMMONS, HENRY TOWER	LCDR	NYC
01926	ACKERMAN, EUGENE BERTHOLD	CAPT	NYC
01927	HALL, ALFRED JOSEPH JR.	CDR	NYC
01928	ELLICOTT, JOSEPH REMINGTON	LCDR	NYC
01929	POWELL, BONNEY MACOY	CDR	NYC
01930	REARDON, JAMES GERARD	CDR	NYC
01931	DRAPEAU, GEORGE (N) JR.	CDR	NYC
01932	MONELL, EDMUND CONVERSE	LCDR	NYC
01933	MC MILLIAN, IRA ELLIS	RADM	NYC
01934	LEEBURGER, FRANKLIN JEFFERSON	CAPT	NYC
01935	SCHWENCK, JAMES EDWARD	LCDR	NYC
01936	HAMBERGER, DEWITT CLINTON ELLIS	RADM	NYC
01937	BURNS, JOSEPH WILLIAM	LCDR	NYC
01938	MC CUE, RAYMOND GERARD	LT	NYC
01939	FOX, WILLIAM JOSEPH	BGEN	NYC
01940	CRUZEN, RICHARD HAROLD	VADM	NYC
01941	DUFFY, MAURICE JOSEPH	ENS	NYC
01942	COLVIN, OLIVER DYER	CDR	NYC
01943	SMEDBERG, WILLIAM RENWICK III	VADM	NYC
01944	MILLS, HARRY LLOYD	CDR	NYC
01945	FELT, HARRY DONALD	ADM	NYC
01946	TATOM, EUGENE (N)	CAPT	NYC
01947	NEALE, EDGAR TILGHMAN	CAPT	NYC
01948	AMBERG, RICHARD HILLER	CDR	NYC
01949	BORKER, WALLACE JACOB	CAPT	NYC
01950	SCHOLTZ, CARL (N)	CDR	NYC
01951	COLIHAN, WILLIAM JOSEPH JR.	LCDR	NYC
01952	TARR, ROBERT JOSEPH	CAPT	NYC
01953	WAINWRIGHT, CARROLL L. JR.	LT	NYC
01954	BURROUGH, JOSEPH GARR	LT	NYC
01955	COLLIHAN, JOHN PATRICK	LT	NYC
01956	MOEBUS, LUCIAN ANCEL	VADM	NYC
01957	JACOBS, RANDALL (N)	VADM	NYC
01958	MC CORMICK, WILLIAM EDWARD	CDR	NYC
01959	BRAYBROOK, WILLIAM MCKENZIE	CAPT	NYC
01960	BROADDUS, CARL ASHTON	VADM	NYC
01961	ANDERSON, OLIVER JOHN	ENS	NYC
01962	COOPER, MAURICE DIEHL JR.	CDR	NYC
01963	HUTCHESON, S. L.	LCDR	AVN
01964	WIRTH, JOHN M.	CDR	AVN
01965	COLEMAN, JOHN BURLINSON A. JR.	CDR	AVN
01966	CARNELL, E. BRADLEY	LT	AVN
01967	PLAYER, C. A. WILLIS	LT	AVN
01968	HOLMES, MACKAY D.	LT	AVN
01969	DRAPER, RALPH C.	LCDR	AVN
01970	JOLLIFFE, ROBERT NELSON	CDR	AVN
01971	DAVIS, CHARLES E. JR.	CDR	AVN
01972	RIDDER, BERNARD JOSEPH	Maj.	AVN
01973	LEONARD, JOHN IRVING	CDR	SFR
01974	WOOD, ERIC WILMER	Lt Col	AVN
01975	SEALY, ROBERT (N) JR.	CAPT	AVN
01976	HARRINGTON, WILLIAM F. JR.	LCDR	AVN
01977	GUTERMAN, HERBERT C.	CDR	AVN
01978	GOODRIDGE, MALCOLM (N) JR.	CDR	AVN
01979	BUCKMAN, C. CLARK	CAPT	AVN
01980	WENMAN, BYRD W., JR.	LCDR	AVN
01981	LANGENBERG, HENRY F.	CDR	AVN
01982	PAUL, JOHNSTON S.	CAPT	AVN
01983	HODGES, WILLIAM V. JR.	LCDR	AVN
01984	FOX, HOWARD A.	LT	AVN
01985	MOORE, BURRESS (N) JR.	CDR	AVN
01986	O'NEIL, AMBROSE P.	LCDR	AVN
01987	WOOD, JOHN WILLIAM	LCDR	AVN
01988	BRUSH, RODERICK MCLEOD	LT	AVN
01989	LEWIS, ROBERT J.	LT	AVN
01990	HALLETTR, JOHN FOLSOM	CDR	AVN
01991	BERRY, LOREN C.	LCDR	AVN
01992	WINTON, W. BREWSTER	LCDR	AVN
01993	SIEGEL, SEYMOUR N.	CDR	AVN
01994	DUPE 0F 1821 (STEPHEN PATRICK MAHONEY)		
01995	SEILER, GEROGE W. JR.	LCDR	AVN
01996	BROWN, ARCHIBALD MANNING JR.	LCDR	AVN
01997	ACHESON, GLEN (N)	CDR	AVN
01998	TILT, ALBERT JR.	CDR	AVN
01999	THORNE, OAKLEIGH L.	CDR	AVN
02000	ADAMS, WILLIAM BARON	LCDR	AVN
02001	PETTIT, KARL D. JR.	LCDR	AVN
02002	GRANT, WILLIAM (N)	LT	AVN
02003	DUPE OF 1608 (JOHN MARE)		
02004	SHIELDS, WILLIAM (N) JR.	CDR	AVN
02005	MUNDY, WILLIAM G.	LTJG	AVN
02006	PITCHER, WILLIAM MORRISON	LT	AVN
02007	MOSIER, HERSCHEL L.	LCDR	AVN
02008	BALLOU, HOSEA CUSHMAN	LCDR	AVN
02009	MACMANNIS, BERTRAM ROBERTS	LT	AVN
02010	BODMAN, LEWIS HENRY	LCDR	AVN
02011	DUPE OF 1513 (GEORGE MICHEL L LABRANCHE JR)		
02012	DRIBBEN, SEYMOUR (N)	CAPT	AVN
02013	FLYNN, NIEL PIERSON	LCDR	AVN
02014	KNIFFIN, HOWARD S.	LCDR	AVN

INSIG	COMPANION	RANK	CDRY	INSIG	COMPANION	RANK	CDRY
02015	COSEL, ROBERT W.	LCDR	AVN	02090	LUNNY, ROBERT MILLER	CDR	NYC
02016	BURNS, JAMES FRANCIS R.	LCDR	AVN	02091	MC GILL, DONALD FORBES	CDR	NYC
02017	DUPE OF 1610 (JOHN HURST PURNELL GOULD)			02092	LEGGETT, WILSON DURWARD JR	RADM	NYC
02018	FELL, JOHN R.	CDR	AVN	02093	SINYEI, LOUIS (N)	LCDR	NYC
02019	LUNDGREN, WILLIAM E.	ENS	AVN	02094	MC CABE, THOMAS EDWARD L.	CAPT	NYC
02020	LYNT, HERBERT E.	LCDR	AVN	02095	SANDERS, HARRY (N)	VADM	NYC
02021	LESLIE, WILLIAM (N) JR.	LT	AVN	02096	MERRITT, EDWARD LESTER	LCDR	NYC
02022	DUPE OF 1624 (PHILLIP THAYER STONEMETZ)			02097	GRAF, DONALD RICHARDSON	LT	NYC
02023	ARNESON, S. RICHARD	LCDR	AVN	02098	PARRY, HENRY LAURENS	CAPT	NYC
02024	HAZZARD, ROBERT PARKS, JR	LCDR	AVN	02099	COOKE, ALMON GOODWIN	CDR	NYC
02025	NILES, WALTER W.	LCDR	AVN	02100	DUPE OF 0780 (HORACE GUION BENENDICT)		
02026	HORGAN, RALPH THOMAS	Col	NYC	02101	KETCHAM, WEAVER VINSON	CDR	NYC
02027	SAGAR, CHARLES PARKER	2ND Lt	NYC	02102	CHRYSLER, JACK FORKER	LT	NYC
02028	ROGERS, WILLIAM OSCAR JR.	Maj.	NYC	02103	GALLAGHER, JOSEPH VINCENT	LT	NYC
02029	PORTER, RALPH LANE	CDR	NYC	02104	VOLK, AUSTIN NICHOLAS	CAPT	NYC
02030	BALDWIN, JAMES TILESTON	CAPT	NYC	02105	GOODNEY, WILLIARD KINSMAN	RADM	NYC
02031	MIDDENDORF, JOHN WILLIAM	LT	NYC	02106	MURPHY, MARION EMERSON	VADM	SWS
02032	OLSON, LOUIS BERNHARDT	RADM	NYC	02107	RICHARDSON, ALBERT BUTLER	LT	NYC
02033	STODDARD, GEORGE CHAFFEE	LT	NYC	02108	THIELE, EUGENE HUGO	CDR	NYC
02034	WATTERS, HARRY JEAN	CDR	NYC	02109	O'LEARY, FRANCIS VINCENT	LCDR	NYC
02035	DELANEY, CORNELIUS JOSEPH	CAPT	NYC	02110	CARLSON, FREDERICK GUSTAV E.	CAPT	NYC
02036	GADE, JOHN ALLYNE	CAPT	NYC	02111	GORDINIER, VIRGIL FRANCIS	CAPT	NYC
02037	LYNN, CHARLES LEIGHTON	CAPT	NYC	02112	HANDLY, ROBERT SHANAMAN	LT	NYC
02038	LANHAM, SAMUEL MARTIN STEPHENS	CDR	NYC	02113	BURBACH, CHARLES MILLER		NYC
02039	DONOHUE, TIMOTHY FRANCIS	RADM	NYC	02114	BENZ, ROBERT PAUL	CDR	NYC
02040	CLAXTON, NORMAN LOUIS	CAPT	NYC	02115	CLEXTON, EDWARD WILLIAM	RADM	NYC
02041	COLLINS, WILLIAM THOMAS II	LCDR	NYC	02116	MATHER, PAUL LUKER	RADM	NYC
02042	LEMLY, FREDERICK WINDEGGER	RADM	NYC	02117	ROFF, EDWARD GIRARD JR.	Lt Col	NYC
02043	JACOBS, CLYDE WEBSTER	LT	NYC	02118	KRAMER, RAYMOND PAUL	LT	NYC
02044	HESS, ROBERT SOL	CDR	NYC	02119	REGAN, WILLIAM FRANK	LT	NYC
02045	DUPONT, ERNEST (N) JR.	CDR	NYC	02120	BRONDUM, HOWARD WILLIAM	LCDR	NYC
02046	JARRETT, HARRY BEAN	VADM	NYC	02121	SNELL, LAWRENCE WORDSWORTH	CDR	NYC
02047	LUSSKIN, HAROLD (N)	CAPT	NYC	02122	MONROE, JACK PENDLETON	RADM	SEA
02048	HIGHFIELD CHARLES FREDERICK	CAPT	NYC	02123	GOLDBERG, JOSHUA LOUIS	CAPT	NYC
02049	TREAT, WILLIAM WARDWELL	ENS	NYC	02124	OKANE, ADRIAN JOHN	LCDR	NYC
02050	RAK, MIKE (N)	LT	NYC	02125	FULLER, HENRY MELVILLE	LT	NYC
02051	AMES, ROBERT THEODORE	LCDR	NYC	02126	PRATT, FREDERICK WILLIAM JR.	LTJG	NYC
02052	MC DILL, ALEXANDER STUART	CAPT	NYC	02127	TYREE, DAVID MERRILL	RADM	NYC
02053	DOBSON, RODNEY HIRAM	LT	NYC	02128	CLEAR, THOMAS LEROY II	LT	NYC
02054	AMES, MORAN PAUL	CAPT	NYC	02129	OKANE, GEORGE HUNTER	CDR	NYC
02055	BAKER, ELLIOT RUSSEL	LCDR	NYC	02130	WALTERS, LOUIS LEONARD	LT	NYC
02056	HITCHINGS, VERNON DAVIS JR.	LCDR	NYC	02131	MC ATEER, "J" EUGENE	LCDR	NYC
02057	TAYLOR, PETER BURR	LTJG	NYC	02132	ANDERSON, EDWARD ROBERT	CAPT	NYC
02058	WATTS, ETHELBERT (N)	CAPT	NYC	02133	BRISCOE, TRAVER (N)	LT	NYC
02059	TAYLOR, WILIAM SHIPLEY	CDR	NYC	02134	MORAN, JOSEPH HENRY II	LT	NYC
02060	HESS, ROBERT TALBOT	LT	NYC	02135	MENDENHALL, WILLIAM K. JR.	RADM	NYC
02061	RORSCHACH, ANTHONY LAWLESS	RADM	NYC	02136	SEWALL, MARSHALL CHRISTOPHER	CDR	NYC
02062	STAR, LEON DAVID	LCDR	NYC	02137	OREM, HOWARD EMERY	VADM	NYC
02063	RINGHAUSEN, ROBERT LEO	CAPT	NYC	02138	MC LEAN, EPHRAIM RANKIN JR.	VADM	NYC
02064	PATE, RANDOLPH, MCCALL	GEN	NYC	02139	HOBBS, ALLEN (N)	CAPT	NYC
02065	MC MANES, KENMORE M, ATHEW	RADM	NYC	02140	DAY, ROBERT EUGENE	CAPT	NYC
02066	BRYSON, WILLIAM (N)	LCDR	NYC	02141	MIDDENDORF, WILLIAM KENNEDY B.	LT	NYC
02067	NOE, HENRY MARTYN	LCDR	NYC	02142	STONE, BROMLEY SCOFIELD	CDR	NYC
02068	TELLER, STEADMAN (N)	CAPT	NYC	02143	ROTH, WILLIAM JAMES JR.	CAPT	NYC
02069	HANSON, THOMAS JOHN	CAPT	NYC	02144	BRACKEN, JOHN PAUL	CAPT	NYC
02070	STUBENBORD, JOHN GEORGE III	CAPT	NYC	02145	CORBETT, MURL (N)	Lt Col	NYC
02071	LANIGAN, JOHN RALPH	BGEN	NYC	02146	WALLIS, FREDERICK HAROLD	CAPT	NYC
02072	LOWANS, WARREN HARDING	CAPT	NYC	02147	NAGER, CHARLES JOSEPH	CAPT	NYC
02073	DRYMALSKI, RAYMOND PAUL	LCDR	ILL	02148	MC COLLUM, ARTHUR HOWARD	RADM	NYC
02074	CARMAN, TRAVERS DENTON	LCDR	NYC	02149	KESSING, OLIVER OWEN	COMMO	NYC
02075	WASHINGTON, JAMES DOWDELL	LT	NYC	02150	COLLINS, LAWRENCE STEPHEN	LT	NYC
02076	VONLEHMDEN, FRANCIS RALPH	LCDR	NYC	02151	TAYLOR, THOMAS HERBERT	RADM	NYC
02077	COTTER, THOMAS ARNOLD JR.	CAPT	NYC	02152	RODGERS, JAMES WILLIAM	CDR	NYC
02078	CALHOUN, AUBRA (N)	CDR	NYC	02153	SUMMERS, CLARENCE GIBBS III	LCDR	NYC
02079	HAWKINS, DAVID DELOS	RADM	NYC	02154	STEINBECK, JOHN MACULEY	CAPT	NYC
02080	CUSTER, BENJAMIN SCOTT	RADM	AVN	02155	SUTTER, EDWIN JOSEPH	LT	NYC
02081	WILLARD, WILLIAM BRADLEY	CAPT	DCA	02156	OSBORN, PHILIP RANSOM	CAPT	NYC
02082	SHAPLEY, ALAN (N)	LGEN	NYC	02157	JACKSON, EDWARD FRANK	RADM	NYC
02083	WAGNER, LOY ARTHUR	LCDR	NYC	02158	ROY, NORMAND YVAN	LCDR	NYC
02084	MC QUEEN, JOHN CRAWFORD	LGEN	NYC	02159	GORDON, WILLIAM RICHARDSON	LCDR	NYC
02085	ANDERSON, GEORGE WHELAN JR	ADM	NYC	02160	SQUIRE, FRANCIS HAGAR	LCDR	NYC
02086	MC KENZIE, JACK RONALD	LT	NYC	02161	WAY, ROBERT LEROY	CDR	NYC
02087	DUDLEY, JAMES ROGERS	RADM	NYC	02162	BRADFORD, LINDSAY (N)	LT	NYC
02088	DUPE OF 1998 (ALBERT TILT JR)			02163	WEIDENHAMMER, CARLTON ANKER	LCDR	NYC
02089	DOWNING, ROBERT ARNOLD	CDR	NYC	02164	KUROVSKY, PAUL (N)	LT	NYC

(l-r) Then Commander General RADM Willaim Merlin, USCG (Ret.), presented the NOUS Rear Admiral Thurston H. James Memorial Award to LTJG Stephen C. Harrington, USN. The plaque was ahnded to him in ceremonies last August with Patrol Squadron 30 at the Jacksonville NAS. The awardee is selected by CNATRA for NOUS.

Lt. (Jg) Doport Wins James Award

In ceremonies at Naval Air Station, Patuxent River, the Naval Order of the United States presented Lieutenant (jg) Kevin R. Doport, U.S. Navy, with its Rear Admiral Thurston H. James Memorial Award.

The award, a handsome chronograph with appropriate accompanting citation, is conferred annually by the Naval Order upon the outstanding graduate of the flight training course at Pensacola, as selected by the Training Command. The award recipient must have demonstrated superlative performance in military achievement and academic standing, and must have evinced the highest order of patriotism. Lieutenant (jg) Doport was the honor graduate selectee of 1981. At subsequent interservice training at Mather Air Force Base, California, he earned a grade-point average of 99.7, highest ever recorded in the history of that program.

Awardee At Patuxent River

Lt. (jg) Doport is currently serving with Air Development Squadron 8 at Patuxent River. Rear Admiral Thurston James, for whom the award is named, served as Commander General of the Naval Order from 1958 to 1961.

Representing the Commander General of the Naval Order in the presentation of the award to Lieutenant (jg) Doport was the Commandery, Vaughn B. Coale, accompanies by members of the Commandery staff: the Vice-Commander, Captain Philip G. Saylor USN (Ret.); the Finance OFficer, Commander Richard R. Bowers USNR; and Immediate Past Commander Russell B. Miller.

Pictured with LTJG Steven S. Vahsen, USN, recipient of the RADM T. H. James Award at NAS Brunswick are the CO and XO of Patrol Squadron 23.

INSIG	COMPANION	RANK	CDRY	INSIG	COMPANION	RANK	CDRY
02165	COOKE, HENRY DAVID	RADM	NYC	02223	SEVERY, DERWYN MARLAND	CAPT	SWS
02166	WINSLOW, SAMUEL RINN	LCDR	NYC	02224	HOYT, JOHN ROBERT	CDR	SWS
02167	FEMONT, JOHN CHARLES	CAPT	NYC	02225	JESTER, ROSS RODERICK	CDR	SWS
02168	HEWITT, ANDERSON FOWLER	LCDR	NYC	02226	DALLAS, NICHOLAS (N)	LT	SWS
02169	ROWE, FRANK WALTER JR.	CAPT	NYC	02227	GARRISON, RALPH STEED	RADM	SWS
02170	SEGAL, STEPHEN MATTHEW	ENS	SFR	02228	JONES, FRANK GILLEAS	RADM	SWS
02171	PRESTON, JOHN PAUL	CAPT	NYC	02229	KASL, DALE ALFRED	CAPT	SWS
02172	SCHWYHART, ROBERT MARION	CAPT	NYC	02230	KIEFER, ORRIN OTTO	CDR	SWS
02173	RUNGE, KURT OTTO	CDR	NYC	02231	ROPE, ROBERT SCOTT	LCDR	SWS
02174	RICHARDSON, LAWRENCE BAXTER	RADM	AVN	02232	STODDARD, SAMUEL WILLIAM	CDR	SWS
02175	OWEN, PERCY (N) JR.	CDR	NYC	02233	SIDENBURG, GEORGE MONROE JR.	CDR	SWS
02176	MILLER, HAROLD BLAINE	RADM	NYC	02234	SMITH, JAMES ROY	CAPT	SWS
02177	JOHNSON, CARL ARTHUR	CAPT	NYC	02235	STAPLES, WILLARD IRVING	CAPT	SWS
02178	HOLSAPPLE, HENRY TAYLOR	CDR	NYC	02236	THOMSON, THEODORE EDWARD	CDR	SWS
02179	SCHOLLE, DONALD WILLIAM	ENS	NYC	02237	DREW, EDWARD JOHN	RADM	SWS
02180	STRACHAN, JOHN ROBERT	LCDR	NYC	02238	TRONOWSKY, OTTO (N)	CAPT	SWS
02181	SMITH, RALPH STONE	CDR	NYC	02239	WESTLAND, JOHN LAWRENCE JR.	CAPT	SWS
02182	JEMAIL, JAMES (N)	CDR	NYC	02240	WINES, RALPH KEN JR.	CAPT	SWS
2182A	VIGUE, DAVID L.	LCDR	MAS	02241	YAMBERT, RALPH FRANKLIN	CDR	SWS
02183	SCOTT, ANDREW HOGG JR.	LT	NYC	02242	WHITE, STEPHEN NOLTING	CAPT	SWS
2183A	VONDERLIPPE, CARL DETLEF	LT	MAS	02243	BACKBERG, FLOYD HENRY	CDR	SWS
02184	GRANDFIELD, FRANCIS JOSEPH	CAPT	NYC	02244	PAXTON, CHARLES NORMAN	RADM	SWS
2184A	SCOTT, ROBERT LIVINGSTON	LCDR	MAS	02245	WAUCHOPE, GEORGE MARKER	RADM	NYC
02185	WORMSER, CHARLES MAILERT	CDR	NYC	02246	MORRIS, WILLIAM LEONARD	LCDR	NYC
2185A	WRIGHT, LEONARD MARSHALL	CAPT	MAS	02247	EXTON, WILLIAM (N) JR.	CAPT	NYC
02186	WINNEY, JUSTIN WILLIAM	CDR	NYC	02248	SHERRY, MARTIN FREDERICK	LCDR	NYC
2186A	REARDON, EDWARD STEPHEN	LTJG	MAS	02249	SEYMOUR, HARRY AUGUSTUS	CAPT	NYC
02187	AUSTEN, WILLARD EMERSON	CAPT	NYC	02250	COWAN, FRANK K.	CDR	NYC
2187A	SPENCER, THAXTER PARKS	CAPT	MAS	02251	FARRELL, JAMES PETER	LCDR	NYC
02188	FRANK, LOUIS LLOYD	Col	NYC	02252	STUHR, BERNARD CANNING	CDR	NYC
2188A	FRACKLETON, JOHN JAMES	ENS	MAS	02253	CORT, CARTER FREDRICK	LCDR	NYC
02189	ROBINSON, WILLIAM (N) JR.	ENS	NYC	02254	MC CORMICK, JOHN JOSEPH	CAPT	NYC
2189A	MC GOVERN, LAWRENCE HAVEN	CDR	MAS	02255	GROHNS, DONALD JOSEPH	LCDR	NYC
02190	DELANEY, HENRY RAYMOND	RADM	NYC	02256	STEWART, OTTO JAMES	CDR	NYC
2190A	PARKER, EDWARD PICKERING	CDR	MAS	02257	SPANGLER, SELDEN BOOTH	VADM	NYC
02191	COLLINS, LUCIUS PATRICK	CDR	NYC	02258	WALKER, ALBERT TRINCANO	RADM	NYC
2191A	MC SWEENEY, MORTIMER PAUL	LCDR	MAS	02259	MAHONEY, JAY EHRET	LT	NYC
02192	RYDER, JOHN FRENCH	CAPT	NYC	02260	HILLBERG, ALBERT GOSTA	CDR	NYC
2192A	KELLEY, STILLMAN FRANCIS II	LCDR	MAS	02261	GUARINI, FRANK JOSEPH	LT	NYC
02193	BRENNER, "J" EDWARD	CAPT	SWS	02262	CONNETT, WILLIAM BREWER JR.	LCDR	NYC
2193A	BUNNELL, WILLIAM BREWSTER	ENS	MAS	02263	ALEXIS, ALGERT DANIEL	RADM	NYC
02194	BROWN, ELMER ELSWORTH	LCDR	SWS	02264	MARTIN, JOHN QUINCY	LCDR	NYC
2194A	HAYWARD, ERNEST TYLER	CAPT	MAS	02265	PETRITZ, JOSEPH SCHMAUSS	LT	NYC
02195	BROWN, NORMAN VICTOR	LCDR	SWS	02266	HOLDEN, EDWIN WESTERMAN	CDR	NYC
2195A	MARCUCELLA, FRANK (N)	CDR	MAS	02267	LYON, NORMAN MORAIS	CAPT	NYC
02196	CASLIN, JOSEPH FRANCIS	CDR	SWS	02268	BARR, FORREST OLIVER	CDR	NYC
2196A	HOWE, HARRY CLIFFORD	CAPT	MAS	02269	RAMSEY, PAUL HUBERT	VADM	NYC
02197	COX, ALVIN STEWART	LCDR	SWS	02270	KERWIN, PASCHAL E.	LCDR	NYC
2197A	WILLESEN, SOREN (N)	LT	MAS	02271	PIRIE, ROBERT BURNS	VADM	AVN
02198	DOLBEN, JOSEPH (N)	LTJG	MAS	02272	GILLETTE, EDMOND STEPHEN	CAPT	NYC
2198A	MERWIN, DAVIS (N)	Col	SWS	02273	O'HARA, EDWARD WILLIAM	CWO	NYC
02199	DAVISON, ROBERT SCOTT	CDR	SWS	02274	MERTZ, JAMES MCCLENAHAN	LCDR	NYC
02200	DENNIS, CLAIR CARDER	CDR	SWS	02275	MOSS, WALTER STEPHEN	LCDR	NYC
02201	DIXON, EDWIN ZANE	CDR	SWS	02276	MORISON, SAMUEL ELIOT	RADM	NYC
02202	ENLOE, KEITH M.	CDR	SWS	02277	WILL, JOHN MYLIN	ADM	NYC
02203	ERDMAN, CALVIN PARDEE	CDR	SWS	02278	DANIELE, EDMUND (N)	CDR	NYC
02204	FARRELL, CHARLES DAVID	LCDR	SWS	02279	HUNT, SANFORD BEEBE JR	Maj.	NYC
02205	FRANCIS, JACK ALBERT	CAPT	SWS	02280	LONGDEN, ROBERT EDWARD	LT	NYC
02206	FRANDSEN, TOM (N)	CAPT	SWS	02281	HAMMOND, MERRILL MILLS	CAPT	ARZ
02207	FRASH, WILLIAM MOURIS	Col	SWS	02282	BUCHANAN, CHARLES ALLEN	RADM	NYC
02208	GILBERT, CARL W.	LT	SWS	02283	BINFORD, THOMAS HOWELL	VADM	NYC
02209	HAYMAN, FRANK TILGHMAN	CDR	SWS	02284	SCHINDLER WALTER GABRIEL	VADM	NYC
02210	HOSMER, HERBERT BUTTRICK JR	CDR	SWS	02285	ENDERTON, OTTO	LCDR	NYC
02211	HUBER, PAUL ROBERT	CAPT	SWS	02286	DIETRICH, NEIL KITTRELL	RADM	NYC
02212	JACKSON, SAMUEL CARSLEY	CAPT	SFR	02287	PHILLIPS, WILLIAM KEARNEY	ADM	NYC
02213	JAMES, THURSTON HALL	RADM	SWS	02288	LAYTON, HARRY EMMONS	LT	NYC
02214	JOHNSON, GEORGE KING	CAPT	SWS	02289	VAUGHN, ROBERT JAMES	CAPT	NYC
02215	KIRKPATRICK, DONALD (N) JR.	CAPT	SWS	02290	SARGENT, CLEMENT DENNY	LT	NYC
02216	MARTIN, JACK DALTON	CDR	SWS	02291	OVERTON, WILLIAM ARTHUR	CDR	NYC
02217	MC COY, DONALD CRAWFORD	LCDR	SWS	02292	HEDERMAN, THOMAS HENRY	CAPT	NYC
02218	MURISON, RICHARD VIVIAN	CAPT	SWS	02293	MARTIN, ORA ALEXANDER	LT	NYC
02219	NAUMANN, ERNEST (N)	CDR	SWS	02294	JUNE, LAURENCE BRIGHAM	LCDR	NYC
02220	RIESTER, LEO BUTTERFIELD	CDR	SWS	02295	DICKERSON, GEORGE ARTHUR	LT	NYC
02221	RYAN, THOMAS SANFORD	CAPT	SWS	2295A	MOHRELD, JOHN HENRY III	CDR	NYC
02222	SCHUBERT, CHARLES EDGAR	CAPT	SWS	02296	PLIMPTON, FRANCIS TAYLOR P. JR.	ENS	NYC

INSIG	COMPANION	RANK	CDRY
02297	ESSTROM, CLARENCE EUGENE	VADM	NYC
02298	TAYLOR, ROSWELL FLOWER	LCDR	NYC
02299	ROSSIER, HARRY AUSTIN	LCDR	SWS
02300	BOGERT, FRANK MITCHILL	CDR	SWS
02301	ALLEN, DONALD EDGAR	LCDR	SWS
02302	BISSELL, ARTHUR DWIGHT	CDR	SWS
02303	BRADLEY, WILLIS WINTER	RADM	SWS
02304	GUTHRIE, JOHN OLIVER	LCDR	SWS
02305	HOLMBERT, JOHN STANLEY	Col	SWS
02306	LLOYD, EDWARD WARREN	LCDR	SWS
02307	NEEFUS, JAMES LEFFERTS	Col	SWS
02308	PETERSON, ROBERT WILLARD	CDR	SWS
02309	ROETHKE, WILLIAM A.C.	CDR	SWS
02310	POWER, TYRONE EDMUND	1ST Lt	SWS
02311	VALENCIA, EUGENE ANTHONY	CDR	SWS
02312	YANCY, SELWYN WILLARD	LT	SWS
02313	COLE, ELWOOD BOURLAND	CAPT	SWS
02314	BOUTROSS, JOSEPH J.	LTJG	SWS
02315	BESCOS, JULIE ANTHONY	LCDR	SWS
02316	ANTHONIDES, JOSEPH WIERDA	CAPT	SWS
02317	BOYD, FLORIAN GILLAR	LT	SWS
02318	BOYD, JOHN PATRICK	CDR	SWS
02319	BURCK, GAIL JOHNSON	CDR	SWS
02320	BURSON, HERCHEL WILLIS	CDR	SWS
02321	CHERNISS, SIDNEY ARTHUR JR.	CAPT	SWS
02322	CONNELL, MYRON FRANCIS	LT	SWS
02323	CORTRIGHT, ANDREW J.	LT	SWS
02324	CRUCHLEY, EDWARD FREDERICK	LT	SWS
02325	FITZEK, DANIEL FREDERICK	LCDR	SWS
02326	GEMMELL, LEROY ARTHUR	LT	SWS
02327	HEIL, ROBERT H. T.	CDR	SWS
02328	HOGAN, RIICHARD JAMES JR.	CAPT	SWS
02329	LUCK, EDWARD JOHN	CAPT	SWS
02330	JAMESON, FRANK GARD	LCDR	SWS
02331	MILLER, W. E. HUTTON	CDR	SWS
02332	PRESTON, CLAUDE LINDSAY	LCDR	SWS
02333	PRUYN, ROBERT LANSING	CDR	SWS
02334	RAGAN, LLOYD ELMER	CDR	SWS
02335	RANNEY, HOWARD CHALMERS	CAPT	SWS
02336	REILLY, ROBERT CHARLES	LCDR	SWS
02337	ROGERS, ARTHUR MAURICE JR.	LT	SWS
02338	SCHOECH, WILLIAM ALTON	VADM	SWS
02339	SMITH, CLIFFORD EDWARD	CAPT	SWS
02340	STEELE, PERCY DAVIS	CDR	SWS
02341	STEWART, GLENN HAYS	CAPT	SWS
02342	STEWART, HENRY ALEXANDER	RADM	SWS
02343	TAYLOR, JOE	RADM	SWS
02344	THURLOW, LEAVITT WEARE	CAPT	SWS
02345	VANDETTE, JOHN JOSEPH	CDR	SWS
02346	VRACIU, ALEXANDER (N)	CDR	SWS
02347	WHEELER, EDWARD GAYLORD	CAPT	SWS
02348	WILLIAMS, JAMES WALTER JR.	CDR	SWS
02349	SHERWOOD, JAMES K. O.	LCDR	NYC
02350	SOUTHARD, MELVILLE	CDR	NYC
02351	FRANKLIN, BENJAMIN III	LCDR	NYC
02352	EATON, EDWIN HARVEY	CAPT	NYC
02353	DUPE OF 1581(HAROLD DUDLEY FREMAN)		
02354	SOLOMONS, EDWARD ALVA	RADM	NYC
02355	MILLS, CHARLES ANTHONY	LCDR	NYC
02356	COHEN, ROBERT HENRY	LTJG	NYC
02357	PETRIE, FRANCIS JOSEPH	CDR	NYC
02358	HOLLOWAY, MILTON THOMAS	CDR	NYC
02359	WILKINSON, ROLAND FIELD	CAPT	NYC
02360	RUSSELL, WILLIAM LETTS JR.	LCDR	NYC
02361	WHITE, WILLIAM RUSSELL	RADM	NYC
02362	CONNORTON, JOHN VINCENT	LCDR	NYC
02363	MILLER, JAY FREDERICK	CAPT	NYC
02364	PIKE, JAMES ALBERT	LTJG	NYC
02365	LARGE, HENRY WHALEN	CDR	NYC
02366	MOORE, FRENCH ROBERT	VADM	NYC
02367	JACKSON, PERRY YATES	CAPT	NYC
02368	REEVES, GEORGE ANDERSON	CDR	SWS
02369	KIELING, ROBERT TAYLOR	CAPT	SWS
02370	VICKERS, RICHARD ANTLIFF	CDR	SWS
02371	BAKER, JAMES ELLIS	CAPT	SWS

INSIG	COMPANION	RANK	CDRY
02372	GOLD, EDGAR ELY	LCDR	SWS
02373	ENLOE, GEEORGE ALBERT	CDR	SWS
02374	CARR, JOHN EDWIN	CDR	SWS
02375	SMITH, CLARENCE WILLIAM	CDR	SWS
02376	KEARNS, WILLIAM EDWARD	CDR	SWS
02377	LANIGAN, EDWARD JONN	CAPT	SWS
02378	KING, WILLIAM C.	CAPT	SWS
02379	MADDOX, LOYAL EDWARD	LCDR	SWS
02380	YOUNG, CARL HAVEN	CDR	SWS
02381	ROBBINS, ALBERT CULBERTSON	CDR	SWS
02382	LONNQUEST, THEO. CLAYTON JR.	CAPT	NYC
02383	HIRONS, GARDNER	CDR	NYC
02384	KANITZ, LOUIS JOHN	CDR	NYC
02385	WALDEN, COY	LCDR	SWS
02386	HAMLETT, JOE DELBHOE	LCDR	SWS
02387			
02388	HUGHES, ARRANDA "A" JR.	CDR	SWS
02389	WILLIS, DANIEL MONROE	LCDR	SWS
02390	DEVITT, ROBERT MICHAEL	LT	SWS
02391	WITHEROW, SIDNEY DANIEL	CDR	SWS
02392	BIGELOW, HERBERT LYMAN JR.	CDR	SWS
02393	STYDAHAR, JOSEPH LEO	LT	SWS
02394	PASCHAL, JOSEPH BENNETT	RADM	SWS
02395	MC CALLEN, MARCUS MARCELLUS	Maj.	SWS
02396	CLAPHAM, WILLIAM TERUCHI	CAPT	SWS
02397	HAYNES, ROBERT MILTON	Lt Col	SWS
02398	HYKA, EDWIN WILLARD	CDR	SWS
02399	HODAPP, JOHN DALE PYE	LCDR	SWS
02400	LARNED, WHARTON E.	RADM	SWS
02401	VIEWEG, WALTER VICTOR RUDOLPH	CAPT	SWS
02402	REYNOLDS, FERRY	Col	SWS
02403	WARD, FRANK TRENWITH JR.	VADM	NYC
02404	GIANNETTI, SANTONIO PASQUALE	LT	NYC
02405	WELCH, EDWARD WILLIAM	CDR	NYC
02406	MADDOCK, CLYDE EUGENE	CDR	NYC
02407	STEWART, ROBERT WAYNE	CDR	NYC
02408	FLYNN, WILLIAM DANIEL	CAPT	NYC
02409	LEONARD, HENRY VIRGINIUS JR.	ENS	NYC
02410	TISZA, THOMAS ERNEST	LCDR	NYC
02411	FENTON, ROBERT GILLESPIE	LT	NYC
02412	SMITH, JOHN LUCIAN	MGEN	NYC
02413	MC KIERNAN, JOHN FRANCIS	CAPT	NYC
02414	WORKMAN, ROBERT DUBOIS	RADM	LM
02415	DUCAN, DONNNNALD BRADLEY	ADM	LM
02416			
02417	BLANDY, WILLIAM HENRY PURNELL	ADM	LM
02418	CLUVERIUS, WAT TYLER	ADM	LM
02419	HALSEY, WILLAIM FREDERICK JR	ADM	LM
02420	HART, THOMAS CHARLES	ADM	LM
02421	HEWITT, HENRY KENT	ADM	LM
02422	HILLENKOETTER, ROSCOE HENRY	VADM	LM
02423	KALBFUS, EDWARD GLIFFORD	ADM	LM
02424	KING, ERNES JOSEPH	FADM	LM
02425			
02426	MC CREA, JOHN LIVINGSTONE	VADM	LM
02427	NIMITZ, CHESTER WILLIAM	FADM	LM
02428	BROWN, JOHN HERBERT JR.	VADM	LM
02429	RAMSEY, DEWITT CLINTON	ADM	LM
02430	RADFORD, ARTHUR WILLIAM	ADM	LM
02431	BERKEY, RUSSELL STANLEY	RADM	LM
02432	FECHTELER, WILLIAM MORROW	ADM	LM
02433	DENFELD, LOUIS EMIL	ADM	LM
02434	LOCKWOOD, CHARLES ANDREWS	VADM	LM
02435	CATES, CLIFTON BLEDSOE	GEN	LM
02436	DUPE OF 1518(JAMES AUGUSTINE FARRELL JR)		
02437	SHEPHERD, LEMUEL CORNICK JR.	GEN	LM
02438	ANDREWS, ADOLPHUS	VADM	LM
02439	INGRAM, JONAS HOWARD	ADM	LM
02440	FORRESTAL, JAMES VINCENT	SEC'Y	LM
02441	CONOLLY, RICHARD LANSING	ADM	LM
02442	WHITNEY, JOHN PERRY	VADM	LM
02443	DUPE OF 2299(HENRY AUSTIN ROSSIER)		
02444	KIRK, ALAN GOODRICH	ADM	LM
02445	DUPE OF 2300(FRANK MITCHILL BOGERT)		
02446	DUPE OF 1214(FREDERIC ROBERT HARRIS)		

INSIG	COMPANION	RANK	CDRY	INSIG	COMPANION	RANK	CDRY
02447	SHERMAN, FORREST PERCIVAL	ADM	LM	02522	NEILL, CLARENCE THOMAS JR.	CDR	SWS
02448	EWEN, EDWARD COYLE	RADM	LM	02523	GODLOVE, WILBUR RUSSELL	CDR	SWS
02449	BIERI, BERNHARD HENRY	VADM	LM	02524	POWERS, HOWARD BRADFORD	LCDR	SWS
02450	FOSTER, EDWIN DORSEY	VADM	LM	02525	MEES, CLIDE LOUIS	CDR	SWS
02451	ROYCE, DONALD	RADM	LM	02526	PHIPPS, ROBERT PRESTON	CDR	SWS
02452	BURROUGH, EDMUND WEIDMANN	RADM	LM	02527	VANDEGRIFT, ALEXANDER ARCHER	GEN	LM
02453	HARRILL, WILLIAM KEEN	RADM	LM	02528	MOREELL, BEN	ADM	LM
02454				02529	SALLADA, HAROLD BUSHNELL	ADM	LM
02455	BADGER, OSCAR CHARLES	ADM	LM	02530	LONNQUEST, THEODORE CLAYTON	RADM	LM
02456	FIFE, JAMES	ADM	LM	02531	PENNOYER, FREDERICK WM. JR.	VADM	LM
02457	STRUBLE, ARTHUR DEWEY	ADM	LM	02532			
02458	MILLS, EARLE WATKINS	VADM	LM	02533	CREESY, ANDREW ELLIOTT	MGEN	LM
02459	FRULONG, WILIAM REA	RADM	LM	02534			
02460	HENDREN, PAUL	RADM	LM	02535	PEPPER, ROBERT HOUSTON	BGEN	LM
02461	DRELLER, LOUIS	RADM	LM	02536	GARDNER, MATTHIAS BENNETT	ADM	LM
02462	BOGAN, GERALD FRANCIS	VADM	LM	02537	HARTMAN, CHARLES CLIFFORD	RADM	LM
02463	HILL, HARRY WILBUR	ADM	LM	02538	COMBS, LEWIS BARTON	RADM	LM
02464	WYNKOOP, THOMAS PILMORE JR.	RADM	LM	02539	BOTTA, RICO	RADM	LM
02465	DURGIN, CALVIN THORNTON	VADM	LM	02540			
02466				02541			
02467				02542	SILVERTHORN, MERWIN HANCOCK	LGEN	LM
02468				02543	BEATTY, FRANK EDMUND	VADM	LM
02469				02544	SPRUANCE, RAYMOND AMES	ADM	LM
02470	COOKE, CHARLES MAYNARD JR	ADM	LM	02545	PALMER, LEIGH CARLYLE	CAPT	LM
02471				02546			
02472				02547	FARLEY, JOSEPH FRANCIS	ADM	LM
02473				02548			
02474	WELLBORN, CHARLES JR.	VADM	LM	02549	WILKES, JOHN	RADM	LM
02475	REDMAN, JOSEPH REASOR	RADM	LM	02550	STUMP, FELIX BUDWELL	ADM	LM
02476	MACKLIN, WILLIAM A. STEWART	RADM	LM	02551	ROBINSON, ARTHUR GRANVILLE	RADM	LM
02477	HAEBERLE, FREDERICK EDWARD	RADM	LM	02552	SOLBERG, THORVALD ARTHUR	RADM	LM
02478				02553	CLARK, DAVID HENDERSON	RADM	LM
02479				02554	NICHOLSON, CHARLES AMBROSE II	RADM	LM
02480	SMITH, EDWARD H.	RADM	LM	02555	HILL, WM. PENDLETON THOMPSON	MGEN	LM
02481	WHITING, FRANCIS ELIOT MAYNARD	VADM	LM	02556	MORSE, FREDERICK ALVIN	LCDR	NYC
02482	KINKAID, THOMAS CASSIN	ADM	LM	02557	PALMER, REICHARD WARE	LT	NYC
02483	GATCH, THOMAS LEIGH	VADM	LM	02558	SUTHERLAND, ROBERT THEO., JR.	CAPT	NYC
02484				02559	KLEM, WALTER	CDR	NYC
02485	WORTON, WILLIAM ARTHUR	MGEN	LM	02560	LYMAN, JOHN BENJAMIN	CDR	NYC
02486	WAGNER, FRANK DECHANT	RADM	LM	02561	KENNEDY, HARRY WILMER JR.	LCDR	NYC
02487	LOWRY, FRANKJACOB	RADM	LM	02562	GOODWIN, HOMER STANLEY	LCDR	NYC
02488	CARLSON, OSCAR LUDWIG	CAPT	LM	02563	BURNHAM, GEORGE HODGMAN	CAPT	NYC
02489	WILL, PRENTIS KING	CAPT	LM	02564	RENN, JOSEPH BRYAN	RADM	NYC
02490	BALLENTINE, JOHN JENNINGS	VADM	LM	02565	GOLINKIN, JOSEPH WEBSTER	CAPT	NYC
02491				02566	LANKENAU, WILFRED ERIC	CAPT	NYC
02492	PRICE, JOHN DALE	VADM	LM,	02567	PERHAM, HERBERT NORTON	CAPT	NYC
02493	CURTIS, MERRITT BARTON	BGEN	LM	02568	SMILEY, CURTIS STANTON	RADM	NYC
02494	SCHOEFFEL, MALCOLM FRANCIS	RADM	LM	02569	GRAHAM, ROBERT WALLACE	RADM	NYC
02495	SHAFROTH, HOHN FRANKLIN JR	VADM	LM	02570	DEHRENS, CHARLES FREDERICKS	RADM	NYC
02496	LOW, FRANCIS STUART	ADM	LM	02571	MCARDLE, DANIEL MICHAEL	LCDR	NYC
02497	BUNKLEY, JOEL WILLIAM	RADM	LM	02572	MARONEY, ARTHUR JAMES	LCDR	NYC
02498	INGERSOLL, ROYAL EASON	ADM	LM	02573	MONTAGUE, WARNER JOHNSON	ENS	NYC
02499	STATON, ADOLPHUS	RADM	LM	02574	GARRISON, GEO. HARTRANFT HALEY	CDR	NYC
02500	YARNELL, HARRY ERVIN	ADM	LM	02575	FORTSON, THOMAS NELSON	CAPT	NYC
02501	FITCH, AUBREY WRAY	ADM	LM	02576	CLAY, HENRY JONES	LCDR	NYC
02502	COOLEY, THOMAS ROSS	VADM	LM	02577	DUCKETT, JOHN PENDLETON	CDR	NYC
02503	KITTS, WILLARD AUGUSTUS III	RADM	LM	02578	KIMMEL, HUSBAND EDWARD	ADM	NYC
02504	BRAND, CHARLES LEES	RADM	LM	02578A	COLEMAN, ARRET STEELE	CAPT	NYC
02505	GLASSFORD, WILLIAM ALEXANDER	VADM	LM	02579	NEYMAN, CLINTON ANDREW	CAPT	NYC
02506	KELEHER, TIMOTHY JEROME	RADM	LM	02580			
02507	KELLY, MONROE (N)	VADM	LM	02581	NOBLE, ALBERT GALLATIN	ADM	NYC
02508	LEAHY, WILLIAM DANIEL	FADM	LM	02582	RUSSELL., PAUL WESLEY	Col	NYC
02509	LAND, EMORY SCOTT	VADM	LM	02583	SULLIVAN, PATRICK JOSEPH	LCDR	NYC
02510	BRAISTED, FRANK ALFRED	RADM	LM	02584	BROYDERICK, LEO JOSEPH	CDR	MAS
02511	RUDDOCK, THODORE DAVIS	VADM	LM	02585	TAISEY, PHILIP CRAWFORD	CDR	MAS
02512	MURCH, JOHN ALLAN	CDR	LM	02586	KEWER, JOHN ROBERT	LCDR	MAS
02513	CALHOUN, WILLIAM LOWNDES	VADM	SWS	02587	BUNTEN, KENNETH ROBERT JR.	LTJG	MAS
02514	NIXON, RICHARD MILHOUS	CDR	SWS	02588	ENGLEMAN, CHRISTIAN LEVIN	CAPT	NYC
02515	BLACKMAN, GEOFFREY ALFRED L.	LCDR	SWS	02589	KNAPP, MICHAEL JOSEPH	CAPT	NYC
02516	BENNETT, HERSHAL EDWARD	LCDR	SWS	02590	DELANY, WALTER STANLEY JR.	CAPT	NYC
02517	CALDER, JAMES WILLIAM	CWO	SWS	02591	FULTON, ROBET C. JR.	LT	AVN
02518	HOLE, JAMES WILLIAM	LCDR	SWS	02592	DUPE OF 1495(CHAUNCEY DEVEREUX STILLMAN)		
02519	KASPARY, JOHN (N)	CDR	SWS	02593	BAKER, MILLS P.	CDR	AVN
02520	COLESON, ROBERT LEE JR.	CDR	SWS	02594	GLENN, BENJAMIN DUKE	CWO	AVN
02521	KOPF, JACK JR (N)	CAPT	SWS	02595	ZIESING, HIBBEN	LCDR	AVN

The Lieutenant Commander Lee W. Douglas Memorial Award

I. **Background.** As Recorder General from 1983 through 1995, LCDR Lee Wayland Douglas rendered singular service to Local Commanderies and individual companions. His reports were diligently documented; his minutes comprehensive and complete. Gifted with an exceptional talent for both writing and research, his legacy includes;

   A. Authorship of the first *NOUS Operations Manual* in 1986 at the request of Past Commander General A. Fred Kempe.
   B. Research and publication of the *Centennial Register of Companions 1890-1990*, in keeping with the suggestion of then Historian General LCDR Russell B. Miller.
   C. Assembly and formatting of the *Naval Order Operations Manual* revised in 1993.
   D. Design of a new, more detailed *Register* of all NOUS Companions, after exhaustive research in federal Archive Repositories.

II. **Award.** Procured annually by the Chairman of the Naval Order Awards Committee.

   A. **Permanent Plaque.** A 12" x 15" mahogany plaque with Naval Order General Commandery Seal in center and flanked by obverse and reverse of the large Naval Order Cross; finished in bronze with raised etching. Recipient Local Commandery name and date is added annually on a ¾" x 3" plate.

   Inscribed:

   NAVAL ORDER OF THE UNITED STATES

   Presents its

   OUTSTANDING LOCAL COMMANDERY AWARD

   In memory of

   LCDR LEE W. DOUGLAS

   In recognition of Exemplary Local Effort and Success achieved in Membership Growth, Internal Communications, Annual Congress Support, Local Commandery Initiatives and National Purpose and Goals. Bravo Zulu!

   (Date) _____

   Commander General

Naval Order Personal Plaque Presented at the Centinnial Congress to Past Commanders General Majka, Carl, Cross, Weber, Bolt, Anderson and Weese (not shown) and to Recorder General Lee Douglas and Historians General Miller and Bonnot.

'Commodore' Thomas J. Lupo accepts the NOUS' service plaque from Commander General Fred D. Carl during the "Bahama '88 Congress". 'Commodore' Lupo was recognized as the organizer of the Florida Keys Commandery and as the Naval Order's number one recruiter during the past year.

INSIG	COMPANION	RANK	CDRY	INSIG	COMPANION	RANK	CDRY
02596	DOUGLAS, ALBERT R.	LT	AVN	02671	DUPE OF 1682(RICHARD BOWERS MORRIS)		
02597	BROWN, NORTON S.	CAPT	AVN	02672	MORRIS, WILLIAM HENRY	LCDR	WNY
02598	DUPE OF 1864(CHARLES WILLIAM DONAHUE)			02673	NICHOLS, JOHN WILLARD	LCDR	WNY
02599	WATSON, PATRICK	ENS	AVN	02674	PAGE, PHILIP EARL	CDR	WNY
02600	HOWE, DANIEL J. JR.	LCDR	AVN	02675	POWELL, JOHN PETER	CDR	WNY
02601	MANTON, STANLEY L.	LT	AVN	02676	RITCHIE, CLARK ALEXANDER	LCDR	WNY
02602	BUBENDEY, PAUL F.	CAPT	AVN	02677	SAUNDERS, WILLIAM VINCENT	RADM	WNY
02603	DUPE OF 1681(THEODORE MANNING STEELE)			02678	SHETTERLY, JAMES OLIVER	LCDR	WNY
02604	CHRISTINE, WILLIAM W.	CDR	AVN	02679	SLODDEN, AINSLIE ALEXANDER	LT	WNY
02605	JUNKIN, JOSEPH DE FOREST III	LCDR	AVN	02680	STEWART, ROBERT EDWARD	LCDR	WNY
02606	COBB, HENRY IVES JR.	CDR	AVN	02681	STURM, HOWARD DANIEL	CDR	WNY
02607	MOONEY, JOHN D.	LCDR	AVN	02682	TAYLOR, JOHN BARRETT	RADM	WNY
02608	CARMODY, EDMUND OLIVER	CDR	AVN	02683	TOWNER, JOSEPH BENJAMIN	LCDR	WNY
02609	TERWILLIGER, DONALD	LCDR	AVN	02684	TOWNSEND, SAMUEL W.	CAPT	WNY
02610	ZIMMERMAN, EDWARD F.	CAPT	AVN	02685	VAN ARSDALE, TALMAN WALKER JR.	LT	WNY
02611	BAKER, RICHARD WHEELER JR.	CAPT	AVN	02686	WACHSLER, HARRY RICHARD	CDR	WNY
02612	GOWLING, ROBERT M.	LCDR	AVN	02687	DUPE OF 1046(ALFRED KENNEDY WARREN, JR)		
02613	WATERBURY, THEODORE EUGENE	CAPT	AVN	02688	WEED, LYLE ALFRED	CDR	WNY
02614	MONTAN, NILS VICTOR	LT	AVN	02689	WELCH, LAUREN GUSTIN	LCDR	WNY
02615	FINUCANE, ROBERT LAWRENCE	CAPT	AVN	02690	WHEELER, PAUL STEPHEN	LT	WNY
02616	NEUMEYER, WILLIAM E.	CDR	AVN	02691	YOUNGMAN, SAMUEL ANTES, JR..	CAPT	WNY
02617	GILMARTIN, MAURICE ANDREW JR.	CAPT	AVN	02692	ZUCARELLI, VICTOR ANTHONY	CDR	WNY
02618	DUY, WILLIAM ELY	ENS	AVN	02693	WENGER, JOSEPH NUMA	RADM	NYC
02619	DUPE OF 2213(THURSTON HALL JAMES)			02694	BARROW, DONALD FRASER	LCDR	NYC
02620	BLUMENTHAL, ANDRE	CDR	AVN	02695	WIRTZ, PAUL CYRIL	CAPT	NYC
02621	AUGHENBAUGH, J. STANLEY	CDR	AVN	02696	HARTNETT, BERNARD MICHAEL	LCDR	NYC
02622	DUPE OF 1296(HARRY GEORGE SEIDEL,JR)			02697	PETERSON, LESTER WILLIAM	LT	SFR
02623	DUPE OF 2080(BENJAMIN SCOTT CUSTER)			02698	DODGE, DOUGLAS WILSON	CWO	SFR
02624	GRETSCH, FRED JR.	CDR	AVN	02699	MATTHEWS, JOHN STANLEY	CDR	SFR
02625	DUPE OF 2174(LAWRENCE BAXTER RICHARDSON)			02700	SHEPARD, ROBERT BURPO	Col	SFR
02626	BALDWIN, DEAN ALLISON	CDR	AVN	02701	CAREY, JAMES OSWALD	LT	SFR
02627	WILDS, WALTER	CDR	AVN	02702	STEELE, LESLIE HUGH	CDR	SFR
02628	RIGHTER, BREWSTER	CDR	AVN	02703	CHAMBREAU, WILLIAM W. JR.	LT	SFR
02629	ROEMER, HENRY C. JR.	LTJG	AVN	02704	DUCEY, JOHN FRANCIS JR.	CDR	SFR
02630	HERRICK, D. CADY II	CDR	AVN	02705	MITCHELL, CHARLES WELLMAN JR.	RADM	SFR
02631	GAVAN, GORDON S.	LCDR	AVN	02706	BARTON, ROBERT RTHUR	LCDR	SFR
02632	HARRISON, JOHN T. JR.	LCDR	AVN	02707	WALLER, RAYMOND RANDOLPH	RADM	SFR
02633	MYERS, RAYMOND F.	CDR	AVN	02708	KOETITZ, ARMIN PAUL	CDR	SFR
02634	PENNOYER, ROBERT M.	LTJG	AVN	02709	MONSALVE, CARLOS ANTONIO	LT	SFR
02635	SMITH, DANIEL F. JR.	RADM	AVN	02710	ABBOTT, WILLIAM RUFUS JR.	LCDR	SFR
02636	TOWERS, CHARLES S.	LT	AVN	02711	RIDLEY, FRANK ELVSON	CAPT	SFR
02637	HANE, HOWARD SPENCER JR.	LTJG	NYC	02712	GANZ, FREDERICK "M"	Maj.	SFR
02638	BRUEN, ARTHUR JACKSON JR.	LT	NYC	02713	WHITLEY, GEORGE COIL	LCDR	SFR
02639	ATWATER, ROGER WITTER	LCDR	WNY	02714	DOLLARD, EDWARD JONN	CDR	SFR
02640	BARNES, WILLIAM FRANKLIN	LCDR	WNY	02715	DUPE OF 1124(EARL GRANVILLE HUTCHINSON)		SFR
02641	BATES, GEORGE FRANCIS	LT	WNY	02716	RAPORT, JAMES H.	LCDR	SFR
02642	BERNARD, EUGENE ALTON	LT	WNY	02717	JONES, WILLIAM WALTER	CDR	SWS
02643	BERRYMAN, MAYNARD WARREN	LCDR	WNY	02718	SIEMINSKI, WILLIAM LUCIAN	ENS	NYC
02644	BORTZ, ERNEST FREDERICK	LCDR	WNY	02719	BUEHLER, MARTIN STOWELL	CAPT	NYC
02645	BURKS, VESPER EARLE	LT	WNY	02720	BLODGETT, GEORGE FRANCIS	CAPT	NYC
02646	DUPE OF 2608(EDMUND OLIVER CARMODY)			02721	VESTAL, FERD SCOTT	CDR	NYC
02647	CITRON, RALPH SEYMOUR	LCDR	WNY	02722	WHEELOCK, ROBERT WEBB	CAPT	NYC
02648	COLGROVE, ARNOLD W.	CDR	WNY	02723	ASCHER, DAVID	LCDR	WNY
02649	CONNELLY, WILLIAM MICHAEL	CAPT	WNY	02724	BARRY, PETER	CDR	WNY
02650	CONNERS, WILLIAM JAMES III	CAPT	WNY	02725	BEHRINGER, CHARLES KENNETH	LCDR	WNY
02651	CONRAD, FRANCIS MINARD	CDR	WNY	02726	CLAUSS, JAMES THOMAS	CDR	WNY
02652	DARROW, JOHN BURGESS	CAPT	WNY	02727	DARROHN, MAURICE DONALD	LCDR	WNY
02653	DODDS, WATSON HAMILTON	CDR	WNY	02728	DODSON, CHARLES OWEN	LCDR	WNY
02654	FISHER, CARLTON ALANSON	BGEN	WNY	02729	DUNN, SEYMOUR BALLARD	CAPT	WNY
02655	GALLINGER, KENNETH DARBY	CAPT	WNY	02730	FLEMING, CARROLL HOLT	CAPT	WNY
02656	GAMBLE, EDMUND ROSS	CAPT	WNY	02731	GEORGE, EDWARD NICHOLAS	CDR	WNY
02657	HAYDOCK, JESSE G. JR.	CDR	WNY	02732	HOWARD, EDWARD DOUGLAS II	LCDR	WNY
02658	HOOPER, HARRY BARTHOLOMEW JR.	Lt Col	WNY	02733	JONES, THOMAS HENRY	LCDR	WNY
02659	HUNTER, ROBERT PACKARD	CDR	WNY	02734	KATZ, SAMUEL EATON	LCDR	WNY
02660	JAMES, RICHARD EDWIN	LCDR	WNY	02735	KELLY, HARRY JOSEPH	LT	WNY
02661	DUPE OF 2213,2219(THURSTON HALL JAMES)			02736	LAWLESS, WILLIAM BURNS JR..	LT	WNY
02662	KATZ, ALVIN EUGENE	ENS	WNY	02737	LAMBERT, JOHN J.	Lt Col	WNY
02663	KIRKWOOD, PHILIP LEROY	CDR	WNY	02738	LEBHERZ, EDWIN JOHN	LCDR	WNY
02664	KWAPISZ, JOHN HENRY	LCDR	WNY	02739	LEET, ERNEST DELOS	LCDR	WNY
02665	LENT, RUSSELL WILLIAM	CAPT	WNY	02740	LIPPSCHUTZ, EUGENE JOHN	CAPT	WNY
02666	MC DANIEL, WILLIAM DEAN	CAPT	WNY	02741	MC CHESNEY, IRVIN G.	CDR	WNY
02667	MC DONALD, WILLIAM FRANCIS	CAPT	WNY	02742	MIRKIN, ARTHUR JOEL	LT	WNY
02668	MC LERNON, RONALD HUGH	LCDR	CDNY	02743	MONTMORE, D. MICHAEL	LCDR	WNY
02669	MORIN, JOSEPH MAURICE	Lt Col	WNY	02744	MURPHY, FRANK DESMOND	CAPT	WNY
02670	MORRIS, JAMES TERRY	CAPT	WNY	02745	NEAL, JOSEPH A. FRANK	CDR	WNY

INSIG	COMPANION	RANK	CDRY	INSIG	COMPANION	RANK	CDRY
02746	POPEN, WALTR MICHAEL	LT	WNY	02821	CONKLIN, BRUCE COX	LCDR	NYC
02747	PROZELLER, NEWCOMB	LCDR	WNY	02822	THACH, JAMES HARMON JR.	ADM	NYC
02748	RICE, HARVEY MITCHELL	LT	WNY	02823	MUNDORFF, GEORGE THEODORE	RADM	LM
02749	SAUSEN, FRANCIS JAMES	LCDR	WNY	02824	NEWBEGIN, ROBERT GOODCHILD III	CDR	NYC
02750	SHEEHY, JOHN WEBB LITTLE	LT	WNY	02825	RUHSENBERGER, JOHN ROGER	CAPT	NYC
02751	STARRETT, HOWARD HAMILTON	LCDR	WNY	02826	WEAVER, ALBERT WRIGHT	CDR	NYC
02752	STEELE, VARIAN	CAPT	WNY	02827	HILTON, JAMES GARRETT	LT	NYC
02753	THOR, HARRY ADAM	LCDR	WNY	02828	LEVENSON, HERBERT BART	MIDN	LM
02754	TISDALE, EBEN DAWES	LCDR	WNY	02829	HOOPER, CONRAD SIDNEY	LT	NYC
02755	TORGLER, ARTHUR FREDERICK JR.	Lt Col	WNY	02830	NORDTROM, LLOYD WALTER	LT	NYC
02756	DUPE OF 1637(STEPHEN TORMA			02831	BOYD, ALSTON MAURY JR.	CAPT	NYC
02757	VELING, THOMAS CLIFFORD	CDR	WNY	02832	MARTIN, ROBERT WADE	LCDR	NYC
02758	WARNER, EDWARD (N)	LT	WNY	02833	GROSS, WEBSTER	CAPT	SFR
02759	WHITE, JAMES J.	LCDR	WNY	02834	RALSTON, BYRON BROWN	CDR	NYC
02760				02835	DUPE OF 1916(WILLIAM GARDNER BLAKE)		
02761				02836	BARNARD, HARRY ALLAN JR.	CAPT	SFR
02762				02837	CARSON, JOHN HAZARD	VADM	SFR
02763				02838	COURSIN, JACK TANNEHILL	CAPT	SFR
02764				02839	GORDON, JOHN NORRIS CURRY	CAPT	SFR
02765				02840	TAYLOR, JESSE DEAN	CAPT	SWS
02766				02841	STEWART, JAMES SETH	LCDR	SWS
02767				02842	SLEE, KENNETH J.	LT	SWS
02768				02843	STERN, WILLIAM WALLACE	CDR	SWS
02769				02844	WHIPPLE, JOWARD THOMPSON JR.	LT	NYC
02770				02845	STROUD, WILLIAM BOULTON DIXON	LCDR	NYC
02771				02846	JAYNE, JOHN KENNON	CAPT	NYC
02772				02847	ENGLISH, DUANE MALLERY	CDR	WNY
02773				02848	MC AULIFFE, CHAS. PATRICK JR.	Maj.	WNY
02774				02849	FLADER, FREDRIC	LCDR	WNY
02775				02850	SMALL, FENWICK GRIFFITH	CDR	WNY
02776				02851	FOSTER, WILLIAM POWELL	Maj.	WNY
02777				02852	FRAUENHEIM, JOHN A.	CDR	WNY
02778				02853	GARDNER, RICHARD WALLACE	LCDR	WNY
02779				02854	KNIGHT, GULICK ZEITLER	CAPT	WNY
02780	ZIMMERMAN, EDWARD JOSEPH	ENS	WNY	02855	HORTON, WILLIAM EDWARD	CDR	WNY
02781	LANG, JOHN FRANCIS	LCDR	NYC	02856	FUSSELL, ROBERT GEORGE	LT	WNY
02782	MAYO, HAROLD EUGENE	LCDR	NYC	02857	BRENNAN, WILLIAM ROBERT	LT	WNY
02783	CHAMPLIN, FRANK JAMES	CDR	WNY	02858	COSGRIFF, FREDERICK WILLIAM	CAPT	WNY
02784	BEU, HARRY JOHN	LCDR	WNY	02859	SUITER, WILIAM ALFRED	LT	WNY
02785	HEIMBURGER, RAY ADELBERT	LCDR	SWS	02860	LAMB, MARTIN MURRAY	CDR	WNY
02786	CHAMBERLAIN, ROY STANLEY	LCDR	SWS	02861	CHAPMAN, GEORGE CHARLES	LT	WNY
02787	HALLORAN, THOMAS FRANCIS	RADM	MAS	02862	CARUANA, ROBERT FRANK	LCDR	WNY
02788	ALEXANDER, WILLIAM T.	RADM	MAS	02863	TALBOT, ROBET IRVIN	LCDR	WNY
02789	DUPE OF 0964(GEORGE CRANDALL CURRIER)		MAS	02864	BUERGER, PAUL THEODORE	LT	WNY
02790	HARBAUGH, AUBREY RUSSELL	CDR	SFR	02865	SHAUGHNESSY, RICHARD JOSEPH	LT	WNY
02791	O'SHEA, JERMIAH FRANCIS	CAPT	SFR	02866	FLEIG, HENRY	LCDR	WNY
02792	WILKINSON, ROLAND CONGDON	CDR	SFR	02867	TOSTLEBE, THEODORE OSCAR	CDR	WNY
02793	WATKINS, CHARLES EDWARD	CDR	SFR	02868	BROWN, LYNN	LT	WNY
02794	CLOUGHLEY, STERLING THOMAS	LCDR	SFR	02869	WALSH, JAMES ELL JR.	LCDR	WNY
02795	GARIBALDI, HERBERT JOSEPH	LCDR	SFR	02870	MC NABB, JOHN WALLACE	LCDR	WNY
02796	GIBBONS, FRED GRAY	CDR	SFR	02871	STICKEL, ROBERT HAMPTON	LCDR	WNY
02797	SHAWK, HARRY ABEL	CDR	SFR	02872	O'CONNOR, WILLIAM FRANCIS	LCDR	WNY
02798	SINCERBEAUX, ROBERT ABBOTT	LCDR	NYC	02873	LAMB, DANIEL WIGHTMAN	LT	WNY
02799	MANLEY, ROBERT RUSSELL JR.	ENS	NYC	02874	BLAKE, ROBERT	MGEN	LM
02800	ARNHEITER, MARCUS AURELIUS	LCDR	NYC	02875	HANSON, EDWARD WILLIAM	RADM	LM
02801	RANDOLPH, VIRGIL PATRICK III	ENS	NYC	02876	TRAIN, HAROLD CECIL	RADM	LM
02802	HYDE, GEORGE WINFIELD	CAPT	NYC	02877	HART, FRANKLIN AUGUSTUS	MGEN	LM
02803	DUNLEAVY, JOHN JAMES JR.	LT	NYC	02878	WOODS, LOUIS ERNEST	LGEN	LM
02804	NEILSON, JOHN JR.	CAPT	NYC	02879	HARDISON, OSBORNE BENNETT	RADM	LM
02805	WALLINE, CHARLES SAYER	CDR	NYC	02880	DAVIS, ARTHUR CAYLEY	VADM	LM
02806	MEARNS, ARTHUR WILLIAM	CDR	NYC	02881	BROWN, DUDLEY SOUTHWORTH	MGEN	LM
02807	LENIHAN, JOSEPH VINCENT	LCDR	NYC	02882	CLEMENT, WILLIAM TARDY	LGEN	LM
02808	BLACK, CLINTON RUTHERFORD JR.	ENS	NYC	02883	STYLER, CHARLES WILKES	RADM	LM
02809	TRAINER, JOHN NEWLIN JR.	CDR	NYC	02884	FAHRION, FRANK GEORGE	ADM	LM
02810	SHENIER, HENRY LEO	CDR	NYC	02885	RIGGS, RALPH SMITH	VADM	LM
02811	MORTHROP, EUGENE STANLEY	CDR	NYC	02886	KENDALL, HENRY SAMUEL	RADM	LM
02812	ROBENSTEIN, ALBERT LEVI	CAPT	NYC	02887	GLOVER, ROBERT OGDEN	RADM	LM
02813	MULLANEY, ROBERT BROWNSON	CDR	LM	02888	BROWN, CHARLES RANDALL	ADM	LM
02814	HOKANSON, EVERT CARL	CDR	SWS	02889	DAVIS, GLENN BENSON	VADM	LM
02815	MOLES, EDWARD WILLIAM	MIDN	NYC	02890	SMITH, OLIVER PRINCE	GEN	LM
02816	LOVEJOY, JAMES DONOVAN	LT	NYC	02891	HUNT, LEROY PHILIP	LGEN	LM
02817	HARVEY, LAWRENCE	LT	NYC	02892	REA, LEONARD EARL	MGEN	LM
02818	MORAN, HENRY GEORGE	RADM	NYC	02893	NOBLE, ALFRED HOUSTON	GEN	LM
02819	STERNE, CECIL MICHAEL	CDR	NYC	02894	HOWARD, SAMUEL LUTZ	MGEN	LM
02820	DILLINGHAM, FREDERIC WILLIAM	LCDR	NYC	02895	KILAND, INGOLF NORMAN	VADM	LM

INSIG	COMPANION	RANK	CDRY
02896	MC CORMICK, LYNDE DUPUY	RADM	LM
02897	CRAIG, EDWARD ARTHUR	LGEN	LM
02898	SCHILT, CHRISTIAN FRANKLIN	GEN	LM
02899	READ, ALBERT CUSHING	RADM	LM
02900 THRU 2999 UNASSIGNED			
03000	ROCKEY, KELLER EMRICK	LGEN	LM
03001	HILL, ROBERT DRAPER	CDR	NYC
03002	NEGRI, PETER JOHN	Col	NYC
03003	CZEHATOWSKI, ADAM WILLIAM	CDR	NYC
03004	MOMSEN, CHARLES BOWERS	VADM	LM
03005	GAEDE, DONALD CORNELIUS	RADM	SWS
03006	MOODY, ROBERT LOUIS	LT	SWS
03007	JOHNSTON, ARNOLD ARTHUR	CDR	SWS
03008	CORNWELL, JOHN DANIEL	CAPT	SWS
03009	GIOVANNONI, JOHN JOSEPH	CDR	SWS
03010	MEGEE, VERNON EDGAR	GEN	LM
03011	MILES, ARTHUR CLARK	VADM	LM
03012	THOMAS, GERALD CARTHRAE	GEN	LM
03013	RUSSELL, GEORGE LUCIUS	VADM	LM
03014	MUNROE, WILLIAM ROBERT	VADM	LM
03015	SCHMIDT, HARRY	GEN	LM
03016	MITCHELL, RALPH JOHNSON	LGEN	LM
03017	LINSCOTT, HANRY DALLAS	BGEN	LM
03018	STEVENS, LESLIE CLARK	RADM	LM
03019	PAINE, ROGER WARDE	RADM	LM
03020	WATSON, THOMAS EUGENE	LGEN	LM
03021	CASSADY, JOHN HOWARD	RADM	NYC
03022	BAKER, WILDER DUPUY	VADM	LM
03023	OSTER, HENRY RICHARD	RADM	LM
03024	CLARK, JOSEPH JAMES (JOCKO)	ADM	LM
03025	FOSKETT, JAMES HICKS	VADM	NYC
03026	WALLACE, WILIAM JENNINGS	LGEN	LM
03027	CUSHMAN, THOMAS JACKSON	LGEN	LM
03028	ROBINSON, RAY ALBERT	BGEN	NYC
03029	PFEIFFER, OMAR TITUS	BGEN	NYC
03030	MAGILL, BRADFORD STEELE	MIDN	NYC
03031	KREUZ, FRANK PETER JR.	RADM	SFR
03032	KINCADE, RICHARD WOOD	CDR	SFR
03033	BUCKLEY, JOHN LAFAYETTE	CDR	SFR
03034	SMITH, ALLAN EDWARD	VADM	LM
03035	JONES, LOUIS REEDER	MGEN	LM
03036	SPRAGUE, THOMAS LAMISON	VADM	LM
03037	WILSON, JULIAN DUBOIS	RADM	NYC
03038	PIXLEY, RICHARD MAYER	CAPT	WNY
03039	BECKER, ADOLPH ERNEST JR.	RADM	WNY
03040	JAMES, CLARENCE WILLIAM	LCDR	WNY
03041	HILL, AUGUST JOHN NORRIS	CAPT	SFR
03042	FLATLAND, RICHMOND JR.	Capt	SFR
03043	TOTH, NICHOLAS	CDR	SFR
03044	FRENCH, THOMAS LOCKWOOD	CDR	SFR
03045	BELCHER, DONALD RAY	HONOR	NYC
03046	GIBBS, WILLIAM FRANCIS	HONOR	NYC
03047	PANNILL, CHARLES JACKSON	HONOR	NYC
03048	PURYEAR, EVARD EWART	ENS	NYC
03049	HERSOM, GIFFORD PERSHING	CAPT	NYC
03050	HERRMANN, LACY BUNNELL	LT	NYC
03051	RICHARDSON, THOMAS FRANKLIN	CDR	NYC
03052	KENNADAY, JOHN MARTIN	RADM	NYC
03053	VAHITALLIE, THEODORE BERTUS	LTJG	NYC
03054	NACRURY, KING	LT	NYC
03055	DONAHUE, THOMAS GERALD	LCDR	NYC
03056	JOHNSON, WARREN WHITNEY	CDR	NYC
03057	COMBS, THOMAS SELBY	VADM	NYC
03058	ATKINS, JAME GORDON	CDR	NYC
03059	UPCHURCH, WALTER MCGOWAN JR.	LT	NYC
03060	CARROLL, JOHN ANSELM	LCDR	NYC
03061	ALER, FRANK VERNON JR..	CDR	NYC
03062	HEARN, REGINALD GORDON	CDR	SFR
03063	GURNEY, MARSHALL BARTON	CAPT	SFR
03064	MC ELLIGOTT, RAYMOND THOMAS	RADM	SFR
03065	MC CREA, JOHN III	CDR	SFR
03066	YOUNG, WILLIAM HENRY	CDR	SFR
03067	PARSONS, CHARLE ANDRUS	LCDR	SFR
03068	QUIGLEY, FREDERICK ANTHONY	LCDR	SFR
03069	GRAMENTINE, JAMES TURNER	CDR	SWS
03070	DEMOND, GERALD EDWARD	LT	SWS
03071	SHELTON, ROBERT REID JR.	LT	SWS
03072			
03073	DOLE, RICHARD WIGGLESWORTH	CAPT	
03076	DUPE OF 1485 (MARTIN JOSEPH WHITE)		
03075	LEUTHI, RALPH W.	HONOR	AVN
03076	BALLEW, JESSE L.	LCDR	AVN
03077	SCHAUFFLER, FREDERICK S.	CAPT	AVN
03078	KAUFFMAN, GARTH EMERSON	LT	AVN
03079	MOONEY, EUGENE H. F.	CDR	AVN
03080	KIRN, LOUIS JOSEPH	RADM	AVN
03081	ZIMMERMAN, FREDERICK W. E.	CAPT	AVN
03082	LAMAR, LAMARTINE VARNDOE	LCDR	AVN
03083	HUTCHINS, ROGER DEXTER	CAPT	AVN
03084	LEONARD, GEORGE STEPHEN	CAPT	AVN
03085	HOPPER, JOHN KIRK	Maj.	AVN
03086	DUPE OF 2465(CALVIN T. DURGIN)		
03087	IDE, JOHN JAY	CAPT	AVN
03088	BEERS, HENRY N.	CDR	AVN
03089	NATION, MILTON ADOLPHUS	RADM	AVN
03090	MARHALL, LEONARD LYON JR.	LT	AVN
03091	MC GEE, ROBERT JOSEPH	LT	SFR
03092	DUPE OF 3028(RAY ALBERT ROBINSON)		SFR
03093	KLING, HERBERT WAYLAND	CDR	SWS
03094	RICH, EDMUND GAINES	CAPT	SWS
03095			
03096	GORTON, EDWARD DEAN	LCDR	WNY
03097	PARKER, ALAN VREELAND	CAPT	WNY
03098	WAHLEN, LESLIE GEORGE	LT	WNY
03099	CAMERON, ROBERT ESDEN	Lt Col	WNY
03100	LANPHERE, NILES EDWARD	CAPT	WNY
03101	WESTFALL, WILBUR WOOD	CAPT	WNY
03102	DENMAN, ANTHONY JOHN	CAPT	AVN
03103	DOAN, FREDERIC GERRY	MAST	SFR
03104	CURRIER, STUART LANE	CDR	SFR
03105	O'BRIEN, WILLIAM ROBERT	LT	SFR
03106	CHURCHILL, ASA GLENN	CAPT	SFR
03107	COSPER, LAVELLE WILLIAM	CDR	SFR
03108	DUPE OF 2355(CHARLES ANTHONY MILLS)		
03109	SHALLOW, WILLIAM JOSEPH	LCDR	NYC
03110	STRUBLE, GEORGE WALLACE	LT	NYC
03111	MICHEL, JOHN J. A.	CAPT	NYC
03112	CRESAP, LOGAN	CDR	NYC
03113	LUCKENBACH, EDGARD FREDK JR.	CAPT	NYC
03114	DESBORDES, LEE HENRY	LT	NYC
03115	PAINE, GEORGE PORTER	LCDR	NYC
03116	OSLER, JOHN N.	LCDR	SWS
03117	HARTFORD, ARNOLD ALFRED	CAPT	MAS
03118	STEVENS, EDWIN P.	LCDR	AVN
03119			
03120	WALKER, JOSEPH SCOTT	CAPT	SWS
03121	KENNEDY, HAROLD MAURICE	LT	NYC
03122	RUSSELL, ERICKSON WHITNEY	CAPT	NYC
03123	O'BRIEN, GEORGE FRANCIS	LCDR	NYC
03124	ANGELL, HORACE MATT	CDR	SFR
03125	SLOAN, FRANCIS GRAIG	CDR	SFR
03126	WASHBURN, EDWARD DAVIS JR.	CAPT	SFR
03127	DUPE OF 2496(FRANCIS STUART LOW)		
03128	BRONSON, RICHARD PORTER	LCDR	SFR
03129	SHEEHAN, WILLIAM WALLACE	CDR	SFR
03130	SIDEMAN, ARTHUR FLORENTINE	LCDR	SFR
03131	SCHMALZ, KENNETH A. H.	LCDR	SWS
03132	THOMASON, "J." HAROLD	CDR	SWS
03133	LEBLOND, HAROLD DONALD (DR)	CDR	SWS
03134	EVERTON, LOREN DALE	Col	SWS
03135	HORGAN, JOHN POOLE	CDR	NYC
03136	MARTIN, MURRAY	CAPT	NYC
03137	WEST, GEORGE EDWARD JR.	LCDR	NYC
03138	WALKER, RAYMOND JOHN	LT	NYC
03139	BEEBE, DANIEL WEEKS	LTJG	NYC
03140	OLIVER, WILLM SETH	LCDR	NYC
03141	RYAN, WILLIAM DOUGLAS	RADM	NYC
03142	THOMPSON BERIH MAGOFFIN	LCDR	NYC
03143	GLOSTEN, EDWARD REINERS	LT	NYC
03144	SHRY, SEPHEN ALLAN	CDR	NYC

Admiral Stanley R. Arthur Selected for NOUS' Top Award

The Naval Order of the United States' Distinguished Sea Service Award will be presenteed to Admiral Stanley R. Arthur, USN (Ret.) at the closing formal banquet of the Order's upcoming New Orleans Congress on Tuesday evening, November 11. The announcement was made by NOUS Commander General, RADM William F. Merlin, USCG (Ret.) who will conduct the presentation ceremony.

Admiral Arthur entered the Navy through the Naval REserve Officer Training Corps (NROTC) Program at Miami University and commissioned in June 1957. His career included many interesting and significant assignments, which prepared him well for the ultimate responsibilities he would be intrusted with during the Persian Gulf War and subsequently.

VADM Fetterman Recieves DSSA

Col William R. Bremer, USMCR (Ret.), Commander General, NOUS, at the 1994 Williamsburg Congress, presented the "Distinguished Sea Service Award", the Naval Order's highest, to Vice Admiral John H. Fetterman, Jr., USN (Ret.) who retired from active duty on March 1, 1993, following a distinguished Naval career of 38 years. Following retirement, the Admiral assumed his current position as President and CEO of the Naval Aviation Museum in Pensacola, FL. His final two active duty assignments were Commander, Naval Air Force, U.S. Pacific Fleet and Chief of Naval Education and Training, respectively. A member through the Southwest Commandery, VADM Fetterman currently serves as a NOUS Vice Commander General-at-large.

The NOUS citation reads: *"In recoginition of unsurpassed and professional leadership and support of the Sea Services of the United States of America. Reflecting singular credit and honor upon himself and his country, and earning gratitude of his fellow countrymen. He stands 'Primus Inter Primos'."*

Admiral Paul Alexander Yost, Jr. (center) immediate past Commandant of the U.S. Coast Guard, accepts the Naval Order's "Distinguished Sea Service Award" from Commander General Wallace H. Lloyd, Jr. (left) at the Congress Banquet. With them is 'Commodore' Thomas J. Lupo who introduced the Admiral.

LT Robert R. Albright, II, USCG, accepts the NAval Order's first annual national award to the outstanding Junior Officer faculty member at the U.S. Caost Guard Academy. The award presentation was made by Commander General Fred D. Carl at the Academy's annual Convocation.

INSIG	COMPANION	RANK	CDRY
03145	SAUGSTAD, EDGAR V.	LT	NYC
03146	LINES, CLIFFORD OWN	LCDR	NYC
03147	TAYLOR, CRITTENBEN BATTELLE	CDR	SFR
03148	CORNELL, WALLACE GORDON	CDR	SFR
03149	MURPHY, JOHN MONTAGUE	CAPT	SFR
03150	ACKERMAN, CHARLES IRVING	HONOR	SFR
03151	ENGLAND, GEORGE M.	CDR	SFR
03152	DUPE OF 2052(ALEXANDER STURART MCDILL)		
03153	REBER, JOHN GIBBONS	Maj.	WNY
03154	UPSON, JAMES JULIAN	LT	WNY
03155	GREEN, FRANK OWEN	CDR	WNY
03156	ABBOTT, FREDERICK MEYER	Maj.	WNY
03157	PRIMERANO, VINCENT A.	CAPT	AVN
03158	LYONS, PAUL A.	LCDR	AVN
03159	MEAD, STATES M.	RADM	AVN
03160	JENKINS, JOHN R.	LCDR	AVN
03161	RUSSELL, EDMUND NELSON	LT	AVN
03162	BOGUMIL, EMIL CASIMIR	LT	WNY
03163			
03164	SCHANZE, EDWIN STANSBURY	RADM	NYC
03165	WILLIAMS, ROBERT EUGENE	LCDR	NYC
03166	BLACK, ORRIN FRANKLIN	LT	NYC
03167	ROGERS, JOSEPH FRANCIS	CAPT	NYC
03168	FURTH, FREDERICK RAYMOND	RADM	NYC
03169	BURR, JAMES KNOX	CDR	NYC
03170	MACHEN, LEO CHARLES	CAPT	NYC
03171	BAGGS, HAROLD EDWARD	CDR	NYC
03172	SHEA, EDWARD CORNELIUS	CDR	NYC
03173	BROCKHOUSE, RICHARD ALLEN	CDR	NYC
03174	KULINSKI, ARTHUR MICHAEL	CDR	NYC
03175	QUIGLEY, ANTHONY JOSEPH	RADM	SFR
03176	DROWN, WILLARD NEWELL	CDR	SFR
03177	CAMPBELL, DOUGLAS MARTIN	CAPT	SFR
03178	TENNEY, FRANK WHITNEY	CDR	SFR
03179	ROGERS, JOHN GARDNER	LCDR	SFR
03180	MC COOL, FELIX JAMES	CWO3	SFR
03181	WESSELS, MERLE EUGENE	LCDR	SWS
03182	SMITH, STEPHEN ELLSWORTH	CDR	SWS
03183	RIDDER, HERMAN HENRY	Col	SWS
03184	ELWELL, JOHN LEE	CAPT	SWS
03185	PEELER, WILLIAM RANDOLPH	CDR	SWS
03186	READ, HENRY RUCKER	CAPT	SWS
03187	STONE, WILLIAM ARTHUR	LCDR	SWS
03188	BREWSTER, ORVILLE DELUE	LCDR	SWS
03189	FARWELL, BYRON HOWES	LCDR	SWS
03190	SCOLE, ALBERT BUDDY	RADM	SWS
03191	PARCELS, WILLIAM HORATIO	CAPT	SWS
03192	WASHBURN, GORGE ARTHUR TAPPAN	RADM	SWS
03193	KERR, ALEXANDER HEWITT	LCDR	SWS
03194	GALLAGHER, BARRETT (N)	LCDR	AVN
03195	ROETGER, RUSSELL P.	LCDR	AVN
03196	CHERNACK, STANLEY I.	CDR	AVN
03197	DUPE OF 0822(WILLIAM A. READ, JR)		
03198	PASHER, FRANKLIN E. III	LT	AVN
03199	MASTAGLIO, JOHN DOUGLAS	CAPT	AVN
03200	ACKER, BENJAMIN AUSTIN	ENS	NYC
03201			
03202	CONNELL, THOMAS PATRICK	CDR	NYC
03203	DUPE OF 2631(GORDON S. GAVAN)		
03204	MC KINNEY, EUGENE BRADLEY	RADM	NYC
03205	HAMBLETT, CYRIL BERTRAM	RADM	NYC
03206	KELLER, DONALD ROSEBOROUGH	CDR	NYC
03207	SCHWASS, EARL ROBERT	CAPT	NYC
03207A	CAMBELL, GEORGE WILLIAM	CAPT	NYC
03208	LEWIS, JOHN STEPHEN (JACK)	RADM	NYC
03209	KING, EDWARD REUBEN	RADM	NYC
03210	GILBERT, RICHARD STUART	CDR	NYC
03211	TRESCOTT, CHARLES EDWARD	CAPT	NYC
03212	BOONE, WALTER FREDERICK	ADM	NYC
03213	ALLMAN, DAVID BACHARACH	LCDR	NYC
03214	CARPENTER, CHARLES LORAIN	RADM	NYC
03215	TEACH, JOHN HENRY JR.	CAPT	WNY
03216	STANLEY, ROBERT M.	LT	WNY
03217	BARNUM, ARTHUR KENNETH	HONOR	WNY
03218	BRONK, DETLEV W.	ENS	AVN
03219	HOLMES, LEMMAN T.	Capt	AVN
03220	MILLARD, THEODORE BALDWIN	Col	SWS
03221	AGGERBECK, JENS CHRISTIAN JR.	Col	SWS
03222	BAKER, ROY MARION (BULLET)	LT	SWS
03223	BARTLETT, RICHARD CALLINOR	CAPT	SWS
03224	BLACK, MAX IRVIN	CDR	SWS
03225	HILL, EDWARD TEMPLETON	MS	NYC
03226	MORRILL, JOHN HENRY	RADM	NYC
03227	MUDORFF, ARTHUR BERTRAM	LT	NYC
03228	SCHANTZ, CURTISS WILLIAM	RADM	NYC
03229	MC NALLY, JAMES ANTHONY	RADM	NYC
03230	RISLEY, RALPH GREENE	CAPT	NYC
03231	WOOD, CHARLES A.	ENS	NYC
03232	HOLLIS, ROBERT PARKER	MGEN	NYC
03233	RABORN, WILLIAM FRANCIS JR. (RED)	VADM	NYC
03234	CURLEY, KYRAN EDWARD B.	LCDR	NYC
03235	MACDONALD, DONALD JOHN	RADM	NYC
03236	GORDON, JOSEPH BERKELEY	LT	NYC
03237	RAWLE, HENRY	CAPT	NYC
03238	FINNEY, HERBERT FRANCIS	LCDR	NYC
03239	LUCAS, CARLTON CHARLES	CAPT	NYC
03240	CHRISMAN, EDWARD WILLIAM	CDR	NYC
03241	ZUNTAG, ALEXANDER ANDREW	CDR	NYC
03242	DEGRAFF, ROBERT WILLIAM	MIDN	NYC
03243	HARLAHAN, JOHN WILLIAM	LCDR	NYC
03244	VOGELER, ROBERT ALEXANDER	ENS	NYC
03245	POHANKA, FRANK SALES JR.	CDR	NYC
03246	DOMBROFF, SEYMOUR	CAPT	NYC
03247			
03248	WRIGHT, IRVIN BROWNING	Maj.	SFR
03249	MILLS, JAMES HERVE JR.	CAPT	SFR
03250	ENZENSPERGER, JOS. GEORGE JR.	CAPT	SFR
03251	BOLLES, FRANK CRANDALL JR.	CDR	WNY
03252	FULLER, JAMES HUGH	CDR	AVN
03253	FONDA, GILBERT CADWALLADER	LCDR	AVN
03254	MC CUTCHEN, JONN CHAPMAN	CAPT	NYC
03255	DODD, JOHN M.	LCDR	AVN
03256	KAUFFMAN, ROLAND PHILIP	RADM	NYC
03257	HALEY, THOMAS BRADLEY	CAPT	NYC
03258	COE, GEORGE VERNON JR.	LCDR	NYC
03259	BERGEN, JOHN JOSEPH	RADM	NYC
03260			
03261	MARE, ANTON LAWRENCE	CAPT	NYC
03262	RYSSY, JOHN WALFRID	CAPT	NYC
03263	LYONS, GERALD EDWARD	LT	NYC
03264	WRIGHT, HAROLD ALLAN	2ND Lt	NYC
03265	MORE, RODERICK M. SCOTT	LCDR	NYC
03266	JENKINS, WALTER TERRY	CAPT	NYC
03267	CLAUSEN, CLAUS KRISTIN RANDLPH	LT	NYC
03268	WHITE, DONALD MORISON	RADM	NYC
03269	GREENWALD, ROBERT CLARK, JR.	LT	NYC
03270	TYLER, GAINES ALBERT	CAPT	NYC
03271	KERR, LLOYD FULTON	LCDR	NYC
03272	BERKLEY, WILLIAM LENEAVE	CAPT	SFR
03273	WHITE, JAMES RIGGS	LCDR	SFR
03274	WOODMAN, WILIAM E.	CAPT	AVN
03275	MURRAY, ALAN K.	LCDR	AVN
03276	AHLBUM, SUMNER P.	LCDR	AVN
03277	MURPHY, LEO J. C.	CDR	AVN
03278	ILIFF, JAMES V.	CDR	SWS
03279	ECONOMOU, CONSTANTINE JAMES	CDR	SWS
03280	COOK, MORTON	LCDR	SWS
03281	DUPE OF 2462(GERALD FRANCIS BOGAN)		
03282	EBERS, CLARENCE HERSHAL	LCDR	SWS
03283	DIXON, JACK PODESTA	LCDR	SWS
03284	WATSON, LAVERNE MONTEITH	CAPT	SWS
03285	MILES, BILL AL	RADM	SWS
03286	BLACK, LEX LEROY	CAPT	SWS
03287	GEISER, KARL FREDERICK	CDR	SWS
03288	MOCK, HAROLD JACKSON	CDR	SWS
03289	WERNER, GERARD LAVELLE	LCDR	SWS
03290	KOPP, JESSE HOBART	CDR	SWS
03291	MC CARTNEY, EDGAR LEE JR.	CDR	SWS
03292	WHALEY, WILLIAM BAYNARD	RADM	SWS
03293	COLBY, JOHN BANCROFT	Lt Col	SWS

INSIG	COMPANION	RANK	CDRY	INSIG	COMPANION	RANK	CDRY
03294	EPPERT, KENNETH WYATT	CAPT	SWS	03369	GLIDDEN , GERMAINE G.	LTJG	AVN
03295	FARRELL, TED LEE	CAPT	SWS	03370	DUPE OF 2694(DONALD FRASER BARROW)		
03296	KROEPKE, EDWARD FRED	LT	NYC	03371			
03297	RIORDAN, CHARLES P. J.	CDR	NYC	03372	MOHAIR, JOHN PAUL	CDR	NYC
03298	KAUFMAN, ROBERT JULES	LT	NYC	03373	RESOR, EDWARD JACKSON	CDR	NYC
03299	RYON, WILLIAM MENDINHALL	CAPT	NYC	03374	HANLON, BYRON HALL	ADM	NYC
03300	HOPKINS, JOSEPH LAWRENCE	CAPT	NYC	03375	BOLGER, JOSEPH FRANCIS	VADM	NYC
03301	HEWITT, JOSEPH ROBERT	CAPT	NYC	03376	LAWTON, THOMAS P.	CDR	NYC
03302	BUNTING, WILLIAM FARNUM	LT	NYC	03377	LEVISON, LEONARD SPENCER	LCDR	NYC
03303	PLUMB, ROBERT JOHNSTON	CAPT	NYC	03378	COLLINS, WILLIAM HOWES	CAPT	NYC
03304	FASHENA, SIDNEY	LCDR	NYC	03379	LEVISON, MURRAY	LT	NYC
03305	MONTGOMERY, JOHN HAMILTON	LT	NYC	03380	HOOKS, ROBERT E.	LCDR	AVN
03306	FOLEY, PAUL JR.	RADM	NYC	03381	WINDALL, OWEN (N)	LCDR	AVN
03307	UEHLING, GORDON ALEXANDER	CAPT	NYC	03382	WELLING, CHARLES H. JR.	LT	AVN
03308	REDMAN, JOHN ROLAND	VADM	SFR	03383	HORNER, MAURICE L. JR.	CDR	SWS
03309	TOWLE, ELMER JAMES	CAPT	SFR	03384	DUPE OF 2716(JAMES H. RAPORT)		
03310	CONLON, EDWARD THOMAS	CAPT	SFR	03385	SINCLAIR, FREEMAN WILLIAM JR.	CDR	SWS
03311	DUPE OF 2543(FRANK EDMUND BEATTY)		LM	03386	OGDEN, LIONEL EDWARD	LCDR	SWS
03312	GROSS, HERMAN ALPHONSE	CAPT	SFR	03387	UNTERBERG, HAROLD	LCDR	NYC
03313	MAZZA, HAROLD RALPH	CDR	SFR	03387A	BOQUA, EDWARD ZELLEKEN	LT	SWS
03314	DECKER, JOSEPH ROY	CDR	SFR	03387B	MC GAFFIGAN, FRANCIS DANIEL	CAPT	SWS
03315	GUMMERSON, EUGENE HOWARD	LT	SFR	03388	EARLE, RALPH JR.	VADM	NYC
03316	DUPE OF 3063(MARSHALL BARTON GURNEY)		SFR	03389	MACK, JOHN BELKNAP	LT	NYC
03317	LEDOGAR, STEPHEN J.	LT	AVN	03390	BRIGGS, JOSEPHUS ASA	RADM	NYC
03318	CLEMENT, STUART H. JR.	LT	AVN	03391	KRAM, HARVEY	LT	NYC
03319	POLLOCK, EDWIN ALLEN	MC	LM	03392	UHLER, EDWARD BARR	LCDR	NYC
03320				03393	GRAVES, JOHN HART	CAPT	SFR
03321				03394	SCRIVNER, JOHN ELMO	CDR	SFR
03322	ALBRION, ROBERT GREENHALGH	HONOR	LM	03395	WILLIAMS, WILLIAM HENRY	LCDR	SFR
03323				03396	WHITEHOUSE, JOHN H.	LT	AVN
03324	THEOBALD, ROBERT ALBERT	RADM	LM	03397	DUPE OF 2067(HENRY MARTYN NOE)		
03325				03397A	O'NEIL, SIDNEY R.	LT	AVN
03326	CRAWFORD, GEORGE CLIFFORD	RADM	LM	03398	RYAN, WILLIAM E.	CDR	AVN
03327				03399	TAYLOR, DAVID S.	LT	AVN
03328	BALDWIN, HANSON WEIGHTMAN	LTJG	LM	03400	BALDWIN, JAMES BARRET	LT	AVN
03329	PULESTON, WILLIAM DILWORTH	CAPT	LM	03401	VAIL, DONALD	CAPT	AVN
03330	SPEAR, NATHANIEL JR.	ENS	LM	03402	TAYLOR, JAMES BLACKSTONE III	LT	AVN
03331	PRODDOW, ROBERT JR.	LCDR	NYC	03403	LUKE, DAVID L. III	Capt	AVN
03332	HUCKINS, THOMAS AVERILL	CAPT	NYC	03404	SONNABEND, A. M.	ENS	AVN
03333	FENTON, CHARLES RUDOLPH	RADM	NYC	03405	GITHENS, WILLIAM FRENCH	CDR	AVN
03334	MAHONEY, JOHN FRANCIS	CDR	NYC	03406	DIECKERT, EUGENE ADOLPH JR.	CDR	NYC
03335	MURTHA, THOMAS VERNON	CDR	NYC	03407	BURGER, JOSEPH CHARLES	MGEN	NYC
03336	BANKERT, BOYD ALLIE	CDR	NYC	03408	HOWARD, HAROLD SMITH	CDR	NYC
03337	COENE, EDGAR THEODORE	CAPT	NYC	03409	DELANEY, JOHN FRANCIS	RADM	NYC
03338				03410	JEWETT, CHARLES HENRY II	ENS	NYC
03339	WILSON, ELWOOD JASPER	CAPT	SFR	03411	MORGAN, JOHN CHAPMAN	CAPT	NYC
03340	PRICHARD, CLIFFORD	Lt Col	SFR	03412	MARTIN, WILLIAM INMAN	VADM	NYC
03341	MURPHY, JOSEPH FANNIN	LT	SFR	03413	SMITH, BERNARD EUGENE JR.	LT	NYC
03342	HILLISON, MORRIS	LT	SWS	03414	GINTY, ROBERT WILLIAM	LTJG	WNY
03343	BUDLONG, DALE HERBERT	LT	SWS	03415	STEIMLE, DOUGLAS B.	LCDR	AVN
03344	SHORT, GILES ELZA	RADM	SWS	03416	STEPHENSON, GEORGE S.	CDR	AVN
03345	COOPER, KENNETH CONRAD	CAPT	SWS	03417	REINBURG, JOSEPH HUNTER	Col	SWS
03346	DANIELS, WILLIAM DALE	LCDR	SWS	03418	AINLEY, JAMES CARPENTER	CDR	SWS
03347	O'BRIEN, THOMAS PATRICK	CAPT	SWS	03419	BAGDANOVICH, MICHAEL PETER	RADM	SWS
03348	GRIFFITH, HOMER OLIVER JR.	CAPT	SWS	03420	KEMPER, FRANKLIN LOYD	Lt Col	SWS
03349	HOCKIN, ARTHUR LLOYD	CAPT	SWS	03421	HILL, EDGAR R.	LT	SWS
03350	SARTORIS, HARRY M.	CAPT	AVN	03422	LOUGHLIN, ALVIN LEWIS	LCDR	SWS
03351	SANDS, JOHN K.	LT	AVN	03423	STINCHFIELD, JOHN EASTWOOD	CDR	SWS
03352	LEAHY, LAMAR RICHARD	RADM	AVN	03424	BUTCHER, GEORGE EDWARD	LCDR	SWS
03353	KIEBERT, MARTIN PETER V. JR.	CDR	NYC	03425	BERTOLDI, JONN B. JR.	CAPT	SWS
03354	HEATLEY, WILLIAM (N)	CDR	NYC	03426	DUFFIELD, MARSHALL DIXON	LCDR	SWS
03355	MC CALL, AMBROSE VICTOR JR.	Maj.	NYC	03427	WHITE, THOMAS FRANCIS JR.	LCDR	SWS
03356	JACOT, JULIUS FREDERICK	CAPT	NYC	03428	CRAWFORD, ROBERT BRACE PENN	CDR	SWS
03357	KANE, RICHMOND KEITH	LCDR	NYC	03429	COOPER, CLIFFORD STEELE	RADM	SWS
03358	BRACE, WILFRED JAMES	LCDR	NYC	03430	CHAPEL, CHARLES EDWARD	1ST Lt	SWS
03359	HOEFER, JOHN HENRY	RADM	SFR	03431	DRAGGE, ALLEN OLIVER	LCDR	SWS
03360	NORMAN, ARVID EDWIN	LCDR	SFR	03432	AINSWORTH, MILO L.	LCDR	SWS
03361	INGRAM, ROBERT STEPHENSON	Lt Col	SFR	03433	BAILEY, JOSLYN RIGBY	Col	SWS
03362	MILES, WILLIAM EDWARD JAXON	CDR	SFR	03434	LAWTON, FRED EMERSON	CDR	NYC
03363	SULLIVAN, J. JOSEPH	CAPT	SFR	03435	KREISER, ALEXANDER WALTER	BGEN	NYC
03364	VANBRUNT, BERGEN HOUSTON	LT	SFR	03436	STOCKHOLM, CARL GEORGE	CDR	NYC
03365	PAYNE, ROBERT MILLER	CAPT	SFR	03437	KENNEY, JOHN DURBIN	LT	NYC
03366	MEREDITH, JOSEPH CARLTON	LCDR	SFR	03438	BLETHEN, WILLIAM KINGSLEY	LT	SWS
03367	PRATT, JOHN LOWELL	LCDR	AVN	03439	BOHMKER, JAMES SHAW	LCDR	SWS
03368	DUPE OF 2583(PATRICK JOSEPH SULLIVAN)			03440	HARWOOD, CHAD MCKINNEY	LCDR	SWS

50

INSIG	COMPANION	RANK	CDRY	INSIG	COMPANION	RANK	CDRY
03441	HARRISON, WALLACE PERSHING	LCDR	SWS	03516	LOVE, JULIAN (N)	CAPT	SWS
03442	GOLDBERG, GEORGE EUGENE	LCDR	SWS	03517	GATES, FREEMAN	LCDR	SWS
03443	HOERNER, HERBERT LISLE	RADM	SWS	03518	BACKLAND, JOHN (N)	CDR	SWS
03444	JORGENSEN, ALFRED VINCENT	Col	SWS	03519	DEWOLFE, ROBERT RATHBUN	CAPT	SWS
03445	FLYNN, THOMAS JOSEPH	CAPT	SWS	03520	MORE, WILFRED NEWTON	LCDR	SWS
03446	SODEN, MARK A.	LT	SWS	03521	HORNE, CHARLES FREDERICK JR.	RADM	SWS
03447	SCARPINO, WILLIAM JOSEPH	CAPT	SWS	03522	BLACK, THOMPSON JR.	CDR	SWS
03448	GANNON, GEORGE DILLON	CWO	SWS	03523	MC KECHNIE, ARNOLD WILFRED	RADM	SWS
03449	NESEN, ROBERT DEAN	LCDR	SWS	03524	WICKETT, RUSSELL MORLEY	LCDR	AVN
03450	GOLENBESKE, JOHN	LCDR	SWS	03525			
03451	WARJONE, HANS WAYNE	LCDR	SWS	03526			
03452	WEST, ERNEST REID	Col	SWS	03527			
03453	MANN, GORDON LEE JR.	LT	SWS	03528	LITTLEFIELD, GORDON ATHORN	CAPT	NYC
03454	DAVIS, JOSEPH I.	ENS	SWS	03529	ROBERTSON, JAMES LOVEJOY	LT	NYC
03455	CANTLEN, JAMES SAMUEL	LT	SWS	03530	MUGGLEY, JACOB MARTIN	CDR	NYC
03456	SWISHER, GUY DAYTON	CAPT	SWS	03531	DUPE OF 3514 (HORACE KENNETH HORNER)		
03457	SCOTT, JACK (N)	LCDR	SWS	03532	DELEHANTY, THOMAS P.	LTJG	AVN
03458	WILLIAMS, LOWELL WINFIELD	CAPT	NYC	03533	GREENE, HARRY C.	CDR	AVN
03459	CRAIG, DONOVAN DONALD	CWO	NYC	03534	MARA, WELLINGTON T.	LCDR	AVN
03460	WEMYSS, WALLY FRANCIS JAMES	LCDR	LM	03535	MC MASTER, JOHN D.	LCDR	AVN
03461	CONROY, VINCENT JOSPEH	LCDR	ILL	03536	VORPERIAN, HARRY G.	LT	AVN
03462	GRAVES, CHARLES COAKLEY	CAPT	NYC	03537	DUPE OF 3408 (HAROLD SMITH HOWARD)		
03463	ROSS, JOHN JUDD	LCDR	NYC	03538	YOUNG, VICTOR KEITH	LT	AVN
03464	WITHINGTON, FREDERIC STANTON	RADM	NYC	03539	DUPE OF 2271 (ROBERT BURNS PIRIE)		
03465	SABIN, LORENZO SHERWOOD JR.	VADM	NYC	03540	WYETH, WALTER F.	CDR	AVN
03466	FITCH, THOMAS SIMON PADDOCK	CDR	NYC	03541	LAWRENCE, GEORGE F.	LT	AVN
03467	HALL, GROVER BUDD HARTLEY	RADM	NYC	03542	JONES, ANDREW B.	CAPT	AVN
03468	HEIDT, EDWARD (N)	CDR	NYC	03543	READ, DUNCAN H.	CAPT	AVN
03469	GISBURNE, EDWARD GEORGE	CDR	NYC	03544	DUPE OF 3158 (PAUL A. LYONS)		
03470	ESPE, CARL FREDERICK	VADM	NYC	03545	BRYAN, JAMES T., JR.	CDR	AVN
03471	MANSFIELD, JAMES ALFRED	LT	NYC	03546	PLACE, JOHN F.	CDR	AVN
03472	HOLDEN, EDWARD CLARENCE JR.	VADM	NYC	03547	ROSE, HUBERT D.	CDR	AVN
03473	MUMMA, ALBERT GIRARD	RADM	NYC	03548	PIERCE, EDWIN LAWRENCE	CAPT	AVN
03474				03549	DUPE OF 1428A (FREDERICK MACKAY TRAPNELL)		
03475	BROOKS, JOHN	Maj.	NYC	03550	DANIEL, PHILIP JAMES	LT	SWS
03476	LANE, FREDERICK ELLISON	CDR	NYC	03551	DUPE OF 1923 (STANLEY LEITH)		
03477	WILDMAN, HENRY VALENTINE	RADM	NYC	03552	TERRY, JOHN MILLER JR.	Maj.	SWS
03478	DECICCO, JOHN MATTHEW	LCDR	NYC	03553	BAYLER, WALTER LEWIS JOHN	BGEN	SWS
03479	KNISKERN, LESLIE ALBERT	RADM	NYC	03554	JAMES, RALPH KIRK	RADM	SWS
03480	WALTERS, JOHN HENRY	LT	NYC	03555	CLARK, ROBET STEWART	LCDR	SWS
03481	WARNER, MACDONALD SPENCER	CDR	NYC	03556	SIMMONS, ARTHUR EDWIN	CDR	SWS
03482	CAPPELLO, HENRY JULIUS	CDR	NYC	03557	HOOVER, JOHN HOWARD	ADM	SWS
03483	STEWART, DAVID HEDLEY	CDR	NYC	03558 – 03579 UNASSIGNED			
03484	STELTER, FREDERICK CARL JR.	RADM	NYC	03580	KIRBY, PETER	CDR	SFR
03485	MILES, MILTON EDWARD	RADM	LM	03581	MARBOURG, EDGAR FOSTER	LT	SFR
03486	KLEIN, IRVING NICHOLAS	CAPT	NYC	03582	HICKS, EDWARD NORTON	CAPT	SFR
03487	MILBANK, THOMS FOWLER	CDR	NYC	03583	TRANSUE, HARRY CURTIS	CDR	SFR
03488	LEVICK, JOHN HARKNESS	CAPT	NYC	03584	JACK, JAMES CLYDE, JR.	CDR	SFR
03489	PERKINS, HENRY CRAWFORD	RADM	LM	03585	FISHER, EVERELL EARL	LCDR	SFR
03490	MASON, REDFIELD	RADM	LM	03586	DAVIS, LEONARD KIER	Col	SWS
03491	ADAMS, SCARRITT	CAPT	NYC	03587	DAVIS, WILLIAM VIRGINIUS JR.	VADM	SWS
03492	FORRESTEL, EMMET PETER	VADM	LM	03588	FORNERO, JAMES E.	CDR	SWS
03493	THOMAS, OLIN PERRY JR.	CAPT	SFR	03589	GARTON, NORMAN FARQUHAR	RADM	SWS
03494	JONES, BERTON FARLEY	LCDR	SFR	03590	GREEN, GEORGE MYRON	CAPT	SWS
03495	KNORP, FRANCIS JOSEPH	Lt Col	SFR	03591	MADSEN, ELWOOD CHRISTIAN	CAPT	SWS
03496	WALTON, ROBERT TOTMON	CDR	SFR	03592	MARSHALL, JAMES PAULL	CDR	SWS
03497	AMES, JOHN GRIFFITH	CAPT	SFR	03593	MOSER, RICHARD P.	LT	SWS
03498	THOMPSON, WALLACE O.	Col	SFR	03594	MURPHY, ROBERT LEE	CDR	SWS
03499	ROLPH, HENRY RENTON	Col	SFR	03595	SCHOTTKE, LORRY S.	CAPT	SWS
03500	DUPE OF 2106 (MARION EMERSON MURPHY)			03596	WELLS, BENJAMIN OSBORNE	RADM	SWS
03501	THEYS, JACK DONALD	LCDR	SWS	03597	DAILEY, FRANKLIN EDWARD JR.	CAPT	WNY
03502	TUTTLE, MELBOURNE WEBB	LCDR	SWS	03598	CAPLAN, STANLEY	CAPT	WNY
03503	TWICHELL, EDMUND C.	CDR	SWS	03599	NEWHOUSE, GORDON LYLE	LT	WNY
03504	LAWSON, HOWARD B. JR.	LT	SWS	03600	PEACOCK, FRANCIS BERNARD	CDR	WNY
03505	LEWIS, DONALD	LT	SWS	03601	BACHMANN, CLARENCE CHARLES	CDR	WNY
03506	ADAMS, DUSTY DWIGHT	CAPT	SWS	03602	NELL, EDWARD RABB	CAPT	SFR
03507	HARPER, JOHN ALDEN	CAPT	SWS	03603	TAGG, WILLIAM LEONARD	RADM	SFR
03508	PRIDE, ALFRED MELVILLE	ADM	SWS	03604	DUPE OF 2212 (SAMUEL CARSLEY JACKSON)		
03509	KAUFFMAN, MAURICE	CAPT	SWS	03605	KANE, JOSEPH LESTER	RADM	SWS
03510	DUPE OF 1890(CLAYTON CHARLES JEROME)			03606	NEWTON, WALTER HUGHES	RADM	SWS
03511	SMITH, HERSCHEL CUTLER	LCDR	SWS	03607	RUPPRECHT, CLAY ARNOLD	CDR	SWS
03512	LUNDBERG, DELTON METZGER	CAPT	SWS	03608	DUPE OF 3063 (MARSHALL BARTON GURNEY)		
03513	MC KINNEY, JOHN REID	RDM	SWS	03609	SCHENCK, WINTHROP B.	LT	AVN
03514	HORNER, HORACE KENNETH	LT	SWS	03610	KISER, JOHN W. JR.	LCDR	AVN
03515	WEBB, LELAND DOTSON	CAPT	SWS	03611	JORALEMON, JOHN L. S.	LT	AVN

USNA Midshipmen Nat'l Award Winners

Three U.S. Naval Academy Midshipmen were honored by the Naval Order of the United States during the Academy's Prizes and Awards Ceremony on May 29 for scoring the highest marks in the annual competitive examination on current national and international affairs. CAPT James F. Brooke, Commander, National Capitol Commandery, represented the Commander General in the awards presentations.

The award recipients were: *Senior Contest:* 1st prize-Midshipman 1/c (now Ensign) Russell J. Coller, Jr. (Naval Order's sword), 2nd Prize-Midshipman 1/c (now 2nd Lt, USMC) John C. McClure (watch). *Junior Contest:* Midshipman 4/c (now 3/c) Ernest D. Miller, Jr. (watch).

Earlier, when the program was being reviewed by the Awards Committee, RADM V. L. Hill, Jr. Superintendant, U.S. Naval Academy, said in a letter:

" Your support of the Academy through the awards program has benefited countless Midshipmen who competed for your prizes over the past fifty six years. The continuing interest on the part of midshipmen is a tribute to your organization's care in maintaining and periodically reevaluating the awards." Further, he said that the awards are "...highly coveted and competition... is keen".

Principals in the annual presentation of the NOUS' Rear Admiral Thurston H. James Memorial Award to the outstanding graduate of the naval flight officers program. From left: RADM Stephen Barchet, who represented the Commander General in the ceremony; LT (jg) Chris Eagle, the awardee; and CDR Ken Bixler, Co, VA-128. The presentation took place at NAS, Whidbey Island, WA last Spring.

LT Atkin Gets NOUS CG Academy Award

LT Thomas F. Atkins, USCG, was the recipient of the Naval Order's 1990 U.S. Coast Academy Junior Officer Instructor Award. The presentation was made by Commander General John C. Rice, Jr. at the Academy's Academic Convocation on August 21 with RADM Thomas T. Matteson, USCG, Academy Superintendent, presiding.

Nominations and voting, in which all cadets and faculty participate, are conducted in late spring. Results are announced only when the citation is read to the thunderous applause of the cadets who are just returning from summer break.

It is a fitting recognition for an officer who himself exemplifies and instills into others the traits expected in Sea Service officers. LT Atkin is a Companion of the Massachusetts Commandery.

INSIG	COMPANION	RANK	CDRY
03612	BENTA, KENNETH LOVELL	CDR	AVN
03613	DENNY, ARCHIBALD M. JR.	LCDR	AVN
03614	ROBERT, ARTHUR H.	LTJG	AVN
03615	GAINES, RICHARD KENNA	CAPT	AVN
03616	DUPE OF 2798 (ROBERT ABBOTT SINCERBEAUX)		
03617	DUPE OF 2295 (GEORGE ARTHUR DICKERSON)		
03618	LYNCH, JOSEPH BERTRAM	RADM	AVN
03619	HATAWAY, CHESTER IRWIN	ENS	NYC
03620	GRELL, WILLIAM FRANK	Lt Col	NYC
03621	CLEAVES, EMERY NUDD	CDR	NYC
03622	CROSLEY, PAUL CUNNINGHAM	CAPT	NYC
03623	BURROUGHS, SSHERMAN EVERET JR.	RADM	NYC
03624	WISE, ROBERT ALFRED	ENS	NYC
03625	CALLAHAN , ROY HANEY	RADM	NYC
03626	STANLEY, REUBEN ELLIOTT	CAPT	WNY
03627	BOWEN, JOHN B. JR.	CAPT	SWS
03628	MILES, MARCUS LINIEL	CAPT	SFR
03629	OMARK, WARREN R.	CDR	AVN
03630	BEYERLY, IRWIN FOREST	RADM	SFR
03631	MARTIN, HENRY JOSEPH	CDR	SFR
03632	O'CONNOR, RICHARD CHARLES	LT	SFR
03633	BELLCHER, FRANK GARRETTSON	CDR	SFR
03634	DICKINSON, EVERETT HOMER	CAPT	SFR
03635	ROSS, CHRISTOPHER THEO WM.	CDR	WNY
03636	ARNESON, RAYMOND LAWRENCE	LCDR	SFR
03637	OAKFORD, MALCOLM I.	LTJG	AVN
03638	BURDEN, HARVEY PAUL	RADM	AVN
03639	LAFLIN, LLOYD ALAN	LCDR	SWS
03640	MAY, DONALD MATHESON	RADM	SWS
03641	DUPE OF 3089 (MILTON ADOLPHUS NATION)		
03642	WESTHOFEN, CHARLES LOUIS	RADM	SWS
03643	MURRAY, WALTER A.	LT	AVN
03644	GALLAGHER, JOHN JOSEPH	LCDR	SFR
03645	RICE, ROGERS J.	LCDR	AVN
03646	BAIRD, WILLIAM CAMERON	LCDR	WNY
03647	OGDEN, HAROLD LEONARD	LCDR	SWS
03648	ROBINSON, BERNARD B.	LCDR	SWS
03649	RIORDAN, WM. FRANCIS JOSEPH	LT	SWS
03650	HABER, NORMAN SHELDON	CDR	SWS
03651	KERRIDGE, PHILIP MARKHAM, JR.	CAPT	SWS
03652	CRAMER, KENNETH JAMES	CAPT	SWS
03653	JOHNSON, ROBERT ELLIOTT	LCDR	SWS
03654	GINN, WILLIAM HENRY	RADM	SWS
03655	QUILTER, EDWARD SINON	CAPT	SWS
03656	WILLCOX, WESTMORE	LT	AVN
03657	DUPE OF 0826 (JONN W. ROSS)		
03658	TURLEY, THOMAS A.	CDR	AVN
03659	WILLIAMS, GEORGE M.	LCDR	AVN
03660	PURVIS, RONALD SCOTT	RADM	AVN
03661	HANFT, SHERWOOD J.	CDR	AVN
03662	BYRNE, PATRICK J.		AVN
03663	WARD, ARTHUR D.	CAPT	AVN
03664	FISCHER, EDWIN A.	CDR	AVN
03665	GREENE, EMMANUEL LEWIS	LCDR	AVN
03666	REARDON, WILLIAM LEO JR.	LCDR	WNY
03667	HULL, CARL FIRMAN	CDR	AVN
03668	MILLER, SHIRLEY SNOW	RADM	AVN
03669	SANDERS, JAMES GILLIES JR.	LT	AVN
03670	GATES, RUSSELL GEORGE	CAPT	SBA
03671	EDMONDS, GEORGE WILLARD	LT	SBA
03672	HUTTON, CURTIS WOOD	LCDR	SBA
03673	PRICE, FRANCIS JR.	LCDR	SBA
03674	MOUTON, EDISON EDWARD	CAPT	SBA
03675	RICE, GILBERT MCKESSON	CAPT	SBA
03676	BUTCHER, HARRY CECIL	CAPT	SBA
03677	SPELLMAN, CLEMENS EUGENE	CAPT	SBA
03678	SCHMOELE, JOHN MOORE	CAPT	SBA
03679	CHURCHILL, E. PERRY	LCDR	SBA
03680	BACKMAN, PAUL OSCAR	CDR	SBA
03681	HOLCOMB, JONN KENNETH	CAPT	SBA
03682	WOOD, CARLETON BALL	CDR	SBA
03683	YOUNG, DAVID BRYAN	CAPT	SBA
03684	WEINGAND, ALVIN CARL	LCDR	SBA
03685	MERRITT, JOHN FREDERICK	LCDR	SBA
03686	LUCKING, WILLIAM ALFRED JR.	LCDR	SBA

INSIG	COMPANION	RANK	CDRY
03687	WESTON, WALLACE HUMPHREY	CAPT	SFR
03688	KINERT, JOHN OSCAR	RADM	SFR
03689	WOOD, RUSSELL ERNEST	RADM	SFR
03690	FRENTRUP, RALPH HUGO	LT	SFR
03691	BRIDGEMAN, HARRY MORRIS	CAPT	SFR
03692	HAUSER, LAWRENCE JOHN	LCR	WNY
03693	CARLO, JAMES NELSON	LTJG	WNY
03694	GRIFFIN, BURGESS H.	LCDR	AVN
03695	THORBURN, DONALDSON BRIDE	CAPT	AVN
03696	DUPE OF 3375 (JAMES FRANCIS BOLGER)		
03697	REMMERT, JOHN L.	CDR	AVN
03698	HENRY, CLEMENT S.	LCDR	AVN
03699	BINGHAM, HENRY P. JR.	CDR	AVN
03700	MOSBY, THOMAS TALFOURD	LCDR	AVN
03701	BOLT, ROBERT BASHFORD	CAPT	SFR
03702	BERKELEY, JAMES PHILLIPS	MGEN	SFR
03703	ARNOLD, MURR EDWARD	RADM	SFR
03704	HAGSTROM, WARREN ANTONE	LCDR	SFR
03705	MISERENDINO, SAMUEL RICHARD	LT	SFR
03706	MEGROZ, JACQUES	LTJG	AVN
03707	DETWILER, JOSEPH MISHLER	LCDR	SWS
03708	WRIGHT, FORD JR.	LT	AVN
03709	GILLETTE, GEORGE C.	LCDR	SWS
03710	JACK, SAMUEL SLOAN	MGEN	SWS
03711	DUPE OF 2122(JACK PENDLETON MONROE)		
03712	WEIR, RAPHAEL LAWRENCE	CAPT	SWS
03713	WILSON, WILLIAM	CDR	SWS
03714	ALDERMAN, JOHN CLEMENT	RADM	SWS
03715	WHEELER, JOHN EDWARD	LCDR	SWS
03716	JAMES, JOHN MERRITT	ENS	SWS
03717	WIRSIG, FRANK HENRY	BGEN	SWS
03718	DUPE OF 3623 (SHERMAN EVERETT BURROUGHS JR)		
03719	DIRKS, DONALD N.	LTJG	AVN
03720	DONOVAN, JOHN JOSEPH JR.	CAPT	SFR
03721	KELLOGG, DAVID MCDOUGALL	CAPT	SWS
03722	MC LAUGHLIN, ROBERT BRIGHT	CAPT	SWS
03723	CALDWELL, HENRY HOWARD	RADM	SWS
03724	CROWDER, JAMES PRICE	CAPT	SWS
03725	NIEKUM, PHILIP JR.	RADM	SWS
03726	FULLERTTON, KENNETH MOORE JR.	LCDR	SWS
03727	DUPE OF 3442 (GEORGE EUGENE GOLDBERG)		
03728	FLAHERTY, EUGENE DEWEY	CAPT	SWS
03729	RUBIN, MORRIS MERRILL	CAPT	SWS
03730	RIPLEY, WILLIAM CHARLES	LCDR	SWS
03731	MEYER, JOHN MELVIN	CDR	SWS
03732	LENTZ, H. L.	Lt Col	SWS
03733	O'NEILL, ROBERT RAYMOND	LCDR	SWS
03734	WEBBER, WILLARD SOUTHGATE	CAPT	SFR
03735	HAWKINS, NORMAN LOFTUS JR.	LTJG	SFR
03736	MOORE, THOMAS ORLAND	CWO4	SFR
03737	TOMLINSON, STANLEY TRACE	LCDR	SBA
03738	POWER, HARRY DOUGLAS	RADM	SBA
03739	MONROE, LYNN "C"	LCDR	SBA
03740	MC COMB, GUY RUTHERFORD JR.	LCDR	SBA
03741	HALL, GEORGE JOHNSON	LT	SBA
03742	HARRIS, GENE MARDEN	CAPT	SBA
03743	WALLER, HENRY TAZEWELL	BGEN	SBA
03744	ROBINETTE, CARL WALDECK	LCDR	SBA
03745	EDMONDS, WARNER, JR.	LT	SBA
03746	MACGILLIVRAY, WM. DONALD	LCDR	SBA
03747	GEORGE, ALONZO GRIFFIN	CDR	SBA
03748	MCNAMARA, DELBERT "H"	CDR	SBA
03749	BELOTTI, ROY THOMAS	LT	SWS
03750	BERNSTEIN, MAURICE EDWARD	LT	SWS
03751	CAMPBELL, NORWOOD AXTELL	CAPT	SWS
03752	FITCH, EDWARD MORRIS JR.	CAPT	SWS
03753	GOOD, GEORGE FRANKLIN JR.	LGEN	SWS
03754	HARTMANN, BENN JAMES	CDR	SWS
03755	JOHNSON, JAMES MAXIMILLIAN	CDR	SWS
03756	MORTON, HUGHES GREGORY	LTJG	SWS
03757	SLOAN, WILLIAM PATRICK	CDR	SWS
03758	WRIGHT, GORDON KENNEDY	LCDR	SWS
03759	CURRIE, FRANCIS	CDR	NYC
03760	MOORE, WAYLAND WILSON	CDR	NYC
03761	CINCOTTA, ANGELO JOHN	Col	NYC

INSIG	COMPANION	RANK	CDRY	INSIG	COMPANION	RANK	CDRY
03762	FELT, CARL ALFRONSO JR.	CAPT	NYC	03837	SCHWANKE, LOUIS CHARLES	CDR	COL
03763	SIEBEL, JOSEPH ALTER	CDR	NYC	03838	SINCLAIRE, REGINALD (N)	CDR	COL
03764	GRIFFITH, PERRY PAUL JR.	LT	NYC	03839	STEWART, BIRGE LAYTON	LCDR	COL
03765	HUTCHINSON, MYRON W. JR.	COMMO	NYC	03840	STOHL, JAMES ROBERT	LCDR	COL
03766	BADGER, JAMES GALVIN JR.	LCDR	ILL	03841	TYLER, WARNER WILLIAM	CAPT	COL
03767	BURK, JEWELL VANDEVER	LCDR	ILL	03842	WACKER, FRANCIS (N)	LCDR	COL
03768	BURROWS, ALBERT COLLINS	RADM	ILL	03843	WIDEMAN, WILLIAM BOMAR	CAPT	COL
03769	CLARKSON, JOHN LEEDS	CDR	ILL	03844	KILKER, JAMES HENRY	CDR	COL
03770	CONRAD, ARTHUR LUCIUS	CDR	ILL	03845	MARK, JULIUS	LCDR	NYC
03771	CUSTER, RUDOLF PRESBER	CDR	ILL	03846	SPRAGUE, WALLACE ARTHUR	CDR	NYC
03772	FOSTER, WILLIAM JOHN	LT	ILL	03847	COLEMAN, JOHN ALOYSIUS JR.	LCDR	NYC
03773	GOODALL, HENRY WILLIAM	RADM	ILL	03848	SMITH, MERCER RICHARD	Maj.	SWS
03774	HALAS, GEORGE STANLEY	CAPT	ILL	03849	OSTERHAUS, HUGO WILSON, JR.	RADM	SFR
03775	HERZMAN, JOSPEH (N)	LCDR	ILL	03850	MCCARTHY JAMES JEREMIAH	CDR	SFR
03776	JAMES, WALTER FRANKLYN	RADM	ILL	03851	HARTFORD, BERTRAM VINCENT	LT	SFR
03777	JOHNSON, ERNEST LEVIN	CAPT	ILL	03852	BRODERICK, PAUL LARKIN	CAPT	SFR
03778	KASSON, CONSTANT BUEL	LT	ILL	03853	DUPE OF 3361 (ROBERT STEPHENSON INGRAM)		
03779	KINSLEY, WILLIAM ALLEN	CDR	ILL	03854	BURRELL, JOHN EDEN	CAPT	SWS
03780	KNIGHT, AUGUSTUS JR.	CDR	ILL	03855	EGELER, PAUL LELAND	LCDR	SWS
03781	KRASS, JOHN CARL	LT	ILL	03856	FIALA, REID PURYEAR	RADM	SWS
03782	KULLMAN, THOMAS BARTON	CAPT	ILL	03857	HINKLE, TRUMAN BRUCE	CAPT	SWS
03783	LACKNER, PETER ROBERT	CAPT	ILL	03858	MC CLOY, WILLIAM MALTBY	RADM	SWS
03784	LAINE, VAINO E.	CDR	ILL	03859	MILLER, ROGER FARRINGTON	CAPT	SWS
03785	LAMBERT, ERIC C.	RADM	ILL	03860	MILLER, WALTER BERNARD	CAPT	SWS
03786	MOORE, JAMES BARTLETT	CAPT	ILL	03861	MOORE, BRUCE EDMUND	LCDR	SWS
03787	DUPE OF 3347 (THOMAS PATRICK O'BRIEN)			03862	TUTTLE, MAGRUDER HILL	RADM	SWS
03788	PURSELL, WARREN BENJAMIN	CDR	ILL	03863	WILSON, ARTHUR LELONG	LT	SWS
03789	ROWE, JOHN EVERETT JR.	CAPT	ILL	03864	BOYLE, PETER FREDERICK	CAPT	SWS
03790	ROSS, JAMES MORTON	RADM	ILL	03865	BUCHAN, ROBERT BOONE	CAPT	SWS
03791	RUTH, PHILIP FREDERICK	CDR	ILL	03866	DOUDNA, CALVIN THOMAS	CAPT	SWS
03792	SAX, SAMUEL WILLIAM	LT	ILL	03867	ECKELMEYER, EDWARD HERMAN JR.	RADM	SWS
03793	SISCO, AUGUST C.	LCDR	ILL	03868	HATTON, GEEEORGE ANTHONY	CAPT	SWS
03794	SMITH, ALLEN JR.	RADM	ILL	03869	HIPPE, ROBERT HOUSE	LCDR	SWS
03795	TASCH, ALLCUIN MARTIN (BUD)	LCDR	ILL	03870	HOLLISTER, WILLIAM WALLACE	CAPT	SWS
03796	TAUSSIG, JOSEPH MAURICE	CAPT	ILL	03871	LEONARD, WILLIAM RICHARD JR.	CDR	SWS
03797	WENDT, GEORGE BERNARD	CDR	ILL	03872	MEYERS, RAYMOND EDWIN	LCDR	SWS
03798	WENDT, GEORGE ROBERT	CAPT	ILL	03873	PAYNE, FREDERICK ROUNSVILLE	BGEN	SWS
03799	WHITE, ROGER QUINCY	CAPT	ILL	03874	SPURGEON, WILLIAM HENRY III	LT	SWS
03800	LITZEWITZ, ELEMER KURZ	LCDR	ILL	03875	BOEMI, ANTHONY ANDREW	LCDR	ILL
03801	TOOLEY, WILLIAM HENRY	LCDR	SFR	03876	BROWNE, ALDIS JEROME JR.	CAPT	ILL
03802	MEGLEN, FRANK DANIEL A.	CDR	SFR	03877	CARVER, LAMAR PEYTON	RADM	ILL
03803	ADKINS, GERALD JACOB	LCDR	COL	03878	CHINNOCK, RONALD JOHN	CAPT	ILL
03804	ATWELL, ROBERT BRISTOL	LCDR	COL	03879	CORBETT, WILLIAM JOSEPH JR.	CAPT	ILL
03805				03880	DENTON, THOMAS KELSEY	CAPT	ILL
03806	BIEBER, ALAN MARK	LCDR	COL	03881	FETRIDGE, WILLIAM HARRISON	LCDR	ILL
03807	BURKE, WILLIAM GLENN	CAPT	COL	03882	FINN, RICHARD B.	LT	ILL
03808	BURRELL, HOMER LINCOLN JR.	LT	COL	03883	FITCH, MORGAN LEWIS JR.	LT	ILL
03809	CALLAHAN, RAYMOND LEONARD	CAPT	COL	03884	HIGGINS, JOHN MARTIN	RADM	ILL
03810	COOK, GEORGE STAFFORD	CDR	COL	03885	JACOBS, LOUIS SULLIVAN	LT	ILL
03811	COOPER, HENRY GIBBONS	CDR	COL	03886	DUPE OF 3639 (LLOYD ALAN LAFLIN)		
03812	CORLISS, WELLS MCGREGOR	CDR	COL	03887	MARKEN, ROY ROCKWELL	CAPT	ILL
03813	DAVIDSON, ADOLPH EUGENE	LT	COL	03888	MC COOL, RICHARD MILES	CAPT	ILL
03814	DOUGLASS, WILLIAM CORBIN II	LT	COL	03889	MEYER, MARSHALL	CDR	ILL
03815	FOLMER, GEORGE WILLIAM	CDR	COL	03890	MOORE, JOHN MAXWELL	LCDR	ILL
03816	FREESTED, ROBERT CHARLES	LCDR	COL	03891	OCK, FRANCIS PAXTON	RADM	ILL
03817	HAHN, JAMES SIDNEY	CDR	COL	03892	OLSON, CARL GIDEON	CAPT	ILL
03818	HALLOCK, WILLIAM HENRY	CAPT	COL	03893	O'REILLY, PHILIP JOSEPH	LCDR	ILL
03819	HENDRIX, HILTON TAFT	CDR	COL	03894	PORETT, LEO I.	CDR	ILL
03820	HOUGHTON, HALEY FRANK	LCDR	COL	03895	SHAHEEN, RAYMOND	LCDR	ILL
03821	HYLAND, THOMAS JAMES	CAPT	COL	03896	WURTZEBACH, EDWARD PAUL	LCDR	ILL
03822	KALTENBACH, JOHN LEE	CAPT	COL	03897	DURKIN, THOMAS CHARLES	CDR	SFR
03823	KORBELIK, ARTHUR "A"	CDR	COL	03898	COOMBS, CHARLES EDWARD JR.	CAPT	SFR
03824	LESHER, DAVID JOHN	LCDR	COL	03899	GRIFFITH, CHARLES WALKER	CAPT	SFR
03825	MC GEE, NEALE STRATTON	LCDR	COL	03900	HOPWOOD, HERBERT GLADSTONE JR.	CAPT	SFR
03826	MONTAGRIFF, BERTRAM PETER	LCDR	COL	03901	CROWN, ROBERT	CAPT	ILL
03827	MOSS, BRYAN WILBUR	LCDR	COL	03902	DUPE OF 1568 (HANS VICTOR VON LEDEN)		
03828	MYERS, ARBRAHAM FRANCIS	CAPT	COL	03903	DOWNEY, WILLIAM WARD	LCDR	ILL
03829	NORGART, MELVILLE JAMES	CAPT	COL	03904	LAMPHIER, JAMES ANDRE	CDR	MAS
03830	OVIATT, ALMON EWING	LCDR	COL	03905	MORRIS, GEORGE NICHOLAS	CDR	MAS
03831	RENO, JOHN SPENCER	CAPT	COL	03906	CAMMISA, JAMES JOSEPH VINCENT	CDR	MAS
03832	REYNOLDS, CLARENCE WILBUR	CDR	COL	03907	BROWNING, HAYS R.	CAPT	DCA
03833	RITTENHOUSE, LEON CLARE	LCDR	COL	03908	WILLIAMSON, DAVID SANFORD	CAPT	DCA
03834	ROBERTS, JAMES LEE	CDR	COL	03909	HILTON, HART DALE	CAPT	DCA
03835	ROBINSON, WILLIAM WALKER	CAPT	COL	03910	CLARK, JOHN EDWARD	RADM	DCA
03836	RUNYAN, ELMO DICKSON	CDR	COL	03911	DUPE OF 3429 (CLIFFORD STELE COOPER)		SWS

54

INSIG	COMPANION	RANK	CDRY	INSIG	COMPANION	RANK	CDRY
03912	FROST, LAURENCE HUGH	VADM	DCA	03987	MILLER, LEIGH GRAYSON	CDR	SFR
03913	GRAY, ROBERT REED	CDR	DCA	03988	FISHER, ALVAN	RADM	MAS
03914	FORTUNE, WILLIAM CHARLES	CAPT	DCA	03989	RAY, CLARENCE "C"	RADM	SBA
03915	GRALLA, ARTHUR ROBERT	VADM	DCA	03990	HOFF, MATTHEW JOHNSON	LCDR	SBA
03916	TENEYCK, JOHN CONOVER	CAPT	DCA	03991	ATWATER, AMARIAH G. COX	CAPT	ILL
03917	SERRELL, ANDREW (N)	CAPT	DCA	03992	BABSON, GUSTAVUS	LCDR	ILL
03918	HOLBROOK, HILLIARD BAXTER	RADM	DCA	03993	BUCKLEY, EDWARD LEONARD	LCDR	ILL
03919	CASWELL, GORDON LEONARD	RADM	DCA	03994	COGHLAN, FRANCIS EDWARD	LCDR	ILL
03920	KALMBACH, KENNETH HENRY	CDR	DCA	03995	GALLERY, WILLIAM ONAHAM	RADM	ILL
03921	JARVIS, WERNINGER	CDR	SFR	03996	HAMPTON, ISAIAH MARTIN	CAPT	ILL
03922	WEIDMAN, HUBERT FKLN (KNUTE)	CAPT	SFR	03997	HASKIN, ENRIQUE D'HAMEL	RADM	ILL
03923	CRANE, JAMES MITCHELL	Lt	SFR	03998	KROCH, CARL ADOLPH	LT	ILL
03924	BOSCA, JOSPEH ROBERT	LT	SFR	03999	O'CONNELL, GEORGE ALOYSIUS JR.	CAPT	ILL
03925	FRIEDENBACH, KENNETH JOSPEH	CAPT	SFR	04000	NORTON, M. C. JR.	CAPT	AVN
03926	ABLAN, JOHN PHILIP	CAPT	SFR	04001	PRINCE, MILTON S.	CDR	NYC
03927	NELSON, CHARLES ROBERT	CAPT	SFR	04002	MC MULLEN, FRANCIS ANTHONY	Lt Col	NYC
03928	SPRAGUE, CHANDLER MONTG'Y II	Maj.	SFR	04003	MENKEN, KENNETH ANDREWS	LTJG	NYC
03929	WILSON, EDWIN MARK JR.	RADM	SFR	04004	LUEDECKE, OTTO RICHARD	CDR	NYC
03930	DEETHS, WILLIAM RICHARD	LCDR	SFR	04005	BERGH, WILLARD ANTON	CAPT	SEA
03931	BITTING, SOULE TRYON	CDR	SFR	04006	CANNON, JOHN EDWARD	LCDR	SEA
03932	MUNGER, MALCOLM TOWNSEND	CAPT	SFR	04007	CULLITON, WILLIAM M.	LCDR	SEA
03933	DALY, CHRISTOPHER LAWRENCE	CDR	SFR	04008	FALLON, WALTER EDDY	CDR	SEA
03934	MC ALISTER, FRANCIS MARION	MGEN	SFR	04009	JONES, WARREN WORTH	CAPT	SEA
03935	HAMILTON, THOMAS JAMES	RADM	SFR	04010	KINSMAN, THOMAS ARTHUR	CDR	SEA
03936	JACOBS, DAVID INKSTER	CAPT	SFR	04011	KRETZLER, HARRY HAMLIN	CAPT	SEA
03937	PRICE, HOWARD CONRAD JR.	CDR	SFR	04012	MONSON, KARL CHRISTIAN	CDR	SEA
03938	MACGREGOR, EDGAR JOHN III	RADM	SFR	04013	ODEGAARD, CHARLES EDWIN	LCDR	SEA
03939	WEBER, LAWRENCE KIRKWOOD JR.	CDR	SFR	04014	SODERBERG, JOHN ALBIN	LT	SEA
03940	ARNER, RADFORD KING	CDR	SFR	04015	VANHORN, PHILIP HUDSON	LCDR	SEA
03941	SWEENEY, WILLIAM EDWARD	RADM	SBA	04016	VOGEL, JOHN L.	CDR	SEA
03942	NORDENSON, JOHN EDMUND	LCDR	SBA	04017	WEBSTER, HOMER FRANCIS	CAPT	SEA
03943	BERRY, FREDERIC AROYCE	RADM	SBA	04018	FREDA, CARMINE	CDR	AVN
03944	HASS, JOHN KELLEHER	Maj.	SBA	04019	DREHER, WILLIAM A.	CDR	AVN
03945	KALLMAN, ROBERT EDWARD	CAPT	SBA	04020	DELEZENE, JAMES ROBERT	CDR	DCA
03946	WAHL, WILLIAM RANDOLPH	Lt Col	SBA	04021	DUVON, JAY	CDR	DCA
03947	PARMELEE, PERRY ORMISTON	BGEN	SWS	04022	SCHUENEMAN, WILLIAM ROBERT	CDR	DCA
03948	BACKUS, STANDISH JR.	CDR	SBA	04023	KLEIN, FREDERICK NELSON JR.	CAPT	DCA
03949	RUDD, RICHARD ORTEN	CDR	SBA	04024	SIMON, THOMAS S.		DCA
03950	JORDANO, JOHN JR.	LT	SBA	04025	BARRICKLO, JOHN ELMER	CDR	SFR
03951	DEAL, CLYDE	LT	NYC	04026	HATFIELD, ROBIN BENJAMIN	CAPT	SFR
03952	MC DOWELL, LESTER LASHELLE	CAPT	NYC	04027	HILL, RALPH PALMER	LT	SFR
03953	DUNN, GILBERT THOMAS	LTJG	NYC	04028	HUBERT, GEORGE HOWARD JR.	CAPT	SFR
03954	MARKS, ANTHONY MICHAEL	2ND LT	NYC	04029	MACRAE, ALLEN DENISON	CDR	SFR
03955	WHITE, KENNETH RUSSELL	CAPT	NYC	04030	DUPE OF 3347 (THOMAS PATRICK OBRIEN)		
03956	ANABLE, ANTHONY	CDR	NYC	04031	WILLARD, CHAUNCEY SHEARER	CAPT	SFR
03957	LOHEED, HUBERT BRADFORD	LCDR	NYC	04032	SANGER, KENNETH JOHN	CAPT	SEA
03958	BAXTER, RAYMOND STANLEY	LT	NYC	04033	BONCUTTER, ALBERT CLAIR	LCDR	SEA
03959	PATTY, ROBERT	CDR	NYC	04034	GUINN, CHARLES GERALD	LCDR	SEA
03960	ACQUAVELLA, FRANCIS JOSEPH	CAPT	NYC	04035	JAMES, FRANK DEXTER	LCDR	SEA
03961	SPERBERG, LESTER WILLIAM	CAPT	COL	04036	KUNDE, NORMAN F.	CDR	SEA
03962	LAPE, EUGENE J.	CDR	AVN	04037	LEIENDECKER, GILBERT LYMAN	CDR	SEA
03963	KUEHN, PAUL G.	LCDR	AVN	04038	RYAN, JOHN LAWRENCE	LCDR	SEA
03964	JEWETT, GARRY WILLIAM JR.	CAPT	SFR	04039	SCHILLER, JOHN ROBERT	CDR	SEA
03965	GLEASON, JAMES JOSEPH JR.	CAPT	SFR	04040	THELEN, GEORGE EDWARD	CAPT	SEA
03966	KOMISAREK, LEONARD	CDR	SFR	04041	SHELLEY, TULLY JR.	RADM	AVN
03967	GAZLAY, RICHARD CLARKE	CAPT	SFR	04042	LYON, HORACE LOCKE	CAPT	AVN
03968	CHAPMAN, WILLIAM KING	LCDR	SFR	04043	CARR, JOHN FRANCIS	CAPT	AVN
03969	DUPE OF 2171 (JOHN PAUL PRESTON)		SWS	04044	SULLIVAN, LEONARD D.	CDR	AVN
03970	GREALISH, JAMES VINCENT	RADM	SFR	04045	SCHAPER, ARMIN N.	LT	AVN
03971	JENKINS, ARTHUR CLYDE	CDR	SFR	04046	RAU, CHARLES E.	CAPT	AVN
03972	DEMAREST, JAMES FRANCIS	CAPT	SFR	04047	REMEY, CHARLES MASON	DESCT	DCA
03973	EVANS, FREDERICK EMMETT	CAPT	SFR	04048	HUNTER, RAYMOND PAUL	RADM	DCA
03974	LARON, JOHN ALBERT	CDR	SFR	04049	RUSSELL, JAMES SARGENT	ADM	DCA
03975	BATES, DANIEL WALKER JR.	CDR	SFR	04050	WHITED, CIRO NEY	CAPT	DCA
03976	LUNDBECK, PAUL JAMES	CDR	SFR	04051	SHARP, ULYSSES "S" GRANT	ADM	DCA
03977	MILLER, MARVIN HERGET	CAPT	SFR	04052	STIVERS, REUBEN ELMORE	CAPT	DCA
03978	MC CLINTIC, WILLIAM S.	CDR	AVN	04053	DUPE OF 1943 (WM. RENWICK SMEDBERG III)		
03979	KASKEL, RICHARD JAY	LCDR	AVN	04054	BOLTHOUSE, DONN CHARLES	CDR	SFR
03980	MAHON, EUGENE J.	LCDR	AVN	04055	VANDERBERG, ROBERT DOYLE	CDR	SFR
03981	AKERS, FRANK	RADM	SFR	04056	LEE, THOMAS AUGUSTUS JR.	CAPT	AVN
03982	ARTHUR, JOHN CALBERT	LCDR	SFR	04057	ROULET, ALFRED LLOYD	ENS	ILL
03983	COLBERT, RICHARD C.	CDR	SFR	04058	KASS, WILLIAM WALLE	Col	ILL
03984	IRISH, ARTHUR STEWART	CDR	SFR	04059	OTIS, JAMES SAUFORD	LT	ILL
03985	KLINE, ROBERT JOSEPH	Capt	SFR	04060	MC DERMOTT, MICHAEL J.	LT	ILL
03986	MARTIN, FREDERICK JOSEPH	LCDR	SFR	04061	HARRISON, RICHARD AHRNELL	CAPT	ILL

NAVAL ORDER of the UNITED STATES

Organized 4 July 1890

WHEREAS, it is well accepted that the illustrious deeds and heroic actions of the great naval commanders and their companion officers-in-arms during the wars of the United States should be forever honored, respected, and recorded, AND

WHEREAS, the undersigned seek to improve naval leadership and enhance military professionalism, with the pronounced intention that it is essential to national security, and that personal readiness will deter aggression and minimize dangers to world peace and make victory in war certain and speedy, AND

WHEREAS, the undersigned do hereby recognize that the fraternal bonds among shipmates are not only unique among men, but are ever enduring, rewarding, and perpetual, and provide for the leadership that is so essential to the well-being of our Navy and our country,

NOW, THEREFORE, we the undersigned Naval officers, survivors, and descendants of the participants in these past conflicts, seek to bond ourselves to the Naval Order of the United States, and do hereby petition the General Commandery to recognize our action and

grant a CHARTER for the

New Orleans Commandery

Charles H. Mayfield
David S. Lindberg

In accordance with the Constitution and Bylaws of the Naval Order of the United States, we the undersigned, serving as duly elected officers of the Order, do hereby certify the grant of this Charter this **THIRD** day of **OCTOBER** **1979**

_____
Recorder General

_____
Commander General

INSIG	COMPANION	RANK	CDRY	INSIG	COMPANION	RANK	CDRY
04062	MANKUS, ROMAN T.	CAPT	ILL	04137	SIEGLER, CARLTON JOHN	LCDR	SFR
04063	BOWMAN, DONALD WALLACE	CAPT	ILL	04138	SMITH, JULIUS ELBRIDGE JR.	CAPT	SFR
04064	DUPE OF 1420A (GARDNER HENRY STERN)			04139	ZAVATERO, ALFRED JAMES	CAPT	SFR
04065	BALLING, GEORGE RAYMOND	CDR	ILL	04140	BLACKBURN, JOHN THOMAS	CAPT	SFR
04066	DALENBERG, JOHN RUSSELL	ENS	ILL	04141	HENNESSY, HARLAND BENSON	CDR	SFR
04067	AMAN, ALBERT EMIL	CDR	ILL	04142	FELDMAN, JESSE	CDR	SFR
04068	TIEKEN, ROBERT	LCDR	ILL	04143	SCHULTZ, ARNOLD FERDINAND	CAPT	SFR
04069	DUPE OF 2073 (RAYMOND PAUL DRYMALSKI)		ILL	04144	ANDERSEN, HANNES MARTIN	CDR	SFR
04070	ELLER, ERNEST MCNEILL	RADM	DCA	04145	BUCHANAN, ERNEST LEONARD	DESCT	SFR
04071	GLOWKA, ARTHUR	LT	AVN	04146	SUMMERS, GEORGE CLYDE	LCDR	DCA
04072	DUBERSTEIN, NORMAN	CDR	AVN	04147	HOTTELL, MARTIN PERRY	RADM	DCA
04073	CALLO, JOSEPH FRANCIS JR.	RADM	AVN	04148	MC ADAMS, FRANK J. JR.	LCDR	ILL
04074	DAVIS, BRUCE G.	LCDR	AVN	04149	ROSBERG, GORDON HARRY	CAPT	ILL
04075	SELBY, JOHN H.	LT	AVN	04150	WASHBURN, G. LANGHORNE	LT	AVN
04076	FOYE, THOMAS J.	CDR	AVN	04151	KIPKE, HARRY G.	LCDR	ILL
04077	WILLIS, CHARLES F. JR.	CDR	AVN	04152	HALPERIN, ROBERT S.	LCDR	ILL
04078	WATTS, JOHN	CDR	AVN	04153	INSULL, SAMUEL JR.	CDR	ILL
04079	ANSCHUTZ, KENNETH J. SR.	CDR	AVN	04154	ELLERTHORPE, THOMAS JAMES	CWO	ILL
04080	CANADAY, HARRY R.	RADM	AVN	04155	MARTIN, EDGAR HARGADON	CAPT	ILL
04081	BACON, GUY NORMAN	LCDR	SBA	04156	GALVIN, JOHN P.	LT	ILL
04082	CONKLIN, ROBERT BREWSTER	CAPT	SBA	04157	RASTALL, PATRIC WILLIAM	CDR	ILL
04083	BURKE, EDMUND JR.	CAPT	SBA	04158	NUNN, IRA HUDSON	RADM	ILL
04084	CHILDERS, KENAN CLARK JR.	RADM	SBA	04159	MARSHALL, DONALD MURRAY	Lt Col	AVN
04085	BOURKE, THOMAS GILMOUR	LCDR	SFR	04160	BACON, NOEL RICHARD	CAPT	AVN
04086	DUPE OF 3548 (EDWIN LAWRENCE PIERCE)			04161	BUCHTENKIRCH, ARTHUR JOHN	LCDR	AVN
04087	TIERNAN, ROBERT PATRICK	LT	SFR	04162	MENDES, JONATHAN DESOLA	Lt Col	AVN
04088	HUMBER, MARCEL BERTHIER	CAPT	SFR	04163	FAY, PAUL BURGESS JR.	SEC'Y	DCA
04089	CHAMBERLAIN, MARTIN NICHOLS	CAPT	SEA	04164	RYAN, WALTER SCOTT	CAPT	ILL
04090	CALLOW, HARRY GRAHAM	LT	SEA	04165	MURPHY, JOSEPH N.	RADM	AVN
04091	WRIGHT, FRED MILTON	LT	SEA	04166	MORRIS, WILLIAM E.	LCDR	SFR
04092	DUPE OF 2271(ROBERT BURNS PIRIE)			04167	BETTS, CONROY FRANCIS DARROW	CDR	SFR
04093	REGAN, ROBERT T.	LT	AVN	04168	ADY, HOWARD PARMELE JR.	CAPT	SFR
04094	DUPE OF 3625(ROY HANEY CALLAHAN)			04169	CAMPBELL, ROBERT KEITH	CDR	SFR
04095	SCHOLER, VERNON EARL	CDR	SEA	04170	THOMAS, ROBERT LANCEFIELD	CAPT	SFR
04096	SWENSON, CARL EDWIN	CAPT	SEA	04171	PERRY, MARK THOMAS	LTJG	SEA
04097	WILLIAMS, ORUS OLIVER	LT	SEA	04172	WILLIAMS, HAYDEN RICHARD	LCDR	SEA
04098	GOLDTHWAITE, ROBERT (N)	VADM	SFR	04173	HOLE, LEGARE R.	LCDR	AVN
04099	WINBECK, ALLEN	RADM	SFR	04174	ESTERLING, GRANT D.	LT	AVN
04100	HARRIS, BEN LOUIS	CAPT	SFR	04175	WEISS, ABRAM	CDR	AVN
04101	ANDERSON, EDWARD SYDNEY	CAPT	SFR	04176	BONVILLIAN, WILLIAM D.	CAPT	AVN
04102	RIEGER, MITCHELL SHERIDAN	CDR	ILL	04177	THAL, WARREN ADOLPH	LT	SFR
04103	MANHOLD, EARL K. JR.	LT	AVN	04178	THISSELL, CHARLES WILLIAM	CDR	SFR
04104	WRIGHTM GEORGE CHARLES	VADM	DCA	04179	CHAPIN, ARNOLD WINFIELD (CHIP)	CAPT	SFR
04105	TAUSSIG, JOSEPH KNEFLER JR.	CAPT	DCA	04180	ROCHE, BURKE BERNARD	LT	ILL
04106	HARLLEE, JOHN	RADM	DCA	04181	MAINLAND, DAVID GRANT	CDR	ILL
04107	HOOVER, WILLIAM HOWARD	CAPT	DCA	04182	MONAHAN, PHILIP CHARLES	1ST Lt	ILL
04108	CHAPIN, ROBERT WILLIAM	CAPT	DCA	04183	QUITTMAN, PHILIP DAVID	CDR	ILL
04109	POOLER, LOUIS GORDON	CDR	DCA	04184	TORNLOF, ALBERT	LT	ILL
04110	TAYLOR, FORD NEWTON	RADM	DCA	04185	KELLY, FRANK EDWARD	LT	ILL
04111	MOREAU, JEAN WILFRED	Col	DCA	04186	LAURITZEN, HAROLD MAX	CAPT	ILL
04112	DUPE OF 2081 (WILLIAM BRADLEY WILLARD)			04187	LEBLANC, ROBERT JACKSON	LCDR	ILL
04113	REID, WILLIAM S.	CAPT	AVN	04188	WILLIAMS, HENRY JR.	CAPT	DCA
04114	DOLSON, LEE STEPHEN JR.	LCDR	SFR	04189	ZRALEK, ROBERT LOUIS	RADM	ILL
04115	MC DONNELL, LAWRENCE RICHARD	CAPT	SFR	04190	BOLLINGER, RUSSELL MOORE	CAPT	ILL
04116	MAHER, EDWARD JOHN	LCDR	SFR	04191	CONLEY, ROBERT F.	Col	ILL
04117	PORTER, NEIL ROBERT	CAPT	SFR	04192	BAUMANN, HENRY RADOLPH	CDR	NYC
04118	PHIPPS, LEROY FORSTER	CDR	SFR	04193	BRENN, HARRY ALLEN	Col	NYC
04119	DUPE OF 3489(HENRY CRAWFORD PERKINS)			04194	BONTER, NORMAN HEDLEY	Lt Col	NYC
04120	MILLIKEN, WILLIAM JENKINS	CAPT	SFR	04195	CRAWFORD, JOHN CLIFFORD	LCDR	NYC
04121	GRAVES, ROBERT MUIR	CDR	SFR	04196	FRALEY, JOSEPH P.	CAPT	NYC
04122	BRACCIA, ANTHONY AUGUSTINE	RADM	SFR	04197	KLAUS, GEORGE H.	CAPT	NYC
04123	BARBERO, EUGENE MICHAEL	CAPT	SFR	04198	KUEGLER, ALEXANDER CHARLES JR.	CAPT	NYC
04124	GNAU, GEORGE LOUIS	CDR	SFR	04199	REED, LOUIS JOSEPH	CDR	NYC
04125	HAMBLIN, WILLIAM HENRY	LCDR	SFR	04200	BRADY, PARKE HOWLE	RADM	NYC
04126	CRAIG, JOHN WILLIAM	CDR	SFR	04201	HARDING, THEODORE PETER	CAPT	NYC
04127	MCWHORTER, JOHN HARDMAN	CAPT	SFR	04202	SCHROCK, VIRGIL E.	CDR	SFR
04128	CARATTO, ROBERT LOUIS	LCDR	SFR	04203	CAMETO, LEON R.	LCDR	SFR
04129	WHYTE, ROBERT MORRIS	CAPT	SFR	04204	SAMPSON, WILLIAM SPOOR	CAPT	SFR
04130	MILLER, WILLIAM R.	LT	AVN	04205	HESS, FRANKLIN GRANT	CAPT	SFR
04131	MARVIL, FREDERICK LINWOOD JR.	CAPT	DCA	04206	SHORTALL, RICHARD COLLINS	LT	SFR
04132	AYTON, WILLIAM JOHN	LCDR	DCA	04207	DOYLE, JOSEPH A.	LT	AVN
04133	CLAGGETT, CHARLES THOMAS JR.	LCDR	DCA	04208	LALLY, BERNARD J.	CAPT	AVN
04134	CHEWNING, WALTER LOUIS	LCDR	DCA	04209	SCHRECKENGOST, VIKTOR (N)	CAPT	AVN
04135	DANIEL, SIDNEY THEODORE	CDR	DCA	04210	BUNTEN, RICHARD COLLINS	CAPT	AVN
04136	MC DOWELL, JOSEPH MATTHEW	CAPT	DCA	04211	HIGGINS, EUENE P.	CAPT	AVN

INSIG	COMPANION	RANK	CDRY	INSIG	COMPANION	RANK	CDRY
04212	HENDRICKS, DANIEL EARLE JR.	CAPT	AVN	04287	CONVERSO, VICTOR E.	1ST Lt	AVN
04213	PAYNE, THOMAS BENJAMIN	CAPT	DCA	04288	DICKSON, CHARLES K.	CDR	AVN
04214	BROWER, EDGAR JAY	CDR	DCA	04289	NEEL, JOHN M.	CDR	AVN
04215	KORTH, FRED	SEC'Y	DCA	04290	MC KNIGHT, THOMAS WESLEY	CAPT	COL
04216	WELLES, CARDER	LCDR	SFR	04291	FLANNERY, WILLIAM ADELBERT	CDR	COL
04217	BERNARD, ROBERT EDMUND	LTJG	SFR	04292	FORBES, JAMES MCMILLAN	CAPT	COL
04218	ENGLAND, ROBERT BARBOUR JR.	DESCT	SFR	04293	MC COLE, FRANCIS PATRICK	LCDR	COL
04219	CLIFFORD, GEORGE MOORE	CAPT	SFR	04294	MOYERS, JACK DEAN	CDR	COL
04220	CURTZE, CHARLES AUGUST	RADM	SFR	04295	NEAR, JESSE LLOYD	CDR	COL
04221	BURGE, JOHN LARRY	CDR	SFR	04296	WILLIS, HAROLD ROBERT	CDR	COL
04222	MERLE, OLIVER VASSEROT	LT	SFR	04297	STENZEL, BERNARD CHARLES	LCDR	COL
04223	GOULD, DALLAS COOPER	CAPT	SFR	04298	HOLLAND, ERICK MARTIN	CDR	COL
04224	VANDEURS, GEORGE	RADM	SFR	04299	GRAHAM, CHARLES EDWARD	CDR	COL
04225	ROEMER, CHARLES EUGENE	CAPT	SFR	04300	HUBKA, FRANK JAMES	Lt Col	COL
04226	BROYLES, NED LEE	CAPT	SFR	04301	GILMOR, ROBERT JR.	LT	AVN
04227	O'MALEY, ROBERT GARTH	CDR	SFR	04302	JAMES, CHARLES G.	LCDR	AVN
04228	SELBY, MALCOLM EDGERTON	CDR	SFR	04303	KENTON, ROLAND H.	CAPT	AVN
04229	GROOM, RALPH ALAN	CAPT	SFR	04304	LAW, RICHARD B.	CAPT	AVN
04230	HALEY, J. FRED	Lt Col	SFR	04305	MC DONALD, ROBERT COLOMB	CAPT	ILL
04231	HILL, RAYMOND EDGAR	CAPT	SFR	04306	HICKMAN, WILLIAM BIBB	CDR	SFR
04232	MC DONALD, JAMES TIMOTHY	LT	SFR	04307	SALEM, LINCOLN A.	LTJG	COL
04233	RUNYAN, LESTER EUGENE	CDR	SFR	04308	STUHLMAN, FRANK WILBUR	Col	AVN
04234	SMITH, MAURICE WILLIAM	CAPT	SFR	04309	DANIELS, FORREST	CDR	AVN
04235	SMITH, HUGH DEMING	LT	SFR	04310	CHILCOTT, RICHARD (N)	CDR	SFR
04236	KOHL, EDWIN PHILLIPS	ENS	SFR	04311	HAMILTON, GEORGE BENJAMIN JR.	CAPT	SFR
04237	CONWAY, JAMES RAYMOND	CAPT	ILL	04312	MC RAE, COLIN CHRISTOPHER	CAPT	SFR
04238	SHRIVER, MARK O.	CAPT	AVN	04313	SMART, WILLIAM RICHARD	Capt	SFR
04239	FEAR, ROBERT FREDERICK	CDR	SWS	04314	BERETON, GEORGE HAROLD	CDR	SFR
04240	RICKARD, HAROLD JAMES	CAPT	SWS	04315	COAKLEY, JAMES FRANCIS	CDR	SFR
04241	CERNY, THOMAS JR.	CDR	SWS	04316	WELLES, PETER SWIFT	2ND Lt	SFR
04242	MADDEN, WALTER FREDERICK	CAPT	SWS	04317	RUEHLOW, STANLEY ERDMAN	CAPT	SFR
04243	BUNKER, FORREST ROBINSON	CAPT	SWS	04318	WARNER, JOHN BYRON JR.	CDR	SFR
04244	CALLAHAN, EDWARD COOPER	CAPT	SWS	04319	RAINEY, CHARLES WILLIAM	CDR	SFR
04245	ARMISTEAD, KIRK	BGEN	SWS	04320	JONES, DECATUR	CAPT	SFR
04246	MILJAN, ROBERT LOWE	CDR	SWS	04321	SHORT, WALLACE CLARK JR.	RADM	SFR
04247	HOY, PATRICK HENRY	LT	ILL	04322	DASMANN, ROBERT EMMET	CAPT	SFR
04248	GILKESON, FILLMORE BOLLING	RADM	SFR	04323	HILLES, FREDCK VANTYNE HOLBRK	RADM	SFR
04249	CATTERTON, GUY BERRY	CAPT	SFR	04324	METZGER, EDWARD FRANCIS	RADM	SFR
04250	DAWSON, PETER L.	LCDR	AVN	04325	HALLIDAY, ALBERT JAMES	CAPT	SFR
04251	DUBUC, CARROLL E.	CAPT	AVN	04326	UHRHAN, ORVILLE WILLIAM	LCDR	SFR
04252	KEYES, COLE JAMES	CDR	ILL	04327	SNYDER, WILLIAM CHARLES	LCDR	SFR
04253	IRELAND, CLEMENT HOWARD	CDR	ILL	04328	COLLINS, DALE EDMUND	RADM	SFR
04254	BRADFORD, EDWARD WAYNE	LCDR	SFR	04329	STAVROS, GUS GEORGE	CAPT	SFR
04255	CARPENTER, DONALD BLODGETT	LCDR	SFR	04330	GLISSON, HIRAM BROADUS JR.	CDR	SFR
04256	GARNEAU, DOUGLAS D.	CDR	SFR	04331	KELLY, DONALD FRANCIS	CAPT	ILL
04257	HAZZARD, WILLIAM HOCKETT	CAPT	SFR	04332	WILLIAMS, JOHN BERNARD JR.	CAPT	SFR
04258	WELSH, DAVID JAMES	RADM	SFR	04333	SMITH, MARSHALL LAWRENCE	LCDR	SFR
04259	JUETTNER, THOMAS RICHARD	LT	ILL	04334	SPRUANCE, EDWARD DEAN	CAPT	SFR
04260	KAHN, HENRY S.	LT	ILL	04335	STRAWMAN, HOWARD DANIEL	CAPT	SFR
04261	DICK, EDISON	CDR	ILL	04336	DUPE OF 3864 (PETER FREDERICK BOYLE)		
04262	HIRSCH, HENRY HAYWARD	CDR	ILL	04337	BLAND, FRANCIS WILLIAM JR.	CDR	SFR
04263	ROTH, DONALD I.	Capt	ILL	04338	KEITHLY, ROGER MYERS	CAPT	SFR
04264	WELLES, DONALD PHELPS	CDR	ILL	04339	BAILEY, JOHN JOSPEH JR.	LT	ILL
04265	LOHR, LENOX RILEY	LCDR	ILL	04340	LAW, HOWARD GOODRICH JR.	CAPT	AVN
04266	LIVINGSTON, HOMER JOHN JR.	LT	ILL	04341	SMITH, GEORGE BENSON	LCDR	SFR
04267	MC WILLIAMS, JOHN CURTIS JR.	LCDR	ILL	04342	LEAKE, JACK HARDEN	LCDR	SFR
04268	CHAY, DONALD SHERWIN	CDR	SFR	04343	DEMING, RICHARD WALLACE	CDR	SFR
04269	MAJKA, STANLEY JOHN	CDR	SFR	04344	OSHEA, JEREMIAH FRANCIS JR.	CDR	SFR
04270	BARNARD, GEORGE HUGH	CDR	ILL	04345	KERRIGAN, JOHN FRANCIS	CAPT	SFR
04271	GALLERY, DANIEL VINCENT	RADM	ILL	04346	RABIN, BERNARD IRVING	CAPT	SFR
04272	LAWSON, EDWARD WILLIAM	LT	ILL	04347	MADDEN, ROBERT FRANCIS	CAPT	SFR
04273	BOCK, GUSTAVUS DENTON	LCDR	SWS	04348	VANKEUREN, MATTHEW SMITH	CAPT	SFR
04274	FIELD, MORRIS HUDSON	CAPT	SWS	04349	HANSEN, HANS PETER	CDR	SFR
04275	REDFIELD, BEN Z.	Col	SWS	04350	LIVINGSTON, PAUL JOSEPH	CDR	SFR
04276	HAARVIG, LAWRENCE MORTIMER JR.	CAPT	ILL	04351	STOKES, HOUSTON HOBSON	CDR	NYC
04277	PAYNE, CHARLES WILLIAM	CDR	ILL	04352	MANZELLA, VINCENT JAMES	CAPT	NYC
04278	COHENDET, WILLIAM AUBRY	ENS	SFR	04353	LARSEN, HAROLD HENRY	CAPT	NYC
04279	JOCKUSCH, JULIUS WILLIAM JR.	CAPT	SFR	04354	NOLAN, WILLIAM HOWARD	CAPT	NYC
04280	HODGDON, ARTHUR JAY	CDR	SFR	04355	ROMANELLI, GUIDO MICHAEL	CAPT	NYC
04281	SNELL, JAMES LAWONN	LCDR	SWS	04356	NEVANS, ROY NORMAN	LCDR	NYC
04282	DUPE OF 1935(JAMES EDWARD SCHWENCK)			04357	GRIFFIN, HAMILTON BROWN	LT	NYC
04283	BENN, WILLIAM W.	CAPT	ILL	04358	MARIADES, JAMES PETER	Lt Col	NYC
04284	GEORGE, CLARK BOWER	CAPT	ILL	04359	CHILCOAT, ALTON B.	LCDR	ILL
04285	MOSES, HAMILTON JR.	LCDR	ILL	04360	LOBBITT, FRANCIS TURNER	CDR Lt	SFR
04286	RUSSELL, NEIL CAMPBELL	LCDR	ILL	04361	IRVIN, WILLIAM DAVIS	RADM	SFR

INSIG	COMPANION	RANK	CDRY	INSIG	COMPANION	RANK	CDRY
04362	HERN, HERBERT ROY	CAPT	SFR	04437	BRASS, SAMUEL YALE	CDR	AVN
04363	WELCH, CLIFFORD ARTHUR	LCDR	SFR	04438	MAGEE, PETER J.	Capt	AVN
04364	KAUFMAN, WILLIAM METCALFE	CAPT	SFR	04439	DREXEL, KARL O. W.	CAPT	SFR
04365	DAVY, LOUIS HENRY	LCDR	SFR	04440	CASSELL, GEORGE LOUIS	RADM	SFR
04366	PLANT, DAVID NESFIELD	LTJG	SFR	04441	HENRY, THOMAS HENLEY	CAPT	SFR
04367	FELDHAUS, BERNARD ROMAN	CDR	SFR	04442	LYALL, JAMES WALKER	LCDR	SFR
04368	MAIENSCHEIN, JOSEPH EUGENE	LCDR	SFR	04443	BALDO, COLUMBUS	CDR	SFR
04369	KETCHAM , FREDERICK ROGERS	CAPT	NYC	04444	SHEA, LINCOLN BRUCE	CDR	SFR
04370	LUNNEY, JAMES ROBERT	CAPT	NYC	04445	GENTRY, WILLIAM WADE	CAPT	SFR
04371	ARCHER, STEPHEN MORRIS	CAPT	NYC	04446	LANCASTER, NORMAN GRAY	CAPT	SFR
04372	ARNOLD, WILLIAM JOHN	CDR	NYC	04447	LUNDGREN, OSCAR BERNDHERD	CAPT	SFR
04373	AUGUSTUS, CHARLES VALENTINE	CDR	NYC	04448	BAHLMANN, WILLIAM FREDERICK	CDR	SFR
04374	AUSTIN, AMORY EARL JR.	CAPT	NYC	04449	MC QUILKEN, JOHN HOWARD	RADM	SFR
04375	BACHMANN, BURTON STANLEY	ENS	NYC	04450	HOWSON, GEORGE OWEN	CAPT	SFR
04376	BOYD, JOSEPH CHARLES	CAPT	NYC	04451	KURZROK, MILTON (N)	CAPT	SFR
04377	BRITTON, AUSTIN R.	CAPT	NYC	04452	JOSE, ROBERT (N)	CDR	SFR
04378	BURKE, JOHN MICHAEL	CAPT	NYC	04453	JOHNS, LLEWELLYN JAMES	CAPT	SFR
04379	BURNS, JOHN SCOTT JR.	CAPT	NYC	04454	QUELLETTE, JOSEPH FRANCIS	CDR	SFR
04380	COLASONO, DONALD JOSEPH	LT	NYC	04455	HOWELL, WILLIAM SMITH	CAPT	SFR
04381	COOPER, GEORGE THOMAS	LCDR	NYC	04456	WILLIAMSON, THOMAS A. JR.	CAPT	AVN
04382	COSGROVE, JOSEPH ALOYSIUS	LCDR	NYC	04457	GRAY, DONALD M.	CDR	AVN
04383	GRAIG, EDWARD WILLIAM	CAPT	NYC	04458	JENSEN, GRADY E.	LTJG	AVN
04384	CUSHING, PRENTICE JR.	CAPT	NYC	04459	MC ANDREWS, CYRIL GREGORY	LCDR	ILL
04385	DAVISON, WILLIAM HALL	CAPT	NYC	04460	WORDELL, HERBERT THURSTON	CAPT	ILL
04386	DAY, CHARLES POPE JR.	CDR	NYC	04461	SMITH, LEO ARTHUR	CAPT	ILL
04387	DRY, MELVIN HULQUIST	CAPT	NYC	04462	MEYER, CARL SHEAFF	CAPT	NYC
04388	EDLUND, TIMOTHY WENDELL	LCDR	NYC	04463	LARSON, ROBERT EDWIN	CAPT	NYC
04389	FISSELL, WILLIAM HENRY	LTJG	NYC	04464	SHELLEY, JOHN FRANCIS	CAPT	NYC
04390	DUPE OF 2408 (WILLIAM DANIEL FLYNN)			04465	DUPE OF 4340 (HOWARD GOODRICH LAW JR)		
04391	FRASER, GEORGE KITRELL	RADM	NYC	04466	FITZMORRIS, HERBERT RICHARD	CDR	NYC
04392	HECK, ALFRED LEON III	CDR	NYC	04467	BJORNSON, ROLF THEODORE	CDR	NYC
04393	HINE, THOMAS LANMAN	CDR	NYC	04468	LAHN, JACKSON AARON	LCDR	NYC
04394	HINMANN, JACK JONES III	CAPT	NYC	04469	DUPE OF 3706 (JACQUES MEGROZ)		
04395	JUNG, JOSEPH WILLIAM	CAPT	NYC	04470	GALLATI, ROBERT RUDOLPH JOHN	CAPT	NYC
04396	KENNEDY, JAMES BEN	CDR	NYC	04471	DUNN, ROBERT L.	CAPT	NYC
04397	KENNY, MICHAEL JOHN	CDR	NYC	04472	SAUER, RALPH W.	CAPT	SFR
04398	KEPPLER, ROBERT BURNS	LCDR	NYC	04473	NEUNZIG, FREDERICK	CAPT	SFR
04399	KIRBY, JOHN M	CDR	NYC	04474	WALKER, THOMAS L.	RADM	SFR
04400	KLING, FRANK	CDR	NYC	04475	BENEDICT, WILLIAM EDWARD	Col	SFR
04401	LAPORTE, LOUIS ROY	RADM	NYC	04476	ROENIGK, JOHN GEORGE	CAPT	SFR
04402	LAYER, WALTER FRANCIS	Col	NYC	04477	FEARS, CHARLES LEROY	CAPT	SFR
04403	MAZZOTTA, JOSEPH	CAPT	NYC	04478	CHAPMAN, JOSEPH ELLISWORTH	CAPT	SFR
04404	MC CAIN, JOHN SIDNEY JR.	ADM	NYC	04479	FABIK, THEODORE JOSEPH	RADM	SFR
04405	MC CUTCHEON, OTIS EDDY	CDR	NYC	04480	GAY, HOBART HORTON	CDR	SFR
04406	MURRAY, FRANCIS WISNER JR.	LCDR	NYC	04481	HODAPP, JOHN DALE PYE JR	CDR	SFR
04407	O'BERLE, GEORGE ALFRED	CAPT	NYC	04482	JOHNSON, WILLIAM HAROLD	CAPT	SFR
04408	ODER, ALLEN DALE	CAPT	NYC	04483	JOHNSTON, FOREST MYRTEN	LT	SFR
04409	OSWALD, ROBERT ANTHONY	CAPT	NYC	04484	KREPELA, MILES CHARLES	CAPT	SFR
04410	POLLARD, ERIC GEO. FREDERICK	RADM	NYC	04485	MONTGOMERY, JOHN ARCHIBALD	CAPT	SFR
04411	PRENDERGAST, JOHN PATRICK	CAPT	NYC	04486	MONTZ, KERMIT WILLLIAM	CAPT	SFR
04412	RAGSDALE, CARL VANDYKE	CAPT	AVN	04487	MURPHY, HUGH ROBERT	CAPT	SFR
04413	REAP, JAMES BURNETT	RADM	NYC	04488	WILLIAMS, GEORGE ATHERTON	CAPT	SFR
04414	ROSS, RICHARD MOORE	RADM	NYC	04489	WEED, WALTER H. JR.	CAPT	NYC
04415	SAMUEL, EDWARD L.	LCDR	NYC	04490	DUPE OF 4384 (PRENTICE CUSHING JR.)		
04416	SCHUMANN, OTHO DOUGLAS	CAPT	NYC	04491	BLACK, ALFRED R.	LCDR	NYC
04417	SIEB, EDWARD FREDERICK	CDR	NYC	04492	BROCKLEHURST, DONALD JAMES	CDR	NYC
04418	SIGEL, CLINTON HENRY	CAPT	NYC	04493	ARNER, JOSEPH	ENS	NYC
04419	SIMON, SIDNEY IRVING	CAPT	NYC	04494	COEN, RICHARD JOSEPH	CAPT	NYC
04420	SKIDMORE, LEMUEL JR.	LCDR	NYC	04495	CARBONARO, ROBERT WARREN	CAPT	NYC
04421	SLYE, ROBERT WEBSTER	CAPT	NYC	04496	CHILDS, HERBERT C.	CAPT	NYC
04422	SOCAS, ROBERTO ENRIQUE	LCDR	NYC	04497	DILLON, WILLIAM WARREN	Maj.	NYC
04423	TREIBER, JOHN CLINTON	LCDR	NYC	04498	DUFFY, BEN KING		NYC
04424	VARNER, ROBERT NOLAN	LTJG	NYC	04499	GARBARINI, ANTHONY PHILIP JR.	CDR	NYC
04425	WERFEL, PHILIP (N)	LCDR	NYC	04500	CROCHOWSKI, RICHARD C.	LT	NYC
04426	WILLWERTH, ROBERT EUGENE	CAPT	NYC	04501	GARIER, GEORGE IRVING		NYC
04427	PUGH, DOUGLAS HAIG	CAPT	SFR	04502	HARDY, ARTHUR H.	CAPT	NYC
04428	DUPE OF 3910 (JOHN EDWARD CLARK)			04503	DUPE OF 2369 (ROBERT TAYLOR KIELING)		
04429	WARD, ROBT. ELWIN MCC (REM)	RADM	SFR	04504	LEBO, HARVEY L.	LT	NYC
04430	LOUGHARY, BLAINE ST CLAIR	CDR	SFR	04505	LYNCH, JOSEPH JOHN	RADM	NYC
04431	SAUNDERS, THOMAS FRANCIS JR.	CAPT	SFR	04506	KURTZ, BARRY D.	LT	NYC
04432	OSTERLOH, EDWIN HERBERT (SAM)	RADM	SFR	04507	DUPE OF 4352 (VINCENT JAMES MANZELLA)		
04433	BURNS, GREY UVALDE	LCDR	SFR	04508	PETERSON, DAVID ROBERT	LCDR	NYC
04434	LEWIS, JOHN GREENOUGH	CAPT	SFR	04509	STOKELY, HUGH LAWSON, JR	LTJG	NYC
04435	FIELD, LEE (N)	LCDR	SFR	04510	SLOAN, DONALD R.		NYC
04436	MULLIGAN, CHARLES EDWARD	CAPT	AVN	04511	TITTERLY, EUGENE FLETCHER		NYC

LCDR Robert C. Brice, Commander of the new Long Beach Commandery, recieves the Commandery's charter from Commander General Fred D. Carl (left). At right is CAPT John Cherensky, USN, Commanding officer of the battleship Missouri (BB-63). CAPT Cherensky was the speaker at the charter night banquet and is a charter member of the new Commandery.

Pictured above are most of the key participants in the charter ceremonies of the new Southeast Florida Commandery. In the center (with charter) is CAPT Milton C. Lapp, Commander of the new Commandery, and Commander General Fred D. Carl, who presented the charter. Others, from left; CAPT Emile L. Bonnot, Historian General Emeritus, RADM Alban (Stormy) Weber, Past Commander General, CAPT John C. Rice, Commander General-Elect, Lapp, Carl, CAPT Charles E. Heiland, Vice Commander General - Membership, CDR Allen D. Oder, Commandery Recorder , and CAPT Austin R. Britton, Commandery Vice Commander - Membership.

(l to r) VADM N. Ronald Thunman, USN (Ret.), guest speaker; CAPT John C. Rice, Jr., Commander General, presenting the Charter to CDR Donald L. Baker, Commander of the noew Philadelphia/Delaware Valley Commandery; and CAPT Fred D. Carl, immediate Past Commander General, at the Charter Dinner held at the Philadelphia Naval Base.

Following the Installation Ceremony, RADM Gordon G. Piche, USCG (Ret.), CDRY Commander, and Diana Larmore, Vice Commander, proudly display the Commandery's Charter with (l) RADM Lester Bob Smith, USNR (Ret.), NOUS Commander General-Elect, and (r) VADM John A. Ryan, USN, Superintendent, Naval Academy.

INSIG	COMPANION	RANK	CDRY	INSIG	COMPANION	RANK	CDRY
04512	TOMAINO, FRANCIS ALBERT	LCDR	NYC	04587	GREER, RICHARD DONALD JR.	CAPT	SWS
04513	WATERS, ODALE DABNEY JR.	RADM	NYC	04588	JOHNSON, JOHN PAULOUS	CDR	SWS
04514	WEBSTER, EUGENE NORMAN	CAPT	NYC	04589	KARABERIS, CONSTANTINE ARTHUR	RADM	SWS
04515	WEINER, WILLIAM	CDR	NYC	04590	LARSEN, WILLARD JAY	CAPT	SWS
04516	NORTON, STANLEY BROWN	LCDR	NYC	04591	LEE, FITZHUGH (N)	VADM	SWS
04517	GLEESON, MORTIMER JOSEPH	CAPT	NYC	04592	MONROE, HENRY STONE	RADN	SWS
04518	ASHFORD, GEORGE WOODSON	RADM	SFR	04593	MORAN, WILLIAM JOSEPH	VADM	SWS
04519	BAILEY, JOHN SHERMAN JR.	CAPT	SFR	04594	PARRISH, GEORGE LANGDON	Maj.	SWS
04520	CANTWELL, RICHARD ANDREW	CAPT	SFR	04595	WAGNER, WILLIAM ROBERT JR.	CDR	SWS
04521	COOPER, FREDERICK WILLIAM	CDR	SFR	04596	WALSTROM, CLIFFORD CHARLES	CDR	SWS
04522	FREBORN, STANLEY BARRON JR.	CAPT	SFR	04597	DAVENPORT, ALLEN GEORGE	CAPT	SWS
04523	HAWKINS, FRED CASE JR	CAPT	SFR	04598	SPAULDING, GEORGE EDGAR JR.	LT	SWS
04524	HERLIHY, JAMES THOMAS	LCDR	SFR	04599	CROSS, RAYMOND EDWARD	LCDR	ILL
04525	LENAHAN, HUGH JAMES	LCDR	SFR	04600	DUTTON, GEORGE REYNOLDS JR.	CAPT	ILL
04526	LUBBOCK, CLYDE GRAYSON	CDR	SFR	04601	ANDERSEN, HARVEY MARVIN	CDR	SFR
04527	MC MAHON, ROBERT JOSEPH	LCDR	SFR	04602	BEHNKE, ALBERT RICHARD JR.	CAPT	SFR
04528	MEILANDT, RALPH LEONARD	CAPT	SFR	04603	BUTCHER, RICHARD EDWARD	CAPT	SFR
04529	ORGINOS, LEONIDAS (N)	LCDR	SFR	04604	CAREY, AMOS CLARK	CDR	SFR
04530	RICARDO, BENNY JOE	CDR	SFR	04605	CLOSE, ROBERT HAMILTON	CAPT	SFR
04531	SILLERS, COLIN BRUCE	CDR	SFR	04606	DAWKINS, M. VANCE	CAPT	SFR
04532	SMITH, RAYMOND KENDALL	CDR	SFR	04607	DODD, EDWIN CURTIS	CDR	SFR
04533	STANKOWSKI, ROBERT JOHN	CAPT	SFR	04608	DREYER, WILLIAM ALBERT	LCDR	SFR
04534	ST JOHN, SHELDON CURTIS	CAPT	SFR	04609	ENTRIKEN, ROBERT KERSEY	CAPT	SFR
04535	WATSON, WALTER JOHNSTON	CDR	ILL	04610	GIBSON, VERNE CYRIL	CAPT	SFR
04536	DANN, MARSHALL WALFORD	CDR	ILL	04611	GOLDBERG, HERSCHEL JOSEPH	RADM	SFR
04537	BIDDLE, RICHARD SPENCER	LCDR	NYC	04612	LYMAN, ANDREW IRVING	Col	SFR
04538	CHRISTIANS, WARD LEONARD	LCDR	NYC	04613	MC CLAIN, WARREN HOWARD	CAPT	SFR
04539	CUSHING, ROBERT H.	CAPT	NYC	04614	MC CUDDIN, LEO BOB	RADM	SFR
04540	DAWSON, HERBERT CHARLES	CAPT	NYC	04615	MULLARKY, HARRY ANTHONY	Lt Col	SFR
04541	FARRELL, WILLIAM JAMES	CDR	NYC	04616	PLASTIRAS, BASIL NICHOLAS SR.	LCDR	SFR
04542	GRIECO, MICHAEL FRANCIS JR.	CDR	NYC	04617	SCHREIBER, ROBERT SPURGEON	CDR	SFR
04543	JEFFERSON, THOMAS LEWIS	CDR	NYC	04618	TOBIAS, ROBERT HAL	CAPT	SFR
04544	KIRKLAND, STUART HALE	CAPT	NYC	04619	WESTCOTT, MALVERN PAUL	CDR	SFR
04545	LYNCH, HAROLD F.	CAPT	NYC	04620	WOODFORD, JAMES GRAHAM	CDR	SFR
04546	VANWERTH, WALTER C.	LCDR	NYC	04621	LONDON, DANIEL EDWARD	HONOR	SFR
04547	WALLACH, LEO	LT	ILL	04622	RITTGERS, HARRY WASHBURN	LCDR	NYC
04548	KEYES, FRANCIS (N) JR.	CDR	ILL	04623	TIEDEMANN, ALBERT WILLIAM JR.	CAPT	NYC
04549	HOLLENBACH, ROBERT CHARLES	CDR	ILL	04624	CONLIN, ROSS M. JR.	LTJG	NYC
04550	OLIVER, SAMUEL CLAY	Lt Col	ILL	04625	DUPE OF 4051 (ULYSSES S. GRANT SHARP)		
04551	MULCAHY, ROBER JOSEPH	CAPT	ILL	04626	ROBERSON, WILLIAM DEAN	Col	SWS
04552	REAVIS, MARSHALL WILSON III	CDR	ILL	04627	BRANNEN, PHILLIP BARRY	CAPT	SWS
04553	SCICHILL, CARL JOSEPH	CAPT	ILL	04628	HUFFMAN, GERALD MARTIN	CDR	SWS
04554	BENDER, CHESTER ROBEY	RADM	SFR	04629	GRIMM, EDWARD ELIAS	RADM	SWS
04555	CALAHAN, HUGH BERNARD	Maj	SFR	04630	SILBERSTEIN, HOWARD JOSEPH	CAPT	SWS
04556	CAREY, CHARLES JAMES	CDR	SFR	04631	ASCHENBRENNER, FRANK ALOYSIUS	CAPT	SWS
04557	EUBANKS, LEON STEWART	CAPT	SFR	04632	SNOWDEN, WILLIAM MELVIN	CAPT	SWS
04558	GROVERMAN, WILLIAM HEALD	RADM	SFR	04633	DUKE, EDWIN LUTHER	CDR	SWS
04559	JENSEN, OLIVER BRINTON	CAPT	SFR	04634	SWARTLEY, JOHN NAYLOR	Lt Col	SWS
04560	KEFAUVER, RUSSELL	RADM	SFR	04635	LIVESAY, MEADE ALDEN	LTJG	SWS
04561	ROBINSON, SAMUEL JAMES JR.	CAPT	SFR	04636	BROWNLEE, ROBERT EARL	CDR	SWS
04562	WHITE, FRANK H.	CAPT	SFR	04637	PARISH, HAYWARD CARROLL JR.	CAPT	SWS
04563	WILSON, BENJAMIN FRANKLIN	LT	SFR	04638	APPLEBY, JACK JESTINY	RADM	SFR
04564	GRIFFIN, JAMES LAWRENCE	LCDR	ILL	04639	ARMSTRONG, HENRY JACQUES	RADM	SFR
04565	ESSLINGER, ROBERT ALLEN	LCDR	NYC	04640	BROWN, SAMUEL ROBBINS JR.	RADM	SFR
04566	RENNER, EDWARD ARTHUR	LCDR	NYC	04641	CONWAY, MICHAEL E.	CDR	SFR
04567	SMITH RAYMOND J.	CDR	NYC	04642	FICK, THEODORE ROBERT	CAPT	SFR
04568	DUPE OF 3205 (CYRIL BERTRAM HAMBLETT)		NYC	04643	HART, CHARLES SAMUEL	CAPT	SFR
04569	JUDSON, THOMAS DAVIS	LCDR	NYC	04644	HEWETT, PAUL N.	CDR	SFR
04570	STONE, EDWARD (N)	CDR	NYC	04645	HOBLITZELL, JAMES JACOB III	CAPT	SFR
04571	HEYEN, GOERGE ALOYS	CDR	NYC	04646	HOLSTROM, ROBERT WM. PERRY	CAPT	SFR
04572	ASHDOWN, CECIL SPANTON	CDR	NYC	04647	HUBBARD, RAYMOND ALBERT	CAPT	SFR
04573	HOSKINS, RICHARD CLARK	CAPT	ILL	04648	KIRKLAND, WILLIAM BAXTER JR.	CAPT	SFR
04574	DUPE OF 4339 (JOHN JOSEPH BAILEY JR)			04649	MANSLE, EDGAR G. J.	CDR	SFR
04575	DUPE OF 3789 (JOHN EVERETT ROWE JR)			04650	ORSER, LYNN STANLEY	CAPT	SFR
04576	DUPE OF 3797 (GEORGE BERNARD WENDT)			04651	RINGHESS, WILLIAM MERRITT	CAPT	SFR
04577	DUPE OF 4189 (ROBERT LOUIS ZRALEK)			04652	RISER, ROBERT DUNLAP	CAPT	SFR
04578	CLAUDIUS, HERBERT GORDON	CAPT	SWS	04653	ROHARKEMPER, HENRY FREDERICK	CAPT	SFR
04579	DRAKE, FRANCIS R.	CAPT	SWS	04654	HALMAN, ROBERT NOEL	CDR	SFR
04580	KLENKE, WILLIAM HENRY JR.	BGEN	SWS	04655	WHITE, VINCENT BERNARD	CDR	SFR
04581	MELVILLE, CHARLES WILLIAM JR.	LCDR	SWS	04656	GRIGGS, AUSTIN CARLISLE	CAPT	SFR
04582	BRANDLEY, FRANK ALBIN	RADM	SWS	04657	MAYER, JAMES HOCK	RADM	SFR
04583	ARENDT, ERIC HARTHAN	CAPT	SWS	04658	POLLICH, GARDINER THOMAS	CAPT	SFR
04584	CORMIER, RICHARD LEE	CAPT	SWS	04659	BOYDEN, JAMES CARLYLE	CDR	SFR
04585	EASTWOOD, EARL RUSSELL	RADM	SWS	04660	CLARK, GROVER VINCENT	CAPT	SFR
04586	FLINT, LAWRENCE EARLJR.	CAPT	SWS	04661	SCHULTZ, JACKSON LEROY	CAPT	SFR

INSIG	COMPANION	RANK	CDRY	INSIG	COMPANION	RANK	CDRY
04662	WHELESS, WILLIAM AUGUSTUS	CDR	SFR	04736	HOLBROOK, JAMES LOUIS	CAPT	SFR
04663	HOLMAN, IRVIN TAYLOR	CAPT	ILL	04737	FERRIS, JAMES VINCENT	RADM	SFR
04664	PERKINS, GEORGE STEPHEN	CAPT	SWS	04738	EVERETT, ROBERT JAMES	CAPT	SFR
04665	BLENMAN, CHARLES JR.	CAPT	SWS	04739	SHARKEY, JOHN I.	LT	AVN
04666	DOSE, ROBERT GEORGE	CAPT	SWS	04740	FLOOD, BOYE JOACHIM	LCDR	NYC
04667	HUMES, RALPH RANDOLPH	CAPT	SWS	04741	BROWNING, BERNARD S.	RADM	SFR
04668	TIGHE, CHARLES	RADM	SWS	04742	WITHEROW, JOSEPH FRANCIS	CAPT	SFR
04669	CONNOR, ROBERT T.	CAPT	NYC	04743	WELL, WADE CANTRELL	CAPT	SFR
04670	JACOBSEN, DOUGLAS ANDREW	CAPT	NYC	04744	PARRY, JOHN COLLINS	CDR	NYC
04671	BARRETT, JAMES JOSEPH	LCDR	ILL	04745	COLE, PHILIP PATTEN	RADM	SFR
04672	BERRY, LOUIS S.	CDR	AVN	04746	COX, DONALD VANCE	RADM	SWS
04673	CLARK, WILLIAM JOSEPH	CAPT	AVN	04747	ROEDER, BERNARD FRANKLIN	VADM	SWS
04674	COMERFORD, GREGORY A.	CAPT	AVN	04748	SALMON, RONALD DEAN	BGEN	SWS
04675	DILLON, JOHN C	LT	AVN	04749	SMITH, GORDON ALLEN	CAPT	SWS
04676	DOLL, RAYMOND E.	CAPT	AVN	04750	WISE, ROBERT EMANUEL	LT	SWS
04677	EISLEY, RICHARD S.	LCDR	AVN	04751	LLOYD, JAMES FREDERICK	LCDR	SWS
04678	FARRELL, GEORGE E.	Lt Col	AVN	04752	MILLER, ROBERT NICHOLAS	CAPT	SFR
04679	FOLEY, WILLIAM JAMES	CDR	AVN	04753	FISHER, ROBERT DEAN	CAPT	SFR
04680	FROTHINGHAM, ROBERT	LCDR	AVN	04754	ALOCCA, LOUIS JOHN	CAPT	NYC
04681	GRAY, WILLIAM H.	LCDR	AVN	04755	PADULA, ARTHUR HENRY	RADM,	NYC
04682	GREENHILL, SAUL H.	LCDR	AVN	04756	MAIER, ROBET JUSTIN	CDR	NYC
04683	HEALEY, TIMOTHY J.	CDR	AVN	04757	DOYLE, HUGH ALOYSIUS	CDR	NYC
04684	HILL, DEAN JR.	LCDR	AVN	04758	DUPE OF 3621 (EMERY NUDD CLEAVES)		
04685	HILT, JOHN W. (DR)	LT	AVN	04759	DUKE, KENNETH BERNARD JR.	LCDR	NYC
04686	JOHNSTON, SAGE MONNISH	CDR	AVN	04760	BISHOP, MAITLAND L. JR.	CDR	NYC
04687	JOSTEN, THOMAS H.	LT	AVN	04761	CAHAN, SAMUEL	LCDR	NYC
04688	KENNY, JOHN JOSEPH	CAPT	AVN	04762	GRILL, JEROME LEONARD	LCDR	NYC
04689	KING, JOHN F. W.	CAPT	AVN	04763	PANETTA, ROCCO RALPH JOSEPH	CDR	NYC
04690	KOHOUT, ANTHONY (N) JR.	CAPT	AVN	04764	WIELERT, JOSEPH VALENTINE	CAPT	NYC
04691	LAMB, GORDON E.	LT	AVN	04765	NASE, HARRY GEORGE	CDR	NYC
04692	LENYO, JOHN A.	LCDR	AVN	04766	KLOECKER, PAUL VINCENT	LCDR	NYC
04693	LEWIS, WRIGHT B.	LT	AVN	04767	NOTCH, MAURICE ANTHONY	CAPT	SFR
04694	LEYDON, JOHN KOEBIG	RADM	AVN	04768	DUPE OF 1433A (RICHARD HOFFMAN WELS)		
04695	LIPPINCOTT, WILLIAM J.	CDR	AVN	04769	WHITE, MARSHALL WILLIAM	RADM	SWS
04696	MC CANN, RICHARD H.	LCDR	AVN	04770	GIFFORD, BROOKS (N)	CAPT	SWS
04697	MEES, JOHN N.	LT	AVN	04771	BAJAK, SIGMUND F.	RADM	AVN
04698	MEIGS, JOSEPH VINCENT	CDR	AVN	04772	CUPPIA, JEROME CHESTER JR.	Capt	AVN
04699	PHILSON, ARTHUR DELONG	LCDR	AVN	04773	GILE, CLEMENT D.	LCDR	AVN
04700	SCHLESINGER, EDWARD S.	LT	AVN	04774	HUHN, JOHN B.	CAPT	AVN
04701	SCHROEDER, CHARLES L.	Lt Col	AVN	04775	KEARNS, WILLIAM H.	LT	AVN
04702	SCHWARTZ, ROBERT P.	CDR	AVN	04776	KEEP, C. RUSSELL	CDR	AVN
04703	SMITH, WILLIAM H. G.	LT	AVN	04777	LEDBETTER, EDWIN L.	CDR	AVN
04704	SMITH, WARREN J. JR.	CAPT	AVN	04778	LEWIS, JAMES LESLIE	LTJG	AVN
04705	TRIBKEN, I. BENNETT		AVN	04779	LUTZ, GEORGE J.	CAPT	AVN
04706	TURLEY, JAMES ANTHONY	Maj.	AVN	04780	PEIRCE, ALLEN F.	CDR	AVN
04707	KNOVALINKA, JOHN W.	LCDR	AVN	04781	PENDRAK, JOSEPH F.	CDR	AVN
04708	WACHSMAN, EDWARD KIEFER	Capt	SFR	04782	PREIL, ALVIN O.	CAPT	AVN
04709	DITMYER, ARTHUR THEODORE	CAPT	SFR	04783	SENFT, DAVID V.	CDR	AVN
04710	DELORENZO, FRANK LEWIS	CAPT	SFR	04784	SYRKIN, MARK WARREN	Maj.	AVN
04711	BECKER, CHARLES (N)	CAPT	SFR	04785	WALKER, SAMUEL SLOAN	CDR	AVN
04712	IVERSON, SELMER ORVIL	CAPT	ILL	04786	GEIS, LAWRENCE R.	RADM	AVN
04713	ALVORD, DONALD B.	LT	AVN	04787	KOPSHAW, GEORGE S.	CDR	AVN
04714	WAYLETT, WILLIAM JAMES	CDR	NYC	04788	VANCOURT, SAMUEL W.	RADM	AVN
04715	WEBER, ALBAN (STORMY)	RADM	ILL	04789	DUPE OF 1425A (WILLIAM JOSEPH JUNKERMAN)		
04716	DECASTRO, JULIAN EDMUND (JED) JR.	CAPT	WNY	04790	STEPHENS, PAGE P.	CDR	AVN
04717	DECASTRO, DONALD R.	ENS	WNY	04791	GETTY, RALPH W.	CDR	AVN
04718	SCHWARTZ, STANLEY P.	CAPT	AVN	04792	KIRK, ROBERT FRANK	CAPT	AVN
04719	VEITH, HAROLD JR.	Capt	AVN	04793	DUPE OF 1059 (FREDERICK CARLETON PECK)		
04720	SELLECK, ZENO EDWIN	CDR	AVN	04794	DUPE OF 1361 (ALEXANDER BOGART LYON JR.)		
04721	PETERSON, FREDERICK WILLIAM	CAPT	NYC	4794A	DUPE OF 4149 (GORDON HARRY ROSBERG)		
04722	NARDI, FRANCESCO PAUL	CAPT	SFR	04795	ROBERTS, SELWYN W. JR.	CDR	AVN
04723	JOHNSTON, BRUCE TODD	CAPT	SFR	04796	STAPLES, NORMAN APPLETON	LT	AVN
04724	FERBER, ARTHUR HENRY	CAPT	NYC	04797	DUPE OF 709 (MARTIN JOSEPH DWYER JR)		
04725	TAYLOR, EDWIN JOHN JR.	CDR	SWS	04798	HEINEMANN, GEORGE A.	CDR	AVN
04726	MAY, SELDEN NORRIS	CDR	SWS	04799	TAYLOR, RICHARD W.	LT	AVN
04727	OKANE, ALBERT EDWARD	LT	SWS	04800	SANCHEZ, ALVARO M.	CAPT	AVN
04728	SEWALL, RICHARD MURRELL	CAPT	SWS	04801	DUPE OF 0829 (GEORGE HAROLD STANTON)		
04729	BREWER, EDWARD VERE JR.	CDR	SFR	04802	GILLSON, GRAY		AVN
04730	WORLEY, JESSE DAVID	CAPT	SFR	04803	DUPE OF 1045 (BECKWITH HAVENS)		
04731	WOODS, DAVID LYNDON	CAPT	NYC	04804	DUPE OF 0793 (GILBERT WILSON DOUGLAS)		
04732	SCHWABA, JOSEPH ROBERT	LT	ILL	04805	ARMOUR, LESTER		CAPT	AVN
04733	BOTTOMLEY, HAROLD SYDNEY JR.	CAPT	SWS	04806	ATHA, STUART K.,	CDR	AVN
4733A	DUPE OF 1280 (JACOB JULIUS (JACK) KLEIMAN)			04807	DUPE OF 0994 (MYERS ELLIOTT BAKER)		
04734	SHAW-CORTHORN, GEORGE	CAPT	SFR	04808	BALLENTINE, HERBERT W.		AVN
04735	BAUMANN, PAUL FREDERICK	CDR	SFR	04809	BARRETT, NORMAN K.	LCDR	AVN

INSIG	COMPANION	RANK	CDRY	INSIG	COMPANION	RANK	CDRY
04810	DUPE OF 0777 (JOSEPH SYDNEY BARR)			04885	FOWLER, LESLIE RALPH	LTJG	COL
04811	DUPE OF 0785 (MILTIMORE WITHERELL BRUSH)			04886	CHAMBERLAIN, LAUREN FELLOWS	LCDR	COL
04812	DEDDISH, MICHAEL RAYMOND JR.	CAPT	AVN	04887	ARONSON, ALICE HENRIETTA	CDR	COL
04813	DUPE OF 0791 (GREGORY FAURE DEMONET)			04888	GRIFFITH, MARY CORNWALL	CDR	COL
04814	DORWIN, O. J.		AVN	04889	ASHWORTH, ARTHUR LYNDON	CDR	COL
04815	DUPE OF 0988 (RICHARD LLOYD FARRELLY)			04890	MORAN, CHARLES RAYMOND	LCDR	COL
04816	DUPE OF 0798 (JOSEPH HEYWOOD GEST)			04891	MC WILLIAMS, THOMAS JEFFERSON	LT	COL
04817	GRUMMAN, LEROY RANDLE	HONOR	AVN	04892	BARTO, ROBERT IJAMS	CAPT	SEA
04818	DUPE OF 0800 &1275 (HARRY F GUGGENHEIM)			04893	HOY, HUGH ALEXANDER	CAPT	SFR
04819	DUPE OF 0804 (CHARLES THOMAS HENRY)			04894	NELSON, WILLIAM EDICK	CDR	SFR
04820	HARRIGAN, WARD D.	RADM	AVN	04895	BRIDWELL, OREN FRANCIS	CDR	COL
04821	HIBBS, SHERLOCK	CDR	AVN	04896	RAMAGE, JAMES DAVID	RADM	SFR
04822	HORN, HERBERT ELMER	CAPT	AVN	04897	WISS, ROBERT EDWARD	RADM	ILL
04823	JOHNSON, STUART H.		AVN	04898	ODDO, SALVATORE EUGENE	CDR	ILL
04824	KING, FRDERICK E.		AVN	04899	LEIKIN, MITCHELL (N)	CDR	ILL
04825	DUPE OF 4792 (ROBERT FRANK KIRK)			04900	DAHLGREN, LAWRENCE J.	LCDR	ILL
04826	MC CAULEY, GEORGE W.	CAPT	AVN	04901	HAWKINS, KENNETH COURTENAY	LT	SWS
04827	MC MILLAN, GEORGE H.	LTJG	AVN	04902	HEDRICK, JAMES GOOLD	CAPT	SWS
04828	MARTIN, SCOVELL M.	ENS	AVN	04903	FREEMAN, CHARLES LAWRENCE	CAPT	SWS
04829	DUPE OF 0718(STERLING MORTON NORDHOUSE)			04904	BURLEM, WILLIAM S.	LTJG	SWS
04830	PACKARD, GUTHRIE W.		AVN	04905	WINDSOR, ROBET WILKS JR.	CAPT	SWS
04831	DUPE OF 0818 (ROLAND PALMEDO)			04906	THACH, JOHN SMITH	ADM	SWS
04832	PAYNE, ROBERT G,	CAPT	AVN	04907	DUPE OF 3910 (JOHN EDWARD CLARK)		
04833	DUPE OF 3508 (ALFRED MELVILLE PRIDE)			04908	LAKE, DONALD HEDGES	CAPT	SFR
04834	DUPE OF 0822 (WILLIAM AUGUSTUS READ)			04909	BUTLER, CLARENCE EDWIN	CAPT	SFR
04835	DUPE OF 0823 (ALBERT FTELEY RICE)			04910	RIDDICK, EUGENE MARSHALL	CAPT	SFR
04836	ROCKEFELLER, WILLIAM A.		AVN	04911	DUPE OF 4225 (CHARLES EUGENE ROEMER)		
04837	ROCKEFELLER, WILLIAM	LCDR	AVN	04912	CARMICHAEL, JOSEPH RIX	CAPT	NYC
04838	DUPE OF 1044 (JOHN JAY SCHIEFFELIN)			04913	DUPE OF 3701 (ROBERT BASHFORD BOLT)		
04839	SMITH, KENNETH R.	CDR	AVN	04914	BEGGS, ROBERT HEDENBERG	LCDR	SFR
04840	DUPE OF 1098 (WILLIAM BRITTON STITT)			04915	HOWELL, WM. ROBERT	CDR	SFR
04841	STRATFORD, W. M.		AVN	04916	KERR, EDWARD EARL	CAPT	SFR
04842	THOMPSON, CLARK WALLACE	Col	AVN	04917	DUPE OF 4892 (ROBERT IJAMS BARTO)		
04843	THOMPSON, EVERETT L.		AVN	04918	DONOHUE, HAROLD PABST	CDR	NYC
04844	VOLCKENING, LLOYD I.		AVN	04919	BECK, GEORGE ALFRED	CAPT	NYC
04845	WEEKS, JOHN K.	LCDR	AVN	04920	COHEN, ROBERT EMANUEL	CDR	NYC
04846	WHITEHEAD, MARCUS A.		AVN	04921	HOLMAN, BUD GEORGE	CAPT	NYC
04847	ZUNINO, FRANK ANTHONY JR.	CAPT	AVN	04922	THOMPSON, GUY BRYAN	CAPT	NYC
04848	BERGER, HERBERFT EVERETT	RADM	NYC	04923	DEADMOND, ROBERT BERLE	CAPT	NYC
04849	ONYX, RAYMOND ROBERT	CDR	NYC	04924	DODGE, BOUGLAS M.	LT	NYC
04850	BRASEL, JOHN R.	CAPT	NYC	04925	MC ALICK, JOHN (N)	CDR	NYC
04851	PECHULIS, JOHN JOSEPH	CAPT	NYC	04926	NULTON, FRANK IRA	LCDR	NYC
04852	KELLY, CHARLES THOMAS	LCDR	NYC	04927	REDDY, JOHN BERNARD	CAPT	NYC
04853	FRAZIER, GRIFFIN GUY	LCDR	NYC	04928	ROBERTSON, HAYWOOD LAWRENCE	1ST Lt	NYC
04854	WILCOX, MARSHAL L. JR.	LT	AVN	04929	VANROSSEM, HENRY NICHOLAS	LCDR	NYC
04855	WILLIAMS, ROBERT STITH JR	LTJG	AVN	04930	FLEMING, ALLAN FOSTER	RADM	SWS
04856	BURR, PAUL JOSEPH	CAPT	AVN	04931	PEARSON, JOHN BARTLING JR.	RADM	SWS
04857	MAHONEY, JOHN WILLIAM	CAPT	AVN	04932	JONES, WILLIAM WEIGOLD	CAPT	SWS
04858	KRANTZ, EDWARD GREGORY	LT	ILL	04933	EVANS, CHARLES RAYMOND JR.	CAPT	ILL
04859	VONLEHMDEN, RALPH FRANCIS	CDR	ILL	04934	RAPP, JEROME ANTHONY JR.	CAPT	SWS
04860	WILKES, HARMAN D. R.	CDR	SWS	04935	YEOMANS, ELMER EUGENE	RADM	SWS
04861	RAAB, FRANK EDWARD JR.	RADM	SFR	04936	DOWD, WALLACE RUTHERFORD JR.	RADM	SFR
04862	OLSON, RONALD WAYNE	CAPT	ILL	04937	WALLER, EDWARD CARSON III	VADM	SFR
04863	DUPE OF 1321 (JOSEPH WILLIAM GROSSELIN)			04938	WARD, JAMES FREDERICK	CAPT	SFR
04864	GINGISS, JOEL DAVID	LT	ILL	04939	ALLEN, HARRY BEMIS JR.	CDR	SFR
04865	HONECK, GLENN WINFIELD	LT	ILL	04940	DUPE OF 4404 (JOHN SIDNEY NCCAIN)		
04866	LAMB, GEORGE GOODRICH	CAPT	ILL	04941	HANIFIN, ROBERT T. JR.	Col	SFR
04867	LUDWIG, BERNARD V.	LCDR	ILL	04942	POND, ROBERT MCHENRY	CAPT	SFR
04868	DUSSAULT, ROBERT FREDERICK	LTJG	SFR	04943	HIRSCH, THOMAS (N)	LT	SFR
04869	MATTER, ALFRED RICHARD	RADM	SFR	04944	RICHTER, JAMES MARION	LT	SFR
04870	SHANKLIN, JOHN HAROLD	CDR	SWS	04945	CARROLL, DENNIS EDWARD	CDR	ILL
04871	THORSON, ROBERT DEAN	CAPT	SWS	04946	SWANSON, HJALMER EUGENE	CAPT	ILL
04872	WEST, HORACE BROSTER	CAPT	SWS	04947	WALTHER, FREDRICK WILLIAM	CAPT	SFR
04873	MACPHERSON, EARL (SGTMAJ)	DESCT	SWS	04948	REYNOLDS, THOMAS CHRISTOPHER JR.	CDR	SFR
04874	ROBINSON, ROBERT HARDING	LCDR	AVN	04949	ROSBERG, GORDON HARRY JR.	CDR	ILL
04875	WALTER, HOWARD LEROY	Col	ILL	04950	SCHMEDER, CHARLES EDWARD	CAPT	SFR
04876	WOODWARD, JAMES FRANCIS JR.	CDR	ILL	04951	LANDON, JAMES LAVERNE	HONOR	SFR
04877	STROHBEHN, WALTER WILLIAM	CAPT	SFR	04952	STILLMAN GUY	LCDR	ARZ
04878	JOHNSTON, CHARLES RICHARD	CAPT	SFR	04953	OLSEN, EYNAR FRANK	1ST Lt	ILL
04879	MEHAFFEY, HAROLD N.	Col	SWS	04954	JACOBSEN, WALTER LINDGREN	ENS	ILL
04880	STOTT, HARRY BARTON	CAPT	SWS	04955	SETZER, BROOKS WALKER JR.	CAPT	SFR
04881	DOZIER, WILLIAM CREAGH JR.	CAPT	SFR	04956	STANSBURY, THOMAS A.	RADM	ILL
04882	WEEKS, RANDALL STANWOOD	LT	ILL	04957	SHEPPARD, HARRY LEON JR.	CAPT	SFR
04883	WHALEN, MARK ALEXANDER	VADM	SFR	04958	BONDS, JOSEPH ELEE	CAPT	SFR
04884	COLLINS, WILLIAM BABCOCK	LCDR	COL	04959	LOEFFLER, HEINZ H.	RADM	ILL

INSIG	COMPANION	RANK	CDRY
04960	FRIZZELL, EDMUND HENRY	CAPT	SWS
04961	SPITEK, CONRAD JOHN	LCDR	ILL
04961A	DUPE OF 4866 (GEORGE GOODRICH LAMB)		
04962	COSTE, JOHN EDWARD	CAPT	ILL
04963	WHEELER, JOHN ROLLINS	CAPT	ILL
04964	EDEL, THOMAS RUDY	CAPT	SFR
04965	KAMM, THOMAS ALLEN	CAPT	SFR
04966	ENNIS, RICHARD JEROME	CAPT	SFR
04967	MC LAUGHLIN, BERNARD (N)	CAPT	ILL
04968	RYAN, PAUL BRENNAN	CAPT	SFR
04969	BARTLETT, RICHARD JAMES	CAPT	SFR
04970	JOHNSON, NELS CLARENCE	VADM	SWS
04971	THRASH, WILLIAM GUY	LGEN	SWS
04972	ANDELSON, ROLAND PERRY	LTJG	SWS
04973	CURTIS, WALTER LOUIS JR.	VADM	SWS
04974	THAPP, EDWIN BASS	CAPT	ILL
04975	WHEELER, MARY CASE	CDR	ILL
04976	ALLSTON, FRANK JAMES	RADM	ILL
04977	BEISANG, ROBERT EUGENE	LCDR	ILL
04978	BARTMES, RUSSELL, JR.	ENS	ILL
04979	REUTER, GEORGE EDWARD	LCDR	ILL
04980	GALLERY, JOHN IRELAND	LCDR	ILL
04981	TRILLICH, LEE (N)	LT	ILL
04982	CROWN, JOANNE	HONOR	ILL
04983	NUSINSON, LOUIS	CAPT	ILL
04984	DUPE OF 1413A (MERCATOR COOPER KENDERICK)		
04985	DUPE OF 1415A (ARTHUR ALEXANDER KNAPP)		
04986	BILGER, LEO VICTOR	CAPT	SFR
04987	CARLSON, ALBERT LEONARD	CAPT	SFR
04988	NEWELL, GEORGE POLK	CAPT	SFR
04989	KERMOIAN, RALPH (N)	CAPT	SFR
04990	THURAU, PAUL JOHN	Capt	SFR
04991	MC CLINTON, ROBERT BROCK	RADM	SFR
04992	DUPE OF 3864 & 4336 (PETER FREDERICK BOYLE)		
04993	SATTERTHWAITE, FRED CHRISTY	CAPT	SFR
04994	KUHN, FRANK STUART	CAPT	SFR
04995	CUMMINGS, EDWARD JOSEPH JR.	CAPT	SFR
04996	STINEMETZ, BROMAN CHAYNE	Col	SFR
04997	BAGG, JOHN HERBERT	LCDR	ARZ
04998	DIBBLE, BEN T.	CAPT	ARZ
04999	MYERS, JOHN RICHARD	CAPT	ARZ
05000	AARDWEG, HENRY THOMAS JR.	LT	ARZ
05001	SUDBECK, GERALD F.	CDR	ARZ
05002	WALDMANN, EDWARD BERNARD	CAPT	ARZ
05003	LENTZ, MALOLM LOUIS	CAPT	ARZ
05004	SHIELDS, WILLIAM SLOAN	CAPT	ARZ
05005			
05006	WILSON, RAY LEE	CW04	ARZ
05007	YAMANOUCHI, HARUTO WILFRED	RADM	ARZ
05008	FLORES, RAYMOND JOHNSON	CDR	ARZ
05009	AXLINE, REA ANDREW	MIDN	SWS
05010	SHILLITO, BARRY JAMES	A-SEC	SWS
05011	OWENS, ROBERT GORDON JR.	MGEN	SWS
05012	SMITH, ROBIN (N)	LTJG	SWS
05013	WILLIAMS, JOSEPH WARFORD JR	RADM	SWS
05014	WARDEN, HORACE DREHER	RADM	SWS
05015	ELDER, ROBERT M.	CAPT	SWS
05016	DUPE OF 4546 (WALTER C VANWERTH)		
05017	HOHLWECK, THOMAS WARREN	CAPT	NYC
05018	FOLEY, DANIEL V.	CDR	NYC
05019	DUPE OF 1669 (JOHN STANLEY CAREY)		
05020	FREIBERGER, HOWARD (N)	CAPT	NYC
05021	DUPE OF 4397 (MICHAEL JOHN KENNY)		
05022	MILLER, JOSEPH D.	CAPT	NYC
05023	MIDBOE, ALBERT M.	CAPT	NYC
05024	DAVIS, DEWITT IV	CDR	NYC
05025	RUSSELL, EDGAR F. JR.	CAPT	NYC
05026	LOOMIS, WILLIAM RAY	CAPT	SWS
05027	LOGAN, ROLAND FRANKLIN	CDR	SWS
05028	BIERI, BERNARD HENRY JR.	RADM	SWS
05029	BARDSHAR, FREDERIC ABSHIRE	VADM	SWS
05030	FEGAN, JOSEPH CHARLE JR	MGEN	SWS
05031	RYAN, RAYMOND E. JR	CAPT	NYC
05032	GARRETT, WILLIAM BRUCE	CAPT	NYC
05033	WALSH, LEO ALOYSIUS	CAPT	NYC
05034	MC CLANAHAN, JAMES FREDERICK	Col	NYC
05035	CHASIS, JOEL "M"	LCDR	NYC
05036	LEAVITT, MORTON (N)	CAPT	NYC
05037	KINNEY, MARGAET MARY (PEG)	CDR	NYC
05038	DUPE OF 3665 (EMMANUEL LEWIS GREENE)		
05039	DEXTER, EDWIN BOARDMAN	RADM	NYC
05040	SMALL, SIDNEY HOWARD	CAPT	NYC
05041	ALEXANDER, THOMAS WILLIS JR.	CDR	NYC
05042	DUPE OF 2054 (MORAN PAUL AMES)		
05043	ROE, JOHN EDWARD	CAPT	NYC
05044	FENNESSY, EAMON TERENCE	CDR	NYC
05045	PERKINS, CHARLES BRUSH	CDR	NYC
05046	JAMES, ROBERT GREGORY	RADM	NYC
05047	BANKS, MYRON CARROLL	CAPT	NYC
05048	DOBBINS, ROBERT	CAPT	NYC
05049	DUPE OF 2045 (ERNEST DUPONT JR)		
05050	DUPE OF 1925 (HENRY TOWER EMMONS)		
05051	BARNES, ROBERT CROZIER	CAPT	SWS
05052	MC LAUGHLIN, JOHN NICHOLAS	MGEN	SWS
05053	ZABLE, WALTER J.	HONOR	SWS
05054	STOECKLEIN, HERBERT GEORGE	RADM	SWS
05055	KOVAL, FRANCIS PETER	CAPT	SWS
05056	FRANCH, ARDWIN G.	CAPT	SWS
05057	ROGERS, WILLIAM KITTREDGE	CAPT	SWS
05058	GALLATIN, ROBERT EUGENE	CAPT	SWS
05059	ARNOLD, JACKSON DOMINICK	ADM	SWS
05060	FOLEY, HARRY JOHN PATRICK JR.	RADM	SWS
05061	WILLIAMS, JAMES WELDON	LCDR	SWS
05062	MYERS, WILLIAM ALBERT III	RADM	SWS
05063	KRULAK, VICTOR HAROLD	LGEN	SWS
05064	BOX, ROGER ELDON	RADM	SWS
05065	GEYELIN, HENRY RAWLE	LCDR	NYC
05066	CHERRY, ALEX HENRY	CDR	NYC
05067	DUPE OF 3266 (WALTER TERRY JENKINS)		
05068	DUPE OF 1450 (JAMES J. LIDDY)		
05069	DUPE OF 2138 (EPHRAIM RANKLIN MC LEAN JR.)		
05070	DUPE OF 1909 (IRVING CARL ROBISHCH)		
05071	REIDER, GEORGE (N)	RADM	NYC
05072	RINALDI, HENRY JOSEPH	LCDR	NYC
05073	BOURNE, KENNETH BARNES JR.	LT	NYC
05074	REARDON, CHARLES WILLIAM	CDR	NYC
05075	KAHN, EVANS (N)	CDR	NYC
05076	DUPE OF 3157 (VINCENT A. PRIMERANO)		
05077	WILSON, HARRELL MARION	CAPT	NYC
05078	CLARK, LEE H.	CAPT	NYC
05079	DUPE OF 2276 (SAMUEL ELIOT MORISON)		
05080	CARL, FREDERICK DANIEL	CAPT	NYC
05081	SCIARINI, LOUIS C.	LCDR	NYC
05082	PARENTEAU, FREDERICK HENRY		NYC
05083	HARRISON, ROBET CLIFTON	CAPT	NYC
05084	MASON, THEODORE TONER	CAPT	NYC
05085	DUPE OF 4378 (JOHN MICHAEL BURKE)		
05086	MUNGER, EDMUND CLOBE		SFR
05087	KEVILLE, FRANKLIN JAMES	CAPT	SFR
05088	DAY, JOHN MARSHALL	LCDR	SFR
05089	MCCLELLAND, JOSEPH J.	VADM	SFR
05090	BERTOLUCCI, LOUIE	LCDR	SFR
05091	BLOHM, HENRY F.	CAPT	SFR
05092	LEWIS, CHARLES HYDE	ENS	SFR
05093	LINSON, ROSS GARNER	CAPT	SFR
05094	STROUD, LISLE ARTHUR JR.	CAPT	SFR
05095	WELLS, AARON LEE	LCDR	SFR
05096	CARMODY, MARTIN DOAN	RADM	SFR
05097	KEENER, BRUCE III	RADM	SFR
05098	ERLY, ROBERT BROUSSARD	RADM	SWS
05099	SERAFINI, ATTILIO	CAPT	SFR
05100	COCHRANE, JAMES DON	LTJG	SFR
05101	BEASLEY, CHARLES BLACK	RADM	SFR
05102	ZIMMERMAN, JAMES ARTHUR	CAPT	SWS
05103	KEMPE, LOUISE A.	HONOR	ILL
05104	O'NEIL, WARREN H.	RADM	ILL
05105	RIEGER, NANCY HORNER	DESCT	ILL
05106	MC GEHEE, JOHN LUTHER	CDR	ILL
05107	RUDDY, RICHARD ALBERT	LT	ILL
05108	SLACK, STEPHEN ROGER	CAPT	ILL

INSIG	COMPANION	RANK	CDRY	INSIG	COMPANION	RANK	CDRY
05109	HALLETT, OLIVER SAWYER	CAPT	ILL	05184	ANZILOTTI, VINCENT JOSEPH JR.	RADM	SFR
05110	CONRAD, CHARLES JOSEPH	LCDR	ILL	05185	HAMILTON, ROLLAND MORRIS	CAPT	SFR
05111	OSSMAN, DANIEL RALPH	CAPT	ILL	05186	HAINES, DOUGLAS MARSHALL	LCDR	SFR
05112	HOTHAM, JAMES ALEXANDER	CDR	ILL	05187	FISHER, GORDON EVERETT	CAPT	SFR
05113	PFLEGER, JAMES WILLIAM	CDR	ILL	05188	CORRIGAN, JOSEPH EDWARD	LCDR	ILL
05114	NANKERVIS, JOHN THOMAS	CDR	ILL	05189	ANDERSON, HERBERT HENRY	RADM	NYC
05115	WEST, KEITH LOUIS	LTJG	ILL	05190	DAWSON, ALBERT LEE	CAPT	NYC
05116	COELHO, JOSEPH RICHARD	CDR	NYC	05191	SINNOTT, GEORGE PATRICK JR.	CDR	NYC
05117	SNEAD, LEONARD ALEXANDER II	RADM	SWS	05192	GINN, VIRGINIA CAMERON	CDR	SWS
05118	PEET, RAYMOND EDWARD	VADM	SWS	05193	FELSOORY, ATTILA (N)	CAPT	SWS
05119	SANTELLI, FRANK	Maj.	SWS	05194	KLEEBERG, FELIX (N)	LCDR	SFR
05120	TURNER, CHARLES HERMAN	CAPT	SWS	05195	SONENSHEIN, NAHAN (N)	RADM	SFR
05121	BLACK, JOSEPH DEAN	RADM	SWS	05196	HORTON, WILLIAM E.	CAPT	SFR
05122	RANKIN, EUGENE PARCHMAN	CAPT	SWS	05197	CONRAD, MARK FRANCIS	LT	ILL
05123	COOPER, DAMON WARREN (HUTCH)	VADM	SWS	05198	GRIBBEN, WALTER JOSEPH	CAPT	ILL
05124	EARLY, FREDERICK JUBAL JR.	CDR	SFR	05199	SACKETT, ALBERT MONROE	RADM	ILL
05125	WEED, OSCAR D.	CAPT	SFR	05200	MOTTERN, JAMES WARREN	CDR	ILL
05126	MORRIS, HENRY ROSSI	Col	SFR	05201	GAMBLE, FRANCIS TREVOR	CAPT	ARZ
05127	LEDBETTER, GARY GLIFFORD	CAPT	SFR	05202			
05128	COUGHLIN, JOHN THOMAS	RADM	SFR	05203	FINN, JOHN (N) JR.	Lt Col	SFR
05129	HANSEN, JULIAN RIAL	CAPT	ILL	05204	HOBSON, ROBERT LOU	CAPT	SFR
05130	PENFIELD, WILIAM FREDERICK	CDR	ILL	05205	CLARKE, WILLIAM FRANKLIN	CAPT	SFR
05131	NARWICZ, CHARLES ANTHONY	CDR	NYC	05206	GILES, FREDERIC POPE	CAPT	SFR
05132	BENSON, WILLIAM TALLMAN	CAPT	NYC	05207	PAGEL, BARTON LOUIS	CDR	SFR
05133	FOSS, NEWTON PERRY	RADM	SWS	05208	FERGUSON, ANDREW JAMES JR.	LCDR	SFR
05134	QUINN, WILLIAM ROBERT	MGEN	SWS	05209	WAGNER, AUSTIN C.	VADM	SFR
05135	ZINE, EDMUND M.	HONR	ILL	05210	LANZIT, JEROME RUTHERFORD	CDR	SFR
05136	DOOLEY, GEORGE ELIJAH	BGEN	SWS	05211	GAMBLE, CARL THEODORE	CAPT	SFR
05137	DUPE OF 1780 (CHARLES STANLEY DOWNEY)		ILL	05212	BRAYER, MICHAEL NICHOLAS	LCDR	SFR
05138	HANSEN, PETER CHRISTIAN	CAPT	ARZ	05213	HANASZ, JOSEPH FRANCIS	LT	ILL
05139	MOORE, ROBERT WALKER	CAPT	ARZ	05214	WHITCOMB, LEE EDWARD	CAPT	ILL
05140	RUDD, ELDON DEAN	Capt	ARZ	05215	VALENTA, JOSEPH RICHARD	CAPT	ILL
05141	JENKINS, WILLIAM CALVIN	CAPT	ARZ	05216	JAVARAS, EFTYHIA IKASSIA	CAPT	NYC
05142	FOSS, JOSEPH J.	Maj.	ARZ	05217	GIRAGOSIAN, NEWMAN HERBERT	CAPT	NYC
05143	JOSEPHSON, JOHN VERNON	RADM	SFR	05218	LAPP, MILTON CHANCEY	CAPT	NYC
05144	GEDDES, WILLIAM WALKER	LCDR	SFR	05219	DUPE OF 4213 (THOMAS BENJAMIN PAYNE)		
05145	REYNOLDS, ROBERT WELDON	CAPT	SFR	05220	REIS, PETER STEVEN	CDR	SFR
05146	ANDRIAND-MOORE, RICHARD N.	CDR	SFR	05221	CLIFT, JAMES CONLAN	CDR	SFR
05147	MC CUNE, JOE DENVER	CAPT	SFR	05222	RAISBECK, CLIFFORD CLINTON JR	CAPT	SFR
05148	PATTERSON, THOMAS J. JR.	RADM	SFR	05223	ROETHE, EDWARD ALBIN	CAPT	SFR
05149	HAZELRIG, PAUL EDWARD	HONOR	SFR	05224	IDLE, CHARLES THOMAS JR.	CDR	SFR
05150	MINO, JOHN ALEC	CWO	SFR	05225	CARR, MICHAEL FABIAN	LCDR	NYC
05151	RENKEN, HENRY ALGERNON	RADM	ILL	05226	VATTER, ROBERT BRYANT	CAPT	NYC
05152	SMITH, HORTON	RADM	SEA	05227	CAREY, FRANCIS MIRIAM NIELSEN	CAPT	ILL
05153	MYERS, ROBERT IRA	CAPT	SWS	05228	MC GLOHN, ROBIN HOLLIE JR.	CAPT	NYC
05154	HOLMQUIST, CARL OREAL	RADM	SWS	05229	GRANDIN, EDWARD SIEBREE III	CAPT	NYC
05155	DARIUS, HENRY ANTHONY JR.	LT	SFR	05230	LYONS, JOHN MICHAEL	LCDR	NYC
05156	PATERSON, THOMAS M.	CDR	SFR	05231	ARDIS, ROBERT B.	CAPT	NYC
05157	DUPE OF 1973(JOHN IRVING LEONARD)			05232	GRUT, D. DE JERSEY		SFR
05158	BRIGGS, CAMERON	RADM	SWS	05233	LEE, EREK ARMITAGE	CDR	NYC
05159	HEDLOFF, ROBERT ARTHUR	1ST LT	SWS	05234	MACPHERSON, ROBERT ANTHONY	RADM	SWS
05160	PIEROZZI, CONSTANTINO NELLO	CAPT	SWS	05235	CONATSER, CHARLIE N.	CAPT	SWS
05161	DUPE OF 4896 (JAMES DAVID RAMAGE)			05236	WALKER, THOMAS JACKSON	VADM	SWS
05162	STOUFFER, RALPH EDGAR	LT	ILL	05237	NEWITT, TERRENCE J.	LT	SWS
05163	SELLERS, CHARLES WILLIAM	CDR	NYC	05238	RENNIE, WILIAM BLAIR	CDR	SWS
05164	WATSON, WILLIAM HENLEY SR.	CAPT	NYC	05239	FEATHERSTONE, CHARLES M. JR.	CAPT	SWS
05165	NEVILLE, LAWRENC E ROBERT	RADM	NYC	05240	IARROBINO, JOHN HENRY	CAPT	SWS
05166	FAINBERG, BERTRAND MARK	CDR	NYC	05241	O'CONNOR, THOMA S MATTHEW	CAPT	NYC
05167	ESTERBROOKS, ROBERT CHARLES	RADM	ARZ	05242	ANDERSON, JOSEPH CORNELIUS	LCDR	NYC
05168	ACQUISTAPACE, TULIO G.	CAPT	SFR	05243	WIRTSCHAFTER, IRENE NEROVE	CAPT	NYC
05169	SLEEPER, DONALD CAMPBELL	CAPT	SFR	05244	COSKEY, KENNETH L.	CAPT	ILL
05170	DUPE OF 4870 (JOHN HAROLD SHANKLIN)			05245	DULACKI, LEO JOHN	LGEN	SWS
05171	FORRESTALL, ARTHUR THOMAS	CAPT	MAS	05246	MURRAY, RAYMOND LEROY	MGEN	SWS
05172	CAREY, JAMES JOSEPH	RADM	ILL	05247	SMOOT, CLEMENT EYER	Maj.	SWS
05173	GOODENOUGH, ROBIN WINCHESTER	CAPT	DCA	05248	HARRINGTON, MERRILL EDWIN	LT	SWS
05174	WULFF, ALDEN THAYER (BUD)	CAPT	ILL	05249	PARTNOY, RONALD ALLEN	CAPT	NYC
05175	KURTIS, WILLIAM HORTON	HONR	ILL	05250	GHORMLEY, ROBERT LEE	CDR	NYC
05176	BENSON, JAMES FRANCIS	CDR	SFR	05251	STACER, RICHARD KENT	CAPT	SWS
05177	CARL, CHARLES LEROY JR.	CWO4	SFR	05252	WHITACRE, PHILIP ARTHUR	RADM	ILL
05178	JOHNSON, CALVIN FREDERICK	CAPT	SFR	05253	GRAHAM, MAC ADAMS	CAPT	WNY
05179	NOLAN, ROBERT LINCOLN	CAPT	SFR	05254	PUTNAM, JOHN G. JR.	CAPT	WNY
05180	QUARG, WILLIAM FREDERICK	CAPT	SFR	05255	FALK, MOSES MURRAY	CDR	WNY
05181	RICHARD, GEORGE LOONEY	CDR	SFR	05256	BRETON, ROBERT WILLIAM	LCDR	WNY
05182	SOINE, JOHN CLARENCE	CAPT	SEA	05257	LEAHY, JOHN HENRY	CAPT	SWS
05183	MOORER, JOSEPH PARK	VADM	DCA	05258	WILLIAMSON, TREN ARTHUR	Col	SWS

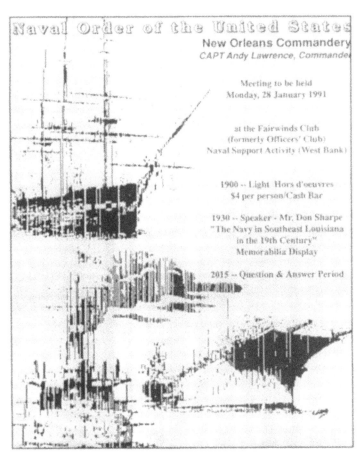

Naval Order of the United States
New Orleans Commandery
CAPT Andy Lawrence, Commander

Meeting to be held
Monday, 28 January 1991

at the Fairwinds Club
(formerly Officers' Club)
Naval Support Activity (West Bank)

1900 -- Light Hors d'oeuvres
$4 per person/Cash Bar

1930 -- Speaker - Mr. Don Sharpe
"The Navy in Southeast Louisiana
in the 19th Century"
Memorabilia Display

2015 -- Question & Answer Period

The former Secretary of the Navy and a Naval Reserve Commander, John F. Lehman, was awarded the New York Commandery's 1989 coveted Samuel Eliot Morison Award for Naval Literature at its Annual Black Tie Banquet last October in the Seventh Regiment Armory in New York City. Secretary Lehman, who was the guest speaker, recieved the award for his book "Command of the Seas". Pictured above with him are (l to r) CAPT Fred D. Carl, Immediate Past Commander General; CAPT John C. Rice, Jr., Commander General, who presented the Secretary; a new Companion, with his NOUS membership certificate; Lehman; CAPT Austin N. Volk, outgoing Commandery Commander, who made the award presentation; and CAPT J. Robert Lunney, incoming Commandery Commander.

LtGen Victor H. Krulak, USMC (ret.) was presented the New York Commandery's prestigious RADM Samuel Eliot Morison Award during it's Annual Dinner in New York City on October 22nd by the N.Y. Commander, CDR Dan V. Foley, USNR (ret.). Pictured on the left is CAPT Fred D. Carl, Carl, USNR (ret.), Commander General Elect, and on the extreme right is CAPT Austin P. Volk, First Vice Commander of the local Commandery. LtGen Krulak is a distinguished writer and was author of the popular book on Marine Corps history, First to Flight. He first gained fame in World War II and was commander of Marines in the Pacific Ocean area during the Vietnam War.

Horner Scholarship Fund Aids Illinois NROTC

As a contribution to the maintenance of high quality in the Navy's officer corps, the Illinois Commandery operates an annual scholarship program aimed at recognizing midshipmen in the 3 NROTC battalions of the state who excell in scholarship and leadership. Known as the Commander M.L. Horner, Jr. Memorial Foundation, the program annually presents a $600.00 check to the Midshipman adjudged best from three universities, and $350.00 to each of the other two. The three schools are Illinois Institute of Technology, Northwestern University and the University of Illinois.

The Foundation was chartered December 9, 1965, four days before Commander Horner's death. it has given them its three scholarships each year since then.

Commanding officers of the 3 NROTC units in the state nominate the candidates. A committee of the Foundation Board interviews the three, selecting the one they consider the best of the three.

Awards are presented to winning Midshipmen at the annual Honors Day ceremonies of each unit.

Head tabel guests at a banquet of the Texas Commandery were: (l to r) CAPT Carl V. Ragsdale, Commandery Commander; RADM Glenn E. Whisler, Commander Amphibious Group TWO, guest speaker; and local Companions CAPT Pihllip C. Pause and RADM S. David Griggs. CAPT Pause was recently awarded the Navy's Meritorious Service Medal and RADM Griggs is the Astronaut who lost his life in a private plane crash in June.

INSIG	COMPANION	RANK	CDRY	INSIG	COMPANION	RANK	CDRY
05259	VITA, HAROLD E.	CAPT	SWS	05334	DUPE OF 5287 (RICHARD JOHN MURPHY)		
05260	SWANSON, LEROY VINCENT	RADM	SWS	05335	PAUSNER, JOSEPH JAY JR.	CDR	SFR
05261	HARRIS, LAWRENCE PEYTON	Col	SWS	05336	O'REILLY, JAMES ARTHUR JR.	CAPT	NYC
05262	HOPKINS, HENRY FREDERICK	CDR	SWS	05337	ELLIOTT, AUGUST WILLIAM	CAPT	SWS
05263	LOWRY, WALLACE MAYNARD	CAPT	SFR	05338	EDGE, DONALD BROWN	CAPT	SWS
05264	BURGER, DONALD J.	Lt Col	SFR	05339	WYAND, DONALD MCKAY	CAPT	SWS
05265	WORCHESEK, ROBERT R.	CAPT	SFR	05340	REED, WILLIAM H. JR.	CAPT	SWS
05266	POHLI, RICHARD ROLAND	CAPT	SFR	05341	CHANDLER, ALFRED WHITE	CAPT	SWS
05267	BREMER, WILLIAM RICHARD	Col	SFR	05342	AGEE, JOHN PELHAM	DESCT	NYC
05268	CANCELLED			05343	ARNDT, EDWARD KENNETH	CAPT	NYC
05269	ROBERTSON, RICHARD ALLEN	CAPT	ILL	05344	BENNETT, MICHAEL CANVILLE	LCDR	NAT
05270	LAUGHEAD, ROBERT R.	CDR	SFR	05345	THOMPSON, GEORGE JARVIS JR.	CW02	NAT
05271	CLANCY, ALBERT HARRISON JR.	RADM	SWS	05346	FERRARO, CARLO JR.	CAPT	NAT
05272	CALDWELL, DAVID CLARK	LCDR	SWS	05347	SAYLOR, PHILIP GEORGE	CAPT	NAT
05273	MC NAMARA, THOMAS WILLIAM	RADM	ILL	05348	BOWERS, RICHARD RONALD	CAPT	NAT
05274	MILLER, JOSEPH HARDY	RADM	NYC	05349	COALE, VAUGHN BAKER	CW04	NAT
05275	THOMAS, DONALD IRVING	CAPT	SWS	05350	CARRICO, JAMES EARL	CDR	NAT
05276	KRUGER, RICHARD JOSEPH	CAPT	SFR	05351	DOUGLAS, LEE WAYLAND	LCDR	NAT
05277	RING, STEWART ANDREW	RADM	SFR	05352	FORREST, JAMES EMERY	RADM	NAT
05278	CHIRURG, JAMES THOMAS JR.	CDR	SFR	05353	WEESE, WINSTON HOLBROOK	RADM	NOR
05279	PRINDLE, CHARLES OBRIEN	RADM	SFR	05354	ALFORTISH, LESTER ANTHONY JR.	CAPT	NOR
05280	LONERGAN, WALTER MANSFIELD	RADM	SFR	05355	PIZZECK, EUGENE ZAVIER	CDR	NOR
05281				05356	BORGMAN, THEODORE JOSEPH JR.	CAPT	NOR
05282	CHRISTOPHER, PHILIP DAVIS	LT	SFR	05357	CAIRE, ALBERT DAVID (GUS)	CAPT	NOR
05283	BENGTSON, BENGT NORMAN	CAPT	ILL	05358	EDWARDS, OLIN MILLER III	CAPT	NOR
05284	BERNHARDT, JOHN WYLLIS	CAPT	ILL	05359	O'CONNER, JAMES JOSPEH	CAPT	NOR
05285	CROSS, RAYMOND EDWARD III	LT	ILL	05360	LINDBERG, DAVID SEAMAN	CAPT	NOR
05286	ERTHEIN, JOHN SCOTT	LTJG	ILL	05361	TAQUINO, MARUCE AUGUSTUS	CAPT	NOR
05287	MURPHY, RICHARD JOHN	1ST Lt	ILL	05362	PHELPS, JAMES COCHRAN	CAPT	NOR
05288	REILLY, FRANCIS X.	LCDR	ILL	05363	STOPKEY, WALDEMAR DMITRO	CDR	NOR
05289	THOMPSON, ARTHUR CECIL	LCDR	ILL	05364	ROBERTS, JAMES GLEN	RADM	NOR
05290	GALLAGHER, WILLIAM SLEICHER	DESCT	ILL	05365	CUCULLU, IRWIN L.	CAPT	NOR
05291	HAYES, JOHN MICHAEL	CAPT	ILL	05366	EICHOLD, BERNARD HERBERT II	CDR	NOR
05292	MILLER, RUSSELL BERNARD	LCDR	NYC	05367	ANDERSON, FRANK HANNUM	RADM	NOR
05293	KARSTROM, JOHN O. JR.	CAPT	ILL	05368	MARTIN, WILLIAM ALBERT	CAPT	NOR
05294	TINLING, JEROME BRUCE	Col	SFR	05369	WILLIS, PARK WEED III	RADM	NOR
05295	TRACY, CHARLES SEDGWICK	Col	NYC	05370	PETRUSEK, BENJAMIN JOHN	CAPT	NOR
05296	SIDEBOTHAM, JOHN PAUL	LT	NYC	05371	MC GINNINS, ROBERT SAMUEL JR.	CDR	NOR
05297	SCHMITT, ROGER MICHAEL LAWRENCE	DESCT	NYC	05372	SEGHERS, PHILIP EDWARD	CDR	NOR
05298	CHERRY, RICHARD H.	DESCT	NYC	05373	ROONEY, WILLIAM EUGENE	CDR	NOR
05299	ERIT, BARTHOLOMEW	CDR	NYC	05374	BOURGEOIS, GERALD PAUL	CDR	NOR
05300	GREER, HOWARD EARL	VADM	SWS	05375	MANGIAPANE, JOSEPH SHERWOOD	CDR	NOR
05301	BRINGLE, WILLIAM F.	ADM	SWS	05376	AKERS, THOMAS GILBERT	CAPT	NOR
05302	LANDSTREET, JAMES COLLINS	RADM	SWS	05377	FARGASON, CRAYTON ANTHONY	CAPT	NOR
05303	DODGE, ELLIOTT GEO.JR. (ACE)	CDR	SFR	05378	KERSTEIN, MORRIS DANIEL	RADM	NOR
05304	LUCIUS, WILLIS RUDOLPH	Col	SFR	05379	PECK, JOSEPH J.	CAPT	NYC
05305	HITCHCOCK, VERNON THOMAS	CDR	SFR	05380	SEMPLE, WILLIAM TUNSTALL	LT	ILL
05306	MC KINNEY, JAMES BRADLEY	CAPT	SFR	05381	SHEPARD, ROGER WHITEN	LCDR	ILL
05307	DIPALMA, MARIO	CAPT	SFR	05382	SHIRLEY, THOMAS WILLIAM	CAPT	ILL
05308	MOORE, DOUGLAS WASHBURN	CAPT	SFR	05383	ERICKSON, ELDON L.	Col	SFR
05309	BERNHARDT, PAUL ARTHUR	CAPT	SFR	05384	TWINEM, FRANCIS PATTON SR.	CAPT	NYC
05310	DALEKE, RICHARD A.	CAPT	SFR	05385	MC GANKA, STEVEN WILLIAM	CAPT	WNY
05311	GRACEY, JAMES STEELE	ADM	SFR	05386	LOFTUS, RAYMOND PATRICK	CAPT	NYC
05312	SHAW, JOHN CLAUDE III	LCDR	SFR	05387	SLOANE, STEPHEN BURTON	CAPT	SFR
05313	DOLENGA, HAROLD EDMOND	CAPT	SFR	05388	ABELSON, NATHANIEL OSCAR	CDR	NYC
05314	SIMPSON, WILLIAM HENRY JR.	CDR	SFR	05389	GUSTAFSON, EMIL	CDR	SFR
05315	HARRIS, ROBERT LEIGHTON	CAPT	SFR	05390	YAHN, GEO. WSHGTN JOSEPH III	ASURG	SWS
05316	SULLIVAN, DONALD KIMBROUGH	LCDR	SFR	05391	MERCIER, FRANCIS PATRICK	LTJG	SWS
05317	KARAS, ROBERT EDWARD	CDR	ILL	05392	PLASCJAK, ANTHONY MARTIN	LT	SWS
05318	FELIX, E. ROBERT	SURG	ILL	05393	SOUSA, MANUEL BENAVIDES JR.	CAPT	ILL
05319	HEAVEY, EDWARD EMMET	LT	SFR	05394	KNUTSON, WILBERT DUANE	CAPT	SWS
05320				05395	DUPE OF 4666 (ROBERT GEORGE DOSE)		
05321	OUTLAND, GEORGE FAULKNER	CAPT	SFR	05396	KANE, THOMAS JOSEPH JR.	LCDR	SWS
05322	WALLACE, DONALD CLINTON	CAPT	SFR	05397	DISQUE, ROBERT W.	LCDR	NYC
05323	FRYER, APPLETON	DESCT	WNY	05398	MAYFIELD, CHARLES HERBERT	RADM	NOR
05324	SPATORICO, JOSEPH SALVATORE	CDR	WNY	05399	CHRISTIANSEN, JOHN SAABYE	RADM	SWS
05325	O'DAY, ANN MARIE	HONOR	WNY	05400	HILL, GEORGE JAMES II	CAPT	NAT
05326	O'DELL, MARY CONCETTA	HONOR	WNY	05401	MILLER, ROBERT LEMUEL	CAPT	NAT
05327	LOUGHRAN, ANTHONY HOOKEY	Col	SFR	05402	DUPE OF 4586 (LAWRENCE EARL FLINT JR)		
05328	O'SHEA, DANIEL DENNIS	DESCT	SFR	05403	HAUCK, FRED PAUL JR.	CDR	SWS
05329	O'SHEA, MATTHEW MICHAEL	DESCT	SFR	05404	MERICLE, RICHARD BARR	CDR	ILL
05330	HUTCHINSON, OTIS HALE	CDR	SFR	05405	SHANAHAN, VINCENT JOSEPH JR.	CAPT	ILL
05331	CARTER, MARSHALL LLOYD	CAPT	SFR	05406	FULTON, MAURICE	LCDR	ILL
05332	SHAVER, NEIL	LT	SFR	05407	COOGAN, ROBERT PAUL	VADM	SWS
05333	RICE, JOHN CHARLES JR.	CAPT	NOR	05408	DUPE OF 4973 (WALTER LOUIS CURTIS JR.)		

INSIG	COMPANION	RANK	CDRY	INSIG	COMPANION	RANK	CDRY
05409	ROBINSON, BOB JOHN	CAPT	SWS	05484	TOWER, DUANE LAMMERTS	LT	WNY
05410	FERREIRA, ALLEN DIETRICK	CDR	NAT	05485	ROBINSON, PAUL H. JR.	LT	ILL
05411	LEFON, CARROLL FAIRFAX	CAPT	NAT	05486	PATTERSON, JERRY RICHARD	LTJG	ILL
05412	BROOKE, JAMES FRANKLIN III	CAPT	NAT	05487	HOKE, HERBERT ALAN	CDR	ILL
05413	GUETTER, PAUL MICHAEL	CDR	SWS	05488	LAMBIN, JAMES THOMAS III	DESCT	ILL
05414	PEARL, HARLAN ROBERT	CAPT	SWS	05489	FLATLEY, JAMES H. III	RADM	ILL
05415	MOREHEAD, JOHN ARLEN	CAPT	ILL	05490	O'GRADY, JAMES WADSWORTH	VADM	SWS
05416	MOORE, DOUGLAS MATTHEW JR.	RADM	SFR	05491	OUTLAW, EDWARD COBB	RADM	SWS
05417	DIRKS, RICHARD ALAN	CAPT	SFR	05492	WILEY, KENNETH RAYMOND	CAPT	SWS
05418	HANDLER, BRUCE HUNT	CAPT	SFR	05493	STIMPSON, CHARLE RUSSELL	LT	SWS
05419	HOUSER, WILLIAM DOUGLAS	VADM	SWS	05494	VINCENT, HAL WELLMAN	MGEN	SWS
05420	MC DONALD, JACK HENRY	LCDR	SWS	05495	LINDELL, JOHN ERIC	CAPT	NOR
05421	HILL, NORDEAN THOMAS	CAPT	ILL	05496	BEARDSLEY, FRKLN HARRISON JR.	CAPT	NYC
05422	PIOTROWSKI, ROMAN EUGN (PETE)	CAPT	ILL	05497	KLONER, WILLIAM (N)	CAPT	NYC
05423	ALEXION, JOHN COULON	CAPT	NYC	05498	BEHRENS, THOMAS REED	ENS	SFR
05424	WHEALY, ROBERT ANDREW	CAPT	NYC	05499	ALBRIGHT, DONALD SEBRING JR.	RADM	SFR
05425	KLEIN, MURRAY JOSEPH	CDR	NYC	05500	HENNING, JOHN FRANCIS JR.	CDR	SFR
05426	EDWARDS, FRANK GARRARD	CAPT	SWS	05501	ROYSTON, LEIGHTON MARION	CDR	SFR
05427	HILL, ALLEN EDWARD	RADM	SWS	05502	OSBORN, PRIME FRCS IV (CHUCK)	CDR	SFR
05428	CHAMBERS, LAWRENCE CLEVELAND	RADM	SFR	05503	BECK, ALAN E.	CAPT	SFR
05429	ROBINSON, WILLIAM ADAMS	CAPT	SFR	05504	COOPER, WILLIAM BURL	CAPT	NAT
05430	SCHRAM, RICHARD WEAVER	CDR	NAT	05505	SPRATT, JOHN S.	CAPT	ILL
05431	HEILAND, CHARLES EDWARD	CAPT	ILL	05506	CUMMINGS, CARL F.	CDR	NAT
05432	SUERSTEDT, HENRY (N)	RADM	SWS	05507	REED, ROBERT LEROY	LTJG	SFR
05433	BALDWIN, ROBERT BEMUS	VADM	SWS	05508	LEGGE, ROBERT BOOLE	CAPT	SFR
05434	MC KELLAR, EDWIN DANIEL JR.	CAPT	SWS	05509	KUHN, GERALD EDWIN	RADM	NAT
05435	MICHAELIS, FREDERICK HAYES	ADM	SWS	05510	BRIDENSTINE, LORNA ELAINE	CW04	NAT
05436	HEALY, CHARLES EDWARD	CAPT	SWS	05511	TIEDEMANN, ALBERT WILLIAM III	LTJG	NAT
05437	EDNEY, LEON ALBERT (BUD)	ADM	SWS	05512	SMITH, PHILIP WESLEY	RADM	NAT
05438	HAVRILLA, KATHRYN MARY RAPOCH	ENS	NYC	05513	DEAR, JOHN WILLIAM JR.	LT	ILL
05439	PALMER, FREDERICK FRASER	RADM	NOR	05514	BANDA, FRANCISCO PERRY	CAPT	NAT
05440	HARRIS, WILLIAM HAROLD	RADM	SWS	05515	KARANJIAN, PHILLIP CARL	CAPT	NAT
05441	GAY, GEORGE HENRY	ENS	NYC	05516	MATHIAS, JOSPEH MARSHALL	CDR	NAT
05442	STAGG, JUDITH SCHANTZ	CDR	NOR	05517	PLEET, ALBERT BERNARD	CAPT	NAT
05443	DRAKE, JOSEPH PAUL	LTJG	ILL	05518	DAVIS, JACK BURTON	CAPT	NAT
05444	BUTLR, GEORGE DAVID	LCDR	ILL	05519	COLEMAN, CURTIN ROBERT II	CAPT	NAT
05445	KIDD, ISAAC CAMPBELL JR.	ADM	NYC	05520	SMITH, MICHAEL PATRICK	LCDR	NAT
05446	DAY, JOHN EDWARD	CAPT	ILL	05521	GIULIANO, CARMINE FRANK	LCDR	SFR
05447	KUDLA, JAMES MATTHEW	LCDR	NYC	05522	BLAKE, ROBERT WALLACE	LCDR	SFR
05448	MEYER, WAYNE EUGENE	RADM	NYC	05523	OSBORNE, ARTHUR MERWIN	CAPT	SFR
05449	LANGENBERG, WILLIAM HENRY	RADM	SFR	05524	PANKO, STEPHEN MATTHEW	CAPT	ILL
05450	ADAMS, DAVID BYRON	DESCT	SFR	05525	SOBALLE, VERNER JENSEN	CAPT	ILL
05451	ANTOFF, JEROME WILLIAM	CAPT	SFR	05526	BOWMAN, JEROME FRANCIS	LT	ILL
05452	BRANSON, JOSEPH ALOYSIUS	HONOR	SFR	05527	TRUMAN, RAMON RODNEY	LCDR	SFR
05453	FIELD, ANDREW MARTIN	DESCT	SFR	05528	FIORITO, JOHN FREDERICK, JR.	LT	SFR
05454	FIELD, KAAR ALEXANDER	DESCT	SFR	05529	BROWNE, MERRICK	DESCT	SFR
05455	DUPE OF 2212(SAMUEL CARSLEY JACKSON)			05530	ORNER, SEYMOUR B.	LT	ILL
05456	MOORE, JAMES KENT	LCDR	SFR	05531	WATKINS, JAMES DAVID	ADM	ILL
05457	CAIN, JAMES B.	CAPT	SWS	05532	FRAUENS, MARIE (N)	LCDR	NAT
05458	DUPE OF 4994 (FRANK STUART KUHN)			05533	ALBRIGHT, PENROSE L (WHITEY)	RADM	NAT
05459	FARREN, JOHN JOSEPH	CDR	SFR	05534	DAVIDSON, FRED (N) III	Lt Col	NAT
05460	CASSADY, RICHARD WESLEY	CDR	SFR	05535	BARLOW, SHIRLEY (N)	CW04	NAT
05461	SHAFER, MARK L.	CAPT	SFR	05536	MC CAIN, JOHN SIDNEY III	CAPT	SFR
05462	GORMAN, RUSSELL WILLIAM	RADM	SFR	05537	MC CAHEY, FREDERICK MILLER	LT	ILL
05463	SHELTON, DONIPHAN BROWN	RADM	SWS	05538	MC PIKE, H. ROGER	Col	SFR
05464	RICHARD JOHN GOUGH	CAPT	NOR	05539	VERLIN, JAMES AUGUSTINE	CAPT	NYC
05465	LILLY, THOMAS GERALD	RADM	NOR	05540	ELLEXSON, STANLEY EDGAR JR.	CAPT	SFR
05466	MADUELL, LOUIS MARION	LCDR	NOR	05541	TREAGY, PAUL EVERETT	CAPT	NAT
05467	BRUGMAN, THOMAS CLETUS	CDR	NYC	05542	QUIGLEY, STEPHEN TIMOTHY	RADM	NAT
05468	FREEMAN, JOHN FRANKLIN	LTJG	NYC	05543	RICHMOND, DONALD GEORGE	CAPT	SFR
05469	BRICE, KAROLLA	CAPT	NAT	05544	APPEZZATO, RALPH JOHN	Col	SFR
05470	QUISENBERRY, ALTON DOYLE	CDR	NAT	05545	ROLLERI, MICHAEL JEROME	1ST LT	SFR
05471	BUSCH, JOSEPH HENRY	CAPT	SFR	05546	KENNEY, JOHN MATTHEW	LT	ILL
05472	PEELLE, MORIS ALBERT	CAPT	SWS	05547	ISAACSON, LEROY VINCENT	RADM	SFR
05473	DAVIS, DONALD COOKE	ADM	SWS	05548	REAGAN, RONALD WILSON	HONOR	ILL
05474	KELLEY, VINCENT FRANCIS	CAPT	SWS	05549	WEINBERGER, CASPAR WILLARD	HONOR	ILL
05475	NERRIE, GEORGE KENNETH	CAPT	SFR	05550	CANCELLED		
05476	POLLARD, BRUCE RALL	CWO	SFR	05551	CRAWFORD, JOHN DAVID	CAPT	ILL
05477	KURTZKE, JOHN F.	RADM	NAT	05552	AUSTIN, JAMES ALBERT	RADM	SDG
05478	DUPE OF 4640 (SAMUEL ROBBINS BROWN JR.)			05553	HARRIS, REUBEN OSCAR	LT	SDG
05479	CHRISTIANS, MARIE (MRS. WARD L)	ASOC	NYC	05554	PARR, WARREN SHERMAN, JR	CAPT	SDG
05480	SOBEL, ARNOLD I.	RADM	ILL	05555	ZIOLKOWSKI, ROMAN GEORGE	RADM	SDG
05481	O'NEILL, MARTIN GEORGE	CAPT	SWS	05556	ROSCOE, JOHN HOBART	Col	SFR
05482	DANIELS, WILLIAM DONALD	RADM	NOR	05557	HOFFMIRE, JOHN SHERWOOD	LT	SFR
05483	HORNE, WILLIAM L.	CAPT	NOR	05558	MERLIN, WILLIAM FIRMAN	RADM	SFR

INSIG	COMPANION	RANK	CDRY
05559	NOWACZYK, MARY LENORE CROSS	LT	ILL
05560	BECHTOLD, JOSEPH ARTHUR JR.	CAPT	ILL
05561	STAAR, RICHARD F.	Col	SFR
05562	STANTON, JAMES EDWARD	Col	SFR
05563	SIMMONS, GUY JOHN	CAPT	NYC
05564	NASH, JOHN FRANCIS	CDR	NYC
05565	HYDE, HENRY J.	CDR	ILL
05566	KELLEY, PAUL XAVIER	GEN	NYC
05567	BLUMBERG, HERBERT KURT	CAPT	NYC
05568	MALONE, WILLIAM NICHOLAS	CDR	NYC
05569	MCAULIFFE, WILLIAM CORNELIUS	CAPT	NYC
05570	SCHELL, NORMAN BARNETT	CAPT	NYC
05571	THOMAS, ARTHUR JOSEPH	CAPT	SFR
05572	WUNDERLICH, LEONARD ARTHUR	Col	SFR
05573	MCNALLEN, JAMES BURL	CAPT	NYC
05574	HOWARD, PAUL LAMAR	CWO4	NAT
05575	OLSON, JAMES ROBERT	LCDR	NAT
05576	CONNELLY, JOHN PETER	RADM	ILL
05577	GALLIANI, WILLIAM RUDOLF	CAPT	ILL
05578	DEXTER, DWIGHT HODGE	RADM	NYC
05579	CLEMENS, WARREN FREDERICK M.	Col	NYC
05580	FOLEY, SYLVESTER ROBERT JR.	ADM	SFR
05581	REID, DONALD FERGUSON	HONOR	SFR
05582	WENGER, MAX (N)	CAPT	NAT
05583	LANDO, ROBERT ELLIS	CDR	SFR
05584	PLANTE, RENE EDMOND	CAPT	SFR
05585	HAGEN, THOMAS BAILEY	CAPT	NAT
05586	DITTES, ROBERT MORRIS JR.	DESCT	SFR
05587	LIPSCOMB, JAMES HORACE III	RADM	SFR
05588	LOCKWOOD, EDWIN JUDSON	CAPT	SFR
05589	MERRICK, ROBERT GREGORY	LCDR	SFR
05590	SHEEHAN, BRIAN TALBOT	RADM	SFR
05591	SPARROW, LEE	Col	SFR
05592	OROURKE, ANDREW P.	CAPT	NAT
05593	JONES, DREW (JOHN ANDREW)	LCDR	SFR
05594	GALLIANI, ROBERT EDWARD	CDR	ILL
05595	FRANK, CARL JOHN	LCDR	ILL
05596	ZIMMERMAN, RONALD LYNN	CAPT	ILL
05597	WITTEBORT, ROBERT JOHN JR.	CDR	ILL
05598	EMANUELE, RICHARD THOMAS	LCDR	NYC
05599	LIPMAN, JOSHUA ROSS	LT	NYC
05600	SMITH, ROBERT EDWARD	CAPT	SWS
05601	STANLEY, THOMAS ALBERT	CAPT	SWS
05602	MANCHEE, FRANK CHARLES	CDR	ILL
05603	HARRIS, GEORGE CARLETON	LT	NAT
05604	ENGEL, JOHN H.	CAPT	NYC
05605	HESTILOW, JACK MARSHALE	CAPT	SFR
05606	HOWE, JOHN WILLIAM	CAPT	SWS
05607	LEEMAN, ROBERT WHITNEY	CAPT	SWS
05608	ENGDAHL, CARL MARCUS	CAPT	ILL
05609	LINDSTROM, JOHN DOUGLAS	CAPT	ILL
05610	FRIEDMAN, HOWARD (N)	CAPT	ILL
05611	VALLEE, ROBERT ANTHONY	Lt Col	SFR
05612	HENDERSON, DAVID EDMUND	CAPT	SFR
05613	ROBINSON, MICHAEL FRANCIS	CAPT	SFR
05614	MERCKEL, CHARLES GEORGE	CAPT	SFR
05615	ALLAN, ROBERT A.	CAPT	SFR
05616	AMME, CARL H.	CAPT	SFR
05617	BANG, HENRY F.	CDR	SFR
05618	BOYD, JAMES (N)	CDR	SFR
05619	BURKY, JOHN D.	CAPT	SFR
05620	CARLSEN, CHARLES R.	CAPT	SFR
05621	CARTER, MALCOM K. JR.	CAPT	SFR
05622	CULLEN, WILLIAM R.	LCDR	SFR
05623	GRAHAM, KENDALL PAUL	CDR	SFR
05624	HAINES, JOHN P.	CDR	SFR
05625	HEMMING, RAYMOND (N)	RADM	SFR
05626	HINE, CHARLES HENRI II	LCDR	SFR
05627	MCCOOK, ALEXANDER (N) JR.	LCDR	SFR
05628	ROBINSON, DUNLAP R.	CAPT	SFR
05629	SKJARET, JALMER H.	CDR	SFR
05630	SNIDER, LEWIS L.	CAPT	SFR
05631	STRUTHERS, JOHN R.	CDR	SFR
05632	WALKER, WILLIAM A. III	CAPT	SFR
05633	BLAKE, WILLIAM C.	CAPT	SFR
05634	ADAMS, RICHARD DONALD	RADM	SFR
05635	DELERY, OLIVER STANISLAUS	LCDR	NOR
05636	HARRELSON, GEORGE DAVID	CAPT	NYC
05637	PUGH, JANET	ASOC	SFR
05638	BATESON, DAVID LINCOLN	LTJG	NYC
05639	COOKSEY, JANET BONE	DESCT	SWS
05640	LEVENSON, LEE EDWARD	RADM	SWS
05641	HARTMAN, MILEVA MARIA	CAPT	NAT
05642	OSBORNE, DONALD VICTOR	CAPT	ILL
05643	ROGERSON, REUBEN G.	RADM	SWS
05644	FISHER, ROBERT WALTER	LCDR	SWS
05645	KIRK, LEONE EDWARD JR.	CDR	SWS
05646	EPES, HORACE HARDAWAY JR.	RADM	SWS
05647	BRETT, ROBERT P.	CAPT	SWS
05648	GILMAN, GEORGE C.	CDR	SWS
05649	HIRR, OTTO ALBERT	HONOR	SWS
05650	RADASCH, ROBERT M.	CAPT	ILL
05651	STECHMANN, DONALD H.	CAPT	ILL
05652	WILLIAMS, DANIEL EUGENE	CAPT	SFR
05653	MCCUE, FRANCIS JOSEPH	CAPT	NYC
05654	STONE, CHARLES LOGAN	CDR	NAT
05655	BAKER, MARK CONWAY	CDR	SDG
05656	DANNI, FRANK R.	CAPT	WNY
05657	GORMAN, DANIEL JOSEPH	CAPT	WNY
05658	HAIN, WILLIAM HART	CAPT	WNY
05659	KENNEDY, DONALD R.	Col	SFR
05660	KLEINSCHMIDT, SHARON KAY	CDR	SDG
05661	KREINER, CHARLES F. JR.	CAPT	WYN
05662	LAIRD, THOMAS FRANKLIN	CDR	WYN
05663	LOOCKERMAN, WILLIAM D.	CAPT	WNY
05664	REEVES, DONALD JOSEPH	CAPT	SDG
05665	RIGHTER, JAMES H.	LCDR	WNY
05666	DUPE OF 3104 (STUART LANE CURRIER)		
05667	THOMSON, NORMAN M.	LT	WNY
05668	TRIFTSHAUSER, ROGER W.	RADM	WNY
05669	WILLIAMS, ROY EDWARD	CAPT	SDG
05670	HAYWARD, THOMAS BIBB	ADM	SWS
05671	RUGGLES, HOWARD EDWIN II	CDR	SWS
05672	LOIDOLD, JOSEPH DRYDEN	LCDR	NOR
05673	BROOKSHIRE, JACK A.	ENS	NOR
05674	FOSTER, RICHARD (N)	DESCT	NYC
05675	GARDINER, ROBERT DAVID LION	LCDR	NYC
05676	MCLINTOCK, GORDON	VADM	NYC
05677	NIXON, CHARLES ESTEVAN	LCDR	NYC
05678	SMITH, ALFRED E.	CDR	NYC
05679	DUPE OF 0670 (WILLIAM EARL DODGE STOKES JR)		
05680	STRASSBURGER, JOHANN A. PETER	CAPT	NYC
05681	STUHR, ROBERT L.	DESCT	NYC
05682	WATTS, HENRY MILLER JR.	CAPT	NYC
05683	BENTZ, ALAN EARL	CAPT	NOR
05684	BUELL, THOMAS BINGHAM	CDR	NYC
05685	CARROLL, JOHN HORNE	Lt Col	SFR
05686	BURNETT, RICH WALT (BURNIE)	CAPT	SWS
05687	CARGILL, LEE BRUELLMAN	CAPT	SWS
05688	KRUPP, LEO (N)	CDR	SWS
05689	HANCOCK, VIRGIL ROLLIN (HANK)	LCDR	SWS
05690	LEGGE, ROBERT FARJEON	CAPT	SFR
05691	BERTAGNA, CAESAR J.	LT	SFR
05692	BEUMER, DELBERT H.	RADM	SFR
05693	DEN-DULK, JOHN DOMINIC	LT	SFR
05694	FITZPATRICK, JULIUS W.	CAPT	SFR
05695	GRAYSON, ELLISON C.	CAPT	SFR
05696	GRIFFIN, DEWITT J.	CDR	SFR
05697	DUPE OF 4362 (HERBERT ROY HERN)		
05698	PECK, PAUL A.	RADM	SFR
05699	SAMARZICH, WARREN N.	CDR	SFR
05700	DODSON, JOHN ROBERT	CDR	NOR
05701	CLAYTON, JOHN WESLEY	CAPT	NOR
05702	SHISSLER, FRANK JAMES	CAPT	SFR
05703	SPERO, PETER J.	CAPT	SFR
05704	VONKEMPF, PAUL	CAPT	SFR
05705	WATTS, DONALD L.	CAPT	SFR
05706	PSIHAS, ANDREW PETER	CAPT	ILL
05707	LARSON, DEAN ROY	CAPT	ILL
05708	THOMPSON, GLYNN MURPHY (PETE)	CAPT	SFR

INSIG	COMPANION	RANK	CDRY
05709			
05710	STENDAHL, STANLEY JOHN	CDR	SFR
05711	LUCCI, PASQUALE R. (PAT)	CAPT	WNY
05712	JEPSEN, EDWARD PETER	LCDR	SFR
05713	POLLARD, ERIC WILTON	CAPT	SWS
05714	BENKO, DAVID FRANK	CAPT	ILL
05715	WILCOX, CHARLES EDSON	CDR	ILL
05716	EASTBOURNE, VELMA STRAWMAN	ASOC	SFR
05717	KIISK, VELLO (N)	LTJG	SFR
05718	MURPHY, JAMES CARL	CDR	ILL
05719	MADDOCK, GEORGE ALBERT	CAPT	ILL
05720	TERRY, WILLIS "E"	1st Lt	ILL
05721	FEDDERN, ROBERT (N)	CDR	SWS
05722	DAY, MARK G.	LCDR	ILL
05723	LENOX, GLEN W.	RADM	SWS
05724	STROOP, PAUL DAVID	VADM	SWS
05725	TANNER, THOMAS W.	LT	SDG
05726	FORTENBERRY, JACK (N)	LCDR	SDG
05727	KLAREN, JOHN CLEMENT	CDR	SDG
05728	OGBURN, EVELYN ROSETTA	ASOC	SDG
05729	WEST, LOYD AVERY JR.	LT	SDG
05730	H'DOUBLER, FRANCIS TODD	LT	NAT
05731	QUAGLINO, JOSEPH (N) JR.	CDR	SDG
05732	CHENOWETH, THEODORE HERSHAL	Lt Col	SFR
05733			
05734	SWANSON, LEONARD PHILLIP	Maj.	SFR
05735	SARGENT, GEORGE KIMBALL II	CDR	ILL
05736	HALL, WALTER JOSEPH	LCDR	SDG
05737	MAXWELL, NEIL LINDSAY	CAPT	SDG
05738	FAULWETTER, WILLIAM CHARLES	CAPT	SDG
05739	MATSON, THOMAS WILLIAM	CDR	SDG
05740	HUFF, HOWARD WILSON	CAPT	NAT
05741	GORDON, DONALD (N)	CAPT	SWS
05742	COMBS, NELSON BROWN JR.	LTJG	SFR
05743	PETTIT, WILLIAM EUGENE	LCDR	NAT
05744	BRIMACOMBE, STUART HOMER	CDR	ILL
05745	SMITH, ARMISTEAD B. JR.	CAPT	SWS
05746	HARDEMAN, CHARLES S.	CDR	SFR
05747	SALMON, EDWARD PATRICK	CAPT	ILL
05748	RUCCI, EUSTINE PAUL	RADM	SWS
05749	FRIZZELL, HELEN C.	LCDR	SWS
05750	PEARSE, JACK F.	RADM	SFR
05751	HAKANSON, GARY EVAN	CAPT	SWS
05752	STEWART, DAVID B.	CAPT	SFR
05753	ZSCHAU, JULIUS JAMES (JAY)	CAPT	NAT
05754	WEESE, STUART CHAFFE BICKNEL	DESCT	NOR
05755	BARTH, JOSEPH JOHN	RADM	SWS
05756	BARRINEAU, EDWIN (N)	RADM	SWS
05757	RINEK, JOHN A.	ENS	SWS
05758	HENNELLY, EDMUND P.	LT	NYC
05759	FUSSELMAN, RAYMOND DENNIS	CAPT	SFR
05760	KAUDERER, BERNARD MARVIN	VADM	ILL
05761	TEWELOW, WILLIAM HARRISON	CAPT	NAT
05762	EASTERLING, CRAWFORD A. (PETE)	RADM	SWS
05763	DALY, HARRY PATRICK JR..	LCDR	NAT
05764	CARVER, ALAN CHARLES	LCDR	SFR
05765	CUCULLU, PATRICIA COLLING	ASOC	NOR
05766	YOUNG, ROBERT JOSPEH	CDR	SFR
05767	CALHOUN, GRANT G.	RADM	SFR
05768	KING, WILLIAM BRUCE	CDR	NOR
05769	DAVIS, LEWIS E.	LCDR	SFR
05770	LUSH, STEPHEN STRINGER	CAPT	NYC
05771	LELAND, ROBERT H.	LCDR	NYC
05772	KRUPP, EDWIN S.	LT	ILL
05773	SOLGAARD, ALBERT LEROY	CAPT	SFR
05774	WILLIAMS, EDMUND M.	Col	SFR
05775	GROWNEY, MAURICE R.	CAPT	SFR
05776	LATHAM, HENRY J.	CAPT	NYC
05777	FANCHER, GORDON CLIFFORD	CAPT	ILL
05778	GULLIVER, VICTOR STANLEY	CAPT	ILL
05779	LAFFERTY, MAURICE DEGILBERT	CAPT	SFR
05780	DOUGLAS, SIMONE CARLIER	ASOC	SDG
05781	OBERG, OWEN HENRY	RADM	SWS
05782	HOLLETT, GRANT THOMAS JR.	RADM	ILL
05783	GILLCRIST, PAUL THOMAS	RADM	SWS

INSIG	COMPANION	RANK	CDRY
05784	TIBBS, JOHN C.	CDR	SWS
05785	HANECAK, RICHARD GEORGE	CAPT	SWS
05786	BOZONIER, EDWIN (N)	HONOR	SDG
05787	BROWN, FREDRICK WILLIAM	CAPT	SDG
05788	HATFIELD, KIRK DANA	DESCT	SDG
05789	GRIGSBY, GILBERT REDMAN JR.	CAPT	SDG
05790	PILGRIM, ALFRED LLOYD	CHPSR	SDG
05791	EMMEL, ROBERT SHAFER	LT	NAT
05792	LIPSCHER, ALLEN SAMUEL	CDR	ILL
05793	POTTER, ELMER BELMONT	CDR	NYC
05794	FAIR, LOUIS, (N) JR.	CDR	ILL
05795	FAIRBANKS, DOUGLAS ELTON JR.	CAPT	NYC
05796	FITCH, WALTER (N) III	LTJG	SWS
05797	KEIL, SIDNEY HAROLD	CAPT	SFR
05798	BROWN, MALCOLM COTTON II	CAPT	SFR
05799	COALE, NAOMI LEE	ASSOC	NAT
05800	DEVILLE, DAVID ALLEN	HONOR	NAT
05801	ASTER, GEORGE HARRY	CAPT	SFR
05802	ONDRICK, ROBERT MARLAN	Col	SFR
05803	EDMANDS, JOHN RAYNER	CAPT	SFR
05804	DETARNOWSKY, GEORGE OLIVER	CAPT	ILL
05805	FRISBIE, JACK MICHAEL	MGEN	ILL
05806	CHURCHILL, JOHN ALFRED	CAPT	ILL
05807	KLAREN, PEGGY EDNA G.	ASOC	SDG
05808	CLARK, HENRY HERMAN	LT	SDG
05809	WALTERS, ROBERT L.	VADM	NAT
05810	KRISER, LOUIS	CAPT	SWS
05811	ANDERSEN, CHARLES WM. (SWEDE)	CAPT	TEX
05812	CHENOWETH, JOHN PRESSLY III	CAPT	TEX
05813	DOLAN, RICHARD MERTON	CAPT	TEX
05814	GOSSE, CLINTON GESSNER	CAPT	TEX
05815	HLOPAK, EDWARD JAY	CAPT	TEX
05816	HOLYFIELD, GEORGE W.	CAPT	TEX
05817	PASSMAN, FREDERICK JAY	CDR	TEX
05818	SMITH, FRANCIS NEALE	RADM	TEX
05819	STERLING, JAMES BENNETT III	LCDR	TEX
05820	BLOCK, MARTIN JOEL	CAPT	TEX
05821	BURR, DAVID SHEPHERD	CAPT	TEX
05822	CRABB, JOE FRED	CDR	TEX
05823	FRAZAR, RICHARD A.	DESCT	TEX
05824	GINN, TAEYONG WALTER	LCDR	TEX
05825	WILSON, DONALD E.	RADM	NYC
05826	GERTH, STEPHEN BROWN	CAPT	ILL
05827	KENNEDY, DAVID N.	LCDR	SFR
05828	ONG, RICHARD EUGENE	CAPT	SFR
05829	SUTTON, JOHN DAVIES	LCDR	SFR
05830	MASON, MARVIN HAWLEY JR.	CAPT	ATL
05831	QUAGLINO, KATHLEEN LENORE	ASOC	SDG
05832	SPARROW, WM. CLAYTON JR.	CAPT	ATL
05833	MAHONEY, HARRY LINWOOD JR.	LCDR	ATL
05834	FRIZZELL, GEORGE E.	CAPT	ATL
05835	THOMPSON, WILLIAM (N)	RADM	NAT
05836	JONES, ROBERT SCARRITT	CAPT	NAT
05837	NELSON, WILLIAM HAROLD	CAPT	ILL
05838	MYATT, KENNETH EDWARD	RADM	ATL
05839	SPRADLIN, LOUIS EDWARD (L.E.)	CAPT	ATL
05840	FELDMAN, JOEL MARTIN	CAPT	ATL
05841	LINDEMAN, JON BURTON	CAPT	ATL
05842			
05843			
05844			
05845			
05846			
05847			
05848			
05849			
05850			
05851			
05852			
05853			
05854			
05855			
05856			
05857			
05858			

INSIG	COMPANION	RANK	CDRY	INSIG	COMPANION	RANK	CDRY
05859				05934	FOOTE, DAVID CALVIN	CAPT	SFR
05860				05935	DROESE, KARL EDWARD JR.	CAPT	SFR
05861				05936	LEE, RICHARD HENRY	Capt	SFR
05862				05937	THUNMAN, NILS R. (RON)	VADM	ATL
05863				05938	OHARA, JACK F.	RADM	SWS
05864				05939	WALTON, JOHN WILLIAM III	CAPT	NAT
05865				05940	WIMMER, RONALD WILLIAM	CDR	ILL
05866				05941	SMITH, CHARLES JACOB	CAPT	NAT
05867				05942	WEBBER, KENT SHEPARD	CAPT	NAT
05868				05943	BROWN, FRANCIS CHRISTOPHER	LCDR	SFR
05869				05944	OLSEN, GORDON B.	HONOR	SFR
05870				05945	YORK, GARY ALVIN	CAPT	SFR
05871				05946	AVERY, FRANCIS ALBERT	CAPT	NOR
05872				05947	LETTEN, JAMES BULLIUNG	LTJG	NOR
05873				05948	MARTIN, RICHARD MASSIE JR.	LT	NOR
05874				05949	NESS, HARRY HEDLEY	CAPT	NOR
05875				05950	RINARD, TOMMIE FRED	RADM	NOR
05876				05951	SULLIVAN, MICHAEL E.	CAPT	TEX
05877				05952	DUNCAN, JAMES WHITNEY	CDR	ILL
05878				05953	PAYNE, CHARLES ALBERT	CAPT	NOR
05879				05954			
05880				05955	LAWRENCE, ANDREW HARRY	CAPT	NOR
05881				05956	STUART, GREGORY (N)	LTJG	NAT
05882				05957	WEED, PETER BERNHARDT	CDR	NAT
05883				05958	CASTELLO, HUGO MARTINEZ	LT	NYC
05884				05959	MOTT, ELIAS BERTRAM (BENNY)	CAPT	NYC
05885				05960	WIRAM, GORDON HUBERT	CDR	SDG
05886				05961	OBRIEN, FRANCIS DONALD	CAPT	ILL
05887				05962	MALONE, GEORGE MARTIN	Lt Col	NYC
05888				05963	HOGAN, EDWARD J. JR.	RADM	SWS
05889				05964	BOLAND, BRUCE RAYMOND	RADM	SWS
05890				05965	MONTGOMERY, HOWARD GROMEL	CAPT	SFR
05891				05966	GIBBS, ANTHONY WAYNE	CAPT	SFR
05892				05967	ANCIAUX, LOUIS NEVIN	CAPT	SDG
05893				05968	RICE, CLAIRE COURREGE	ASOC	NOR
05894				05969	BADER, JACK HOWELL	LT	ATL
05895				05970	GILMORE, JOHN (N)	CAPT	NAT
05896				05971	BERRYMAN, ERIC J. C.	CDR	NAT
05897				05972	SMITH, WALLACE DEAN SR.	CDR	NAT
05898				05973	STEWART, GERALD CLOUSTON	LCDR	SFR
05899				05974	DECKERT, WARREN PAUL	CAPT	NOR
05900				05975	RODRIGUEZ, ANTONIO JOSE	CAPT	NOR
05901				05976	CALHOUN, JOHN F.	RADM	ILL
05902				05977	STODDARD, ROY CHARLES	CAPT	NOR
05903				05978	LABOUISSE, JOHN PETER III	CAPT	NOR
05904				05979	SIZEMORE, WILLIAM GENE	RADM	ILL
05905				05980	RAM, EDWARD JOHN JR.	LCDR	ILL
05906				05981	OBRECHT, DONALD FREDERICK	LTJG	NAT
05907				05982	WELCH, KENNETH JOHN	CAPT	NAT
05908				05983	AVERY, JOHN FRANCIS	LTJG	NOR
05909				05984	RAMSEY, WILLIAM EDWARD	VADM	ILL
05910				05985	DUNN, ROBERT FRANCIS	VADM	NAT
05911				05986	KARLSSON, CARL RICHARD	CAPT	ILL
05912				05987	TURPIN, ROBERT (N)	CAPT	ARZ
05913				05988	POPELL, CHARLES WILLIAM	LT	SDG
05914	LICKO, RICHARD JERRY	CAPT	ILL	05989	LACEY, WINFIELD MARVIN	CAPT	SDG
05915	BENNETT, DAVID MICHAEL	RADM	ILL	05990	MILLER, ALAN SCOTT	CAPT	ILL
05916	WHITACRE, ROBERT GEAN	CAPT	ILL	05991	HINTON, VON JARRIET	CDR	ATL
05917	CLARK, JOHN EARLE (JACK)	CAPT	ATL	05992	MADUELL, AUDREY S.	ASOC	NOR
05918	HIGGINSON, JOHN JOSEPH	RADM	SWS	05993	BROWN, LORIN W.	CAPT	ILL
05919	SERVICE, JAMES EDWARD	VADM	SWS	05994	WARD, WILLIAM RAY	DESCT	SFR
05920	KRAUSE, ALAN LEON	CDR	SWS	05995	ROAKE, JOHN FRANCIS	1ST Lt	SFR
05921	WINKLER, MICHAEL WESLELY	LCDR	TEX	05996	RICHARDSON, CHARLES WILLIAM	LT	SFR
05922	LUTHER, JOHN ALEXANDER	LTJG	ILL	05997	SHANAFIELD, HAROLD ARTHUR	CAPT	ILL
05923	MULKEEN, MARTIN JOSEPH	CAPT	SFR	05998	NEWMAN, ALVIN SIMMERMAN	RADM	SWS
05924	WILLEY, MICHEL FREDERICK	CAPT	SFR	05999	LEHMAN, BEN J.	RADM	SFR
05925	HAYWARD, OLIVER STODDARD	LCDR	SFR	06000	LUPO, THOMAS JOSEPH	COMO	NOR
05926	RODER, PETER STEVAN	CAPT	SFR	06001	WOOD, PHILLIP RAY	CAPT	SWS
05927	WOOD, JOHN RANDOLPH	LT	SDG	06002	COSTELLO, JOHN D.	VADM	SFR
05928	SMITH, THOMAS JOSEPH (J.T.)	CW04	SDG	06003	TONEY, ROBERT LEE	RADM	SFR
05929	WHITE, ROBERT DOUGLAS	Col	SDG	06004	ANSELMO, GUY (N) JR.	CDR	DCA
05930	STONE, RAYMOND M.	CAPT	SFR	06005	LAWRENCE, MARY C.	ASOC	NOR
05931	MAY, DAVID THOMAS	CAPT	SFR	06006	CONNALLY, ROBERT FRANKLIN	CAPT	TEX
05932	WHITE, JOHN ALEXANDER	Col	SFR	06007	ANDERSON, GERALD DUANE	CAPT	ILL
05933	RHETT, WILLIAM MEANS SMITH	CDR	SFR	06008	SCHLOZ, JOHN MICHAEL	CAPT	TEX

NEW YORK COMMANDERY
NAVAL ORDER OF THE UNITED STATES

ANNUAL DINNER

Rear Admiral Samuel Eliot Morison Award for Naval Literature

WEDNESDAY 18 OCTOBER 1989

Reception 18:30 — Dinner 19:30

Guest of Honor

HONORABLE JOHN F. LEHMAN, Jr
Secretary of the Navy, 1981 — 1987

Author

COMMAND OF THE SEAS:
Building the 600 Ship Navy

7th REGIMENT ARMORY
643 Park Avenue at 67th Street
New York, New York

The SS Jeremiah O'Brien
Historic Plaque

The engraving of the name

Naval Order of the United States

on this historic plaque was ordered by

Naval Order of the United States
San Francisco Commandery of the Naval Order

January 12, 1994

The National Liberty Ship Memorial

SS Jeremiah O'Brien

S.S. Jeremiah O'Brien
Historic Plaque

This is to certify that the name

Naval Order of the United States

has been inscribed forever into history
aboard the World War II Liberty ship, S.S. Jeremiah O'Brien.

The SS Jeremiah O'Brien, an armed merchant vessel, is the lone
survivor of the great Allied armada that stormed the
Beaches of Normandy on D-Day, 1944.
She is an historic National Landmark.

Your name will be seen and honored by millions of visitors
from around the world for generations to come.

Your contribution has helped preserve this historic vessel
as a tribute to the spirit of freedom.

Rear Admiral T. J. Patterson
Chairman
Normandy '94 Committee

Robert F. Wake
Chairman
National Liberty Ship Memorial

January 10, 1994

The National Liberty Ship Memorial

Above: The S.S. Jeremiah O'Brien is the only Liberty ship to survive World War II. In keeping with the Mission of the Order, the General Commandery and the San Francisco Commandery sent a combined donation.
Right: 1994 Bonnot Award winner Author Barrett Tillman

NAVAL ORDER OF THE UNITED STATES

Phila/Del Valley CDRY Presents Awards

The feature at the Philadelphia/Delaware Valley CDRY's October dinner, at the Orion Officer's Club at the Willow Grove Naval Air Station, was the presentation of its two annual awards. The CDRY's ADM David Glasgow Farragut Award went to MGen James E. Livingston, USMC (Ret.). A Congressional Medal of Honor recipient, MGen Livingston distinguished himself above and beyind the call of duty in action against enemy forces while serving as the Commanding Officer, Co. E, 2nd Battalion, 4th Marines, on May 2, 1968.

David Sullivan of Rutland, MA, recieved the CAPT Emile Louis Bonnot, USNR, Memorial Award for Naval writing. In 1994, Sullivan was the first recipient of the Certificate of Appreciation for his "personal contribution to the advancement of professional education and leadership development at the Marine Corps University."

INSIG	COMPANION	RANK	CDRY	INSIG	COMPANION	RANK	CDRY
06009	MOTT, WILLIAM CHAMBERLAIN	RADM	NYC	06084	CHALBECK JOHN ARVID	CAPT	FKY
06010	THOMPSON, DONALD CHAS. (DEESE)	VADM	NYC	06085	WOODRUFF, JESSE L.	CW04	FKY
06011	DOWLING, ARTHUR L.	CDR	TEX	06086	SAMUEL, JOSEPH RAYMOND	CDR	NOR
06012	MARSHALL, PAUL EUGENE	CAPT	TEX	06087	THOMAS, ALEXANDER BRAST	CDR	ILL
06013	HILL, CAL DEAN JR.	CAPT	TEX	06088	LEIRD, WILLIAM ARCHEY	LCDR	FKY
06014	BARCHET, STEPHEN (N)	RADM	NOR	06089	VAUPEL, DAVID KARL	CDR	FKY
06015	ONEILL, HELEN GERALDINE	Lt Col	NAT	06090	KERWICK, RICHARD PATRICK	CDR	FKY
06016	BESKIND, ROBERT LETAW	CAPT	NAT	06091	CODDINGTON, KEITH (N)	LCDR	FKY
06017	JUSTICE, JOHN RODMAN	DESCT	SDG	06092	RECK, RONALD DAVID	CDR	FKY
06018	LELAND, WALTER TED	RADM	SFR	06093	CHAMBERS, RICHARD KENNER	RADM	NOR
06019	SPANE, ROBERT JOHNSON	RADM	SFR	06094	BAIR, GARY (N)	CAPT	ILL
06020	VAUGHT, CLARENCE THOMAS	CAPT	SFR	06095	KOCH, EDGAR JURGEN	CAPT	ILL
06021	MALONE, SUSAN LYNN	Lt Col	NYC	06096	SCHNEIDER, JAMES GORDON	LT	ILL
06022	BLOCK, L. JACK	HONOR	SFR	06097	TAYLOR, ALLEN J.	CAPT	NYC
06023	MOZELESKI, JAN (N)	CAPT	TEX	06098	HANSON, HARVEY HAROLD	HONR	SFR
06024	BRIGGS, FRANKLIN HENRY	CAPT	SDG	06099	BOWSER, PETER ADAMS	CAPT	SFR
06025	FROEHLICH, EDWARD WILIAM JR.	CAPT	NYC	06100	BASHOR, TIMOTHY MORROW	MAJ	SFR
06026	COLDREN, CLARKE L.	LCDR	TEX	06101	SHREWSBURY, JOHN MICHAEL	CDR	TEX
06027	SERWICH, THOMAS GREGORY II	CDR	NOR	06102	PAGE, LOREN HOWARD	CAPT	NOR
06028	JACKSON, DENNIS JAMES JR.	Maj.	ILL	06103	SKOTTY, DONALD RAYMOND	CDR	TEX
06029	OCONNOR, WILLIAM JOS. MICHAEL	RADM	ILL	06104	DURAZO, MARLENE LUCILLE	CDR	FKY
06030	CHURCH, SPENCER CHAPIN	CAPT	SDG	06105	FARRINGTON, RICHARD STANLEY	CDR	FKY
06031	WOLENSKY, IRENE (N)	CAPT	NAT	06106	LYTTON, EUGENE RAYMOND	LT	FKY
06032	WESTERFIELD, JOHN HENRY	CAPT	SEF	06107	MILLIGAN, ROBERT FRANK	LGEN	FKY
06033	STOHR, RICHARD JACOB	CAPT	NAT	06108	PITTS, ANDREW JOSEPH	CDR	FKY
06034	BRESNAHAN, MAURICE JOSEPH JR.	RADM	TEX	06109	SHUFORD, JACOB LAWRENCE	CDR	FKY
06035	WILLIAMS, TYLER EDWARD JR.	CAPT	NAT	06110	ARMSTRONG, JAN VINCENT	CAPT	SFR
06036	WALSH, JAMES P.	HONOR	NAT	06111	FITZGERALD, WILLIAM EDWARD	CAPT	NOR
06037	JOHNSON, JOHN DAVID	VADM	NAT	06112	CARLSON, RICHARD ALBERT	CDR	NOR
06038	MCCLINTOCK, WILLIAM R.	CAPT	NAT	06113	CARL, MURIAL HODGES	ASOC	ILL
06039	GIBFRIED, CHARLES PHILIP	CAPT	SWS	06114	MIGUEL, THEODORE (N) JR.	CAPT	FKY
06040	ORTEGA, JOSEPH JESUS (JAY)	CAPT	SWS	06115	KING, GEORGE JACK	Lt Col	FKY
06041	DUPE OF 5064 (ROGER ELDON BOX)			06116	LEACH, GEORGE HENRY	CDR	FKY
06042	DOBBS, GARY RONALD	LCDR	SWS	06117	THOMAS, CREED COX	CAPT	ILL
06043	DUNCAN, JOHN GARD	CAPT	SWS	06118	LILES, HUGH ALLEN	CDR	NOR
06044	HERNANDEZ, DIEGO E.	VADM	SWS	06119	MERICAS, EVANGELOS C.	CDR	NOR
06045	KEMPF, CECIL JOSEPH	VADM	SWS	06120	CUMMINS, RONALD HARRY	CDR	NOR
06046	MYERS, LOWEL RICHARD	RADM	SWS	06121	WEISNER, MAURICE FRANKLIN	ADM	FKY
06047	PEDERSEN, DAN ARTHUR	CAPT	SWS	06122	MORSE, JACK H.	CDR	SDG
06048	STEELE, TED CHARLES	RADM	SWS	06123	DAVIS, FRANK LAWSON JR.	CAPT	SDG
06049	STRICKLAND, JAMES MERRILL	RADM	SWS	06124	SMITH, MILLARD (N) JR.	LT	SDG
06050	BATZLER, JOHN RICHARD	RADM	SWS	06125	LOUGHRIDGE, EVERETT ALLEN	CAPT	NOR
06051	JANIEC, ROY THOMAS	CAPT	SWS	06126	ROBBINS, CLYDE E.	VADM	SFR
06052	YATES, CHRISTOPHER BARRETT	CDR	NAT	06127	KONETZNI, ALBERT HENRY JR.	CAPT	ATL
06053	BLANK, BILLY D.	CAPT	SDG	06128	WAYLETT, AGNES FREAR	ASOC	NAT
06054	BRICE, ROBERT CURTIS	LCDR	SDG	06129	CORMIER, WARREN GEORGE	CAPT	SDG
06055	MAJORS, MARY JOSPEHINE	CDR	SDG	06130	NAKASONE, HARRIET H.	CAPT	SDG
06056	ANDERSON, ROY CARL	LCDR	FKY	06131	FURLONG, GEORGE MORGAN JR.	RADM	FKY
06057	BEVER, JERRY DONALD	LCDR	FKY	06132	BECKWITH, RONALD LEE	MGEN	FKY
06058	BROWN, THOMAS WILLIAM	CAPT	FKY	06133	BOOMER, WALTER EUGENE	MGEN	FKY
06059	BUTLER, FRANK HALBERT JR.	Col	FKY	06134	COPE, WILLIAM DELOACH	LT	FKY
06060	DENNING, WILLIAM JAMES	CAPT	FKY	06135	HARFORD, JOSEPH LEO	CAPT	FKY
06061	DURAZO, MANUEL YGNACIO JR.	CDR	FKY	06136	HAYS, RONALD JACKSON	ADM	FKY
06062	ERLENBUSCH, PETER MICHAEL	LT	FKY	06137	KATZ, JOSEPH THEOPHILE	CAPT	FKY
06063	FANDREI, DENNIS ERVIN	CAPT	FKY	06138	KNUTSON, ALBERT EUGENE	CAPT	FKY
06064	FLENNER, JAMES A.	LCDR	FKY	06139	LANSDEN, HUMPHREY BAYLOR	CAPT	FKY
06065	FOULK, DONALD LAMAR	CDR	FKY	06140	LIVINGSTON, WILLIAM HAROLD	RADM	FKY
06066	GUARDENIER, EDGAR VANHORN (NED)	LT	FKY	06141	LUPO, ALVENA FLORENCE SMITH	ASOC	FKY
06067	HAMILTON, STEPHEN H.	CAPT	FKY	06142	WILLIAMS, JOSHUA FRANK	CDR	FKY
06068	HAMMERTON, GEORGE ARTHUR	LCDR	FKY	06143	BRESEE, MILES HABERLE JR.	CAPT	SFR
06069	KNIGHT, EDWARD B.	LTJG	FKY	06144	TEWELOW, ANN L.	ASOC	ATL
06070	MCCLAIN, ROY RUSSELL	LT	FKY	06145	DOEGE, ARTHUR GUSTAV	LCDR	NAT
06071	SAUNDERS, NORMAN THOMAS	CAPT	FKY	06146	RINGELBERG, JOHN MICHAEL	CAPT	NAT
06072	SHEWCHUCK, WILLIAM MICHAEL	CAPT	FKY	06147	DANIEL, ANNETTE J.	ASOC	NAT
06073	WEINTRAUB, ALLAN PAUL	LCDR	FKY	06148	FRANK, CHARLES WILLIAM JR.	CAPT	NOR
06074	WONG, HENRY KINGSY	CAPT	FKY	06149	MCCLAVE, ROSS RODES	CDR	NOR
06075	MARTIN, GEORGE HOYT	LCDR	SFR	06150	OBRIEN, MICHAEL JOSEPH	CAPT	SEF
06076	MAZLOUM, SILVANO GEORGE	HONOR	SFR	06151	LAIRD, JOHANNA MARIA	ASOC	WNY
06077	TASCA, ANTHONY V.	1ST Lt	SFR	06152	CHESLOCK, WILLIAM BERNARD	CAPT	
06078	ELLIOTT, RICHARD EDWARD	CAPT	NOR	06153	HORNER, MAJORIE LOUISE MCN.	2ND LT	LBE
06079	DAVIS, TERESA (N)	CDR	NOR	06154	OCONNELL, MARGARET M. YOUNG	LT	ILL
06080	CLARKE, FRANCIS MANN JR.	CAPT	NAT	06155	COUTURE, RAYMOND R.	RADM	ILL
06081	CUMMINGS, GERALD EDWARD	CDR	FKY	06156	COLAN, VINCENT J.	CAPT	ATL
06082	HAMBRIGHT, THOMAS LEROY	LCDR	FKY	06157	HERMANN, EDWARD PHILIP	CDR	TEX
06083	HAWKINS, ARTHUR RAY	CAPT	FKY	06158	ZANGAS, CHARLES LOUIS	Lt Col	SWS

INSIG	COMPANION	RANK	CDRY	INSIG	COMPANION	RANK	CDRY
06159	MCDONALD, JAMES MICHAEL	CDR	NOR	06234	PIOTROWSKI, LUKE EDWARD	DESCT	ILL
06160	MCDONALD, WESLEY L.	ADM	FKY	06235	NEWELL, BYRON BRUCE	RADM	NAT
06161	MOORER, THOMAS HINMAN	ADM	FKY	06236	KAUFFMAN, DANIEL GEORGE	CAPT	NAT
06162	BEESLEY, JOHN ROBERT	LT	FKY	06237	GARNER, FRED STANTON	CAPT	HRD
06163	MORGAN, G. THOMAS	CAPT	NYC	06238	FETTERMAN, JOHN HENRY JR.	VADM	SWS
06164	KRAUSS, GORDON WALTER	CAPT	NAT	06239	KOEHR, JAMES ELMER	RADM	NOR
06165	JOHNSON, ROY LEE	ADM	FKY	06240	MOODY, ROY BEDFORD JR.	CAPT	SEF
06166	SCOBIE, ROBERT WILLIAM	CAPT	FKY	06241	MEEHAN, KAREN ANN	CAPT	TEX
06167	WAYTENA, JAMES RICHARD	CAPT	FKY	06242	SAUNDERS, RICHARD SCOTT	LCDR	SDG
06168	KRIZ, EDWARD DEAN	CDR	FKY	06243	BLISH, NELSON ADRIAN	CAPT	TEX
06169	SKELLY, ARTHUR RICHARD	CAPT	FKY	06244	ROHRBACH, CLAYTON JOHN JR.	LT	SEF
06170	GITLIN, ALLEN REYNOLD	CAPT	FKY	06245	HEYER, NORA FRAIN	LTJG	SEF
06171	ROSENBLATT, JOHN J.	CDR	SDG	06246	PRENDERGAST, FINIS HOMER JR.	CAPT	TEX
06172	ALLEN, ERICA WENDY	DESCT	SDG	06247	HALBERT, ROBERT HARLAN	LT	NOR
06173	GLINDEMAN, HENRY PETER JR.	RADM		06248	MATTESON, THOMAS T.	RADM	FKY
06174	ANDERSON, RUSSELL FREDERICK	CAPT	ILL	06249	STOWE, CHARLES ROBINSON B.	CDR	TEX
06175	YOST, PAUL ALEXANDER JR.	ADM	FKY	06250	INGWERSEN, WILLIAM FRED	CAPT	LBE
06176	HOLLOWAY, JAMES LEMUEL III	ADM	FKY	06251	INGWERSEN, DARLENE WILLIAMS	ASOC	LBE
06177	HAFFNER, JOHN GRAHAM JR.	CDR	SFR	06252	CROUCH, "W L" LAMON	LCDR	ILL
06178	LANGLEY, ROLLAND AMENT JR.	CAPT	SFR	06253	FORSTER, ROBERT DOUGLAS	CDR	NAT
06179	WONDER, ROY L.	LCDR	SFR	06254	KRONBERGER, ROBERT SAMUEL	CDR	LBE
06180	STROLE, DENNIS SILVER	CAPT	SWS	06255	SIMER, MURICE MARLIN	CAPT	TEX
06181	HEYER, NELSON OTTO	RADM	NYC	06256	IRWIN, JAMES C.	VADM	FKY
06182	AMMON, WALTER RESOR	1ST LT	SFR	06257	MEYER, CONRAD (N) III	LT	FKY
06183	WEBER, ALBAN III (CHIP)	LT	NAT	06258	LAKSER, LAWRRENCE J.	CDR	FKY
06184	SERLES, JAMES CRAIG	CAPT	LBE	06259	CROSS, WILLIAM V. II	CAPT	FKY
06185	BENNETT, HARRY HOFFMAN	CAPT	LBE	06260	BREWER, ROBERT GEORGE JR.	CDR	FKY
06186	LEARSON, HAROLD WENDELL	CAPT	MAS	06261	SHRADER, GLENN EVANS	CAPT	SEF
06187	SMITH, LEIGHTON WARREN	RADM	FKY	06262	SPEYER, CARLOS ERIK	CDR	SEF
06188	PIENO, JOHN ANTHONY	CAPT	FKY	06263	MORRIS, THOMAS E.	RADM	SEF
06189	NOWACZYK, TIMOTHY IRVIN	LT	ILL	06264	ELKINS, JOHN THOMAS JR.	CAPT	SEF
06190	DECKER, PETERSEN NILES	LT	ILL	06265	WESTFALL, ALAN RAY	CAPT	TEX
06191	WEAVER, KEITH THOMAS	CAPT	NAT	06266	ELSTON, ROBERT "G"	CDR	TEX
06192	KASTNER, WILLIAM JOSEPH	CAPT	NAT	06267	KLOTZ, JOHN WILLIAM	CAPT	NOR
06193	BEPKO, JOHN JOSEPH III	CAPT	NAT	06268	CHERNESKY, JOHN JOSEPH JR.	CAPT	LBE
06194	DONNELL, JOSEPH S. III	VADM	FKY	06269	BURLINGAME, GEORGE EDWARD	LT	ILL
06195	HARDISTY, HUNTINGTON (N)	ADM	FKY	06270	DUNNE, JAMES MORGAN	CAPT	SEF
06196	KELSO, FRANK BENTON II	ADM	FKY	06271	COHUNE, JAMES SHELDON	CDR	SFR
06197	LUSK, CLYDE THOMAS JR.	VADM	FKY	06272	THOMAS, RANDOLPH WOODSON	DESCT	SFR
06198	SCHOULTZ, ROBT. FRCIS (DUTCH)	VADM	FKY	06273	BUNCH, PETER A.	RADM	SFR
06199	SMITH, RICHARD HILMAN	CDR	FKY	06274	KELLY, WM. CHRISTOPHER JR.	CAPT	MAS
06200	WATERBURY, WILLIAM JOHN	LCDR	FKY	06275	POCK, ARNOLD (N)	CAPT	ILL
06201	STEELE, ROBERT ALFRED	CAPT	SDG	06276	FARRELL, VINCENT DEPAUL	CAPT	NYC
06202	HEPPE, FRANCES ZOE	LT	LBE	06277	WOOD, DANIEL ANDRAE	CAPT	NYC
06203	METZ, ROBERT JOSEPH	LT	WNY	06278	GRAVELY, SAMUEL LEE JR.	VADM	NYC
06204	BAKER, JAMES B.	CAPT	WNY	06279	KOSS, ANDREW JAMES	CDR	FKY
06205	BECK, RICHARD EDWARD	CDR	WNY	06280	HAMEL, WILLIAM ROGERS	LCDR	FKY
06206	DANIELSON, LARRY ROBERT	CAPT	LBE	06281	DUNLEAVY, RICHARD MICHAEL	VADM	FKY
06207	DANIELSON, BRENDA MAYERS	ASOC	LBE	06282	DISHER, JOHN STEPHEN	VADM	FKY
06208	REMUS, THOMAS ALLAN	CAPT	SFR	06283	ACOSTA, ANNEMARIE	LT	LBE
06209	GOTTSCHALK, ROBERT GEORGE	CAPT	SFR	06284	GORLA, THOMAS WAYNE	CDR	LBE
06210	REINKE, SHARON FERNANDO	CAPT	NAT	06285	SUDHOLZ, HERMAN OTTO	CDR	MAS
06211	HUHN, S. PETER	CAPT	NAT	06286	TRUSSELL, GRAYSON LEE	CAPT	TEX
06212	WRIGHT, SAMUEL FISKE	CDR	NAT	06287	CRAIGE, DANNY DWAINE	CDR	TEX
06213	WELLS, DONALD MASON	CAPT		06288	CHUNG, DAVID YUIK	LT	LBE
06214	HILL, THOMAS JAMES	CAPT	ILL	06289	AUSLANDER, STANLEY ERNEST	LCDR	NYC
06215	MILLER, JAMES EDWARD	RADM	HRD	06290	FINK, EDWARD ROBERT	CAPT	SEF
06216	WILLIS, EDMUND PHILIP	CAPT	NYC	06291	RUEHLIN, JONN HENRY	RADM	SWS
06217	MCCARTHY, JOHN JOSEPH	CAPT	SFR	06292	ABLESON, BRADFORD EDWARD	LT	SFR
06218	SANDS, ROBERT J.	CAPT	SFR	06293	HARDY, HUGH WILSIE	MGEN	TEX
06219	ZAGANO, PHYLLIS (N)	LCDR	NYC	06294	DUKE, JOHN M.	CAPT	NOR
06220	EAGLETON, HUGH EDWARD	CAPT	NAT	06295	STOPKEY, DOUGLAS WILLIAM	LTJG	NOR
06221	MYRICK, DAVID GEORGE	CAPT	NAT	06296	STANDER, CHARLES JOSEPH	Col	NAT
06222	SIEGEL, KENT RODNEY	CAPT	NAT	06297	EDWARDS, THOMAS HAINES	CDR	TEX
06223	GILL, HARRY ROSS II	LCDR	SWS	06298	AILOR, RONALD GARTH	CAPT	TEX
06224	SPENCE, DALE WILLIAM	Col	TEX	06299	SULLIVAN, ARTHUR EDWARD JR.	LCDR	NAT
06225	ROSENBERG, DAVID ALAN	LT	TEX	06300	SLONIM, GILVEN MAX	CAPT	NAT
06226	SIMON, WILLIAM JAMES	CAPT	WNY	06301	POPP, RALPH WILLIAM	LCDR	NAT
06227	HERNANDEZ, JESSE J.	RADM	SFR	06302	SEELEY, JIMMIE WAYNE	RADM	FKY
06228	BENHAM, ARTHUR GEORGE	LT	SFR	06303	DUPE OF 5437 (LEON ALBERT (BUD) EDNEY)		
06229	ACKERT-BURR, CHERI NORTHCUTT	LTJG	TEX	06304	ROBERTS, NASH CHARLES JR.	LT	FKY
06230	WILLENBROCK, ERIC FREDERICK	CDR	TEX	06305	BERNSEN, HAROLD JOHN	RADM	FKY
06231	GOLDHAMMER, STEPHEN EDWARD	CAPT	TEX	06306	LEWIS, WILLIS IVAN JR.	RADM	FKY
06232	PELTIER, WILLIAM H.	CAPT	ILL	06307	MORAN, WILLIAM THOMAS	CAPT	NAT
06233	JOHNSON, CLINTON BERNARD	CAPT	ILL	06308	COBB, CALVIN H. JR.	LTJG	NAT

INSIG	COMPANION	RANK	CDRY	INSIG	COMPANION	RANK	CDRY
06309	SMOLEN, THEODORE FRANCIS	CDR	MAS	06384	TAYLOR, JAMES E.	RADM	FKY
06310	HOECK, JEANNE FRANCES	CAPT	LBE	06385	CANCELLED		
06311	MCKERNAN, JAMES MICHAEL JR.	CDR	ILL	06386	MORRIS, DAVID ROLAND	RADM	FKY
06312	WILKINSON, JOSEPH BARBOUR JR.	VADM	FKY	06387	SMITH, VERNON CHARLES	RADM	FKY
06313	RIEDER, ALBERT EUGENE	RADM	FKY	06388	LOFTUS, STEPHEN FRANCIS	RADM	FKY
06314	BUTCHER, MARVIN EVERETT JR.	CDR	FKY	06389	WHITE, THEODORE G. III	CDR	TEX
06315	DEKKER, JON KAREL	CDR	SWS	06390	ROHR, JOHN ANTHONY	CDR	HRD
06316	FRANKLIN, LARRY BRUCE	RADM	TEX	06391	FREY, HERMAN S.	LCDR	NAT
06317	STRITTMATTER, LAWRENCE RICHARD	CDR	NAT	06392	UMBERGER, JAMES ALEXANDER	CAPT	NOR
06318	METCALF, JOSEPH (N) III	VADM	NAT	06393	WINTERTON, BOYD "W"	CDR	LBE
06319	TURK, JAMES DONALD SR.	LCDR	TEX	06394	GARBER, PAUL WILLIAM	CAPT	MAS
06320	LYONS, RICHARD BRODERICK	CAPT	SFR	06395			
06321	ABBOTT, DONALD ROBERT	LTJG	SDG	06396	BURNS, ROBET FRANCIS	HONOR	SDG
06322	ZUNIGA, GUILLERMO (WILLIE)	CAPT	SDG	06397	WILLIAMS, WILLIAM LLEWELYN	HONOR	SDG
06323	HARTER, ROGER KARR	Col	ILL	06398	ALBRIGHT, ROBERT REITER II	LT	MAS
06324	LEWIS, FLOYD COLVIN	Col	ARZ	06399	KOHL, ERNEST JAMES	CAPT	PDV
06325	NELSON, RAYMOND L.	HONOR	TEX	06400	FITZPATRICK, MICHELE (N)	LT	MAS
06326	JEFFORDS, JAMES MERRILL	CAPT	NAT	06401	MASSE, STEPHEN J.	CAPT	MAS
06327	SMART, DAVID OLIVER (D.O.)	RADM	NAT	06402	TUTTLE, JERRY OWEN	VADM	FKY
06328	HENDEL, RICHARD WILLIAM	CAPT	LBE	06403	BEST, JAMES BRUCE	RADM	FKY
06329	HIGGINSON, JOHN FRANCIS	LCDR	LBE	06404	KARALEKAS, S. STEVEN	CAPT	FKY
06330	CAMPBELL, RICHARD BRUCE	CAPT	NOR	06405	ORRIK, FREDERICK JOHN	CAPT	FKY
06331	PLAZA, JOSEPH BREWER	Maj.	TEX	06406	LEWIS, FREDERICK LANCE	RADM	FKY
06332	TAYLOR, JIMMIE WILKES	RADM	FKY	06407	GORDON, JOHN E. (TED)	RADM	FKY
06333	DENNEY, JAY RONALD	RADM	FKY	06408	SCHIFF, ALBERT JOHN (BUD)	CAPT	FKY
06334	WATERS, MITCHELL J.	MGEN	FKY	06409	PUTO, MICHAEL HILARY	HONR	FKY
06335	KILCLINE, THOMAS JOHN	VADM	FKY	06410	MAGALIS, RICHARD L.	CAPT	TEX
06336	WHEELAHAN, HAROLD MENTON JR.	CDR	FKY	06411	WHITING, ARTHUR A. III	CDR	TEX
06337	DUPE OF 4049 (JAMES SARGENT RUSSELL)			06412	FELDMAN, LEE RUSSELL	LTJG	SEF
06338	FINKELSTEIN, JIMMIE BENNIE	RADM	FKY	06413	HAMMER, LEON (N)	CAPT	MAS
06339	PRUEHER, JOHN WILSON	RADM	FKY	06414	FLYNN, STEPHEN EDWARD	LT	MAS
06340	WEBB, JAMES HENRY JR.	Capt	FKY	06415	TYLER, H. DAVID	LCDR	HRD
06341	SULLIVAN, RAYMOND FRANCIS	CAPT	FKY	06416	FORBES, BERNARD BROWN JR.	VADM	HRD
06342	MICHELL, ALBRO P. (PERE)	CDR	NOR	06417	KLAHR, OWEN ALLEN	CAPT	HRD
06343	MICHELL, ALBRO P. (FILS)	DESCT	NOR	06418	FANNING, TIMOTHY ONEIL JR.	CAPT	PDV
06344	MICHELL, JACQUES BLAISE	DESCT	NOR	06419	TRAWEEK, BILLY BANKS	CAPT	TEX
06345	PEARSON, JEREMIAH WMS. III	MGEN	NOR	06420	DUPUIS, CHARLES THOMAS	CAPT	NAT
06346	RINARD, ELAINE J.	ASOC	NOR	06421	KIME, STEVE FRANCIS	CAPT	NAT
06347	SMITH, MYRON LORENZO JR.	LCDR	MAS	06422	WOOD, LELAND EDWARD JR. (BUD)	CAPT	NAT
06348	MILLER, PAUL DAVID	VADM	FKY	06423	CRONLEY, MAUREEN PATRICIA	LTJG	NAT
06349	MULQUEEN, MICHAEL PATRICK	BGEN	FKY	06424	HIGGINS, EARL JAMES	CDR	NOR
06350	HILL, CLARENCE ARTHUR JR.	RADM	FKY	06425	MCDANIEL, EUGENE BARKER (RED)	CAPT	FKY
06351	MARTIN, EDWARD HOLMES	VADM	FKY	06426	RAPPS, RICHARD EDWARD	CAPT	ATL
06352	LYNCH, JARVIS DERBY JR.	MGEN	FKY	06427	ROTHSTEIN, JEROME PHILIP	CAPT	JAX
06353	BERNING, RONALD CHARLES	CAPT	FKY	06428	MILLER, DANIEL ARTHUR	LTJG	ILL
06354	RAUSA, ROSARIO M.	CAPT	FKY	06429	HANAWALT, EDWARD ALAN (TED)	CAPT	NOR
06355				06430	DUNCAN, RICHARD GRAVES	CAPT	LBE
06356	HOUTING, PETER ROMAN	CDR	NOR	06431	BAUER, THOMAS GEORGE	CDR	SDG
06357	SMITH, LESTER ROBERT	RADM	NOR	06432	ALLEN MEREDITH JULIE	DESCT	SDG
06358	VAHSEN, STEVEN SCOTT	LTJG	MAS	06433	CRILLY, EUGENE RICHARD	CDR	SDG
06359	HOFFMEYER, JOHN THOMAS	CAPT	NYC	06434	SIDLER, NORMAN FRAZIER JR.	CAPT	ILL
06360	MILLER, HARVEY S.	LT	MAS	06435	CROWELL, DUGLAS WOODS	CAPT	NAT
06361	WATSON, THOMAS CAMPBELL JR.	RADM	FKY	06436	HOLMES, SIDNEY LAWRENCE JR.	CAPT	NAT
06362	JEREMIAH, DAVID E.	ADM	FKY	06437	DRENNEN, CHRISTOPHER JOHN	LT	NAT
06363	MARRYOTT, RONALD FRANK	RADM	FKY	06438	DAVIE, CLINTON WILLIAM	CAPT	ILL
06364	PARTINGTON, JAMES WOOD	RADM	FKY	06439	HOLLER, ANN FLYNN	CDR	SDG
06365	GALLO, SALVATORE FRANK	RADM	FKY	06440	FALCONA, SAMUEL FRANK	CDR	ILL
06366	READY, JOHN KENNETH	VADM	FKY	06441	OMALLEY, THOMAS FRANCIS JR.	Col	ILL
06367	PEARSON, JOHN DAVIS	RADM	FKY	06442	OBRIEN, GLENN PAUL	CDR	ILL
06368	BALL, WILLIAM LOCKHART III	LCDR	FKY	06443	DUPE OF 4155 (EDGAR HARGADON MARTIN)		
06369	ENSCH, JOHN C.	CAPT	FKY	06444	WILLIAMS, JOHN ALLEN	CDR	ILL
06370	MCDUFFEE, FRANK WILLIAM	Col	FKY	06445	TAYLOR, HARVEY ALBERT	LCDR	ILL
06371	RAMSEY, DAVID G.	RADM	FKY	06446	WULFF, ELIZABETH WILLIAMS	ASOC	ILL
06372	ROE, EDWARD K.	CAPT	TEX	06447	MILLS, JON MARTIN	CDR	LBE
06373	KENDALL, WILLIAM THEODORE	CDR	TEX	06448	BALOK, LARRY JAMES	CAPT	ILL
06374	FOSTER, PATRICK LYMAN	LT	SFR	06449	MITCHLER, ROBERT WALTER	HONR	ILL
06375	LAZO, LEO MICHAEL	CAPT	MAS	06450	HARNESS, FRANCIS WILLIAM	CAPT	ILL
06376	FITZGERALD, DAVID RAYMOND	CDR	MAS	06451	SWEENEY, JOHN JOSEPH	RADM	PDV
06377	LAPP, MARGRET M.	ASOC	SEF	06452	LINDER, JAMES BENJAMIN	RADM	HRD
06378	MOODY, BARBARA G.	ASOC	SEF	06453	BROWN, LEROY A.	CDR	HRD
06379	KURTH, RONALD JAMES	RADM	FKY	06454	MOSLEY, DON EARL	Lt Col	HRD
06380	WILLCOX, LAWRENCE GERMAN	ENS	FKY	06455	BEASLEY, CHARLES JAHNS	CAPT	SFR
06381	JOHNSON, JEROME LAMARR	VADM	FKY	06456	ROY, LARRY WAYNE	CAPT	TEX
06382	MILLER, EDWARD JOHN	LGEN	FKY	06457	BLOUNT, THOMAS EDWARD	CDR	FKY
06383	DAVISON, HOLLIS E.	MGEN	FKY	06458	GILLEN, ROBERT LEO	CDR	MAS

USS HOUSTON (CA 30)

Monument to Honor the Ship and Her Gallant Crew
Commissioned: June 17, 1930
Sunk: March 1, 1942 at Sunda Strait

Monument Erected by the USS Houston Foundation
A Project of the Naval Order of the U.S. Texas Commandery
Dedicated: Navember 11, 1995 in Sam Houston Park
The Heritage Society Museum, 1100 Bagby St., Houston Texas

INSIG	COMPANION	RANK	CDRY	INSIG	COMPANION	RANK	CDRY
06459	WALKER, EDWARD KEITH JR.	RADM	HRD	06533	MELVIN, ALBERT ANTHONY	CDR	LBE
06460	GRACE, ELDON WAYNE	LT	HRD	06534	PETERS, JOHN CHARLES	CDR	SDG
06461	PIOTROWSKI, MARY TERESA KELLY	ASOC	ILL	06535	LEVERONE, ROBERT MICHAEL	CAPT	MAS
06462	LEHMAN, JOHN FRANCIS JR.	CAPT	FKY	06536	BENJAMIN, JUNE G.	ASOC	SEF
06463	HAYDEN, WILLIAM BUFORD	CAPT	FKY	06537	FELDMAN, STACEY HOPE	ASOC	SEF
06464	BUTCHER, PAUL D.	VADM	FKY	06538	CAMPBELL, NORMAN DEAN	RADM	SWS
06465	VANDIVORT, WALTER DERRIS	CAPT	ILL	06539	WHITTEN, ROBET CRAIG	CDR	SFR
06466	HYDE, ROBERT TODD JR.	CDR		06540	ELLIOTT, JAMES ROBERT II	DESCT	LBE
06467	BRADLEY, DAVID MICHAEL	LT	LBE	06541	FARLEY, JAMES PARKER	HONOR	NYC
06468	CASHMAN, DAVID MATTHEW	CDR	MAS	06542	MURPHY, WILLIAM AUGUSTINE	CDR	NYC
06469	CARGILL, DENNY BRUCE	RADM	FK	06543	DUSSMAN, THOMAS RAYMOND JR.	CDR	ILL
06470	KRAMEK, ROBERT E.	RADM	FKY	06544	DOHNER, DAVID EDMUND	CAPT	TEX
06471	JOHANSON, ROBERT LOUIS	RADM	FKY	06545	NARVA, WILLIAM M.	RADM	FKY
06472	KELLY, ROBERT JOSEPH	RADM	FKY	06546	GROESBECK, DEBORAH (N)	CDR	TEX
06473	LESS, ANTHONY ALBERT	RADM	FKY	06547	FULLING, ROGER WILLIAM	HONOR	SEF
06474	YOW, JOHN SAMUEL	RADM	FKY	06548	WISCHMEYER, WILLIAM DOUGLAS	Col	NOR
06475	CIANCAGLINI, DAVID EMIL	RADM	FKY	06549	KORCHOWSKY, GEORGE WILLIAM	LT	NAT
06476	LINFORD, JOHN HERBERT	LCDR	NYC	06550	RENFREE, EDWARD WILLIAM	LT	NYC
06477	THORSEN, HOWARD BENTON	VADM	NYC	06551	ALFORD, ZEB DICKEY	CAPT	TEX
06478	COVINGTON, MICHAEL BRUCE	CAPT		06552	COLT, MARSHALL (N)	CDR	LBE
06479	ZIMBLE, JAMES A.	VADM	NAT	06553	FELTON, DONALD ARTHUR	CW04	LBE
06480	GANTHER, ROBERT JOSEPH	LTJG	SEF	06554	TOLLISON, THOMAS MICHAEL	CAPT	NAT
06481	CARLSON, GEORGE ROBERT	CDR	SWS	06555	BARALDI, WILLIAM JOSEPH	CAPT	NOR
06482	VORBACH, JOSEPH EDWARD	RADM	FKY	06556	MEEHAN, CONAN J.	LCDR	TEX
06483	BULL, LYLE FRANKLIN	RADM	FKY	06557	TURNBULL, STEVEN SCOTT	CDR	ILL
06484	GRIGGS, KAREN FRANCES	ASOC	TEX	06558	STEVENSON, WALLACE JOSEPH	LT	NYC
06485	HAMPTON, PHILLIP MICHAEL	CAPT	TEX	06559	MAYER, EARL HERLAN JR.	CDR	WNY
06486	HESLOP, ROBERT WILLIAM	LT	SEF	06560	RICE, SONDRA SCIBILIA	LCDR	NOR
06487	BRENNAN, LAWRENCE BRIAN	CDR	NYC	06561	NELSON, RICHARD HALE	LCDR	SEF
06488	ABRAMSON, HARVEY (N)	CAPT	NYC	06562	HENLEY, DAVID CLEMENT	CDR	NAT
06489	FREIN, JANE VERLIN	DESCT	NYC	06563	YOUNG, CHARLES "K"	CDR	HRD
06490	FITZGERALD, REGINA AGNES V.	DESCT	NYC	06564	LADD, PAUL VON BOSE	CAPT	NOR
06491	STEINHAUER, JULES VERNE	LCDR	NYC	06565	WARD, GLENN HOWARD	CDR	SDG
06492	CORCORAN, JOHN DANIEL ZAVIER	CDR	NYC	06566	ENGLER, ROYCE ALAN	CDR	TEX
06493	PRICE, STEPHEN ROBERT	LCDR	ATL	06567	SMITH, JUDY GAIL	Capt	NAT
06494	JONES, JAMES JERROLD	CDR	ATL	06568	JANES, DAVID ANTHONY	RADM	LBE
06495	MARCH, DANIEL PETER	RADM	FKY	06569	JONES, MEADE ADDISON JR.	CAPT	NAT
06495A	INGERSOLL, FREDERICK THOMAS	CAPT	SDG	06570	MCKINLEY, KEVIN JAY	LT	NAT
06496	LEE, BOBBY C.	RADM	FKY	06571	SULLINS, WILLIAM DAVID JR.	RADM	NOR
06497	BERAN, ARNOLD BRUCE	VADM	FKY	06572	PAIGE, MITCHELL (N) (MOH)	Col	TEX
06498	KOENEMAN, ALVIN BERTHOLD	RADM	NAT	06573	ROBERTSON, JOHN SHERROD	LCDR	TEX
06499	MUMMERT, DALE ROBERT	CAPT	SWS	06574	KROELL, HUGH SCOTT JR.	LT	ATL
06500	KAYE, ALBERT SCOTT	CAPT	NAT	06575	KENDALL, JULIUS (N)	LCDR	MAS
06501	HENN, ARTHUR EUGENE	RADM	FKY	06576	INGRAM, CHARLES MARSHALL	CDR	NOR
06502	ACKLIN, ERNEST BOYD	RADM	FKY	06577	KING, KEVIN L.	ENS	SEA
06503	UNRUH, JERRY LEE	RADM	FKY	06578	TACKITT, PATRICIA ANN HYLAND	CDR	NAT
06504	ILG, RAYMOND PAUL	VADM	FKY	06579	TACKITT, ROBERT DUANE	CAPT	NAT
06505	ROGERS, DAVID NEIL	RADM	FKY	06580	ELLIS, ROSALIND K.	HONOR	ILL
06506	GRAVES, KENNETH ERNEST	CAPT		06581	DELLAVALLE, JOHN ROBERT	Capt	PDV
06507	FLINT, WILLIAM KINMONT	CAPT	SFR	06582	DELLAVALLE, SUZANNE ARLENE	ASOC	PDV
06508	KESSELRING, WAVERLEY DALE	CAPT	SFR	06583	GERSON, JOE ROSS	LT	PDV
06509	CLARKE, LAURENCE BREEN	LTJG	NYC	06584	COX, JOEL CAPRON	LT	PDV
06510	DEVITO, VINCENT NICHOLAS	CAPT	NYC	06585	HANFT, GEORGE JOSEPH	LT	PDV
06511	DUFFICY, THOMAS JOSEPH	CAPT	NYC	06586	KATZ, GILBERT (N)	ENS	PDV
06512	BUNTING, CYRENUS GARRITT	LTJG	SEF	06587	KILEY, LEO ANTHONY	LT	PDV
06513	WILKINS, RICHARD STUART	LCDR	SEF	06588	KRAMER, ROBERT (N)	LT	PDV
06514	ROBERTS, TIM HAL	CAPT	ATL	06589	KULP, NED KNIPE	CAPT	PDV
06515	LAWRENCE, KENT BECKWITH	CDR	MAS	06590	LAMBERT, DAVID (N)	ENS	PDV
06516	DAVIS, ROBERT EDWARD	CDR	FKY	06591	MILLER, ANITA FELT	DESCT	PDV
06517	PULEIO, DANIEL THOMAS	LCDR	TEX	06592	RAUSCH, HARRY ANTHONY	CAPT	PDV
06518	LEGG, WILLIAM EMERY	CDR	SEF	06593	SCHLUSSEL, PHILIP M.	ENS	PDV
06519	DOGGETT, BURTON LEE	LCDR	NAT	06594	SEMET, ROBET JOHN	CAPT	PDV
06520	MCDEVITT, MICHAEL ALLEN	RADM	NAT	06595	SLOTE, ROBERT KILEY	LTJG	PDV
06521	MICHAELIS, FREDERICK HAYES JR.	CDR	NAT	06596	WEBER, FREDERICK C. JR.	LT	PDV
06522	SAYLOR, NAN ALIN	DESCT	NAT	06597	CLANCY, THOMAS L. JR.	HONOR	PDV
06523	WOODWARD, GEORGE PHELPS JR.	CAPT	NAT	06598	BLADH, JAMES CARL	LCDR	NAT
06524	FIELD, MICHAEL EDWARD	CAPT	ILL	06599	WATERS, JAMES P. D.	LT	MAS
06525	VIERZBA, EDMUND ALAN	CDR	LBE	06600	LEARSON, JOHN RICHARD	LCDR	MAS
06526	BOURNE, DOUGLAS J.	LTJG	TEX	06601	BOWERS, JOHN H.	Col	SFR
06527	DAVENPORT, JOSEPH D.	CAPT	NOR	06602	PADGETT, WAYNE W.	LCDR	SFR
06528	HOLM, KENETH CLARK (K.C.)	CAPT	SFR	06603	MERRILEES, GEORGE ROBERT	RADM	SFR
06529	GREALISH, KENT MICHAEL	CDR	SFR	06604	TRAUT, JULES R.	2AENG	ILL
06530	SUFFRIDGE, BUFORD JOSEPH	CAPT	SEF	06605	HATFIELD, BETTY CAMERON	ASOC	SDG
06531	NEWBERG, ERIC GEORGE JR.	CDR	NYC	06606	CHRISTY, DONALD EDWARD	Col	SFR
06532	PAUL, ROY LESLIE	LCDR	LBE	06607	SCHUTZ, GEORGE WILBUR	CDR	SFR

Rear Admiral Miller

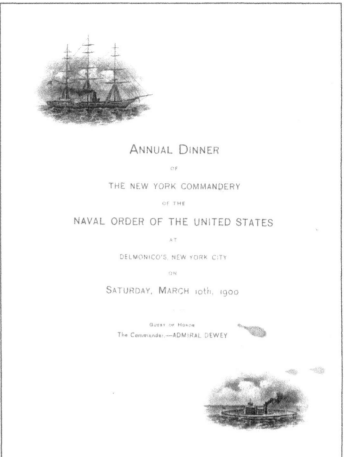

ANNUAL DINNER

OF

THE NEW YORK COMMANDERY

OF THE

NAVAL ORDER OF THE UNITED STATES

AT

DELMONICO'S, NEW YORK CITY

ON

SATURDAY, MARCH 10th, 1900

GUEST OF HONOR
The Commander,—ADMIRAL DEWEY

MENU

HUÎTRES

Potages
CONSOMMÉ COLOMBUS
BISQUE DE CRABES

Hors D'Oeuvre
RADIS   OLIVES   CELERI

Poisson
SAUMON À LA VÉNITIENNE
POMMES DE TERRE À L'ANGLAISE

Relevé
SELLE DE MOUTON SAUCE COLBERT
TARTELETTES D'ÉPINARDS

Entrées
POULARDE À LA VIENNOISE
MACÉDOINE À LA CRÈME

RIS DE VEAU MODERNE
POINTES D'ASPERGES

SORBET "OLYMPIA"

Rôts
PLUVIERS
SALADE DE LAITUES

Entremets de Douceur
GLACES DE FANTAISIES
FRUITS   PETITS FOURS
FROMAGE
CAFÉ

TOASTS

I. The President of the United States
    Music, HAIL COLUMBIA

II. Ourselves—just a few words
    LEONARD CHENERY, U. S. N.
    Vice-Commander, N. Y. Commandery

III. Our Commander—the Admiral
    GEO. WILLIAMSON SMITH, D.D., LL.D.
    General Chaplain

IV. Our Old Navy
    Rear-Admiral GEO. E. BELKNAP, U. S. N.
    Commander, Mass. Commandery

V. Our New Navy
    Captain H. C. TAYLOR, U. S. N.
    of the General Council

VI. Our Navy in the Future
    Captain A. T. MAHAN, U. S. N.

VII. Our "Empire State"
    Lieutenant-Governor TIMOTHY L. WOODRUFF

MUSIC

INSIG	COMPANION	RANK	CDRY	INSIG	COMPANION	RANK	CDRY
06608	HAUG, DAVID HENRY	LT	SFR	06683	WESENDORF, CAROLYN M.	ASOC	PDV
06609	BITOFF, JOHN WILLIAM	RADM	SFR	06684	BOLICK, JEROME WILSON	LT	COL
06610	KNIGHT, JEFFERY ROBERT	LT	SFR	06685	GEER, JOHN J.	CAPT	COL
06611	DUFF, CHERYL DIANE	LCDR	SFR	06686	MADSAGER, DENNIS LEE	CAPT	COL
06612	BRANNING, DELOS JOHN (JACK)	CAPT	SFR	06687	BARNETT, ANDREW FLOWERS	CAPT	HRD
06613	CARLSON, DUDLEY LOUIS	VADM	NAT	06688	ROUGHEAD, GARY (N)	CDR	HRD
06614	MORENCY, DONALD CHARLES	CAPT	NAT	06689	MORGAN, JAMES WALKER JR.	CAPT	TEX
06615	FRAZIER, ROBERT BRUCE	CDR	TEX	06690	HANNA, ALVIN TERRY JR.	CDR	NOR
06616	BUROW, ROBERT JOHN JR.	LCDR	ILL	06691	BRESEE, WILLIAM FREDERICK	CDR	LBE
06617	BARBER, JAMES ALDEN JR.	CAPT	FKY	06692	CAMPBELL, JOHN FRANCIS	CAPT	PDV
06618	LAMBDIN, PHILIP EUGENE	CAPT	FKY	06693	SHEFFIELD, BRIAN EDWARD	CAPT	NAT
06619	LAWRENCE, WILLIAM PORTER	VADM	FKY	06694	STUCKEY, JAMES EDWIN II	LTJG	TEX
06620	MURRAY, GORDON LAWRENCE JR.	CAPT	FKY	06695	MICHAEL, KIRK BURTON	CDR	TEX
06621	WICKERSON, STEPHEN FRANCIS	LT	TEX	06696	COUNTS, STANLEY THOMAS	RADM	SDG
06622	GASTON, ALEXANDER (SANDY)	HONOR	NYC	06697	CLARK, CHARLES RICHARD	LTJG	COL
06623	SAYLOR, NILA ASH	ASOC	NAT	06698	LANCASTER, HAROLD MARTIN	CDR	COL
06624	ALBUS, JOHN PATRICK	CDR	TEX	06699	MAYNARD, DONALD JAMES	CAPT	COL
06625	ATKIN, THOMAS F.	LT	MAS	06700	OZMUN, RICHARD RANDALL	CDR	COL
06626	DYKE, JAMES RONALD	CAPT	SFR	06701	HUGGARD, JOHN PARKER	CDR	COL
06627	FINGERHUT, ALFRED F. (TOM)	LT	SFR	06702	COOPER, MATTHEW T.	MGEN	NOR
06628	HAYWARD, WINCHELL THRALL	LCDR	SFR	06703	VERMILYEA, CLYDE LAVERNE	MGEN	NOR
06629	ODEGAARD, RICHARD E.	CDR	SFR	06704	GAMBOA, JOHN FRANK	CAPT	NAT
06630	GNERLICH, CHARLES HENRY	CAPT	NYC	06705	WATSON, WILLIAM HENLEY JR.	LCDR	COL
06631	LEWIS, WILLIAM RICHARD	LTJG	ILL	06706	FELGER, DANIEL GENE	CDR	NAT
06632	COLEMAN, JOE THOMAS JR.	CDR	TEX	06707	DENTCH, JONATHAN MICHAEL	LT	HRD
06633	KIME, JOHN WILLIAM	ADM	FKY	06708	LEWIS, JOHN BAKER JR.	CAPT	COL
06634	LOY, JAMES M.	RADM	FKY	06709	HUSHING, WILLIAM COLLINS	RADM	SEF
06635	DAVIS, WALTER J. JR.	RADM	FKY	06710	NEILL, JAMES STUART	CAPT	SFR
06636	APPLETON, DANIEL SIDNEY	CAPT	SDG	06711	ST.GERMAIN, ROBERT DONALD	CDR	TEX
06637	ORZECH, JAMES KENNETH (OTTO)	CAPT	SDG	06712	NUTWELL, ROBERT MICHAEL	CAPT	FKY
06638	REBER, PETER MICHAEL	CAPT	SWS	06713	MUR, RAPHAEL (N) (RAY)	CAPT	NYC
06639	BUTTNER, PATRICK ELLIOTT	CAPT	SFR	06714	KIRK, DAVID QUENTIN	CAPT	NYC
06640	HAIGWOOD, PAUL BENTLEY	Col	SFR	06715	RUSCH, THOMAS A.	CDR	ILL
06641	GIBBS, JOHN EDWARD	LT	ILL	06716	MYERS, MARTINE ROBINA	LCDR	TEX
06642	MUNDY, CARL EPTING JR.	LGEN	FKY	06717	KELLEY, WILLIAM EMANUEL	CAPT	NAT
06643	MCKINNEY, HENRY CLAYTON	RADM	NAT	06718	LONG, BRYON DEFLYNN	CDR	ATL
06644	CROWE, WILLIAM JAMES JR.	ADM	NAT	06719	BOBRICK, EDWARD ALLEN	CAPT	ILL
06645	GUTHRIE, WALLACE NESSLER JR.	RADM	NAT	06720	ADAMS, JOSEPH PETER	BGEN	FKY
06646	CONNALLY, ALTHEA M.	ASOC	TEX	06721	HARMEYER, KAREN ANN	CDR	ILL
06647	CAMPBELL, ROBERT E.	CDR	ILL	06722	REILLY, MICHAEL JOSEPH	CAPT	ILL
06648	MARCH, JOSEPH H.	LCDR	NAT	06723	MCVOY, JAMES LEONARD	CAPT	NAT
06649	HORNE, CHARLES FREDERICK III	RADM	NAT	06724	PETERSON, HARRY EDWIN	LT	NYC
06650	BRINSON, ZEB CEIGHTON	CAPT	NAT	06725	RITZENBERG, PHILLIP (N)	CDR	NYC
06651	STAIGER, ROGER P. JR.	CAPT	NAT	06726	DOUGHERTY, CHARLES WILBUR	CAPT	NAT
06652	STREETER, GREGORY F.	CAPT	NAT	06727	ZIMMERMAN, JOHN DANIEL	LCDR	MAS
06653	YOUNG, BRUCE A.	CAPT	NAT	06728	ZWALL, RICHARD (N)	CAPT	SDG
06654	HARVEY, RAY WILSON JR.	CAPT	NOR	06729	MCCARDELL, JAMES ELTON	RADM	NOR
06655	LLOYD, WALLACE HOWARD III	LT	NAT	06730	CATRON, DELBERT FRANKLIN	LT	LBE
06656	GRANT, HAROLD ERIC	CAPT	COL	06731	LIEPIN, OTTO LEON	LTJG	PDV
06657	BROWN, SARAH LOUISE	LCDR	COL	06732	RAVITZ, ROBERT ALLAN	RADM	NYC
06658	GREGORY, HOWELL JACKSON	CAPT	COL	06733	ENGELSTATTER, GEROLF HERBERT	LT	RAL
06659	MARTIN, JAMES NELLO	CAPT	COL	06734	BACKUS, RICHARD PAUL	1ST Lt	NYC
06660	WIEHAGE, JAMES WALTER	CAPT	TEX	06735	MCLEOD, WALTER JAMES III	CAPT	RAL
06661	CLARK, TERRELL IRVIN	CAPT	NAT	06736	ALEXANDER, JAMES MORTON	LTJG	RAL
06662	PYTEL, RONALD JOSEPH	CAPT	NAT	06737	GLASS, FRED STEPHEN	RADM	RAL
06663	PATAFIO, JOHN J. JR.	CDR	NYC	06738	COOPER, DAVID JACKSON JR.	CDR	RAL
06664	MARKS, JOHN JULIO	LT	NYC	06739	BURNETT, WESTON DYER	CDR	RAL
06665	COHEN, PAUL ROBERT	LTJG	SEF	06740	SIEGEL, JAY MARTIN	CAPT	RAL
06666	CALLAN, CAROL J.	LTJG	PDV	06741	CHURCHILL, WINSTON GILES	CAPT	SFR
06667	COPELAND, HARRIE EDMOND III	CDR	PDV	06742	MONTOYA, BENJAMIN FRANKLIN	RADM	SFR
06668	CUMMINS, SAMUEL AMSPOKER	RADM	PDV	06743	GOORJIAN, PAUL MIKE	CAPT	SFR
06669	FARLEY, RADCLIFFE WILCOX	LT	PDV	06744	INSKEEP, GEORGE WESLEY	LT	SFR
06670	GILSEHAN, JOHN SMITH	CAPT	PDV	06745	PENDLETON, ROBERT LEON	CAPT	SFR
06671	GORIN, FREDERICK (FRANK)	Capt	PDV	06746	SHAWKEY, RICHARD SUTHERLAND	CDR	SFR
06672	GOSHOW, JOHN PHILLIP	CAPT	PDV	06747	FELL, JOHN CORRY	DESCT	SFR
06673	KINDSVATTER, ANNE LORETTO	CDR	PDV	06748	RIEDELL, WILLIAM ALBERT	CAPT	NYC
06674	KOEHLER ERHARD WILLIAM JAMES	3AENG	PDV	06749	KEANE, FRANK WILLIAM	RADM	NYC
06675	MALAY-KOEHLER, LINDA ANNE	3AENG	PDV	06750	KRAFT, LEONARD HERBERT	CDR	NYC
06676	MAYO, WILLIAM R.	LCDR	PDV	06751	CRISTOL, "A" JAY	CAPT	NYC
06677	MURRAY, ANTHONY H. JR.	RADM	PDV	06752	BOWERS, CHARLOTTE LUCRETIA	ASOC	NAT
06678	SHIELDS, CHARLES D. JR.	CAPT	PDV	06753	MATHESON, DONALD CAMERON	CAPT	LBE
06679	STIMPSON, JEFFREY SCOTT	Capt	PDV	06754	GOODWIN, NORMAN (N)	CDR	LBE
06680	STODDARD, HWD, SANFORD (SANDY)	CAPT	PDV	06755	GILBERTSON, ROGER GEORGE	RADM	NAT
06681	WATTS, JAMES THOMAS	CAPT	PDV	06756	DEFRAITES, VIRGINIA ALEXANDRIA	ASOC	NOR
06682	WESENDORF, LEONDARD E.	CDR	PDV	06757	BOWMAN, MICHAEL LEE	RADM	FKY

Centinnial Banquet—Foreground: Past CDR Gen Robert Bolt and RADM/Mrs Lester R. Smith. Head table: CDR Gen at podium Past CDRs Gen E. Armstrong, Fred Carl, Stan Majka and Vice CDR Gen RADM W. M. Merlin

INSIG	COMPANION	RANK	CDRY	INSIG	COMPANION	RANK	CDRY
06758	PEAVEY, MICHAEL PENDEXTER	CDR	RAL	06833	BECKER, KELLY LYNN	LT	NAT
06759	BAKER, EVAN SMITH	LT	SFR	06834	MILLER, DALE ROBIN	LCDR	TEX
06760	KELLER, DONALD HENRY JR.	LT	SFR	06835	PATTISON, JAMES WYNN	CAPT	WNY
06761	MASLIN, CHARLES WALTER	LT	NYC	06836	SAMSON, JOHN WILLIAMS	LT	FKY
06762	CHASE, HARRY EUGENE (REV)	CWO	NYC	06837	TOURTELLOT, WARREN ESTUS JR.	LT	PDV
06763	FORDHAM, ROBERT JOHN	CAPT	NYC	06838	NADOOLMAN, MILTON (N)	LT	NYC
06764	ALLEN, PRICE PHILIP HANDSMAN	DESCT	SDG	06839	BARR, JON MICHAEL	RADM	NAT
06765	ALLEN, SETH ANDREW HANDSMAN	DESCT	SDG	06840	ISKRA, DARLENE MARIE	LCDR	FKY
06766	MILLER, ROBET REISCH	CDR	NAT	06841	BOUSHEE, FRANK LAWRENCE	CAPT	RAL
06767	RICHARDSON, DANIEL CHARLES	RADM	PDV	06842	DECASTRO, SAMUEL FLETCHER	DESCT	WNY
06768	CONN, ROBERT HENRY	CAPT	FKY	06843	GASTON, MACK CHARLES	RADM	FKY
06769	LAIL, GRAHAM LEROY	LT	RAL	06844	IVES, JOHN GORDON JR.	CAPT	NYC
06770	ADAMS, JOHN WARREN	RADM	SWS	06845	SCARPA, JOSEPH (N)	LCDR	NAT
06771	MORRIS, ROBERT E.	CDR	SWS	06846	DENT, THOMAS AUGUSTINE	LT	NYC
06772	WILLIAMS, DAVID DANIEL	CAPT	SWS	06847	GRASKE, THEODORE WESLEY JR.	CAPT	NYC
06773	WILSON, JOHN RAYMOND	RADM	SWS	06848	JOSEPH, MARK RICHARD	CAPT	NYC
06774	HOOVER, ROBERT CLEARY	DESCT	SFR	06849	BUELL, HAROLD LLOYD	CDR	TEX
06775	BAUER, LYNTON G.	CAPT	NMX	06850	BRUBAKER, HERBERT MINETREE	CDR	SEF
06776	VERZINO, WILLIAM JOHN JR.	CAPT	NMX	06851	WISE, CLETUS F.	CAPT	NAT
06777	SEIGEL, SIGMUND LEE	CAPT	PDV	06852	GRAVES, GUY DUNNING	LT	TEX
06778	CHRISTIAN, DAVID ALAN	HONOR	PDV	06853	MILLER, THOMAS HULBERT	LGEN	FKY
06779	BANNING, WILLIAM PECK	2ND LT	PDV	06854	JINDRICH, CHARLES ANTHONY	CAPT	ILL
06780	HRYSHCHYSHYN, MICHAEL HARRY JR.	LCDR	PDV	06855	BACKUS, DAVID PAUL	Capt	NYC
06781	CUERONI, RICHARD PAUL	RADM	FKY	06856	KRIMMER, LEE ALBERT	LT	NYC
06782	FULTON, DONALD M.	CAPT	NMX	06857	GROJEAN, CHARLES DAVID	RADM	TEX
06783	SCHMIDT, MARGARET MCCORMICK	CAPT	NMX	06858	WALKER, DAVID MATHIESON	CAPT	TEX
06784	LEMOYNE, IRVE CHARLES	RADM	TEX	06859	MCCLAVE, ROSCOE PARKE JR.	LCDR	NOR
06785	EGAN, GREGORY TOWNSEND	LTJG	TEX	06860	HOOPER, JOHN DAVID	LCDR	PDV
06786	ALAIR, GENE LYLE	CAPT	NAT	06861	MCCANN, AGNES FRANCES	LTJG	NYC
06787	TOMKA, THOMAS GEORGE	CW03	LBE	06862	PERKERSON, THOMAS ROBERT	LCDR	ATL
06788	BOWERS, CHARLES HATHAWAY	CAPT	ILL	06863	DUFFY, THOMAS EDWARD JR.	CAPT	SDG
06789	SMITH, LEWIS MONROE	CAPT	ILL	06864	BUBLITZ, ROBERT ENRIGHT	CDR	NYC
06790	KELLY, PATRICK THOMAS	LCDR	MAS	06865	CIAFFA, PHILIP ROBERT	LT	NYC
06791	MIXSON, RIELEY DEWITT	RADM	FKY	06866	SKERCHOCK, PETER (N)	CAPT	NYC
06792	TAYLOR, RAYNOR ANDREW KENT	RADM	FKY	06867	ROLAND, KENNETH LEEROY	CDR	ILL
06793	GEE, GEORGE NICHOLAS	RADM	FKY	06868	HINSON, WILLIAM HARLAN JR.	CAPT	ATL
06794	SEIDENSTEIN, WILLIAM ROY	LCDR	NYC	06869	BARTELS, STANLEY LEONARD	LCDR	PDV
06795	BLACK, BRUCE ALLEN	RADM	NMX	06870	RYAN, MICHAEL JOSEPH	LT	SDG
06796	MICUCCI, PATRICK ANTHONY	LT	ILL	06871	KEHOE, JAMES WILLIAM	CAPT	NAT
06797	ORTHLEIB, LARAINE FRANCES	COMMO	FKY	06872	HODGE, SHARON LEE	CDR	TEX
06798	MURRAY, DWIGHT HARRISON JR.	CDR	SFR	06873	MACPHERSON, RONALD GARY	DESCT	SWS
06799	WOOD, ROBERT ALLEN	LCDR	SFR	06874	SANDERS, WADE ROWLAND	CAPT	SDG
06800	BARTELS, WILLIAM L.	Capt	SDG	06875	HOLLER, EDWARD MORLEY	ASOC	SDG
06801	GRAY, ALFRED MASON JR.	GEN	NAT	06876	KISER, COLIN LEE	LT	TEX
06802	TOWNSEND, EDWARD JOHN	Maj.	SDG	06877	GREGORY, FREDERICK DREW	HONOR	TEX
06803	LIVINGSTON, JAMES EVERTTE (MOH)	MGEN	FKY	06878	HULSEBOSCH, ADRIAN PETER	LT	SEF
06804	BURNETT, HOWARD JEROME	LT	PDV	06879	LLOYD, LOIS RUSSELL	ASOC	ARZ
06805	ALLARD, DEAN CONRAD JR.	CDR	CDR	06880	REED, WILLIS EVERETT	CAPT	SEF
06806	BODOUR, HAIG (N)	CAPT	NMX	06881	ADDICOTT, RAYMOND WALTER	CAPT	SEF
06807	BRINSFIELD, ORVILLE PAGE	CAPT	PDV	06882	MCCUNE, HARRY D.	Capt	SFR
06808	TARLTON, LEE ALEXANDER	CAPT	NAT	06883	STEFANKI, JOHN (N)	LT	SFR
06809	CLINKSCALES, HULAN FERRELL	CAPT	SEF	06884	KNICK, WILLIAM DALE	LT	SFR
06810	DONOVAN, FRANCIS RAYMOND	VADM	WNY	06885	SABER, RICHARD ARTHUR	LT	SFR
06811	WILMOT, LOUISE CURRIE	RADM	FKY	06886	WILSON, JAMES GERALD	CAPT	SFR
06812	BAKER, JOSEPH WILLIAM	CAPT	PDV	06887	WOOLEVER, GERALD FRANCIS	RADM	SFR
06813	CLOAK, STEPHEN PETER JR.	LT	PDV	06888	COVERT, JOHN J.	1ST LT	SFR
06814	RIZEN, BRIAN KENNETH	LCDR	PDV	06889	DAVIDSON, GEORGE THOMAS D.	LTJG	SFR
06815	DONOHOO, STANLEY FRANCIS	CAPT	SEF	06890	HURLEY, JEFFREY ALAN	CDR	ATL
06816	SILVERMAN, JOSEPH (N)	CAPT	SEF	06891	DUNNE, ELIZABETH ANN C.	DESCT	SEF
06817	SRITE, DAVID ALAN	CAPT	NMX	06892	CUPSCHALK, JOHN FRANCIS VANCE	LT	NYC
06818	TIERNEY, GLENN PATRICK	CDR	NAT	06893	LITTMAN, LEON (N)	CAPT	NYC
06819	OLSON, JAMES D. II	RADM	FKY	06894	WALLACE, GEORGE ALLEN	CDR	TEX
06820	OTTO, BERTON REED (BUD)	CAPT	NAT	06895	KUHN, ALVIN ROLAND	LTJG	SFR
06821	CASSIDY-BEPKO, KATHLEEN MARY	ASOC	NAT	06896	OCHELTREE, JAMES REED	LT	SFR
06822	DONNELLY, RICHARD FINLAY	RADM	ATL	06897	REED, OLOF PAYNE	LT	SFR
06823	KAINE, LEONARD PAUL (SKI)	CAPT	SWS	06898	WILLIAMS, LEWIS IRVING JR.	CAPT	SFR
06824	MONROE, PHILIP ALVAH	CAPT	SWS	06899	HOWELL, TERRY LAWSON	LCDR	SFR
06825	ADAMS, JOSEPH ALLEN	CAPT	RAL	06900	UNTERMEYER, CHARLES GRAVES (CHASE)	LT	FKY
06826	WALDRON, JAMES LEROY	CDR	NAT	06901	READDY, WILLIAM FRANCIS	CDR	FKY
06827	HAFER, DALE VINCENT	LCDR	NAT	06902	COURSEY, ROGER WARREN	CAPT	TEX
06828	SALATIELLO, PETER PAUL	LCDR	NYC	06903	BADGLEY, EDMUND KIRK JR.	LT	NMX
06829	AMBOS, JOHN FRANCIS	LCDR	NYC	06904	ARTHUR, STANLEY ROGER	ADM	FKY
06830	HANLEY, ROBERT ALOYSIUS	LTJG	NYC	06905	GERNES, DEBORAH SUE	CDR	FKY
06831	PURDY, DELBERT CHURCHILL	CAPT	NYC	06906	RIFFLE, DONALD LEE	CAPT	FKY
06832	ST.GEORGE, GREGORY JOHN	LTJG	ILL	06907	KURTH, MICHAEL MARK	Col	FKY

The Dewey Monument in downtown San Francisco. Above Left: Shown adjusting the Naval Order wreath are Centinnial Congress co-chairs Companions Robert Laugnerd and Edward Jepsen. Photos courtesy Companion Chuck Heiland.

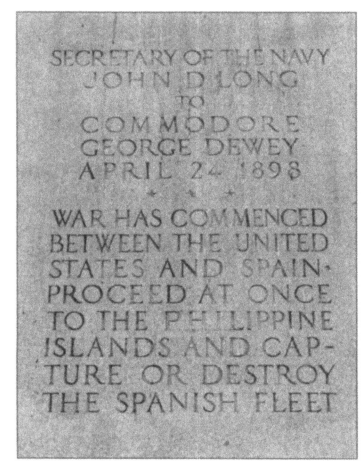 

INSIG	COMPANION	RANK	CDRY	INSIG	COMPANION	RANK	CDRY
06908	REYNIERSE, PETER JAMES	CDR	NAT	06983	KOVITZ, BERNARD (N)	LT	PDV
06909	RIPA, CARL VAUGHAN	LT	NAT	06984	BABICH, JACK WOOD	LTJG	PDV
06910	WASSMAN, EDWARD ROBERT	LCDR	NYC	06985	OLAUGHLIN, FRANCIS MICHAEL III	CAPT	NOR
06911	LEE, PATRICIA LOUISE	DESCT	PDV	06986	RAZZETTI, EUGENE ANTHONY	CAPT	NAT
06912	RAUCH, KENNETH NORBERT (DUTCH)	CAPT	FKY	06987	OCONNER, JOHN CORNELIUS III	LTJG	MAS
06913	KERR, BAINE PERKINS	Maj.	TEX	06988	HIGGINS, ROBIN L.	Maj.	FKY
06914	FRANKE, KELLY JUNE	LT	FKY	06989	BURGESS, ROBERT EDWARD	CAPT	SFR
06915	BUCKNER, RHONDA LOUISE	LT	FKY	06990	DICHOV, MARIA ELIZABETH	LCDR	SFR
06916	TURNEY, PATRICIA ANNE	LT	FKY	06991	PACHECO, RNALD EDWARD	CDR	SFR
06917	GRAY, DAVID JUDSON	CAPT	MAS	06992	MCGANN, BARBARA ELIZABETH	CAPT	SFR
06918	OKEEFE, JAMES GEORGE	CDR	MAS	06993	CARMICHAEL, EDWARD WILLIAM	Maj	SFR
06919	SOLOMON, RACHEL E.	CDR	NAT	06994	KESSLER, ROBERT ROTH	CDR	SFR
06920	SAVAGE, WARREN HENRY JR.	CW04	NAT	06995	MAJKA, PEGGY JUNE	ASOC	SFR
06921	HONTZ, EDWARD BRIGHAM	CAPT	NAT	06996	STONE, RAYMOND WOODBURY	DESCT	SFR
06922	JOHNSON, JOHN MICHAEL	CDR	ILL	06997	THOMAS, CAROLYN BEAL	DESCT	SFR
06923	SMITH, ROBERT (N) III	RADM	FKY	06998	MOELLER, JOHN WILLIAM	CAPT	SFR
06924	GILLETTE, ROBERT CHARLES	CAPT	NAT	06999	MURPHY, JOSEPH FRANK	LCDR	SFR
06925	PECK, EDWARD ROBERT JR.	CAPT	SFR	07000	SPARKS, BENNETT SHER (BUD)	RADM	SFR
06926	CRAIG, ROBERT MARSHALL	LCDR	TEX	07001	DUNCAN, STEPHEN MARK	CAPT	FKY
06927	MILLER, RICHARD HENRY	CAPT	NMX	07002	PITMAN, CHARLES HENRY	LGEN	FKY
06928	WALSH, FRANCES (FRANKIE) KAY	LCDR	NMX	07003	LANGE, WALDEN ALFRED	CAPT	SDG
06929	NAVA, EDWARD JOHN	LT	NMX	07004	WENZE, GLORIA ANN TANSITS	CAPT	NMX
06930	MARKETTE, ANTHONY CARMEN	DESCT	PDV	07005	HALL, LYLE ROSS	RADM	SEF
06931	MILLER, FLOYD HARRY	RADM	PDV	07006	GOSLER, JAMES RAYMOND	CDR	NMX
06932	SAPERA, LEONARD JOSEPH	CAPT	SEF	07007	CANEPA, LOUIS ROBERT	CAPT	SWS
06933	SUTHERLIN, BENJAMIN THOMAS	CAPT	LBE	07008	CONNELL, EARL WAYNE	CDR	SWS
06934	TOMASKI, JULIUS WILLIAM	LCDR	TEX	07009	DYKES, ROBERT ANDREW	CAPT	SWS
06935	HUSS, WILLIAM WEISSMAN	CAPT	LBE	07010	ELLIS, JAMES LEONARD	CDR	SWS
06936	ROBINSON, WILLIAM ALAN	CDR	TEX	07011	KOHN, EDWIN RUDOLPH JR.	VADM	SWS
06937	READE, RICHARD S. JR.	CAPT	NYC	07012	MCCAULL, JOHN WAYNE	CAPT	SWS
06938	GROSSO, LOUIS JOHN (LCOL)	HONOR	NYC	07013	MCCULLOUGH, MARTIN LIENTZ	CAPT	SWS
06939	MYHRE, JOHN SILAS JR.	CAPT	NYC	07014	SHEPPARD, CHRISTOPHER GERARD	CAPT	SWS
06940	BRACKETT, EDWARD BOONE	LCDR	NYC	07015	SWARTZ, THEODORE ROBERT	CDR	SWS
06941	PETERSON, GLENN GUY	LT	ILL	07016	CAMPILLO, FRED GROVER	LCDR	ILL
06942	HINGER, ERIC RICHARD	LCDR	FKY	07017	MCLANE, WILLIAM BAYARD	DMC	ILL
06943	STEWART, RODNEY LEE	CAPT	NMX	07018	WILHITE, DOYLE (N)	CAPT	ILL
06944	BOLSHAZY, ROBERT STEPHEN	CDR	SDG	07019	LUISI, GERARD HENRI	HONOR	NYC
06945	BUNDO, NEAL GEORGE	LCDR	SDG	07020	POSNER, ANTON CALLIAS	ENS	NYC
06946	BUTTRON, WAYNE RICHARD	HONOR	SDG	07021	HERMAN, ROBERT LEWIS	CDR	PDV
06947	HERR, PHILIP LEONARD	CAPT	SDG	07022	DALY, EDWARD JOSEPH (CAPT)	HONOR	PDV
06948	BYERS, LARRY JON	LCDR	NOR	07023	WARRICK, JAMES CRAIG	CAPT	SEF
06949	GIRON, LAWRENCE J.	CDR	NMX	07024	DYER, CHARLES ARNOLD	CAPT	SFR
06950	GUTIERREZ, ARIEL J.	LT	NMX	07025	SWINDAL, FREDERICK LEROY JR.	CDR	ARZ
06951	MYNARD, CHARLES RANDALL	CAPT	NMX	07026	JENSEN, CHRISTINE EVE	LT	ARZ
06952	PEREZ, ANTHONY HERMAN	CDR	NMX	07027	MOORE, ROBERT WILLIAM	LCDR	ARZ
06953	BARRON, GARY ROBERT	LT	LBE	07028	PECK, MICHAEL DAVID	LT	TEX
06954	KLINGELBERGER, MARY CLARE	CAPT	LBE	07029	KNUTSON, RODNEY ALLEN	CAPT	SWS
06955	CLARKE, WALTER LEWIS JR.	CAPT	ILL	07030	SMITH, ALBERT LEO	LCDR	NMX
06956	KALLERES, MICHAEL PETER	VADM	NAT	07031	FOSTER, MARVIN REED	LTJG	SFR
06957	MURTHA, JOHN PATRICK JR.	Col	PDV	07032	STUBBS, CAMPBELL LAWRENCE III	LCDR	RAL
06958	HUGYA, JOHN ANTHONY	Col	PDV	07033	GREENE, WILLIAM MORRIS ARL	RADM	RAL
06959	KING, "W" "O"	CAPT	ILL	07034	MORGAN, CRAIG WALKER	LTJG	TEX
06960	EDWARDS, MICHAEL BRUCE	CAPT	SFR	07035	JONES, HARLEY THORTON	CAPT	ATL
06961	MOTT, HARRY JAMES III (BGEN)	HONOR	NY	07036	SCHWARZ, OTTO CARL (BMC)	HONOR	TEX
06962	GORCZYK, FREDERICK JOHN	CDR	NYC	07037	HAYNES, KENNETH GEORGE	RADM	NAT
06963	TRAKAS, GEORGE NICHOLAS (LCOL)	HONOR	NYC	07038	TURPIN, THOMAS JEFFERSON JR	CAPT	NAT
06964	HALL, THOMAS FORREST	RADM	FKY	07039	EVERSON, CHRISTOPHER LESLIE	LCDR	ATL
06965	GIEDRAITIS, JOHN BENJAMIN	CDR	ARZ	07040	KAUDERER, HOWARD TODD	CDR	NAT
06966	CULBERTSON, CAROL (EEN) CHANG	CDR	ARZ	07041	JUNGE, WILLIAM PATRICK	CAPT	SFR
06967	LAWRENCE, WILLIAM HENRY JR.	CDR	ARZ	07042	VERA, ALBERT JESSSE	CDR	TEX
06968	LICHTSINN, JOHN WILLIAM	CDR	ARZ	07043	NICHEL, HOWARD JULIUS	LCDR	TEX
06969	ZUMWALT, ELMO RUSSELL JR.	ADM	RAL	07044	BURKE, THOM WALTER	LT	SFR
06970	BACKUS, MARY REED	ASOC	NYC	07045	RUCK, MERRILL WYTHE	RADM	SFR
06971	BACKUS, JANE LESLIE	ASOC	NYC	07046	WIKLINSKI, STANLEY EZECHIEL	CDR	NYC
06972	COHEN, HARVEY RICHARD	CAPT	NYC	07047	MOORE, JAMES JOSEPH	DESCT	NYC
06973	RIZZI, LOUIS LEON	CAPT	NYC	07048	WEINBERGER, JACK (N)	ENS	PDV
06974	CARTNER, JOHN AUBREY	CAPT	NAT	07049	OBRIEN, KEVIN GERARD	LT	PDV
06975	MCGIFFIN, JOHN GIRVIN III	CAPT	SEF	07050	BOCKSTRUCK, LLOYD DEWITT	DESCT	TEX
06976	KINNEBERG, PAUL WILLIAM	CAPT	ILL	07051	TOOLE, MORTON EGNER	RADM	NAT
06977	KOPP, JAMES EDGAR	CAPT	SEF	07052	RUSSE, LAURENCE PRINCE II	LCDR	RAL
06978	SZEKRETAR, ALLEN ROBERT	LT	NYC	07053	LEESTMA, DAVID CORNELL	CAPT	TEX
06979	SMITH, ROBERT GEORGE JR.	LTJG	NYC	07054	BERNARD, CAROL (N)	Col	SEF
06980	METZ, ROGER "C" JR.	CAPT	ILL	07055	BRENT, GERALD PAGE	CDR	NAT
06981	MILLER, ROBERT BRUCE	CAPT	SEF	07056	PYLES, STEVE (N)	CDR	ANN
06982	GILLESPIE, JOHN CLEMENT	CAPT	PDV	07057	SMITH, DOUGLAS HENDERSON	CDR	ILL

RADM Jack Coye, USN (Ret.), a reknown submarine commander of World War II was the speaker at the San Diego Commandery's Pearl Harbor Day annual banquet at the South-Western Yacht Club. Shown to the right is Commander General Fred D. Carl congratulating him while CAPT Roy E. Williams (center), Commandery Commander,, presents the Commandery's Certificate of Appreciation to him.

Commanderies Remember
Pearl Harbor

TO RENDER HONORS AND CEREMONIES TO OUR HEROS WHO DIED AT PEARL HARBOR BECAUSE OF THE SNEAK JAPANESE ATTACK AND THE RESULTING WAR THAT FOLLOWED, COMPANIONS OF THE MASSACHUSETTS CDRY GATHERED ON BOARD THE DESTROYER CASIN YOUNG, DD-793. MOORED IN THE OLD NAVY YARD, CHARLESTON MA NOT FAR FROM WHERE THE NAVAL ORDER WAS FOUNDED IN BOSTON, JULY 4, 1890, SHE WAS NAMED AFTER CAPT CASSIN YOUNG WHO EARNED THE MEDAL OF HONOR AT PEARL HARBOR AND LATER PERISHED IN THE BATTLE FOR GUADALCANAL.

On December 7th the National Capitol Commandery held a wreath placing ceremony in Arlington National Cemetery at the Naval Order's memorial, which is inscribed "To all seafarers who have served this nation." Shown here with CAPT Charles J. Smith-(c), Commandery Commander, are two past Commanders CAPT Lisle "Art" Stroud Jr. on left and CAPT James F. Brooke who is also a past Vice Commander General.

Texas CDRY Companions salute the Flag abroad the TEXAS during the Pearl Harbor Day commemoration.

The Massachusetts commemoration included remarks and prayers by CAPT Leo M. Lazo, CDRY Commander, and the tossing of flowers into the sea by CDR Robert L. Gillen, former Commanding Officer of the CONSTITUTION, which is moored nearby.

INSIG	COMPANION	RANK	CDRY
07058			
07059	HARRINGTON, JOHN PATRICK JR.	LT	TEX
07060	LANIER, ROBERT CLAYTON	LTJG	TEX
07061			
07062	CARLETTI, JAMES SILVIO	CAPT	SDG
07063	DURBIN, JAMES LANIUS JR.	CAPT	SWS
07064	LATHROP, MITCHELL LEE	CAPT	SDG
07065	CARES, JEFFREY RICHARD	LCDR	NPT
07066	NEWMAN, JESSE DAVID	MR	SEF
07067	SCUDI, JOHN TURNER	RADM	NAT
07068	EISENBERG, ROBERT ALLEN	LT	NAT
07069	CHRISTOPHERSON, RUTH ANN	LCDR	NAT
07070			
07071			
07072	DOLLASE, STEVEN WALTER	LCDR	NAT
07073	GOUDREAU, JAMES CHRISTOPHER	LT	MAS
07074	BROWN, THOMAS RUSSELL JR.	CAPT	ATL
07075	REYNOLDS, JOHN MANNING	CAPT	SFR
07076	HEMLEY, EUGENE ADAMS	CAPT	NYC
07077	DEVEAU, PAUL EDWARD	LT	NAT
07078	KOTLARZ, CARL JAMES	LT	ARZ
07079	SHEPHERD, CHARLES WILLIAM	CAPT	ILL
07080	TROST, CARLISLE ALBERT HERMAN	ADM	NAT
07081	BROWN, WILLIAM TIMONTHY	CAPT	HRD
07082	BELLAIRS, JACQUES TERHUNE	CAPT	HRD
07083			
07084			
07085	HUGHES, DAVID CHARLES	LT	HRD
07086	FREDERICK, STEPHEN EDMUND	CDR	ATL
07087	DARBY, MICHAEL MEADOWS	CDR	HRD
07088	OLECH, MARSHALL STANLEY	LT	ILL
07089			
07090			
07091	BONDI, PETER ALBERT	RADM	NAT
07092	RYAN, MARGARET ANNE (PEG)	LT	ILL
07093	SAREERAM, RAY RUPCHAND	RADM	MAS
07094	BERCK, HENRY FRED JR.	CAPT	HRD
07095	NORDGREN, ROBERT CARL	CAPT	SWS
07096	MARTIN, ALFRED JOSEPH JR.	CAPT	NMX
07097	DEFRANCESCO, JOHN BLAZE JR.	CDR	ILL
07098	REHER, RAYMOND ROBERT	Capt	SFR
07099	HOPKINS, STEWART WRIGHT	RADM	SFR
07100	STACK, ROBERT COLE	RADM	TEX
07101	ROGERS, RICHARD SPALDING	CAPT	TEX
07102	MELLISH, WILLIAM JOSEPH	CDR	SFR
07103	ARMSTRONG, THOMAS FREDERICK	CDR	RAL
07104	ANDERSON, KAREN MAE	CDR	LBE
07105	NEAL, ROBERT PAUL	LT	ILL
07106	DONDERO, ROBERT THOMAS	CDR	SFR
07107			
07108	LINDSAY, GILBERT MOORE	CAPT	SWS
07109	BREMER, MARGARET HERRINGTON	MRS	SFR
07110	BRUMME, HERMAN (N) JR.	CAPT	TEX
07111	HILL, VIRGIL LUSK JR.	RADM	PDV
07112	REDMAYNE, RICHARD BANKS	CAPT	SEF
07113	HARGREAVES, ANDRE' CHARLES	LCDR	NAT
07114	GARBARINI, "V" "A" (GINGER)	CDR	HRD
07115	JANOSCO, KATHRYN MARY	LCDR	HRD
07116	JOHANSON, RAYMOND ROGER	CDR	HRD
07117	PRIEST, FENTON FURR III	CAPT	HRD
07118	KENNEDY, RONALD WILLARD	CAPT	SEF
07119	BAXTER, VALERIE LYNNE	LCDR	TEX
07120	BRUYERE, THOMAS EDGAR	CAPT	NAT
07121	ALLEN, MERRITT HAMILTON	LT	NAT
07122	DAVIDSON, MICHAEL LEROY	MR	SFR
07123	KEEFE, DANIEL STANTON	CDR	NYC
07124	MILLER, JAY RALPH JR.	RADM	SFR
07125	GARVIN, VAIL PRYOR	DR	PDV
07126	GANNON, FRANCIS XAVIER	CAPT	SEF
07127	ISRAEL, STEPHEN SEABROOK	RADM	TEX
07128	ROBERTSON, MONRE WAYNE	LTJG	TEX
07129	KEOUGH, ROBERT PAUL	LT	WNY
07130	KIRSTEN, GEORGE JERALD	CAPT	SFR
07131	OCONNOR, JOHN JOSEPH JR.	LCDR	ATL
07132	TANINBAUM, WARREN (N)	LCDR	ATL

INSIG	COMPANION	RANK	CDRY
07133	RENTON, WILIAM J.	CAPT	LBE
07134	WENDT, LORETTA MARY HOWARD	MRS.	ILL
07135	BACHOWSKY, PETER DIMITRI	MR	PDV
07136	HALL, DAVID EDSON	LCDR	TEX
07137	WIMBERLY, TOMMY CHARLES	CAPT	TEX
07138	WATTS, VAN (N)	CW04	LBE
07139	WALTZER, JACK ROBT.(ORIG JACOB)	CDR	NYC
07140	FLUCKEY, EUGENE BENNETT	RADM	ANN
07141	BENCHER, DENNIS LEO	CDR	NYC
07142	SILVIS, JON BRADLEY	MR	ILL
07143	KIRKPATRICK, JOHN HENRY	RADM	NAT
07144	RICHARDS, THOMAS ANDREW	Lt Col	SDG
07145	SAX, KARL (N) II	LCDR	NAT
07146	ETHRIDGE, STEPHEN ARTHUR	LCDR	SFR
07147	SPASEK, EDWARD JOHN	Col	SFR
07148	WELLS, LISALEE ANNE	CAPT	LBE
07149	HAZEN, PETER CARL	CDR	WNY
07150	CZERWONKY, JAMES HARVEY	CAPT	NAT
07151	MORRISON, VANCE HALLAM	CAPT	NAT
07152	BACHELLER, JOSEPH HENRY III	LT	SFR
07153	HILL, CHARLES HILTON	CDR	SFR
07154	BEACH, EDWARD LATIMER (NED)	CAPT	NAT
07155	BERGE, JAMES HALLARD (HAL) JR.	BGEN	NAT
07156	RYAN, JOAN SCHREIBER	MRS	SEF
07157	BODOR, GUY HUBERT	CW04	ILL
07158	DECASTRO JULIAN EDMUND III	MR	WNY
07159	ROSEN, ROBERT ARNOLD	CAPT	NYC
07160	SANDKNOP, JOHN BENJAMIN	CAPT	ILL
07161	MILLER, ROBERT BRUCE	LCDR	NAT
07162	BRECKNER, ANTHONY JACOB	CDR	WNY
07163	MONAGHAN, MARK ERIC PAUL	LCDR	NAT
07164	BROWN, GARY ESTLE	BGEN	SEF
07165	MEAD, LAWRENCE CAMPBELL	LT	JAX
07166	STEINBAUCH, CHARLES JAMES	CDR	NOR
07167	EVANS, MARSHA JOHNSON	RADM	MON
07168	OWENS, WILLIAM ARTHUR	ADM	SDG
07169	OLD, HAROLD EVANS JR.	CAPT	ILL
07170	FAMME, JOSEPH BORTNER	CDR	NAT
07171	MACH, LUDWIG FRANK	CAPT	HRD
07172	MOBILIA, ROSS FRANK	LCDR	NAT
07173	BURROWS, JOHN SHOBER JR.	CAPT	NYC
07174	TRITTEN, JAMES JOHN	CDR	HRD
07175	DURHAM, FREDERICK (N)	Capt	ILL
07176	LAMBING, CLARENCE LAWRENCE	CDR	MON
07177	ORSINI, LOUIS JOHN	CDR	NAT
07178	WADDELL, JOHN WILLIAM	CAPT	NAT
07179	BAUER, FRANK GEORGE	CAPT	ANN
07180	ANDERSON, LISA ANNE	LT	ATL
07181	CIOE, MARIAN (N) (MARY)	CDR	ILL
07182	POTTS, ANTHONY VINCENT	LCDR	ILL
07183	D'ORSO, JAMES NICHOLAS	CDR	ILL
07184	SCHLESINGER, EDWARD SAMUEL	LT	NYC
07185	HARDY, JOHN PAUL	Maj.	SFR
07186	MORRIS, GERALD MITCHELL	LTJG	TEX
07187	HARRINGTON, JAMES JOSEPH	CAPT	TEX
07188	GHOMLEY, RALPH MCDOUGALL	RADM	NAT
07189	CONWAY, JOHN JOSEPH	CAPT	SFR
07190	DONOVAN, ROBERT WILLIAM	LTJG	ILL
07191	MCCAFFERY, THOMAS FRANCIS	CDR	NAT
07192	COLE, BERNARD DAVID	CAPT	NAT
07193	KOMOROWSKY, RAYMOND ANTHONY A.	CAPT	NAT
07194	MCCLEASEY, KEVIN BRIAN	CAPT	HRD
07195	WILLIAMSON, CHARLES THOMAS	Col	NAT
07196	HIGGINS, JOHN JOSEPH	CDR	NAT
07197	SUTHERLAND-HALL, FRANK SHELTON	MR	TEX
07198	MASON, RAYMOND MULFORD	LT	SDG
07199	WINDLE, WILLIAM WOODARD	LT	TEX
07200	MCCAMERON, JAMES DAVID	CAPT	SFR
07201	SHARKEY, WILLIAM RICHARD III	CDR	SFR
07202	FEERICK, JAMES PAUL	MR	ILL
07203	FEERICK, JOHN PAUL	CAPT	ILL
07204	BOORDA, JEREMY MICHAEL	ADM	NAT
07205	HULSEBOSCH, JESSICA (N)	MRS.	SEF
07206	DODGE, WINIFRED JOHN O'LEAL	MRS.	SFR
07207	WEBBER, MICHAEL JON	CAPT	SWS

Pearl Harbor Observances

Top Far Left: The Naval Order is committed to helping all citizens to remember that "Day of Infamy" to honor those Americans who made the supreme sacrifice and as a reminder that maintaining our military preparedness is essential. In a message to Local Commanderies, the Commander General said: " I am very concerned that the light of freedom surfacing in Europe, not to be allowed to eclipse the lamp of eternal vigilance. The lesson of December 7th must not be forgotten. It must be our beacon, guiding us to steer a true and safe course."

In Chicago, the Illinois Commandery conducted its annual ceremony at the Daley Center. The participation of Major Richard Daley this year added to occasion, covered by major news media. Following his remarks the Major jioned CAPT Roman Piotrowski, Commandery Commander, in placing a wreath at the Sternal Flame after which a Navy bugler sounded taps. The program was attended by representatives of of several local military commands, Companions from the Commandery, including immediate Past Commander General Fred D. Carl, and some two hundred pedestrians who stopped for it. A City Council resolution said in part "...and urge all citizen and public buildings to fly their U. S. Flags in order that we never forget Pearl Harbor Day—a day which has become a part of our American heritage..."

Top Right: Framed by the Commandery's wreath at Chicago's eternal flame, Captain George R. Dutton, Jr., Immediate Past Commander of the Illinois Commandery, pays a December 7 tribute to the men and women who last their lives at Pearl Harbor 40 years before.

Such a tribute is an annual affair of the Illinois Commandery. It is always followed by the Commandery. It is always followed by the Commandery's Pearl Harbor Day banquet. Rear Admiral James H. Flatley III USN, Commander of the U.S. Naval Training Station ay Great Lakes, was the principal speaker for the 1981 event.

Left: Admiral Carlisle A. M. Trost, Chief of Naval Operations, and CAPT Milton C. Lapp, Commander, Southeast Florida Commandery, at the Pearl Harbor Day commemorative luncheon in Palm Beach, FL.

Below: The 86 Companions and guests who attendeed the San Francisco Commander's annual Pearl Harbor Day stag banquet. Principal speaker was Rear Admiral P.T. Smith USN, Commander Patrol Wings, U.S. Pacific Fleet.

INSIG	COMPANION	RANK	CDRY	INSIG	COMPANION	RANK	CDRY
07208	KELLY, ROGER VAN	Maj.	SFR	07283	JOHNSON, KENNETH MAINE	LCDR	MON
07209	SATTERFIELD, GARY THOMAS	CAPT	NAT	07284	BRIGGS, STEVEN RUSSELL	RADM	LBE
07210	SWINGER, ALAN WILLIAM	CAPT	NAT	07285	COX, KENNETH EUGENE	CAPT	NAT
07211	LINFORD, HELEN ROBERTSON	MRS	NYC	07286	DAVIS, CHARLES EDWARD	CDR	NAT
07212	MCNAMARA, JOSEPH H.	Lt Col	NYC	07287	RENO, WILLIAM JAMES	LCDR	NYC
07213	VISCOGLIOSI ANTHONY GAETANO	LT	NYC	07288	MERRITT, BROOKS PALMER JR.	CDR	MON
07214	WALKER, LEWIS MIDGLEY JR.	CDR	NYC	07289	BECK, BARRIE LEE	MRS.	SEF
07215	KING, MICHAEL JAMES	CAPT	SFR	07290	SENCINDIVER, JAMES DANIEL	CDR	NAT
07216	MOORE, GEORGE MALCOLM	CAPT	SFR	07291	LEWIS, CHARLES A. JR.	LT	RAL
07217	POWELL, JOHN DOUGLAS-ROBERT	CAPT	SFR	07292	WILLIAMS, SUZANNE BARWICK	MS	NAT
07218	RICE, KINGSLEY LORING (JIM) JR.	LT	SFR	07293	PIGNOTTI, DENNIS ALEXANDER	CAPT	NAT
07219	TEMPEST, MARK JACQUOT	CAPT	TEX	07294	RICE, CHARLES LANE	CAPT	ILL
07220	HOFFMAN, PAUL MYLTON	CDR	MON	07295	GALINDO, ROBERT AUGUSTUS	LT	SFR
07221	PERKINS, FRANK ALLAN	CAPT	MON	07296	PENICK, ANDRICO QUINNTRAL	LT	SFR
07222	MAUCK, CHARLES JOEL III	CAPT	MON	07297	SHETENHELM, PHILIP EMERSON	CAPT	MON
07223	GANTER, JANICE PATRICIA MORRIS	MRS	NAT	07298	CROCCO, FRANCIS BARTHOLOMEW	CAPT	SEF
07224	GOODALL, THOMAS DAVID	CDR	JAX	07299	LINCOLN, CHARLES TURNER	PNCS	PDV
07225	ROSER, H. GARY	COL	MON	07300	SIMPSON, DAVID MILES	CDR	ATL
07226	HOUSTON, WILLARD SAMUEL JR.	CAPT	MON	07301	HALL, GEORGE N.	Capt	SFR
07227	LAMBING, JANE WILLIAMS	MRS	MON	07302	WATTS, ROBERT DARRYL	CAPT	PNS
07228	SPOWART, DAVID JOSEPH	CDR	MON	07303	BREMER, WILLIAM RICHARD JR.	MR	SFR
07229	BERC, HAROLD THANE	LT	ILL	07304	DEMY, TIMOTHY JAMES	CDR	NPT
07230	ARNOLD, JOHN ELWIN	CAPT	NAT	07305	KVAALEN, ARNE KRISTIAN	LTJG	NAT
07231	GRANT, RICHARD LEE	CDR	SWS	07306	EISENBERG, ROBERT ALAN	LT	NAT
07232	MCNITT, ALLEN LAWSON JR.	CAPT	SFR	07307	MORRELL, JAMES MICHAEL	CAPT	SDG
07233	ANDERSON, WILLIAM WARNER JR.	LT	SFR	07308	STEPHENS, GREGORY FRANKLIN	LCDR	TEX
07234	PEKARSKY, SARA JEAN	LCDR	MON	07309	WEIGEL, CHARLES JOSPEH II	LT	TEX
07235	MAUZ, HENRY HERRWARD JR.	ADM	MON	07310	MADDONALD, JOHN FRANKLIN	CAPT	ILL
07236	ROBINSON, CHARLES LEON	CAPT	NAT	07311	STEAGALL, WILLIAM FRANCIS JR.	CAPT	ILL
07237	BLOCK, CHARLES ERNEST	CAPT	ANN	07312	FESLER, DIANE MARIE	LT	ILL
07238	CRAGIN, CHARLES LANGMAID III	CAPT	NAT	07313	SKOWRONEK, LESLIE JEANNE	CAPT	NAT
07239	WEST, MICHAEL CHRISTOPHER	CDR	NAT	07314	KINNEY, GILBERT FORD	CAPT	MON
07240	BEGBIE, ALBERT JOSEPH	CAPT	MON	07315	BENOIT, ARTHUR EDWARD	CDR	MON
07241	NEVIUS, JOHN HOWARD	LCDR	SEF	07316	OLDEN, KEVIN WILLIAM	CAPT	SFR
07242	CAREY, GERARD MARTIN	LTJG	NYC	07317	NORTON, JOHN JEROME	Col	SFR
07243	STROH, GREGORY FRANCIS	LCDR	NAT	07318	LA COURSE, ANTHONY LAWRENCE	LT	MAS
07244	PARCELL, PAUL WHITNEY	RADM	HRD	07319	MCALILEY, JOHN RICHARD III	LT	ATL
07245	NESTLERODE, WILLIAM AUSTIN	CAPT	TEX	07320	TURNER, JAMES ROGERS JR.	LCDR	SDG
07246	TAYLOR, DEAN (N) JR.	CAPT	MON	07321	CATENA, EMANUELA NELLIE MARIE	CDR	SFR
07247	DEL TORO, CARLOS	CDR	SDG	07322	STEINMETZ, JOHN JUTHER	CDR	SFR
07248	BEIN, GEORGE EDWARD	LCDR	MON	07323	COLLINS, BOBBI LORRAINE	LCDR	MON
07249	ARCHAMBAULT, GUY ANDRE'	CAPT	NPT	07324	BAUMGARDNER, HUGH WIRTH	CAPT	NAT
07250	NELSON, RICHARD NORMAN	CAPT	NAT	07325	THOMPSON, RICHARD ALLEN	CAPT	NAT
07251	DUNHAM, RICHARD CLYDE ALLAN	LT	SFR	07326	PYKOSH, HENRY PAUL	CAPT	NAT
07252	STANSFIELD, PATRICK JOHN	LCDR	NAT	07327	SEIGEL, LEONARD MITCHELL	CAPT	SEF
07253	ZILINSKY, THOMAS JOHN	CAPT	TEX	07328	MEHRHOFF, WILLIAM ROBERT	CAPT	PDV
07254	EMIL, ARTHUR DAVID	LTJG	NYC	07329	PACE, JOHN RAY	LTJG	TEX
07255	POULTON, WILLIAM LAWRENCE	CDR	NYC	07330	VON SAUNDER, RAYMOND OSCAR	CDR	NAT
07256	LUNDEBERG, PHILIP KARL	CDR	NAT	07331	LAWRENCE, JAMES FUGATE	BGEN	NAT
07257	CAUDILL, MICHAEL RAY	LCDR	NAT	07332	JONES, WILBUR DAVID JR.	CAPT	NAT
07258	LEVIEN, FREDERIC HOWARD	CDR	MON	07333	FALGE, FRANCIS M.	CAPT	MON
07259	NAKAGAWA, GORDON ROSS	CAPT	MON	07334	WORRELL, HAROLD LENFORD	CW03	SDG
07260	WILSON, JACQUELIN GATES	MRS.	MON	07335	RUD, GILMAN EVERETT	CAPT	SWS
07261	JAFFE, WILLIAM IRVING	LCDR	SEF	07336	DUDLEY, WILLIAM SHELDON	LT	ANN
07262	WENDROW, BERNARD (N)	ENS	ILL	07337	HICKEY, ROBERT PHILIP	RADM	SWS
07263	HAMMOND, WELDON WOOLF	CAPT	TEX	07338	WEDVICK, DWYER QUENTIN	Capt	NYC
07264	QUINONES, ABEL MACARIO	WO	MON	07339	MOFFITT, LLOYD WILLIAM	RADM	SEF
07265	LIMBERG, DANIEL BERNARD	LT	MON	07340	JONES, HENRY JR.	CDR	MON
07266	BALDWIN, JOHN FRANCIS	CAPT	MON	07341	MILLER, CHRISTINE MARIE	CDR	NAT
07267	PALKO, DANIEL ANTHONY	LCDR	PDV	07342	PHILBIN, WILLIAM JOSEPH	Maj.	ANN
07268	RUBISON, LAURA LEE	LT	NAT	07343	SAUNDERS, NORMAN THOMAS	RADM	FKY
07269	HALL, JAMES BENNETT	CDR	MON	07344	THOMAS, GARY MICHAEL	LCDR	NAT
07270	DUGAN, SCOTT EDWARD	LT	MON	07345	EDWARDS, WILLIAM EVERETT	Capt	NYC
07271	THORNTON, MICHAEL EDWIN	LT	TEX	07346	WILSON, CHRISTOPHER TODD	CAPT	SWS
07272	MERCER, THOMAS ALEXANDER	RADM	MON	07347	JAEGER, RICHARD JOSEPH III	CAPT	SWS
07273	HAMMOND, TERRENCE EUGENE	LT	MON	07348	ROBINSON, DAVID BROOKS	VADM	TEX
07274	HEALD, JOSEPH FRANK	CAPT	SFR	07349	ZALUDEK, GEORGE MICHAEL	CAPT	SWS
07275	HUGHES, WAYNE PHILO JR.	CAPT	MON	07350	ENCH, JOHN (JACK) CLYDE	CAPT	SWS
07276	BLOCH, ROY STEPHEN	LCDR	MON	07351	NIBE, RICHARD JEROME	RADM	NAT
07277	SPENCER, LARRY HOWARD	CDR	MON	07352	ROGERS, DAVID NEIL	RADM	SWS
07278	GOVER, JOHN BARRETT	LTJG	JAX	07353	KOETJE, FREDERIK ENRICO	CAPT	NAT
07279	HOSHKO, JOHN (N) JR.	CDR	NAT	07354	STONE, JAMES HIRAM	1ST Lt	NOR
07280	SASS, ARTHUR HAROLD	CAPT	NAT	07355	GREER, ROBERT COLLINS IV	CDR	SEF
07281	HACKER, BENJAMIN THURMAN	RADM	HRD	07356	LOREN, DONALD PATRICK	CAPT	NAT
07282	JOHNSON, DENNIS JOY	LT	MAS	07357	COLLINS, JAMES EDWARD	CAPT	NAT

Key figures in the Southwest Commandery's banquet held in connection with its annual Pearl Harbor Day weekend program at the Racquet Club in Palm Springs, CA: From left – Incoming Commandery Commander, CAPT Donald B. Edge; VADM John H. Fettermann, Jr., USN, Commander, Naval Air Force, U.S. Pacific Flett; VADM Diego E. Hernandez, USN, Commander U.S. Third Flett and guest speaker; CAPT Fred D. Carl, Commander General NOUS; and outgoing Commandery Commander, CAPT H. Robert Pearl.

CAPT Frad D. Carl, Commander General Elect, and CDR Sid Daniel, Commander, National Capitol Commandery, hold up new Naval Order flag in front of recently planted blue spruce tree after unveiling the marble marker during dedicatory services in Arlington National Cemetery on July 4th. The bronze plaque on top is inscribed "To all seafarers who served our country"–"Naval Order of the United States".

CAPT John C. Rice Jr., Commander General, NOUS, and CAPT John Lawrence, Pres., Pearl Harbor Survivors Association, accompanied by a member of the Honor Guard, return to their places after laying their wreath at the Tomb of the Unknowns in Arlington National Cemetery.

(1-r)Jim Balcer, a Marine veteran and Director of Veterans Affairs, representing Chicago Mayor Daley, CAPT George R. Wendt; Illinois Commandery Commander, and Arlandres L. Dixon, a Pearl Harbor survivor, salute during the playing of taps following the placing of the wreath by CAPT Wendt at the eternal flame in Daley Center Plaza. The public ceremony, annually sponsored by the Illinois Commandery, marked the 51st anniversary of the bombing of Pearl Harbor. In his remarks, Mr. Balcer reminded the audience of the necessity for the nation to remain militarily prepared RADM William Thompson, President; Navy Memorial Foundation, was the guest of honor and speaker at the Commandery's Formal Dinner Banquet

INSIG	COMPANION	RANK	CDRY	INSIG	COMPANION	RANK	CDRY
07358	CAPEN, GEORGE SIGURD	LT	SDG	07433	BOOMER, WALTER E.	GEN	NAT
07359	OLECHNOWICZ, STEPHEN MYRON	CDR	NAT	07434	SMITH, CARMEN M.	MRS.	TEX
07360	TALLEY, DARRELL LEE	LCDR	TEX	07435	FRATARANGELO, PAUL A.	MGEN	SFR
07361	HEARNEY, RICHARD DAVIS	GEN	NAT	07436	CIARDELLO, CARMEN A.	RADM	PNS
07362	WOOD-HARVEY, DARLENE R.	CDR	NAT	07437	CASINI, VINCINZO	CAPT	NAT
07363	BURKE, ROBERTA	MRS	NAT	07438	NIETO, WILLIAM JR.	CAPT	ANN
07364	SMITH, ALBERT GEORGE	CDR	SFR	07439	PROKOP, PAUL JEFFREY	CAPT	NOR
07365	REMUS, THOMAS ALLAN	CAPT	SFR	07440	LOEFSTEDT, WILLIAM JOSEPH	CAPT	NOR
07366	GARCIA, MARCIAL EDWARD	CDR	SFR	07441	DEWEY, ROBERT AUSTIN	MR.	PDV
07367	KING, DANIEL GEORGE	MR	NYC	07442	CUNY, THOMAS BACON	LCDR	TEX
07368	WAGGENER, ANNA THOMPSON	CDR	MOB	07443	HETHERINGTON, DONALD LEROY	CAPT	TEX
07369	BERNARDO, JOHN JOSEPH	LCDR	MOB	07444	SLOANE, STORY JONES JR.	MR	TEX
07370	ROSENTHAL ROBERT NATHAN	LT	SFR	07445	ROOKS, HAROLD REDFIELD	MR	TEX
07371	WITT, KENNETH HENRY	HONOR	SEF	07446	SWANK, JAMES ROBERT	LTJG	TEX
07372	WEBB, SOLON DALE	CAPT	SFR	07447	FREESE, RALPH FRANCIS	CDR	NAT
07373	SETTLE, PETER MICHAEL	CAPT	SFR	07448	STOEHR, LEONARD ARTHUR	CAPT	NAT
07374	HUFFINE, DONALD HARRIS	CAPT	SFR	07449	COILE, RUSSELL CLEVEN	Col	MON
07375	KIRSCHTEN, JOSEPH DICKEN (DICK)	LTJG	NAT	07450	FINERTY, GARY THOMAS	CAPT	MAS
07376	FISHER, JOHN RICHARD	RADM	ARZ	07451	BUCK, NICHOLAS VINCENT	LCDR	NAT
07377	BURROWS, MARION DUVAL	MRS	SEF	07452	CONROY, THOMAS LOUIS	CAPT	MON
07378	MCCAFFREE, BURNHAM CLOUGH	RADM	NAT	07453	PICKETT, CHARLES DELOSS	CAPT	SWS
07379	ANCELL, ROBERT MANNING	LCDR	NAT	07454	FREEBORN, GUY HERBERT	CDR	SWS
07380	GRIFFITHS, CHARLES HENRY	VADM	NAT	07455	PEARSON, LARRY GLENN	CAPT	SWS
07381	HILTON, JACK	CAPT	NAT	07456	ARRIVEE, KIM ARTHUR	LCDR	SFR
07382	MURRAY, TON REED II	CAPT	NAT	07457	TINLING, JESSIE GUNDRY	MRS.	SFR
07383	AMES, FRED LEWIS	RADM	SFR	07458	STONE, SUE LINNIA	MRS	SFR
07384	KAHN, GREGORY WALTER	LCDR	NOR	07459	FELGER, JEAN HERZ	MRS.	NAT
07385	DAVIS, DONALD ALEXANDER	CAPT	TEX	07460	MOSCOSO DEL PRADO, FERMIN	CAPT	NAT
07386	PEHL, CHARLES EDWARD SR.	CAPT	TEX	07461	CAMPBELL, VICTOR SCOTT	LTJG	NYC
07387	JOHNSON, KENNETH ALBIN	CAPT	NAT	07462	SHERMAN, WILLIAM GEORGE	LT	SWS
07388	STUBBS, WILLARD BACON	LCDR	NPT	07463	SASSEN, GRANT WILLIAM	CAPT	SWS
07389	NORTH, ROBERT CLYDE	RADM	NAT	07464	KELLEY, JERRY ROBERT	CAPT	TEX
07390	WATSON, ANTHONY JOHN	RADM	NAT	07465	HERB, MARION ATHEARN	MS.	SFR
07391	LAUTENBACHER, CONRAD C. JR.	VADM	NAT	07466	SIMMONS, ROBERT DON	LT	MON
07392	HOMAN, JAMES ARTHUR	Col	ILL	07467	HAVNEN, CHARLES RANSOM	CDR	NOR
07393	SPENCER, THOMAS FREDERICK	LT	NYC	07468	BESAL, ROBERT EUGENE	CAPT	HRD
07394	LEE, BRUCE (N)	MR	NYC	07469	BOLT, MARGARET HEWETT	MRS.	SFR
07395	NEVANS, ROY NORMAN	LCDR	NYC	07470	DUNNE, JACK HARRY III	Lt Col	PDV
07396	HENNESSEY, JAYNE CECELIA	LCDR	NOR	07471	BREAST, JERRY CREIGHTON	RADM	SWS
07397	HENNESSEY, ALOYSIUS GONZAGA JR.	CAPT	NOR	07472	PALMER, JERRY DALE	CAPT	SWS
07398	SANDS, JACK BAIR	MR	NOR	07473	JOSIAH, TIMOTHY WILLIAM	VADM	NOR
07399	LILES, RAEFORD BRILEY	LTJG	NYC	07474	DEVAULT, RICHARD HERBERT	CAPT	NOR
07400	ROLLINS, BRYAN LEE	CAPT	SWS	07475	EVANS, FRANK GARRETTSON	Capt	TEX
07401	BOENNIGHAUSEN, ROGER PAUL	CAPT	SWS	07476	SOMERVILLE, JOY ELENWOOD	1ST Lt	SFR
07402	BROWN, DAVID LYNN	CDR	NAT	07477	KRAUSE, DEIRDRE ANNE	CDR	SEF
07403	JOHNSTON, FRANCIS XAVIER III	CAPT	SFR	07478	RESEDEAN, PETER ROBERT	CDR	PNS
07404	ZEZULKA, KENNETH HARRY	CAPT	NOR	07479	SCHEYE, EDWARD H. JR.	CDR	PNS
07405	WHIDDON, WILLIAM DAVID	CAPT	NOR	07480	REYNOLDS, ROBERT FRANCIS	1ST Lt	SFR
07406	RITTER, RONALD AIRES	CDR	SDG	07481	GERFIN, ANDREW LOTZ JR.	CAPT	NOR
07407	MUIR, MALCOLM JR.	MR	NAT	07482	MOLANO, WALTER THOMAS	LCDR	NYC
07408	BOWELL, JOHN HOWARD	CAPT	NAT	07483	KINYON, WILKINSON OWEN	MR	ILL
07409	BROOKE, MARGARET WOODALL	MRS.	NAT	07484	KINYON, PAUL JOSEPH	MR	ILL
07410	EISNER, EDWARD THOMAS	LT	ARZ	07485	KINYON, JOHN HOEY	MR	ILL
07411	MCDAVID, ELIJAH LLEWELLYN	CDR	NAT	07486	KEITH, STEPHEN THOMAS	RADM	NOR
07412	WHEELER, WAYNE CABLE	LT	SFR	07487	MORRIS, MARK FRANKLIN	CDR	TEX
07413	WOODBURY, BARBARA JOHN	MS	SWS	07488	ERIKSON, MICHAEL SCOTT	LCDR	HRD
07414	WHITE, JOHN STANTON	CAPT	NOR	07489	LANGE, ROBERT JOHN	CDR	NOR
07415	SINCOX, JAMES JOHN	MR	PDV	07490	KAVANAGH, COLEMAN ANTHONY	CAPT	TEX
07416	LANGSTON, ARTHUR NAVARRO III	RADM	SWS	07491	GRIPPI, JOHN AMBROSE	CAPT	SFR
07417	MERLIN, ALICE VOLK	MRS.	TEX	07492	DEVINEY, JAMES RAYMOND	CDR	PNS
07418	HOLBEN, NEIL EDWARD	CAPT	NAT	07493	WHALEN, DAVID ALOYSIUS	CDR	PNS
07419	LLOYD, DOUGLAS LYNN	CDR	NOR	07494	LINDSEY, ANDREW EDGAR	CAPT	PNS
07420	FARRELL, WILLIAM JOSEPH	MR	NYC	07495	FIDLER, NEVIN LLOYD JR.	CDR	SFR
07421	JONES, JONATHAN CORNWELL	LT	NYC	07496	ROSS, SHARON FITZGERALD	CDR	SEF
07422	ADAMS, JOHN QUINCY	CDR	NYC	07497	GUTHRIE, BRUCE BRADFORD	LCDR	NAT
07423	ADELAAR, WILLIAM RONALD	LT	NYC	07498	SOMMER, JAMES ALOYSIUS	LT	WNY
07424	HAWKINS, KATHERINE P.	MRS.	SFR	07499	MCTIGHE, ROGER PAUL	CDR	SWS
07425	CLARK, RICHARD R.	CAPT	SFR	07500	WALSH, DAVID EDWARD	LCDR	SWS
07426	LUPONE, DONALD F.	CAPT	PNS	07501	O'REILLY, ARTHUR MICHAEL	Col	PNS
07427	BRINSON, FRANCES W.	MRS.	RAL	07502	KRUCKE, HANS HERMANN	CAPT	PNS
07428	PHILLIPS, HENRY L.	CAPT	ANN	07503	TREIS, ROBERT ENLOW	CAPT	PNS
07429	READY, JOHN K,	VADM	SWS	07504	REINWALD, CHARLES ANTHONY	LTJG	SEF
07430	CARL, JANET MACINTOSH	MRS.	SEF	07505	MCLOONE, HUGH EDWARD	CAPT	SFR
07431	MCGINNISS, HUGH JOHN	MR.	PDV	07506	CATO, CARL SALOMON	LT	NAT
07432	JEREMIAH, DAVID E.	ADM	NAT	07507	MCDOUGALL, THOMAS DONALD	LCDR	NAT

Above: Chief of Naval Operations ADM Vern Clark spoke to Companions of the Southeast Florida Commandery at their annual Pearl Harbor Day luncheon. Shown with the CNO are past Commander General CAPT Fred Carl on the left and Commandery Commander RADM Julian R. Benjamin. Left: J. William Middendorf II. While serving the public as Ambassador to the Netherlands, and as Secretary of the Navy, has also been active as

a composer, having written over thirty marches, several symphonies, concerti, piano and violin solos, and a opera.
Being the patriotic American that he is, mr. Middendorf has written and dedicated his marches to great Americans and to great American musical orgenizations. His "Old Ironsides" march was written for and dedicated to Arthur Fiedler, who premiered the work with the Boston Pops Orchestra. To honor the Sea Services, "Brave Marines", "Navy On The Go" and "Coast Guard March" were written while he served as Secretary of the Navy.

Conductor Score

To Admiral of the Navy George Dewey
and Companions of the Naval Order,
Past and Present

The Naval Order March

for

Concert Band

first played at the Navy Memorial, Washington DC September 27, 1799

by

J. Wm. Middendorf, II

Instrumentation List

4 - Pic / Flute	2 - Cornet 1	1 - Trombone 1
2 - Oboe	2 - Cornet 2	1 - Trombone 2
	2 - Cornet 3	1 - Trombone 3
2 - Clarinet 1		2 - Euphonium (TC/BC)
2 - Clarinet 2		3 - Tuba
2 - Clarinet 3		1 - String Bass
1 - Bass Clarinet	2 - French Horn 1/2	1 - Snare Drum
2 - Bassoon	2 - French Horn 3/4	1 - Bass Dm./Cym.
2 - Alto Sax 1/2		1 - Bells
1 - Tenor Sax		
1 - Baritone Sax	1 - Conductor Score	

CIMARRON Music & Productions
Dallas, Texas 75247

INSIG	COMPANION	RANK	CDRY	INSIG	COMPANION	RANK	CDRY
07508	PALMER, GARY WAYNE	CAPT	NYC	07583	REDSHAW, MICHAEL DENNIS	CAPT	ANN
07509	GUBSER, CHARLES SAMUEL	MR	NAT	07584	REDSHAW, MARY COTTRELL	LCDR	ANN
07510	CHAVEZ, RUBEN	Capt	ANN	07585	ANDERSON, BARBARA L.	MRS	FKY
07511	MCNABB, JERRY ELVIN	CAPT	PNS	07586	JORDON, JOSEPH CORNELIUS	MR	SFR
07512	MCCLAIN, JOSEPH ADOLPHUS	CAPT	TEX	07587	PICKETT, LARRY JAMES	CAPT	JAX
07513	HERRMANN, LACY BUNNELL	MR.	NYC	07588	KARONIS, JEFFREY KEY	CDR	NAT
07514	ABBOTT, FREDERICK FRASER	LT	ILL	07589	EDONE, JOSEPH CHARLES	LT	LBE
07515	BEARSS, EDWIN COLE	MR	NAT	07590	KELLER, ALBERT PETER II	LT	TEX
07516	WHITE, THOMAS RICHARD	CDR	SFR	07591	WIGHT, RANDY LEE	CDR	MON
07517	WILEY, TOVA PETERSEN	CDR	SFR	07592	MCCULLOUGH, STUART WILLIAM	CAPT	SFR
07518	SCHULTZ, JAMES RICHIE	LT	SFR	07593	WHITKOP, ROBERT NILS	CDR	JAX
07519	DOVE, LARRY EUGENE	CDR	LBE	07594	IRELAN, DENNIS WAYNE	CAPT	SWS
07520	WEDDING, GREGORY LOUIS	CAPT	ATL	07595	HUGHEY, LORRAINE DONNA	MS	SFR
07521	ARTKE, CALVIN	MR.	NYC	07596	MEZZADRI, FRANK XAVIER	CAPT	SWS
07522	GORMAN, THOMAS JOSEPH	CDR	NYC	07597	CLARK, JACK C.	CDR	SWS
07523	CUTLER, THOMAS JOSHUA	LCDR	ANN	07598	EVERT, RICHARD DOWNEY	CAPT	SWS
07524	LANSING, JAMES CATHER	LT	SFR	07599	O'DOWD, MARGARET DEMPSEY	LTJG	MON
07525	DORION, ROBERT CHARLES	LTJG	NAT	07600	SEKKEL, RONALD PETER	LT	MON
07526	ROHRBACH, CAROLEE M.	MRS.	SEF	07601	WALKER, WILLIAM BENJAMIN JR.	CAPT	RAL
07527	MANNING, JOHN JOSEPH	LT	NAT	07602	VISTICA, MARGARET MAY	MRS	SFR
07528	PORTO, JOSEPH ANTHONY	LCDR	TEX	07603	ORR, WILLIAM STEWART	CAPT	SWS
07529	OLSEN, ALLEN N.	CAPT	MON	07604	TRAFTON, WILBUR COBB	CAPT	SWS
07530	LANGE, ROBERT JOHN JR	MR	NAT	07605	DAVIS, JOHN RAY	CAPT	SWS
07531	BALDWIN, GEORGE HEISLER	CAPT	SEF	07606	BOYER, JAMES CHARLES	CAPT	TEX
07532	POPE, ROSE HELEN	LCDR	ATL	07607	STERLING, PHILIP HAMILTON	MR	TEX
07533	HANTHORN, RUSSELL LEROY	Col	SDG	07608	KAPLAN, BRADLEY JAY	CAPT	NAT
07534	BROWNING, ROBERT MONROE JR	MR	NAT	07609	MORRISON, JULIAN KNOX III	LT	NAT
07535	FOWLER, JAMES LOFTUS	Col	NYC	07610	ATKINS, HAROLD TURNER	CDR	NYC
07536	HAYMAKER, WILLIS GRAHAM JR.	LT	SFR	07611	REY, WILLIAM JOHN	MR	ARZ
07537	WALSH, BERNARD	CAPT	PNS	07612	LANT, JAMES HAWTHORNE	CAPT	ANN
07538	MARQUIS, JACK STEWART	LCDR	PNS	07613	LARMORE, DIANA GOFF	MR	ANN
07539	KOWALCZYK-BECKWORTH, JOAN ANN	CAPT	SDG	07614	CREEKMAN, CHARLES TODD	CAPT	NAT
07540	PICKAVANCE, WILLIAM WILSON	RADM	SWS	07615	WARKENTIEN, DAVID JEFFREY	CDR	SEF
07541	PETERSEN, ROY DAVID	CAPT	ATL	07616	STEMPER, MARION FRAIN	LT	NYC
07542	KAISER, DAVID GORDON	CAPT	NAT	07617	BOORDA, ROBERT NATHAN	LCDR	NAT
07543	MCKINNEY, HENRY CLAYTON	RADM	NAT	07618	SHEFFIELD, JULIA SPANN	MRS.	JAX
07544	HOWARD, VICTOR	LT	SFR	07619	DAVIS, STEPHEN FAIRBANK	LCDR	JAX
07545	MOREY, DAVID BARNETT	Lt Col	NOR	07620	RONCOLATO, GERALD DAVID	CDR	JAX
07546	DANIELSEN, ARNOLD MELVIN	RADM	CON	07621	SOBECK, DENNIS JAMES	CDR	JAX
07547	BROWN, JOHN EDWARD	CAPT	SWS	07622	AVERILL, ROBERT CAMERON	CDR	JAX
07548	BUCKLEY, JOHN THOMAS	LCDR	SFR	07623	HEWETT, RONALD EDWARD	CAPT	NAT
07549	ARTHUR, STANLEY ROGER	ADM	NAT	07624	KLINE, EDWARD CHARLES JR.	CAPT	NAT
07550	NEATHERY, JAMES WESLEY	CAPT	SDG	07625	LAPKIN, STEVEN ANTHONY	LT	SFR
07551	HOWELL, PAUL NEILSON	RADM	TEX	07626	FURUKAWA, ROBERT JON	LCDR	NOR
07552	THOMPSON, WILLIAM GLENN	LCDR	TEX	07627	DANNER, ANN SUBLETTE	LCDR	ANN
07553	MOORE, LOUIS MOREIRA	LTJG	TEX	07628	PIROTTE, STEVEN JOHN	LT	ANN
07554	CLIME, ROBERT HENRY	CAPT	NAT	07629	BERGSTROM, ROBERT WILLIAM	LT	ARZ
07555	SCHNEIDER, STEPHEN EVERETT	LT	SFR	07630	DAUS, RUDOLPH HALOUK	CAPT	NAT
07556	ANDERSON, H. SCOTT	ENS	SFR	07631	NOVACK, PAUL DAVID	HONOR	SEF
07557	GOODALE, SARAH E.	MS.	ARZ	07632	WALSH, CHRISTOPHER	LT	NAT
07558	BERGER, RICHARD K	MR	NYC	07633	KARLE, EDWARD WILLIAM	LTJG	NYC
07559	WEBER, HELMUT ERNST	MR	SDG	07634	GIES, ERIC PATRICK	LT	SFR
07560	PALERNO, PAMELA BLANCHE	MS.	TEX	07635	GARRETT, PATRICK MARTIN	CAPT	SDG
07561	PILIE, JOSEPH MAURICE	LTJG	NOR	07636	MC LEAN, EDWARD SMITH	MR	ANN
07562	MASSIMI, ROBERT FRANCIS	CAPT	NOR	07637	ZANIN, ERIC FRANCIS	LT	NPT
07563	PILIE, MILDRED FORTIER	MRS	NOR	07638	MC COMB, DENNIS NEILL	CAPT	ARZ
07564	SEEGER, ISRAEL GENALYAH	LCDR	NYC	07639	THOMPSON, PETER MICHAEL	CDR	NAT
07565	KENTON, ROLAND H.	CAPT	NYC	07640	BUDAI, DONALD MICHAEL	CAPT	LBE
07566	SILLMAN, JAMES HENRY	LCDR	NAT	07641	RYTELL, FRANK EUGENE JR.	CAPT	SDG
07567	FROEHLICH, EDWARD WILLIAM JR.	CAPT	JAX	07642	INGRAM, RICHARD CAMERON	CAPT	NAT
07568	BRUNELLI, JOHN FRANCIS	RADM	NOR	07643	KENNEDY, JACK MARTIN	CAPT	NAT
07569	MCMULLEN, WILLIAM THOMAS	RADM	TEX	07644	BULLER, WARREN ROSS II	LT	NAT
07570	VISTICA, GREGORY THOMAS	MR	SFR	07645	HEYER, THOMAS N.	MR	ANN
07571	DUNLOP, DAVID BARTLETT	CAPT	JAX	07646	WENZ, CARL ROBERT JR.	LT	NAT
07572	WILLANDT, THEODORE AUGUST	CAPT	JAX	07647	COLLINS, WINIFRED QUICK	CAPT	NAT
07573	DAUBENSPECK, DAVID GRANT	CAPT	PDV	07648	ISRAEL, THOMAS JEFFERSON	LCDR	ANN
07574	BLANCHARD, GEORGE KILBEY JR.	CDR	NOR	07649	FITZGERALD, JOHN WILLIAM	CAPT	JAX
07575	JONES, JEANNE RENEE	CAPT	NAT	07650	LIND, JAMES JAY	CAPT	ARZ
07576	PICHE, GORDON GRANT	RADM	ANN	07651	WALSTON, JOHN DALE	MR.	TEX
07577	STUART, WAYNE SHELTON	CAPT	NOR	07652	WARE, STEPHEN GILKEY	CAPT	SFR
07578	HICKERSON, ROBERT (N)	Col	TEX	07653	KITCHEN, KENNETH STANLEY	Col	SFR
07579	PHILIPP, DOUGLAS TYLER	CDR	TEX	07654	HOPE, PETER RAWSON	LT	SFR
07580	ROCHON, STEPHEN WAYNE	CAPT	NAT	07655	ALEXANDER, ROBERT CHESTON	CAPT	SFR
07581	WILTSHIRE, GLENN ALLEN	CAPT	WNY	07656	BROADBEAR, DAVID GEORGE	LT	SFR
07582	KALLERES, MICHAEL PETER	VADM	JAX	07657	FRANCIA, DANILE AUGUSTO	Col	NAT

INSIG	COMPANION	RANK	CDRY	INSIG	COMPANION	RANK	CDRY
07658	RHODES, RANDY EDWIN	LCDR	ANN	07733	THOMPSON, HADWICK ALVIN	MR	SFR
07659	ROSENFELD, GABRIEL IRA	MR.	NYC	07734	LEGG, BRUCE MICHAEL	MR	ANN
07660	SHEFFIELD, CAROLINE CONNORS	MS.	JAX	07735	BAIRD, CLAYTON DEWARD	LT	TEX
07661	TEAGUE, FREDERIC	MR	SFR	07736	HOADLEY, JEFFERY SCOTT	LCDR	JAX
07662	GAUHRAN, FRANCES MARY	LTJG	SFR	07737	WITTER, RAY COWDEN	RADM	NPT
07663	BLAND, NORA ELIZABETH	MRS.	SFR	07738	DICKSON, EPHRIAM D. III	MR	TEX
07664	WANZENBERG, FRITZ WALTER	LCDR	NYC	07739	WILLOUGHBY, CHARLES WILLIAM	Capt	ARZ
07665	RAINEY, DANIEL LAWRENCE	CAPT	SWS	07740	SMITH, PHILIP ALLEN	CDR	NPT
07666	HOGG, JAMES ROBERT	ADM	NPT	07741	FUCHS, LEONARD RICHARD JR.	Col	ARZ
07667	MARTIN, GEORGE JOSEPH	CDR	NYC	07742	BARNES, LEONARD EDWARD JR.	CW04	MON
07668	HARMS, JOEL EDWARD	LT	SFR	07743	MC COY, DENNIS FREDERICK	RADM	NPT
07669	CARNES, CLIFF BERTRAM III	LTJG	NAT	07744	MC ENNESS, JOSEPH FRANCIS	MR	NPT
07670	POOLE, MICHELE ANN	LTJG	JAX	07745	EDWARDS, JONATHAN PHILLIPS	CAPT	NPT
07671	LARSON, KEITH HOWARD	CAPT	HRD	07746	ELLIS, WINFORD GERALD	RADM	NAT
07672	POWELL, WILLIAM HOWARD	LTJG	ILL	07747	PAUSNER, JOANN FRANCES	MS	SFR
07673	VERMILYEA, CLYDE LA VERNE	MGEN	TEX	07748	LEECH, EDWARD LAWRENCE	CAPT	SFR
07674	CALLAHAN, ROY HOWARD	CDR	NPT	07749	TREJO, PAUL EDGAR	CAPT	MON
07675	WYLIE, ELIZABETH GORDON	CAPT	NPT	07750	O'NEIL, JOHN EDWARD JR.	CAPT	JAX
07676	RAPKIN, JEROME (N)	CAPT	ANN	07751	HIRSCH, RICHARD MILES JR.	Capt	ARZ
07677	WAGES, CLARENCE JORDAN, JR.	CAPT	PNS	07752	BROWNE, MICHAEL JOSEPH	CDR	ILL
07678	CALVANO, CHARLES NATALE	CAPT	MON	07753	DOUD, HOWARD RAYMOND	CDR	ILL
07679	ATKINSON, ROBERT CLARK	MR	SFR	07754	WALKER, WILLIAM BRUCE	CAPT	ILL
07680	RICHTER, MARY	MRS.	SFR	07755	EGLER, VICKI LEA	MRS	ILL
07681	MCLAY, DEIDRE LOREEN	LT	NPT	07756	EGLER, GERARD THOMAS	CDR	ILL
07682	DAY, JAMES KEVILLE	MR	MAS	07757	BROWN, MARTHA CAROLINE	LTJG	SFR
07683	MCCARTHY, EDWARD TIMOTHY	CDR	MAS	07758	DREES, LINDA JEAN	MRS	TEX
07684	WRIGHT, CHESTER ARTHUR	MR	SFR	07759	POSS, EVELYN VALDERINE	MRS	TEX
07685	MAROLDA, EDWARD JOHN	1ST LT	NAT	07760	CAULEY, BRUCE ALLEN	LTJG	NYC
07686	O'KEEFE, TIMOTHY ROBERT	CAPT	NAT	07761	BROWN, EDWIN RICHARD	MR	NAT
07687	TUCKER, RONALD D.	RADM	ARZ	07762	MAYNARD, MICHAEL JUDE	CDR	NYC
07688	HOCKING, JAMES ROBERT	LCDR	NYC	07763	LOCHRIDGE, WILLARD FISKE IV	Capt	NYC
07689	HANEY, RICHARD LEE	LT	SFR	07764	BRIGIANI, WILLIAM GUY	LCDR	NYC
07690	MC CABE, THOMAS JOHN JR.	CAPT	SFR	07765	STILLWELL, PAUL LEWIS	CDR	ANN
07691	HALLETT, FREDERICK HOWARD	CAPT	ANN	07766	NUGENT, JOHN JOSEPH	BM2	HRD
07692	DUNCAN, MAX CARSON	CAPT	ANN	07767	TINKER, GORDON EDWIN	LTJG	TEX
07693	ROBERTS, TIM HAL	CAPT	JAX	07768	IEVA, RONALD ANTHONY	LCDR	NYC
07694	MONSON, ARTHUR C.	CAPT	TPA	07769	MORRISON, WILLIAM DAVID	Capt	ARZ
07695	OBRIEN, ANTHONY THOMAS	LCDR	HRD	07770	RABIL, DANIEL JOSEPH	Maj.	ARZ
07696	ANDOLSEK, TIMOTHY GEORGE	LCDR	TEX	07771	GALLUS, DENNIS EDWARD	MR	NAT
07697	WATKINS, JOHN FRANCIS	LTJG	TEX	07772	PERKINS, JAMES BLENN	VADM	NAT
07698	HAWKS, DONALD RAY	CDR	SFR	07773	SHORT, MARY IRENE	MS	SEF
07699	KEMPNER, WILLIAM CLYDE	LT	NYC	07774	BLADES, DANIEL WESLEY	MR	NAT
07700	HARRISON, DONALD KAY	LTJG	ARZ	07775	MARTIN, JOSEPH THADDEUS	PS2	SFR
07701	REINIGER, PETER DAVID	CAPT	ARZ	07776	MC DOUGALL, CRAIG ALLEN	Lt Col	SFR
07702	KNIGHT, GLENN BRUCE	MR	PDV	07777	TEMPLETON, ROBERT ERNEST	CAPT	SFR
07703	WEISE, WILLIAM	BGEN	PDV	07778	BROWN, ELBERT LEON	LT	SFR
07704	CASEY, MICHAEL KIRKLAND	MR	NAT	07779	BROYLES, NED LE E.	CAPT	SFR
07705	HALL, DAVID HOWARD	CAPT	NAT	07780	CREECH, JONN WILLIAM JR.	LCDR	SFR
07706	CLEERE, GAIL SUSAN	MRS	NAT	07781	CONLEY, DENNIS RONALD	RADM	NAT
07707	MCCARTHY, GEORGE EDWARD	LCDR	TEX	07782	SODERHOLM, RICHARD CARL	CDR	SFR
07708	WHISLER, GLENN EDWARD JR.	RADM	NPT	07783	MC CARTHY, CAMPBELL JOSEPH	LCDR	JAX
07709	YOUNG, JOHN WESLEY JR.	CAPT	NOR	07784	ROSITZKE, ROBERT HUGH	CDR	NAT
07710	CLANTON, PETER WILLIAM	LCDR	NAT	07785	BAKER, STEPHEN CLARK	LCDR	NAT
07711	RUOTOLO, ANTHONY PAUL	LCDR	SEF	07786	CHADBOURNE, CHARLES CUMSTON III	CAPT	NAT
07712	SULLIVAN, DAVID MICHAEL	MR.	PDV	07787	JONES, CONWAY BENJAMIN JR.	Col	SFR
07713	DOWNEY, JOHN BERNARD	CAPT	SFR	07788	BRANCH, THOMAS LIVINGSTON	CAPT	SFR
07714	LUTZ, GERALD GILBERT	CAPT	SFR	07789	MC CARTHY, HELEN MARY	CAPT	MAS
07715	MC MAHON, ROBERT JOSEPH	LCDR	SFR	07790	MONTGOMERY, MARK CONNON	LCDR	NAT
07716	MC CANN, JOHN FRANCIS	CAPT	NYC	07791	FRENCH, ROBERT CALHOUN	CAPT	SFR
07717	NATHAN, BRUCE ALFRED	LT	NYC	07792	GREEN, FRANK LOYD	MR	SFR
07718	LOWERRE, WARREN PELHAM	CDR	TEX	07793	KEMPER, JACKSON (N)	MR	NAT
07719	AUSTRAW, JAMES DAVID	CAPT	JAX	07794	EMMONS, GEORGE DANIEL	CAPT	NAT
07720	HEWELL, CHARLES LEE	CAPT	TEX	07795	HAUSER, CHRISTOPHER BLAIR	Maj.	NAT
07721	MARCH, WAYNE PAUL	Lt Col	ARZ	07796	EGAN, JOHN MAURICE	CPL	SFR
07722	COUGHLIN, JOSEPH CHRISTOPHER	LCDR	NAT	07797	JOHNSON, RICHARD GORDON	CPO	SFR
07723	MAHNKEN, THOMAS GILBERT	LT	NPT	07798	SUTTON, FRANK WALTER	LT	SFR
07724	HOOS, E. LOU	CAPT	NAT	07799	O'NEILL, FRANCIS JOSEPH	Capt	SFR
07725	FOX-MCINTYRE, MARLENE ELIZABETH	MS	NAT	07800	WOODWARD, WILLIAM JASPER JR.	CDR	TEX
07726	KANE, EDWARD JAMES	CDR	NAT	07801	LANG, ROBERT HARRY JR.	CAPT	ILL
07727	ZUCKER, CHANNING MOORE	CAPT	HRD	07802	LANG, LESLIE JUNE	CAPT	ILL
07728	SCOTT, STANLEY REED	Col	SFR	07803	ARMSTRONG, CRAIG STEVEN	CAPT	JAX
07729	LOCKWOOD, HANFORD NICHOLS	CAPT	SFR	07804	NASH, ROBERT IRVING	MR	ILL
07730	LOCKWOOD, MICHELE HUGHES	CAPT	SFR	07805	KRASNITZ, MARTIN (N)	LTJG	ILL
07731	GORELL, NANCY FLORENCE	MRS.	SFR	07806	FERN, JOSEPH MICHAEL	CAPT	ILL
07732	THOMPSON, LILY ANN	MRS	SFR	07807	PARSONS, WILLIAM DUVAL	CAPT	ILL

INSIG	COMPANION	RANK	CDRY	INSIG	COMPANION	RANK	CDRY
07808	PULEIO, DANIEL THOMAS	LCDR	TEX	07883	BUCCHI, TONEY MICHAEL	RADM	TEX
07809	AUSTIN, STEPHEN WILLIAM	Maj.	TEX	07884	RAGAN, ALBERT DENIS	LT	SFR
07810	LONSCHEIN, ALLAN JEROME	LT	NYC	07885	DARST, DAVID MARTIN JR	MR	NYC
07811	DEITZ, ROBERT JOSEPH	BGEN	SFR	07886	REAGER, WILLIAM REARDON	CDR	SWS
07812	ROY, ELMON HAROLD	DR	NAT	07887	BOO, GARY WILLIS	LCDR	SFR
07813	WERTHEIM, ERIC MICHAEL	MR	NAT	07888	WEBSTER, HUGH LARIMER	RADM	SDG
07814	PAULSEN, ALBERT GEORGE	RADM	NAT	07889	NUCKOLS, DONALD BERT JR.	LCDR	HRD
07815	LAPLANTE, JOHN BAPTISTE	VADM	NAT	07890	BAUM, RUSSELL ALTON JR.	ENS	NAT
07816	PAGE, PAUL	MR	SWS	07891	DE BRINE, RICHARD ALLEN	1ST Lt	SFR
07817	CAVINESS, SUSANNE MARIE	CAPT	NAT	07892	PHILLIPS, RALSTON DALE	MR	ANN
07818	RYAN, EDWIN MILES	LTJG	NAT	07893	LASOWSKI, DONALD THOMAS	CDR	NAT
07819	DANIEL, THOMAS RAYMOND JR	CAPT	NAT	07894	ROTHRAUFF, THOMAS BENEDICT JR.	CAPT	HRD
07820	FARGO, DENNIS KENNETH	CDR	NAT	07895	ABELL, WILLIAM JAMES	LCDR	SFR
07821	KOWACK, ERIC PAUL	LT	CON	07896	MAGEE, TERRY EDWARD	CAPT	SWS
07822	NEAL, MACK ELLIS	MR	TEX	07897	PEAKE, THADDEUS ANDREW	CDR	ATL
07823	SEGER, CHRISTIAN NILES	LTJG	TEX	07898	MC GILL, JAMES FIJUX	LT	SFR
07824	CHINN, JAMES ALTON	CDR	LBE	07899	STINNETT, ROBERT	MR	SFR
07825	CURTIS, ARTHUR WALLACE	LCDR	SFR	07900	BRAITHWAIRE, KENNETH JOHN	CDR	PDV
07826	BARNSDALE, WILLIAM JORDAN	LTJG	SFR	07901	KEMERY, FRANCIS XAVIER	CDR	PNS
07827	NICELY, KIP WILSON	CAPT	NMX	07902	NAUGHTON, RICHARD JOSEPH	RADM	SWS
07828	GALLOTTA, RICHARD ARNOLD	CAPT	NAT	07903	ZAJICEK, RICHARD GENE	CAPT	SWS
07829	HICKEY, DENNIS JOHN IV	CAPT	JAX	07904	PENTIMONTI, RICHARD JOSEPH	CAPT	SWS
07830	DERVAY, JOSEPH PAUL	CAPT	TEX	07905	DORMAN, MERRILL HERRICK	CAPT	HRD
07831	RANARD, HARVEY EDGAR JR.	CDR	SDG	07906	SHERMAN, JOHN EDWARD	CAPT	HRD
07832	MALLOW, EDWARD SCOTT	CDR	JAX	07907	HODGE, QUINCY MICHAEL	CDR	TEX
07833	BELL, CHRISTOPHER LANE	LT	JAX	07908	YARSINSKE, RAYMOND JEROME JR.	LCDR	HRD
07834	KURTA, ANTHONY MICHAEL	CDR	JAX	07909	YARSINSKE, AMY WATERS	MRS	HRD
07835	DAVIDSON, MARK HAROLD	CDR	NAT	07910	STEIN, FREDRIC CONRAD	CDR	HRD
07836	HOLBROOK, JAMES LOUIS	CAPT	SWS	07911	BROOKS, JENNIFER ELLYN	CDR	NAT
07837	DERR, JOHN FREDERICK	CAPT	SEA	07912	LONG, JOHN EDWARD	CDR	TEX
07838	ULSETH, RONALD RICHARD	LCDR	ILL	07913	RESNIK, EDWARD DONALD	Col	SEF
07839	KRUGER, WAYNE KEITH	CAPT	ILL	07914	WILLS, ROBERT EMMETT II	Capt	TEX
07840	WALSH, JOSEPH FRANCIS	CAPT	NAT	07915	PETTITT, JOHN ALLEN	CAPT	SWS
07841	JOHNSON, RONALD ERNEST	CAPT	HRD	07916	SNYDER, HARRY CALVIN	WRE	ARZ
07842	EMMERT, ALEXANDER JOHN	MR	NAT	07917	BELL, DENIS JOSEPH	CAPT	SWS
07843	EMMERT, FREDRIC ALAN	MR	NAT	07918	WHITE, ROBERT EDMUND	CAPT	SWS
07844	BURROWS, HERMAN DUVAL	MR	NYC	07919	MC CUISTION, JAMES HARVEY	Lt Col	TEX
07845	MILLS, LESLIE EUGENE	MR	MAS	07920	NELSON, DAVID LEON	Capt	TEX
07846	BRUNO, SALVATORE T.	MR	SFR	07921	NAHRA, RALPH JOHN	MR	HRD
07847	BRUNO, REBECCA GRACE	MRS	SFR	07922	HALVORSON, THOMAS GRAHAM	LCDR	NAT
07848	MUELLER, MICHAEL GENE	LT	ANN	07923	KUCHEM, ROBERT	CAPT	SFR
07849	HARLEY, AL BOYCE JR.	Capt	NAT	07924	MC NICHOLAS, THOMAS MICHAEL	CAPT	HRD
07850	HILL, LEE BALMER	CDR	JAX	07925	LORD, MICHAEL WILLIAM	CDR	ANN
07851	KETTERSON, JEFFREY CLAYTON	CAPT	NYC	07926	SEELYE, THOMAS TAYLOR JR.	LCDR	NYC
07852	KEOTHER, BERNARD GUSTAVE II	LTJG	NYC	07927	CHISHOLM, DONALD WILLIAM	MR	NYC
07853	MC CARTHY, JAY ALAN	RADM	SWS	07928	JENKS, SHEPHERD MARTIN	CAPT	SFR
07854	MASERANG, DAVID LEE	CAPT	TEX	07929	SILVA, EUGENE ALAN	LT	NAT
07855	FARGO, THOMAS BOULTON	ADM	TEX	07930	ROBARDS, FRANK BENJAMIN	CDR	NAT
07856	WILLIAMSON, DONALD EDWARD	CDR	TEX	07931	BOWDON, WILLIAM GEORGE III	MGEN	SWS
07857	ZOEHRER, HERBERT ALFRED	CAPT	SWS	07932	WYNKOOP, PETER	CAPT	JAX
07858	COUFAL, JERRY WAYNE	CDR	TEX	07933	KING, JEFFREY AYRES	CDR	TEX
07859	LIESKE, DON DAVID II	CDR	TEX	07934	BENEDIKT, CYNAN JOSEPH	LCDR	TEX
07860	TOBIN, PAUL EDWARD JR.	RADM	NAT	07935	MARFIAK, THOMAS FLETCHER	RADM	ANN
07861	HOLBROOK, HEBER A.	CW02	SFR	07936	BAKER, ROBERT KENNETH	CDR	TEX
07862	BARNSDALE, WILLIAM JORDAN JR.	MR	SFR	07937	KITTLER, JOHN LOGAN	CAPT	HRD
07863	GALASINAO, PETER DIMATTEO	LCDR	NYC	07938	JOHNSON, WILLIAM SPENCR IV	CAPT	NAT
07864	REESER, JOHN DAVID	LCDR	PDV	07939	SOLIDUM, JOSEFINO B.	CAPT	NAT
07865	BAIR, JOHN SCOTT	MR	NOR	07940	SOLTOW, PAUL CARL JR.	Capt	SFR
07866	BERLISS, ARTHUR DAVID SR	CAPT	NYC	07941	GLAZER, JACK HENRY	CAPT	SFR
07867	MC GILL, CHARLES HARY III	LT	NYC	07942	MENELOW, DAVID JACOB	LT	TEX
07868	NILES, HARRISON PAUL	LCDR	NYC	07943	ZULLINGER, CHARLES FREDERICK	CDR	SWS
07869	MOORE, DANIEL EUGENE JR.	CAPT	NAT	07944	ENGLAND, CHRISTOPHER STEPHEN	LTJG	SDG
07870	BOCKSEL ARNOLD ARMAND	ENS	NYC	07945	WHEELER, HERBERT KING	CDR	SFR
07871	PORTER, JOHN COLLIER	CDR	SWS	07946	DAVIS, JAMES HOWARD	Capt	TEX
07872	VEIGELE, WILLIAM JOHN	LT	SDG	07947	SEARS, RAYMOND SANFORD	LT	NAT
07873	HAMBY, JANICE MARIE	CAPT	JAX	07948	KEAST, DONALD GEORGE	Lt Col	SWS
07874	OLIVER, DANIEL TRANTHAM	VADM	NAT	07949	DELGADO, PHILIP ANDREW	LCDR	NAT
07875	WILLIAMS, ELMER ROYCE	CAPT	SWS	07950	CHRIST, CHARLES JOSEPH	MR	NOR
07876	DUNKELBERGER, THOMAS EDWIN	Col	HRD	07951	RANKIN, ERIC DAVID	CAPT	NAT
07877	SHELLEY, MARKE ROBERT	RADM	NAT	07952	PLUTA, PAUL JOSEPH	RADM	NOR
07878	MARVIN, RICHARD BRUCE	CAPT	NAT	07953	SNYDER, WILLIAM CHARLES	CAPT	LBE
07879	JENKINS, ROBERT DONALD III	CAPT	NAT	07954	COULON, RICHARD ANTHONY	CAPT	NOR
07880	FERGUSON, JOHN KIRK	CDR	NAT	07955	SCOTT, JUD	RADM	SFR
07881	VANZELOTTI, S. ELLEXSON	CAPT	SFR	07956	MELVIN, CHARLES DALTON	LCDR	JAX
07882	GREENE, ELIZABETH	CDR.	NAT	07957	THOMPSON, DONALD LEROY	LCDR	ILL

INSIG	COMPANION	RANK	CDRY	INSIG	COMPANION	RANK	CDRY
07958	COLLINS, JAMES MATTHEW	Col	SWS	08033	KAIN, GEORGE FREDERICK JR.	CAPT	NAT
07959	MIRICK, ROBERT ALLEN	CAPT	NAT	08034	HOWARD, MARY ROWAN	MRS	NPT
07960	BESANCON, MICHAEL D.	CAPT	ILL	08035	JEBBER, PAUL WILLIAM	CDR	NPT
07961	WEDEKIND, ALICE W.	MS.	NOR	08036	HOWARD, JOHN HAMILTON	LCDR	NPT
07962	VITTER, DAVID	HONOR	NOR	08037	CZECH, THEODORE THOMAS	CDR	NPT
07963	DUFFY, THOMAS MICHAEL	CDR	NYC	08038	LONDON, J. PHILLIP	CAPT	NAT
07964	STEIGMAN, DAVID SIDNEY	CDR	NAT	08039	BOGLE, WILLIAM THOMAS	CAPT	SWS
07965	JACOBS, JOEL HARRY	CAPT	SWS	08040	PROUTY, TREVOR JOHN	ENS	NAT
07966	VAN DER HULST, LEE DOUGLAS	MR	ILL	08041	WAGNER, LILIEN AUDREY	MIDN	NAT
07967	LINDEMAN, ELLEN NOEL	MRS	SEF	08042	HUFFMAN, FRANKLIN LEE	ENS	NAT
07968	TUCKER, NELLIE SUE	LCDR	NAT	08043	BURKETT, DONALD CARL JR.	RM2	NAT
07969	BROWN, HARRY WAYNE	CAPT	TEX	08044	LOUGHRAN, JOHN XAVIER III	Col	SFR
07970	MAUCK, LINDA SUE	MRS	MON	08045	CUMMINGS, TIMOTHY CHRISTOPHER	BT3	TEX
07971	NICHOLSON, DAVID RICHARD	RADM	NAT	08046	CHICKERING, HOWARD ALLEN	LCDR	NAT
07972	FREDO-CUMBO, JOSEPH M.	CAPT	NYC	08047	POWERS, ROBERT ROLAND JR.	CDR	JAX
07973	RISSEEUW, HUGH JOSIAS	CDR	SWS	08048	HILL, CLARENCE EBBERT	CAPT	JAX
07974	PRUEHER, JOSEPH WILSON	ADM	NAT	08049	JORNLIN, ROBERT DENNIS	LT	ILL
07975	HALE, MORRIS DOYLE	Maj.	TEX	08050	YANCEY, DIANA RAYE	MS	NAT
07976	TICHENOR, AUSTIN KENT	CAPT	SFR	08051	HARRIS, JAMES DANIEL	CAPT	NAT
07977	SCHREIBER, CHRISTA MARGRET	MRS	SFR	08052	MC CRATH, J. MICHAEL	CDR	JAX
07978	FITZSIMONDS, JAMES RUSSELL	CAPT	NPT	08053	CRAWFORD, JOHN DAVID	CAPT	ILL
07979	HATTENDORF, JOHN BREWSTER	LT	NPT	08054	PETRIK, JOHN FERDINAND	Maj.	NAT
07980	BLUM, MICHAEL ALEXANDER	CW04	NPT	08055	ZINNI, ANTHONY CHARLES	GEN	HRD
07981	NEIMEYER, CHARLES PATRICK	Lt Col	NPT	08056	DITZLER, THOMAS FREDERICK	MR	NAT
07982	BAER, GEORGE W.	MR	NPT	08057	LEHMAN, JOHN	CAPT	NYC
07983	HARDEMAN, EDWARD LEE	CAPT	NPT	08058	GUARINO, JOSEPH MICHAEL	LT	TEX
07984	GRANT, DOROTHY KENDALL	CAPT	NPT	08059	NESTLERODE, ROBERT NORMAN	CAPT	TEX
07985	MANKO, MICHAEL BRADLEY	LCDR	JAX	08060	NESTLERODE, SAMYE MOTT	MRS	TEX
07986	FALLON, WILLIAM JOSEPH	ADM	HRD	08061	PEDIGO, ROBERT EUGENE	CDR	SFR
07987	BUNYAN, DENNIS JENKINS	LCDR	ARZ	08062	MAXWELL, GEORGE WALTER III	CPL	NAT
07988	PARKER, LOUIS HUDSON	YN2	SFR	08063	BORGNINE, ERNEST	GMC	LBE
07989	TREVINO, ROBERT CAMPOS	CAPT	TEX	08064	WENSING, KEVIN MICHAEL	CAPT	NAT
07990	WHITE, EDWARD DOUGLAS III	CDR	SFR	08065	GORELL, FREDERICK REIMER	CDR	SFR
07991	JOLLY, MARTIN EDWARD	LCDR	NAT	08066	AGMAN, ROBERT S.	CDR	HRD
07992	SHARKEY, CARROL JEANNE	MRS	SFR	08067	MACGREGOR, JOHN LINDSAY	CAPT	HRD
07993	MADSEN, JOHN WILLARD	CAPT	NYC	08068	LUDMER, CHRISTOPHER LYLE	LT	NAT
07994	HAYLOR, ROBERT WARD JR.	CAPT	NAT	08069	COYNE, BRIAN JOSEPH	HM3	NYC
07995	RAITHEL, ALBERT LAWRENCE JR.	CAPT	NAT	08070	STREETER, RICHARD JOHN	LT	JAX
07996	BARON, WILLIAM CARL	LT	NAT	08071	FINN, MICHAEL PATRICK	CAPT	NAT
07997	SIMSON, DAVID FREDRIC	1ST LT	NYC	08072	LETHCOE, BRYAN JEFFERY	LCDR	TEX
07998	DODGE, JEFFREY NATHAN	MR	SFR	08073	POBAT, MICHAEL JOSEPH	EWC	NAT
07999	FULTON, ROBERT BURWELL	RADM	TEX	08074	CHINN, BARBARA WILLIS	MRS	LBE
08000	CEBROWSKI, ARTHUR KARL	VADM	NPT	08075	GILLILAND, GREG ALLAN	CAPT	TEX
08001	LOEWENTHAL, ROBERT GORDON	CAPT	NPT	08076	DEVINE, ROBERT JAMES	MR	TEX
08002	JENKINS, ROBERT DONALD IV	MDTN	ANN	08077	MELHUISH, CHRISTOPHER ALLAN	CAPT	HRD
08003	ATWOOD, ANTHONY DEWEY	YNC	SEF	08078	MYATT, JAMES MICHAEL	MGEN	SFR
08004	HICKS, GREGORY LAWRENCE	LCDR	MON	08079	LANDAUER, DONALD ARTHUR	MR	SFR
08005	ANDRUS, PETER LEVERETT	RADM	TEX	08080	LLOYD, ALAN STANLEY	MR	TEX
08006	PRESSWOOD, RONALD G.	LT	TEX	08081	KELLAR, MICHAEL ALLEN	DR	NAT
08007	MC ANALLY, ROBERT GARY	PNCS	JAX	08082	KEEN, RALPH	MR	NAT
08008	MURTAUGH, EDWARD JOHN	LCDR	NPT	08083	NELSON, ROBET WAYNE JR.	CAPT	NAT
08009	ALLEN, W. SLATER JR.	AT1	NPT	08084	LABAK, STANLEY JOSEPH	LT	NAT
08010	NELSON, WALTER THOMAS	LT	JAX	08085	HERBERT, FRANK REY	CAPT	LBE
08011	KASTL, ROBERT THOMAS	CPL	SFR	08086	SOKOLOWSKI, STEVEN	LT	HRD
08012	STONECIPHER, CHARLES ANDREW	MR	NAT	08087	BURKART, MELVIN GERALD	CAPT	ARZ
08013	SNELL, HOWARD LINWOOD	STC	TEX	08088	STOCKDALE, JAMES BOND	VADM	TEX
08014	ROSE, JOHN D. JR.	LCDR	SEF	08089	MORRIS, JOHN WILLIAM III	MR	JAX
08015	MERRILEES, G. ROBERT	RADM	SEF	08090	GLYNN, WILLIAM CHARLES	CAPT	ILL
08016	JOHNSON, ALAN ALFRED	PN2	TEX	08091	STOCKINGER, ZSOLT THOMAS	LCDR	NAT
08017	GLORIOSO, GLENN STEPHEN	MR	NAT	08092	JOHNSON, RUTHERFORD BARRY	MR	ATL
08018	HASKINS, MICHAEL DONALD	VADM	NAT	08093	GOEDEN, GERALD EDWARD	BMCM	NAT
08019	SAMCHUCK, GERALD MONT	LT	NYC	08094	WOOTEN, DAVID ROBERT	MR	NAT
08020	GIFFIN, HENRY COLLINS II	VADM	HRD	08095	GROESBECK, GEOFFREY ALANPETER	MR	MAS
08021	LANDERSMAN, STUART DAVID	CAPT	SDG	08096	KOENIG, ALAN WALTER	Maj.	SFR
08022	RECKNER, JAMES RICHARD	LCDR	TEX	08097	DEMOTT, DANIEL LEE	MR	SEF
08023	DUDEK, THEODORE EDWARD	CPO	HRD	08098	ROTHROCK, JOHN GRAYSON	LT	NAT
08024	JONES, THOMAS LEVATTE	CAPT	NAT	08099	MC NAIR, MARTIN BENNETT	CAPT	SFR
08025	PLATT, DAVID NICOLL	LT	NYC	08100	LEACH, DONALD BENJAMIN	CDR	NAT
08026	TAYLOR, SANDRA JOHNSON	MS	JAX	08101	WEEKS, STANLEY BYRON	CDR	NAT
08027	STENBERG, WILLIAM VERMONT	CDR	TEX	08102	SMITH, JOSEPH THOMAS JR.	MR	SFR
08028	BERRY, CHARLES LEWIS III	LT	TEX	08103	DOLGIN, STEPHEN MARK	LTC	SFR
08029	EVANS, ROBERT WILLIAM	ABE3	NAT	08104	CARMAN, JOHN W.	CAPT	HRD
08030	MENNIS, JAMES FINBARR	CAPT	JAX	08105	WERTHMULLEFR, ROY WALTER SR.	CAPT	HRD
08031	POLING, KERMIT WILLIAM	REV	NAT	08106	WONG, GARY CHARLES	MR	SFR
08032	JANSEN, ADRIAN JOHAN	CDR	NAT	08107	JACOBS, TIMOTHY LESTER	MR	NAT

94

INSIG	COMPANION	RANK	CDRY
08108	MARKARIAN, RONALD HENRY	Col	SFR
08109	STEWART, CARL JOSEPH	CDR	SFR
08110	ZANGER, FRANCIS CHARLES	LT	JAX
08111	COUCH, HUGH RICHARD	CAPT	TEX
08112	PEACOCK, WILLIAM ELDRED	Col	SFR
08113	RUHM, THOMAS FRANCIS	LT	NYC
08114	WONG, CHRISTINA JEAN	MIDN	SFR
08115	BECKER, WILLIAM DAVID	MR	NAT
08116	SHIMP, DAVID KEITH	CAPT	NAT
08117	SIMS, WILLIAM MALCOLM JR	CAPT	NOR
08118	GRIFFIN, CHARLES CALVIN	LTJG	ARZ
08119	CHERAMIE, CRAIG MICHAEL	HM3	NOR
08120	SCHMIDT, WILLIAM HENRY	HM2	NYC
08121	WARREN, ROBERT HAGEN	CAPT	LBE
08122	MOSHER, WILLIAM DEAN	MR	NAT
08123	GREEN, KRISTIN LEE	CDR	NAT
08124	BITTER, MARCUS K,	LCDR	MON
08125	WARD, BARRY JOHN	MR	TEX
08126	O'LEARY, TIMOTHY STUART	CDR	TEX
08127	DUNN, JAMES ANDREW	SK1	NYC
08128	LUCAS, CHARLES C. JR.	DR	NYC
08129	PARNHAM, HAROLD ATHAERTON JR.	CDR	NYC
08130	HOLT, JOHN ALBERT III	CDR	TEX
08131	BULL, NORMAN SPRINGER	CAPT	NAT
08132	NAGELIN, THOMAS FREDERICK JR	CAPT	NOR
08133	WAYLETT, EVA CHLOE		NAT
08134	MORGAN, STEPHEN LEE	LCDR	ATL
08135	HARRELL, JOHN MICHAEL	LCDR	NAT
08136	ROTHE, ERNST	LT	NYC
08137	POLK, EDWARD MARTIN		ARZ
08138	FERGUSON, JOHN CRAIG	SSGT	TEX
08139	GILLIS, ELIZABETH ANNE	MIDN	ANN
08140	AYERS, GEORGE WILLIAM	Col	NAT
08141	SCHULD, DODNALD WILLIAM	RD3	NYC
08142	BOSWORTH, WILLIAM POSEY	CAPT	JAX
08143	NELINSON, JEROME WILLIAM	S1/C	HRD
08144	BADER, DAVID ERNEST	JO2	NOR
08145	MERCURIO, SUSAN MARIE	LT	NAT
08146	JENSEN, WOLLOM ALLEN	CAPT	NAT
08147			
08148	BESAG, FRANK PAUL	DR	JAX
08149	HEMMING, BARBARA ANN		SFR
08150	MONTOYA, MARCO	CAPT	TEX

INSIG	COMPANION	RANK	CDRY
08151	KOMOROWSKI, MARY ELLEN		NAT
08152	WOHLERT, EARL ROSS	LCDR	NAT
08153	SANDERS, GILBERT OTIS	CAPT	TEX
08154	WARREN, JAMES MARION	CDR	NAT
08155	GATELY, JOHN BRENDON	LT	HRD

COMMANDERY

ANN	ANNAPOLIS
ARZ	ARIZONA
ATL	ATLANTA
AVN	AVIATION
CAL	CALIFORNIA
COL	COLORADO
CON	CONNECTICUT
DCA	DISCTRICT OF COLUMBIA
FKY	FLORIDA KEYS
HRD	HAMPTON ROAD
ILL	ILLINOIS
JAX	FIRST COAST FLORIDA
LBE	LONG BEACH
MAS	MASSACHUSETTS
MON	MONTEREY
MPN	MOBILE/PENSACOLA
NAT	NATIONAL CAPITOL
NMX	NEW MEXICO
NOR	NEW ORLEANS
NPT	NEWPORT
NYC	NEW YORK CITY
PDV	PHILADELPHIA/DELAWARE VALLEY
PEN	PENNSYLVANIA
RAL	RALEIGH N C
SBA	SANTA BARBARA
SDG	SAN DIEGO
SEA	SEATTLE
SEF	SOUTH EAST FLORIDA
SFR	SAN FRANCISCO
SWS	SOUTHWEST
TEX	TEXAS
TPA	TAMPA
WDC	WASHINGTON DC
WNY	WESTERN NEW YORK

Significant Civil War Engagements

When one recalls the original intent of our three Founders, who were concerned that 25 years after the War Between the States, the U.S. Congress focus on military needs was still directed toward the Grand Army of the Republic to the virtual exclusion of maritime needs of the Republic, the importance of this first step taken by the Founders is truly visionary.

Merchant Mariners plying their trade were active from the early 1600s. Prior to the Revolutionary War many served under Letters of Marque or Warrant issued by the individual 13 colonies. Their efforts were to continue under the Continental Congress and subsequently under the U.S. Congress through not just the War of the Revolution but also in suppressing the Barbary pirates and during the War of 1812.

Yet the U.S. Congress in 1890, perhaps reflecting the view of most citizens focused on the land engagements. Overlooked was the tremendous loss inflicted on U.S. Commerce by marauders in the early 1860s.

Many had heard of the outstanding successes of Confederate naval forces especially the hated CSS *Alabama* and CSS *Merrimac*. The latter was bested by the USS *Monitor* and the former sunk by the USS *Kearsarge*.

Apparently with this threat ended, the nation's mind could return as it always has to peaceful pursuits. Overlooked entirely were the lessons which should have been brought to the nation's attention about essential changes needed to insure America's right to the sea unencumbered by obsolescence.

Here presented are personal accounts of participants and eye witnesses. Read of the heroic action of the skipper of the *Monitor*. John L. Worden and his executive officer who took over when Worden was incapacitated. Read the XO's personal account of the transit of the untested *Monitor* to Hampton Roads and Lt. Greene's exceptional performance.

In the crucible of conflict, Naval ship design would forever be changed. America, however, was not being told this story in an insightful manner. But three New England patriot mariners set out to tell Congress and the Nation. What is reproduced here is what they knew must be told. There could be no going back. America must move forward and prosper. To do this she needed new maritime policies and funding. In a sense we can say proudly they fired the salvo heard across the nation. Their action ranks with those of the minutemen at Concord and Lexington.

PENNSYLVANIA COMMANDERY OF THE NAVAL ORDER OF THE UNITED STATES

At the meeting of the Pennsylvania Commandery, Naval Order of the United States, held at the Hotel Bellevue, on the evening of March 9, 1898, on motion of Henry M. Dechert, Esq., it was

RESOLVED, 'That the description of the fight between the *Monitor* and *Merrimac* on the 9th of March 1862, given by Major R.S. Collum, U.S.M.C., and the copy of the letter written by Lieutenant S. Dana Greene, the Executive Officer of the *Monitor*, to his father and mother, be published, and that a copy be sent to each member of the Senate and House of Representatives of the United States.'

"The memorable action between the *Monitor* and the *Merrimac* in Hampton Roads on March 9, 1862, was commemorated at the Hotel Bellevue, Philadelphia, on the evening of March 9, 1898, by a dinner given by the Pennsylvania Commandery, Naval Order of the United States.

"The distinguished guests were Hon. C.A. Boutelle, Chairman of the House Naval Committee, Rear Admiral Bancroft Gherardi, U.S.N., and Hon. Charles F. Warwick, Mayor of Philadelphia.

"The following description was given by Major R.S. Collum, the Historian of the Pennsylvania Commandery, who was an eye witness of the historic struggle:-

'On the 8th of March, 1862, a great disaster overtook the Union in Hampton Roads, filling the country with dismay, and even bringing the people to doubt the success of the cause for which they had labored so hard.

'When our officers set fire to the buildings of the Norfolk Navy Yard it was supposed that every precaution had been taken to destroy everything of value. The *Merrimac* had been sunk, but the lower part of her hull and her engines and boilers were not injured. This vessel was raised by the Confederate authorities. Both ends for a distance of seventy feet were covered over, and when the ship was in fighting trim were just awash. On the midship section, a length of 170 feet was built over, the sides being at an angle of 55 degrees, a roof of oak and pitch pine extending from the water line to a height of seven feet above the gun deck. Both ends of this structure were rounded, so that the pivot guns could be used as bow and stern chasers, or quartering; over the gun deck was a light grating, making a promenade twenty feet wide.

'The wood backing was covered with iron plates rolled at the Tredagar works in Richmond. These plates were eight inches wide and two inches thick. The first covering was put on horizontally; the second up and down, making a total thickness of iron of four inches, strongly bolted to the woodwork and clinched inside.

'The ram was of cast-iron, projecting four feet, and, as was found subsequently, was badly secured. The rudder and propeller were entirely unprotected. The pilot-house was forward of the smokestack and covered with the same thickness of iron as the sides.

'Her battery consisted of two 7-inch rifles, which were the bow and stern pivots, in broadside two 6-inch rifles and six 9-inch smooth bores; in all ten heavy guns.

'She represented at the moment the most powerful fighting ship in the world.

'When this formidable vessel on the 8th of March got under way and proceeded down Elizabeth River, the following vessels composed our fleet at anchor off Fort Monroe: The *Minnesota*, of 40 guns, Captain Van Brunt; *Roanoke*, of 40 guns, Captain Marston; *St. Lawrence,* 50 guns, Captain Purviance; and several army transports. Seven miles above, off Newport News, lay the *Congress*, 50 guns, and the *Cumberland*, 30 guns. Newport News was well fortified and garrisoned by a large Union force.

'I will not take up your time by a description of the appalling disaster to the Union arms on that fatal day. Our re-union tonight is to celebrate the most gallant encounter between two fighting machines, a pigmy and a giant, and which marked a new era in naval warfare.

'At sundown when the *Merrimac* returned to Sewall's Point and anchored, an avenger was then approaching from the sea, destined to revive the drooping spirits of loyal hearts and turn the tide of victory to defeat for the Confederates.

'At 9 o'clock at night Ericsson's little *Monitor*, under the command of Lieutenant John L. Worden, arrived from New York, after experiencing trials and difficulties sufficient to have appalled an ordinary officer.

'It was a great relief to the officers and men of the squadron to know that an iron-clad of any description was at hand to assist them, but when they saw the little 'nondescript,' her decks level with the water, and appearing above it only her pilot-house and a small turret, in which latter were two 11-inch guns, they could not feel very sanguine of the result of the coming conflict.

'Lieutenant Worden was ordered to proceed at midnight and take position alongside the *Minnesota* to be ready to receive the *Merrimac*.

'The morning dawned clear and bright, and it was difficult to realize that 250 men had on the previous day lost their lives in the defense of their flag in a hopeless contest.

'The flag still floated from the *Cumberland*, while the smoke from the *Congress* ascended to heaven. The *Minnesota* lay hard and fast aground, while the *Roanoke* and *St. Lawrence* were a few hundred yards down towards the fort, the officers and men at their quarters, where they had been all night; marks of the destructive shot and shell from the *Merrimac* visible. At 8 A.M. the *Merrimac* was perceived approaching.

When she had come within a mile of the *Minnesota* that vessel opened upon her and signaled the *Monitor* to attack. Then came the contest which was to exert so important an influence upon naval architecture. Running down the wake of the frigate, the tiny *Monitor* placed herself alongside of her huge antagonist and fired gun after gun, which were returned by whole broadsides without effect. After a time the little vessel began maneuvering, shooting by her antagonist and sending her shots first into the bow, and again raking her stern, while broadside after broadside was fired from the *Merrimac*, either passing quite over, or, if they struck, glancing harmless from her bomb-proof turret.

'The *Merrimac* attempted to ram her antagonist, but before the vessel could gather headway the *Monitor* turned, and the prow of the *Merrimac* gave a glancing blow, which did no harm whatever. The *Monitor* came upon the *Merrimac's* quarter, her bow actually against the ship's side, and at this distance fired twice. Both shots struck about half way up the *Merrimac's* armor, abreast of the after pivot, and so severe was the blow that the side was forced in several inches.

'It is said that Lieutenant Jones, the Executive Officer of the *Merrimac*, having occasion to visit the gun deck, saw a division standing at ease, and inquiring of the officer in command why he was not firing, that individual replied: 'After firing for two hours I can do the enemy about as much damage by snapping my fingers at him every two minutes and a half.'

'Finding that she could make no impression on the *Monitor*, the *Merrimac* again gave her attention to the *Minnesota*, returning a tremendous and futile broadside from the frigate with a shot from her rifled bow gun, which went crashing through the vessel, bursting in the boatswain's room, and setting fire to the ship. The fire was, however, promptly extinguished. The second shell exploded the boiler of the tug alongside. The *Monitor* by this time came between the contending vessels, forcing the *Merrimac* to change her position. In doing this she grounded. As soon as she got off she stood down the bay, chased at full speed by the *Monitor*. Suddenly she turned and made for her antagonist, and for a time the contest between this seemingly ill-matched pair was again hot and furious. After a time the *Merrimac* seemed to tire of the fray, and again headed towards the frigate. It was a trying moment for the *Minnesota*, fast aground and badly crippled, but the enemy had no mind to renew the experience of the morning, and it being shortly after noon, retreated to Sewall's Point. During the night Captain Van Brunt succeeded in getting his ship afloat, and next morning was safely anchored at Fort Monroe. Towards the close of this terrific engagement a

An interior view of the turret of a sea-going Monitor.

percussion shell exploded against the look-out of the pilot-house of the *Monitor*, where Lieutenant Worden, who so brilliantly fought his vessel, and who thus made himself in a few hours the hero of the day, was stationed during the engagement. The result was a serious injury to the eyes of that officer, which, with the effects of the concussion, so disabled him as to oblige him to place the vessel in command of Lieutenant S. Dana Greene, the Executive Officer.

'The *Monitor* saved not only the squadron but the honor of the nation, and her gallant commander is fully entitled to the honors he received.

'Thus ended this remarkable engagement, which, in the bravery and ability displayed on both sides has never been excelled.'

"In response to the toast, "The *Monitor*, her Officers and Crew," A.C. Oliphant, of Trenton, N.J., read a copy of a letter from Lieutenant S. Dana Greene, the young officer who took charge of the Monitor after Lieutenant Worden was wounded. This letter was written on March 14, 1862, to Lieutenant Greene's mother, and is considered the best account of the battle and the perilous trip of the *Monitor* from New York to Hampton Roads, extant."

Remodeling the Merrimac *at the Gosport Navy Yard*

"My dear Mother and Father:

I commence this now but I don't know when I shall finish, as I have to write it at odd moments, when I can find a few minutes rest. When I bade Charley good-night on Wednesday, the 5th, I confidently expected to see you the next day, as I then thought it would be impossible to finish our repairs on Thursday, but the mechanics worked all night and at 11 A.M., on Thursday, we started down the harbor in company with the gun-boats *Sachem* and *Currituck*. We went along very nicely and when we arrived at Governor's Island the steamer *Seth Low* came alongside and took us in tow. We went out past the Narrows with a light wind from the west and very smooth water. The weather continued the same all Thursday night. I turned out at 6 o'clock on Friday morning, and from that time until Monday at 7 P.M. I think I lived ten good years. About noon the wind freshened and the sea was quite rough. In the afternoon the sea was breaking over our decks at a great rate, and coming in our hawse pipes, forward, in perfect floods. Our berth deck hatch leaked in spite of all we could do, and the water came down under the tower like a water fall. It would strike the pilot house and go over the tower in most beautiful curves. The water came through the narrow eye-holes in the pilot house with such force as to knock the helmsman completely round from the wheel. At four o'clock the water had gone down our smoke-stacks and blowers to such an extent that the blowers gave out, and the engine room was filled with gas. Then, Mother, occurred a scene I shall never forget. Our engineers behaved like heroes, every one of them. They fought with the gas, endeavoring to get the blowers to work, until they dropped down apparently as dead as men ever were. I jumped in the engine room with my men as soon as I could and carried them on top of the tower to get fresh air. I was nearly suffocated with the gas myself, but got on deck after every one was out of the engine room, just in time to save myself. Three firemen were in the same condition as the engineers. Then times looked rather blue, I can assure you. We had no fear as long as the engine could be kept going, to pump out the water, but when that stopped, the water increased rapidly. I immediately rigged the hand pump on the berth deck, but as we were obliged to lead the hose out over the tower, there was not force enough in the pump to throw the water out; our only resource now was to bail, and that was useless as we had to pass the buckets up through the tower, which made it a very long operation. What to do now we did not know. We had done all in our power and must let things take their own course. Fortunately, the wind was off shore, so we hailed the tug boat and told them to steer directly for the shore in order to get in smooth water. At eight P.M. we managed to get the engines to go, and everything was comparatively quiet again. The Captain had been up nearly all the previous night, and as we did not like to leave the deck without one of us being there, I told him I would keep the watch from eight to twelve, he took it from twelve to four and I would relieve him from four to eight. Well, the first watch passed off very nicely, smooth sea, clear sky, the moon out and the old tank going along five and six knots very nicely. All I had to do was to keep awake and think over the narrow escape we had in the afternoon. At twelve o'clock things looked so favorable I told the Captain he need not turn out; I would lay down with my clothes on, and if anything happened I would turn out and attend to it. He said very well, and I went to my room and hoped to get a little nap. I had scarcely got to my bunk, when I was startled by the most infernal noise that I ever heard in my life. The *Merrimac's* firing on Sunday last was music to it. We were just passing a shoal and the sea suddenly became very rough right ahead. It came up with tremendous force through our anchor well, and forced the air through our hawse pipes, where the chain comes, and then the water would come through in a perfect stream clear to our berth deck over the ward room table. The noise resembled the death groans of twenty men, and certainly was the most dismal, awful sound I ever heard. Of course the Captain and myself were on our feet in a moment and endeavoring to stop the hawse pipe. We succeeded partially, but now the water commenced to come down our blowers again, and we feared the same accident that happened in the afternoon. We tried to hail the tug boat, but the wind being directly ahead they could not hear us, and we had no way of signaling to them as the steam whistle which Father recommended had not been put on. We com-

menced to think then the *Monitor* would never see daylight. We watched carefully every drop of water that went down the blowers, and sent continually to ask the fireman how the blowers were going; his only answer was 'slowly, but could not be kept going much longer unless we could stop the water from coming down.' The sea was washing completely over our decks and it was dangerous for a man to go on them, so we could do nothing to the blowers. In the midst of all this our wheel ropes jumped off the steering wheel (owing to the pitching of the ship) and became jammed. She now commenced to sheer about at an awful rate, and we thought that our hawser must certainly part. Fortunately, it was a new one and held on well. In the course of half an hour we fixed the wheel ropes and now our blowers were the only difficulty. About three o'clock on Saturday morning the sea became a little smoother, though still rough and going down our blowers to some extent, and the never failing answer from the engine room 'blowers going slowly, but can't go much longer.' From four o'clock until daylight was certainly the longest hour and a half I ever spent. I certainly thought old Sol had stopped in China and never intended to pay us another visit. At last, however, we could see, and made the tug boat understand to go nearer in shore and get in smooth water, which we did at about eight o'clock A.M. Things were again a little quiet, but everything wet and uncomfortable below. The decks and air ports leaked and the water still came down the hatches and under the tower. I was busy all day making out my station bills and attending to different things that constantly required my attention. At three P.M. we parted our hawser, but fortunately, it was quite smooth and we secured it without difficulty. At four P.M. we passed Cape Henry and heard heavy firing in the direction of Fortress Monroe. As we approached it increased, and we immediately cleared ship for action. When about half way between Fortress Monroe and Cape Henry we spoke a pilot boat. He told us the *Cumberland* was sunk and the *Congress* was on fire, and had surrendered to the *Merrimac*. We did not credit it at first, but as we approached Hampton Roads we could see the fine old *Congress* burning brightly, and we knew then it must be so. Sadly indeed did we feel to think those two fine old vessels had gone to their last homes, with so many of their brave crews. Our hearts were very full and we vowed vengeance on the Merrimac if it should ever be our lot to fall in with her, At nine P.M. we anchored near the frigate *Roanoke*, the flag ship, Captain Marston (the Major's brother). Captain Worden immediately went on board, and received orders from Newport News to protect the *Minnesota* (which was aground) from the *Merrimac*. We immediately got under way and arrived at the *Minnesota* at eleven P.M. I went on board in our cutter and asked the Captain what his prospects were of getting off. He said he should try to get afloat at two A.M., when it was high water. I asked him if we could render him any assistance, to which he replied no. I then told him we should do all in our power to protect him from the attacks of the *Merrimac*. He thanked me kindly and wished us success. just as I arrived back to the *Monitor*, the *Congress* blew up and certainly a grander sight was never seen, but it went straight to the marrow of our bones. Not a word was said, but deep did each man think, and wish he was by the side of the *Merrimac*. At one A.M. we anchored near the *Minnesota*. The Captain and myself remained on deck waiting for the *Merrimac*. At three A.M. we thought the *Minnesota* was afloat and coming down on us, so we got under weigh as soon as possible and stood out of the channel. After backing and filling about for an hour, we found we were mistaken, and anchored again. At daylight we discovered the *Merrimac* at anchor with several vessels under Sewall's Point. We immediately made every preparation for battle. At eight *A.M.* on Sunday, the *Merrimac* got under way, accompanied by several steamers, and started direct for the *Minnesota*. By this time our anchor was up, the men at quarters, the guns loaded, and everything ready for action. As the *Merrimac* came closer, the Captain passed the word to commence firing. I triced up the port, run the gun out, and fired the first gun, and thus commenced the great battle between the *Monitor* and the *Merrimac*.

'Now mark the condition our men and officers were in. Since Friday morning (48 hours)they had had no rest and very little food, as we could not conveniently cook. They had been hard at work all night, and nothing to eat for breakfast except hard bread, and were thoroughly worn out. As for myself, I had not slept a wink for fifty-one hours and had been on my feet almost constantly. But after the first gun was fired we forgot all fatigues, hard work and everything else, and went to work fighting as hard as men ever fought. We loaded and fired as fast as we could. I pointed and fired the guns myself. Every shot I would ask the Captain the effect and the majority of them were encouraging. The Captain was in the pilot-house directing the movements of the vessel. Acting Master Stodder was stationed at the wheel which turns the tower, but as he could not manage it he was relieved by Stimers. The speaking trumpet from the tower to the pilot house was broken, so we passed the word from the Captain to myself on the berth deck, by Paymaster Keeler and Captain's clerk Toffey. Five times during the engagement we touched each other, and each time I fired a gun at her and I will vouch the 168 lbs. penetrated her sides. Once she tried to run us down with her iron prow but did no damage whatever. After fighting for two hours we hauled off for half an hour to hoist shot in the tower. At it we went again as hard as we could. The shot, shell, grape, canister, musket and rifle balls flew about us in every direction, but did us no damage. Our tower was struck several times and though the noise was pretty loud it did not affect us any. Stodder and one of the men were carelessly leaning against the tower when a shot struck the tower exactly opposite to them and disabled them for an hour or two. At about 11:30 the Captain sent for me. I went forward and there stood as noble a man as lives, at the foot of the ladder of the pilot-house. His face was perfectly black with powder and iron and be was apparently perfectly blind. I asked him what was the matter. He said a shot had struck the pilot-house exactly opposite his eyes and blinded him, and he thought the pilot-house was damaged. He told me to take charge of the ship and use my own discretion. I led him to his room and laid him on the sofa and then took his position. On examining the pilot-house I found the iron hatch on top had been knocked about half-way off and the second iron log from the top on the forward side, was completely cracked through. We still continued firing, the tower being under the direction of Stimers. We were between two fires. The *Minnesota* on one side and the *Merrimac* on the other. The latter was retreating to Sewall's Point and the *Minnesota* had struck us twice on the tower. I knew if another shot should strike our pilot-house in the same place our steering apparatus would be disabled and we would be at the mercy of the batteries on Sewall's Point. The *Merrimac* was retreating towards the latter place. We had strict orders to act on the defensive and protect the *Minnesota*. We had evidently finished the *Merrimac*. As far as the *Minnesota* was concerned, our pilot-house was damaged and we had strict orders not to follow the *Merrimac* up; therefore, after the *Merrimac* had retreated, I went to the *Minnesota* and remained by her until she was afloat. General Wool and Secretary Fox, both have complimented me very highly for acting as I did, and said it was the strict military plan to follow. This was the reason we did not sink the *Merrimac*, and everyone here capable of judging says we acted exactly right.

"The fight was over now, and we were victorious. My men and myself were perfectly black with smoke and powder; all my under clothes were perfectly black and my person was in the same condition. As we ran alongside the Minnesota, Secretary Fox hailed us and told us we had fought the greatest naval battle on record and behaved as gallantly as men could. He saw the whole fight. I felt proud and happy then, Mother, and felt fully repaid for all I had suffered. When our noble Captain heard the *Merrimac* had retreated he said he was perfectly happy and willing to die, since he had saved the *Minnesota*. Oh, how I love and venerate that man. Most fortunately for him his classmate and most intimate friend, Lieutenant Wise, saw the fight and was alongside immediately after the engagement. He took him on board the Baltimore boat and carried him to Washington that night. The *Minnesota* was still aground and we stood by her until she floated, about 4 P.M. She grounded again shortly and we anchored for the night. I was now Captain and 1st Lieutenant, and had not a soul to help me in the ship as Stodder was injured and Webber useless. I had been up so long, had had so little rest and been under such a state of excitement that my nervous system was completely run down. Every bone in my body ached; my limbs and joints were so sore that I could not stand. My nerves and muscles twitched as though electric shocks were continually passing through them, and my head ached as if it would burst. Sometimes I thought my brain would come right out over my eyebrows. I laid down and tried to sleep, but I might as well have tried to fly. About 12 o'clock, acting Lieutenant Frye came on board and reported to me for duty. He lives in Topsham, opposite Brunswick, and recollects father very well. He immediately assumed the duties of 1st Luff, and I felt considerably relieved. But no sleep did I get that night owing to my excitement. The next morning at 8 o'clock we got under weigh, and stood through our fleet. Cheer after cheer went up from frigates and small crafts for the glorious little *Monitor*, and happy indeed did we all feel. I was

Captain then of the vessel that had saved Newport News, Hampton Roads, Fortress Monroe (as General Wool himself said) and perhaps your Northern ports. I am unable to express the happiness and joy I felt to think I had served my country, so well, at such an important time. I passed Farquhar's vessel and answered his welcome salute. About 10 A.M. General Wool and Mr. Fox came on board and congratulated me upon our victory, etc., etc. We have a standing invitation from General Wool to dine with him, but no officer is allowed to leave the ship until we sink the *Merrimac*. At eight o'clock that night Tom Selfridge came on board and took command, and brought the following letter from Fox to me:

'U.S. Steamer 'ROANOKE'
Old Point, March 18th.

My Dear Mr. Greene:
'Under the extraordinary circumstances of the contest of yesterday and the responsibility devolving upon me and your extreme youth, I have suggested to Captain Marston to send on board the *Monitor* as temporary commander, Lieutenant Selfridge, until the arrival of Commodore Goldsborough, which will be in a few days. I appreciate your position and you must appreciate mine, and serve with the same zeal and fidelity.'
With the kindest wishes for you all,
Most truly,
G.A. FOX.

'Of course I was a little taken aback at first, but on a second thought I saw it was as it should be. You must recollect the immense responsibility resting upon this vessel. We literally hold all the property ashore and afloat in these regions, as the wooden vessels are useless against the *Merrimac*. At no time during the war, either in the navy or army, has any one position been so important as this vessel. You may think I am exaggerating somewhat because I am in the *Monitor*, but the President, Secretary, General Wool,—all think the same, and have telegraphed to that effect, for us to be vigilant, etc., etc.

'The Captain receives every day numbers of anonymous letters from all parts of the country suggesting plans for him, and I think some people north of Mason and Dixon's Line have a little fear of the *Merrimac*. Under these circumstances it was perfectly right and proper in Mr. Fox, to relieve me from the command, for you must recollect I had never performed any but midshipman's duty before this; but between you and me I would have kept the command with all its responsibility if I had my choice, and either the *Merrimac* or the *Monitor* should have gone down in our next engagement. But then you know, all young people are vain, conceited and without judgment. Even the President telegraphed to Mr. Fox to do so. Mr. President, I suppose, thinking Mr. Fox rather young, he being only about forty. Mr. Fox, however, had already done what the President telegraphed to him, several hours before.

'Selfridge was only in command two days until Lt. Jeffers arrived from Roanoke Island. Mr. Jeffers is everything desirable; talented, educated, energetic and experienced in battle. Well, I believe, I have about finished. Buttsy, my old room-mate, was on board the *Merrimac*; little did we ever think at the Academy we would be firing 150 lb. shot at each other, but so goes the world. Our pilot house is nearly completed. We have now solid oak, extending from three inches below the eyeholes in the pilot-house, to five feet out on the deck. This makes an angle of twenty-seven degrees from the horizontal. This is to be covered with three inches of iron. It looks exactly like a pyramid. We will now be invulnerable at every point. The deepest indentation on our sides was 4 inches; tower 2 inches, and deck 1/2 inch. We were not at all damaged except the pilot-house. No one was affected by the concussion in the tower, either by our own guns or the shots of the enemy.

'This is a pretty long letter for me, for you recollect my writing abilities. With much love to you all, I remain.
'Your affectionate son and brother,
'Dana.'
(copy)
"I certify that this is a correct copy of the original letter now in my possession, written by my father, the late Captain S. Dana Greene, U.S. Navy, shortly after the fight between the *"Monitor"* and the *"Merrimac."* The fight took place in Hampton Roads, Va., March 8th, 1862; at that time my father was executive officer of the *"Monitor,"* having been ordered to her when she first went into commission. He was twenty-two

years old on February 11th, 1862, and had had a Lieutenant's commission for about six months, although only graduated from the U.S. Naval Academy in June, 1859.

(Signed) S. Dana Greene
Schenectady, N.Y.
February 26th, 1898"

Colonel Porter then introduced Congressman C.A. Boutelle to respond to "The Navy." Mr. Boutelle thanked the president for the kindly words with which he had introduced him, and said that they more than compensated for the detraction which "a momentary spasm of wildness that seemed to have taken possession of a portion of our press could have inflicted upon us."

He paid a high tribute to Lieutenant Greene, whose intrepid valor had entirely missed fitting recognition in "the rapid hastening and thickening of events of such a critical character that they obliterated each other as do succeeding waves."

Coming to the subject of the development of our modern navy, Mr. Boutelle said: "Standing as we do at peace with all the world, but still within the shadow of hostilities, I am glad to be able to congratulate you upon the magnificent progress that has been made within the last ten years. There has been no domain in which the magnificent power and resources and splendid adaptability of the American people has been exhibited so marvelously as it has been in the rehabilitation of the American navy.

"When I went to Congress in 1883," he continued, "the United States had not one flag floating above a modern battleship. We have today nine first class battleships, completed and under construction. The *Massachusetts* is believed to be able to fight any ship built, and if she can't, the *Iowa* will. The fundamental principle on which our battleships are constructed is that they must be able to distance any ship that can whip them, and whip any ship that can catch them. I have come over to Philadelphia tonight to meet with some of my old naval comrades, and assure them that I have been doing a little something at my end of the line."

THE USS KEARSARGE VS THE ALABAMA
SHOWDOWN OFF CHERBOURG

Showdown off Cherbourg, by John M. Taylor recounts the final encounter of the *Alabama*, which was destroyed by the *USS Kearsarge*. Raphael Semmes, skipper of the *Alabama*, had sunk 55 Yankee vessels in the Civil War and hence was hated and hunted by the Yankee Navy, none more doggedly than CAPT John Winslow of the *Kearsarge*. Rules of engagement were different then and civilities observed which are not in evidence today.

The abbreviated text presented here is from a publication intitled "Yankee" and printed in July, 1984. The original was uncovered among periodicals in a used book store outside Annapolis, Maryland.

The Reader's attention is also invited to *The Century Illustrated Magazine*, November 1885 to October 1893. Talisman Press, P.O. Box 5485 of Auburn, CA 95604, describes it: " In the Civil War era, the *Century Illustrated Magazine* was a widely read and respected publication both here and abroad". Pages 280-298 is an excellent piece describing the origin, design and development of the *Monitor*. Also "The Loss On The *Monitor*", written by a survivor, pages 299-300, and "The Duel Between The *Alabama* and the *Kearsarge*", by the surgeon of the *Kearsarge*, John M. Browne, pp. 923-934.

"On June 11, 1864, the residents of the French port of Cherbourg were intrigued to see a sleek black-hulled cruiser steaming slowly past the breakwater, perhaps the most famous ship afloat – the Confederate raider *Alabama*, a British built warship that had destroyed 55 Yankee merchantmen in the Civil War at sea. The Union Navy, embarrassed by the Alabama's depredations, had no higher priority than to bring the Rebel "pirate" to bay.

"Skipper of the *Alabama* was Maryland born Raphael Semmes, a career Navy man. The combative Semmes would have preferred fighting the Union Navy to harassing Northern shipping. When acting as a commerce raider he fought by the rules; there had been virtually no loss of life aboard the Yankee merchantmen he had overtaken and destroyed. After 22 months at sea Semmes could no longer postpone a refit, and he hoped that France would prove a politically hospitable host.

"Some 300 miles northeast, at the Dutch port of Flushing, Captain John Winslow of the USS *Kearsarge* received electrifying news: the no-

torious *Alabama* had been seen to enter port at Cherbourg. Winslow, who had spent two years pursuing the *Alabama*, wasted no time in getting under way, and by June 14 the *Kearsarge* was off Cherbourg. Winslow and Semmes had been messmates in the old Navy, now they were enemies and spoiling for a fight.

"The *Kearsarge* and the *Alabama* were almost equal in size and fighting power. Both were screw steamers of about the same tonnage, and while equipped for sail, depended primarily on two coal-fired engines. The *Alabama* carried a crew of 149 and mounted eight guns; the *Kearsarge* had a complement of 163 and seven guns. The outcome of the battle would depend heavily on the skill of the commanders. Twenty-year-old William Alsdorf, a native of Hamburg, Germany, may have had only a limited understanding of the war, but he knew an exciting battle when he saw one, and five months after the *Kearsarge* took on the *Alabama*, William set down his version of what transpired.

"We steamed up with our signal flags flying from stem to stern as a challenge for the *Alabama* to come out and meet us...

"(On June 14 a boat flying a white flag came to our vessel bearing Lieutenant Kell of the *Alabama*. He presented the challenge for our Captain Winslow.

"Capt. Winslow, after reading the challenge, told the Lieutenant of the *Alabama* that he would meet Capt. Semmes with pleasure. Kell saluted Capt. Winslow and returned to his boat and rowed back to the *Alabama*. Capt. Winslow gave orders to unlimber guns, get ammunition ready, and be in order for immediate action.

"We cruised within the three-mile limit, keeping a close watch on the Alabama, as we suspected that the *Alabama* might leave the harbor at night.

"In the meantime our opponent, the *Alabama*, was busy completing repairs, taking on coal, supplies, and ammunition in order to be ready for a trip.

"Considering the *Alabama's* need of an overhaul, Semmes may appear to have been unduly eager to take on the *Kearsarge*. If he were to remain in Cherbourg, the Yankees would send so many fighting ships that the *Alabama* would probably be blocked the remainder of the war. Far better a fair fight in which the *Alabama* might bring new glory to the fledgling Confederate Navy!

"Unknown to Semmes, the enterprising Winslow had made imaginative use of his ship's chains, draping them along vulnerable portions of the hull and concealing them behind wood paneling.

"On Sunday the 19th, about 9 a.m. the bell had just tolled for service, and our captain was ready to commence the reading. His first sentence was just finished when the look-out hailed "Ship ahoy!"...

"Our officer of the deck spied a vessel with a Brazilian flag leaving the port. Next the large French iron vessel and after it the *Alabama*.

The clash was pure theater. Everyone in France wanted to view what would prove to be the last single-ship duel of the era of wooden ships. Excursion trains and throngs of small craft hovered for a closer view of the hostilities. Semmes did make a speech to his crew, reminding them that "the name of your ship has become a household word throughout the civilized world," and asking rhetorically, "Shall that name be tarnished by defeat?" His men shouted back, "Never!"

"As soon as we saw the *Alabama* approaching, every man sprang to his station. The guns were unlimbered ready for action long before the long roll of drum and fife (called) us to quarters. We heaved around until we were headed straight for our opponent...

"We were within 1,200 yards of our opponent. She gave us a volley of seven guns, and one shot struck the waterline. The next shot struck the water and cut off some of the rigging. We were going at the fullest speed towards the *Alabama*. As we were unable to fire any of our guns, the captain shouted, "Lay down, boys," as the *Alabama* had a raking bulls eye on us, and if one of his 100 pound rifle balls would sweep our deck it would be a great loss of life.

"Many thought Capt. Winslow intended to run into her. But he intended to run at her stern to give her raking shots in return. The captain of the *Alabama* sheared to starboard, parallel to our starboard side. As soon as Semmes came around, enabling us to bear our side guns on him ... the boys shot off their guns.

"Winslow hoped to run under the *Alabama's* stern and there deliver a broadside, but Semmes turned away to prevent this. The result was an engagement in which the two antagonists fought in a circular track, each with his starboard side engaged, at a distance of from one-quarter to one-half mile.

"Whilst we were thus engaged a shell struck amidships and exploded, setting the side on fire. The fire squad soon extinguished the fire. Jack Dempsey came along with one arm dangling loose at his side. He threw his other arm towards the *Alabama* and said, "Take this one, too."

"Lt. Weaver hollered, "Fire, Fire, Fire!" And our shot went through the *Alabama's* side and we saw the coal fly through the air midships. (Another shot) struck midship and exploded on the *Alabama's* starboard side, bursting open her deck.

"The firing now became very hot," Semmes wrote, "and the enemy's shot soon began to tell on our hull, knocking down, killing, and disabling a number of men ... in different parts of the ship." According to some accounts, Semmes offered a reward to the gun crew that could silence the two 11 inch Dahlgrens – one of them Alsdorfs – that were wreaking such havoc aboard his ship.

"The two antagonists offered contrasts in marksmanship. The *Kearsarge* fired a total of 173 rounds. Onlookers estimated that the *Alabama* fired about twice that many, but of the 28 shots that struck the Union vessel - many in the rigging - only two or three caused significant damage. Of the *Kearsarge's* three casualties, only one, William Gorwin, would eventually die of his wounds.

"Both of our ships were completely enveloped in smoke, but as we were fighting in a circle we soon ran out of it, and then the shells flew thick and fast. After one hour's fighting the *Alabama's* fire slackened, and then she tried to make sail and run for shore. As her fires were out and her engine useless, she began sinking. Her ensign ... was shot down early in the engagement... They now fired their lee gun to leeward in token of surrender which we acknowledged. Our Captain ordered (us) to cease firing but to stand by our guns.

"After we ceased firing a few moments, two shells came booming at us. Capt. Winslow shouted, "Give it to them, boys – they are playing us a trick!"

"Then we noticed a white flag as a sign of second surrender. They lowered a boat at the stern that came along with a Lieutenant Wilson. Our Lieutenant Thornton asked him if he surrendered. He stated, "I have no orders to that effect but to ask you to take these wounded men on board." He desired to pick up those men struggling in the water and to deliver them to us on board. In the meantime the *Deerhound* came along our bow, and Winslow spoke to the captain. "Will you please, in the name of humanity, pick up those men from drowning?" Aye Aye came the answer and the *Deerhound* lowered her boats and picked up all they could find struggling in the water.

"Nothing in the action would prove more controversial than the action of the English yacht, which shortly sailed off to Britain with the rescued Semmes, his first officer, and 38 other "pirates" saved from the English Channel.

"Lieutenant Wilson returned with his boat loaded with saved men. He surrendered and presented his sword to Lieutenant Thornton, who would not receive it and stated, "Never mind, keep your sword."

"The only gentleman among the pirate officers was Lieutenant Wilson. As soon as the *Deerhound* had our prisoners safe on board she steamed rapidly away for England with 40 prisoners, Capt. Semmes and 14 officers among them. Capt. Semmes and his officers had thrown their swords into the sea when they abandoned their sinking ship.

"Capt. Winslow called all hands to muster He read a prayer and said, "We have won the battle without loss of life, and God must be on our side. Our boats, with the aid of two French pilot boats, picked up 65 men and five officers ... You are requested to give them some of your clothing and report any expense to me. These men have surrendered and I want you to treat them as brothers and shipmates.

"The two commanders in the *Kearsarge-Alabama* duel both survived the war. Semmes returned to the Confederacy and commanded an army brigade in the closing months of the war. John Winslow was slow in getting recognition for his feat in destroying the *Alabama*. The Navy Department complained that Winslow's report on the battle was insufficiently detailed. Nevertheless, his victory over the *Alabama* brought about Winslow's promotion to Commodore. After the war he became an admiral(sic)."

USS KEARSARGE VERSUS THE ALABAMA–SHOWDOWN OFF CHERBOURG

Right: "Old Beeswax" Semmes had captained the Confederate cruiser Alabama *to world fame, sinking 55 Yankee vessels in the Civil War at sea. For two years Bostonian John Winslow held the* Kearsarge *in dogged pursuit. On June 19, 1864, the two brave crews played out the final act as thousands of spectators looked on. By John M. Taylor*
Left: "Destruction of Alabama *by* Kearsarge*" an 1864 oil painting by British artist Edwin Hayes, depicts the rescue of* Alabama *survivors by a boat from the* Kearsarge

Special Stories

S. J. Majka, CDR, USNR(Ret.)

We ran into a typhoon which lasted for 36 hours. We lost all our airplanes off the flight deck and the ship had undergone great stress. It had rolled up to 38 degrees from normal, which, for an aircraft carrier, was almost at the overturning point. The wind was so terrific that we had rolled up the metal curtains on each side of the hanger dack to save them from damage. One of our chiefs was passing an open area near the forward elevator when a great gust of wind whipped him into the rolling ocean. Luckily of him, the ship rolled to port, (his direction) and a couple of pilots, who had gone to the flight deck to see what was transpiring and who had been forced to lie prone on the deck, holding onto the arresting gear deck cleats for dear life, happened to see the chief's body floating by. They reached out, grabbed him, and pulled him aboard before he was swept out past the rear port side of the flight deck and out to sea. Whew! There is a man definitely living his second life! Except for this rare set of circumstances, there was absolutely no way of picking him up–ever!

CDR Stanley J. Majka as V-2 Division Officer while aboard the aircraft carrier CVL-26, USS Monterey, 1944.

Fighter Friends –By Van Watts

Mike did it all, boxed, wrestled, refereed, acted and founded Hollywood's Cauliflower Alley Club. One day he was returning from somewhere in a 347 when the chap in the seat next to his introduced himself as Jeff Botton, President of the Navy League's Hollywood Council.

"Navy?" said Mike. "Do you know Van Watts?"

"Why, he's a member of our council!" said Jeff, whereupon Mike explained I was a member of his club. But Mike Mazurki is only one of many friends from the ring. Some years back a Navy fighter flew into town looking for the fellow who, in the early fifties, had starred him on radio and television. Bill Brennan had been one of my Original Sailors of the Week, the famed "nautical celebrities" who inspired Sailor of the Week, Month, and Year Programs Navy-wide. A "nautical celebrity" with a punch, Bill had just become President of the World Boxing Association.

And I must tell you about Kid Chissell. A Hollywood area couple, who came to know us both, thought we two old Navy fellows ought to get together. And that's where Bob Hope, another ex-fighter, found us the day he put together the cast for his latest NBC-TV Special starring the new World Heavyweight Champion, George Foreman.

Back in1932, Kid had won the All-Navy middleweight Boxing Title, and subsequently carved out a career in Hollywood, appearing in twenty of Bob's NBC-TV Specials, and winning an award for parts, big and small, in over a thousand films. Consequently, if there was anyone in Hollywood he didn't know, I can't imagine who it was.

But you can imagine what it was like accompanying Kid around Hollywood. We never once had lunch together but one or more actors or actresses would come over to our table to share memories of the movies they had made with Kid. One lady remembered making a shoot'em-up-western with him twenty years earlier.

"Why if it isn't Kid Chissell!" she had exclaimed.

But walking or talking, some actor or actress up in years was sure to barge in with "Why, if it isn't Kid Chissell!" It was a little like a long series of flashbacks into Hollywood's Golden Era.

Bob depended on the former All-Navy Champ to put fighters at ease whenever he had one on his show during the long four-hour taping of his two-hour specials. And having gotten the entire cast together except Chissell, Bob had been told he was "over at Van Watt' place". And there we were telling sea stories and sipping coffee when the phone rang, but it often rang for Kid Chissell. In what must have been an endurance record, Kid would average twenty films a year for fifty years. In the very week Bob's NBC-TV Special aired, he would also appear on the Julie Andrews Hour and in a rerun of "To Tell The Truth".

"Chissell! What a name for a fighter!" Bob would say of my old friend. But how about Bell?

And chances are, I never would have met Archie Bell had he been behaving himself and not partying in his eighties. Though to my knowledge he never held a world title, "He was some fighter!" My barber remembers. But who could forget? Especially after his last fight, at a local mall.

It seems Archie was taking a stroll in broad daylight when a couple of young fellows jumped him. After all, he was an old white-haired man, shrunken a little to about five foot six. What possibile trouble could he give a couple of young fellows who only wanted his wallet?

So easing around him, one was about to crush his skull with a black-jack, when ringwise Archie, sensing they were up to no good, suddenly turned and his neck muscles took the impact of the weapon. Their crotches took the impact of Archie's orthopedic shoes as each in turn crashed screaming to the floor of the mall, in the process one of them dropping the blackjack.

"Look at the old man beating uo those two young punks," said bystanders at the mall, as he pounded them into submission with their own weapon. And that was the situation when the police arrived.

Born Al Brown in New York City in 1906, Archie says he came up fighting to survive. You can tell his old friends back there that here in Hollywood, Archie is still surviving. And I am glad that he survived long enough to become the most recent, but I hope not the last, of my fighter friends. Cheers!

From the Walpole Gazette, February 7, 1992

July 22, 1997
Dear Ed:
These fellows both entertained servicemen throughout World War II. They had known each other since back in the late 1920's when Hope and Chissell had trained in Cleveland's famed Marriot's gym which had turned out the likes of Gene Tunney. Via vaudeville and radio,

Two of Van Watts' "Fighter-Friends" in Hollywood: Bob "Packy-East" Hope is at right, with Noble "Kid" Chissell, the 1932 All-Navy Middleweight Boxing Champ. The scene is from the 1940 Paramount Pictures release, "The Road to Rio".

Hope would end up in Hollywood and in the movies! But Chissell would beat him to it! At Great Lakes Naval Training Center he would become known as Popeye the Sailor when he knocked a professional prize fighter cold! In 1932, he would become the Navy's All-Navy Middleweight Boxing Champ and two years later would be helping Hollywood make those great fight pictures of the 1930's–and that's what he would be doing when his old friend from Cleveland arriving in Tinsel Town! Kid Chissell starred and co-starred in some of those fight pictures. In others he just trained guys like Robert Taylor to look like fighters!

Then Bob took him along on USO tours and gave him parts in his "ROAD" shows, and thirty television shows, including 20 of his NBC-TV Specials. When Kid passed away at 93 in 1987, interred on Veterans Day, of all days, Bob was in Washington presiding over Veterans ceremonies. If much of Hollywood had shown up for Chissell's funeral, the biggest bunch of flowers came from Bob Hope–if I had beaten him to the punch with the first!

The closest of Kid's hollywood buddies, ten years later I have told the curator of the new Great Lakes Naval Museum that, if they will do the job, I will provide the memorabilia for a permanent memorial for the Great Lakes Popeye the Sailor!

Van Watts

Lt. Kenneth A. Menken, USNR

During the summer of 1953, I was serving as an Ensign abroad a tanker with the Sixth Fleet in the Mediterranean. The ship lay at anchor for a few days taking a break from fueling formations. We were in Golfe Juan near Cap d' Antibes, and several of us junior officers were granted shore leave to Eden Roc, to this day an elegant resort on the Riviera.

Going over by motor whaleboat, we were dropped off at the base of a shallow cliff guarding the restaurant and pool area. It was a glorious day, we had our bathing suits and we soon found ourselves surrounded by a college of Europe's elite, not to mention Gregory Peck and his gamine co-star Audrey Hepburn, having just completed *Roman Holiday*. In Navy parlance, it was a hundred and eighty degrees from our usual shipboard routine.

After basking in the sun, swimming and taking photographs, we repaired to the window-framed dining room overlooking the bay, and our ship, and settled in for lunch. The previous winter, we had called at Aruba, NWI, and it's Lago refinery to take on oil. The island was a relative wasteland compared with its tourist attractions today, but pausing for refreshment, we discovered a delightful Dutch brew called Heineken's. It was not for sale in the States; so when we saw it on the restaurant menu, our table was soon laden with the green bottles. The Navy did have some redeeming features.

As we dined, a smiling chap approached our group, clearly wanting to make conversation and, as we told him who we were, he introduced himself as Freddy Heineken. He had recently married an American and was on a brief honeymoon. Finding him most agreeable and entertaining, it soon became apperant that he was engaging in a bit of market research. How and where had we come by his beer? Does it really suit our tastes in the land of the Bud and the Schlitz? As the conversation proceeded, he insisted on sending a case out to our ship amidst protests that, unlike the Royal Navy, ours had a strict policy of *No Booze Aboard*. After awhile, he parted with a cheery wave, and we prepared to return to the ship.

The following afternoon I had the quarterdeck watch, in other words I was the duty gatekeeper on board. As I stood looking fondly at Juan Les Pins and back at Eden Roc, a small boat pulled alongside, announcing that a package was being delivered to Ensigns Brace, Garrison, Menken and Spivey. As I peered over, a sizeable box wrapped in white paper was being held up marked Electric Trains. I smiled inwardly, allowed it to be brought aboard, and after extending our thanks, ordered it stowed away. Weeks later, on our return to the States, our small group gathered at a table near the Norfolk Naval base and reminisced over, I don't think I have to tell you, Freddy's thoughtful kindness.

The incident would have been all but forgotten except for news headlines three decades later announcing the kidnapping of one Alfred Heineken, scion of the Dutch brewery family, and his chauffeur (for ransom). They were shortly thereafter released. Never having the chance to communicate with Freddy after sailing off with his gift, it struck me to write a much belated note of thanks, also expressing relief at his safe return from captivity. I did so, exercising a little poetic license by including my long since scattered shipmates as well wishers, and a photograph of us that distant afternoon.

Satisfied with my gesture, a few weeks passed unnoticed when a letter arrived from Amsterdam. To quote, Freddy had responded:

April 5, 1984

Dear Mr. Menken,

I feel a little guilty that I did not answer your letter of February 13 sooner. The reaon for the delay is that I had to anwser several thousands of letters (seriously) upon my liberation, and that I decided to anwser the "special" ones when I got through the bulk of correspondence.

So, here I am at last.

I vaguely remember the incident at Eden Roc some 30 years ago and feel rather proud of the fact that I kept my promise to send a case of beer to the ship. Had I been you, I would have been very unhappy not to recieve an electric train but beer instead, even if it was our famous product.

I am returning your photograph since I'm not sure you have a copy yourself. I do know that the girl in the white bikini in the background is my wife, and I even believe that I am the one standing between her and the man in the white shirt. I look alot worse now.

Thank you very much for your letter.

Kindest regards,

yours sincerely,

That left me feeling quite gratified, and even more so when a few days later our office receptionist announced a visitor carrying an unusual looking package for me. Moments later, a messenger from the Heineken New York distributor appeared at my door extending personal thanks from Freddy. He placed a case of Heineken on my desk, shook my hand and left. When I pried the case open, I uncovered a magnificent set of Markel electric trains.

By Kenneth A. Menken

USS Houston (CA-30)Pride Of The Asiatic Fleet

USS *Houston* (CA-30) was sunk at the beginning of World War II on March 1, 1942, at a place called Sunda Strait between the Indonesian islands of Sumatra and Java. She was in company with the Australian light cruiser HMAS Perth attempting to steam south through Sunda Strait to reach Australia before the strong Japanese fleet in the Java Sea to the north could destroy them. Dutch air reconnaissance reported that the strait was clear for their night transit. However, a large Japanese force had started to make a major landing on the northwestern tip of Java. Both ships fought valiantly before both were sunk about midnight.

USS *Houston* was one of eight heavy cruisers of the Northampton class. She had nine eight-inch guns in three turrets. Her secondary battery was eight 5-inch/25-caliber guns in single mounts. She was 603 feet long and 66 feet 1 inch in beam. Originally she was built with a six-tube 21-inch torpedo mount, but this was later removed. She also carried four seaplanes.

In 1927 Mr. William A. Bernrieder, who was a Naval Reserve officer and an aide to Mayor Oscar Holcombe, energetically pursued a campaign to have one of the eight heavy cruisers authorized by Congress named in honor of the city of Houston. The school children of Houston wrote over 50,000 letters requesting that one of the cruisers be named for the city. The campaign was successful and the ship was named for the city and was commissioned on June 17, 1930. She visited Houston that year and received a gift of their silver service. She was President Franklin Delano Roosevelt's favorite ship, having made four cruises aboard her.

Just before the outbreak of the Pacific war with Japan the USS *Houston*, which was the flagship of the Asiatic Fleet, was in Cavite Navy Yard near Manila. She was ordered to leave there on December 1, 1941 and proceed to Ilo Ilo on the south side of the island of Panay. On December 7 after the Pearl Harbor attack, she manned her guns and got underway and cleared the harbor staying in the shadow of the mountains just in time to see Japanese planes bomb the harbor and attack and sink a large transport anchored there which the Japanese thought was the USS *Houston*. This was the first time the Japanese reported that they had sunk her. It happened subsequently in the vicinity of Java, which led to the ship being called the "Galloping ghost of the Java Coast."

After leaving the Philippines on December 7, USS *Houston* steamed south through the South China Sea and the Java Sea and served as a convoy escort between Java and the northern port of Darwin, Australia during December and January 1942. The Japanese, by this time, had conquered most of the area north of Java.

USS *Houston* operated out of the port of Surabaja on the northeast coast of Java. On February 4, 1942, USS *Houston* and the light cruiser, USS *Marblehead* were operating in the Madura Strait north of Bali and were attacked by 54 land based Japanese bombers. The rudder of the *Marblehead* was severely damaged. USS *Houston* was struck by a large bomb on her number three turret that killed 48 men and knocked the turret out of action. The *Houston* gunners were accurate against the attacking aircraft, but only about 20-30% of the antiaircraft shells were exploding because the ammunition was outdated.

On February 10, 1942, USS *Houston* left Java for Darwin, Australia to escort a convoy of four troop ships, which were going to attempt to reinforce the troops on the island of Timor. Japanese aircraft attacked the convoy but Houston was able to defend herself and the convoy. However, the convoy was ordered to return to Darwin. On February 17, 1942, *Houston* left Darwin for Surabaja, Java, to join a multi-national fleet being formed of about 14 Allied capital ships to counter Japanese forces converging on Java from two directions with large naval forces.

The Japanese fleets were converging from the north through the South China Sea and the Makassar Strait east of Borneo. This Allied fleet of ABDA forces (American, British, Dutch and Australian) was placed under a Dutch admiral, Rear Admiral Karel Doorman. This fleet suffered from the fact that they had never operated together and the commander spoke a different language than that of the English-speaking crews. Many of the Dutch ships had no English-speaking interpreters. The Allies formed this fleet in hopes of giving time to build up the defenses of Australia. The Battle of the Java Sea was fought in a single day and night action on February 27, 1942. It was the first surface-to-surface action of the Pacific War, the first large surface action since the Battle of Jutland in World War I.

The eight-hour battle took place north of Surabaja in the Java Sea. The superior Japanese forces sank a total of 12 Allied capital ships. Surviving the action were the two cruisers: HMAS *Perth* and USS *Houston*.

The Dutch admiral in charge, Rear Admiral Karel Doorman, went down with one of the Dutch cruisers. The commanding officer of the Australian light cruiser HMAS *Perth*, Captain Hector M.L. Waller, became the senior officer remaining and took charge of *Perth* and *Houston*. He ordered the two cruisers to disengage and made a feint to the southeast, but then turned into the western port of Batavia for refueling prior to making an attempt to escape to Australia. Captain Albert H. Rooks, USN, was the commanding officer of USS *Houston*. The Battle of Sunda Strait took place on the northwestern tip of Java near a bay called Banten Bay. Although the air reconnaissance reports indicated that Sunda Strait was free of enemy shipping, it was far from that. The two cruisers had run directly into the middle of a large Japanese landing force, which was landing troops on Java. The two cruisers fought valiantly but could not overcome the sheer power of numbers. The *Perth* sank shortly after midnight after having been hit by four torpedoes. *Houston* fought on alone until sinking at about 12:22 a.m. on March 1, 1942, after being hit by a fourth torpedo. *Houston* was listing to starboard when Japanese destroyers formed a semi-circle and illuminated her with searchlights while firing their batteries at her. The Commanding Officer of *Houston*, Captain Albert H. Rooks, USN, was killed by shrapnel on the bridge. The abandon ship order was given just a few minutes before the ship sank.

The two cruiser captains have been highly praised for the magnificent manner in which the two cruisers were fought and handled. For his extraordinary heroism Captain Rooks was awarded the Medal of Honor posthumously. *Houston* had a crew of 1,068 men assigned at the beginning of the battle. Only 368 men survived to become prisoners of war. Of the latter number, 79 died at the hands of their captors from starvation, disease and mistreatment. The survivors from the POW camps totaled 289 after 3-1/2, years of captivity until their liberation in September 1945.

The fate of the *Perth* and *Houston* was not known to the outside world until the end of 1944. At that time U.S. submarines picked up large numbers of Allied survivors from Japanese transports they had sunk. Among the survivors were four enlisted men from *Perth* who told what had happened to both ships during the battle and also the inhuman treatment they had received as prisoners of war while working on the Burma-Siam railway. The Burma-Siam railway was built by the prisoners of war to take supplies from Bangkok, Thailand, to Burma to support the Japanese war effort there. The bridge over the River Kwai was a part of this railway. The railway was 262 miles long, much of it through very thick jungle growth.

The Japanese forced about 200,000 natives to work on the railway as slave labor after "liberating" them from their Dutch and British "colonial oppressors." The Japanese supplied the prisoners with very few tools. The labor had to be performed with brute force. The only clothing furnished to the prisoners was some diaper-like shorts. The prisoners lived in huts constructed of bamboo poles and leaves. Allied prisoners working on the railway numbered 61,000 and approximately 16,000 died. Of the 200,000 native workers only 30,000 ever were accounted for after the project completion. The Japanese were never able to use the railway because the Allies bombed the bridges as soon as they were repaired.

In the spring of 1942, after it was known that the *Houston* was lost with a crew of more than one thousand men, the people of Houston initiated a drive to collect funds for a new USS *Houston*. More than $85 million was raised from contributions of the school children of Houston, major corporations and the public, which covered the cost of a new cruiser and a new small aircraft carrier. The two new ships were USS *Houston* (CL-81) and USS *San Jacinto* (CVL-30). On May 30, 1942, a public swearing in ceremony was held on Main Street in downtown Houston to swear in one thousand Texas volunteers to replace the gallant crew of the lost USS *Houston*. A small monument depicting this event exists on the west side of Main Street between Lamar and McKinney Streets.

By Carter B. Conlin, CAPT, USN (RET)
Naval Order of the United States, Texas Commandery

Biographies

WILLIAM RONALD ADELAAR, LT, USNR, was commissioned as ENS, USNR, after graduating from Dartmouth College and completing the Contract NROTC program in 1963. His two years active service were spent aboard the ice breaker USS ATKA (AGB-3) with deployments to McMurdo Sound, Antarctica (Operation Deep Freeze 1964) and to Baffin Bay, Greenland (Operation SUNEC 1964). He was honorably discharged from the Navy as LT, USNR, in 1974.

After his active service, he attended graduate school and participated in a bank training program before joining Adelaar Bros., Inc. in 1968. He completed his MBA degree in the evening at Fordham University in 1972.

He worked for Adelaar Bros. for 18 years and became chief operating officer and treasurer. The firm was wound down in 1986 after 52 years of successful operations. Since 1986 he has been a private investor based in New York.

FRANK JAMES ALLSTON, RADM (0-8), born Oct. 2, 1930, New Bern, NC. He has AB degree in Journalism and Political Science (1952) and MBA degree from University of Chicago (1988).

Allston joined the USNR Feb. 7, 1951 and was commissioned June 6, 1952. Active duty: NSCS, Bayonne, NJ, 1952-53; BuSandA Navy Dept., 1953-54; and reserve duty in New York, North Carolina, New Jersey and Illinois.

Units served with include NR Ships Supply Off. Div. 3-3, (1968-69); NR Supply Co. 6-7 (1969); and NR SPCC Mechanicsburg 1013 (1974-77).

Memorable experiences: directed Naval Reserve Supply Development and Readiness Project, 1978-85; received two Centurion awards for making 215 Sea Power presentations in 11 states and Canada; researched and wrote *Ready For Sea,* the bicentennial history of the USN Supply Corps, 1795-1995.

RADM Allston retired from the USNR in 1985. His awards include the Navy Meritorious Service Medal, Legion of Merit and Armed Forces Reserve Medal w/2 Hour Glasses.

He married Barbara French Brown and they have two children, James Frank and John Pierson, and three (soon to be four) grandchildren: Pierson John, Christine Loraine and Nathan Lenard.

As a civilian he was employed with General Electric (mgr.), Bunker Ramo Corp. (dir.), IC Industries (dir., fin. comm.) and Illinois Central Railroad (VP, corporate affairs). Retired from ICRR in 1989.

RICHARD "RICH" ANDRIANO-MOORE, CDR, born May 25, 1932, Petaluma, CA. He received his commission as Ensign, USNR, in 1957, upon graduation from the Officer Candidate School, Newport, RI. He received his BA degree from San Jose State University, his MBA degree from Pepperdine University, and attended several Navy schools, including the Naval War College.

A Surface Warfare Officer he served aboard ships in both the Atlantic and Pacific Fleets.

Shore assignments, included command of several Naval and Marine Corps Reserve Centers; duty on the staff, Commandant, 11th Naval District, San Diego, CA; Director of Administrations and Operations Officer, National Committee for Employer Support of the Guard and Reserve; and as Commander, Naval Reserve Recruiting Region One (Ten Western States). Commander Andriano-Moore completed his Naval career as Chief of Staff, Naval Reserve Readiness Command Region Twenty, Treasure Island, San Francisco, CA, retiring on Aug. 31, 1985.

He is a member of the San Francisco Commandery, NOUS, the Naval Reserve Association and the Retired Officers Association.

His decorations and awards include the Defense Meritorious Service Medal, Navy Commendation Medal (2 awds.), Navy Expert Pistol Shot Medal w/Silver E, two Gold Wreaths for recruiting excellence, Office of the Secretary of Defense Identification Badge, Command Ashore Insignia and the Surface Warfare Insignia.

After retirement CDR Andriano-Moore resided in Petaluma, CA. He now lives in Santa Rosa, CA with his two children, Erika and Stephen, who attend Santa Rosa Junior College. CDR Andriano-Moore is listed in *Who's Who of California* and Marquis *Who's Who of the West, In America,* and *the World.*

HENRY JACQUES "HEINIE" ARMSTRONG JR., RADM, USN (RET), born in Salt Lake City, UT on June 14, 1903. He graduated from USN Academy in 1927. During WWII he served in the Aleutians as Commanding Officer, USS *Waters* (DD-115), 1940-41.

As CO of USS *Spence* (DD-512) he performed convoy duties off North Africa. Thence to the Pacific area, joining Destroyer Squadron 23 (Arleigh Burke's "Little Beavers"). This renowned group participated in the Solomon Islands campaign and the battles of Empress Augustus Bay and Cape St. George. Awarded two Navy Crosses, the Silver Star and the Bronze Star w/Combat V.

While CO of USS *Adams*, and participating in the Okinawa Campaign, the ship was struck twice by Japanese kamikaze, destroying the rudders. After minor repairs, Adams escorted the

USS *Chicago* from Guam back to Pearl Harbor, maintaining station using only the twin propellers for steering; awarded second Bronze Star w/Combat V.

At cessation of hostilities, as Commander Mine Division 8, he volunteered to organize and command a group of damaged cargo ships, known as the Guinea Pig Squadron. The ships were rigged with remote control from bridge to the engine and fire rooms, fully loaded and by reversing the degaussing gear, maximum electrical effect was achieved to explode possible mines. The ships operated in formation, steaming through already "mine swept" Japanese channels to ensure safety of the occupation ships. Awarded the Legion of Merit w/Combat V.

Served as Naval Attaché with US Embassy in Venezuela, 1946-48, and awarded the Order of Bolivar; Head, Mine Warfare and Harbor Defense, CNO, 1948-51; commanded Destroyer Squadron 15, patrolling Korean waters and bombarded shore facilities, 1951; awarded a second Legion of Merit w/Combat V. Retired in 1956 as Rear Admiral.

Remained active in civic organizations and is a member of the San Francisco Commandery and Past Vice Commander General NOUS.

He is father of Capt. Jan V. Armstrong, USNR (Ret) and Derik V. Armstrong. RADM Armstrong passed away in 1989.

JAN V. ARMSTRONG, CAPT, USNR (Ret), born April 11, 1935, Annapolis, MD. She graduated from Barat College of the Sacred Heart, 1957, and was commissioned ensign in 1958. She is the daughter of the late RADM Henry J. Armstrong Jr.

During her nine years of active duty, assignments included tours of duty with the Bureau of Ships; Operational Test and Evaluation Force, Virginia; District Intelligence Office, Hawaii; recruit training for women, Maryland; and Navy Correspondence Course Center, New York.

After leaving active duty, she affiliated with the Naval Reserve serving in various capacities including: Assistant Chief of Staff for Administration and Senior Inspector, REDCOM 20; CO of VTU 2011; BIOMED Emergency Response Unit 120; XO of PERS MOB Team 220, and RADCW ERTPAC 120; and Coordinator Command Assistance Team, Alameda. CAPT Armstrong retired in 1991.

In civilian life she was a management services officer with the University of California, retiring in 1992.

She is the Registrar General of NOUS and a member of the San Francisco Commandery, the Naval Reserve Association and the University of California Faculty Club. Hobbies include raising and training her German Shepherd dogs.

She resides in Oakland, CA.

JOHN ELWIN "JAY" ARNOLD, CAPT, born Sept. 7, 1931, Maud, MS. Attended the University of Mississippi, BBA, 1953; US Naval Postgraduate School, certificate, 1963; George Washington University, MS, 1967. Joined the

USN and was commissioned NROTC, May 30, 1953.

Military stations: USS *NOA* (DD-841); USS *Galveston* (CLG-3); USS *Engage* (MSO-433); USS *Duncan* (DDR-874); USS *Joseph Strauss* (DDG-16); USS *White Plains* (AFS-4). Units served with: DESLANT, CRULANT, OPNAV, SECNAV, NAVMAT. Commands held: MSO-433, DDG-16, AFS-4.

Discharged June 30, 1983, with the rank of Captain. Awards and medals include Vietnam Service Medal w/5 stars, Korean Service Medal, UN Service Medal, Legion of Merit w/Gold Star, Meritorious Service Medal and Meritorious Unit Commendation.

Memorable experiences: sailed around the world (including a WESTPAC deployment from Norfolk, VA) in the USS *NOA* (DD-841), 1953-54.

Married Anne V. Risley and has two sons, CDR Thomas E., USN, and CDR David R., USN. Two of his brothers were also naval officers. Grandchildren are Emily, Andrew, Caroline and Elisabeth. Civilian employment included Director, Government Relations, UNISYS Defense Systems. He retired June 30, 1990.

GEORGE H. ASTER, CAPT, USNR (Ret), born April 22, 1932, in Detroit and raised in Grand Rapids, MI, CAPT. Aster enlisted in the Naval Reserve as a Seaman Recruit May 1, 1951. By the time of his graduation from the University of Michigan in 1955 with a Bachelor of Architecture degree, he had advanced to the rate of CT3.

Commissioned as Ensign USNR through the ROC program at Newport, RI in August 1955, he was ordered to USN Station, Argentia, Newfoundland, where he served successively as Communications Watch Officer, Personnel Officer and Special Services Officer.

Released from active duty in August 1957, he migrated to San Francisco, where he worked many years as an architect. In San Francisco he affiliated with the Naval Reserve Intelligence program, and during the following 23 years advanced to the rank of Captain.

He retired from the Naval Reserve on June 1, 1981 and from his civilian employment with Pacific Gas & Electric Co., May 1, 1992. CAPT Aster and his wife Pat reside in Larkspur, CA. They have two sons and, as of 1996, five grandchildren.

GARY BAIR, CAPT, USNR, born Feb. 9, 1939, Pleasantville, NY and educated at Phillips Exeter Academy and Amherst College. Commissioned from OCS in 1962.

Stationed at San Diego, Santa Monica, Seattle, Philadelphia, Great Lakes and New Orleans.

Units include USS *Providence* (CLG-6), Seventh Fleet Flagship, 1962-65; USS *Richard S. Edwards* (DD-950), 1966-68; Destroyer Division 12, 1969-71; XO, USS *McKean* (DD-784), 1975-76; Destroyer Squadron 37, 1977-79; and CO USS *Corry* (DD-817), 1979-81.

His shore tours include Reserve Coordinator, Commander Naval Surface Forces Pacific, 1981 and Pacific Representative Naval Surface Reserves, 1985; and CO at Santa Monica, CA, 1971-72; at Encino, CA, 1973; Naval Support Activity, New Orleans, 1991-93; Deputy Commander, Naval Surface Reserve Forces, 1988-91.

Memorable was the first 15 of 18 years at sea; command of USS *Corry*; as Deputy Commander, Naval Surface Reserve Force, and personally directing the recall of 15,000 reservists for Operations Desert Shield and Desert Storm.

Personal decorations include three Legions of Merit, two Meritorious Service Medals, Navy Commendation Medal w/Combat V and Navy Achievement Medal. CAPT Bair retired Sept. 1, 1993.

He is married to the former Norma Jean Hardin of Ivanhoe, CA and they have sons, John and Paul.

DONALD L. "DON" BAKER, CDR, USNR, born July 19, 1927, Philadelphia, PA. He is New York State Maritime Academy Graduate; Amherst College, AB degree; Harvard Business School, MBA degree; New York University, GBA, MBA plus credits for Ph.D. in business administration; the New School for Social Research, MA, international economics, plus Ph.D. credits.

Served active duty in USNR, MMR; USS *Rockwall* (APA-230) during Korean War; and sailed in Merchant Marine as licensed deck officer. He attended National War College and numerous service schools; commanded USNR Surface Divisions; USMCR Intelligence Unit; served on Group Command Staffs and other line units; annually served on Afloat ACDUTRA. Discharged in October 1974.

CDR Baker is a life member of NRA and appointed to and served on national committees; held chapter and district offices, including president. He is active in community activities and is a member of numerous military and civic organizations.

As a civilian he has held corporate top management positions with Sears Roebuck and Co., Continental Can Co., H.E. Lavffer & Co. and Design Rearch & Co.

He is the father of five children: Wendy, Jeffrey, Donald II, Sarah and David, and grandfather of three: Halley, Graham and Jane.

JOHN FRANCIS BALDWIN, CAPT, born Sept. 14, 1933, Chicago, IL to John T. and Marie Spielvogel. He attended St. Clare Parochial School, Quigley High School Seminary and received BA and MA degrees from St. Mary of the Lake Seminary, Mundelein, IL. He was ordained to the priesthood by Cardinal Albert Meyer on May 7, 1959 and assigned to Resurrection Church on Chicago's west side, then transferred in 1964 to St. Joseph's, Round Lake, IL.

Having been commissioned as a Navy Reserve Chaplain in January 1967, he entered on active duty in October 1968. His naval assignments were Amphibious Squadron One home ported in San

Diego, 1968-70; NAS, Lakehurst, 1970-74; 3rd MarDiv (2/9 and 12th Marines, Okinawa), 1974-75; Coast Guard Alameda, 1975-78; USS *Guam* (LPH-9) Norfolk, 1978-80; Chaplains' School Newport, 1980-81; Naval Station Treasure Island/Coast Guard Alameda, 1981-84; Marine Corps AS Iwakuni, Japan, 1984-86; NETC Newport, RI, 1986-89; Fleet Chaplain, CINCUSNAVEUR, London, England, 1989-91, Naval Postgraduate School, Monterey, CA, 1991-95.

Retired from active duty Sept. 1, 1995, Father Baldwin entered on a sabbatical which included extensive time in Europe and study at TANTUR Ecumenical Institute in Jerusalem. He now continues an active ministry in Alameda, Monterey/Carmel in California and in Chicago.

Military awards include the Legion of Merit, Meritorious Service Medal and Coast Guard Achievement and Commendation Medals.

CAPT Baldwin saw service in Vietnam making two deployments with the "gators" of Phibron One. He has a Master's in Theology from Princeton Seminary and faculties as a Roman Catholic priest from the Archdiocese of Chicago.

JAMES A. BARBER JR. attended University of Southern California, BA in economics, 1955; Vanderbilt University, MA in economics, 1960; Stanford University, MA in International Relations, 1964 and Ph.D. in political science, 1965; U.S. Naval War College, Command and Staff Certificate, 1970 and Naval Surface Warfare Certificate in 1971; Senior Officers Ship Material Readiness Course, Idaho Falls, 1978.

Military stations: 1955-58, USS *Lexington*; 1958-60, Northwestern University, instructor; 1960-62, USS *Lowry* (DD-770); 1962-65; Doctoral studies, Stanford University; 1965-66, USS *Henry W. Tucker* (DD-875); 1966-68, USS *Hissem* (DER-400), Commanding Officer; 1968-71, U.S. Naval War College; 1971-72, USS *Schofield* (DEG-3); 1973-75, Strategic Plans and Policy Division; 1975, Executive Assistant to Commander-in-Chief, U.S. Naval Forces Europe; 1975-76, Executive Assistant and Naval Aide to Undersecretary of the Navy; 1976-77, Systems Analysis Div. (OP-96), Navy Dept.; 1977-79, USS *Horne* (CG-30), CO, two Pacific Fleet deployments; 1979-82, Politico-Military Policy and Current Plans, Navy Dept.; 1982-84, Strategic Concepts Development Center; presently, Chief XO and Publisher, U.S. Naval Institute.

He has held many ancillary positions, 1969-present and is the author of numerous publications and two books.

Military awards include the Defense Superior Service Medal, Bronze Star w/Combat V, Legion of Merit, Meritorious Service Medal, Vietnam Service Medal (6 awards) and others. He also received the Navy League Alfred Thayer Mahan for literary achievement.

GARY R. BARRON, LT, USNR-R, born March 30, 1958, San Pedro, CA. He received an Associate of Science in Aeronautics from Long Beach City College in 1980; a BS in business computer methods from California State University Long

Beach in 1982; and MBA from University of Phoenix in 1985. In June 1988, LT Barron received a direct commission as an Ensign in the USNR and was designated an Intelligence Officer.

Upon commissioning, LT Barron affiliated with Reserve Intelligence Area Four (RIA4) at NAVAIRES San Diego and was assigned to Fleet Intelligence Rapid Support Team Pacific 0919 (FIRSTPAC 0919) as an intelligence analyst in geo-political and special warfare studies. In November 1990 he was selected to become the first Air Intelligence Officer for Tactical Air Control Squadron 1294 (TACRON 1294). In November 1993 he joined COMNAVSURFPAC 0994 where he is currently drilling as an amphibious intelligence analyst, Asst. Training Officer and OIC of the COMPHIBRON 3 DET.

Attending the Direct Commission Officer Course at NAS Pensacola, LT Barron graduated top in his class and received an outstanding student award from the Naval Aviation Schools Command. He also attended Basic Intelligence Training Course and Image Interpretation Course at FITCPAC San Diego, graduating top in his class with honors for both courses. In July 1994 LT Barron graduated with honors from the Basic Naval Operational Intelligence Course at NMITC in Dam Neck, VA. Lt. Barron has participated in Yama Sakura XXIII 1993 in Sendai Japan, Cobra Gold 95 in Korat Thailand, FLEETEX 92-IM and PAC JTFEX 96-1 aboard the USS Tarawa off the coast of Southern California.

In January 1989 LT Barron joined the NRA as a life member and is currently President of the 11th Dist. and past; National VP of Junior Officer Affairs, National VP Education and Chapter Activities, President of the South Bay Chapter, VP Junior Officer Affairs for the NRA 11th Dist. and past VP Budget & Finance/Treasurer of the South Bay Chapter.

In 1990 he was the recipient of the 11th Dist. Outstanding Junior Officer Award and in 1992 he was selected as the NRA's Naval Reserve Junior Officer of the Year (Selected Reserve). LT Barron is also a Life member of the NOUS and Commander of the Long Beach Commandry, life member of the USN Institute, Navy League of the US, Naval Intelligence Professionals, ROA and a member of the USS Arizona Reunion Assoc.

His decorations include the Navy Achievement Medal, National Defense Service Medal, Expert Rifleman Medal and Expert Pistol Shot Medal.

He is married to the former Pamela J. Baune (a chiropractor) of San Pedro, where they live with their 9-year-old daughter Jessica and 6-year-old son Jonathan. LT Barron is presently employed as a senior manager at McDonnell Douglas in Long Beach, CA, working as the C-9D program manager leading the McDonnell Douglas efforts to replace the USN's C-9B Fleet Logistic Support Aircraft.

EDWARD ALBERT BASDEKIAN, CAPT, born Nov. 21, 1928, George-town, WA, DC. Education includes BS, FlaSoCol; BSP/DPhm, University of Florida; MA (MBA/MHA) Central Michigan University; NatlWarCol, NDU; IdustColArmed Forccs, NDU; NROS6-11; 20170thUSAR Schl, NDU; NavWarCol, NAS JAX.

Joined the USAR, August 1947 and the USN in November 1949. He was commissioned in May 1960. Military stations include NAAS Oceana; NAS JAX, FL, USS Saipan (CVL-48); USNHCS PTSMTH, VA; USNH Beaufort, Camp

Lejeune; MCS Quantico; NARTU JAX; USS JFK (CVA-67); NAS ROTA, SP; NAS Wash; FSO, Athens, Greece; NAS El Centro; NAS Sigonella; USS Saratoga (CV-60); COMNAVFORV Staff, USS Newport News (CA-148); RR PR FASRON Three; VF 42; 1st and 2nd MarDiv; 4th FSSG; VP-742; VR-60FI; AWS-74.

Commands held include 4th MAWMED; NRMC 1608, NAVMEDCOM/SERegion; OIC BRCL NAS Whiting. He participated in MAAG/COMNAVFORV in April 1972.

Memorable was first flight in a TBM; advisor, USAID/Laos; COMNAVFORV (MAAG); FLTSUPPOFF, Athens GR; project officer, USS JFK (CVA-67) under construction, Newport News, VA; DepSpecialAsst, SGN (ResAffairs) and Dir., TemAc Prog, OP-13 (MED).

CAPT Basdekian decorations include the NCM, MSM, Good Conduct, CombatAxn, PUC, NUC, USNRMSM, NavOccup(Euro), NDSM w/ 3 stars, VnSvcMed (FMF Insig & CampStar), ArmForResMed w/3 HG, RVN Gallent w/palm, RVN CivAxnMed and RVN CampSvcMed w/ scroll.

Married to the former Alice Louise Thompson; they have no children. Civilian employment as Dean and professor (Emeritus), pharmacy; adjunct prof., graduate programs; asst. prof., pharmacy; MedProgAdvisor, USAID/Laos.

HUGH W. BAUMGARDNER, CAPT, USNR (Ret), born in Akron, OH and spent his youth in Chillicothe, OH. Following graduation from Marietta College in Ohio, he attended Aviation Officer Candidate training in Pensacola, FL and was commissioned an Ensign in 1963.

His first tour was with the Navy Hurricane Hunter Squadron, VW-4, based in Puerto Rico where he was designated as a Naval Flight Officer and collateral duty Intelligence Officer. In 1967 he was assigned to RCVW-4 and later to LATWING ONE located in Jacksonville, FL before leaving active duty.

He affiliated with the Naval Reserve in 1970 and was redesignated as a Special Duty (Intelligence) Officer. Subsequently, he served as an Air Intelligence Officer with RTU-62, VP-1407 and VP-62 until 1977 when he was assigned to DIAHQ 0408.

In 1979 he was recalled to active duty at the Naval Intelligence Command in Washington, DC and upon completion of active duty, was assigned to DEFATTACHE 0166. In 1981 he was assigned as XO and later in 1983 as CO of the National Military Intelligence Center Naval Reserve Unit, DIACURRENTINTEL 0166 in the Pentagon.

Baumgardner was assigned in 1986 as CO of the Naval Reserve Headquarters unit of the Naval Investigative Service, NISHQ 0166 and in 1989 as XO of the Defense Technology Security Administration Naval Reserve Unit, OSD TECH TRANSFER 0166 within the Office of the Secretary of Defense. In 1990 he was recalled to active duty during Operation Desert Shield/Storm and served as Deputy Assistant to the Director of Naval Reserve for Legislation, Liaison and Information.

He retired in 1993 with 30 years of commissioned service and is authorized to wear the Meritorious Service Medal, Joint Commendation Medal, Navy Commendation Medal, Joint Unit Commendation (second award), National Defense Medal (second award), Armed Forces

Reserve Medal (second award), Navy Overseas Service Ribbon and Battle Efficiency Ribbon.

Capt. Baumgardner was awarded a JD degree from George Mason University School of Law in 1980 and is a member of the Virginia Bar.

He lives with his wife, the former Molly Allison Rahe, a Commander in the Naval Reserve, and son Mark in Arlington, VA.

GEORGE A. BECK, CAPT, USNR (Ret), a long-time resident of Westport, CT, attended the University of Virginia, receiving his BA degree.

Ordered to the YMS-183, he transited the Panama Canal to the South Pacific, receiving three Battle Stars. He then attended the Naval Mine Warfare School, serving as Operations Officer and instructor afloat.

After WWII he was Vice President of the Wallach Laundry, Inc. and later became executive Director of Pi Lambda Phi Fraternity, retiring in 1992. Capt. Beck was awarded the National Interfraternity Conference Gold Medal for Distinguished Service to youth. He has been a member of NOUS since 1972.

JULIAN R. BENJAMIN, RADM, born Aug. 24, 1926, Chicago, IL. Received his JD degree from University of Miami in 1949, Cum Laude. Joined the USNR on March 20, 1944 and was commissioned Oct. 1, 1951.

Stationed at Great Lakes for boot camp; attended electronic tech service schools in Chicago, IL, Del Monte, Treasure Island, NOB #230 Adak, AK.

Served with Naval Reserve Law Units, 1949-84; Naval Reserve Law Company 6-3, 1953-58; Director, Naval Reserve Law Programs, 1980-84.

Retired June 1, 1984 as RADM (08) JAGC. Awards include Legion of Merit, Naval Reserve Medal, Armed Forces Reserve Medal, American Defense and WWII Victory.

He had a great career as a Navy lawyer; had leadership roles in Naval Reserve Association, local Naval Order Commandery and many in bar associations; and was President (1978) Judge Advocates Association.

Married June and they have two children, James Scott and Jeffrey Steven, and four grandchildren: Kaitlyn, Courtney, Rachel and Hayley.

He has been a practicing attorney from 1949 to date.

JAMES FRANCIS BENSON, CDR, SC USNR (Ret), born in Stockton, CA. During WWII, CDR Benson served in the Merchant Marine, beginning as dishwasher and ending as a junior Third Officer. He participated in the Southern France invasion and earned the Pacific, Atlantic, Mediterranean Service, Victory medals and the Combat Ribbon.

Between WWII and the Korean War, he returned to school, graduating from the University of California, Berkeley, 1952.

During the Korean War, he served as Disbursing Officer and assistant to the Comptroller of the Military Sea Transportation Service, Washington, DC.

CDR Benson affiliated with Marine Terminal Management Unit 12-1, the Aviation Supply and Readiness Project (ASDARP), and as Commanding Officer Supply Company 12-1.

After leaving active duty, he began a civil service career with the Navy, at various commands, in budgeting and project management. He retired in 1981 from the Naval Facilities Engineering Command, San Bruno, CA as a GS-13.

He is currently engaged in tax preparation and financial counseling.

Life member of the Naval Reserve Association, NOUS, ROA, TROA and member of ANA, NOAC and Marines' Memorial Club. He has served as a national officer of NRA and NOUS as Treasurer and VP for Budget and Finance. Additionally, he has served as treasurer of several NRA National Conventions, Naval Order Congresses, and ANA National Conventions. He is on the Board Chairman of the Crestmont Conservatory of Music.

He resides in San Carlos, CA with his wife, Gloria. They have two children, James Jr. and Darcy, and two grandchildren, Joseph and Gianna.

JOHN J. BEPKO III, RADM, born and raised in Milford, CT. After graduation from the University of Connecticut, he enlisted in June 1968. Then, Seaman Bepko was selected for Officer Candidate School and commissioned in September 1969.

His assignments include: Gunnery Officer, USS *Orleck*; Combat Information Center Officer, USS *Orleck*, Operations Officer, USS *Bausell*; Counter-intelligence Officer, US/Taiwan Defense Command; XO, USS *Preserver*.

Received master's degree in manpower/personnel training analysis from the Naval Postgraduate School; XO, USS *Excel*; XO, USS *Pyro*; CO, USS *Kiska*; Deputy Director, Surface Warfare Manpower and Training Requirements Division (OP-39).

Received his master's degree in national security and strategic studies, and was CO, USS *Supply*.

Bepko's first assignment following selection to Rear Admiral is Commander, Logistics Group Western Pacific.

LOUIE BERTOLUCCI, LCDR, born Aug. 6, 1918, Stockton, CA. Attended two years at San Francisco Junior College. He joined the service (Line) Jan. 2, 1942 and was commissioned July 28, 1943.

Stationed at Armed Guard, Treasure Island, San Francisco; USS *Wileman* (DE-22) and NSD, Clearfield, UT.

Memorable Experience: Pearl Harbor was their first stop on their way to the South Pacific

in August 1943 and it was bustling with ships. After a brief visit to the PX, he went aboard an already loaded boat that would take him to his ship; the coxswain was having some problem getting underway. Suddenly, as he looked up, there was a yard Oiler bearing down on them. Being close to the helm, he stood up and shouted, "Full steam ahead" and they barely cleared the Oiler. As he looked up he could see the Chief shaking his fist at them. Later, he figured out that he was the senior officer aboard and was in "command."

LCDR Bertolucci was discharged June 27, 1946. His awards include the WWII Victory Medal, American Campaign and Asiatic-Pacific Ribbon.

Employed Accoc. Oil Co., clerk; Acme Beer Co. (salesman) Schlitz Beer; retired Aug. 6, 1984. Married Regina Annita and they have three children: Kathleen Marie, Ronald Louis and Marcia Jean; and seven grandchildren: Dustin, Ahmon, Shawna, Monica, Christine, Regina and Michayla.

JOHN W. BITOFF, RADM, USN, (Ret), born May 9, 1936 in Brooklyn, NY. Graduated from the Maine Maritime Academy and was commissioned an Ensign in June 1958. He initially served in the Merchant Marine, participating in Operation Deep Freeze in the Antarctic during the International Geophysical Year 1958-59.

He began active service in January 1960 and spent the major portion of the next 13 years in sea duty assignments which included USS *Spiegel Grove* (LSD-32), USS *Springfield* (CLG-7), USS *Bristol* (DD-857), USS *DeLong* (DE-684), USS *Charles P. Cecil* (DD-835) and the USS *Blakely* (FF-1072).

In January 1970 he began his first shore assignment in the Pentagon as a CNO Operations Briefer. Later that year, he was among the first group of Lieutenant Commanders selected to command ships in what was known as the "Mod Squad" concept. Then LCDR Bitoff was ordered to command USS *Blakely*.

Following two years in command he attended the National War College and graduated in the Class of 1976. He returned to the Pentagon in the Office of the Assistant Secretary of Defense for International Security Affairs. Next came a tour on the staff of the CNO where he headed the NATO Office and the Strategy and Concepts branch.

In the summer of 1980 he was assigned as Executive Assistant and Senior Aide to the Commander-in-Chief, Allied Forces Southern Europe in Naples, Italy. In October 1983 he returned to the US and assumed command of the Fleet Combat Training Center, Atlantic at Dam Neck, VA. In July 1985 he was ordered to Camp H.M. Smith, HI as Executive Assistant to the US Commander-in-Chief Pacific Command. This tour was interrupted in September, when he was ordered to Washington, DC to become Executive Assistant to the chairman, Joint Chiefs of Staff.

In November he was selected for promotion to Rear Admiral.

Adm. Bitoff reported to HQ, US European Command, Stuttgart, Germany in November 1986 and became director for Plans and Policy (J-5). One of his primary responsibilities was the implementation of the INT Treaty. From January 1989 to October 1991, Adm. Bitoff served as Commander, Combat Logistics Group ONE and Commander, Naval Base San Francisco. It was during this assignment that he led the rescue and recovery operations following the Loma Prieta Earthquake. In addition to his year of study at the National Defense University, Admiral Bitoff did graduate work at the Catholic University of America and earned an MS from Golden Gate University. The university later conferred upon him the degree of Doctor of Laws, Honoris Causa for his work as "a soldier statesman."

His personal military awards include the Defense Distinguished Service Medal w/OLC; Defense Superior Service Medal; Legion of Merit w/2 Gold Stars; Defense Meritorious Service Medal; Navy Commendation Medal w/Gold Star and a Navy Meritorious Unit Citation.

Adm. Bitoff is married to the former Maureen L. Collins of Portsmouth, NH. They have one daughter, Elizabeth.

BRUCE A. BLACK, RADM, born Aug. 20, 1936, Albuquerque, NM. Received his BS degree in 1959; MS, 1964; and Ph.D., 1983; all in geology. He joined the USNR in high school as a Seaman Recruit in January 1955; graduated from Texas Western College, BS in geology, 1959; and received his commission from OCS Newport, RI in July 1959.

He was the Air Intelligence Officer for VP-50 in Iwakuni, Japan until June 1961 when he reported to the Pacific Fleet Air Intelligence Training Center in Alameda, CA. Released from active duty on July 24, 1962, RADM Black affiliated with NAIRU D1 in Dallas, TX, while he attended graduate school at the University of New Mexico, receiving his MS in geology, May 1964. He worked for Shell Oil Co. in California, New Mexico and in Denver.

In 1971, RADM Black founded Colorado Plateau Geologic Services, a geologic consulting firm. In 1973 he received his Ph.D., geology, University of New Mexico. Then from 1973-74, CG 1319, Albuquerque, NM; NRIP Area 5, NORAD HQ unit; NICHQ 0118, 1977-79; CO, AFAITC 0171, 1979-80; CO, FIRSTPAC 0571, 1980-81; Chief of Staff, RIAC FIVE, IVTU

0118, 1981-83; RIAC FIVE, NICHQ DET 0187, 1983-85, and again in 1987; IVTU 0111, Dallas, TX, COMNAVRESINTCOM, 1987-91; promoted to Rear Admiral and assumed command of the Naval Reserve Intelligence Command, 1992.

RADM Black retired July 27, 1996. His decorations include the Legion of Merit, MSM, Navy Commendation Medal w/2 Gold Stars, National Defense and Armed Reserve w/HG devices. He is a Life member of the NRA, ROA, Naval Intelligence Professional Association and is a former Blue and Gold Officer.

He is owner and president of Black Oil Co. He is an active member of local and national geologic societies and has been active in the Civil Air Patrol and other civic activities. He is an avid private pilot with over 5,000 hours of flying experience. He is married to the former Marjorie Manget Watkins. They have a son, Capt. Bruce Harmon Black and daughter, Leigh Helen Black Irvin.

ROBERT BLAKE, MajGen, USMC, born Aug. 17, 1894, Seattle, WA. Received BA in history, University of California in 1917; attended Marine Corps Schools, Quantico, company and field courses; Graduate School, University of Salamanca, 1931-32; Naval War College, 1941.

Commissioned in the USMC April 17, 1917; trained at Mare Island and Quantico, then served overseas in France, Luxembourg and Germany.

Between WWI and WWII he had shore duty at Quantico, Mare Island, Goat Island, Nicaragua (3 times), Spain, Panama and Washington DC, Naval War College. Sea duty in USS *Henderson, Pennsylvania, Trenton, Memphis, Omaha* and *San Francisco.*

Battles and campaigns during WWI include Belleau Wood, Soissons, St. Mihiel, Aisne-Marne and Meuse-Argonne; WWII includes Solomons, New Georgia, Marianas and Okinawa.

Awards include Navy Cross w/Gold Star, Distinguished Service Cross, Silver Star, Legion of Merit w/Gold Star and Combat V, French Croix de Guerre w/Gold Star and Bronze Star, Belgian Order de la Couronne, Nicaraguan Medal of Merit w/Silver Star, Ecuadoran Abdon Calderon Star First Class, WWI Victory Medal w/clasps, Army of Occupation of Germany Medal (WWI), Second Nicaraguan Campaign Medal, American Defense Service Medal w/Bronze Star, WWII American Campaign Medal, Asiatic-Pacific Campaign Medal w/4 Bronze Stars and WWII Victory Medal.

He served with various units and held several commands as Captain, Major, Lieutenant Colonel and as Colonel. Was deputy island commander, Guam; Marine deputy chief of staff, 10th Army on V-J Day; Commanding General, Occupation Forces Truk (after V-J Day) and Inspector General, USMC, 1946 to retirement June 30, 1949.

After retirement he served on numerous boards and committees of civic organizations in Santa Barbara and San Francisco. Gen. Blake died Oct. 2, 1983 and is buried in Golden Gate National Cemetery, San Bruno, CA. Widowed twice, he had one son Robert Wallace Blake.

ROBERT WALLACE "BOB" BLAKE, LCDR, born May 24, 1921, Quantico, VA, son of MajGen Robert Blake, USMC. Received BS degree in aeronautical engineering, MIT, 1941, USN V-5 Program; graduate study at Columbia Grad School of Business and Navy War College. He joined the USNR April 7, 1944 and was commissioned Jan. 1, 1947.

Military locations include USNPFS St. Marys, NAS Glenview, NAS Corpus Christi, NAS Memphis, NAS Pensacola, NAS New York, NAS Quonset Pt., NAS Oceana, NAS Cecil, NAS Seattle, NAS Rota, USS *Saipan,* USS *Gilbert Islands,* USS *Lloyd Thomas,* BUWEPS Washington, Hartford, El Segundo, Burbank, CINCUSNAVEUR.

At NAS New York he served with VF-841, VA-833, VA-832 flying TBM, FG1-D, F9F-7 aircraft, BARTU 832, WEPTU 832 and NARS-W2. At Paris France with NRCC NAVEUR-2 and at NAS Seattle with WEPTU 891 and NARS-T1.

Memorable experience was meeting CDR John Thach as an Aviation Cadet, then (20 years later) serving under VADM Thach at CINCUCNAVEUR as LCDR. Also memorable was initial jet qualification in the F9F-7 and visit to Aden and Jedda aboard USS *Lloyd Thomas.*

He was released to inactive duty Jan. 29, 1947, transferred to Retired Reserve in July 1971 and retired in June 1981. Awards include American Defense Medal, WWII Victory Medal, Naval Reserve Medal and Armed Forces Reserve Medal. He is a Life member of NOUS, USNI, NRA and Marine Memorial Association.

Employed 41 years with Pan American World Airways as engineer, pilot, director of operations engineering, airport manager, factory rep and VP of operations planning. After retirement in 1982, he served as a consultant, writer and lecturer.

Active throughout his career in industry and professional society committees and working groups of AIAA, SAE, ATA, IATA, ICAO and RTCA. He has articles published in SAE Transactions, Seattle Times, Seattle P-I, Navy War College Review, Naval Institute Proceedings, professional society publications.

His wife Ruth passed away in 1989 - no children.

ROBERT BASHFORD "BOB" BOLT, CAPT, born March 20, 1917, Berkeley, CA; graduated from Stanford University in 1940; USN Midshipmen's School, Northwestern University, Chicago, IL, 1940-41; and attended USN PG School, 1945-46. He joined the service Sept. 6, 1940 and was commissioned in March 1941.

He served in USS *Indianapolis,* 1941, in the Pacific; Naval Armed Guard, 1941-43, SS Exhibitor, USAT, SS Argentina, Atlantic, Indian Ocean, Bay of Bengal, North Sea; Mediterranean-North Africa, 1942; Destroyer Escorts (26, 13, 54, 238), 1943-45; USS *Duluth,* 1946-47, in Pacific.

Capt. Bolt was discharged in April 1983. His awards include the Silver Star, Navy Commendation (4), SecNav Distinguished Public Service, Armed Forces, Reserve, all theaters of WWII, Korea and China.

His memorable experiences include Philippine Liberation, 1946; Shanghai Station Ship, 1946; attack by Japanese in Bay of Bengal, April 3, 1942; landing in North Africa in 1942; and North Atlantic Convoy Escort duty, 1944-45.

Employed as officer with several insurance companies, 1953 until retirement in March 1977. He is licensed in 12 states as nonresident broker.

Married Margaret Kingsland (Winks) Hewitt and has one child, Leslie Topliff Bolt Dennis, and two grandchildren, Jeffrey Mercer Dennis and Brian Bolt Dennis.

He served as National President of the NRA, 1967-69; Commander General of the NOUS, 1975-77; and continues to be affiliated with NRA, Naval Order, Navy League, ROA, MOWW, FRA, Naval War College, Naval Institute and Stanford Alumni Assoc.

EMILE L. BONNOT, CAPT, USNR (Ret), born May 11, 1907, Orange, NJ and graduated Rutgers University with BA degree in 1929.

Served in the Pacific during WWII as a member of ships company in various billets aboard the USS *Fremont* APA/RAGC 44 including Executive Officer.

He was a plankowner of the *Fremont* which served as a flag ship of Admirals Blandy, Fechteler and Commodore Loomis through a number of invasions including Saipan, Pelelieu-Anguar, Leyte, Linguyan, Iwo Jima and Okinawa.

In addition to the Navy flag officers and their staffs, the *Fremont* carried the Army Commanding Generals and their staffs of the 27th Div., 81st Div. (twice), 6th Div., 1st Cav. Div. and the Marine 5th Div.

Being in command of the beachheads, the *Fremont* stayed from the initial landing to when the islands were declared "secured." They survived shelling, strafing, bombing, kamikazi attacks, under water swimmers, a crippling engine room fire and typhoons. Bonnot was the first Allied serviceman ashore on Ulithi and on Samar in the Philippines.

Bonnot is active with many Naval organizations including the NOUS in which he was Commander of the New York Commandery, Vice Commander General, Historian and Historian General Emeritus.

In civilian life he was vice president of the Prentice-Hall Corporation System, a wholly owned subsidiary of Prentice-Hall, Inc.

He resided in Teaneck, NJ with his wife Dorothy.

KENNETH BARNES BOURNE JR., LT, USNR, born Feb. 27, 1932, New York, NY. Earned BA degree, Brown University and Ensign, USNR (NROTC) at Brown University, graduating in 1954. He joined the USNR and was commissioned in 1954.

Military stations include USS *Formoe* (DE-509), Newport, RI and San Diego, CA.

LT Bourne was discharged June 24, 1956. His medals include the National Defense, China Service Medal and Korean Service Medal.

Memorable experience was losing both anchors, one while refueling at sea as they collided with a cruiser from which they were taking on fuel and the other while anchoring in Atami off the coast of Japan.

Married Carole Nimmo Bourno and has two children, Peter Clark and Nancy Hathaway. Employed as a marketing director, international group until retirement in 1978.

NOUS commissioned ancestor: LCDR Kenneth Barnes Bourne, USNR (deceased).

WILLIAM RICHARD BREMER, COL, USMCR, born Jan. 5, 1930 in San Francisco. Bill received his BS in Business Administration from Menlo College in February 1952 and headed for Quantico, VA, as a Marine Private assigned to the Fourth OCC. When commissioned, he completed the 14th SBC and Air Control School, then ordered to Korea as a GCI Air Controller, MGCIS-1, Kunsan. He was assigned as an exchange controller to the 608th AC&W Sqdn., USAF, Chodo Island, and recorded eight enemy aircraft intercepts. Released from active duty in 1954, he stayed in the Marine Corps Reserve holding a variety of billets and commands through February 1982, whereupon he retired from the Marine Corps. He holds the Meritorious Service Medal and Combat Action Ribbon.

After receiving his JD from the University of San Francisco School of Law in 1958, he was admitted to the California Bar in January 1959 and has been in the private practice of law ever since. He serves as a Hearing Officer for the County of Marin, as a Judge Pro Tem for the County of Marin and the County of San Francisco and as an Arbitrator for both.

He was a board member and president of the Marines' Memorial Club, San Francisco. He is a life member of the Navy League and was San Francisco Council President, Northern California State President and a National Director for 12 years, and is presently a National Deputy Judge Advocate. He is a life member of the NOUS and has served as San Francisco Commandery Commander, Judge Advocate General and Commander General (1993-95). He was elected a Councilman and Mayor of the town of Tiburon. He has served as an officer and director of the Marshall Hale Memorial Hospital Board, San Francisco Children's Hospital Board, The Bridgeway Plan for Health, and as a director for Bay Area USO, and the Center of the Pacific Rim, University of San Francisco. He is a life member of MCROA and Naval War College Foundation, where he served as a Regional

Vice President, Association of Naval Aviation, ROA, TROA and Naval Reserve Association. He is a past Commodore of the Corinthian Yacht Club and currently president of Tiburon Belvedere Rotary Club.

He is married to the former Margaret "Peggy" Herrington, also a Life member of the Naval Order. They have three children: Karen, William Jr. and Mark (dec.)

KAROLLA "KAY" BRICE, CAPT, USN (Ret), born April 3, 1920, Bridgeport, CT. She graduated from nurses training Feb. 5, 1942 and joined the USNR Jan. 28, 1943. She stayed on active duty for seven years and seven months. Augmented to the Regular Navy in 1946.

During WWII she had many duty stations and one tour on a hospital ship, where she met her husband. They were married in 1947. In 1947 she resigned her commission and returned to civilian life. In April 1948 the Bureau of Naval Personnel asked her to re-enlist in the Naval Reserve, and she went back on active duty from January 1949-January 1951.

She was then released from active duty and returned to a drilling Reservist for the next 29 years. Her rank progressed from Ensign to Captain.

She retired from all naval duty April 3, 1980. Her medals include the Asiatic-Pacific Campaign w/battlestar, Philippine Liberation Medal, American Theater Medal, WWII Victory Medal and the Reserve Medal.

She has been a certified Registered Nurse Anesthetist for 35 years. Her nursing career was 50 years long.

Married Robert C. Brice and has two stepchildren, Barbara and Irene Johnson; grandchildren: Randy, Ricky, Debbie, David, Stephen and Kathy.

MERRICK BROWNE, LTJG, born Feb. 18, 1926, Lake Forrest, IL. Graduated the University of San Francisco with a BS degree in 1950. Joined the USNR in February 1945 and commissioned in September 1950.

Stationed in San Diego; Bainbridge, MD; and San Francisco. LTJG Browne was discharged in 1950. Awards include the WWII Victory Medal.

NOUS commissioned ancestor is his father, RADM Davenport Browne, USN (Ret).

DONALD M. BUDAI, CAPT, born Nov. 22, 1937, Chicago, IL. Received his BS, MS and law degrees. Joined the USN July 29, 1959 and was commissioned Feb. 3, 1960.

Military stations include OCS; Naval Degaussing Station, San Diego; Naval Electronics Laboratory, San Diego; Mine Warfare, Charleston; USS *Black* (DD-666); USS *Shields*; USS *Marsh*; Naval Ordnance Div. 11-1 and 11-2 Commands; Naval Sea Systems Command 519 Command; Naval Industrial Mobilization 319 Command; Fleet Training Group, San Diego.

Awards include Meritorious Service Medal, Navy Commendation Medal, National Defense Service Medal, Armed Forces Expeditionary Medal, Armed Forces Reserve Medal (2 subsequent awards).

CAPT Budai retired Sept. 1. 1990; served as degaussing and deperming officer, navy diver and Explosive Ordinance qualified, Surface Warfare qualified and Naval Engineer.

Married Margaretta and has children: Blair, Blake and Brooke Budai, Beth Roach, Kathleen Houston, Kerry McDaid; and grandchildren: Andrew, Joseph, Hannah and Patrick Budai; Caela and Megan Roach; Parker Houston and Aidan McDaid.

JOHN SHOBER "JACK" BURROWS JR., CAPT, USNR (Ret), born Dec. 31, 1911, Norfolk, VA. Graduated Taft School, 1931; Yale, 1935; Ensign, D-V(G)USNR, 1937 BFA, Yale School Fine Arts, Yale Fellow Europe. Joined the USN in 1931 and was commissioned in May 1935.

Military locations/stations: Office CNO, 1941; Washington, DC Dir. Naval Communications, 1942; CO USS PC-496, 1943; CO USS PC 1078 Attu, Kiska Ops. CO USS *Edmonds* (DE-406), 1944-45; Comp Unit Scarsdale, NY, 1946.

Battles/Campaigns: Neutrality Patrol, Atlantic Coast, 1942; Aleutians, 1943; Pacific (5), 1944-45.

CAPT Burrows retired Nov. 1, 1959. Awards include Legion of Merit w/Combat V, Naval Reserve Medal and a Gold Star in lieu of second Legion of Merit.

Memorable experience was the night of Feb. 21-22, 1945 when he directed the rescue of 378 survivors of the sinking USS *Bismark Sea*.

Married since 1938 to Marion Duval and has three children: Capt. J.S. Burrows, USN (Ret), Bonnie Gandleman and H. Duval Burrows; grandchildren are Ensign J.S Burrows, USCGR; Debora and Donna Burrows. Civilian employment as partner, Urban Brayton Burrows, Architects, 1950-60, and sole proprietor, 1961-79.

ALBERT D. "GUS" CAIRE, CAPT, USNR (Ret), attended Tulane University NROTC, 1939-43, commissioned ensign upon graduation and began a career that would span 33 years of naval service.

Active duty began as a commissioning plankowner and Assistant Gunnery Officer aboard the USS *Evans* (DD-552). Her operations and engagements include the Marshall Islands; Marianas Operation, including capture and occupation of Saipan, Tinian, and Guam; Battle of the Philippine Sea (Marianas Turkey Shoot); 2nd Bonins Raid; the West Caroline Island Operation, including capture and occupation of the Palau Islands Peleliu-Anguar, the assault on Philippine Islands, on Yap and Leyte Operations; assault and occupation of Iwo Jima followed by Okinawa Gunta.

The *Evans* is credited with lobbing over 2,000 shells into a single sector at the base of Mount Suribachi in one night, accounting for up to 2,000 Japanese casualties. Gus and his gunnery group bagged a destroyer record of 26 Japanese planes. At Okinawa the *Evans* was hit by four kamikaze aircraft crashes and two 500 lb. bombs. *Evans* received a Presidential Unit Citation.

Duty also included USS *English* (DD-696), USS *W.L. Lind* (DD-763), and update enhancement training at Flight Gunnery School, Washington, DC; Damage Control in San Francisco; ASW in Key West; Advanced Weapons in Key West and Charleston; and Senior officer Tactics AAW at Dam Neck.

Gus was awarded the Outstanding Reserve officer of the Center plaque for his leadership and performance. He served as Admin/Pers Off, XO and CO of SURFDIV 8-29(L) (8-29 won the

8th Naval District (5 state) Commandant's cup three year's running and captured the Forrestal Trophy (first among 600 SURFDIVs). Tours followed as Battalion 8-8 Chief of Staff, SURFDIV 8-12, XO and Mob Team CO.

CAPT Caire shaped the careers of most of the Naval Reserve officers at N&MCRTC New Orleans as senior instructor in the NROS course program; chairman of the Counseling Board; Naval Reserve Group Command 8-1(L) CO and received the Group Command Award Plaque.

Gus is a Life member of both NRA and the Naval Order, a plankowner of the New Orleans Commandery of the Naval Order and Past Companion of the NOUS General Council.

Gus married the late Beth Glass Caire. Their children are Jennifer Caire Wein (mother of Ashley and Collin Wein), A. David Caire Jr. (father of James and Jason Caire) and Miles Hand Caire.

FRED GROVER CAMPILLO, LCDR, born Dec. 24, 1956, Inglewood, CA. Attended the El Camino College, CA, 1978, AA, psychology; California State University, Long Beach, 1980, BA, psychology; Naval Postgraduate School, 1987, MS, financial management; Texas Christian University, 1998, MA, liberal arts.

He joined OCS, Jan. 15, 1981, was commissioned in May 1981 and joined NRA, Jan. 7, 1991.

Military stations were Long Beach, CA; Manama, Bahrain; Monterey, CA; Newport, RI; Pearl Harbor, HI; Agana, Guam; Decatur, IL; Norfolk, VA; Dallas, TX

Units served with were USS *Racine* (LST-1191); USS *LaSalle* (AGF-3); USS *Badger* (FF-1071); USS *Niagara Falls* (AFS-3); NAVRESCEN Decatur, IL; USS *George Washington* (CVN-73); REDCOM 11.

Participated in Operation Earnest Will (Iran-Iraq War); Operation Desert Shield (Gulf War); Operation Desert Storm (Gulf War); Operation Southern Watch (Gulf War); Operation Deny Flight (Bosnia).

Decorations include Meritorious Service Medal, Navy Commendation Medal, Combat Action Ribbon, Navy Unit Commendation w/ Bronze Service Star, Meritorious Unit Commendation w/2 Bronze Service Stars, Navy Combat Efficiency "Battle E" Ribbon, National Defense Service Medal, AFEM, Southwest Asia Service Medal w/3 Bronze Campaign Stars, Armed Forces Service Medal, Humanitarian Service Medal, Sea Service/Deployment Ribbon w/3 Bronze Service Stars, Reserve Sea Service Ribbon, AFRM, Kuwait Liberation Medal (Saudi Arabia), Kuwait Liberation Medal (Kuwait), Rifle Marksmanship Ribbon, Expert Pistol Shot Medal. Rank achieved was Lieutenant Commander.

Memorable experiences include sailing on a frigate nose-to-nose with a Russian battle group across the Sea of Okhotsk; rescuing dying Vietnamese refugees adrift in the South China Sea; being on TAO watch in the Persian (Arabian) Gulf when the call went out for the cruise missile launches that marked the transition from Desert Shield to Desert Storm; giving the keynote address before a capacity crowd and local news cameras as part of the 1991 Memorial Day commemoration in Decatur, IL; and the many, many nights on watch at sea.

Married to Chris Andrea Cherches, he has one daughter, Madeline Elaine Campillo.

FRED D. CARL, CAPT, USNR (Ret), born in Washington, DC., June 16, 1920. Graduated from American University in June 1947. He enlisted in the Navy in March 1942, served for 18 months at the Washington Navy Yard Communication Office and advancing to the rate of Yeoman 2/c. He was commissioned an Ensign in December 1943 upon completion of Northwestern University Midshipman School in Chicago.

His first sea duty was aboard the USS *Eldridge* (DE-172), operating in the Atlantic and Mediterranean.

Following training at the Sub Chaser Training Center in Miami, he reported aboard the USS *Waters* (APD-8), former DD- 115), which carried Underwater Demolition Teams; and soon became the Communication Officer. During the year and a half he was aboard, the *Waters* was engaged in combat throughout the Iwo Jima and Okinawa campaigns.

Following WWII, he served in Reserve Surface Warfare assignments, including that of Group Commander. Capt. Carl retired in 1976 after 34 years of service.

His professional career was with the YMCA in Washington, Indianapolis, New York City and nationally. He retired in 1986 as the National Executive Director, Armed Services YMCA of the USA. Capt. Carl was the National President of the NRA, 1977-79. He previously served as national Vice President, Surface Program and National Treasurer and President of the Stephen Decatur Chapter. He was the Commander General of the NOUS, 1987-89, after first being the Commander General-elect and Treasurer General, and has served for 13 years as the managing editor of its newsletter. Between 1993-95, Capt. Carl was the National Chairman, USN Sea Cadet Corps. He was a national Vice President of the Navy League of the US, 1990-95, and earlier was the President of the Chicago Council He currently serves as a national Director and as chairman of its Youth Program Committee.

Decorations include the Navy Commendation, Navy Superior Public Service, Navy Meritorious Public Service, Coast Guard Meritorious Public Service, American, Pacific w/2 stars and European Theaters, WWII Victory, National Service and Naval Reserve.

Capt. Carl and the former Janet A. MacIntosh were married in 1996 and reside in Indialantic, FL. He has two married daughters, Cheryl C. Hughes and Sandra C. Barber, by his deceased wife of 45 years, Murial H. Carl.

CAPT JOSEPH R. "MIKE" CARMICHAEL, CAPT, USNR (Ret), born June 13, 1915, Eureka, UT. He is a graduate of the University of Washington with a degree in forestry and an Ensign commission in the Naval Reserve. He was first employed in the Oauchita National Forest in Arkansas but soon answered a call from the Navy for Reserve officers to train for submarine duty and was ordered to New London. When he finished the course, there was a call for officers to man old WWI destroyers being recommissioned and he was assigned to the USS *Clemson*, a 1200 ton flush decker then at Brooklyn.

The *Clemson* home ported in Coco Solo, Panama and operated on both coasts of South America and in the Caribbean, tending PBY planes in Brazil, Trinidad and the Galapagos and in between patrolling for enemy submarines. Following his promotion to Lieutenant he was designated the ship's Chief Engineer and he served as such until detached in late 1942 to go to the USS *Elizabeth C. Stanton*, an Attack Transport, fitting out in Brooklyn for the invasion of North Africa. Until the regular Captain arrived he was acting CO and went to Africa as the senior watch officer. There at the amphibious landings he was given command of a captured French trawler in which he carried troops and cans of gasoline under fire to the docks in Fedala.

On return to New York the *Stanton* made a round trip to the Mediterranean after which Carmichael was detached to go to Boston as a member of the *Bunker Hill's* commissioning detail. In this ship he went to the Pacific in the engineering department a "B" Division Officer. In due course he was promoted to Lieutenant Commander and advanced to Assistant Engineer and then to be Chief Engineer of the *Bunker Hill*. It was in this latter capacity that he was serving on May 11, 1945 when the ship was damaged by kamikaze attack. For his services on this occasion he was awarded the Navy Cross.

In May 1946 having been detached from the *Bunker Hill* he returned to the Naval Reserve until his retirement from the Navy in 1975. Ribbons and medals include Navy Cross, Presidential Unit Citation, American Defense, American European Theatre, Asiatic-Pacific w/11 stars, Victory Medal, Philippine Liberation w/2 stars, Philippine Presidential Unit Citation, North Africa w/ 2 stars

Following the war he joined the Irving Trust Co. at One Wall Street managing the bank's real estate in 12 countries as a vice president. He retired in 1980.

Carmichael is married to the former Jeanne Dunn, the widow of James E. Dunn, who also served in the *Bunker Hill,* and they live in Manhattan. He has two step-children, Linda Hamer and William Dunn; and step-grandchildren, Cole and Jenna Hamer.

DONALD BLODGETT CARPENTER, LCDR, born Aug. 20, 1916. Entered USNR Sept. 8, 1942; completed indoctrination training, Newport, RI; and commissioned Ensign, Nov. 6, 1942.

Stations include Communication's Liaison Officer in Asiatic-Pacific Theater; USS *Atakapa* (ATF-149) USS *Lyra* (AK-101); USS *Bayfield* (APA-33); USS Wisconsin (BB-64); and USS *Spica* (AK-16) when WWII ended.

Returned to States, Feb. 26, 1946 and remained in Reserves. LCDR Carpenter retired June 30, 1968. Awards include SECNAV Letter of Commendation w/Ribbon, COM 12 Letter of Commendation, WWII Victory Medal, Naval Reserve Medal, American Theater Campaign Ribbon and Asiatic-Pacific Campaign Medal.

Life member of American Legion, Past Commanders Club of California, NRA, Navy League, ROA, MOWW, NOUS, Naval Institute, Vice President of National Association of Fleet Tug Sailors (1990), plankowner, USS *Wisconsin*, and member of National Navy Memorial Foundation. A real estate appraiser, Carpenter retired Dec. 31, 1988. He is single.

JOHN A. CHALBECK, CAPT, USN (Ret), born Sept. 30, 1926, Chicago, IL. Joined the USN in 1944 and was commissioned in 1948.

Duty assignments include 1944-47, flight training at Iowa City, Glenview, Corpus Christi and Pensacola; 1947, AT-6, F4U, NAS Cecil Field; 1947, VF-1A F8F, F6F, NAS North Island, USS *Tarawa*; 1948, VF-11, NAS *Cecil Field*, VF-721, F8F, NAS Glenview (Reserve); 1949, VF-721, F4U F9F, NAS North Island, USS *Boxer*, Korea (active duty, 55 missions); 1951, VRF-32, NAS North Island; 1954, TPS NATC Patuxent River 1955, Armament Test NATC Patuxent River; 1956, USNPGS Monterey; 1957 USS *Yorktown*; 1959, VA-56 A4, NAS Miramar, USS *Ticonderoga*; 1961, Aviation Safety School, USC, RCVW-12, NAS Miramar; 1964, VA-112 A4, NAS Lenore, USS *Forrestal*; 1966, Naval War College, Newport; 1967, NAVAIRLANT staff; 1967, RCVW-4, NAS Cecil Field; 1968, COMCW-10, NAS Cecil Field, USS *Intrepid*, Vietnam (60 missions); 1969, CNARESTRA, NAS Glenview staff; 1971, Director, Flight Test, NATC Patuxent River; 1975 CO NARU Jacksonville.

CAPT Chalbeck retired from active duty in November 1977. Medals include Distinguished Flying Cross (2), Bronze Star (1) and Air Medals (10).

He and his wife Sybil have three children: Michael, Kirk and Steve, and grandchildren John, Bill and Angela.

As a civilian John was chief pilot, Monroe County, Fl.

WINSTON G. CHURCHILL, CAPT, joined the Coast Guard in 1958 and served on Ocean Station Ships and Buoy Tenders in both Atlantic and Pacific Fleets. He attained the rating of Chief Quartermaster before assignment to Officer Candidate School in 1967. He served on 13 cutters including duty as Executive Officer of *Valiant* and *Jarvis* and CO of Cape Starr and Taney.

Assignments include serving as Deputy Commander of Coast Guard activities in Europe with headquarters in London; Coast Guard HQ in Washington; Pacific Area Command in San Francisco; 14th District Office in Honolulu; and as CO of Coast Guard Support Center, Alameda, CA.

He has served six tours of duty with the Navy; Fleet training Group, Pearl Harbor; Naval Material Command, USS *Pharris*; staff of the Commander-in-chief, US Pacific Fleet; Operational Test and Evaluation Force in Norfolk; and staff of Commander US Naval Central Command embarked in USS *La Salle*. Churchill was also

the officer-in-charge, Coast Guard forces Middle East during the latter part of Operation Desert Storm.

He is a graduate of Chaminade College of Honolulu and the Armed Forces Staff College. Awards include the Meritorious Service Medal w/2 Gold Stars, Coast Guard Commendation Medal w/Gold Star, and Coast Guard Achievement Medal w/Gold Star.

Married to the former Merri Lynne Stevenson, a Navy Reservist and daughter of a career Marine. He is a member of Central Union Church of Honolulu, the Nautical Institute of London and the NOUS.

WARREN FREDERICK MARTIN CLEMENS, LTC, born April 17, 1915, Aberdeen, Scotland. Attended Bedford School, England, 1924-33; Christ's College, Cambridge, 1933-38 and Imperial Defense College. He joined the service at Solomon Island in February 1942 and commissioned in March 1942.

Military stations include Guadalcanal, Munda, Solomon Islands and coast watches. Served with the 1st U.S. Marine Division, XIV Corps, both as British liaison officer, US Army. He was CO, Special Service Bn. and Solomon Island Defense Force.

LtCol Clemens was discharged July 28, 1945. He is the author of *Alone in Guadalcanal*.

He and his wife Adelaide have four children: Charlotte, Victoria, Alexandra and Mark. Civilian employment: British overseas service, 1938-60; 1966-99, served on various boards, business, agricultural and charitable.

CLARKE L. COLDREN, LCDR, USNR (Ret), born Jan. 24, 1926 in Uniontown, PA. He joined the Navy V-12 program at Cornell University in 1943 and commissioned from the NROTC program at Georgia Tech in June 1945.

He served in USS *Indiana* (BB-58) as secondary gun battery director from August 1945 to April 1946 and as Officer-in-Charge, GM diesel section SPPC, Mechanicsburg until released to inactive duty in July 1946. He served in several Reserve companies, including Research Co. 12-5 as CO. LCDR Coldren retired in July 1970.

He completed his education as a chemical engineer with a BS from Penn State in 1948 and MS and Ph.D. from Illinois in 1950 and 1954. He joined Shell in 1952 in San Francisco as research engineer and subsequently held a number of research and business management positions in various Shell companies in New York, Houston and the Netherlands, including chief planner for Shell Chemical and manager of their epoxy resins business. He holds five patents and has published numerous papers. He retired in 1984.

He is active in civic, business and political affairs in Houston and Texas, including the Executive Service Corps of Houston, Navy League, NOUS, USS Houston (CA-30) Foundation and the Republican Party.

Divorced, he has four children: Sharon, Anne, Kathryn and Eleanor.

ROGER W. COURSEY, CAPT, born in Millen, GA, in 1949. He graduated with honors from the Coast Guard Academy in 1971 and initially served in USCGC Boutwell (WHEC-719) on weather patrols. Upon graduating from Naval Flight Training (CG Aviator No. 1619, Helicopter Pilot No. 987) in 1973, he was assigned to CGAS Elizabeth City, NC.

Other assignments in aviation included tours in Polar Operations Division at ATC Mobile, AL; instructor duty with TRARON Two at NAS Whiting Field, FL; CGAS Detroit, MI; instructor duty and Chief, Training Division at ATC Mobile, AL; Deputy Group Commander/Air Station executive officer at North Bend, OR; and CO, CGAS Houston, TX.

He retired as a Captain in 1994 while serving as Chief, Search and Rescue of 5th CG District at Portsmouth, VA.

Roger earned an MBA from the University of West Florida in 1980. Since retirement, he has been a Naval Science Instructor in the Navy Junior ROTC program. He taught at Aiken High School, Aiken, SC; Sol C. Johnson High School, Savannah, GA; and South Effingham High School, Guyton, GA. He has four children.

CHARLES L. CRAGIN, CAPT, USNR, a Portland, ME, native, enlisted in the USN in 1961 and served on active duty until 1964. He was separated as a Communications Technician second class. In 1968 he was commissioned as Ensign (Public Affairs) and currently serves as the Naval Emergency Preparedness Liaison Officer to the First Continental US Army. He previously served as CO of USACOM 506 and NAVINFO 101 as well as Reserve Special Assistant (Public Affairs) to the Chief of Naval Operations.

CAPT Cragin earned bachelor of science and doctor of law degrees from the University of Maine. He was the 1982 Republican nominee for governor of Maine and later served as chairman of the Budget Committee of the Republican National Committee. In 1988, he served as sergeant-at-arms of the Republican National Convention.

In February 1991, CAPT Cragin was confirmed by the Senate, for a six year term of office, following nomination by President Bush to be the first presidential appointed chairman of the Board of Veterans' Appeals. In this assistant secretary-level position, CAPT Cragin is the chief executive and operating officer of the Board which decides veterans' appeals of VA claims adjudication actions.

EDWARD J. "ED" CUMMINGS JR., CAPT, USN, born Aug. 28, 1920, in Baltimore, MD. Received a BS degree from the US Naval Academy; master's degree in International Affairs from George Washington University; Naval War College.

Joined the USN June 28, 1938 and commissioned June 19, 1942. Stations include Naval Intelligence School, Washington DC; Admiralty, London; OPNAV, Washington DC (3); COMASWFORPAC, Pearl Harbor and COMCRUDESPAC, San Diego.

Served in USS *Buck*, (DD-420); USS *Missouri* (BB-63); USS H.S. *Ellison* (DD-864); USS *Cromwell* (DE-1014); USS *Somers* (DD-947); COMDESDIV 252 and COMDESRON 21.

Battles/Campaigns: WWII Atlantic Convoys, North Africa, Sicily, Italy, Iwo Jima, Okinawa, raids on Japan, and Vietnam.

Awarded the Legion of Merit, Bronze Star w/ V, Purple Heart, Meritorious Service Medal and Navy Commendation Medal. CAPT Cummings retired July 1, 1972.

Memorable experiences include making Ensign; leaving his sinking ship; being aboard the *Missouri* from Sept. 2, 1945 until end of WWII; briefing Lord Mountbatten when he was notified that King George VI passed away; taking the USS *Somers* through Soviet Baltic Fleet exercise; and rescuing downed aviators off Vietnam.

Civilian employment was in construction and development as well as being project manager to the president. Retired in 1993.

Married Ethel and they have one daughter Candace and two grandchildren.

PRENTICE "CUSH" CUSHING JR., CAPT, born Feb. 27, 1924, New York City, NY. Attended Cornell University, BEE; and the US Naval Academy. He joined the service Nov. 22, 1942 and was commissioned April 25, 1945, USN.

Military stations include Boston Navy Yard, USN Underwater Sound Lab; USS *Cythera* (PY-31), USS *Cubera* (SS-347), USS *Sirago* (SS-485). Held commands aboard the *Sirago*, NAVRES SURFDIV 3-77; and NAVRES SUBDIV 3-55.

Participated in battles and campaigns in the Atlantic and Europe. Capt. Cushing retired Feb. 27, 1984. He received all the usual WWII and Korean awards and decorations.

Memorable: In the summer of 1952, off NORVA, during USNA Midshipman Demo. The mission was to proceed on surface between two carriers on which were embarked Midshipmen so that they could see what a submarine looked like on surface, diving, snorkeling and surfacing.

Everything went according to Hoyle until it became time to surface at which point the Commodore thought it would be a good show to do a battle surface. Having no deck guns, They'd never done one, so Cush was asked if he thought he could do it - no problem. They started to blow and hold her down with the planes. Everything went well until the Commodore, who'd never had any experience with a Guppy, got nervous because they were only at 2/3 Ahead, so said, "Go to Full Ahead" which the helmsman did (when a Commodore gives

an order who's going to wait for the Diving Officer?). Down they went like a yo-yo with a broken string, about 30° down angle, so blow like hell and back full. As the stern popped out of the water with the screws making like high-speed turbines, their air-manifold Auxiliaryman Cooper went ass over teacups to the forward end of the control room, wrench in hand, and lying on his back shouted, "Well, we ain't got no deck guns so we cut'em up with our screws." The famous Commodore said, "Let's get the hell out of here," and they did, full ahead (on the surface, this time).

Cush and his wife Barbara have three children: William, Susan and Joanne (Higgins); and four grandchildren: William, Ryan, Kelly Ann and Connor. He was president of G.K. Heller Corp., Las Vegas, NV; President, Cesco Inc., Floral Park, NY; and retired February 1997.

HENRY DARLINGTON JR., LT, USNR, born Jan. 8, 1925, New York City, NY. Joined the service Dec. 23, 1942 and was commissioned June 1, 1945.

Attended V-12 Unit, Cornell University; Pre-Mid, Asbury Pk., NJ; Midshipman's School, Cornell University; Adv. Line School, Miami, FL; West Coast Sound School, San Diego, CA; Columbia College, AB, 1949 and honorary LHD, St. Paul's College.

Duty as Executive and Gunnery Officer, Navigator, and Commanding officer of USS *Rosewood* (AN-31).

Lt. Darlington was discharged July 12, 1946. He received the American Theater and WWII Victory Ribbon.

He has been retired since Sept. 30, 1992.

FRED DAVIDSON III, COL, USMCR (Ret), Life member and a native of Indianapolis, he attended Central State University, Howard University School of Law and received the LHD degree from the National University in San Diego. He is also an associate alumnus of the US Naval Academy and a life member of the New York Naval Militia Association.

He began his naval career in 1963 at the USMC Officer's Candidate School in Quantico. Upon his commissioning, he reported to Camp Lejeune for training with continuing orders to WESTPAC. While in Vietnam, he was assigned to the First Marine Aircraft Wing.

After the completion of his various logistical and legal assignments at the group level, he was again assigned to Quantico. Lt. Davidson was released from active duty in December 1969 and immediately affiliated with various OMCR units.

Reserve assignments included: Executive Officer 4th Communication Support Company (FMF), USMC Advisor NAVRESRESCOM Region 13, MTU HQMC Training officer Congressional Reserve Unit, and served as the State Emergency Preparedness Officer, USMC Representative, Office of the Governor and State Adjutant General, State of Indiana.

In 1991, Col. Davidson was recalled to active duty for Operation Desert Storm and served

as Executive Officer of RTB-7. In July 1993, he retired from the Marine Corps.

His military education includes various staff schools with both LFTC (LANT) and (PAC), the Amphibious Warfare School, Command and Staff College and the Armed Forces Staff College.

As a civilian, Secretary Davidson held several senior positions in private industry, was elected to public office and served in the administrations of Presidents Kennedy and Johnson as a White House intern and President Reagan as the Deputy Assistant Navy Secretary (RA).

In 1985, he was granted knighthood in Oslo, Norway. Additionally, he was awarded the Distinguished Civilian Service Award SECNAV, Meritorious Public Service Award USCG, and received a letter of appreciation, Office of the Secretary of Defense RFPB. Finally, Secretary Davidson was elected as a Trustee of the US Naval Academy Foundation.

GEORGE T. DAVIDSON, LT(JG), participated in the last convoy from Manila Nov. 27, 1941, consisting of the transports, *Scott* and *Coolidge*, three destroyers and the cruiser *Louisville*. The convoy headed south between Australia and New Guinea, passed the Solomons on December 7 and landed in SF, Christmas 1941, the first wounded from Pearl.

Birthday Oct. 13, 1942, V-1, V-12, University of California Fall 1942; Spring 1943, Pre-Midshipman's School, Asbury Park, Midshipman's School at Notre Dame (60 days), Ensign "C(L)" Aug. 4, 1943.

Rejected for sea duty - PTS, Landing Craft and Destroyers. He was determined to fight for friends captured by the Japanese in Manila and Hong Kong, and finally realized solution to problem was to memorize the eye chart, he became Ensign "C."

Rejecting shore duty N.D., COM 11, CincPac, boarded *Rodman* (DMS-21) (DD-456) Pearl Harbor, January 1944.

Ultihi, Eniwetok, Okinawa, pre-invasion minesweeping, shore bombardment, depth charging, radar picket line. April 16, 1944, 300 kamikaze attacked all afternoon. Took three planes, shot down nine, almost sank (Naval Letter of Commendation).

Charleston, SC long repair. Tactical Radar School Hollywood Beach, CIC officer, V-J Day.

Torpedo Target Providence. Released to inactive duty June 16, 1946 as LTJG.

CHARLES POPE "CHARLIE" DAY JR., CDR, USNR (Ret), born. Sept. 7, 1932, in New York City. He joined the USN July 2, 1954 and was commissioned through Princeton NROTC in 1954, receiving BA degree in sociology and psychology.

He served aboard USS *Dortch* (DD-670), 1954-56, Newport, RI, receiving his MA from Vanderbilt in 1959.

First active in Naval Reserve Composite Company 3-6, he transferred to Naval Reserve Intelligence Division 3-1 in 1964, where he served on Division Staff, NYC Units, and the Washington Attaché Unit until retiring in 1980.

Service medals include WWII European Occupation, National Defense, Navy Expert Rifle and Pistol, and Armed Forces Reserve w/Hourglass. CDR Day was discharged from active duty in June 1956 and retired from service in July 1980.

He is a Life member of the NOUS since 1963 (Companion No. 4386), the NRA, ROA, Military Order of Foreign Wars, and the National Rifle Association; he is also a member of Naval Intelligence Professionals, TROA, and the Army and Navy Club in Washington, D.C.

Divorced, he has one daughter Margaret Genevieve Mary Day. Civilian employment as vice president and director, Joseph Day, Inc., real estate auctioneers. He is a writer and lobbyist for pro-gun causes.

VIRGINIA ALEXANDRIA DE FRAITES, LT, born Dec. 1, 1938 New Orleans, LA. She graduated from the University of Alabama, School of Dentistry, Division of Dental Hygiene in 1958. From a Navy family, she has actively participated in many Navy associations, primarily initiating the Navy Weekend in Colorado Springs for many years. This also involved establishing the first female cheerleaders at the US Naval Academy. In 1966 she acquired the code name "Mother Goose" from her volunteerism with the midshipmen.

A long time member of the Navy League, she served as a vice president with the Colorado Springs Council, Coast Guard Liaison and social chairman for the Orange County Council, founder and president of the Bayou Council.
She received the rank of Lieutenant as OPS Officer for the NAVSTAR Division of the US Naval Sea Cadet Corps.

She is a member of the Naval Reserve Association, an honorary Navy Recruiter, and received the DOD Distinguished Service Medal from the Employer Support of the Guard and Reserve.

Residing in Houma, LA, she is active in Public Relations with her brothers' firm of Gulf South Engineers, Inc. and numerous parish volunteer commissions. Her two children, both born at the US Naval Academy, are David and Pamela, who is currently president of the South San Diego Council of NOUS. Her grandson by David is Nicholas.

"Mother Goose" joined the New Orleans Commandery as an associate member in 1991, was Vice Commander, Historian, and a member of the National Public Relations, Credentials and 1997 Congress Committees.

ELLIOTT "ACE" DODGE JR., CDR, born July 1, 1915, Narberth, Philadelphia, PA. Received his AB in 1938, Union College, Schenectady, NY; graduate work at Northwestern University, Chicago, IL; and Case Institute of Technology, Cleveland, OH.

Joined V-7 USNR on Sept. 9, 1940 and was commissioned March 15, 1941. Military locations and stations include the USS *New York* (BB-34), Atlantic; USS *Vulcan* (AR-5), (Caribbean, Iceland, Oran, Algeria); USS *Dutchess* (APA-98), Navigator-Pacific.

Units Served With: ATLANTIC-COMSERVLANT; PACIFIC COMPHIBPAC.

Commands Held: Founder and CO, USNTC Lorain, OH 1946-49, Ninth Naval District.

Battles and campaigns include the USN's April 1, 1945 landing on Okinawa, which proved to be the last and greatest air battle in the Pacific. The Japanese in their deeply dug, honey combed underground defenses fully intended to make this fight another Dunkirk. By May 1 when his ship, the USS *Dutchess* (APA-98), arrived at Orange Beach to off load 2,000 Marines, 1st Mar. Div., they were subject to constant attack by hundreds of Japanese kamikazes and suicide dive bombers for eight days. By June 30, after fierce fighting, their victory was assured in the Pacific.

Memorable experiences: 1) "In September 1941, Vulcan entering Hvalfjordhur, Iceland from the vast Atlantic, to establish a base as senior officer present afloat (SOPA) for next two years to assist our fighting ships and convoys in war against German U-boats."

2) "Landing in Algiers mid-1943 prior to establishing a base at Oran to support allied invasion of Anzio, Italy from North Africa."

3) "Flight in April 1944 as naval courier from Oran, Algeria to Cairo, Egypt via RAF and American Transport Command (ATC) where he flew over battle fields where British 8th Army fought Rommel's German Panzer Divisions to a stand still in the North African Desert campaign. Their DC-4 set down at Benghasi Airbase in the Sahara for the night then proceeded to Cairo arriving Easter morning. At dinner they greeted the British and Aussies at the world famous Sheppard Hotel and toured the ancient City of the Dead. En route to Algiers they spent the night at the Translantique Hotel Tunis which just months before was German Headquarters."

4) "My safe arrival home after 61 months of foreign sea duty. I wrote *Five Years at Sea Around the World in 1996*, published in *World War II Reminiscences* by John H. Roush Jr., USA Ret., sponsored by the ROA of the US, Department of California, memorializing the history of WWII 50 years ago."

CDR Dodge was discharged July 16, 1966 and retired July 16, 1975. Awards and medals include American Defense w/Fleet A, American Campaign, EAME Campaign, Asiatic-Pacific Campaign, WWII Victory, Navy Occupations Service, National Defense Service, Armed Forces Reserve, Naval Reserve and Philippine Liberation.

He was a founder of the Marin County Council, San Rafael, CA; Life member of NOUS (his wife is also a member), NRA, Navy League of the US, TROA, Association of Naval Aviators and Naval Officers Association of Canada.

His first wife, Anita Weymouth Vieth, passed away April 15, 1977. He married Winifred O'Leal Dewey, Jan 2, 1981. His children are Elliott G. III, Randall D., Nancy C., Jeffrey N. (Naval architect, Pearl Harbor); stepchildren are Jo Anne, Leland D., Linda Joy, Mark D. and Gail C. O'Leal.

He retired in 1976 from a full 30-year career as an executive in operations, sales and engineering departments of the US Steel Corp. Retired March 1, 1976.

ARTHUR GUSTAVE "REDD" DOEGE, LCDR, born July 31, 1938, Bronxville, NY. Attended the University of Rochester, BSME; USN Test Pilot School, Patuxent River, and Defense Systems Management School, MSMN, USC. Joined the USN in 1956 and was commissioned June 6, 1960.

Military stations were Pensacola, FL; Corpus Christi; Key West; HS-3, Norfolk, VA; VP-10, Brunswick; C-121, Argentia; NavAirSysCom, NATC. Units served with: HS-3, VN-13, VP-10, NASC an NATL.

Participated in the Cuban Crisis, Vietnam, TH-57 BIS/NPE, P-3C, NPF/BIS and LAMPS I, II and III Design.

LCDR Doege was discharged June 6, 1980. Memorable experiences include creating the design for LAMPS on the back of envelopes while assigned to VP-10 in Sigonella. He forwarded the design to NASC and became first NASC design engineer for LAMPS. He designed and managed the SQR-17 Lamps MKI, LOFAR processor; designed the anti-submarine warfare suite for the sea control ship; managed the creation and integration of the first prototype on board the USS *Guam*; created the first successful CRT ASW display with electronic analysis aids; and created the Navy's ALL-DIFA2 submarine location tactics.

He is divorced and father of Wayne, Peter B., Johanna Marie and Christyna Michelle. Owner and CEO of ETS Inc. Action Chemicals. He designed the improved processor and display system for Naval Reserve P-3A and B aircraft; designed the
SQR- 17A Lamps DIFAR processor; designed the AQH9/I1 Mission Data Recorder and Replay System and obtained funding for all.

R.G. DOSE, CAPT, USN (Ret), born Jan. 9, 1915, St. Louis, MO. During WWII his brother Richard Herman Dose served in RCAF and was flying a Spitfire from England when shot down over Holland. Dose attended Washington University, School of Engineering and Flight Training in Pensacola, 1936-37.

Stations: 1937-Torpedo Squadron Three, NAS North Island, San Diego, attached to USS *Saratoga*; 1940-Corey Field, Pensacola; 1942-Corpus Christi; Dec. 7, 1941-Pearl Harbor and WWII; 1943-North Island, San Diego, where he joined Fighting TWELVE; 1944-NAAS Green Cove Springs, FL; 1945-USS *Gilbert Islands*; 1945-Alameda as Commander, Carrier Air Group 14; 1946-Air Group 14 decommissioned; took command of CAG 81 in Norfolk attached to USS *Princeton*; 1947-Line School, Newport; 1948-Ass't Head, Air Branch, Office of Naval Research, Patuxent; 1950-Training officer, Staff, COMFAIRJAX; 1952-Ass't Training officer, Staff, CNATRA; 1954-XO, USS *Kearsarge*.

From 1955-57, CO, Air Development Squadron Three, NAS Atlantic City, NJ; he was the first fleet pilot to fire a Sidewinder; made the first mirror landing on a US Carrier, Aug. 22, 1955; was the first pilot in the fleet to have to eject from an F8U "Crusader" and on June 6, 1957, he and a wing man established a transcontinental speed record, flying from the *Bonhomme Richard* 50 miles west of San Diego and landing on the new *Saratoga* (CVA-60), 50 miles east of Jacksonville, in three hours and 28 minutes. The record still stands, as of 1991.

1957-Naval War College, Newport, RI; 1958-Cecil Field; 1960-CO, USS *Mispillion*; 1961-CO, USS *Midway*; 1962-Pentagon as head of Op-56, Naval Air Training in the office of CNO; 1965-CO, Military Assistance Advisory Group, the Netherlands.

Retired from the Navy in July 1968. Returned home to Solana Beach, CA. His decorations include the Legion of Merit, three DFCs, seven Air Medals and a British Combat Commendation.

Married Laura Elizabeth Curtis of San Diego on Jan. 25, 1941. They had four children: Carole Lynn, Curtis Richard, Diane Michele and George Robert (died in March 1997) and five grandchildren and four great-grandchildren. Capt. Dose passed away Sept. 27, 1998.

LEE WAYLAND DOUGLAS, LCDR, USNR (RET) was born in 1931. He completed his college studies at Harvard University, where he majored in International Relations, with minors in English and Journalism. He was commissioned in 1953 through the Regular ROTC Program at Harvard, afterwards serving on three Amphib ships, in a Beachmaster Unit, the COMPHIBGRUWESTPAC Staff, as a Reserve Center CO, and COMEIGHT Classification and Mobilization Officer.

His initial primary avocation was the Naval Reserve Association, which he joined in 1966, becoming a Life member in 1970. He eventually became National VP Membership and National Statistician, and from 1979-93 National Historian. He  joined the Naval Order on Oct. 17, 1979, becoming Companion #5351 as a charter member and first Recorder of the National Capitol Commandery. Life Member Douglas served the Naval Order as Recorder General from 1983-95, one of the longest tenures in the Order's history.

He was author of the first NOUS Operations Manual in 1986. In recognition of his services, he received the General Commandery Certificate of Appreciation at the 1985 Williamsburg Congress; in Galveston the NOUS bronze plate with NOUS cross was presented in 1987; Long Beach in 1989 saw a large ship's wheel plaque with the NOUS seal; at the Centennial he received the same type plaque as did all Past Com-

manders General; and in 1991 he was presented a wristwatch bearing the USN logo on the dial.

He passed away in 1995.

STANLEY EDGAR ELLEXSON JR., CAPT, USNR (Ret), born July 4, 1929, Tacoma, WA; grew up in Sumner, WA. Graduated from the University of Washington (BA in Education), commissioned Ensign in NROTC in 1952.

Served two years active duty on USS *Orca* (AVP-49). Primary duty was station ship Hong Kong with seven tours of one to three months. In between he had goodwill tours to Saigon, Bangkok, Penang, Indonesia and several ports in the Philippines. Various duties on board and ending tour as 1st Lieutenant Gunnery Officer. While in Hong Kong the second year he served as senior Shore Patrol Officer.

Affiliated with several Naval Reserve Units including SUR-DIV 11-45(M), Santa Barbara, 1955-57; SUR-DIV 11-37(L), Pasadena, 1958; various units at Treasure Island, 1959-83, with one year at NAS Alameda Group Command 12-1(L). Commands included SUR-DIV 12-20(M); Mobilization Team 12-4(L) at Treasure Island. From 1970-83 he was involved primarily with the USN Sea Cadet Corps; CO, COWELL Div. 12-4, 1970-75, winning first place of 152 units in 1972-73; attached to training and support 12-36, 11-67 and REDCOM 20 as Sea Cadet Officer inspecting all 20+ units annually, 1975 through retirement until 1995 in REDCOM area.

Joined the NOUS in 1982 and became Life member in 1983, Companion #5540. Served as chairman, Credential Committee, 1992-present; Assistant Treasurer, General Regalia, 1997; Master-at-Arms General, 1997-present; Commander, San Francisco Commandery, 1997-present; life member of NRA, Navy League and Naval Order.

Capt. Ellexson retired Aug. 23, 1983. Awards include Navy Commendation Medal, China Service Medal, National Defense Medal and Armed Forces Reserve Medal w/2 HGs. He is still involved with the USN Sea Cadet Corps as Senior Vice President, 1985-present. Was the fourth awardee of the NSCC Chairman's Medal, the Sea Cadets highest award in 1990.

Divorced, no children, he is self-employed at Big Stan's Coffee Shop, Richmond, CA.

JAMES ROBERT ELLIOTT II, born on Feb. 18, 1932, in Kansas City, MO. He graduated from Princeton University, magna cum laude, in 1953. He is a descendant member, joining NOUS in 1990. His other lineage societies include, General Society of Colonial Wars, Deputy Governor General and Past Governor of the California Society, holder of the California Distinguished Service Medal; National Society Sons and Daughters of the Pilgrims, Deputy Governor, Southern California Branch; Colonial Society of Pennsylvania; National Society Sons of the American Revolution, President of the Pasadena Chapter, holder of the Silver and two Bronze Good Citizenship Medals; Sons of the Revolution; Aztec Club of 1847; Military Order of the

Loyal Legion; Military Order of Foreign Wars, Past Commander of the California Commandery, holder of the Distinguished Service Award; also past president and honorary member of the Orders and Medals Society of America, holder of the Distinguished Service Medal, Meritorious Service Medal and Literary Medal. He wrote the section on Orders, Decorations and Medals in the *World Book Encyclopedia* and is a holder of the Order of Polonia Restituta and the Cross of Merit, I Class of Poland.

His career included vice president of Walt Disney Music of Canada, Ltd., and national sales manager of Record Division for Walt Disney Productions. Also served as director of the Tape Division at A&M Records, producing a highly suc-  cessful album entitled, *Halloween Horrors*.

Mr. Elliott is married to the former Delores Anderson. They have three sons: James Robert III, William Carlyle and John Newman and a granddaughter, Suzanne.

DOUGLAS FAIRBANKS JR., CAPT, born Dec. 9, 1909, New York City, NY. Attended Bovee School, Collegiate School, Knickerbocker Greys Cadet, Polytechnic School, Harvard Military School; and was privately tutored in London and Paris.

Joined the USNR and was commissioned in 1941. Sea Duty (1941-44): Office of Naval Intelligence (ONI) Navy Dept., Washington, D.C.; USS *Ludlow*; USS *Mississippi*; at sea with Minesweeper Patrol; assigned to staff of commander, US TF-99 in USS *Washington*; TDY, USS *Wasp* on convoys from Scapa Flow and Glasgow to Malta; USS *Wichita*; assigned to Rear Adm. Lord Louis Mountbatten's Combined Operations HQ, London and later as Commander of Flotilla of Amphibious Raiding Craft, (only US officer so assigned). From late 1942-44 assigned various special operational and staff duties.

After invasion of France in 1944, he transferred to Strategic Plans Division and later to Post War Plans Division of the HQ of the Chief of Naval Operations and of the CinC, US Fleet, Washington, D.C., as liaison between Chiefs of Staff and Department of State. Returned to inactive duty in February 1946.

Received the Silver Star, Legion of Merit w/ V, Distinguished Service Cross, Chevalier of the National Order of the Legion d'Honneur, Croix de Guerre w/Palm, War Cross for Military Valor, USNR Medal w/8 stars, American Defense w/A, EAME w/6 stars, Victory Medal, US Joint Chiefs of Staff Badge, USN Expert Pistol, numerous citations and commendations for military service and decorations for diplomatic, public or philanthropic services.

Married Lucille Le Sueur (Joan Crawford), 1929-34, divorced; Mary Lee Epling, 1939 until her death Sept. 14, 1988, and Vera Lee Shelton, May 30, 1991. He has three children: Daphne, Victoria and Melissa; eight grandchildren: Anthony, Natasha,  Dominick and Nicholas Fairbanks-Westonl; Barend and Elizabeth Van Gerbig; Crystal and Joseph Morant; and three great-grandchildren: Aislinn, Georgina and Benjamin Fairbanks-Weston.

He is an actor, producer and writer and has received numerous civilian medals, citations, honorary degrees, fellowships and military memberships.

VINCENT D. FARRELL, CAPT, born Aug. 12, 1929, Jersey City, NJ. Attended St. Mary's College, KY (BA degree) and St. John's Law School (JD degree). He joined the USN June 30, 1947, was commissioned Nov. 16, 1972 and served on active duty for nine years.

Military duty includes USS *Midway*, 1951-55, making two Med cruises and a world cruise; USS *Coral Sea* and USS *Boxer* during Inchon invasion in Korea and various stations in the States. He played on the Bainbridge and Lakehurst baseball teams.

In the Naval Reserve he served as CO of six NR units and as SJA. Capt. Farrell retired Aug. 12, 1989. Awards include the Navy Commendation (2), China Service, Good Conduct (2), Korean Service, PUC, Korean PUC, Naval Unit Citation, MUC, UNSM, European and Japanese Occupation, Armed Forces Reserve, Expert Pistol and Rifle.

He is an attorney with Farrell, Farrell & Burke, which includes his son Ed and daughter, Patty Burke. He is married to Margaret O'Brien, a professor at Nassau Community College, and they have two other children, David and Maureen. Grandchildren are Kevin and Conor Burke.

JOHN PAUL "JACK" FEERICK, CAPT, born Aug. 15, 1950, New York City, NY. Received his BS in 1972 and MD in 1978 from Georgetown University, Washington, D.C. Joined the USN in April 1979.

Stations include NAF, Washington, D.C.; MCALF-15, Bogue Field, Cherry Point; NAS Pensacola, FL (NAMI); NS Keflavik, Iceland; London, UK; and BuMed, Washington, D.C.

He served with the following units: 2nd Marine Air Wing; MEDCRU 404; Fleet Hospital 250 (combat zone) 7D; NMCRRC, Columbus, OH; and Code 25, operational medicine and fleet support, BuMed, Washington, D.C.

A Captain in the Selected Reserves, his decorations include the Navy Commendation Medal, Meritorious Unit Commendation, National Defense Service Medal and Armed Forces Reserve Medal.

Memorable experiences include flight training at Pensacola (aerospace medicine), service in Iceland and flights to the North Pole, and flying from carriers, *Lexington* and *Nimitz*, during cruises.

Married Patricia and has four children: John, Meaghan, Catherine and Thomas. He is a neurologist, stroke researcher and editor in chief, *Neurore Habilitation News*.

Memberships: A Companion of the NOUS, also NRA, ROA, chapter officer; USNI, AMSUS; and National Maritime Historical Society.

NOUS Ancestor: Albion Burnham, CDR of USS *Carnation*, 1865, So. Atlantic Blockade Sqdn.

DANIEL G. FELGER, CDR, USN (Ret), born Sept. 5, 1939, Mishawaka, IN. He was commissioned an Ensign in June 1961 following graduation from the University of Kansas with a Bachelor's degree in Journalism. He served as CIC officer of USS *McDermut* (DD-677), including the ship's assignments to the Taiwan Patrol and as an escort for a San Diego based PHIBRON during the Cuban Missile Crisis.

His assignment as Executive Officer and Navigator of USS *Embattle* (MSO-434) included a total of eight months of Operation Market Time, the counter infiltration patrol of the Republic of Vietnam. Lt. Felger transferred to the Naval Reserve in 1967.

He worked as a general assignment reporter on *The Cleveland Press* until recall to active duty and augmentation in 1970. LCDR. Felger was the Engineer Officer and a Tactical Action Officer of USS *Fox* (DLG/CG 33) from 1971-72. During this period *Fox* became the first US warship to enter the Sea of Okhotsk since the end of WWII and later destroyed two North Vietnamese fighter aircraft in the Tonkin Gulf using the ship's assigned CAP.

From 1972-75 he was the Officer-in-Charge of the initial COMNAVSURFLANT ship propulsion mobile training team. A Naval Institute Proceedings article he wrote during this period that documented training and material problems with 1200-PSI steam plants sparked congressional inquiry and was a major factor in the Navy's reprogramming of funds to improve propulsion plant conditions for steam-powered cruisers and destroyers.

He was Executive Officer of USS *Jonas Ingram* (DD-938) from 1975-77. Subsequent tours included DD-963 class fleet introduction, recruiting and Pentagon billets. In 1979 the Naval Institute published CDR Felger's book, *Engineering For The Officer Of The Deck*, which was used in the engineering curricula at the Naval Academy and NROTC universities and aboard ships of the fleet.

His final assignment involved development and introduction of the former destroyer USS *Barry* (DD-933) as the Washington Navy Yard display ship.

Cdr. Felger retired in 1984. His decorations include the Meritorious Service Medal, Armed Forces Expeditionary Medal, Vietnam Service., Medal, RVN Campaign Medal and National Defense Service Medal.

He is married to the former Lydia Jean Herz. He and his wife are life members of the Naval Order. They have two married children, Sara L. Sherwood and Anne Mary Felger; and two grandchildren, Ellen and Joseph Sherwood.

Dan was employed as senior engineer and project manager from 1985 to retirement in 1998.

LYDIA JEAN HERZ-FELGER, born Dec. 21, 1943, Palo Alto, CA. She received a BA in history from Stanford University in 1965 and a MPA from Harvard University JFK School of Government.

Her father, Maj. Ludwig E. Herz (US Army Air Corps), was killed in the Pacific Theater in November 1944. Maj. Herz, who had been a professor of marine biology at San Francisco State College, had three daughters.

Jean is a member of the WWII Orphans Network and an Associate Life Companion of the Naval Order. She is married to CDR Daniel G. Felger, USN (Ret) and the mother of Sara Sherwood and Anne Mary Felger. Grandchildren are Ellen and Joseph Patrick Sherwood

Civilian Employment: GS-14 Chinese Programs Manager, Office of International Aviation Federal Aviation Administration.

JOHN RICHARD "JACK/SILVERFOX" FISHER, RADM, born Dec. 28, 1924, Columbus, OH. Attended the USN Academy, BS degree; Renselaer Polytechnic Institute, BCE and MCE; Advanced Management Program, Harvard Business School; and Armed Forces Staff College. He joined the USN in June 1943 and commissioned June 5, 1946.

Military stations included NAS Barbers Point, HI; BUDOCKS, Washington, DC; Naval Powder Factory, Indian Head, MD; Atlantic Missile Range, Cape Canaveral, FL; Southeast Div. BUDOCKS, Charleston, SC; Department of Defense, Washington, DC; Naval FAC Engr. Comd., Washington, DC, Manila, Philippine Islands; Chesapeake Div., NAVFAC, Washington, DC; and Pearl Harbor, HL

Served in USS *Kearsarge* (CV-33); USS *Plover* (AMS-33); Naval Mobile Const. Bn. 4; 30th Naval Const. Regt. and held commands in OICC, Cape Canaveral, FL; OICC, Southwest Pacific, Manila, Philippine Islands; 30th Naval Const. Regt., Vietnam; COMDR, Chesapeake Div., NAVFAC, Washington, DC; COMDR, Pacific Div., NAVFAC, Pearl Harbor; and COMDR Pacific Fleet Seabees.

Participated in battles and campaigns in Vietnam, 1968-69; Vietnam, Cambodia and Laos, 1975.

RADM Fisher retired May 1, 1977. Decorations include the Distinguished Service Medal, Legion of Merit (2) w/Combat V, Joint Service Commendation Medal, Navy Commendation Medal, Vietnamese Gallantry Cross w/Gold Star; Antarctica Service Medal, Combat Action Ribbon, WWII Victory Medal, National Defense Service Medal, American Theater Medal, Vietnamese AF Honor Medal and Navy Unit Commendation.

Memorable experiences include the construction of the Atlantic Missile Range tracking stations; construction of base facilities in Philippines, Australia, Antarctica and New Zealand; visiting the South Pole; design of modernization of the Naval Academy; being responsible for Presidential security facilities at Camp David; being in command of 8,000 Seabees in support of Marines and Army in I Corps, Vietnam; closing down defense facilities and offices in Vietnam, Cambodia, Laos; construction of Diego Garcia by Seabees; construction of Vietnamese Refugee Camp for 20,000 on Guam; construction of Corregidor Memorial.

NOUS Ancestor: Great-Uncle Commodore Wilson W. Buchanan, USN (d. 1927).

Married Kitson Overmyer and has two children, The Rev. Scott O. Fisher and Mrs. Lani F. Browning; grandchildren are Charleen, Shane and Rebecca Fisher and Skylar and Lilia Browning.

Civilian employment as executive vice-president, Raymond International. Inc., Houston, TX, retiring May 1, 1986; and president of Chama Inc., retiring Dec. 31, 1995.

EDWARD M. FITCH JR., CAPT, born Aug. 26, 1920, Phoenix, AZ. Graduated high school; completed two years of junior college; and two years at USC, receiving his BA in business. Joined the USNR March 31, 1941, and was commissioned in January 1942.

Military stations and units include NAS Long Beach, Corpus Christi, USS *Saratoga* (CV-3), USS *Bataan* (CVE-29), VTN 42-52-63; USS *Bonhomme Richard*, VT(N)42, VT(N)53, VT(N)63 and VF781.

Participated in battles and campaigns in Okinawa (USS *Saratoga),* Japan (USS *Bataan),* and Korea (USS *Bonhomme Richard).* He was officer in charge, Parachute Loft at Corpus Christi.

Discharged in December 1945 at the end of WWII and again in July 1952, after Korea. After 20 years CAPT. Fitch retired from the Naval Reserve.

As a civilian he was an insurance broker, going from mail-boy to president.

RAYMOND J. "RAY" FLORES, CDR, born in Miami, AZ on March 11, 1922, to Aurelio Flores and Rosa Johnson. He graduated from MHS in 1941 and left for Arizona State University. WWII interrupted his schooling and he enlisted in the USAAC in August 1942, serving as a Draftsman until separation 41 months later. He was commissioned in the USNR in August 1958.

On return to Phoenix he enrolled at the American Graduate School for International Management (AIFT) and earned BA degree in foreign trade. He completed BA and MA degrees in Education, 1949-50 and served as an educator for 35 years, retiring June 30, 1985.

Service in the Army and commissioned service in the Naval Reserve totaled 28+ years. Went from E-5 to 0-5 in 10 years and retired as a Commander in 1982. His awards include the National Defense, American Theater, Army Good Conduct and USN Meritorious Service Medal.

Commanded units for NAVSECGRU for nine years in Phoenix and Tucson and is a Life member of NOUS Commandery in Arizona. Memorable was being privy to factual data regarding national and international concerns and Naval Service "E" for USNR NSG Div 11-8.

Married Leota Resler Dec. 26, 1951, and has six children: Deborah, Rebecca, Raymond, Roderick, Kathryn and Gregory; 10 grandchildren: Christopher, Jared, Brady and Shawn McGonigle; Travis, Alina, Leah, Ryan and Nicholas Flowers; Toby Kajan; and one great-granddaughter Samantha McGonigle.

His American commissioned ancestor is J.R. Johnson (CAPT, Union Army) circa 1864-5, New Mexico Vol.

PAUL A. FRATARANGELO, MGen., born Feb. 24, 1943, Corning, NY. Graduated from Niagara University and was commissioned a 2nd Lieutenant in the USMC in June 1964. He is a designated Naval Aviator and has flown over 5,900 hours, including 485 combat missions and 263 carrier landings, primarily in F-4, F-14, A-4 and F/A-18 aircraft.

Gen. Fratarangelo's 33 years active service as a Marine Officer include nine years in command as a Squadron, Aircraft Group, Aircraft Wing, Air Station and Joint Task Force Commander. His staff assignments include serving as the Commander, Forward Headquarters Element/Inspector General for the U.S. Central, and as an Operations Analyst with the Office of the Secretary of Defense. He also served as the senior U.S. Representative for the successful POW repatriation negotiations following the Gulf War. During his final active duty assignment as Commander, Marine Corps Air Bases, Western Area, he developed successful Master plans for the closure of El Toro and Tustin, and the standup of MCAS Miramar.

His personal decorations include the Navy Distinguished Service Medal, Defense Superior Service Medal, Defense Meritorious Service Medal, Air Medal w/Gold Numeral 2 and Bronze Numeral 33, Joint Service Commendation Medal, Navy Commendation Medal w/Combat V and the Vietnam Gallantry Cross w/Gold Star.

Maj. Gen. Fratarangelo is married to the former Andrea Hetzel. They have two daughters Linda Ann Steer and Lori Ann Pratt; and five grandchildren: Hailey, Heather, Andrea, Amanda and Audrey. He was president of Contrail, Inc. until retirement July 1, 1997.

JOHN FRANKLIN FREEMAN, LTJG, born June 23, 1925, Philipsburg, PA. Received his BA (arts and letters), MA (secondary ed.) and PhD (ed. admin.) degrees. Joined the USNR June 17, 1943 and was commissioned March 10, 1949.

Military stations were NAS Olatha, KS; Ohio Wesleyan University, prep flight training, Delaware, OH; Central Michigan College, Mt. Pleasant, MI, WTS Flight Ground School training; University of Iowa, Iowa City, IA, pre-flight training; NAS Ottumwa, IA, primary flight training; NAS Corpus Christi, TX, intermediate flight training; NAS Kingsville, TX, advanced flight training.

Held commands of NAVCAD officer on each of the above stations. He was about ready for wings and commission when the war ended and he was sent home in the Reserve status and discharged Sept. 6, 1959 as LTJG.

Memorable was all phases of naval flight training during WWII, 1943-45; his association with great officers, fellow NAVCADS and Navy support personnel; serving as a cadet officer on each of his stations.

Married Kelly Dee and has three children: William C., Kathleen Freeman Hensley, Susanne Freeman Cottrell; and two grandchildren, April and Laura Hensley. John is a public school teacher, counselor and administrator; college dean of education; and YMCA executive director.

He is a life member of Assoc. of Naval Aviation, MOWW, Navy League of US, NOUS, ROA; a member of Military District of Washington Officer's Club, American Legion and numerous professional, civic and charitable affiliations and has served as an officer (including president) in many of them.

NOUS Commissioned Ancestors: His father, Charles E. Freeman, served as 2LT, USA, in WWI and with AEF in France; his great-grandfather, John Kelly, served as a Capt. in Union Army, Civil War; he also has Revolutionary War ancestors.

RALPH F. FREESE, CDR, USN (Ret), born in 1930 in Hugoton, KS, and grew up in Colorado. He graduated from high school in Julesburg, CO. Entered the USN Academy on a competitive appointment in 1949, graduated in 1953 (BS degree), and commissioned Ensign in the Supply Corps. Attended the Navy Supply Corps School in Bayonne, NJ and George Washington University (MA degree).

Military Stations: USS *Magoffin* (APA-199) assigned to Pacific Fleet and took part in the evacuation of Vietnamese refugees from North to South Vietnam; 1954, USS *Roberts* (DE-749), Norfolk, VA; Navy Exchange Officer, Ports-  mouth Naval Shipyard and London, England; 1961, Office of the Chief of Naval Operations; 1964, USS *Francis Marion* (APA-249), Atlantic Fleet; 1966, staff of the Inspector General, Supply Corps, Washington, D.C.; Customer Service officer, Navy Foreign Aid Program; OinC, Navy Exchange Charleston.

CDR Freeze retired with 20 years service. Military decorations include Korean Service Medal, PUC, China Service Ribbon, UN Service Ribbon, National Defense Service Medal w/star, Joint Service Commendation Medal, Secretary of the Navy Commendation, Turkish Navy Commendation and as Supply Officer received the E for an outstanding supply department.

After retirement from the Navy, he purchased and operated two Hallmark card stores in northern Virginia from 1973-90. Sold them and went to work at the USN Memorial and in 1996 accepted the position of operations manager of Yesterday's Rose, a thrift shop operated by volunteers from various organizations. He was president of the Old Dominion Chapter of DESA until 1997 when he became the executive administrator.

Married in 1954 to Trianne Lampkin and they have three grown children and four grandchildren.

HOWARD FREIBERGER, CAPT, born April 2, 1921, New York, NY. received his BS degree from CCNY in 1941 and MA from Columbia University in 1949. He joined the USN June 28, 1944, and was commissioned July 8, 1948.

Military stations include Great Lakes, Chicago, Gulfport, Yokosuka, Sasebo and Panama City, FL. Served with COMFLTACT, Yokosuka; COMPHIBPAC, Mine Countermeasures Station. Held commands of CO, NR Communications Div. 3-1, 1961-64; CO, NR Officers School 3-2, 1969-72.

Participated in the Occupation of Japan, 1945-46; Korean War, 1951-52.

CAPT Freiberger retired April 2, 1981. Decorations include the WWII Victory Medal, Korean Presidential Unit Citation, UN Medal, USNR Medal, Navy Occupation Service (Japan), and various area awards.

Memorable experiences include teletypewriter repairman (radio technician); occupation of Japan; Mediterranean cruise in USS *Leary*, 1948; Guantanamo and Panama Cruise in USS *Wisconsin*, 1947; St. John, NB cruise in USS *Albany*, 1949.

Worked as chief of the Research and Development Division, VA Prosthetic and Sensory Aids Service until retirement in 1982.

F. TREVOR "TRIG" GAMBLE, CAPT, USNR (Ret), born July 10, 1928 in Vermont, grew up in upstate New York and attended Colgate University under the Holloway Plan. Following flight training as an Aviation Midshipman flying SNJs and ADs at Pensacola and Corpus Christi, he was designated a Naval Aviator in 1950.

Capt. Gamble's active duty assignments during the Korean War included a three year tour with Air Anti-Submarine Sqdn. 26 flying the TBM Avenger with deployments aboard several Atlantic Fleet CVE and CVL aircraft carriers. Thereafter in 1954, following graduation from Aviation Electronics School (Officer) in Memphis and Guided Missile School in Jacksonville, he served as Guided Missile Officer aboard the USS *Shangri-La* (CVA-38). The WestPac deployment of the Shangri-La with Task Force 77 in 1996 marked the first deployment of an aircraft carrier with air-to-air guided missile capability.

Joining the Naval Air Reserve in 1957 he flew FJ, F2H, S2F, P2V and SNB aircraft at Niagara Falls, South Weymouth, Grosse Ile and Detroit. He commanded Air Anti-Submarine Sqdn. 36Y1 (1969-71) as well as an NAS augmentation unit and a VTU.

CAPT Gamble holds a Ph.D. in physics from Connecticut and served on the faculty of Denison University from 1963-96 teaching physics, astronomy and downhill skiing. He has published a number of research papers on magnetic resonance in solids and on optical information processing. He is married to the former Carolyn Barber and has three children and seven grandchildren.

PATRICK M. GARRETT, CAPT, commissioned in 1972, University of Utah NROTC and received MA degree in 1992, Naval War College. Sea duty included USS *Chewaucan* (AOG-50), USS *Horne* (DLG-30), USS *O'Brien* (DD-975), USS *Leahy* (CG-16), USS *Worden* (CG-18), Destroyer Sqdn. 25, Commander 3rd Fleet. Commanded USS *Rathburne* (FF-1057), USS *Leftwich* (DD-984) and Destroyer Sqdn. 23. Sea Combat Commander, USS Carl Vinson battle group.

Served ashore on staff Surface Warfare Officer's School, staff deputy CNO (surface warfare), Executive Assistant to Deputy Commander in Chief, U.S. Space Command and CO, Pacific Board of Inspection and Survey.

Awarded Defense Superior Service Medal, two Legions of Merit, Bronze Star w/Combat V, three Meritorious Service Medals, two Navy Commendation Medals, Navy Achievement Medal and Combat Action Ribbon. Honolulu Navy League's Adm. Bernard A. Clary Leadership Award winner in 1991.

Married to the former Kathleen Roll. They have two children.

ALEXANDER "SANDY" GASTON, QM3/c, born Oct. 26, 1946, New York, NY. He completed one semester of college at Hofstra University in Hempstead and graduated from New York Institute of Photography in June 1970.

Joined the USNR Oct. 31, 1963 and served with USS *Princeton* (LPH-5) in 1967 and USS *Wexford County* (LST-1168) in 1968. He was involved in various amphibious operations between March-May 1967 and between December 1967-May 1968.

He achieved the rank of Quartermaster 3/c. Decorations include the National Defense Medal, Vietnam Service Medal, Vietnam Expeditionary Combat Action Medal, Meritorious Unit Commendation and the Meritorious Public Service Award by Secretary of the Navy John Dalton in June 1996 "...for exceptional service in support of the Navy and the Navy League of the U.S..."

He has been active in Navy League since 1971 with a life membership since 1976; holds membership in four Councils; and is honorary plankowner in last five CVNs plus numerous other warships. He was discharged Oct. 31, 1969.

Memorable experience occurred when the Viet Cong shore battery began firing while his ship, the USS *Princeton* (LPH-5), was offloading ammunition by DMZ on his last day in Vietnam.

NOUS Ancestor is his father, Maj. John Gaston who served with the USMC during WWII. Alexander Gaston never married.

DALLAS COOPER "COOP" GOULD, CAPT, USNR (Ret), born March 27, 1912, Alton, CA.

Graduated high school and business college. Joined the USN in 1942 and commissioned same year.

Military stations were NAS Jacksonville, FL; NAS Norfolk, VA; NAS Key West; NAS Memphis, TN; NAS Oakland, CA; NAS Glenview, IL. Served with Phase NATTC, Jacksonville, FL; O&R off., Key West, FL; CO, NAS San Julian, Cuba; a/c Maint. Officer, NAS Memphis; a/c Maint. Officer, NAS Oakland; Assistant Maint. Officer, administration staff, NAS Glenview, IL. CAPT Gould retired March 27, 1972.

Memorable was decommissioning San Julian Air Station and returning the field to the Cuban Government.

He was a real estate broker and sales manager, retiring Oct. 1, 1994. Coop and Rita married in 1937 and have three children: Robin, Fredric and Beverly. Grandchildren are Heather, Lori, Natalie, David, Gerry, Lisa, Sandra; and two great-grandchildren.

JAMES V. "JIM" GREALISH, RADM, born Aug. 8, 1920, San Francisco, CA. He graduated from the University of San Francisco in 1942 with a degree in accounting. He enlisted in the USN in 1942, reporting to USNR Midshipman's School, from which he was commissioned an Ensign on March 5, 1943.

His WWII service included duty aboard the USS *North Carolina* (BB-55), USS *Waters* (APD-8) and as CO of USS *Cronin* (DE-704).

In 1951 he was recalled to active duty for the Korean Conflict and served as Executive Officer of the USS *Nawman* (DE-416) and USS *Cushing* (DD-797). Remaining active in the USNR, he held shore and afloat command billets, including Commander. Naval Reserve Readiness Command, Region 20.

RADM Grealish retired July 1, 1979, after 37 years of service. Among his awards and decorations are the Legion of Merit, Navy Meritorious Service Medal, Asiatic-Pacific Theater Ribbon w/7 Battle Stars, Philippine Defense, Korean Service, Navy League Distinguished Service Award and the Order of the Malta Cross of Merit.

Since again returning to civilian life in 1953, he has served in financial management positions and presently is chairman of Protected Investors of America, a full service investment planning firm founded in 1934.

Married Jean B. and has three children: Kent M. (CAPT, SC USNR, Ret), Kathleen Ciardella and Susan Flanigan; grandchildren: Tony, Todd, Jon, Nicole, Danielle, Meaghan, Kaitlin and Kelly. Jim was chairman of Protected Investors of America at the time of his retirement on July 1, 1979.

WALLACE N. "WALLY" GUTHRIE JR., RADM, USNR (RET), born Feb. 22, 1939, New York City, NY. Attended US Naval Academy - BS in 1961; Rollins College, Winter Park, FL - MS in management, 1974 and EdS in 1981.

Shore Duty included USNA, Annapolis, MD, July 1957 to June 1961; SUBSCOL NLON, CT, July-December 1961; sea duty from January

1962 to December 1963; shore duty, NAVGMS, Dam Neck, VA, January to April 1964; sea duty from May 1964 to September 1967.

Reserve assignments from October 1967 to April 1986 were at various locations in Florida with units NROS 6-14, NRSD 6-48, SERVSCOL 308, SUBRON 3408 (ATK), COMSUBRON 4-408, COMSUBGRU 8 DET 208, CNET HQ DET 108, USREDCOM 108, REDCOMREG 8; April 1986 to present, member of Naval Reserve Flag Support Unit.

Recalled to active duty to serve as Deputy Director of Naval Reserve from July 1989 to October 1992. He served through duration of Desert Shield/Desert Storm.

RADM Guthrie retired Sept. 1, 1994. Decorations include the Defense Superior Service Medal, Legion of Merit, Defense Meritorious Service Medal and Navy Meritorious Service Medal.

Wally and his wife Ginny three children: Wallace, Gail and Virginia; and five grandchildren: Christopher, Kevin, Kristen, Brent and Justine.

THOMAS BAILEY HAGEN, CAPT, USNR (Ret), of Erie, PA, is a recognized business executive, community leader and public official. His first association with the Navy was as a youngster through his grandfather, Frank J. Bailey (1874-1961), Captain, NYNM and Lieutenant Commander, USNR, a charter member of New York Naval Militia and USNR who served in both World Wars.

Capt. Hagen joined the inactive Naval Reserve in January 1957 while in college. He was called to active duty in June 1958 following graduation, as an OCSA in Class 34 of the Navy Officer Candidate School, Newport. He was commissioned an Ensign, Supply Corps, USNR on Nov. 1, 1957, taking the oath of office from his grandfather who presented him the sword given him when he was commissioned in 1909. CAPT Hagen carried that sword throughout his 30 year Naval Reserve career.

He attended Navy Supply Corps School, Athens, GA, graduating May 1958. He was ordered to independent duty as supply and disbursing officer of USS Harwood (DDE-861) home-ported in Newport with Destroyer Squadron 24 assigned to ASW Task Group Bravo.

In January 1960, he reported to Navy Supply Depot, Newport as Issue Control and Fleet Liaison officer. Upon detachment from active duty as a LTJG in October 1960, he affiliated with the Naval Reserve Center, Erie, PA, until his retirement on Dec. 1, 1986. He was promoted to Captain on June 1, 1985.

His Naval Reserve assignments included: logistics officer of Mobilization Team 4-10, assistant Joint Petroleum Officer of CINCLANT Detachment 105 and senior officer of a Voluntary Training Unit. Active duty for training included: Navy Finance Center, Cleveland; various mobilization exercises; Navy Supply Center, Norfolk; Naval Activities, UK and CINCLANT logistics staff.

A life member of the Naval Reserve Association and NOUS, CAPT Hagen was born in Buffalo, NY, on Sept. 19, 1935 and moved to Erie, PA, in 1943 where he attended public schools and Penn State-Erie, The Behrend College, 1953-55. He is past chairman of the College Council of Fellows, and in 1988, received the prestigious and lifetime Penn State Alumni Fellow Designation. Capt. Hagen graduated from The Ohio State University in 1957 with a BS degree in commerce. He was a Griffith Scholar, member of Phi Kappa Psi and received the Alunmi Citizenship Award. In 1996, Edinboro University of Pennsylvania conferred the honorary degree of Doctor of Public Service.

Capt. Hagen had a distinguished business career spanning more than 40 years with Erie Insurance Group where he rose from part-time file clerk to chairman and CEO. He continues as a member of the board of directors. He is also a board member of: GPU, Inc., Pennsylvania Housing Finance Agency, Team Pennsylvania, and chairman of The Team Pennsylvania Foundation. Additionally, Capt. Hagen is a board member of The Athenaeum of Philadelphia, board member and past president of The Pennsylvania Society, honorary director of Erie Conference on Community Development, honorary director and past president of Erie Philharmonic, past chairman of Insurance Federation of Pennsylvania, trustee emeritus of Griffith Foundation at Ohio State, and past president of Erie Council of the Navy League.

Capt. Hagen is a former board member of Pennsylvania Business Roundtable, Pennsylvania Chamber of Business and Industry, First National Bank of Pennsylvania, Union Bank and Trust Company, Chautauqua Hotel Company, Erie Western Pennsylvania Port Authority, and Preservation Pennsylvania.

From 1995-97, Capt. Hagen served in the Cabinet of Governor Tom Ridge of Pennsylvania, as Secretary of Commerce and then as First Secretary of Community and Economic Development. He was a member of the Governor's Executive Board and past chairman of Pennsylvania Industrial Development Authority, Pennsylvania Economic Development Finance Authority, and Ben Franklin/Industrial Resource Centers Partnership.

Long identified with community revitalization, Captain Hagen earned the "Pennsylvania Preservationist of the Year Award" and the "Honor Award" of the Pennsylvania Society of Architects for contributions to the profession by a non-architect. He also received the "Outstanding Community Service Award" in Erie and was named a "Distinguished Pennsylvanian" by both Greater Philadelphia Chamber of Commerce and William Penn Society of Gannon University, Erie. He is listed in Who's Who in America and Who's Who in the World.

DAVID E. "DAVE" HALL, LCDR, born Aug. 7, 1957, Fort Worth, TX, and was raised in Quitman, TX. Received his commission at the NROTC Unit at Rice University on Dec. 19, 1980. He gradu-

ated from the University of Saint Thomas with a BA in meteorology.

Active duty assignments include Communications Officer, Naval Communications Station, Iceland; Implementations and Plans Officer, Naval Telecommunication Command, Washington, DC; Assistant Electronic Materials Officer, USS America (CV-66); Maintenance and Material Control Officer, NAS New Orleans; and Assistant Maintenance Officer, VA-85.

Reserve units include Maintenance and Material Control Officer, VR-56; maintenance officer, NR USS Kitty Hawk 0170; and training officer, NR Naval Air Warfare Center 0170.

Awards include two Navy Achievement Medals, Navy Unit Commendation for Operations of Libya, two Meritorious Unit Commendations, National Defense, Armed Forces Expeditionary Medal, Sea Service, Overseas Service, Armed Forces Reserve Medal and Navy Expert Pistol Shot Medal.

In civilian life, he is a police officer, with the US Treasury Department and lives in North Richland Hills, TX LCDR Hall is single.

E H. HANDLER, CAPT, USNR (Ret), served in the OCS Class 40 (1958); Patrol Sqdn. 40 (1959-61); NFO, 0-in-C, CIO, CDO, customs officer, Armed Forces courier, Survival Officer and narcotics and blood chit custodian, special escort and interpreter for CINCPAC; COMNAVDEFEASTPAC, CWSF, CINCPACRESFLT (1962); and assistant N-2/ASSO/flag briefer.

Reserve service consisted of non-pay politico-military experimental unit, 1963; CO, 1979-85 and 1987-89; AT and SPECAT: COMPHIBPAC, COMNAVDEFEASTPAC, OPNAV (OP-06), OASD/ASA, OSD/ISA, US Dept. of State (PM/ MC, PM/ISO, et al.) and policy planning staff, US/OAS, US Dept. of Commerce (BXA), US MBFR DEL Vienna, USCINCEUR/EUCOM, SHAPE, NATO/IMS, CSCE and National Security Council (White House), among other assignments. Representational duties for SECDEF, SECNAV and other agencies. Acting Chief of Mission (Ambassador) US/EC. Special projects and studies for various federal departments.

Awards include the French Order of National Merit (Knight), Order of Merit of the Italian Republic (Knight), US Legion of Merit and Armed Forces Expeditionary Medal, inter alia Badges: US JCS and NATO IMS.

JULIAN R. "JULES" HANSEN, CAPT, born Aug. 7, 1927, Chicago, IL. Received his JD degree in 1952, University of Chicago, Order of COIF. Joined the USNR May 3, 1945 and commissioned Sept. 12, 1948.

Military stations were Ottumwa, Corpus Christi, Pensacola, Jacksonville, North Island, Miramar, Glenview and the USS Essex. Units served with while on active duty include VF-111, 1948-49; VF-143, 1952-54; and with the Reserves VA/VF-727 and NAS ADAR, NASRV-7.

Retired from the service in 1987 with the rank of Captain. Received the WWII Victory Medal, Korean Service Medal and UN National Defense Medal.

Memorable experiences include flying over Dien Bien Phu when the French departed; being a member of the Reserve Jet Demonstration Team Air Barons," first Reserve flight non-stop, NAS Glenview to Guantanamo.

Married to Barbara and has two children, Jane and Dicie; and two grandsons, Christopher and Andrew Miller. He is an attorney-at-law.

LAWRENCE P. "SLEEPY" HARRIS, COL, born Aug. 30, 1918, Mannering, WV. He graduated University of Virginia; joined the USMC in June 1941 and commissioned Nov. 1, 1941.

Military stations include Quantico, VA; New River, NC; Samoa; Guadalcanal; Australia; New Guinea; New Britain; Naval War College, Newport; White House aide, Washington, DC; San Diego; Japan; China; Quantico; Camp Lejeune, NC; Navy Congressional Liaison, Hawaii; Charleston, SC; Okinawa; NROTC, Georgia Tech, Atlanta.

Units/Commands include lst, 2nd and 3rd Mar. Div.; E-2-7, CO, lst Bn., 8th Marines; CO, NROTC, Georgia Tech. Participated in battles and campaigns at Guadalcanal, New Guinea and New Britain.

Col. Harris retired July 1, 1968, his decorations include the Silver Star and two Presidential Unit Citations.

Memorable experiences was serving with the 1st Mar. Div. in Guadalcanal, New Guinea, Cape Glouchester, New Britain, China, Japan, Okinawa; being a White House Aide for Roosevelt and Truman; Navy Congressional Liaison; professor of Naval Science and CO, NROTC, Georgia Tech; G-3, 2nd Mar. Div.; and G-4, 3rd Mar. Div.

Married Jeanne and has three children: Lawrence Jr., Shelley and Gibbs; and four grandchildren: Lawrence III, Ashley, Sloane and Lindsay Harris. Worked as an administrator for North Point, San Francisco, CA, until retirement in September 1983.

FREDERICK C. "FRED" HAWKINS, CAPT, born Oct. 12, 1928, Los Angeles, CA. Attended the University of California, Berkeley, for his BS degree. Joined the USN March 7, 1947 and was commissioned Nov. 11, 1950.

Served as Chief Purser, US Merchant Marine with direct commission in Supply Corps, USNR. Served aboard the USS Princeton, Supply Dept., Bremerton, WA. Was CO, Ship's Supply Officer, Div. 12-1; Supply Officer, COMNAVAIR and participated in action in Korea.

Capt. Hawkins was discharged May 18, 1952. He received the Navy Commendation Medal.

Memorable experiences include serving as Commander S.F. Commandery, NOUS, 1995-97, and being elected Vice Commander General, NOUS, 1997.

Married Patricia and has two daughters and four grandchildren. As a civilian he worked in direct sales/marketing with Kansas Packing Co., New York City, until retirement July 1, 1982.

EUGENE ADAMS "GENE" HEMLEY, CAPT, USN (Ret), born Feb. 20, 1918, Brooklyn, NY. Graduated Columbia, 1935; US Naval Academy, 1936-40, BSEE; and George Washington University, 1968, MS in International Affairs. Joined the USN July 15, 1936 and was commissioned June 6, 1940.

Military Stations: CO, US Naval Communications Station, Japan; Office of CNO Director Fleet Communications Div., director, War Gaming Dept., US Naval War College.

Served in USS Nashville (CL-43); USS Sea Dragon (SS-490); USS Greenling (SS-213); USS Bang (SS-385), CO; USS Volador (SS-490); USS Bristol (DD-857); USS Taconic (AGC-17); and USS Northampton (CC-1).

Battles/Campaigns: North Atlantic convoy to Iceland, Doolittle Campaign, Aleutian Islands, Solomon Islands and five sub war patrols off Japan.

CAPT Hemley retired May 1, 1970; his decorations include the Silver Star Medal, Submarine Combat Insignia w/3 stars, Asiatic-Pacific w/6 stars and the Philippine Liberation Medal.

Memorable experiences include being left topside when the sub dived during a Japanese air attack; being a host to President Lyndon Johnson and family, 20 governors, senators, etc. aboard the USS Northampton; Black Belt, Aikido, in Japan; and Hawaiian area Navy tennis doubles championship where he was runner-up in singles, 1948.

Married Charlotte and has four children: Philip, Paul, Anne and Margaret; and six grandchildren: Lauren, Scott, Charlotte, Michael, Elliot Seth. Worked as executive director for International Trade Facilitation Council; business advisor, UN Econ. Comm. for Europe; and president of FEDA Realty Corp., 1994-97. Capt. Hemley has been semi-retired since June 15, 1994.

JOHN HIGGINSON, RADM, USN (Ret), born Oct. 24, 1932 in St. Louis, MO. In 1990 he retired from a 34 year Navy career where he attained the rank of Rear Admiral.

His Navy career saw him qualified as a Naval Aviator with extensive expertise in anti-submarine and amphibious warfare. He served in seven command positions, mostly afloat, and in his last assignment was the senior officer and only flag officer in the Long Beach/Los Angeles Area, leading 17,000 active duty Navy personnel responsible for the 38 ships assigned to the area for homeport.

He earned degrees from St. Mary's University, the Naval Postgraduate School and George Washington University. He is the co-author of Sea and Air, The Marine Environment, 1968, 2nd Ed., 1973, a text in meteorology and oceanography, and has taught at the university level these and other subjects. He participated in five Apollo astronaut recoveries as a pilot of a Recovery Team Helicopter.

Civilian employment as president/CEO, American Gold Star Manor until retirement in 1995. He was president of Long Beach, CA, Chamber of Commerce, 1990-92. He lives with his wife Nancy in Long Beach, CA.

GEORGE JAMES HILL, CAPT, MC, USNR (Ret), born Oct. 7, 1932, Cedar Rapids, IA. After graduation from Yale University and the Harvard Medical School and a career in academic medicine in 1996, he was appointed Emeritus Professor of Surgery at the New Jersey Medical School.

Capt. Hill was a Corporal in the USMCR from 1950-52 and a Lieutenant in the U.S. Public Health Service Reserve from 1960-68. He transferred to the USNR as Lieutenant Commander in 1968 and was promoted to Commander in 1969 and Captain in 1976.

Capt. Hill is entitled to wear the Meritorious Service Medal, Navy Unit and Meritorious Unit Commendation ribbons, National Defense Service Medal (three awards), Vietnam Service Medal w/campaign star, Armed Forces Reserve Medal w/Hourglass Device, two Vietnam Meritorious Unit Citations, Navy and Marine Corps. Parachutist Badge and USMC Rifle Expert Badge (two awards). He was awarded the Gorgas Medal in 1991 by the Association of Military Surgeons of the U.S. He retired from the Navy Reserve in 1992.

He and his wife, Dr. Helene Zimmerman Hill, live in West Orange, NJ. They have four children.

VERNON THOMAS "TOM" HITCHCOCK, CDR, USNR (Ret), born Feb. 21, 1919, Selma, IN. Graduated from Purdue University in 1940 with BSA and from Stanford with JD in 1953. Joined the USNR July 16, 1941 and commissioned July 13, 1942.

Military stations were USNRAB, St. Louis; NAS New Orleans; NAS Corpus Christi; NAS Alameda; NAS Oakland; NAS Olathe; NAS Moffett; NAS Honolulu and Naval Air Transport Service.

Units served with include VR-2, VR-3, VR-4, VR-I1, VR-24, VR-65, VR-873, ASW VP-875 and aboard the USS Midway. He held the command of transport plane commander, NATS.

CDR Hitchcock was discharged Dec. 12, 1945. Memorable experiences include flying the NATS schedules when the weather shut down civilian airlines and being a member LT(jg) to Lieutenant Officer Selection Board, 1961.

Married Betty Kathryn and has five children: Brenda, Linda, Nancy, Debra and Randolph; and 10 grandchildren: Ryan and Christopher Nixon; Nathan, Zachary and Brittany Taralson; Alexis, Brett, Erik and Arianna Hanson; and Cooper Hitchcock.

Civilian employment: pilot for Southwest Airlines, 1946; TWA, 1947-51; practiced law, 1954-55; deputy attorney general, California, 1956; deputy county counsel, Sonoma County, CA,

1957-63; Executive Director, Libyan Aviation Co., 1966-67; Sonoma County School's legal counsel, 1967-82. Retired July 1, 1982. He is the author of *The Airline to Infinity;* plays trumpet in concert band, Ham Radio KB6UOJ, and is a private pilot.

EDWARD J. "ED" HLOPAK, CAPT, USNR (Ret), born Sept. 18, 1942, Stratford, NJ. He graduated from the US Naval Academy in 1965 with BS degree and from Babson College with MBA.

Upon commissioning, he completed Submarine School, Nuclear Power School and nuclear power prototype training before reporting to the USS *Henry L. Stimson* (SSBN-655) (Blue) in April 1967. He made six FBM deterrent patrols and was designated "Qualified in Submarines."

Captain Hlopak left active service in 1970, accepted a commission in the Naval Reserve, then served in NRSSD 1-11; NSSF 101; NSSF NLON DET 301; Readiness Command Region One and Ten Staffs; VTU G 1007; NRMTF HQ 110; and the DSW N87 unit at the Pentagon. He also commanded NSSF NLON DET 201, AS37 Dixon DET 3710, CSS 1 DET 110, Readiness Unit "Delta" Houston, and Readiness Unit "Alpha" San Antonio, and was a Navy Blue and Gold officer for 10 years during his 25 years in the Reserve from which he retired on June 30, 1995.

His personal decorations included the Navy Commendation Medal, Navy Meritorious Unit Commendation, National Defense Service Medal and the Armed Forces Reserve Medal (with hourglass). He also wore submariners gold Dolphins and the SSBN Strategic Deterrent Patrol Insignia with one Silver and one Gold Star.

CAPT Hlopak married the former Dorothy Marie Atkinson of Gloucester, NJ. They currently reside in Houston, TX and have two children, Edward II, a West Point graduate, and David, an alumnus of Texas Tech University, a daughter-in-law, Holly, and a granddaughter, Hannah.

His civilian experience includes more than 19 years, and positions, in engineering, business development and management at two major architect-engineering/constructors, Stone & Webster Engineering Corp. and Ebasco Services Inc., and for four plus years with Destec Energy, Inc., a leading independent power project developer. He is currently president of Visitech, Inc., a small company which designs and manufactures high technology electronic products for the traffic industry. He has an MBA from Babson College and is a registered professional engineer.

ROBERT L. "BOB" HOBSON, CAPT, USNR (Ret), born July 10, 1935, Gary, IN, is a native of Crown Point, IN. He graduated from Wabash College in June 1957 (BA degree), entered OCS at Newport and was commissioned an Ensign in March 1958.

After attending Fleet Sonar School Key West, he was assigned to the US Naval Facility, Coos Bay, OR, and then to the US Naval Facility, Big Sur, CA. He was reassigned to Coos Bay as the CO before being released from active duty.

CAPT Hobson graduated from the University of California, Hastings College of the Law in June 1964 (JD degree). During that time and thereafter he affiliated with several Naval Reserve units in the San Francisco Bay area, serving as CO of

seven Reserve Units and as Assistant Chief of Staff for the Naval Reserve Readiness Command, San Francisco and in other assignments with the Readiness Command Region 20. Capt. Hobson was assigned for three years to the National Naval Reserve Policy Board by the Secretary of the Navy.

CAPT Hobson retired July 1, 1988 and currently practices law in San Francisco in tax and estate planning. His family consists of wife Mary, a school counselor, and two sons, Steve and Mike, both graduates from the University of California.

KENNETH C. "KC" HOLM, CAPT, born Dec. 19, 1920, Bozeman, MT. Received his BS degree from USC and his Master's in Internal Affairs from George Washington University. Joined the USN Dec. 11, 1941 and commissioned Feb. 27, 1946.

Military stations were the Receiving Station, San Diego; NROTC, USC, Los Angeles; Electronics School, Treasure Island; Sub School, New London, CT; GMS, Dam Neck, VA; PG School, Monterey, CA; USNA, Annapolis, MD; NWC, Newport, RI; and OP42, Washington, DC.

Served in the USS *Denver* (CL); USS *Bremerton* (CA); USS *Rochester* (CA); USS *Carp* (SS); USS *Bream* (SS); GMU-90 (SS); USS *Carpenter* (DD); USS *Joyce* (DER); USS *James C. Owens* (DD); USS *Pyro* (AE).

Commands held: USS *Joyce,* GMU-90, USS *James C. Owens* and *Pyro* (AE-24).

CAPT Holm was discharged Sept. 1, 1970. Decorations include the China Service, South Pacific w/3 stars, Vietnam Occupation, UN Service Medal, WWII Victory Medal, Philippine Independence, American Service, Korean Service and Vietnam Service medals.

Married to Zayna and has two children, Ken Jr. and Laura Holm Hogan; and five grandchildren: Tom and Rose Hogan; Jessie, Kellie and Rachel Holm. He has written an article that was published in a book called *World War II Reminiscences*

GEORGE W. HOLYFIELD, CAPT, USN (Ret), a native of Kansas City, KS, currently residing in Houston, TX, attended the Kansas City, KS, Junior College and the University of Kansas. Appointed a midshipman in the Naval Reserve Officer Training Corps, he graduated in 1955 with a degree in Civil Engineering and a naval commission. Following flight training at NAS Pensacola, FL and NAS Hutchinson, KS, he was designated as Naval Aviator in 1956.

Captain Holyfield was ordered to AEW Sqdn. 14 at NAS Barbers Point, HI, flying EC-121 aircraft.

Released from active duty in 1958, he joined Reserve Transport Sqdn. 883 at NAS Olathe, KS. He was designated as Transport Aircraft Commander in both C-54 and C-118 aircraft at that station.

Employed by Chevron, USA, Capt. Holyfield transferred to Dallas, TX in 1967 where he joined Transport Sqdn. 704 at NAS Dallas. He served as Executive Officer and CO of several flying units at NAS Dallas and in 1976 assumed

command of Fleet Logistic Support Squadron 53 at NAS Memphis and NAS Dallas. During his tenure as CO, VR-53, he was awarded the Noel Davis Trophy for Excellence.

Capt. Holyfield has been awarded the National Defense, Armed Forces Reserve, Vietnam Campaign, Navy Commendation and Meritorious Service Medals.

A Life member and charter member of the Texas Commandery, Capt. Holyfield has served on the National Executive Committee, Awards Committee and the Site Committee. After serving as Vice Commander, Capt. Holyfield assumed the office of Commander, Texas Commandery in January 1997.

He has two sons, Kevin and Kyle.

E. LOU HOOS, CAPT, born in Muskegon, MI. He is a graduate of Michigan State University and obtained a JD degree from Wayne State University Law School. He entered the USN via USN Officer Candidate School. Newport, RI, and was commissioned an ENS in June 1962.

Hoos first served aboard the USS *Kitty Hawk* (CVA-63) as an Assistant Navigator, Air Transportation Officer and Officer of the Deck (fleet operations). He served two tours in Vietnam and participated in the conflict between communist mainland China and the Taiwanese nationalists involving the shelling of Matsu and Quemoy Islands. During Desert Storm he served with Commander, Military Sealift Command, Far East, Yokohama. Japan.

He served as CO of the following Naval Reserve Commands: Naval Reserve Surface Div. (9-96M), USS *Pharris* (FF-1094), Naval Liaison Officer to the state of Michigan and the Michigan National Guard Adjutant General and Military Sealift Command Office Middle Pacific 113.

During his career he has served in the USS *Havre* (PC-877); USS *Compton* (DD-705); USS *Hyman* (DD-732); USS Vulcan (AR-5); USN Justice School, Newport, RI; USS *Shreveport* (LPD-12); USS *America* (CVA-66); USS *Lexington* (CVT-16); USN War College, Industrial College of the Armed Forces; USS *Vogelsong* (DD-862), Naval Base, Norfolk, VA; USS *Meredith* (DD-890) and Shore Intermediate Maintenance Activity,

Newport, RI; Readiness Command Region 13, NTC Great Lakes, IL; USN Training Center, Great Lakes, IL; Lowry AFB, Denver, CO; Naval Construction Bn. HQ Gulfport, MS; Robbins AFB, Macon, GA; CINCLANTFLT, Norfolk, VA; Commander Military Sealift Command Pacific, Oakland, CA; Michigan National Guard Camp Grayling; CINCPACFLT, Pearl Harbor, HI; Military Sealift Command Office, Pearl Harbor; Commander, Military Sealift Command Far East, Yokohoma, Japan.

Capt. Hoos was designated as a Surface Warfare Officer and awarded the Meritorious Service Medal, Army Commendation Medal, Navy Unit Commendation Ribbon, Navy Meritorious Unit Commendation, Navy "E" Ribbon, National Defense Service Medal, Armed Forces Expeditionary Medal, Vietnam Service Medal, Armed Forces Reserve Medal, RVN Campaign Medal, Navy Rifle Expert Medal and Navy Pistol Expert Medal.

He is a Life member of the NRA, American Legion, Veterans of Foreign Wars and Vietnam Veterans of America and is president of the NRA Adm. VanKammen Chapter in Grand Rapids, MI. He is a practicing attorney in Grand Rapids, MI and a member of the American Bar Association, State Bar of Michigan and the Grand Rapids Bar Association. He and his wife, Marty, have three children: Jennifer, Stephanie and M. Bradley.

GEORGE W. HYDE, CAPT, born July 4, 1912, Jersey City, NJ. Attended public schools through high school; New York University, BA and LLB. Joined the USN April 7, 1942 and was commissioned same day.

Military locations and stations were the Local Defense Force; State Pier, New London, CT; Mine Warfare, USS *Acme* (AMC-61); USS *Sentinel* (AM-113); Naval Mine Warfare School, Yorktown, VA; Chief of Naval Operations, mine warfare section, minesweeping desk, Washington, DC; Minecraft Training Center, Little Creek, VA; USS *Capable* (AM-155), Mine Division 29, COMPAC.

Battle and campaigns include minesweeping east coast from Newport through New York. Stationed at Tompkinsville, Staten Island, NY; convoy duty North Atlantic and Mediterranean, Sicilian Invasion; convoy duty Pacific Saipan to Ulithi to Seattle to Alaska; Defense Council at General Court Martial, San Diego, CA.

Received a spot promotion to Lieutenant from LTJG after Sicilian campaign. LCDR Hyde was discharged Dec. 26, 1945. He joined the Naval Research Reserve Unit 3-1 on July 31, 1949 and achieved rank of Captain. He retired July 4, 1972.

Memorable experiences include the sinking of the USS *Sentinel* (AM-113) off Lacata, Sicily, during the invasion of that island.

Married Anne Shropshire. He has private law practice and firms Pendry, Schneider and Hyde; and Garfunkel and Hyde.

LOUIS SULLIVAN JACOBS, LTJG, born Jun. 11, 1914, Chicago, IL. He received a BS in architecture from Armor Institute of Technology; MS in Industrial Engineering from Illinois Institute of Technology; Ph.D. in engineering and ScD in Safety Engineering from Indiana Northern University.

Jacobs joined the Navy Jan. 25, 1942, and commissioned Mar. 27, 1942. He was stationed at Pearl Harbor; San Diego Navy Installation; Edgewood Arsenal, Baltimore, MD; and Great Lakes, IL. He served with Passive Defense Unit at Pearl Harbor and aboard USS *North Carolina*, USS *Altomitar*, USS *Coral Sea* and the SS *Grant*.

Jacobs was involved in various naval campaigns in SW Pacific. He was awarded the American/Pacific Campaign Medal and achieved the rank of Lieutenant(jg). Jacobs was discharged April 17, 1946.

His most memorable experience occurred when he assisted in raising sunken battleships, the California, West Virginia, etc., at Pearl Harbor between April and June 1942.

Jacobs never married. He had a private practice as an architect and engineer; a professor of architecture at Loop College in Chicago, IL and was a professor of Industrial Engineering at Illinois Institute of Technology.

KENNETH A. JOHNSON, CAPT, USN (Ret), a native of California, graduated from the University of Southern California in 1960, and received his commission through OCS in 1960. During the 10 years following his commissioning he served aboard four combatants, USS *St. Clair County* (LST-1096), USS *King* (DLG-10), USS *Preble* (DLG-15) and USS *Jouett* (DLG-29). During this period, he served an operational tour on the staff of Commander, Destroyer Flotilla Five and later as an advisor to the Vietnamese Navy.

The next three years of Capt. Johnson's career were spent in advanced study, first at the Armed Forces Staff College, then the Naval Postgraduate School at Monterey, CA, where he received his Master's degree in management in December 1973.

In May 1974, he took command of USS *Bagley* (FF-1069) homeported in San Diego, CA. He then served as Surface Operations Officer on the staff of Commander, Carrier Group Five, CTF-70, CTF-77, homeported in the Republic of the Philippines.

Three successive tours in the Washington, DC area followed. First as naval aide to the Chief of Naval Operations; then additional studies at the National War College; and later as communications section head in the Office of the Chief of Naval Operations.

Following his Washngton tours, he served as the current Operations Officer to the Commander in Chief, US Pacific Fleet from 1982-84. In August 1984 he took command of the Naval Communications Station Stockton, Stock-

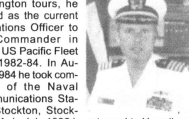

ton, CA. In July 1986 he returned to Hawaii and assumed the duties of the Assistant Chief of Staff for Communications to the Commander in Chief US Pacific Fleet. In June 1989 he assumed the duties as director for Command, Control and Communications Systems Directorate (J6), US Atlantic Command. He retired June 30, 1991, following over 31 continuous years on active duty in the USN.

CAPT Johnson is a proven subspecialist in the areas of command and control, and communications systems. He has also been designated a joint duty specialist by the Secretary of Defense. His personal decorations and awards include the Defense Superior Service Medal, Legion of Merit w/Gold Star, Meritorious Service Medal, Navy Commendation Medal w/Combat V and Gold Star, RVN Honor Medal 1st Class, and the Armed Forces Expeditionary Medal in addition to numerous service and campaign medals.

He is a life time member of the NOUS and of the Navy League of the US. Capt. Johnson is married to the former Judith Gay Helwig of Topeka, KS and they have a grown daughter, Nancy.

KENNETH M. JOHNSON, LCDR, USN (Ret), born Feb. 15, 1930, Cedar Rapids, IA. Enlisted in the USN Aug. 13, 1947 and completed recruit training, Electronics Material and Electronics Technician Schools at Great Lakes. He was promoted to ET2.

Kenneth served in USS *Furse* (DDR-882), recommissioned and served in USS *Barton* (DD-722). Discharged in May 1950, he enlisted in the USNR and was recalled to active duty in August 1950. Served in the USS *Xanthus* (AR-19). Subsequently served as Station keeper (TAR). Graduated from Submarine School in November 1956. Served in USS *Crevalle* (SS-291) and qualified in submarines.

Ordered to the University of Colorado as Naval Enlisted Scientific Education program student and graduated in June 1961 with a BA in chemistry. Graduated from OCS and commissioned Ensign, USN, November 1961.

Served in USS *Elakamin* (AO-55), commissioned and served in USS *Richmond K. Turner* (DLG-20), activated and served as O-in-C, River Section 542 (PBRs) in Vietnam, May 1966-May 1967. Graduated from Naval Post Graduate School. Served in USS *Luce* (DLG-7) and Staff Amphibious Sqdn. 11. Final duty was at Naval Communications Station Honolulu.

LCDR Johnson retired in March 1973. Decorations include the Bronze Star w/V, Commendation Medal, Combat Action Ribbon, two Navy Unit Commendations, Meritorious Unit Commendation, Good Conduct Medal w/star, National Defense Service Medal w/star, Armed Forces Expeditionary Medal (Cuba), Vietnam Service Medal w/4 stars and Vietnam Campaign Medal. Enlisted Submarine Dolphins and is qualified Surface Warfare Officer.

Memorable experiences include commissioning USS *R.K. Turner* (DLG-20); River Patrol Section 542; USS *Barton* (DD-722); decommissioning USS *Luce* (DLG-7; and COMPHIBRON II.

He is a widower.

HENRY JONES, born Sept. 17, 1957, North Kingstown, RI. Graduated Naval Academy, Class of 1979. Stations include USS *Bradley* (FF-1041), NAVOCEANCOMCENJTWC Guam, OIC, NAVOCEANCOMDET Kadena, USS *Missouri* (BB-63), NRL Washington, DC and CNO(N096). Served aboard as Ships Oceanographer/ OA Division Officer from November 1989-December 1991.

Surface Warfare and Navy Parachutist Designators. Awarded Meritorious Service Medal, Navy Commendation Medal, Navy Achievement Medal, Combat Action Ribbon, Navy Unit Commendation w/3 stars, Navy E Ribbon, National Defense Service, SWA Service w/2 stars, Saudi Arabia and Kuwait Liberation Medals, Sea Service Deployment Ribbon w/2 stars, Overseas Service Ribbon w/2 stars, Navy Recruiter Gold Wreath. He is currently a military instructor/ oceanography lecturer at the Naval Postgraduate School, Monterey, CA.

ROBERT E. "BOB" KARAS, CDR, born May 25, 1934, in Chicago, IL. Earned his BSCE degree at Marquette University, advanced science, and attended US Postgraduate School, Monterey. He enlisted in the service June 1956.

His military locations and stations: 1956-58, Harbor Defense Units, San Francisco and Yokosuka, Japan; USS *Laffey* (DD-724); 1961-62,

Postgraduate School, Monterey, CA and Steam Engineering School, San Diego, CA; 1962-64, USS *Wasp* (CVS-18); 1964-65, Chief of Staff and Material Officer Commander Destroyer Sqdn. Two; 1965-67, engineering head, staff of Commander Training, Command Atlantic Flt.; 1967-69, Executive Officer, USS *Noa* (DD-841); 1969-71, Staff Analysis and Project Officer, Center for Naval Analysis; 1971-73, Commanding Officer, USS *Henderson* (DD-785); 1973-76, Staff OP-03, Washington, DC; 1976-80, Commanding Officer Naval Reserve Center, Chicago and Forest Park, IL.

He participated in the 1962 Cuban Crisis aboard the USS *Wasp* and Vietnam Cruise aboard the USS *Henderson*, 1972-73.

CDR Karas retired in June 1980. He was awarded the Navy Commendation Medal, Second Award w/Combat V, Combat Action Ribbon, Navy Unit Commendation, National Defense Service Medal, Vietnam Service Medal w/3 stars, Armed Forces Expeditionary Medal, RVN Gallantry Cross Unit Citation and RVN Campaign Medal. Authorized to wear: Surface Warfare Device, Command at Sea Device and Major Command a Shore Device.

He married the former Barbara E. Falbe. He was employed as manager, technical market, Everpure, Inc. until his retirement in July 1996.

WILLIAM C. "BILL" KEMPNER, LT, born Nov. 21, 1954, New York, NY. Received his BA, University of North Carolina, Chapel Hill; MPA, Long Island University; and is a graduate of College of Command and Staff, U.S. Naval War College. Joined the USN Oct. 1, 1982; and commissioned Feb. 11, 1983.

Military Stations: USS *Belleau Wood* (LHA-3), USS *Pigeon* (ASR-21); U.S. Naval Weapons Facility, RAF, St. Mawgam, Naval Weapons Station, Concord, CA. Served with the 42nd Sqdn., RAF-Desert Storm. Battles and campaigns include Operation Desert Storm and service with the Royal Air Force at RAF Akroti Cypress.

Retired Feb. 1, 1994, with the rank of Lieutenant (0-3). Received the Air Force Commendation Medal w/OLC, Navy Achievement Medal w/Gold Star, Qualified Special Operations Officer, Surface Warfare Officer, Deep Sea Diving Officer, Naval Parachutist, USAF Master Parachutist and US Army Air Assault Badge.

Bill and his wife Diane live in Roslyn Heights, NY. He is a hospital safety officer for North Shore University Hospital.

FREDERICK ROGERS "ROG" KETCHAM, CAPT, born Aug. 24, 1916, Fort Slocum, NY. Graduated high school, attended the University of Virginia two years, DNG. Joined the USCG in 1942 and commissioned the same year.

Military stations were the US Coast Guard Academy, Manhattan Beach; Alaska; Coast

Guard Headquarters, Washington, DC. He served with the USCG Cutter *Onan-daga* (LST-26), Var. Vol. Reserve Units. Was CO of the USS LST-26 and of VTU, Governors Island, NY. Participated in the Aleutian Campaign, South Pacific, Battle of Leyte Gulf and Zambango Island.

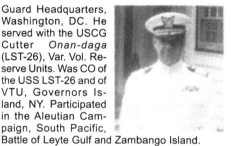

Released to the Retired Reserves with the rank of Captain. Received the American Campaign, Asiatic-Pacific, National Defense Service Medal, WWII Victory Medal, China Service Medal, Philippine Liberation Medal and Navy Occupation Medal.

Memorable experiences include the Battle of Leyte Gulf; typhoon in Okinawa; and landing at Zambango under heavy mortar fire.

His wife is deceased. He has three children: F. Rogers Jr., Dale and Kathleen; and six grandchildren: Matthew, Rebecca, Sarah, Elizabeth, Paul and Hillery. He is senior vice president of a construction corporation.

JERALD KIRSTEN, CAPT, born Sept. 13, 1924, Portsmouth, OH and reared in Stockton, CA. He graduated from Weber Grammar School, Stockton High School and College of the Pacific with AB degree in accounting, June 1947.

Joined the USNR Dec. 12, 1942, as a Naval Aviation Cadet. The war ended while in flight training and he received a direct commission Aug. 17, 1958.

Military stations were V-12(a), University of California, Berkeley; USNPFS, St. Mary's College, CA; NAS Norman, OK; NRID 12, San Francisco. He served with various units and held the position of CO with FIRSTPAC 1387. CAPT Kirsten retired Feb. 1, 1981

Married Claudine Estep June 28, 1944, and again June 28, 1990. They have three children: Claudia Styles, Kenneth and Susan Kirsten; six grandchildren: Lisa, Lynn and Lora Kirsten, Dolores Kolb, Christopher deMelo and Billy Styles.

Self-employed CPA, 1954-91; member, Board of Directors, Stockton Savings Bank, 1975-present; real estate investor, 1962-present.

He is active in his community and numerous civic and professional affiliations and has served in many capacities including president. In 1965, 1967 and 1969 he served as mayor, city of Lodi. He is a member of Stockton Scottish Rite Bodies, Tokay Shrine Club and others.

SHARON "SHERRY" KLEINSCHMIDT, born Dec. 29, 1936 in Minnesota and has a Bachelor of Science degree. Joined the USN on Oct. 2, 1959 and commissioned in February 1960.

Was a charter member of the San Di-

ego Naval Order and served in responsible positions. Remained in the Reserve active status until retirement Dec. 29, 1996.

Civilian employment as a home economics teacher and has one son, AJ.

FRANK KLING, CDR, born Dec. 2, 1916, in New York, NY. Joined the US Navy April 10, 1942 and commissioned Jan. 5, 1946. During WWII he was stationed at Eastern Sea Frontier HQ, CINCLANT, aboard the USS *Vixen* (PG-53), Western Sea Frontier HQ. During Korean War he served with 3rd Naval District.

CDR Kling retired May 1, 1968, with the rank of commander. His decorations include the Commendation Medal from CINCLANT.

Married Consuelo A. and they have two children, Frank W. and Michael A., and four grandchildren: Andrew, Caroline, Margaret and Michael. Employed in investment management until retirement May 10, 1989.

GLENN B. KNIGHT, MSGT, born Oct. 24, 1944, Lancaster, PA. Received his BS in Political Science, University of the State of New York. He joined the service Aug. 14, 1962.

Military stations: USS *Independence*; 2nd Marine Div., Camp Lejeune, NC; Parris Island, SC; Maxwell AFB, AL; Incirlik, CDI, Turkey; Ft. George G. Meade, MD. He served with the 2nd Marine Div. and at Naval Academy Prep School.

Participated in battles and campaigns in Dominican Republic in 1965. MSGT Knight was retired from the USAF April 1, 1984. Decorations include the Meritorious Service Medal, Combat Action Ribbon, Navy Unit Commendation, Armed Forces Expeditionary Medal, Humanitarian Service Medal and others.

Memorable experience was being the first Marine combat correspondent in the Dominican Republic in 1965; Public Affairs staff for "Operation Inland Seas, and joint Navy/Marine public relations tour of the Great Lakes.

Married Beverly D. Walker (CPL, USMC) and has two children, Christopher and Marianne (LCPL, USMC), and two grandchildren, Evin and Brittnee. Civilian employment as historian, researcher, author, webmaster, and biographer of ADM William Reynolds, USN.

F. STUART "STU" KUHN, CAPT, bom July 31, 1928, Dubuque, IA. Attended Yale University for his BA and Stanford University for his MBA. He joined the USN in June 1952 and was commissioned in November 1952.

Military stations include OCS, Newport, RI; CIC Officers School, NAS Glenview, IL, and USS *John R. Craig* (DD-885). He held Reserve commands only.

Capt. Kuhn was discharged in October 1955 and retired July

31, 1988. His awards include the China Service, UN Service Medal, Korea Service, Reserve Medal and Sharpshooter.

Divorced, he has five children: Jeffrey, Lisa, Kristina, Katherine and Stephen; and seven grandchildren: Diana and Alex Hall; Hillary, Spencer and Sophia Kuhn; Patrick and Michael McCartney. He is chairman of Presidio Charter Trust, Inc.

ARNE K. "THE BEAR" KVAALEN, LTJG, born Jan. 22, 1923, Lambert, MT. Received his BA from Concordia College and MFA from University of Iowa. He joined the USNR Oct. 28, 1942 and was commissioned March 17, 1944.

Military stations and locations were Amphibious Base, Fort Pierce, FL; Maui, HI; and the USS *Blessman* (APD) Served with the Navy Combat Demolition Teams, Team 15; held command of Underwater Demolition Team 15, 3rd Plt. officer. Participated in battles and campaigns at Lingayen Gulf, Philippines, Iwo Jima and Troop Landing on Korea in September 1945.

LTJG Kvaalen was discharged Oct. 28, 1945. Awards include the Silver Star.

Memorable experiences include kamikazes in the Philippines (Lingayen Gulf); swam reconnaissance of Blue Beach, Iwo Jima on D-Day minus 2; led first wave of marines into Blue Beach on D-Day; experienced bombing of their ship USS *Blessman*, D-Day minus 1 with 40% casualties (ship subsequently had to be towed to Saipan).

Married Ruth and has three children: Virginia, Kristin and Eric; and nine grandchildren: Shira, Elisabeth, Ada Renee, Samuel, Laura, Virginia, Rachel, Arne and David.

Civilian employment included Professor, Dept. of Creative Art, Purdue University. He retired in June 1993, but is still working full time as an artist.

WILLIAM H. "BILL" LANGENBERG, RADM, born Aug. 26, 1928, New York, NY. Attended US Naval Academy for his BS, Carnegie Institute of Technology for MS, University of California-Davis for MA, and California State University-Haywood for BA. He joined the USN July 3, 1947 and was commissioned June 1, 1951.

Military stations include US Naval Academy; USS *Lewis Hancock* (DD-675) and USS *Oglethorpe* (AKA-100). He served with the 14th Naval Reserve Unit and held seven commands, the last one being the Naval Reserve Readiness Command Region 20.

Participated in the Korean Theater, 1952-53. Decorations include the Legion of Merit, Meritorious Service Medal and Navy Commendation Medal. ADM Langenberg retired Aug. 1, 1983.

Memorable experiences: Naval gunfire

support, rescuing downed aviators, dodging floating mines, and launching submarine attacks during Korean Theater.

Bill and his wife Mary have two children, Robert and Janet. He is president of Langen Corp.

ROBERT E. "BOB" LANDO, CDR, born Sept. 18, 1920, San Diego. He has a BS and MA degrees in teaching. Joined the USN April 7, 1942 and was commissioned in January 1944.

Military stations include COMINC, 1944; BJ units 8G, 1944; BJ units, 6-7, 1944-45; navy yard, Annapolis, 1945; advance training in Florida, 1945; Barbers Point, 1949; COMNAVFE, 1950-52. Participated in action in the Asiatic-Pacific, Philippines and Korea.

CDR Lando retired in 1976 with 20 years of military service and 10 years Naval Reserve duty.

Memorable experiences: New Guinea battle between the US and Australian citizens; Japanese bombing tanker; Palau final conquest; Philippines 0+4 to Mendoro; watching Lyganian invasion fleet pass; and Korean coastal interdiction.

Worked as an elementary class room teacher until retiring in 1980. Retired from the military in 1985. He is divorced. His NOUS commissioned ancestor is Capt. Ellis Lando (Class of 1907).

THOMAS G. "TOM" LILLY, RADM, born Sept. 17, 1933, Belzoni, MS. Attended Tulane University for his BBA in 1955; University of Mississippi for his LLB in 1960 and JD in 1968. Joined the USNR and was commissioned May 31, 1955.

Was stationed aboard the USS *Betelgeuse* (AK-260); Service Force Atlantic Fleet; NAS, Sanford, FL. Commands held were NR, Advance Supply Base 109, New Orleans, LA; and NR, Cargo Handling Force.

RADM Lilly was released from active duty May 31, 1958. Retired Sept. 17, 1993. Awards include the Legion of Merit, Navy Commendation Medal, Navy Occupation Service Medal (Europe) and Armed Forces Reserve Medal.

He married Constance Ray Holland and had two sons, Thomas G. Jr. and William H.; a daughter, Carolyn Ray Lilly Wilson; and two grandchildren, Thomas B. Lilly and Ella Katherine Lilly Wilson.

He worked as an associate with Stoval & Price, attorneys, Corinth, MS, 1960-62; assistant US Attorney, Oxford, MS, 1962-66; associate, Wise, Carter Child and Calawey, attorneys, Jackson, MS, 1967, and as member from 1967-94; and member, Lilly and Wise, attorneys, Jackson, MS, 1994-present.

JAMES E. LIVINGSTON, MajGen, USMC, was born on Jan. 12, 1940 in Towns, GA. He was commissioned a Second Lieutenant in June 1962, following graduation from Auburn University and promoted to Captain in June 1966.

Gen. Livingston served as the Commanding Officer of the Marine detachment aboard the aircraft carrier USS *Wasp,* before joining the 3rd Marine Division (Reinforced) in the Republic of Vietnam in August 1967. On May 2, 1968, while serving as the Commanding Officer, Co. E, 2nd Bn., 4th Marines, he distinguished himself above and beyond the call of duty in action against enemy forces and earned the Congressional Medal of Honor.

In March 1975, on his second tour of duty, he served as the Operations Officer for the Viet-

nam evacuation operations which included Operation Frequent Wind, the evacuation of Saigon. He commanded the 6th Marines before joining the Joint U.S. Assistance Group in the Republic of the Philippines. After commanding the 1st Marine Expeditionary Brigade, he was advanced to Major General on July 8, 1991 and assumed command of the 4th Marine Division (Reinforced). In July 1992 he assumed command of the newly created Marine Reserve Force.

He retired on Sept. 1, 1995 following over 33 continuous years on active duty in the USMC. His decorations include the Medal of Honor, Navy Superior Service Medal, Distinguished Service Medal, Silver Star Medal, Defense Superior Service Medal, Bronze Star Medal with Combat "V," Purple Heart (third award), Defense Meritorious Service Medal and Meritorious Service Medal.

PAUL J. LUNDBECK, CDR, born Oct. 9, 1918, San Francisco, CA. Received his BA from Stanford University in 1940. Joined the USN in April 1942 and commissioned Ensign in August 1942, Cornell University.

Military Stations: 1943, stationed at Panama, CZ; USS *Dortch;* 1944, JCTC, Miami, FL, commissioned (plankowner) USS *George E. Davis* (DE-357), ASW officer; 1944-45, 7th Fleet, Leyte Gulf; 1946-50, various Reserve billets; 1950-53, recalled to active duty for Korean War and boarded USS *Higbee* (DDR-806) as Ops Officer and later XO; 1953-68, RTC, Treasure Island, San Francisco, CA.

Participated in liberation of Manila, Peleliu and Okinawa; escorted first troop ship to Sasebo, Japan after surrender; three years, 1953-68.

CDR Lundbeck retired in 1968 with 27 years of service. Decorations include the National Defense, American Campaign, Asiatic-Pacific Campaign, Philippine Liberation, China Service, Asia Occupation Service, WWII Victory Medal, Naval Reserve Medal, Armed Forces Reserve Medal, Korean Service, UN Korean Medal, War Veterans Medal and three Bronze Stars

Memorable experiences: becoming plankowner of USS *George E. Davis;* while refueling in the Leyte Gulf the USS *Minneapolis* arrived and waved them off so they could refueling. The *Minneapolis* was half-way through refueling when a Japanese kamikaze plane headed for it and crashed through the bridge of the tanker, then into the empty #2 oil hold. The bridge was destroyed, killing and wounding many personnel. His ship spent the rest of the day picking up sailors out of the water.

He is a widower with no children and has worked in sales, contract, marketing executive and wholesale distribution until retirement in 1975.

PHILIP KARL "PHIL" LUNDEBERG, CDR, born June 14, 1923 in Minneapolis, MN. He attended Duke University for his AB and MA degrees (1944) and Harvard University for his PhD in 1954. He's a graduate of USNR Midshipmen's School, New York (Columbia University), 1944 (following graduation from Duke in February

1944). He had subsequent training at Sub Chaser Training Center, Miami; Fleet Sound School, Key West; and Damage Control School, Philadelphia.

Joined the USNR Dec. 29, 1942 and commissioned June 29, 1944. Served aboard the USS *Frederick C. Davis* (DE-136); USS *McCoy Reynolds* (DE-440); CNO, OP-29, Office of Naval History; Dept. of English, history and government, US Naval Academy, 1955-59, where he taught diplomatic and naval history. Was CO of the Naval Reserve Intelligence Unit 5-1-2, Baltimore and Operation Teardrop, March-May 1945, in the North Atlantic.

CDR Lundeberg retired June 14, 1983. Decorations include the Bronze Star w/Combat V and the Purple Heart.

Memorable experiences include being the youngest of three officer survivors of the *Frederick C. Davis* that sunk in the North Atlantic on April 24, 1945, by U-546, being the last USN vessel lost in the Atlantic during WWII Subsequently he served with RADM S.E. Morison in OP-29, preparing history of US Naval Operations in the Atlantic, 1943-45. As a Naval Historian he has written extensively on the history of undersea warfare.

Married Eleanore Berntson in 1953 and has one son, Karl Fredrik, and one granddaughter, Marika Julia. He worked as Assistant Professor of History at St. Olaf College, 1953-55; US Naval Academy, 1955-59; Curator of Naval History, Smithsonian Institution, 1959-84, and is currently Curator Emeritus. He retired Nov. 1, 1984.

J ROBERT "BOB" LUNNEY, CAPT, JAGC, USNR (Ret), born Dec. 15, 1927, New York City and resides with his wife Joan and son Alexander in Bronxville, NY. He served in the Naval Reserve from May 1, 1945 to Dec. 15, 1987.

Enlisting in the Naval Reserve at 17, he served on occupation duty with the Naval Amphibious Forces, Pacific (Eniwetok, Kwajelein, Saipan, Guam, Iwo Jima) 1945-46, as a Quartermaster 3/c. During the Korean War, 1950-51, he served with the US Merchant Marines as a staff officer (Inchon Landing and Hungnam Evacuation).

His awards include the Navy Commendation Medal, Asiatic-Pacific Campaign Medal, Korean Service Medal (2 stars), Merchant Marine Gallant Ship Citation and the Korean Presidential Unit Citation.

His Gallant Ship Citation commends Capt. Lunney for courage and resourcefulness in participating in "one of the greatest marine rescues in the history of the world" at Hungnam, North Korea during the Chosin Reservoir campaign, December 1950.

In February 1994, Hon. John H. Dalton, Secretary of the Navy, decorated CAPT Lunney with the Dept. of the Navy Distinguished Public Service Award. The citation commends CAPT Lunney for exceptionally outstanding service to the Navy for over four decades and especially for his dedication and leadership in improving the strength and readiness of the Navy and the capabilities of the Dept. of Defense to carry out essential wartime missions.

He received his BA degree (1950) from Alfred University, Alfred, NY and his Doctor of Law degree (1954) from Cornell Law School, Ithaca, NY. By appointment of the US Attorney General he served five years with the Dept. of Justice as an assistant US Attorney in New York (1955-59). In 1968, after eight years with the New York firm of Shearman & Sterling, he founded his own law firm, now Lunney & Murtagh, LLC specializing in litigation.

CAPT Lunney has been a member of the NOUS since 1965 and has served as the Commander of the NY Commandery (1989-91). CAPT Lunney has also served as the 22nd National President (1991-93) of the Naval Reserve Association. His other civic and charitable activities include the Sovereign Military Order of Malta (American Association), Sons of the Revolution in the State of NY (past president), Lavelle School for the Blind, New York City (bd. dirs.), Navy League of US, NY Council (bd. dirs.), NY Naval Militia (RADM), The Chosin Few (past national director) and Military Order of World Wars (vice commander, NY Chapter).

L. FRANK MACH, CAPT, born, Aug. 2, 1941, Chicago, IL. Received his BS degree from the University of Illinois in 1964; attended the Naval War College in 1990; National Defense University, Washington, DC; and Naval Transportation School, Oakland, CA.

Joined the USN July 27, 1964 and was commissioned Feb. 5, 1965, OCS, Newport, RI. Active duty aboard the USS *Robert L. Wilson* (DD-847) to OPS Dept. Head, December 1967. Reserve duty as CO in USS *Leahy* (CG-16).

Served with the Support Unit; CO, MilSeaLiftCmd Norfolk, VA; CO, MSC Southwest Asia. Participated in battles and campaigns in Dominican Republic and was CO of the unit deployed to Desert Storm, 1990-91.

CAPT Mach retired June 1, 1995. Awards include the AF Expeditionary Medal, Navy and Joint Unit Commendation, Joint Service Commendation and Meritorious Service Medal.

Memorable experiences include being Officer in Tactical Command, Commodore, CTU 48.1.16 Joint Logistics Over The Shore (JLOTS, 1988) and Commodore, OTC CTU 48.1.18, Solid Shield (JLOTS, 1989).

Married Connie Kight Dec. 9, 1967 and has three children: Vallie Lynn, Mandy Anne and Hunter Lewis. Works for US DOT, Maritime Administration, South Atlantic Region. Projected retirement to 20 years government service, October 2005.

STANLEY J. "STAN" MAJKA, CDR, USNR, born Jan. 28, 1919, Three Rivers, MA. He gradu-

ated from Wocester Polytechnic Institute with a BS degree in Mechanical (aeronautical) Engineering. Stan joined the service April 19, 1941.

Navy service includes Massachusetts Institute of Technology, BuAer, USS *Monterey* (CVL-26), Aircraft Sqdn. VC-30 (VF and VT), US Naval Attache, US Embassy, Belgrade, Yugoslavia and Naval War College. He engaged in nine major Pacific battles aboard CVL-26, starting with Makin and Tarawa through the battle of the Philippines.

Most memorable experience occurred on Dec. 18, 1944, when CVL-26, was struck with a typhoon lasting 36 hours. They lost all planes off the flight deck due to winds of unbelievable strength followed by a hangar deck fire which disabled the carrier's forward elevator. The maximum roll was recorded at 38 degrees. They were a part of ADM Bull Halsey's Task Force.

CDR Majka was discharged June 30, 1967. His awards include the Navy Commendation Medal, Pacific Theater w/9 stars, European Theater and Philippine Liberation Medal.

Stan, his wife Peggy June and sons, Paul and Stanley Jr. are life members of NOUS. Stan is also a Past Commander of NOUS. He was employed by Chevron, USA for 32 years and is a certified financial planner with 27 years experience and still active.

JOHN J. MARKS, CDR, born Nov. 2, 1946, Boston, MA. Received his associates in occupational studies and BS in business management. Joined the USCG Sept. 9, 1964; and was commissioned July 1, 1984.

Military stations were Ist CG District, 14th CG District and 3rd CG District. He served with CGC CASCO (WAVP-307), Boston, MA; Commander, 1st CG District (p), Boston, MA; CGC Planetree (WLB-370), USCG Captain of the Port, Honolulu, HI; Reserve Group 3rd CG District, New York; Reserve Group Sandy Hook, Highlands, NJ; Reserve Unit Manasquan, Point Pleasant, NJ; Reserve Unit captain of the Port New York, NY; Group/Captain of the Port New York, NY; Commander, USCG activities New York; Commander, 1st CG District (oax-sr); and Group/Marine Safety Office, Long Island Sound, New Haven, CT.

Commands held: Reserve Unit Manasquan Inlet, 1991-92, Point Pleasant, NJ. He achieved the rank of Chief Petty Officer Yeoman (Enlisted) and Commander (Commissioned Service).

Awards include the USCG Commendation Medal, Commandant's Letter of Commendation w/operational device, Meritorious Team Commendation w/operational device (6 awards), Unit Commendation w/operational device (3 awards), Meritorious Unit Commendation Award w/operational device (2 awards), Cutterman's Award, Reserve Enlisted Good Conduct Medal (3 awards),

Military Civilian Volunteer Award, Armed Forces Reserve Medal w/M Device Roman Numeral II and Hourglass Device. He is presently in a drilling status with an expected retirement date of June 1, 2006.

Memorable Experiences: selection as the 1992 Junior Officer of the Year, USCGR, award presented by the ROA; selection of Reserve Unit of the Year, 1st CG District, 1991, Reserve Unit Manasquan; advancing to Chief Petty Officer with nine years of service.

Married Christine Anne Kusek and has two sons, Stephen John and Edward. Currently employed by the Court of Common Pleas, Northampton County as official court reporter. SELRES (presently in drilling status – expected retirement date of June 1, 2006)

BURNHAM C. MCCAFFREE JR., RADM, born Sept. 28, 1931, San Diego, CA. Received his BS in Naval Engineering, US Naval Academy, Class of 1954. Joined the USN Sept. 29, 1948 and was commissioned June 10, 1954.

Stations and Units served with include the USS *Midway* (CV-41); USS *Newport News* (CA-148); USS *Gearing* (DD-710); USS *Traverse County* (LST-1160); USS *Rich* (DD-820); COMOPTEVFOR; NSA DaNang RVN; COMPHIBGRU Two; OPNAV; USS *Johnston* (DD-821), USS *Shreveport* (LPD-12), COMPHIBRON TWO and COMPHIBGRU ONE.

Participated in battles and campaigns in Vietnam. RADM McCaffree retired Aug. 1, 1988. His awards include the Legion of Merit (5), Meritorious Service Medal and Navy Commendation Medal.

Married Erlend "Lynn" Carlton and has two married daughters, Elizabeth Anne Antanitus and Debora Lynn Hagwood; and four grandchildren: Emily, Alison, Rachel and Robert. He is a member of the research staff, Center for Naval Analysis and Institute for Defense Analysis.

FRANCES M. "FRAN" MCDONALD, CAPT, born Aug. 29, 1942, Clinton, IA and attended the University of Iowa for his MA degree. Joined the USNR in April 1963 and was commissioned in June 1964.

His military stations include the Military Sealift Command, Desert Storm.

CAPT McDonald is single.

ROBERT JOSEPH "MAC" MCMAHON, LCDR, born July 5, 1921, Carrollton, IL. Attended Harvard for his BA and MBA degrees and Los Angeles, USC for his CPA. He joined the USN Sept. 15, 1939 and was commissioned in 1943.

Military stations include USS *Oklahoma* (sunk at Pearl Harbor); USS *Enterprise* (CV-6); USS *Kenmore* (APA-32); USS *Wedderburn* (DD-684); USS *Cushing* (DD-246); USS *Cushing* (DD-797). Held commands DESRON 53 (nine destroyers).

He participated in all battles in the South Pacific and retired Dec. 6, 1959. LCDR McMahon awards include Navy Cross, two Presidential Citations and 15 Battle Stars.

Memorable experiences: his son's birth; his first commissioning as a Warrant Chief Boatswain; his commission as a Lieutenant, USN; being in the 8th Winter Olympics as housing and community relations director with the U.S. Olympic Committee.

He was owner-president of McMahon Accounting in Sacramento, 1978-89 and McMahon Realtors, 1975-89. He a widower with three children: Michael, Mary Ann and Lori Sue; and has two grandchildren, Jennifer and Jeremy.

Commissioned ancestors: Hugh McMahon, Lt. Gen., U.S. Army, 1864; and Thomas McMahon, Admiral, USN, 1869.

WILLIAM J. MELLISH, CDR, CEC, USNR (Ret), born Feb. 26, 1922, west of the Allegheny River in Bradys Bend Township, Armstrong County, PA. Graduated from East Brady High School in June 1940. On Sept. 16, 1942, while attending Grove City (PA) College, he enlisted in the Naval Reserve as an Apprentice Seaman. In June 1943 the Navy placed him in the V-12 program at Brown University where he continued until November 1944 when he was transferred to the 22nd class of Midshipmen at Columbia University.

Upon commissioning as a line officer (1105) Ensign, March 8, 1945, he was assigned to the heavy cruiser USS *Columbus* (CA-74) in the engineering department and immediately sailed to the Pacific Theater. Following duty in Japan, after the surrender, the *Columbus* spent the winter of 1945 in Tsingtao and the spring of 1946 in Shanghai, China.

Upon release from active duty in September 1946 he returned to Brown University and graduated in June 1947 with a BS degree in Engineering. As a Ready Reservist he was recalled for Korean duty aboard USS *Missouri* (BB-63). When not in Korea or Japan during this two-year tour of sea duty, the battleship visited England, Norway, France, Cuba, Haiti and Hawaii.

In 1955 he changed his designator from line to Civil Engineer Corps (5105) to match his Naval Reserve service more appropriately with his civilian occupation as a highway construction engineer with the state of California. As a Selected Reservist from July 1964-July 1967 he was CO of Reserve Mobile Construction Battalion 28. Personnel for this battalion came from the northern halves of California and Nevada plus Utah. When a shortage of officers developed in July 1969 he volunteered to return for a

third two-year tour of active duty as head of the Seabee Reserve Program for the 12th Naval District located at Treasure Island, San Francisco, CA.

His campaign and service medals are China Service, American Campaign Service, Asiatic-Pacific Campaign, WWII Victory, American Occupation Service, National Defense Service, Korean Service w/3 Bronze Stars, Armed Forces Reserve, Naval Reserve, Korean Presidential Unit Citation, United Nations Service and Navy Rifle Marksmanship. He retired from the Navy in July 1971 after 29 years of honorable service.

He retired from state highway construction in September 1987 after 40 years. As a Life member of the Naval Order, he has given many hours of service promoting the Order's programs. He is also a Life member of the Naval Reserve Assoc., the Association of Naval Aviation and the Navy League.

He will always be outranked by his wife, CAPT Lucille Mellish, NC, USNR (Ret). The family consists of son Markham, daughter-in-law Roslyn, and grandchildren, Alan and Alison.

KENNETH A. MENKEN, LT, born Jan. 8, 1931, Vienna, Austria. Graduated from Hutchkiss in 1947, Duke in 1952, completed his MBA degree at Penn (Wharton) in 1956; and Columbia in 1957 (no degree). He joined the NROTC in 1948 and was commissioned in 1952.

Stations and units served include Atlantic SERVRON, Norfolk, VA, Sixth Fleet, USS *Merrimack* (TAO-37), USS *Nantahala* (AO-60) and Navigator (AO-60).

After completing his MBA degree he moved to New York and joined Telecomm Censorship Div. 3-1 Reserve Unit as a Lieutenant. He served with this unit for several years, shortly before its dissolution, and resigned, maintaining his interest in the Navy through the NOUS.

LT Menken was discharged in 1965. His awards include the European Occupation Medal and National Defense Service Medal.

After several decades on Wall Street, he became founder and CEO of Managers' Capital Development, a marketing consulting firm serving alternative asset financial assets managers.

Married Joan Buck and they plan semi-retirement within the next few years to Landfall, near Wilmington, NC.

NOUS ancestors: Midshipman Benjamin Nones, USN, USS *Constitution*, 1812.

JOSEPH DOUGLAS "DOUG" MILLER, CAPT, born Dec. 23, 1918, Detroit, MI. Received his AB and MBA from the University of Michigan. Joined the USN and was commissioned in June 1941. CAPT Miller retired in 1983.

Doug and his wife Nancy have three children: Charles, Steven and David, and seven grandchildren: Robert, Andrew, Sarah, Nathan, Joshua and Abigail. He retired in 1988.

SENATOR ROBERT W. MITCHLER, (Ret), born June 4, 1920, Aurora, IL. Graduated East Aurora High School and Aurora University with BS degree in 1953. Enlisted in the USN as Yeoman 3/c, Nov. 17, 1941 with recruit training at NTC Great Lakes. Shore duty was at NAS Sand Point, Seattle and NTC Farrragut, ID.

Sea duty in Pacific with amphibious force in USS *Oxford* (APA-189) and minesweeping in USS *Scoter* (AM-381) and USS *Endicott* (DMS-

35). Participated in the Philippines and Okinawa campaigns.

Honorably discharged May 15, 1946, with the rate of Chief Yeoman. He re-enlisted in the USNR, serving on the USS *Wisconsin* (BB-64). On Sept. 2, 1950 he was recalled to active duty during the Korean Conflict to staff UN Blockading and Escort Force (CTF-95) with RADM Allen E. Smith and RADM George C. Dyer, serving on the USS *Dixie* (AD-14), USS *Prairie* (AD-15), USS *Piedmont* (AD-17), USS *Missouri* (BB-63), USS *New Jersey* (BB-62), USS *Toledo* (CA-133), USS *Manchester* (CL-83), USS *Helena* (CA-75), USS *Bataan* (CVL-29), USS *Massey* (DD-778), USS *Forest Royal* (DD-872), USS *Fechteler* (DD-870), USS *Kidd* (DD-661), USS *Burlington* (PF-51), USS *Jason* (ARS-1), USS *Haven* (AH-12).

Transferred Nov. 22, 1951, to Staff UN Delegation Peace Conference at Pamnunjom Korea. Transferred in January 1952 and honorably discharged.

Civilian employment with CB&Q Railroad, 1937-54; Better Boxes, 1954-58; Northern Illinois Gas Co., 1958-75. Served five terms in Illinois State Senate, 1965-81, and 10 years Illinois Dept. Veteran Affairs, 1981-91. Appointed to rank of Captain, Illinois Naval Militia, serving as military and Naval Aide to Gov. Jim Edgar, 1991-99, and Gov. George H. Ryan, 1999-present.

Married the former Helen Drew of Aurora, IL and they reside in Oswego, IL. They have two sons, one daughter and seven grandchildren.

MARK E.P. MONAGHAN, LCDR, born July 2, 1960, Chestnut Hill, PA. Education: Jacksonville University in Florida, BA in April 1982; Worcester State College in Massachusetts, M.Ed. in May 1988; SWOS basic and graduated from ASW Officer School; Naval War College and Command and Staff College, June 1995. He was commissioned from NROTC at Jacksonville University, April 1982 as Ensign, USN.

Stations include USS *Samuel Eliot Morison* (FFG-13) Mayport, FL, as ASW officer; NROTC Unit, College of the Holy Cross, Worcester, MA, as Administrative Officer, and a Naval Science Instructor; COMNAVSURFGRU FOUR, NETC, Newport, RI; SWOS Department Head School; USS *Boone* (FFG-28), Mayport, FL; USS *Nashville* (LPD-13), Norfolk, VA; Inter-American Defense Board & College, Washington, DC, January 1993-96; USS *Nimitz* (CVN-68), Bremerton, WA, as Assistant Combat Direction Center Officer.

Participated in Operation Urgent Fury, 1983 invasion of Grenada; Operation Earnest Will, 1984 and 1989, FFG-13/28 escort missions for US flagged tankers in and out of the Persian (now Arabian) Gulf; participated in Drug Interdiction Operations in USS *Boone*; Operation Desert Storm; Operation Southern Watch with COMFIFTHFLT, deterrent air patrol of Southern Iraq in support of the United Nations; Maritime Interdiction operations against Iraq.

Awards and medals include Defense Meritorious Service Medal, Navy Commendation Medal, Navy Achievement Medal, Joint Meritorious Unit Commendation, Meritorious Unit Commendation (2 awards), National Defense Medal, Armed Forces Expeditionary Service Medal w/3 Bronze Stars, Southwest Asia Service Medal w/ Bronze Star for Operation Desert Storm, Sea Service Deployment Ribbon w/3 Bronze Stars, NOUS, Inter-American Defense Board Medal w/ 2 Gold Stars, Kuwait Liberation Medal and the Navy Expert Rifle Medal. Highest rank achieved was LCDR, USN.

Married Patricia Louise Kosakowski, April 24, 1982, in Cheektowaga, NY. Children are Katherine Louise Monaghan and Theresa Ann Monaghan.

WILLIAM T. MORAN, CAPT, USNR (Ret), a native of San Francisco, CA, he enlisted in the USNR in January 1951 while in high school. He was an economics major at Stanford University, completing ROC program and commissioned an Ensign in 1955.

Ordered to the Naval Air Technical Training Center, Memphis, TN and graduated with distinction, Naval Justice School, Newport, RI. Returned home in October 1958 to NRSD 12-20. Recalled to active duty as a Lieutenant in the Training Administration Reserve (TAR) Program, 1959. Served in the USS *San Joaquin County* (LST-1122) as 1st Lieutenant/Navigator and for the second year as Executive Officer/Navigator. In November 1962 he was assigned as Commanding Officer of the Naval Reserve Center, Lake Charles, LA.

Transferred to the USNR Manpower Center, Bainbridge, MD, as head of Mobilization Branch for shore activities in November 1965. In July 1966 was fleeted up to head of the Processing Department. In March 1968 he transferred to the USS *Hermitage* (LSD-34) as Operations Officer.

Served in the Bureau of Naval Personnel as head of the Surface/Subsurface Programs Branch and also the Special and General Programs Branch, 1970-74. In 1973 he became Director of Mobilization for all aviation, surface and subsurface programs of the Naval Reserve.

Graduated with distinction from the senior course, Naval War College, Newport, RI, 1975. Served in the Pentagon under the director of Naval Reserve as head of the Surface Plans, Policy and Programs Branch, 1975-76.

Served one day as Commander, Cleveland Readiness Command and two years as commander, Naval Reserve Readiness Command Region Five. Retired October 1981 after three years as Special Assistant for Reserve Affairs to the ASN (M&RA) and recorder for the Secretary of the Navy's National Naval Reserve Policy Board. His awards include the Legion of Merit, Meritorious Service Medal, Naval Reserve Meritorious Service Medal, Naval Reserve Medal (3) and National Defense Medal(2).

Was NJROTC Department Head and instructor, Northwestern High School, Adlephi, MD, 1981-88. Was executive director, The Master Builders' Assoc., Inc., and executive director, Construction Contractors Council, 1988-95. Re-tired in 1995 to serve as a consultant for Labor Relations, and also sits as a board member on a number of Union Trust Funds.

Married to the former Mitzi Carole Brummel of Union City, TN. They live in Fairfax Station, VA, and have two daughters, Tina (md. Richard A. Buckingham) and Shari (md. Joseph A. Trotter III); and three grandchildren: Joshua and Amy Buckingham and Michael Trotter.

VANCE H. MORRISON, CAPT, USN (Ret), born Aug. 25, 1938, New London, CT, the son of a submarine Commanding Officer. He attended the University of Virginia for BA in physics, and the University of Southern California for MS in systems management. Upon graduation in 1962, he was commissioned through the NROTC Regular Program.

He first served in USS *Herbert J. Thomas* (DDR-833), then USS *Weiss* (APD-135), participating in two combat deployments to Vietnam. After language instruction in Chinese, he was assigned to US Naval Security Group Activity, Hakata, Japan.

His next assignments were as operations officer in USS *Reeves* (CG-24) and on the J-2 Staff, USCINCPAC. He then reported to USS *Somers* (DDG-34) as Executive Officer in 1975. A tour on the OPNAV Staff (ASW Division) was followed by assignment as CO of USS *Francis Hammond* (FF-1067). He was a branch head in OP-60, then CO, USS *Richmond K. Turner* (CG-20) with a deployment to the Mediterranean during the Libyan Campaign in 1986.

He served as US Naval Attaché in Beijing, China, observing the Tiananmen Incident in 1989. His last tour on active duty was as Senior Navy Planner for the CNO during Desert Shield/Desert Storm.

CAPT Morrison retired in January 1992. His decorations include the Defense Superior Service Medal, Legion of Merit (2), Meritorious Service Medal (2), Joint Service Commendation Medal (2), Navy Commendation Medal and various other decorations.

Captain Morrison is married to the former Liberty Anne Paterson. They have two sons, Douglas and Robert; daughter, Katherine; and two grandchildren, Tiffani and Heather. He is a division director for SWL/GRCI.

ROBERT P. NEAL, LT, served 1957-61 and honorably discharged as ET2-P2. He re-enlisted in 1978 under APG program as ATI with VR-51 at Glenview NAS. Flew more than 1,000 hours as flight communications operator on the C-118 and more than 1,000 hours as flight attendant on the C-9, all with VR-51 while serving as work center supervisor and division chief.

He earned the rank of ATC and authorized to wear Air Warfare Wings and subsequently (through the LDO program) was commissioned Ensign in 1987. Promoted to LTJG in 1989 and full Lieutenant in 1991.

He served as division officer, then Maintenance/material Control Officer with many collateral duties including PAO and weight and balance Officer. He was awarded a Navy Achievement Medal in 1994.

From VR-51s decommissioning date September 1994 until June 1996, he was attached to VTU-1314G, to NAVINFO Midwest and VTU-7272G. He was then assigned to NR Adak, AK, as division officer/PAO, and when the unit was changed to NR NSA Souda Bay, Crete, he was assigned as Training Officer and Public Affairs Officer where he continues to serve.

Lt. Neal continues to reside in Wadsworth, IL, with his wife Pat. They have five children and four grandchildren. He is a life member of NERA, NRA, Naval Order, USN Public Affairs Alumni Association, Navy League (serving on chapter board), Bluejackets Association (serving as national president) and ROA (serving as legislative chairman for Illinois).

WILLIAM A. "BUD" NESTLERODE SR., CAPT, born Feb. 9, 1923, Chicago, IL. Received his BA in physics, BA in Engineering and MA in Physics. Joined the USN Dec. 14, 1942; and commissioned Feb. 24, 1944.

Military stations included Amphibious Base, Solomon, MD; USS LCS(L) 381, South Pacific. Units served with were 3rd Fleet and 5th Fleet.

Commands held: (Reserve) ORGSURFDIV 9-234; NROS 9-2; and NRGC 8-26. Battles and campaigns: Kerama Retto and Okinawa Gunto (radar picket patrol).

CAPT Nestlerode's awards include the Naval Reserve, American Theater, Asiatic-Pacific w/star, WWII Victory Medal, Philippine Liberation, Japanese Occupation, Armed Forces and NOUS.

Memorable experiences: outfitting and commissioning USS LCS(L) 381, November 1944, Portland, OR; picket patrol, two kills: one Val and one Betty, one assist and one Oscar; Occupation of Japan; sailing their ship back to Portland, OR; as Group Commander, introduced War Gaming to Houston Readiness Command with HOUNAVEX 1-74, which included all Reserve units under NRGC 8 26.

Married Dr. Samye Mott and they have four children: William A. Jr., Robert N., Eleanore L. and Victoria R. Harvey; grandchildren are Karl, Robert and Austin Nestlerode; Sam, Jacob and Haley McGuffie.

Civilian employment includes field engineer, Continental Oil; machinery representative, Bethlehem Supply Co.; president, Lynes International; vice-president, Baker Oil Tools-Baker Eastern; managing director, Baker Oil Tools-Hong Kong; and president, Nestlerode and Assoc. Oilfield Services. He retired July 1, 1975.

ERIC G. NEWBERG JR., CDR, born July 6, 1919, Mt. Vernon, NY. Received his MS and ME from MIT. Joined the USN May 26, 1941 and was commissioned Aug. 1, 1961.

Military stations: Navy Dept. (BUORD); MIT; NOP, Forest Park, IL; CTD, Newport, RI; Buweps (MUC Ord); Bupers, Scranton, PA; and NWREP, Sacramento, CA. Held commands at all except BUORD and Bupers. CDR Newberg received service ribbons only.

Memorable experiences: representative at Operation Teapot test site in Nevada; open trench, walked to ground zero in 1955.

Married Georgette and has three children: Elizabeth, Eric and Enid; and grandchild. He was primarily an engineering supervisor, Boeing, CSC (OS-15), Northrop, McLaughlin Research Corp. Retired Aug. 1, 1961.

MARGARET "PEGGY" DEMPSEY O'DOWD, LTJG, born Jan. 14, 1922, Chicago, IL. She received a BS in Education and a MA in Guidance counseling. Peggy joined the USNR in October 1943 and was commissioned in December 1943.

Military stations include Smith College, Mt. Holyoke officer training and communications training. She served with the Western Sea Frontier as a Communications Officer during WWII.

Memorable experience was being a volunteer at the US Naval Post Graduate School, 1992-97 in the Public Affairs Office. She was discharged in December 1945 with the rank LTJG.

Her husband, Lt. Frank E. O'Dowd, USN, is deceased. Children are Frank Jr., Peg, Tom, Kathie, John, Maureen, Gerald, Patricia and Michael. There are 15 grandchildren. Civilian employment with Hines Lumber Co., National Building Materials Distributors Association.

FRANCIS M. "RED" O'LAUGHLIN III, CAPT, USNR, born in Norfolk, VA in September 1946. He graduated from Texas A&I University with a BS in chemistry, 1969, then entered Aviation Officer Candidate School. He was commissioned in October 1969 and designated a Naval Flight Officer in May 1970.

He reported to Patron Six and had deployments to Vietnam, Japan, Guam, Philippines, Okinawa and Thailand. In November 1973 Capt. O'Laughlin left active duty and affiliated with the Naval Reserve, reporting to Patron Nine One. Additional Reserve assignments included Patron Nine Four, Mobile Inshore Undersea Warfare Unit 108, Maritime Defense Zone Atlantic Sector Eight and Readiness Command Region Ten.

Capt. O'Laughlin was recalled to active duty several times from 1994-97 in various capacities with Maritime Defense Zone Atlantic and Pacific.

His civilian employment included quality assurance, reliability and logistics management positions at National Semiconductor, Memorex, Basic Four, Dresser Magcobar Data, NL McCullough, Boeing Petroleum Services and Source Production and Equipment Co. He obtained an AA degree from DeAnza College (quality control, 1977), MS degree from the University of Southern California (systems management, 1979), Master of Business Administration from the University of Houston (international business, 1984) and graduated from the Naval War College in 1995.

O'Laughlin has been a principal consultant with European Quality Connection since 1995. He holds professional accreditation as a certified quality engineer, certified reliability engineer and certified professional logistician. He has published papers in international journals and conducted professional seminars throughout the US. His personal awards include the Air Medal, Navy and Marine Corps Commendation (2) and numerous other unit and campaign awards.

He is married to the former Marilyn Huggins of Corpus Christi, TX, and has two children, Michelle Yvonne and Francis M. IV, and one grandchild.

RONALD A. PARTNOY, CAPT, USNR (Ret), born Dec. 23, 1933 in Norwalk, CT. He graduated from Yale University with a BA degree (1956), Harvard Law School with LLB (1961) and from Boston University with LLM (1965). He joined the service and was commissioned Ensign in 1956.

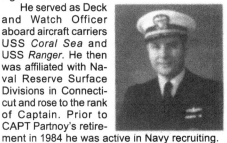

He served as Deck and Watch Officer aboard aircraft carriers USS Coral Sea and USS Ranger. He then was affiliated with Naval Reserve Surface Divisions in Connecticut and rose to the rank of Captain. Prior to CAPT Partnoy's retirement in 1984 he was active in Navy recruiting.

In civilian life he has been general counsel of Remington Arms Co. and senior counsel of the DuPont Co. He has served as Naval Reserve Assoc., 3rd District president, Navy League national director and Connecticut state president and Naval Order Companion of New York Commandery. He is listed in Who's Who in America, Who's Who in Finance and Industry, and Who's Who in American Law.

He and his wife Diane reside in Kennett Square, PA.

ROMAN E. "PETE" PIOTROWSKI, CAPT, SC, USNR (Ret), enlisted in the Navy in 1952. His duties at NSD Yokosuka, Japan, were different from most enlisted men and included public affairs, assistant for management planning and as a War Plans Administrator. He received three Letters of Commendation for his work, the first of which was awarded for "a heroic act above and beyond the call of duty."

Upon release, he became active in the Naval Reserve and was commissioned in 1961. His Reserve units included NRED 9-29, Executive Officer; SSOD 9-1, Executive Officer, DCASR613; Assistant Logistics Officer; REDCOM13 and CINCUSNAVEUR DET 513.

His ACDUTRA included tours on five Navy ships, at DCASMA's Chicago and Milwaukee, NAVWEPSUPCEN Crane, DLA HQ, Alexandria, NAVSUPSYSCOM HQ, Washington, NAVPERS

LCDR-LT Selection Board and COMFAIRMED Naples, Italy,

His military awards include the Joint Service Commendation Medal, Good Conduct Medal and various other service awards. A Life member of the Naval Order, he served as chairman of the 1993 Congress in Chicago. He has been awarded the General Commandery Certificate of Appreciation and the Commander General's Medal.

Pete and his wife, Mary, reside in Glenview, IL and have two sons and a daughter.

ARNOLD "ARNY" POCK, CAPT, born July 19, 1934, Chicago, IL. Graduated from the Scholl College of Podiatry Medicine in June 1956. He joined the USNR (active duty) June 27, 1956, under a two year enlisted program, inasmuch as commissions for podiatrists were closed. Discharged in 1958, he entered private practice and joined a Naval Research Unit at Northwestern University.

One year later, he received a commission in the Medical Service Corps as Ensign, USNR, coupling his private practice in Podiatry with Naval Reserve assignments. He excelled in both and rose through the ranks, delivering foot care at Navy and Marine Corps Recruit Training Commands throughout the country.

In 1989 Dr. Pock acquired a Master's degree in Management and human resources and propelled himself even farther in areas of administration and command responsibilities. He served as CO of NR Naval Hospital Great Lakes, Unit 313, and multiple tours as Staff Administrative Officer and Staff Medical Officer, Readiness Command, Region 13, Great Lakes. He served four years at NRREDCOMREG13GLAKES as director of health services. Capt. Pock served as Surgeon General of the Naval Order.

In August 1991 Capt. Pock was recalled to active duty (BUMED) for four years. He served as Special Assistant for Reserve Integration, assigned to the dental division (MED-06) and double hatted in Reserve Matters (MED-07). Dr. Pock also conducted a foot clinic at BUPERS which he equipped and organized independently. His tour at BUMED was eventful. He orchestrated important changes in Chapters 6 and 15 of the Manual of the Medical Department which paved the way for Reservists to secure complete physicals and four year dental examinations. NPQ status for dental neglect was a paramount achievement.

130

He was awarded the Legion of Merit in July 1994 for his tour at BUMED. He also received the Meritorious Service Medal, Navy Achievement Medal, Expert Pistol and Rifle Medals, National Defense Medal and Gold Wreath Award for Medical Department Recruiting during his career.

Dr. Pock is married and has two children. His daughter, Arnyce, is a physician (LTC) in the USAF, currently assigned to the Surgeon General's staff at Bolling AFB, Washington, DC. His son, David, is a social worker in Chicago, IL. Capt. Pock and his wife are retired and reside in Pensacola, FL.

RICHARD R. "DICK" POHLI, CAPT, born Aug. 16, 1929, San Pedro, CA. Received his BS degree, USNA, 1952, and post-graduate, NWC, 1968. He joined the USN June 14, 1948 and was commissioned June 6, 1952.

Stations include USS *Pickaway* (APA-222); FITRON 53; USS *Laws* (DD-558); BuPers; USS *Vireo* (MSC-205); USS *Eversole* (DD-789, two tours); CINCPACFLT, OPNAV, Treasure Island; AWSNA, New Delhi, India, NWC.

Held commands aboard the Viero, Eversole, NAVSUPACT Treasure Island.

Participated in battles and campaigns in Korea (two stars) and Vietnam (8 stars). CAPT Pohli was discharged Sept. 1, 1980. Awards include the Bronze Star (2) (V), Navy Commendation Medal (2), Joint Service Commendation Medal, Meritorious Service Medal and Vietnam Honor Medal 1/c.

Dick is divorced and has two children, Robert and Krista, and five grandchildren: Michael, Heather and Jennifer Pohli and Brandon and Jesse Rose. Civilian employment as president of Invest-In-America Council, Inc.

IRVING SHERWOOD "SCOTTIE" PRESTON, LCDR, born Dec. 16, 1911, East Orange, NJ. Graduated Georgia Tech in 1934 plus a short Seminar at Oxford, UK. Joined the USNR in 1943 and was commissioned July 3, 1943.

Military stations include Atlanta INSMAT, Birmingham RINSMAT, Little Creek, VA and Pearl Harbor. Served with the Amphibious Force; Atlantic Fleet and Pacific Fleet. Commands held: USS LSM-230, group commander.

Participated in independent duty out of Pearl Harbor. LCDR Preston was discharged in 1954. He received several awards and medals.

Memorable experiences include the deluxe cruises with all expenses paid by Uncle Sam, including personal stewards mate and private stateroom.

Married Frances Taylor, who is descendent of signer of Declaration of Independence. They have two children, Bruce Mackelvie (also a Navy vet) and Craig; and five grandchildren: Anthony, Athena, Samuel, Elizabeth and Emily. Worked mainly as executive of companies he formed. Retired in 1950 and has been cruising ever since.

ALTON "DOYLE" QUISENBERRY, CDR, USNR (Ret), is a native of Amarillo, TX. He graduated

from Amarillo College (AAS), West Texas A&M (BS), Pepperdine University (MA). Enlisted in the USNR in 1947, called to active duty in 1950 during Korean conflict and served in USS *Skagit.*

Released from active duty in 1951 and completed Reserve Officer Candidate Program. Returned to ACDU in 1953 and served as XO and Chief Engineer, USS *Teaberry* during Korean conflict.

Left Navy, taught industrial arts in various Amarillo junior high schools, 1956-61. TDY, Service School Command, San Diego, summers of 1957, 1959 and 1960. In 1961 selected for TAR program and was Chief Engineer, USS *George Clymer,* off coast of Vietnam in 1964.

Logistics officer, staff, Commander Amphibious Group Two, embarked in flagship USS *Pocono,* USS *Francis Marion,* USS *Austin* and in USS *Guam* during 1970 Jordanian crisis. CO, Naval and Marine Corps Training Center, Amarillo, 1964-65, staff duty (NRA) at COMFIVE, COMSIX, COMEIGHT, COMTHIRTEEN, ADDU and instrumental in development of first USNR Readiness Command, Baltimore.

Upon retirement in 1996 was employed BUPERS, transferred to Staff Commander-in-Chief, US Atlantic Fleet in 1978, retiring in 1993 as a GM-13.

Significant accomplishments: architect, Naval Reserve Logistic Task Forces, Atlantic and Pacific, 1992, and Naval Reserve Cargo Rig Teams, 1991; key role in development of wartime maintenance support at bare bases overseas for deployed NATO and US Maritime Patrol Aircraft; instrumental in development of mobilization readiness measurement of NR Inshore Undersea Warfare Units and funding to equip them in 1970; also allocation and proper outfitting of selected merchant ships to augment Navy Combat Logistic Forces following Operation Desert Shield/Desert Storm.

Life member #72 and past national officer of the NRA (received the NRA "Twice-a-Citizen" and National Membership awards, ROA Silver Minuteman (life member and past president of ROA Dept. of Virginia); member of NOUS and Eagle Scout.

Formal awards include Navy Civilian Superior Service Award and Medal (2), Navy Civilian Meritorious Service Award and Medal, Dept. of Navy Desert Shield/Desert Storm Award, Navy Commendation Medal (2), MUC, NDSM (2), AFEM, VSM, RVNCM w/device, Naval Reserve Medal, Armed Forces Reserve Medal and authorized to wear the Surface Warfare and Command of Shore Activity insignia.

Married Edna "Frances" Hudson in 1950 and has two sons, Bob and Kerry.

CARL V. RAGSDALE, CAPT, born on May 16, 1925 in Illmo, MO. He attended Washington University, St. Louis, MO, 1942-43; enlisted in the Navy V-5 Program in at Denison University, OH, transferred to the V-12a Program and commissioned an Ensign at USNMS Fort Schuyler, NY, July 1945.

He served CINCPAC Staff, XO Pacific Fleet Camera Party, O-in-C Western Pacific Fleet

Camera Party, 1948-49. Returned to the Naval Reserve and graduated from Denison University in June 1950.

Recalled to active duty for Korea, 1950-53, onboard the USS *Eldorado* (AGC-11) and Pacific Fleet Combat Camera Group and as director and producer at the Naval Photographic Center. Returned to the Reserves and worked as a director and producer in the motion picture industry in New York City, 1954-76.

He was a pioneer in the production of television commercials, and was awarded every motion picture award for excellence, including the Academy Award Oscar in 1966. He was nominated for another Oscar in 1967. He founded Carl Ragsdale Associates, and owned Sun Dial Films, Inc., a division.

Carl joined the New York Commandery of the Naval Order in 1962. He joined the Aviation Commandery in 1965, serving as Treasurer until 1976. He moved to Houston in 1976 where he continued his film and Naval Reserve careers. As a Commander, he put into commission the first Naval Reserve Combat Camera Group at the NAS, New York. As a Captain, he was CO of the Naval Reserve O1 Det 202 in NYC and at the same time organized the O1 Det 310 in Houston and served as CO. He retired in May 1985. Carl was the most senior Captain in the Navy at the time of his retirement.

In 1986 he organized the Texas Commandery of NOUS with 15 Reserve and Active Duty officers. He served as Commander of NOUS in Houston for six years and was named Commander Emeritus. Today the Texas Commandery has over 120 members and is one of the most active chapters. Carl served as Vice-Commander General of NOUS in 1987.

In addition to his Commandery duties, he served as chairman for many Navy related programs e.g., the USS Houston first port visit, Chairman Recruiting District Assistance Council (6 years), Vice Chairman USS *San Jacinto* Commissioning Committee, Chairman USS Houston Memorial Monument Foundation.

Carl was awarded the Silver Anvil Award from the Public Relations Society of America for the best community relations program of 1983. CAPT Ragsdale retired from the Navy in May 1985 with 41-1/2 years of active duty and Naval Reserve service. He was awarded the Navy Meritorious Service Medal, Navy Meritorious Public Service Medal, Navy Commendation Medal w/Gold Star, Navy Unit Commendation Ribbon w/3 Bronze Stars, and 10 other service ribbons for duty in WWII, Korea (7 battle stars), China, the Atlantic and Pacific. In 1998 he was awarded the Texas Commandery's highest award for leadership, the "Fleet Admiral Chester W. Nimitz Leadership Award."

Carl is retired and lives in Montgomery, TX with his wife Dr. Diane Ragsdale. They have two children, John and Susan, and six grandchildren.

EDWARD J. "ED" RAM JR., CDR, born Feb. 23, 1955, Teaneck, NJ. Received his BS in Economics, Wharton School, University of Pennsyl-

vania, 1977; MBA, University of Chicago, 1982. Joined the USNR and was commissioned May 22, 1977.

Military stations include Naval Station Brooklyn; Naval Support Activity, New Orleans; NAS Glenview; NARA Chicago; USS *Dyess* (DD-880), CNAVRES, NRNAVAIRLANT DET 0172 and NR DCASR DET 613.

CDR Ram was discharged June 30, 1999. His awards include the Navy Commendation Medal and Joint Service Achievement Medal.

Memorable experiences: passing under the Brooklyn Bridge and by the Statue of Liberty while on sea detail in the *Dyess* (DD-880); as battle watch captain at forward Logistics Support Base, Andoya, Norway.

Married Sharon and has two children, Carson and Garrett. Civilian employment: Andersen Consulting, consulting manager; and Allegiance Healthcare, senior supply chain manager.

NOUS commissioned ancestors is CAPT Frederick Rambousek, USNR.

RICHARD S. READE JR., CAPT, enlisted in 1942. Member first Tarmac Bn., Olathe, KS, 1943; received wings at Pensacola, 1945; search team for Flt. 19 (Bermuda Triangle); Fort Lauderdale OP Training; Torpedo 4, WestPac (USS *Tarawa*).

Joined the Reserves in 1947. He has over 3,000 hours fixed and rotary wing (TBF, F4U, F6F, AD, AM, HUP, SH-34 and SH-3) shipboard and at Reserve Stations Floyd Bennet, Dallas, Akron, Grosse Ile, Willow Grove and Lakehurst; CO of HS-752 (Noel Davis Trophy), NWS-704, NAL-275, AWS-75; retired 1981.

US School of Naval Justice, Naval War College (2x), tours in NAVAIR and Pentagon; and a Sikorsky Rescue Award. Helped conceive and inaugurate MOBS Program tying Reservists to their MoBillets.

Civilian career as engineer, project/program manager of aerospace programs at Bell, Sikorsky, Goodyear, Gyrodyne, and Grumman (helo development; DASH; F-14; E-2/C-2) after MME from Cornell University 1952. Life member of NRA. He now resides in Old Field, LI, NY with his wife of 43 years, nee Thomasine Hocart of Montclair, NJ.

FRANCIS X. REILLY, LCDR, USNR (Ret), born Sept. 18, 1916. A graduate of Dartmouth College and Harvard Law School, he was commissioned as an Ensign, USNR, in April 1943. Assigned to the Office of General Counsel, Navy Department, Washington, DC, he served as Assistant Counsel, BuPers and later BuAer, until separation from active duty in July 1946 as a Lieutenant Commander.

Following law practice in Massachusetts, Francis joined Wilson & Co., Inc. as counsel, later becoming treasurer. Subsequent positions held were vice president, LTV Corporation; vice president and treasurer of B.F. Goodrich Co.; vice president and treasurer of Katy Industries; and vice president and general counsel of Rollins Burdick Hunter.

A Life member of the Naval Order, he has served as commander of the Illinois Commandery, National Recorder General, and National Vice Commander, and received a plaque for outstanding leadership at the 1993 Congress.

A widower, Francis has a daughter, son, and three grandchildren.

JOHN M. REYNOLDS, CAPT, born Sept. 11, 1938, Oakland, CA. Received his BS degree in Mechanical Engineering (1961) and MS in engineering economic systems (1993), both at Stanford. He joined the USNR, NROTC in September 1956 and was commissioned in April 1961.

Served on active duty in the USS *Lynde McCormic* (DDG-8); Reserve duty at Naval Control Shipping Office (NCSO), San Francisco; NCSO, MidPac; Military Sealift Command Office (MSCO), Oakland; MSCO, Concord; and Volunteer Training Unit, San Bruno.

CAPT Reynolds retired in August 1991. His awards include the Navy Meritorious Service Medal, Armed Forces Reserve, National Defense and Marksman Medal.

Memorable was working with an extremely capable and dedicated group of Naval Reservists.

Married Dee Dee and has three children: Sarah, Julia and Patrice; and two grandchildren, Brandon and Cassidy. Worked as an engineering manager, Pacific Bell, then Principal Decision Consulting Associates.

JOHN C. RICE JR., CAPT, USNR (Ret), upon graduation from Loyola University of New Orleans, he was commissioned through OCS in 1953. ACDU followed at NAVCOMMSTA Boston and USS *Taconic* (AGC-17) in communication, Mobilization and Planning billets.

After RAD, he held several billets in Advanced Base Planning Unit 8-3; Group CMD 8-1(L) Admin.; SURDIV 8-21(M) CO; Group CMD War Gaming; Fleet Processing (Mobilization) Team CO, Force Area Commander Staff; REDCOM Team Retention/IG; Merchant Marine Div. CO; and Navy staff liaison to State Adjutant General followed.

John Rice was elected to the Naval Order in 1979 sponsored by companions, Fred Kempe and Bob Laughead, and soon became a Life member. At the request of CDR Gen. Kempe, he and RADM Winston Weese co-founded the New Orleans Commandery in 1979, and John served as its first commander and companion of the General Council.

As Commander General Elect 1987-89, he produced new design formats for General Commandery Awards. As Commander General 1989-91, he organized and chaired the Centennial Congress. John personally rewrote the Operations Manual, and with Recorder General Lee Douglas (now deceased) completely revised the computer program for membership records and billing. A Centennial Log was authored by John to commemorate the Centennial and three new commanderies were chartered.

CAPT Rice's interest in Naval history was whetted and fed by Historian General Emeritus Emile Bonnot and his successor LCDR Russell Miller. In preparation for the Centennial he undertook to locate Naval Order files placed in depositories in various states and to collect, preserve and collocate them. Working from those records he assisted Recorder General Lee Douglas to compile a complete and accurate listing of all companions since 1890. As an outgrowth, he serves the Order today as National Historian.

CAPT Rice was married to the late Claire Courrege Rice who had been an Associate Life member since 1985.

WAYNE ROBERTSON, LTJG, born July 20, 1923, Dallas, TX. Received his BBA from the University of Texas, joined the USNR July 1, 1943 and was commissioned March 17, 1944.

He served two years on the USS *Rall* (DE-304) in the Western Pacific during WWII; and served six months in USS Fargo (CL-106) in Atlantic. He supported the invasion of Iwo Jima and Okinawa. Also convoyed carriers, troop ships and second tankers.

Discharged July 1, 1946, with the rank of LTJG. He received the Pacific Theater Ribbon WWII and Presidential Unit Citation for *Rall*.

While on the *Rall* they sank a Japanese submarine at Ulithi Atoll. They also shot down four Japanese aircraft at Okinawa and were hit by a Japanese kamikaze airplane off Okinawa in the Pacific during WWII.

Married Virginia Lee and has two children, Monroe Wayne Jr. and Robert Guy; and three grandchildren: Randall, Tiffany and Kiara Robertson. He spent 35 years with Texaco, Inc. and retired as region supervisor, July 1, 1982.

RICHARD SPALDING ROGERS, CAPT, USN, after graduation from the Naval Academy in 1937, ENS Dick Rogers spent two years in the heavy cruiser *San Francisco* where he was given two Letters of Commendation for duties in the Gunnery and Engineering Departments before departing for flight training.

In the spring of 1940, he left Pensacola with orders to Fighting Squadron Three aboard the carrier USS *Saratoga*. VF-3 was the first to fly the Brewster Buffalo, the Navy's original monoplane fighter. A year later, LTJG Rogers was transferred to Composite Squadron One to fly the Buffalo off our first escort carrier, *Long Island*.

On Dec. 7, 1941, Long Island, having just completed a neutrality patrol, lay at anchor in Bermuda's sound. Her aircraft were shore-based nearby. Planes were ordered aboard without delay. Dick's was one of the five Brewster F2A's that were recovered aboard the small carrier without incident while Long Island remained at anchor.

Reassignment in 1942 to Composite Squadron Nine in the Escort Carrier *Bogue* brought Anti-Submarine Warfare duty flying F4Fs. Bogue's Hunter-Killer operations helped turn the tide against German U-Boats and won the ship and VC-9 the Presidential Unit Citation. LT Rogers participated in five aerial attacks against submarines in this period.

In mid-1943, he was ordered to the Pacific to commission and command Composite Squadron Sixty Eight. As Squadron CO, he flew combat missions in both the Wildcat fighter and

Avenger torpedo planes off the Escort Carrier *Fanshaw Bay*. LCDR Rogers flew combat air patrols, close air support, and air coordinator missions in the Marianas Invasion and in the Leyte Landings and led air strikes against heavy vessels of the Japanese fleet that were firing on ships of *Fanshaw Bay's* Task Unit Oct. 25, 1944. His ship received battle damage in both operations while he was airborne.

After return to the US with his damaged carrier, he reported for duty with the Joint Chiefs of Staff and two years later, CDR Rogers was ordered to command Fighting Squadron 11 aboard the newly commissioned carrier *Valley Forge*. In 1948, *Valley Forge* and her Air Group left Pearl Harbor for an unusual circumnavigation of the world, visiting seldom seen ports including Sidney, T'Sing Tao, Singapore, Trincomalee, Ras Tanura, a high speed transit of the Suez, Bergen, Norway, and into the Pacific via the Panama Canal. His fighter squadron won the coveted AIRPAC Battle Efficiency Award that year.

In 1949, Dick was made Executive Officer of Air Transport Squadron Three and flew in the Berlin airlift. A year later he was ordered to the Bureau of Aeronautics' Armament Division followed by command of Carrier Air Group One. He was on the bridge of the carrier *Wasp* when *Wasp* and the destroyer escort *Hobson* collided at night off Iceland. Dick volunteered to remain behind with *Wasp's* rescue boats while the ship stood on to recover aircraft. All his boats were hoisted back aboard in heavy seas by dawn the next day.

CDR Rogers subsequently served at NAS Atlantic City, as Executive Officer of the carrier *Midway*; and on the staff of COMCARDIV 14 where he received his promotion to Captain. He then became Chief of Staff to COMFLEET AIR HAWAII before attending the State Department's Language School with orders to Turkey as Naval Attaché.

During 30 years service, he was awarded the Silver Star Medal, four Distinguished Flying Crosses, four Air Medals, three Presidential Unit Citations and four Letters of Commendation. He has flown nearly 10,000 hours in Naval aircraft, mostly fighters, and has made over 350 carrier landings.

His wife of more than five decades is Dorothy Marilyn "Lynn" Rogers, who is the daughter of RADM Cecil D. Riggs, M.C., USN.

Dick is a fifth generation Texan. His forebears fought against Mexico in Texas' War of Independence. He is a member of The Sons of the Republic of Texas and a member of NOUS and has been given special recognition by the Governor of Texas.

EDGAR FARR "ED" RUSSELL JR., CAPT, USNR (Ret), born May 9, 1927, Washington, DC. He was appointed Midshipman, Merchant Marine Reserve, USNR, May 1, 1945. After completion of Plebe Year at the U.S. Merchant Marine Cadet School, Pass Christian, MS, including assignment to the USN SC-1305 served at sea as deck cadet in U.S. Merchant ships: SS *Brazil Victory,* TES *Quirigua,* and SS *Del Sud.* Assigned to U.S. Merchant Marine Academy, Kings Point, NY as Second Classman in July 1947 and graduated from US Merchant Marine Academy June 15, 1949 with BS degree, Commissions as ENS, US Maritime Service; ENS, USNR and USCG Unlimited License as Third Mate. Attended Georgetown University as ADM McNulty Scholar, 1949-51, and received Master of Arts degree in International Relations in 1955.

Served as naval officer on active duty for training in USS *Kiowa* (ATF-72), USS *Roanoke* (CL-145), and USS *Robert F. Keller* (DE-419).

From May 1951 to June 1952, he served on active duty in US Maritime Service. On June 14, 1952, he married Miss Jean Neely Peake of Rock Hill, SC. Two weeks later he entered active duty in USN and assigned to Postgraduate Course, USN Intelligence School. Upon graduation he was assigned to intelligence duty in Charleston, SC.

Upon release from active duty in June 1954, he was employed as Intelligence Analyst by Office of Naval Intelligence. In 1963 he transferred to Defense Intelligence Agency. Three years later, selected to attend the 10-month Senior Resident Course in Naval Warfare, U.S. Naval War College from which he was graduated in June 1967. In June 1972, appointed Administrative Assistant to Member of Congress. One year later, returned to Naval Intelligence and served as Naval Reserve Intelligence Program coordinator, Naval Intelligence Support Center from which position he was retired Dec. 26, 1987.

Four years prior, on July 1, 1983, he had been retired from USNR as a Captain after 38 years of service. Commands held were Commanding Officer, Naval Intelligence Command Reserve Unit 406 and Commanding Officer, Naval Reserve Intelligence Volunteer Training Unit 106. Recognition as a Merchant Marine Cadet included award of a sextant as the Outstanding Deck Cadet-Midshipman of the Fourth Class at the Merchant Marine Cadet School in 1946 and the Admiral Richard R. McNulty Scholarship and the Marine Insurance Award, an inscribed gold wrist watch, upon graduation from the U.S. Merchant Marine Academy in June 1949.

Personal Navy decorations consisted of the Meritorious Service Medal, the Navy Commendation Medal, and the Navy Superior Civilian Service Medal. Service awards included the American campaign Medal, World War II Victory Medal, National Defense Service Medal, Armed Forces Reserve Medal (2 awards), Naval Reserve Medal, Merchant Marine Atlantic War Zone Medal, Merchant Marine World War II Victory Medal, and Navy Expert Rifleman Medal.

Ed and Jean have two sons, LtCol Edgar Farr Russell III, USAF (born 1954) and Frazier Neely Southey Russell (born 1957), a published poet and the assistant director of The Writer's Studio in New York City.

ARTHUR H. "ART" SASS, CAPT, USN (Ret), born Nov. 22, 1928, Bronx, NY. Graduated University of New York at Oswego with BS degree and Rutgers University with Ed.M. He joined the USN March 19, 1952 and was commissioned July 24, 1952.

He served at US LSMR-512, Little Creek, Oct. 3, 1952-Dec. 23, 1953; Merchant Marine Reserve officer Training Facility, December 1953 to September 1955; NAVSEASYSCOM, August 1953-November 1955; Reserves, NARTU-LAKEHURST; WEPTU, CO; BuPers Personal Unit; NAVWEP Station, EARLE (WEPTU). Was CO of WEPTU, NAVWEPSTA-EARLE.

He was recalled to Active Duty in August 1983 to December 1985 as the Academic Director for Naval Reserve Engineering Duty Officer School.

CAPT Sass retired Nov. 26, 1985, with the rank of Captain. Awards include the National Defense Service Medal, Armed Forces Reserve Medal (3), Navy Commendation Medal, Meritorious Unit Commendation, Surface Warfare Badge and Navy Recruiting Badge w/Crest.

Memorable experiences include OOD at sea; developing and implementing program for BuPers placement and assignment officers; developing standards and evaluation criteria for naval instructors; serving as academic director of the Naval Reserve Engineering Duty Officer training program; supervising complete overhaul of a naval vessel.

Married Eleanore; has four children: Nancy Threlfall, Arlene Sells, Susan Sass and Eric Sass; eight grandchildren; and one great-grandchild. Civilian employment included teaching, principal, superintendent of schools; director of education and training, Naval Research Laboratory; and President DEVPRO, Inc. (consultant). He is a Life member of the NRA, ROA and Navy League of US.

RICHARD SCOTT SAUNDERS, CDR, born June 13, 1955, Richmond, VA. Received his BS in psychology and MS in business management. Joined the USNR in February 1978 and was commissioned Feb. 10, 1978.

Military stations were NAS Pensacola, flight training; NAS Meridian, MS, flight training; NAS North Island, squadron tour; RAG instructor tour, S-3 SAU director; NAS Norfolk, Reserve Pgm. Director; NAS Memphis, Squadron OIC tour; NSA New Orleans, COMNAVAIRESFOR Staff tour, NAS New Orleans, Executive Officer of NAS.

Served with VT-3; VT-19; VT-7; VS-33, VS-41; NAVAIRES San Diego; VR-56; VR-60; NAVAIRES Norfolk; COMNAVAIRESFOR, NAS New Orleans. He participated in Desert Shield.

CDR Saunders is still on active duty; his awards include the Navy Achievement Medal, Navy and Marine Corps Commendation Medals and Meritorious Service Medal.

Memorable experiences include the first solo night flight as a student in the TA-4, halfway through hop had main gear unsafe indication and went NorDo. On 1981 cruise in the S-3A, on an ugly dark stormy night with only the one wire rigged, had six bolters and lost five pounds.

Married Denise Enneking and has three children: Robert, Samuel and Rachel.

JAMES G. SCHNEIDER, born Aug. 24, 1925, Kankakee, IL. Took Navy V-12 nationwide test, April 2, 1943; ordered to active duty, Milligan College Navy V-12 Unit, Milligan College, TN, July 1, 1943; March 1944, Duke University V-12 Unit; November 1944, Asbury Park Pre-Midshipmen's School; January 1945, Midshipmen's School, Northwestern University, Chicago.

Commissioned Ensign, May 24, 1945; after Tactical Radar and Fighter Director Schools,

went aboard USS *Hornet* (CV-12), 1945-46; district Communications Office, 5 ND, 1946 to inactive duty; recalled to active duty as LTJG, Oct. 8, 1950, Glenview NAS, Precommissioning Detail, USS *Essex*, Bremerton Naval Shipyard, 1951-52, aboard *Essex*; 1952, Naval Station, San Diego, followed by inactive duty until discharge in 1957.

Graduated University of Iowa, BA, 1948 and JD, 1953. Married Phyllis Jordan, Aug. 12, 1950 and has three children: Holly, Scott and Thomas. After Phyllis' death in 1991, he married Suzita Cecil Myers, Aug. 22, 1993. Suzita died in 1995. Married Gail Barnes Nicholas June 21, 1997.

From loan officer to president/CEO, Kankakee Federal Savings & Loan Assoc., 1954-90; chairman/CEO, Kankakee Bancorp, Inc., 1993- present. Filmed and edited an hour video, "USS Essex: From Recommissioning to the End of its First Korean Cruise, January 1951 to March 1952 "He is the author of The Navy V-12 Program: Leadership for a Lifetime.

MARK L. SHAFER, CAPT, born June 27, 1929, Berwick, PA. Received his BS degree in Ocean Transportation from US Merchant Marine Academy and MBA, Sophia University, Tokyo. Joined the USNR, midshipman in 1947 and commissioned in 1951.

Military stations were Inchon, Korea, MSTS; Yokosuka Navy Base, MSTS; USS *Radford* (DD-447/449); USS *Dixie* (AD-14); Iwo Jima; Sacramento (AOE-1); Shasta (AE-33); COMNAVFOR, Japan; COMNAVMARIANAS, Guam; COMNAVPHIL, Manila. Was CO, Naval Reserve, VTU, Yokohama, Japan; Politico, Military Affairs Co. 2011, San Francisco.

Participated in battles and campaigns in Korea and Vietnam, for which he received several medals and awards.

The best two years of his life were on active duty in Korea and Japan; at Inchon with MSTS and at Yokosuka Navy Base, Japan with MSTS,

Married Dulce Dease and has three children: Carol Lynn Wesley, Deborah Shafer and Charles Shafer; and three grandchildren: Paul, Shaele and Cullen. Worked for Pacific Far East Line Inc., area manager Far East Matson Navigation Co., vice president of agencies and sales. Retired in 1989

CHARLES WILLIAM "BILL or "SHEP" SHEPHERD, born July 12, 1929, Pontiac, IL. Earned his BS degree at the University of Illinois and his MS degree at New York University.

Joined the US Merchant Marines in 1951. Enlisted in the USN in 1951 and served as CO. Graduated Class A Communications Technician School (both R and 0 branches), Bainbridge Island, WA, in 1952. In 1953 he served at Yokosuka, Japan to Kami Seya and advanced to P03 (CTR). He graduated OCS, ENS, CO. Assigned Washington, DC, OPNAV 202, Naval Security Gp. HQ, assistant department head. Was promoted to LTJG, department head in 1954 and transferred to Bremerhaven, Germany.

In 1955 was sent on 12-month TAD to 6th Fleet as assistant O-in-C, NavSecGru Det. and served aboard the USS *Salem,* USS *Newport News,* USS *Northampton,* and USS *Coral Sea.* Was one of eight Reserve officers fleetwide selected for Regular Navy Augmentation in 1956.

Declined Regular Navy Augmentation and released from active duty in Bremerhaven in 1957. In 1958 he joined Clifton, NJ, NavSecGru Reserve Unit NSGD 3-7 as Training Officer and promoted to LT, USNR. Clifton unit won national NavSecGru competition in 1959.

Joined New Rochelle, NY NavSecGru Reserve Unit NSGD 3-11 as Executive Officer in 1962. In 1965 affiliated with Chicago NR Public Affairs Co. 9-2. Joined Chicago NavSecGru Unit 9-2 as Training Officer. Maintained dual participation in both units until the Public Affairs Co. was decommissioned in 1979. Joined Illinois Naval Militia and Militia officers Mess. Promoted to CO, Chicago NavSecGru Div. 9-2 in 1969. In 1971 was CO, Forest Park NavSecGruDiv 9-17. Served as Public Affairs Officer, Gp. Command Staff and promoted to Commander, USNR in 1974.

In 1975 served as Executive Officer, NavSecGru Command and Control Unit 913, Chicago. Was CO, NavSecGru DIRNSA Unit 913, Chicago and Forest Park in 1977 and promoted to Captain, USNR, in 1979. Served with Readiness Command 13 as project officer in 1980; NavSecGru program officer in 1981; and project officer in 1983. In 1984 was CO, NavSecGru DIRNSA 1013. As CO, NavSecGru VTU 1311 in 1987 he was recalled to active duty for 90 days as acting Reserve forces advisor to director, National Security Agency. In 1989 served as NavSecGru liaison and project officer, Readiness Command 13 VTU 1310. Retired from USN on 60th birthday at Great Lakes as senior cryptologic officer in Midwest.

Awards include the American Spirit of Honor Medal, Korean War Medal, UN Medal, European Occupation Medal, National Defense Medal, Armed Forces Reserve Medal w/2 Hourglasses, Naval Reserve Meritorious Service Medal, Naval Security Group Meritorious Service Award, Readiness Command Region 13, Meritorious Service Award and numerous Reserve Unit citations and commendations.

He married the former Lorraine Hirvonen and has four children: John, Jennifer, Joan and Barbara; and one grandchild, Abigail. Civilian employment as field PR director with New York Life from which he retied Nov. 1, 1985.

KENT R. SIEGEL, CAPT, USN (Ret), born Jan. 4, 1935, Wausau, WI. Received his USNR commission via NROTC from University of Wisconsin in 1957 (BS in geology). His first duty was in USS *James E. Kyes* (DD-787) followed by training as a Deep Sea Diving Officer and service in the submarine rescue ship, USS *Tringa.* He then entered submarine training and was augmented into the Regular Navy, subsequently serving in the diesel submarines USS *Thornback,* USS *Segundo,* USS *Volador* as Executive Officer, and

USS *Pickerel* as CO; and as Chief Staff Officer for COMSUBRON FOUR.

He opted to "surface" in 1975 and went on to further sea duty as Executive Officer in the 6th Flt. flagship, USS *Little Rock* (CG-4), and in the amphibious navy in command tours in USS *Cleveland* (LPD-7) and USS *Tarawa* (LHA-1), and as Chief of Staff for COMPHIBGRU THREE.

Other assignments have included study at the Naval Postgraduate School (BS in meteorology, 1966) and the Royal College of Defense Studies in London, instructor duty at the Naval Academy, and staff duty for Commander Navy Recruiting Command and the Deputy CNO for Surface Warfare in the Pentagon.

Capt. Siegal retired in December 1986. Awards include the Legion of Merit, Meritorious Service Medal (2) and Navy Commendation Medal (2).

Since retiring he has worked as a logistics manager with M. Rosenblatt and Son, Inc., a naval architecture and marine engineering firm. He joined the Naval Order in 1988, becoming active in the National Capitol Commandery where he served as Commander from 1993-96. He and his wife Addie reside in Fairfax County, VA, near Washington, DC; they have three daughters: Gretchen Gianneli, Jennifer and Julie Siegeland two grandchildren, Stefan and Lara Gianneli.

LESLIE J. SKOWRONEK, CAPT, USN, born Aug. 2, 1950, New York, NY, daughter of Helen W. and Lester J. Skowronek. She is a 1972 University of Colorado graduate. Completing Women Officer's School, Newport, RI, she was assigned to Naval Facility Bermuda. She served at Commander, Oceanographic System Atlantic from 1974-77, transferring to Naval Facility Cape Hatteras.

In 1982, she completed an MS degree in Engineering Acoustics from Naval Postgraduate School. She was Executive Officer of Naval Facility Centerville Beach, Ferndale, CA, from 1983-85 before transferring to the Naval Military Personnel Command in Arlington, VA. From 1987-91, in the Undersea Warfare Program of the Space and Naval Warfare Systems Command, she served as Deputy Program Director. She commanded the Naval Ocean Processing Facility, Dam Neck, VA, until 1993 when she became Inspector General for the Chief of Naval Technical Training in Millington, TN.

Capt. Skowronek is currently CO, NROTC Unit, The Ohio State University. Awards include the Navy Commendation (2) and Meritorious Service (3) Medals. She is single.

SIDNEY HOWARD SMALL, CAPT, USNR (Ret), born Dec. 8, 1920, Wilkes-Barre, PA. Enlisted in the USN Dec. 8, 1941 and attended boot camp in Newport, RI. He helped put Coddington Point in commission. Left Newport to join Bobcats.

In January 1942 he was sent to Bora Bora. The Bobcats became part of first construction battalion which built oil tanks and air strip on Bora Bora.

In August 1943 he was accepted for V-12 and sent to Colgate University. Received commission from Northwestern University, May 24, 1945. Assigned to the USS *Saratoga* as assistant to lst Lieutenant. At the war's end he participated in Magic Carpet operation which returned servicemen from the Pacific to San Francisco.

Released from active duty in February 1946. In December 1950 he was recalled and served as Chief Engineer on USS *D.H. Fox* (DD-779). He spent seven months in Korea where the ship earned two Battle Stars. Released from active duty in December 1952.

From 1953-75 he was a drilling Reservist and held three commands including Group Commander of largest Group in 3rd Naval District. The Small family consists of wife, Molly; sons, Jay and Charles; daughter, Faye; and grandsons,

CHARLES J. "CHUCK" SMITH, CAPT, born Sept. 11, 1936, Frankfort, IN. Received his BS degree, USNA, 1958; MS, USNPGS, 1964; Nuclear Power, Eng., CO; Commander, National Capitol Commandery, NOUS, Washington, DC, 1971-73; joined the USN June 27, 1954 and commissioned June 6, 1958.

Military stations were USNA; Pearl Harbor, HI; San Diego, CA; Monterey, CA; Vallejo, CA; West Milton, NY; Long Reach, CA; Idaho Falls, ID; Coronado, CA; Norfolk, VA; and Washington, DC. Served with USS *Taylor* (DDE-468); USS *Hartley* (DE-1029); USS *Long Beach* (CEN-9); USS *Truxtun* (CGN-35).

Participated in the Formosa Straits patrol; Vietnam PIRAZ Station, four deployments (total 25 months); Iranian hostage crisis and Desert One rescue attempt.

Memorable Experiences: 1968 deployment to Tonkin Gulf in USS *Long Beach;* 1978 South Pacific Good Will Cruise as CO in USS *Robinson;* 1981 Around the World – IO deployment as CO of USS *California;* and shooting down of two MiGs.

Retired July 1, 1988, with the rank of CAPT, USN. Also, position of Commodore, Destroyer Squadron Commodore and Convoy Commodore. CAPT Smith was released from active duty Sept. 30, 1988. He received the Legion of Merit w/2 Gold Stars, Navy Commendation Medal, Meritorious Service Medal, Navy Unit Commendation, Meritorious Unit Commendation w/star, Armed Forces Expeditionary Medal, Navy Ex-

peditionary Medal, Battle E Award, National Defense Medal w/star, Sea Service Ribbon w/star, Vietnam Service Medal w/6 stars and Vietnam Campaign Medal.

Married to Elizabeth, March 1963-November 1993; married Tamara in November 1993. Has six children: Daine, Derrick, Andrew, Don, Dianne and Grant; and one grandchild, Andrew. Worked as an executive director for American Society Naval Engineers; and coordinator for STEP AHEAD, Clinton County, IN. Retired April 1, 1994.

T.J. SMITH, CWO4, USNR (Ret), born at Leavenworth, KS, Oct. 11, 1939. Joined the Navy at Wilmington, CA Sept. 30, 1957. After boot camp at NTC San Diego, he completed Interior Communication Electrician "A" and Motion Picture Operator "C" Schools. Assigned to USS *Barton* (DD-722), at Norfolk, VA (August 1958 to December 1959). Barton made a six month Mediterranean cruise and was awarded the Engineering "E."

Transferred to USS *Wren* (DD-568), at Galveston, TX (December 1959 to March 1960). *Wren* completed underway training at Guantanamo Bay, Cuba. After completing basic Submarine and Nuclear Power Schools, at New London, CT, he attended prototype training at SIC Windsor Locks, CT. Assigned to USS *George Washington* (SSBN-598), Gold Crew, at Holy Lock, Scotland as a reactor control operator. Completed six FBM deterrent patrols from August 1961 to August 1965, mainly standing IC watches forward. Qualified in submarines May 6, 1962, and as a scuba diver on June 12, 1964.

Transferred to USS *Angler* (AGSS-240) at New London, CT (August 1965 to August 1966). Left active duty Aug. 13, 1966, as IC1(SS)(DV).

Joined the Naval Reserve Sept. 17, 1966, as Company Commander for recruit training program in Submarine Div. 11-6. Chief Petty Officer Smith was selected to become a Warrant Electrician (WO1) on Dec. 15, 1970. He was a plankowner of the Reserve unit for Submarine Support Facility, San Diego, CA (SUBSUPPFAC 519), becoming the first Reservist to qualify as Command Duty Officer. CWO Smith served as CO of Naval Reserve Mobile Mine Assembly Group Unit 2419 from Dec. 16, 1976, to Sept. 30, 1979. Later, he served as the unit's Executive Officer and Mine Assembly Officer from Feb. 1, 1982 to Sept. 30, 1987. "Gunner" Smith was designated as BN1 in Mine Warfare on May 27, 1983. Mr. Smith also served in the following Reserve Units: SURDIV 11-3(L), SUPDIV 11-1, SUBSUP 11-6, and SUBSUPPFAC 119. He retired on June 1, 1988, as a Chief Engineering Technician (CWO4). A life member of the Naval Reserve Association, Mr. Smith served as the 1983-84 President of the Terminal Island Chapter. Presently, he is active in the Sutter Chapter. He has been a life member of the NOUS since 1987, serving as the 1990 commander of the Long Beach Commandery.

Married to the former Brenda Hanson, RNC, DNS, from Santa Clara, CA. They have two children, Kari (Girl Scout Gold Award) and Victor (Eagle Scout). On his retirement from the US

Bureau of Prisons, as a unit manager on June 2, 1990, he changed his name to Hanson-Smith. Currently a volunteer in the Golden Empire Council Boy Scouts of America, serving as the Rio Del Oro District Commissioner. Mr. Hanson-Smith has earned his Wood Badge Beads (1992), been awarded the Silver Beaver (1996) and in 1996 completed a 70 mile Philmont High Adventure Trek.

THOMAS F. SPENCER, LT, born November 1948, Somerville, NJ. Received his BA, Union College, and MBA, University of Pennsylvania, Wharton. He joined the US Navy in April 1968 and was commissioned in August 1968.

Military stations: USS *Dupont*, Norfolk and WestPac Cruise; USS *Manley*, Charleston, SC; RID 43, Vietnam, Mekong Delta.

He held commands of senior advisor, RID 43, Vietnamese River Unit. Participated in miscellaneous battles and campaigns.

LT Spencer was discharged in August 1971. Awards include the Navy Commendation, Purple Heart, Vietnam Campaign, Vietnam Service, National Service, Combat Action, Foreign Medal-Vietnam (Valor).

Memorable experiences: rats in Vietnam; dangers and risks on the rivers of the Mekong Delta.

NOUS commissioned ancestor is his uncle, Robert Burchard, Army Air Corps, KIA, WWII, North Africa; Navy Surgeons Mate Cogswell, Revolutionary War, Propositus, Soc. of the Cincinnati-Mass. Chapter.

He is divorced.

PETER J. SPEROS, CAPT, born May 25, 1919, Salt Lake City, UT. Voluntary enlistment March 13, 1933, DIO, 12ND, SF, Y2C. Early 1943 assigned to Naval Attaché, Cairo, Egypt and governments of Greece and Yugoslavia. While there, obtained and translated the operation report of Greek navy by ADM Alexandris, for which he received Letter of Commendation from the Admiral and shortly thereafter a spot commission to Ensign.

In the interim, he volunteered to be parachuted in northern Greece, but Normandy invasion changed that to Japanese Language School in Boulder, CO, subsequently attending special schools in Platsburg, NY and Miami, FL. Assigned as Deck and Gunnery Officer, USS *Shipley Bay* (CXVE-85); was in charge of motor whale boat #2 and picked up Officers and crew of a Catalina patrol bomber (about 130 miles south of Wake Island on January 19) who had been adrift in the Pacific for more than 12 hours—to this date he can still see the smiles of those 13 men delivered to Pearl Harbor.

Discharged in 1946 but remained in the Reserves until called to duty for the Korean War in January 1951. Attended six months Naval Intelligence School, and later assigned to CNO, Pentagon, for release and receipt of information to foreign governments and classification control. In 1953 back to civilian life. Retired June 30, 1969, as CO NRID 12-1 having been appointed

Captain Sept. 1, 1966. Following his dad's advice to all of them, "Your first duty is to your family, and second to your country," well said for a Greek immigrant.

Peter and his wife, Mary, have four children: John (retired commander), Chriss, Peter Jr. and Tia Ann; and four grandchildren: Jeromie, Peter J., James and Benjamin. His civilian employment includes: editing, *Business Digest;* executive secretary, CSPE; and president, Allen-Spero Corp.

LOUIS E. "L.E." SPRADLIN, CAPT, USNR, born Jan. 13, 1940, Ropesville, TX. Received his BA in Mathematics, University of Texas in Austin; MS in Management, Pace University in New York. Joined the Naval ROTC (Regular) in September 1958 and commissioned ENS, USN, June 1, 1963.

Stations include: student at USN Submarine School, New London, June 1963-January 1964; USS *Harder* (SS-568), January 1964-March 1966; staff commander Submarine Sqdn. Four at Charleston, April 1966-June 1967; released from active duty as LT, USNR.

Served as Operations Officer and Training Officer in Naval Reserve Surface Div. 6-32M at Charleston, July 1967-June 1970; Operations Officer, Reserve Underway Training Unit 6-15 and continued when the unit changed names to Fleet Training Group 107, in July 1974 and served until November 1974; prospective XO for Naval Reserve Surface Unit 6-11, December 1974-January 1975; XO, USS *Orion* (AS-18) Det. 107, February 1975-September 1977 and CO from October 1977-September 1979; Center Training Officer, Volunteer Training Unit 0705, Columbia, SC, October 1979-September 1981; CO, Naval Reserve Commander Submarine Sqdn. 16, Det. 1208, October 1981-September 1983; and drill commander, Voluntary Training Unit 080IG in Atlanta, October 1983-86.

CAPT Spradlin was discharged Sept. 30, 1990. One of his memorable experiences was at Guantanamo when a poker game was broken up by an attractive, "thought to be naive" Guantanamo School teacher who bluffed their self proclaimed poker master Executive Officer out of the biggest pot of the evening.

Married Mary Helen Moore on Aug. 26, 1966 and they have children: Helen Keels Spradlin Jorn (physician) (Bernard C. Jorn, minister and hospital chaplain) and Susan Elizabeth Spradlin (artist). Employed for 28 years with BellSouth, holding 16 different positions in five cities from New York to Miami, and retired in July 1995 as vice president of sales, The Carolinas for BellSouth Business Systems. Currently he is self-employed in consulting and networks and having a great time.

JOHN STRICKLIN SPRATT, CAPT, born Jan. 3, 1929, San Angelo, TX. Earned the following degrees: AS, BS, MSPH and MD, Diplomate American Board of Surgery and FACS. He joined the service Sept. 19, 1952.

Active duty stations include Chest Service, USNH, Oakland, CA, 1953; Field Medical Training School, Camp Pendleton, CA, 1953; Arctic Weather Training, Cold Water, CA, 1954: 1st Mar. Div., Korea; USNH, Great Lakes, IL, 1955; NRMC, Guam, 1982; USNH, Portsmouth, VA, 1984; and National Naval Medical Center, Bethesda, MD, 1985-90.

Spratt attended many schools throughout his career at Bethesda, MD; Corpus Christi, Fort Sam Houston and Camp Bliss, TX; Great Lakes, IL; Albuquerque, NM, Rochester, MN; Newport, RI; Yokosuka, Japan; Minneapolis, MN; Pensacola and Jacksonville, FL; Colorado;

Washington, DC; Gulfport, MS; Charleston, SC; San Diego and Coronado, CA; Alexandria, VA; New Orleans, LA; Mediterranean; and Millington, TN. He also completed numerous NR Officer Correspondence Courses from 1954-92.

Reserve assignments were at St. Louis and Columbia, MO, Louisville, KY; Medical Officer, 3rd Inf. Bn., USMCR, 1956-59; MOB Team OIV 9-28, 1959-61; NRMC 9-1, 1961-62; representative of the Commandant, 9th Naval Dist., Ensign 1915 Program, 1961-68; Medical Officer, 3rd Inf. Bn., USMCR, 1962-67; Medical Officer, USN Reserve Research Co., 9-28, 1967-72, Naval Representative of the Commandant, 9th Naval Dist., Military Support Planning Office, HQ, MONG, 1972-74; XO, USN Regional Medical Center, 1975-77; CO, USNR Surgical Team 118, 1977; CO, USNR G-5 Station Hospital 118, 1977-79; CO, USNR Medical Contingency Response Unit 209, 1979-81; Medical Officer, MEDCRU 209, Louisville, KY, 1981-83; Medical School Liaison Officer, University of Louisville, 1977-93; Medical Officer, NR USNH Camp Lejeune, Det. 309, 1983-84; OIC, PRIMUS (NR FH 500 COMMZ-11 DET P-6509), University of Louisville School of Medicine, 1984-92; and NR volunteer, Training Unit 0909, NMRC, 1992-93.

Spratt was awarded the NUC, NDM w/Bronze Star, KSM w/Marine Corps Emblem, AFRM w/3 HG Devices (for 40 years of uninterrupted satisfactory Federal service as a NR officer), UN Medal, Navy Expert Rifleman Medal, Gold Wreath Award w/Letter of Commendation, Silver Star in lieu of second Gold Wreath, Conspicuous Service Medal, Letters of Appreciation and Commendation, medals for life membership in The Naval Order, The Association of Military Surgeons of the US, TROA and NRA. He was appointed Admiral for the Commonwealth of Kentucky in 1977 and military advisor to the University of Louisville School of Medicine. He is a member and a past-president of Commodore Club of Navy League and in 1991 received a Letter of Commendation for seventh Gold Wreath Award from Naval Recruiting Command. He transferred to the NR Retired List with pay July 1, 1993.

He and his wife, Beverly, have three children: John A. Spratt, CDR Shelley S. Young, and LCDR Robert Spratt; and six grandchildren: John Robert, Madelyn, Abigail, Austin, Molly and Thomas. Civilian employment as clinical professor of surgery, F. Edward Hebert School of Medicine, Uniformed Services University of the Health Sciences, Louisville, KY, 1988 to present.

RICHARD K. "DICK" STACER, CAPT, born May 19, 1921, in Oregon. Received his BA, Willamette University and LLB, University of Washington Law School. Joined the USN in 1943 and commissioned same year.

Naval stations include USS *Knox* (APA-46), JAG Staff, 1950, Staff ComSixthFlt, COM 13 ND, Alaska Sea FRON, COMTHREE JAG Staff, ComPhibPac Staff.

Participated in battles and campaigns at Saipan, Tinian, Leyte, Luzon and Iwo Jima.

CAPT Stacer was discharged in 1972. Awards include the Meritorious Service Medal.

Memorable experiences: Naval Advisory Group to UN Ambassador; represented EXO of Pueblo; JAG of Naval Order; and NOUS Executive Committee.

ROBERT C. "BOB" STACK, RADM, a Raleigh, NC, native, graduated from the University of North Carolina with an AB and NROTC commission in June 1965. After active duty from 1965-68 on board the USS *Fox* (DLG-33) and USS *Sproston* (DD-577), he attended the University of Virginia receiving his MBA degree in June 1970.

As a Reservist, he drilled on board USS R.K. *Huntington* (DD-781) and USS *Fiske* (DD-842), and served as CO of Reserve Cargo Handling BN 7, Navy Petroleum Office Fleet DET 211, NSC, Charleston HQ A 107 and DCMD Atlanta B811. Promoted to Rear Admiral in June 1993; his mobilization billet was Deputy Commander, Aviation Supply Office (later Naval Inventory Control Point). As president, Navy Supply Corps Foundation from 1987-96, he was responsible for awarding over $1 million in scholarships to dependents of Supply Corps officers and supply Enlisted ratings while increasing the investment account from $1.2 million to $2.6 million.

A NRA life member since June 1976, he has been awarded the Legion of Merit, Defense Meritorious Service Medal, Meritorious Service Medal, Joint Service Medal w/2 Gold Stars and Combat Action Ribbon. He is qualified as a Naval Aviation Supply Officer and Surface Warfare Supply Corps officer.

RADM Stack is executive vice-president of Texas Commerce Bank in Dallas, TX, where he lives with his wife, Debbie.

ROGER POWELL STAIGER, born Nov. 23, 1921, Trenton, NJ. Graduated from Ursinus College, Collegeville, PA, and was immediately appointed an Instructor in Chemistry at Ursinus to teach Navy V-12 students during WWII. Joined the USN in August 1944 and was commissioned same year.

Training assignments were to the Subchaser Training Center at Miami, FL; Tactical Radar School at Hollywood, FL; *Walter S. Gorka* (APD-114) for its commissioning at Hingham, MA and shakedown cruise to Guantanamo

Bay, Cuba. Returned to Boston Navy Yard for refitting for combat service in the North Atlantic when VE Day occurred. Reassigned to the Norfolk, VA, Navy Yard for a re-fitting for South Pacific duty. The ship's last assignment was to the mothball fleet at Green Cove Springs, FL, on the St. Johns River. Released from active duty on May 22, 1946.

After the war he returned to Ursinus College as a chemistry instructor. Received his Ph.D. in chemistry from the University of Pennsylvania. Served as the chairman of the chemistry department at Ursinus from 1964-68. At various times during his career he performed consulting and research work for the Maumee Chemical Co., the Althouse Chemical Co., and the Pennsalt Chemical Co.

Married Margaret Klauder "Peggy" Brown on Aug. 17, 1944 and they enjoy traveling. In 1988, they retired to their summer home on Shaws Road, Newcastle, Nevis, Leeward Islands, West Indies where Roger operates a nine hole pitch and putt golf course. They have one son, Roger P. Jr., who was in the Navy during the Vietnam War.

DONALD HENRY "THE BARON" STECHMANN, CAPT, born Dec. 9, 1933, in Zumbrota, MN. Attended pre-engineering at University of Minnesota prior to Naval Cadet flight training in September 1953. Received his BA in Political Science, Naval Postgraduate School, Monterey, CA, 1967.

A Veteran Navy carrier pilot, he flew off eight of our nation's aircraft carriers. During a 32 year career, he held numerous flight instructor and staff assignments including aide to Commander Second Fleet. He was Commander of Navy Recruiting District Minneapolis; the Sixth Fleet Naval Support Activity, Souda Bay Crete, Greece and the Naval Training Center, Great Lakes, IL.

Medals awarded include Battle Efficiency Award, National Defense Service (one star), Navy Commendation, Meritorious Service and the Legion of Merit. He retired with the rank of Captain in 1985.

Since retirement he served for four years as president of the Lake County, IL, Navy League and employed in Illinois real estate military relocation. Married in 1959 to Marjean; they have three children: Dana, Kurt and Erik (LCDR, USNR); and four grandchildren: Erin, Cara, Nicholas and Jacob.

JULES VERNE "JV" STEINHAUER, LCDR, born Aug. 25, 1925, Brooklyn, NY. Received his BA degree from Tufts University; MBA from City University (Baruca College) of New York. Joined the USNR May 5, 1943 and was commissioned July 5, 1945.

Stations/Units: Navy V-12 Program (Tufts); Navy V-7 Program (Columbia University); seven months of service ashore, Subic Bay, 1945-46; LCI-749; SC-773; various diesel submarines; NavAirRes as ASW advisor.

Last unit was Air Wing Staff 83, NAS New York. Commands held were Engineer, LCI-749 and XO, SC-773.

Discharged in 1971 with the rank of Lieutenant Commander, he received the Asiatic-Pacific, American Theater, WWII Victory Medal, Naval

Reserve Medal, National Defense Service Medal and Armed Forces Reserve Medal.

Memorable experience was achieving qualification in diesel and electric submarines (June 1951).

Married Eleanor - no children. Worked as a systems analyst for New York Telephone, 1955-85. Retired June 6, 1985.

JAMES B. STERLING III, CDR, USNR (Ret), born in Anahuac, TX, in 1948. He graduated from Texas A&M University in 1971, having been a member of the Fighting Texas Aggie Band, and received a Navy commission and USCG license.

After serving on several ships in the Merchant Marine, he entered the family funeral business. He is currently chairman of the First National Bank of Dayton and owns two Century 21 Real Estate franchises.

During his Naval Reserve career, he commanded five Reserve units and volunteered for Operation Desert Storm, where he served as Executive Officer of the Dover Port Mortuary, earning the Navy Commendation Medal. He was Commander of the Texas Commandery NOUS in 1993, and served on the USS Houston Bell Committee.

A retirement ceremony was held for CDR Sterling in 1994 on the battleship *Texas*. CDR Sterling recently organized a Sons of Confederate Veterans Camp, which he commands.

He lives in Liberty, TX, with his new bride, Sandra, three cats and two step-cats.

RAYMOND M. STONE, CAPT, NOAA (Ret), born Dec. 26, 1914, in Riverhurst, Sask., Canada. He received his BS degree in Civil Engineering at the University of California at Berkeley in June 1940 and commissioned Ensign on Dec. 15, 1940, at the US Coast & Geodetic Survey HQ in Washington, DC.

After a brief orientation, he proceeded to Guantanamo Bay, Cuba, and reported to the USC&GS *Hydrographer*, his first ship assignment. The *Hydrographer*, at that time, was engaged in making geodetic, hydrographic and topographic surveys of the Mayaguana Island area in the West Indies, in preparation for the US to make that barren island area a military base.

From this assignment he was transferred to other USC&GS ships in the Atlantic and Pacific, each engaged in providing needed surveys for the US military forces.

Some of his earlier experiences on these assignments included: 1941, the survey of a 100 square mile area off the Delaware Coast for submarine dive-testing maneuvers; 1942, the survey of Casco Bay, ME, to establish an anchorage for the Navy's 7th Fleet; 1943-45, conducting extensive surveys of the Western Aleutians at a time when Japanese forces were still occupying the islands of Kiska and Attu.

He served as CO of the ship *Marmer* and the ship *Hydrographer* at the conclusion of his 10 ship assignments.

In September 1963, following 18 years at sea, he was transferred to USC&GS HQ in Washington, DC, to become the Assistant Chief of Operations, Office of Hydrography & Oceanography. In the three years that followed, he advanced to the position of Chief Of Operations, and then director of that division.

He retired March 31, 1972, following 32 continuous years of active duty in the USC&GS (now

NOAA). His decorations include the Defense Service Ribbon w/Bronze Star, Atlantic War Zone Ribbon and Pacific War Zone Ribbon.

Married Frances Woodbury and had two children, Raymond and Edward Stone, and one granddaughter, Jeanene Stone Doolin. He is currently married to Sue L. Mulborn.

RAYMOND W. STONE, TMC, born Dec. 12, 1943, Seattle, WA. He is the son of NOAA CAPT Raymond M. Stone (Ret) (his NOUS ancestor). He received his AA in business management, Northwood Institute, 1987; BBA with a Major in Management from Northwood Institute, 1988 (graduated Cum Laude); and MS in Management from Troy State University, 1990. He joined the USNR May 28, 1963.

Military stations include NRED 6-49, 1963-64; SUBDIV 5-8, 1964; NR AS-18 Orion DET 406, 1975; NR AS-37 Dixon DET 3710, 1978.

Units served with include USS *Sea Cat* (SS-399), USS *Carp* (SS-338), USS *Grampus* (SS-523), USS *Runner* (SS-476), USS *Drum* (AGSS-228), USS *Torsk* (AGSS-423), USS *Trumpetfish* (SS-425), USS *Picuda* (SS-382), USS *Sirago* (SS-485) USS *Haddock* (SSN-621) and Trieste II (DSV-1).

In September 1985, Raymond was voluntarily recalled to active duty, to serve as a technical consultant to the Deputy Chief of Staff for Information Systems (COMNAVRESFOR Code 10) at Naval Reserve Headquarters, in New Orleans. He also served as Defense Data Network (DDN) Host Administrator and LAN Manager for staff headquarters. He was the architect of the BBS hub installed at CNRF HQ. During his tour, he served on the Force Master Chief Board of Advisors at NERA National Conferences (1987, 1988, 1989) as an expert in Naval Reserve ADP issues. In October 1990, Raymond returned to the Washington, DC area to continue his civilian career in information systems management.

He retired from USNR in September 1991 as TMC(SS). Awards include the AFRM w/star, Good Conduct Award, Navy Achievement Medal, Expert Pistol Medal, Marksman Rifle Medal, National Defense Service Medal, Naval Reserve Meritorious Service Medal w/4 stars, Navy Commendation Medal and qualified SS Designator.

He is currently a program manager for VISTA Computer Services, Inc. and resides in Springfield, VA. Raymond is divorced and has one daughter Jeanene Lynn Doolin.

LISLE A. (ART) STROUD, CAPT, born Feb. 12, 1936, Mitchell, SD. Received his BA in Business Administration with a Marketing major from the University of Washington, Seattle, WA. Joined the USNR in April 1954 and was commissioned in June 1958.

Served with the USS *Hassayamra* (AO-145), Pearl Harbor, WestPac; USS *Washburn,* San Diego, WestPac; Bureau of Naval Personnel, Washington, DC; Naval Reserve Readiness Command, New Orleans, LA; Office of Chief of Naval Operations.

Commands held: CO, Naval Reserve Cen-

ter, Hunters Point, San Francisco, CA; CO, Naval Reserve Center, San Mateo, CA; CO, Navy Personnel Support Activity, New Orleans, LA.

Participated in battles and campaigns at Quemoy MATSU, Vietnam, and numerous other WestPac deployments.

CAPT Stroud retired in August 1982. Awards include the Meritorious Service Medal, Navy Commendation Medal, Navy Achievement Medal, Vietnam Cross of Gallantry w/5 stars, Vietnam Campaign Medal, Armed Forces Expeditionary Medal w/star, Naval Reserve Service Medal w/Hourglass and National Defense Service Medal.

Married Mary and has three children: Helen S. Krupp, Laurie S. Schneider and son, Frederick. There are five grandchildren: Christina Stroud; Garrett, and Allison Schneider; Gretchen and Emily Krupp. Worked at Metrocall (paging and celluar) as vice-president, June 1983 to retirement in April 1993.

RAY "JACK" STRUTHERS, CDR, born June 6, 1916, San Francisco, CA. Received his BS degree from the University of California-Berkeley. Joined the USNR in November 1940 and was commissioned in July 1941.

Stationed at NAS Pensacola, Oakland, Alameda, New Orleans, Jacksonville, Cape May, Seattle, San Diego, Saipan and USS *Bennington* (CV-20).

Units served with were Training Command, VB-82, VBF-8, VC-11 and VF-121. He was CO of VF-878. Participated in American and Asiatic-Pacific campaigns.

CDR Struthers was discharged in 1962. His awards include the American Defense, Naval Reserve, American and Asiatic-Pacific Campaign Medals.

Married Beatrice and has two children, John and Joyce; and eight grandchildren: Elizabeth, Matt, Kate, Emilie, Haley, Leslie, Jody and Mary. Worked as a civil engineer until retirement in 1978.

GREGORY STUART, LT, USNR, CHIEF ENGINEER, born Dec. 27, 1962, Long Branch, NJ. Received his BS in Marine Engineering, Kings Point, 1987. Joined the USN in July 1952 and was commissioned June 23, 1987.

After graduating USMMA he sailed as Merchant Mariner, maintaining commission USNRMM until 1995. Participated in battles and campaigns in the Persian Gulf, Desert Shield; Operation Restore Democracy, Haiti.

LT Stuart was discharged Oct. 1, 1995, with the rank of LT, USNR, Chief Engineer. Received the Merchant Marine Expeditionary Medal (Desert Shield).

Memorable experiences: before and during the Persian Gulf War, sleepless days and nights; dragged old junk ships from lay-up fleet and applied enough bubble gum and duct tape to make them run again.

Gregory and wife Coleen have one son, Blake (born April 22, 1985). Gregory is a marine engineer and still sailing.

WILLIAM DAVID "DAVID" SULLINS JR., RADM, MSC, USN (Ret), born Aug. 3, 1942, Athens, TN. He earned a BS degree, Tennessee Wesleyan College and OD, Southern College of Optometry. He joined the USN May 1, 1967 and was commissioned a LTJG in the USN Medical Service Corps on April 1, 1966.

Upon his release from active duty in December 1969, he continued his Naval Reserve career as an Optometrist providing primary eye care.

From 1982-85, Health Services Support Officer, 4th FSSG; 1985-86, CO, NR NAVHOSJAX-108; 1986-88 CO 4th Med. Bn., 4th FSSG, 4th Mar. Div.; 1988-89, Executive Assistant OP-093R, NR OPNAV-093-106 the Pentagon; 1989-90, principal advisor BUMED Code 07, Bureau of Medicine and Surgery. He was selected for Flag 1989. He was Deputy Director, Medical Service Corps and Assistant Chief BUMED 04 (Logistics).

RADM Sullins is the first medical representative to Marine Corps Reserve Officers Association and first MSC representative to the Navy Reserve Medical Dental Flag Council. Currently he is president of a professional corporation, Eyecare Clinics, P.C. of Athens, Madisonville and Etowah, and chief of Eye Services at Woods Memorial Hospital, Etowah, TN; past president, former chairman, of the board of trustees of the American Optometric Association. He retired Aug. 5, 1995.

Married Leslie Methvin and they have two sons, William David III and Stuart Andrew, both optometrists.

THOMAS W. TANNER, LT, USNR, (Ret), born May =19, 1930, Los Angeles, CA. He majored in Business Administration and Marketing at the University of Southern California.

LT Tanner enlisted in the Naval Air Reserve at NAS Los Alamitos, CA, in 1950 and was assigned to Sqdn. VF-784. By March 1952, he became a Naval Aviation Cadet at NAS Pensacola, FL, Class 13-52. Many training assignments led to his commission as an Ensign and a naval aviator in September 1953.

With the first Special Weapons Squadron deployed in the fleet, his unit, VA-95, flying AD Skyraiders, served aboard the USS *Hornet* (CVA-12), rounding the world for service in Korea. During his final year of active duty, March 1955 to March 1956, he was a Primary Flight Instructor, Basic Training Unit (BTU) 1N at NAAS

Whiting Field, Milton, FL. He remained active in the Naval Reserve until retirement, July 1, 1974.

A life member of the NOUS, Tanner served as Commander of the Long Beach Commandery. Beside the NOUS, Tanner holds life memberships in the Air Force Assoc., Assoc. of Naval Aviation, Combat Pilots Assoc., Marines Memorial Assoc., Naval Reserve Assoc., ROA and the Tailhook Assoc.

Thomas is divorced with two adult children, six grandchildren. He currently resides in Long Beach, CA.

DEAN TAYLOR JR., CAPT, born April 12, 1923, Mason, MI. He graduated from high school and attended college at Michigan State University; BS from US Naval Academy Class 48A; and PhD from Case Institute Tech. He joined the USN in December 1942 and was commissioned June 6, 1947.

Stationed in the CONUS Pacific and Far East aboard the USS *Helena* (CA-75) and the submarines *Pickerel, Guitarro, Menhaden; Atlantic Barracuda, Conger,* COMSUBDIV, USNA (Faculty) and Nuclear Power School (Faculty). Units served with were Com First Fleet Staff Communications.

Commands held were *Barracuda, Conger,* COMSUBDIV 82 and *Chara* (AE-31). Participated in campaigns in Korea (aboard the *Pickerel*) and Vietnam (aboard the *Chara*).

CAPT Taylor was discharged June 30, 1977 and received all the standard military medals. In 1957 he received the Cyanamid Research Award from the American Chemical Society in 1957.

Memorable experiences include his research in physical chemistry at Case Tech, assignments to naval research and development projects, and resolving racial problems in the *Chara*.

Married Barbara Davis and they have a son Whitney and daughter Jill. His civilian employment was with Montery Institute (assistant to the president), California Student Aid Comm.

WILLIAM H. "BILL" TEWELOW, CAPT, USN (Ret), born May 25, 1935, in Wilmington, DE. He earned a BA degree from the University of Delaware, a Master's in Educational Psychology (summa cum laude), AGS in international relations (both from Boston University).

Entered the USN July 9, 1954, as a Seaman Recruit, accepted a commission in 1963 and served aboard the USS *Fremont* (APA-44); USS *Colleton* (APB-36) in-country Vietnam and NSA Naples, Italy. After affiliation with the Naval  Reserve he served as Force Comptroller with the Seabees, ILO CENTCOM, CO ASB(M) 108, XO, NSC Jacksonville, and Logistics Officer, VTU-6767.

CAPT Tewelow retired June 30, 1994; his awards include two Navy Commendation Medals and 23 other decorations.

He retired as president of the Tewelow Agency, Inc. in Mableton, GA, where he resides with his wife, the former Ann Lamborn of West Grove, PA. They have three children: Beau, Valeri and John; and two grandchildren, Trey and Devin. Retired Jan. 1, 1996.

ALEXANDER BRAST "TOMMIE" THOMAS, CDR, born April 28, 1914 in Cincinnati, OH. He attended Lehigh University for his BS degree in Civil Engineering. On Aug. 29, 1942, he was appointed an Assistant Civil Engineer with the rank of ENS in the USNR of the USN.

On Jan. 2, 1943, he reported to Camp Allen, Norfolk, VA and was assigned duty with the then forming Naval Construction Battalion 68. Following commissioning of the battalion and training on the east coast, Companies C and D and one half of the HQ Co. were detached to form Construction Bn. Det. 1008 who together with some 110 Navy doctors and nurses boarded the USS *Henderson* in Port Hueneme, CA for transport to Port Purvis and Tulagi in the southern Solomon Islands. Their mission included the construction of hospital, base and harbor facilities on Tulagi and Florida Island for the Fleet Anchorage in Purvis Bay.

In January 1945 he was assigned duty with Base Construction Depot Det. Navy 131 in Noumea, New Caledonia as OinC of rebuilding and repairing battalion construction equipment for movement to forward areas as needed. In  June 1945, he returned Stateside and was assigned duty in the Public Works Department of the Charleston Naval Shipyard, Charleston, SC, as assistant Yard Transportation Officer and the OinC of Crane and Rail and of Automotive Transportation. Following release to inactive duty on June 26, 1946, he joined Naval Reserve Seabee Division 5-5 and 5-6 and was promoted to the rank of Commander Feb. 1, 1957. He continued to serve in the CB Reserve until his retirement April 28, 1974.

Memorable was the problem solving capabilities and "can-do, let's get it done now" attitude of the men with whom he was privileged to serve.

Married Barbara Ann Scherr Wiles. Children are Julie, Joseph, Kirk and Lisa Wiles; grandchildren are John and Chris Gorrell and Patrick and Philip Wiles. Civilian employment as president and CEO, Thomas Company, Inc.

JAMES JOHN TRITTEN, CDR, USN (Ret), entered the USN in 1965 and was commissioned and designated an aviator via the NAVCAD program. His fleet assignments primarily included carrier-based ASW.

CDR Tritten was selected for three educational tours of duty at civilian universities where he earned a BA, MA and PhD. He served at RAND, in OPNAV, OSD/Net Assessment, and

as the chairman of the National Security Affairs Department at NPS. His highest personal award was the Defense Superior Service Medal. He earned subspecialty ratings in ASW general and nuclear strategic planning, joint intelligence, and area studies.

Since he retired in 1989, CDR Tritten has been employed as a naval civil servant teaching at the NPS, as academic advisor at the Naval Doctrine Command and most recently at the USACOM JTASC. He has been awarded the Navy Superior Civilian Service Award and the Alfred Thayer Mahan Award from the Navy League.

RAMON R. "RAY" TRUMAN, LCDR, born June 25, 1932, San Francisco, CA. Received his BA degree in world business, San Francisco State College; graduate study at Golden Gate College, School of Traffic Management; California Maritime Academy, Continuing Education Div.

He joined the USNR Aug. 20, 1949 and was commissioned July 1, 1961. Stationed at NavSta Treasure Island; USS *Grady, Daniel A. Joy* and *Naifeh* as leading Radarman; USNAS Oakland, New York, Alameda and Moffett Field; and USS *Uhlmann* (DD-687). He made two deployments to Korea during the Korean War and was a unit intelligence officer for eight years.

Battles and campaigns: Wonson Harbor; 41st Parallel, North Korea, landed 30 guerrilla warfare ROK marines and civilians above Chonjin, North Korea at night in clandestine warfare ops during Argentine War of 1982; Falkland Islands, served as intelligence briefing team to IPAC at Camp Smith, Oahu, Hawaii on staff of CINCPAC during ACDUTRA.

Retired July 1, 1982, with the rank of Lieutenant Commander. Received the Korean Presidential Unit Citation, China Service, Korean War w/4 Battle Stars, UN Service Medal, National Defense, Naval Reserve, Armed Forces Reserve Medal w/Hourglass Device.

Memorable was serving as President of Naval Reserve Association, FADM Nimitz, Golden Gate Chapter, 1981-82; one month in Wonson Harbor, North Korea in 1951 assigned to TF-95 for close-in shore bombardment - ship was hit by shore gunfire in fall of 1951 from a Korean railcar mounted Howitzer gun. During second deployment in 1952 ship was again taken under fire with one man seriously wounded and ship damaged by small arms fire off coast of North Korea. He served 12+ years as Radarman, and in 1961 was selected for Ensign under the first program for Limited Duty Officers in the Naval Reserve. Served 21 years as a commissioned line officer in Naval Air Reserve Billets in various command and control units as ASW Watch Officer, Training Officer, Division Officer and finally as Intelligence Officer for ASWOC and OPCON units in 3rd and 7th Fleets. Retired in 1982 after 33 continuous years.

Married Benita Camicia and has two children, Scott and Laurie, and two grandchildren, Danielle and Dominic. He was vice-president, Project Cargogs and consultant in marine transportation. Retired Jan. 30, 1997.

THOMAS J. "TOM" TURPIN, CAPT, USN (Ret), born Dec. 8, 1935, Miami, FL. After graduating from Florida State University, he was commissioned ENS, USNR, July 7, 1959 at OCS. He was ordered to USS *Van Voorhis* (DE-1028), at Newport as CIC officer, ultimately "fleeting up" to Operations Officer. He was then reassigned to the CIC School, Glynco, GA, as a surface ASW instructor. He was promoted to Lieutenant in 1963 and "augmented" to USN, whereupon he was ordered to USS *Worden* (DLG-18) at San Diego, as Missile Officer and Gunnery Assistant.

During this tour, *Worden* deployed twice to WestPac, operating first on Dixie Station, then Yankee Station, after the second Tonkin Gulf Incident. In July 1966, LT Turpin assumed command of USS *Sunnadin* (ATA-197), an ocean tug at Pearl Harbor. The ship deployed to WestPac as a unit of TF-73 engaged in towing and salvage operations, principally in the Mekong Delta.

He was then reassigned to CINCPACFLT Staff as fleet scheduler. He was honored by the Honolulu Navy League as the Outstanding Junior Officer on CINCPACFLT staff in 1968, promoted to Lieutenant Commander, and shortly thereafter reported to Naval War College as a Command And Staff Course student.

Upon completion, LCDR Turpin became executive officer, USS *Sellers* (DDG-11) at Charleston and deployed to the Mediterranean. His next assignment was as development coordinator for Surface Missile Systems, Office of the CNO (OP-982).

In August 1975, he was promoted to Commander and took command of USS *Buchanan* (DDG-14), at San Diego. Most of this tour was spent in overhaul and pre-deployment workup. In August 1977, he reported to NAVSEASYSCOM as program manager for the MK 71 8"/55 major caliber lightweight gun. When the program failed to survive FY79 President's budget deliberations, Commander Turpin was reassigned as director, Gun Weapon Systems Div. (SEA 62Y1). He subsequently became placement officer for the Navy Material Command in BuPers. He was promoted to Captain in 1979 and returned to NAVSEA as director, Long Range Missile Weapon Systems Div. (SEA 62Z1).

After a short tour as Executive Officer, NAVSTA Mayport, he took command of USS *Dale* (CG-19). Dale deployed to the Mediterranean and represented and supported COMSIXTHFLT in celebration of the 40th Anniversary of the Allied Liberation of France in Cannes. Capt. Turpin subsequently returned to Washington as deputy AEGIS program manager (PMS-400A).

He retired Aug. 1, 1986. His decorations include Legion of Merit, Meritorious Service Medal w/stars in lieu of second and third awards, Navy Commendation Medal, Vietnam Campaign Medal and various campaign medals.

Memorable experiences include Yankee Station, Tonkin Gulf Search and Rescue Operations, and towing and salvage operations in the Mekong Delta, VN.

He is married to the former Carolyn Davis. They have three sons: Thomas J. III, Christopher and Cameron; and a grandson, Thomas Nolan Turpin. Civilian Employment: vice president of the Federal Services Div., Advanced Systems Technology, Inc.

EDWARD B. WALDMANN, CAPT, born Feb. 6, 1926, Council Bluffs, IA. Received BS in medi-

cine, Creighton University, 1946; Doctor of Medicine, Creighton University School of Medicine, 1948; MS, cardiovascular physiology, Creighton University Graduate School, 1950; DNB, 1950; and ABIM, 1956.

Military Positions: 1945, Student SV-12(S), Creighton University School of Medicine, Omaha, NE; 1949-50, Battalion Medical Officer 9-38, Omaha, NE; 1951-51, student at School of Aviation Medicine, Pensacola, FL; 1951-52, Group Flight Surgeon, Marine Air Group 16; 1953-59, Wing Flight Surgeon, WS-81, NAS Minneapolis, MN; 1959-82, several billets, Phoenix (AZ) Navy and Marine Reserve Training Center; August-March 1977, CO, Navy Regional Medical Center, Phoenix, AZ; 1980-82, CO, Medical Contingency Response Unit 1119, Phoenix; 1945-82, Captain, Medical Corps, USNR and Naval Flight Surgeon, Ready Reserve, USN.

Industrial and aviation medicine and medical administrative positions from 1949-84 as assistant track physician, assistant health director, assistant medical director, consultant in aviation medicine, employee health director, wing flight surgeon, member of board, director, commanding officer, chairman and member of numerous committees. His last position was as medical reviewer, Health Services Advisory Group, 1985-90.

Life member of the NRA and NOUS, Reserve Officers of Naval Service, Society of USN Flight Surgeons, TROA, American Legion, AMVETS and life member of Marines Memorial San Francisco.

FREDERICK WALTER "FRITZ" WANZENBERG, LCDR, USNR, born July 28, 1918, Aumuhle, Germany. He joined the USNR in 1934 as an Apprentice Seaman, took NROTC at Northwestern University and graduated from Purdue in (Tectonic) Metallurgy in 1940. He received his Ensign commission Dec. 8, 1941.

Stationed at Cape Henry, VA; Baltimore, Key West, Fantan I and II, Fiji Archipelago, San Pedro, Terminal Island, CA. Unit he served with was ANZACS.

LCDR Wanzenberg received commendations for building and commanding the replacement for Pearl Harbor.

Memorable experience was in a jungle outpost where Adm. Nimitz personally commissioned Wanzenberg to build the replacement for Pearl Harbor at Nandi, Vatakoula, Fiji. When the harbor was ready the Pacific Fleet steamed in. The deep screws of the carriers and battleships churned the black magmatic bottom mud. Water-borne, this magma cloud registered a signature on his fluxmeter chart indicating it contained supermagnetic, superconducting metallic glass defined as complex gold silicon. The chemical formulae are 80Au.20Si, 80Pt.20SiC etc.; its complexed metals refractory to all known metallurgical processes, except by methods of this serendipital discovery as expressed by the U.S. Department of Interior who attended our U.S. Senate Testimony on this globally vital tectonic discovery.

He married Nancy Wheelock and has four children: F. Wheelock, Kimball, Mark Brooks and

Carolyn Leland; and one grandchild, Alexis.

Civilian employment as director, Booz Allen & Hamilton Applied Research Corporate Staff, AMAX; co-responsible for upgrading Navy ships and nukes.

VAN WATTS, Naval Philosopher and Sea Power Advocate Supply Corps, CWO W4, USN (Ret), born Aug. 26, 1920, in Mooers, NY. He joined the USN Dec. 15, 1937 and was promoted to Chief Disbursing Clerk at 22 years, two months and five days on Nov. 1, 1942, while serving aboard USS *Mackinac* (AVP-13) during the Battle of Guadalcanal.

Promoted to SC Warrant Officer at age 23 years, three months and 19 days, Dec. 15, 1943, while serving as deputy paymaster at Milne Bay during the Battle of New Guinea. Retired Oct. 1, 1962, as SC CWO4. He declined higher promotion but CO entered recommendation for LCDR in his official record.

Originator/producer of TV and radio Navy slanted shows from Norfolk in early 1950s. Founded Navy's Sailor of the Week, Month, Quarter and Year programs which implemented his ideas and philosophy acquired coming up through the ranks throughout the Navy in 1952.

Created Norfolk's big ship welcoming ceremonies called by CHINFO "The centerpiece of Norfolk-Navy relations," 1954. Enrollment of all TV and radio media in area to promote Norfolk-Navy goodwill inspired formation of Navy League's Hollywood Council, or "media division" of which he is a life member, in 1954.

Recipient of numerous honors including city of Norfolk official thanks in 1954 and Royal Mace Pin in 1988. Hollywood Council Navy League's Gold Plaque for the founder of programs that spread around the globe with three of his nautical celebrities returned from Persian Gulf duty for ceremonies at Bob Hope Hollywood USO 1988.

Inspired by Maury, Mahan and Dana, Watts came into the Navy well prepared to continue their work and is today honored for his own contributions to the sea service throughout the Navy. "Much of the positive civilian awareness of the role and value of the Navy can be attributed to Van Watts." Naval historian, Kit Bonner, in *Treasure Island Museum Association Newsletter,* Fall of 1993.

Decorations include the National Defense Service, American Defense Service, American Campaign, Asiatic-Pacific Campaign, WWII Victory Medal, Navy Occupation, Armed Forces Expeditionary, Guadalcanal and New Guinea Battle Stars.

Member of USN Institute, Naval Hist. Found., Navy Sup. Corps Assoc. Guadalcanal Campaign Vets Assoc., VFW, FRA, Hollywood Council Navy League, Botsford Family Historical Assoc. and the New Hampshire Hist. Sec.

CHARLES JOSEPH WEIGEL II, LT, born May 24, 1932, Chicago, IL. Received his BA, JD and LL.M degrees. Joined the USN Sept. 13, 1953 and commissioned in January 1954.

Stationed at OCS, Newport, RI and served in the USS *Kearsarge* (CVA-33). He participated in the China Service.

He married Barbara Lewis and they have four children: Susanna, Charles III, Victoria and Garry; and too many grandchildren to name here.

Civilian employment: private law practice, FTC, law professor for 32 years.

TREN A. WILLIAMSON, COL, born Jan. 22, 1931, Ketchikan, AK. Col. Williamson was reared in Seattle. He attended Franklin High School, 1945-49, followed by University of Washington, 1949-53. During his senior year at the university, as the result of an accidental gun shot wound, he was physically disqualified for commissioning in the Naval services and dis-enrolled from the Naval ROTC.

After graduation he enlisted in the Marine Corps, serving four years as an Infantryman, rising to the rank of Sergeant.

On release from active duty in 1957, he returned to Seattle, applied for and received an appointment as a 2nd Lieutenant in the Army Reserve in April 1958. Subsequently, he returned to active duty in 1962, serving initially at Fort Polk, LA, as CO of a recruit training company and later as a staff officer with the faculty group.

During 1965-66 he served in the 7th Inf. Div. in the Republic of Korea. On completion of that 13-month tour, he was transferred to Fresno, CA, assuming command of the Fresno Armed Forces Examining and Entrance Station, responsible for the enlistment and induction of individuals into our Armed Forces.

From Fresno in 1967, he transferred as a Captain to the Marine Corps. His first assignment was as a Company Commander, 28th Marine Regt. at MCB, Camp Pendleton, CA. During the TET Offensive of 1968, he shipped out to the Republic of Vietnam with the 27th Marine Regt., serving initially as a Company Commander and subsequently as a Staff Officer on being promoted to Major.

Released from active duty in 1971, he remained active in the USMCR until his retirement as a Colonel, July 1, 1989, serving nearly 36 years of active and Reserve duty as an Enlisted member of the USMC, and as an Officer in both the USA and USMC, exclusive of his nearly four years as Midshipman, USNR. His assignments included command and staff in the combat arms, logistics and intelligence.

As a civilian, he was an investigator initially in 1972 with the Bureau of Narcotics and Dangerous Drugs, subsequently renamed the Drug Enforcement Administration, US Department of Justice. He retired from the Defense Investigative Service, Department of Defense in November 1990. He earned graduate degrees in Management and Business from West Coast University and the University of Southern California.

Williamson survives his wife of 31 years, the former Helen W. Keith, who passed away in July 1993. He married second the former Miss Karen Jean Strandberg of Seattle and Bainbridge Is-

land, Washington State. They both have children from previous marriages.

EDMUND P. WILLIS, CAPT, USNR (Ret), graduated from the NROTC Program at the University of Wisconsin, Madison in 1955. Ordered to duty aboard USS *Samuel B. Roberts* (DD-823). ENS Willis served as DCA and OOD underway. USS *Roberts* cruised the Mediterranean in 1956 and took station with the Mid-East Force in the Persian Gulf.

LTJG Willis transferred to *Rochester* (CA-124). As 6th (Gunnery) Division officer and OOD underway he sailed to WestPac in 1957 where *Rochester* served as 7th Fleet flagship, making port calls in Sydney, Yokosuka, Kobe, Hong Kong, Manila, Keelung and Saigon.

In 1958, Willis left active duty and enrolled in graduate studies at the University of California, Berkeley. He served in the inactive Reserve aboard USS *Alvin C. Cockrell* (DE-366) at Alameda, and was recalled to active duty in 1961 during the Berlin Crisis. *Cockrell* patrolled off Vietnam in 1962. During that period, Lt. Willis served as Naval Liaison Officer in Danang, Vietnam.

Returning to inactive status in 1962, Willis took the doctorate in history from UC, Berkeley. As assistant professor of history he taught at Moravian College from 1964. In 1967, he joined York College, City University of New York. An associate professor, he taught history and chaired a special studies program.

In 1980, Willis established Kinsale Mangers, Inc., a recruiting firm serving Wall Street. He headed the operation until 1993 when he became historian and political analyst with the Joint Warfare Analysis Center in Dahlgren, VA. He left JWAC in 1996.

In New York, Willis served in the Reserve afloat program, moving up to Prospective CO of *Moale* (DD-693). Next he was Chief Staff Officer of Reserve Destroyer Division 3ND. He then served as Program Coordinator with Readiness Commander Two. Upon promotion to Captain he took command of Naval Control of Shipping Office NY 102. During these years he served concurrently with the New York Naval Militia, He retired in 1983 after 28 years naval service.

CAPT Willis has two daughters and lives in Alexandria, VA.

RAY L. WILSON, CWO4, USNR (Ret), born Aug. 7, 1912, in Phoenix, AZ. Inducted into active duty in March 1941, his permanent duty station was the Pearl Harbor Navy Yard Dispensary. At the time of the attack he was on detached duty at the "Old Naval Station Dispensary." It was on the water front in Honolulu and was a dispensary for dependents of naval personnel.

He, along with two doctors, was dispatched to Pearl Harbor to give all aid possible to the causalities and he shall never forget that eight mile ride. The Japanese were strafing the highway; USN was stenciled all over their car, but fortunately they were not hit.

He was ordered aboard the USS *Platte*, a fleet oiler, similar to its sister ship the USS *Neosho*. The *Neosho* was in Pearl Harbor at the time of the attack.

They were active in the Coral Sea battle, the occupation of Guadalcanal, the Midway battle

and the occupation of Attu in the Aleutian Islands. In the Coral Sea battle, the *Neosho* had just relieved the *Platte* when it was attacked and sunk.

His shore duty stations were San Diego and Great Lakes Naval Training Stations, San Bruno, CA, Advance Base Personnel Depot. At the end of the war he was stationed back in Pearl Harbor as the personnel officer of the hospital.

The *Platte* received 11 Battle Stars for WWII, six Battle Stars for Korea, and five Battle Stars for Vietnam.

His personal awards include the Good Conduct Medal, Naval Reserve, American Defense Service w/Base Clasp, Asiatic-Pacific w/Bronze Star, American Campaign, WWII Victory Medal and Armed Forces Reserve Medal. He retired on Aug. 7, 1972 from the USNR.

His wife is deceased. He has five granddaughters and six great-grandchildren. In civilian life he is a registered pharmacist.

IRENE N. WIRTSCHAFTER, CAPT, born in Elgin, IL, daughter of David A. and Ethel G. Nerove. She attended Columbus University – BCS, Philadelphia Board of Realtors (appraiser) Insurance Broker, CPA Review, and other continuing education courses. Commissioned ENS, USN, 1944, Supply Corps. Retired with rank of Captain in 1976.

Sea duty as Assistant Supply Officer, 1956; CO Supply Unit, 1973-75; Honorary Chief USN, 1973; National Treasurer, Naval Reserve Assoc., 1975-77; National Advisory Committee, Naval Reserve Assoc., 1978-date; appointed by Secretary of the Navy to the Secretary of the Navy's Advisory Committee for Retired Personnel, 1984-87; elected National Trustee, Assoc. of Naval Aviation, 1984-date; founder and comptroller ANA Banana River Sqdn., 1985-date; appointed to Veterans Administration Advisory Comm. On Women Veterans, 1986-89; Navy Liaison officer, Commanders Retirees Council, Patrick AFB, 1985-88; ROA, past chapter officer; TROA, Florida Conference Committee, 1987; Golf Committee, 1997-date; Naval Order, past D.C. Commandery officer, charter member three commanderies; WAVES National, Board Member Space Coast Chapter, 1990-date; Tailhook Assoc.; Navy League; Guest of Honor, 1124th Recruit Revue, Orlando Naval Training Station.

Career: Internal Revenue Agent, US Treasury, Office of International Operations, International Banking Specialist; Real Estate Associate; Real Estate Appraiser, Insurance Broker; Statistician; Accountant; and Amway Distributor.

Active in numerous civic programs and committees and recipient of many awards and Certificates of Appreciation. Also, commercial instrument pilot SEL and SES and owner of Cessna Skyhawk.

She was widowed in 1966 and lives in Cocoa Beach, FL.

KENNETH HENRY WITT, born Nov. 2, 1939, in Bedford, VA. Attended California State University at Los Angeles for his BA degree. He joined the USNR Aug. 19, 1964.

Stationed at Los Angeles and Los Alamitos, CA; Bremerton, WA; San Diego, CA; San Francisco, CA, and Vietnam. Served in special services and weapons. Served in the USS *Kitty Hawk* (CVA-63), aircraft carrier and the USS *St. Paul* (CA-73), cruiser.

Discharged Jan. 7, 1968, his awards include the Good Conduct Medal, National Defense Service Medal, Vietnam Service Medal and RVN Campaign Medal.

Married Marcia DeSarro and they have two

children, Sonya and Tanya (twins). Civilian employment as educator and real estate.

NOUS commissioned ancestors: Lt. Henry Jeter and Lt. Henry Stratton.

CHESTER A. WRIGHT, Master Chief Petty Officer SDCM(SS), born May 3, 1922, Hope, AR. He attended Merritt College, Oakland, CA, for his AA degree, 1963; San Francisco State College, BA in social welfare, 1965; Master's degree in Social Work, UCLA, 1968. Joined the USN July 2, 1940.

Military stations include U.S. Naval Academy, Morto Torpedo Base 15, Tulagi; British

Solomons, ComNav l2 (flag); naval magazine Port Chicago; NAS Kodiak, AK; USS *Princeton* (CVA-37); CornSubPacAdmin, Mare Island, USS *Salmon* (SSR-573).

Participated in battle and campaigns in British Solomons, Admiralty Islands and Philippines during WWII, and in USS *Princeton* in Korea and during the Cold War.

Discharged April 5, 1967, with the rank of Master Chief Petty Officer SDCM(SS), he received the National Defense, American Defense, Asiatic-Pacific Campaign, WWII Victory, China Service, Korean Service, UN Service, Philippine Liberation, Korean Presidential Unit Citation, Superior Civilian Service Award.

Memorable experience was in 1942 at the USNA when he met President Franklin D. Roosevelt.

He married Billie Gale and has four children: LaShon Caldwell, Terra M. Lofton, Sadaya Z. and J. Zimmerle; and one grandchild, Zackary Zimmerle. Civilian employment as a faculty field and classroom instructor, Case Western Reserve University, assistant professor of social psychology, Naval Post Graduate School, Monterey, CA.

INDEX

9 781681 621586